Deliverance from Error

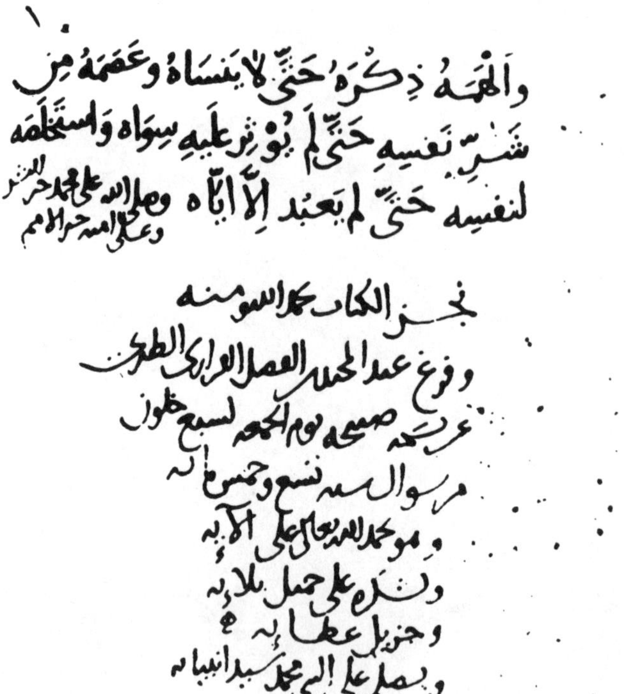
والهمه ذكره حتى لا ينساه وعصمه من
شر نفسه حتى لم يؤثر عليه سواه واستخلصه
لنفسه حتى لم يعبد الا اياه
وصلى الله على محمد خير البشر وعلى امته خير الامم
نجز الكتاب بحمد الله ومنه
غرة … صبيحة يوم الجمعة لسبع خلون
من شوال سنة تسع وخمسمايه
وجزيل عطائه
وعلى آله وسلم
بسم الله الرحمن الرحيم

Last page of the ms. of the *Munqidh min al Ḍalāl* contained in no. 1712 of the Sehid Ali Pasa of Istanbul. The colophon is dated 509 A.H. [=1115–1116 A.D.]

DELIVERANCE FROM ERROR

AN ANNOTATED TRANSLATION OF
al-Munqidh min al Ḍalāl
AND OTHER RELEVANT
WORKS OF

AL-GHAZĀLĪ

by

RICHARD JOSEPH MCCARTHY, S.J.
A.B. (Holy Cross), M.A. (Boston College), D.Phil. (Oxon.)

INCLUDING:

THE CLEAR CRITERION FOR DISTINGUISHING BETWEEN
ISLAM AND GODLESSNESS,

THE INFAMIES (ENORMITIES) OF THE BĀTINITES AND THE
VIRTUES (MERITS) OF THE MUSTAẒHIRITES,

THE CORRECT BALANCE,

THE NOBLEST OF AIMS IN THE EXPLANATION OF GOD'S FAIREST NAMES,

THE BOOK OF THE MARVELS OF THE HEART

FONS VITAE

Original Edition entitled FREEDOM AND FULFILLMENT
Twayne Publishers, 1980.

This edition printed and distributed by Fons Vitae, Louisville, KY

Printed in Canada

Library of Congress Catologing in Publication Data

Ghazzālī, 1058–1111
Freedom and fulfillment
p. cm.
Includes bibliographical references and indexes
ISBN-1-8057-8167-6
1. Islamic theology—Early works to 1800. 2. Ghazzālī, 1058–1111. 3. Muslims—Islamic Empire—Biography. I. McCarthy, Richard Joseph. II. Title

Fons Vitae
49 Mockingbird Valley Drive
Louisville, KY 40207-1366
email: fonsvitaeky@aol.com
website: www.fonsvitae.com

Contents

FRATRIS AMICISQUE
VIVIS
ILSE-THERESE-EDWARD-AUSTIN
ATQUE DEFUNCTIS
MICHEL-RICHARD-HARRY-JOSEPH

In Loving Memory of
Reverend Richard J. McCarthy, S.J.
Arabist and Islamic Scholar
1913–1981

Baghdad College	1938–41, 1951–59
Oxford University	1947–51, 1969–77
Al-Hikma University	1959–68

President of Al-Hikma University, Baghdad, Iraq
1965–68

May his scholarly dedication live on in his students and readers

Editor's Preface

From the original Twayne edition of this work

CLASSICAL Arabic Literature is still almost inaccessible to most scholars, and is even less read and enjoyed by the general educated public. Neither the range of its subjects—from poetry and folklore to historiography, religious speculations and philosophy, not to mention scientific works of all kinds—nor the skill and artistry of the writers are generally recognized outside the small circle of specialists. The nonspecialist does not always realize that Arab literature flourished far earlier than did most European literatures and that it reached its zenith (and, one might say, began to stagnate) at a time when the latter were just beginning their ascent. Not all of the authors, nor even a majority, were Arabs; they used Arabic as the *lingua franca* of the medieval Muslim empire.

The Library of Classical Arabic Literature aims at making the work of the Arabic-writing thinkers and literati available to those scholars and lovers of literary works unable to read them in the original. Translations of some works into various European languages, including English, have appeared. Most of these, however, lacked grace by adhering slavishly to peculiarities of the Arab style; they failed to express the idiom used in the original by its equivalent in the language of translation. Others, by paraphrasing, deviated so far from the original text that the scholar could not always be sure of the correct rendering of the author's thought. Memorable modern exceptions to this statement are Enno Littmann's German translation of the *Arabian Nights,* Sir Hamilton Gibb's translation of Ibn Baṭṭūṭa's *Travels,* and the most recent version of the Koran by A. J. Arberry.

This series plans to present readable and enjoyable versions which, though cast into idiomatic English, will remain true to the author's own thoughts. They will be introduced by an essay on the work and its author, his life and *oeuvre,* his rank and role in medieval Arab literature and scholarship. Full scholarly and interpretative notes will give added help and information.Thus, the historian, the sociologist, the literary critic or the humanist, as well as the philosopher may find valuable research material for his own field.

But these works should—and can—be read for their own sake. This series differs from previously offered translations in that it will, whenever applicable, emphasize the relevance of the thought contained in these ancient writings for our own culture and times. It is hoped that this approach will enrich its value and provide an added dimension for our generation in the understanding of the ideas of a brilliant civilization of the past.

The [original edition of this] volume was prepared for the press during the weeks of the Islamic Revolution in Iran. The religious frenzy of the masses, stirred by the "holy man," the Ayatullah Ruhullah Khomeini, bewildered the Western observer who watched millions of men and women follow him as if in a trance, unquestioning, declaring themselves willing to die for him and the cause he represented. We wondered whence he received his power—not only over the masses, but for himself. Perhaps the following pages, transmitting the thought of a twelfth-century Muslim spiritual leader—philosopher as well as mystic—may help to explain in a certain measure the phenomenon of Muslim spirituality in the twentieth-century world, the differences between Ghazālī's Sunni convictions and the Ayatullah's Shiᶜism notwithstanding.

However, in this instance *"tout comprendre"* is not *"tout pardonner."*

ILSE LICHTENSTADTER
Harvard University

Introduction

1 "With the time came the man." These words are the introductory sentence of the chapter on Ghazālī in Duncan Black Macdonald's famous book *Development of Muslim Theology, Jurisprudence and Constitutional Theory.* Even in my first reading of them I seemed to hear in their background a flourish of trumpets: philosophical and theological and mystical trumpets, trumpets of strife and battle, trumpets on this side and from the other side, trumpets of death and of life. With the time came the man. The time was the period encompassed by the years 1058–1111 A.D. [450–505 A.H.: the Muslim calendar]. The man was Abū Ḥāmid Muḥammad son of Muḥammad son of Muḥammad al-Ghazālī.

2 The time in which Ghazālī lived and labored was, politically speaking, a time of agitation and turmoil. According to the historian Abū l-Fidāʾ the Abbassid Caliphate was in a state of abasement and decline, the Arab rule in Baghdad had passed away, or nearly passed away, Spain was revolting against its Muslim rulers, Peter the Hermit was summoning men to the Crusades, men were divided into Shiʿites and Sunnīs by religious and political differences, and Ashʿarism and the "Scholastic Philosophy" in Islam, with the support of the Seljuqs, were opposing the Muʿtazilites. The political regime in Baghdad was complicated and confused. On the one hand there was the Caliph, whose dominion seems to have been limited to the mention of his name in the canonical prayer in the mosques, and on the other there was the Seljuq Sultan, who dominated the army and politics.

3 The Caliphs who supported Ghazālī were al-Muqtadī Billāh [d. 487 A.H.] and al-Mustaẓhir Billāh [d. 512 A.H.], and he was backed by the Sultans ʿAḍud al-Dawla [d. 465 A.H.], Jalāl al-Dīn Malikshāh [d. 485 A.H.], Nāṣir al-Dīn Maḥmūd [d. 487 A.H.], Rukn al-Dīn Abū l-Muẓaffar Barkiyārūq [d. 498 A.H.], Rukn al-Dīn Malikshāh al-Thānī [d. 498 A.H.], and Muḥammad son of Malik-shāh [d. 511 A.H.]. At the Sultan's side was his Wazīr [Minister], who usually held the reigns of power. One of these powerful Wazīrs was Niẓām al-Mulk, who was able to dominate the state for nearly a quarter of a century. This man had a great influence on the cultural life of the time because it was he who founded the renowned

Niẓāmiyya Schools. He was a contemporary and fellow student of Ghazālī. And it was Fakhr al-Dawla, the son of Niẓām al-Mulk, who urged Ghazālī, toward the end of the latter's life, to return to teaching in the Niẓāmiyya [School] of Nīsābūr.

4 In farthest North Africa, the State of the Veiled Ones [tribes whose men veiled their faces] was ruled by Yusuf son of Tashfin, and after him by his son. In another part of North Africa the Berbers ruled, the most famous of them being Tamīm son of al-^{c}Izz son of Bādīs and Yaḥyā son of Ghanīm. The Fāṭimids reigned in Egypt. Their most famous caliphs who were contemporaries of Ghazālī were al-Musta^{c}lī Billāh Abū l-Qāsim Aḥmad son of al-Mustanṣir and al-Āmir bi Aḥkām Allāh ^{c}Alī al-Manṣūr son of al-Musta^{c}lī.

5 Ghazālī witnessed, or rather heard of, the disaster which befell the Islamic world in the last years of his life. This was the incursion of the Crusaders, which led to their founding princedoms in Rahā [in the Euphrates valley] in 490 A.H. and in Antioch in 491. Jerusalem was conquered in 492 and Tripoli [of Lebanon] in 495. There is no mention of these events in any of Ghazālī's writings, a fact for which he has been criticized by Zakī al-Mubārak. But Farīd Jabre found an excuse for that in the fact that Ghazālī was in Khorasan, far from the battle, and the Islamic regions were all at that time embroiled in dissensions and plots, while the princes' battles for power were unceasing—something which distracted Muslims in one country from the affairs of those in the other countries.

6 At this time, too, the Bāṭinite peril was on the upswing. It reached a high degree with their assassination of Niẓām al-Mulk in 485 and of his son Fakhr al-Dawla in 500 and of the Wazīr of the Sultan Barkiyārūq in 495. The Bāṭinites imposed a kind of terrorism on the eastern zones of the Islamic world. Behind their movement were the Fāṭimids, who exploited the political anarchy and the lack of outstanding leaders to cause general havoc. I need not dwell here on the Bāṭinites since the reader will find much more information about them and about Ghazālī's preoccupation with them in the text of my translation and the notes and references attached thereto, and especially in Appendix II.

7 In the days of Ghazālī the Islamic world was subjected to various cultural influences. In addition to the pure Islamic element different cultural currents affected the thinking of the Muslims. Perhaps the most influential was that of Greek culture. As Dr. al-Ṭībāwī has declared: "It was the Greek culture which prevailed in the milieu of this East of ours from the time of Alexander's conquests, and it continued to progress with time and had added to it various factors in varying times and it became

mixed with Indian, Persian and Egyptian philosophy; but it remained clear and dominant until the coming of the Muslims, who worked energetically after the consolidation of their rule to take over the civilization of those who had preceded them: and they found Greek culture within easy reach."

8 After the mingling of the pre-Islamic Greek culture with the other cultures and its being tinged with a Christian mode of metaphysical thought, Neo-Platonism made its appearance in the third century A.D. and it had a great influence on Islamic thought, especially in the area of Sufism. The influence of Persian philosophy was not less than that of Indian philosophy. Its greatest effects were on the extremist Shiᶜite beliefs concerning the divine right to rule and the "descent" [indwelling: *ḥulūl*] of God into the body of the Imam. Mention may also be made of the pagans of Ḥarrān, who are said to have hidden behind the name of the Sabaeans mentioned in the Qurᵓān.

9 The Egyptian scholar ᶜAbd al-Karīm al-ᶜUthmān declares that the ᶜAbbassid ages can be divided into three eras: the first era is that of the stage of transition and expansion and creation and innovation by way of translation [of Greek philosophy and science] and the mingling of the Arab culture with other cultures. The second is the stage of application and the effort to reconcile philosophy and religion. The third (the era of Ghazālī) was marked by the appearance of a new flare-up, viz. that of religion's fury against philosophy. In this third era Ghazālī played a leading role, a role for which he was well equipped by his own Sufi experience and his study of philosophy and, above all, by his authentic Muslim spirituality.

10 As a natural consequence of these different cultural factors, often mutually opposed, this age was characterized by a kind of intemperateness in thought and an unruliness in imagination which led to an extraordinary confusion and a curious concern with religions and sects and movements, with each tongue and pen going its own ideological way. There was conflict between the partisans and the opponents of the ancient Greek philosophy, while the *mutakallimūn* [Muslim theologians] were split between Ashᶜarism and Muᶜtazilism. The Sufis, discontented with the general state of affairs, created their own trends—and were themselves influenced by elements from the doctrines of Persians and Indians and Greeks.

11 With the time came the man: what little I have been able to set forth here must suffice as a very sketchy description of "the time." It will be supplemented somewhat by the rest of this book, and the interested reader will find many references to sources which will provide a much more detailed and ample picture of an age which, in some profound respects, was not entirely unlike our own. Now we must turn to a brief consideration of "the man."

12 If Ghazālī or one of his friends, had been able to compile a kind of proleptic scrapbook of adulatory references, or "rave reviews," it would have contained some rather remarkable items. Here are some random examples to illustrate this point.

1) "If there had been a prophet after Mohammed, it would have been Al-Ghazali"—al-Suyūṭī, cited by Zwemer.

2) ". . . The greatest, certainly the most sympathetic figure in the history of Islam, and the only teacher of the after generations ever put by a Muslim on a level with the four great Imams."—D. B. Macdonald.

3) "Al-Ghazālī has sometimes been acclaimed in both East and West as the greatest Muslim after Muḥammad, and he is by no means unworthy of that dignity"—W. M. Watt.

4) ". . . A man who stands on a level with Augustine and Luther in religious insight and intellectual vigour"—H. A. R. Gihb.

5) "He was the pivot of existence and the common pool of refreshing waters for all, the soul of the purest part of the people of the Faith, and the road for obtaining the satisfaction of the Merciful. . . . He became the unique one of his own day and for all time among the Moslem learned"—Jamāl al-Dīn; and another nearly contemporary: ". . . An Imam by whose name breasts are dilated and souls revived, in whose literary productions the ink horn exults and the paper quivers with joy, and at the hearing of whose message voices are hushed and heads are bowed."

6) "Ghazali is without doubt the most remarkable figure in all Islam"—T. J. DeBoer.

7) "This man, if ever any have deserved the name, was truly a 'divine,' and he may be justly placed on a level with Origen, so remarkable was he for learning and ingenuity, and gifted with such a rare faculty for the skillful and worthy exposition of doctrine. . . . He was the first of the Mohammedan divines"—Dr. August Tholuck.

8) "I saw the Prophet in a dream, and he was contending with Moses and Jesus regarding the superiority of excellence of the Imam Al-Ghazālī and saying to them: 'Have you had in your sects such a learned and righteous man?' alluding to Al-Ghazālī and they both replied, 'No.'"—al-Damīrī, cited by Zwemer.

9) "'Muḥammad son of ᶜAbdallāh—God bless him and grant him peace!—is the lord of the Prophets, and Muḥammad son of Idrīs is the lord of the Imams and Muḥammad son of Muḥammad son of Muḥammad al-Ghazālī is the lord of the writers [*al-muṣannifīn*]"—al-Ḥaḍarī.

10) "When I was sitting one day, lo, I perceived the gates of heaven opened, and a company of blessed angels descended, having with them a green robe and a precious steed. They stood by a certain grave and brought forth its tenant and clothed him in the green robe and set him on the steed and ascended with him from heaven to heaven, till he passed the seven heavens and rent after them sixty

veils, and I know not whither at last he reached. Then I asked about him, and was answered, 'This is the Imam Al-Ghazālī.' That was after his death; may God Most High have mercy on him!"—al-Zabīdī, cited by Zwemer.

11) "There was in our time a person who disliked al-Ghazālī and who used to censure and calumniate him in Egypt. Then he saw the Prophet—God bless him and grant him peace!—in a dream, and beside him Abū Bakr and [c]Umar, and al-Ghazālī sitting in front of him and saying: 'O Apostle of God, this person speaks against me.' And the Prophet—God bless him and grant him peace!—said: 'Bring the whips!', and he commanded the man to he beaten on account of al-Ghazālī. And this man awoke from sleep and the marks of the whips were still on his back—and he was wont to weep and to recount this to people."—al-Subkī.

12) "The Proof of Islam and the Way of Religion by which one attains the Abode of Peace; collector of [or: uniter of] the scattered parts of the sciences, surpassing in the traditional and the rational. . . . He was a lion, before whom [all other] lions shrank and disappeared; and a perfect full moon, save that its guidance illumined by day; and a man among men, but he the high and towering mountain; and a part of creation, but as pearls set in order are a part of the stones; he came when men stood in greater need of the refutation of the philosophers than the darknesses of the lights of heaven and in greater want than the arid land of drops of water. He fought for the True Religion with the charm of his utterance and defended the area of religion without being stained by the blood of those who passed the boundary of his blades until religion was firmly consolidated and the darkness of doubts were routed and became only fabricated prattle. In addition to this, his heart enclosed a piety and a solitude in which his chosen companion was none other than obedience to God and a denudation [*tajrīd*] which makes him visible, for he indeed was unique in the sea of unification [*tawḥīd*: or, proclamation of God's unity; this and *tajrīd* have Sufi overtones]—

> He cast down the page to lighten his luggage,
> And his provisions, and even his sandal he discarded.

He left the world behind him and devoted himself to God, dealing [only] with Him privately and publicly."—al-Subkī in what Jabre calls *"une longue introduction dans le style décadent de l'époque."*

13 Such is a sampler of the items which the proleptic scrapbook of Ghazālī or of one of his friends might have contained. But it was not all sweetness and light of adulation. Ghazālī had his critics, and even his detractors and vilifiers, as we shall see. But enough has been said to indicate that he was a very extraordinary man. Extraordinary, yes: but also a man. And what can be said about the man Ghazālī? [c]Abd al-Karīm, al-[c]Uthmān has published a compilation of the principal Arabic biographical sketches of Ghazālī under the title *Sīrat al-Ghazālī.* It includes the

earliest, that of ᶜAbd al-Ghāfir al-Fārisī, who died in 529 (1138), eighteen years after the death of Ghazālī, followed by those of Ibn ᶜAsākir al-Dimashqī [d. 571/1175], Abū l-Faraj son of al-Jawzī [d. 597/1200], Yāqūt al-Ḥamawī [d. 681/1282], Ibn Khillikān [d. 681/1282], al-Dhahabī [d. 748/1347], al-Yāfiᶜī al-Yamānī [d. 768/1366], al-Subkī [d. 771/1369], and al-Zabīdī [d. 1205/1790]. Usually, the more recent the biography, the longer it is, and also, in most cases, the less informative. What I propose to do here is to give a translation of the earliest biography of Ghazālī, that of ᶜAbd al-Ghāfir al-Fārisī, who actually knew Ghazālī. Some further notes will be added from other sources.

ᶜAbd al-Ghāfir's Life of Ghazālī

14 Abū l-Ḥasan ᶜAbd al-Ghāfir son of Ismāᶜīl, the Khaṭīb [the preacher] al-Fārisī [wrote the following biography of Ghazālī]: "The Khaṭīb of Nīsābūr, Muḥammad son of Muḥammad son of Muḥammad Abū Ḥāmid al-Ghazālī, the Proof of Islam and the Muslims, the Imam of the Imams of Religion, whose like eyes have not seen in eloquence and elucidation, and speech and thought, and acumen and natural ability, in his childhood in Ṭūs, acquired some learning in jurisprudence from the Imam Aḥmad al-Rādhkānī. Then he went to Nīsābūr where, with a group of youths from Ṭūs, he frequented the lectures of the Imam al-Ḥaramayn [the Imam of the two sancturies, i.e. Mecca and Medina, so called from his enforced sojourn there]. He worked so hard and seriously that he finished his studies in a short time. He outstripped his fellows and mastered the Qurᵓān, and became the best reasoner [*anẓar*] of the men of his time and matchless among his fellows in the days of the Imam al-Ḥaramayn. The students used to derive profit from him, and he would instruct them and guide them and work hard himself [or: formulate his own independent judgments]. He finally reached the point where he began to compose works. The Imam, despite his high rank and lofty diction and the speed of his flow in speech and discussion, did not have a sincere private regard for Ghazālī because of his dislike for his speed in expression and his natural ability, nor was he pleased by his literary undertakings, even though Ghazālī had been trained by him and was associated with him, as is not unknown regarding human nature; but he made an outward show of pride in him and esteem for his position, contrary to what he hid in his heart. And Ghazālī continued thus until the end of the Imam's days.

15 "Then Ghazālī left Nīsābūr and went to the ᶜAskar [usually: *al-Muᶜaskar*—camp-court, political and military base] and was officially

[or: warmly] welcomed by Niẓām al-Mulk. And the Master [i.e. Niẓām] took an interest in him because of his high rank and conspicuous name and his excellence in disputation and his command of expression. And His Excellency was the stopping-place of the ulema and the goal of the imams and the literary men. So there befell Ghazālī some fine encounters from contact with the imams and meeting tough adversaries and disputing with luminaries and arguing with the distinguished, and his name became known in distant lands. He took the fullest advantage of that until circumstances led to his being appointed to go to Baghdad to take charge of the teaching in the blessed Nīẓāmiyya School there. He went off to Baghdad and his teaching and disputation delighted everyone and he met no one like himself, and after holding the Imamate of Khurāsān he became the Imam of ᶜIrāq.

16 "Then he looked into the science of the "roots" [*ᶜilm al uṣūl*—i.e. the roots, or bases, or sources, of jurisprudence] and when he had mastered them he composed some books on that science; and he refurbished the school [of jurisprudence: the Shāfiᶜite] and wrote works on it; and he molded *al-khilāf* [i.e. the branch dealing with differences in jurisprudential matters] and also composed new works on that. His rank and entourage (?) in Baghdad became so great that it surpassed the entourage of the notables and the princes and the residence of the caliph. Then, from another aspect, the matter was turned around.

17 "After studying the subtle sciences and applying himself to the books written about them, he was overwhelmed and followed the path of asceticism and godliness, and he gave up his entourage and cast away the rank he had attained to devote himself to the causes of piety and the provisions for the afterlife. So he left his occupations and repaired to the House of God and performed the Pilgrimage. Then he entered Damascus and remained in that region for nearly ten years, wandering about and visiting the venerated religious shrines, and he began to compose the renowned works to which no one had preceded him, such as *The Quickening of the Religious Sciences* and the books abridged therefrom, such as *The Forty* [Chapters] and others of the treatises which, if one reflects on them, he will know the man's place vis-à-vis the branches of learning.

18 "He began to battle against self and to regulate his character and to improve his qualities and to rectify his life-style. Thus the devil of frivolity and of seeking leadership and fame and of taking on bad qualities was transformed into serenity of soul and nobility of qualities, having done with [outward] forms and rites. He took on the apparel of the godly and reduced his hope and devoted his time to the guidance of men and to

summoning them to what concerned them regarding the afterlife and to making the world and preoccupation with it hateful to those in via [i.e. to the afterlife], and to preparation for the departure to the everlasting abode and obedience to everyone in whom he saw a promise of or smelt the fragrance of [spiritual] succor or alertness to any glimmer of the lights of [mystical] vision until he became pliant and supple regarding that.

19 "Then he returned to his native land where he kept fast to his house, preoccupied with meditation, tenacious of his time, a godly goal and treasure for hearts to everyone who repaired to him and visited him. That went on for some time, and [his] works appeared and [his] books circulated. In his own day there appeared no opposition to what he was doing nor did anyone object to what he prescribed. Finally the office of Minister [Wazīr] came to the most venerable Fakhr al-Mulk [son of Niẓām, assassinated by a Bāṭinite in 500]—may God encompass him with His mercy! Khur was adorned with the latter's entourage and government. He had heard of and verified Ghazālī's position and rank and the perfection of his superiority and his standing and the purity of his belief and his social intercourse. So he sought a blessing from him and had him brought and listened to what he had to say. Then he asked Ghazālī not to let his breaths and useful lessons remain sterile, with no one profiting from them or learning from their lights, and he went all out in importuning and suggesting until Ghazālī agreed to go forth. He was transported to Nīsābūr—and the lion was absent from his lair, and the matter was hidden in the veiled and secret decree of God. Then Ghazālī was invited to teach in the blessed Niẓāmiyya School [of Nīsābūr]—God grant it length of days! He could not but yield to his master. By bringing forth that with which he had busied himself he aimed at guiding the trained [educated, those with learning] and benefiting the seekers [of learning] without going back to what he had been divested of, viz. seeking honor and wrangling with his peers and condemning the headstrong.

20 "How often was he attacked by opposition and defamation and calumniation regarding what he did not or did and slander and vilification: but he was unaffected by it and did not busy himself with answering the slanderers nor did he manifest any distress at the calumny of the confused [or: the muddle-headed, or: the scheming]. Indeed, I often visited him, and I did not find in him what I had formerly been familiar with in his regard, viz. maliciousness [or: peevishness] and making people uneasy and regarding them disdainfully and looking down upon them out of haughtiness and arrogance and being dazzled by his own endowment of skill in speech and thought and expression, and his quest of glory and high status: he had

become the exact opposite and had been cleansed of those impurities. I used to think that he was wrapped in the garment of constraint [or: affectation] and "blessed" by what he had achieved [the phrase is ambiguous: it perhaps has the nuance of "having his head turned by good fortune" (?)]. Then I realized, after reflection and examination, that the matter was not as I thought, and that the man had recovered from madness.

21 "He related to us on certain nights how his circumstances had been from the beginning of his manifest following of the path of godliness and the victory of the mystical state (?) over him after his delving into the sciences and his behaving arrogantly toward all by virtue of his [superiority in] discourse [or: arguing], and the readiness with which God favored him in the acquisition of the various kinds of knowledge, and his capability for investigation and speculation until he became dissatisfied with preoccupation with the sciences alien to conduct and he reflected on the outcome and on what was profitable and useful regarding the afterlife. He had begun in the company of al-Fāramdī and learned from him the beginning of the Way, and he followed what he suggested to him, viz. the performance of the offices of worship and intentness on works of supererogation and seeking to practice *dhikr* [remembrance of God; or the practice so designated] continuously and assiduity and diligence in the quest for salvation until he traversed those steep paths and undertook those hardships—but he did not attain the goal of his questing.

22 "Then he related that he reviewed the sciences and waded into the [various] branches and applied anew his assiduity and diligence to the books on the subtle sciences, and he so acquired their interpretation that their doors were opened to him. For a while he remained preoccupied with their details and the counterbalancing of the proofs and the different sides of the problems. Then he related that there was opened for him a door of fear to such an extent that it distracted him from everything and compelled him to abandon all else with the result that it became easy for him, and so on and so on until he became fully practiced [in religious matters] and truths were manifest to him and what we used to think was manipulation [?] and put-on [?] became [his] nature and ascertainment [conviction]. That was a sign of the beatitude decreed for him by God.

23 "Then we asked him how he had come to wish to leave his house and to return to what he was summoned to, viz. the business of Nīsābūr. In defense of that he said: According to my religion I could not conceivably hold back from the summons and the utility of benefiting the seekers [of knowledge]. It was indeed imperative for me to disclose the truth and to speak of it and to call to it—and he was truthful in that.

24 "Then he forsook that before being himself forsaken and returned to his house. He set up nearby a school [*madrasa*] for the seekers of knowledge and a place of sojourn [*khānqāh:* a kind of monastic dwelling (?)] for the Sufis. He apportioned his time to the tasks of those present, such as the recital of the Qurʾān and keeping company with the men of hearts [sufis, or, sufi masters (?)] and sitting down to teach, so that not a single one of his moments or of those with him was profitless. [This went on] until the eye of time attained him and the days begrudged him to the men of his age. Then [God] translated him to His gracious proximity after his endurance of the varied attacks and opposition of his adversaries and his being led to kings [?].

25 "And God protected him and preserved him and guarded him from being seized by vexing hands or from having his religion defiled by any slips. The conclusion of his affair was his applying himself to the Tradition[s] of the Elect—God's blessing and peace be upon him!—and frequenting the company of those devoted to it [i.e. Tradition] and reading [or: studying] the two *Ṣaḥīḥs* of al-Bukhārī and Muslim [the two "Sound," or collections of sound Traditions, compiled by the authors mentioned], who are the Proof of Islam. Had he lived, he would have outstripped everyone in that discipline in a small number of the days in which he would have made every effort to acquire that. Doubtless he had heard Traditions in former days, and at the end of his life he busied himself with hearing them, but he did not happen to relate them. There was no disadvantage [or: harm, i.e. he certainly] in what he left behind him of books written on the roots and the branches [of jurisprudence] and all the other kinds [of books] which immortalize his memory, and it is owned by all the students who have profited from them that he did not leave his like after him.

26 "He passed to the mercy of God on Monday, the fourteenth of Jumādā II, in the year 505 [Dec. 18, 1111 A.D.]. He was buried in the outskirts of the citadel (?) of Ṭābarān. And God favors him with various marks of esteem in his afterlife, just as He favored him with various kinds of learning in his life here below. He left only daughters. He had of the means of subsistence, by inheritance and by his earnings, what provided him with a sufficiency and the support of his household and his children. He was not at ease with [or: beholden to (?)] anyone regarding temporal [secular] affairs; wealth had been offered to him, but he did not accept it and shunned it and was content with the amount which would preserve his religion [i.e. keep him independent] and with which he would not need to address himself to asking and receiving from others." [End of the biographical account]

27 The last short section of ᶜAbd al-Ghāfir al-Fārisī's account is devoted mostly to answering some criticisms which were directed at Ghazālī—grammatical weaknesses, his use of some Persian words, and occasional injudicious writing which might harm those not capable of understanding it properly. This section need not detain us here, for we shall have more to say about Ghazālī's critics later.

28 Such is the oldest, and perhaps the most authentic, biography of Ghazālī. It is sober and brief, and it does not tell us much that we should like to know. Even the *Munqidh* is more informative, though more *l'histoire d'une âne* than *l'histoire d'un homme.* But, as in so many other cases in Islamic history, the simple account was greatly expanded during succeeding generations. I have no intention of entertaining—or wearying—the reader with details of little real value. Fortunately we possess the considerable corpus of Ghazālī's authentic writings. These more than reveal his charm and his greatness and his significance for Muslims and non-Muslims, both his contemporaries and ours. Here I merely mention the valuable articles by Macdonald and Jabre and the books by Margaret Smith and Samuel Zwemer. In these, and in many other obvious items mentioned in the Annotated Bibliography, the interested reader may pursue his quest for the "life" of Ghazālī: I am more interested in trying to understand and appreciate his "spirit"—or what he himself might refer to as his *qalb* [cf. Appendix V].

Ghazālī's Works

29 At this point I propose to offer some general remarks on Ghazālī's literary output before dealing in detail with the work which is of primary interest in this book. Like certain other Muslim polymaths and more specialized writers, Ghazālī left behind him a rich legacy of works. It is not my intention to try to list all his works here, or to discuss the status of those which are of doubtful authenticity. Father Maurice Bouyges has dealt most competently with Ghazālī's works and their chronological order, and I refer the interested reader to his book as edited by the much regretted Father Michel Allard [cf. Annotated Bibliography]. Even the casual reader will be struck by the abundance and the variety of Ghazālī's writings. His primary function, during his teaching periods, was to teach *fiqh* [Islamic jurisprudence]. But he was also thoroughly versed in *kalām* [the basically polemic theology of Islam] and philosophy and mysticism [Sufism].

30 Of Ghazālī's books on jurisprudence I am not qualified to speak with any authority, but some of them have remained renowned right down to our own day. Incidentally, I may observe here that anyone seeking the

quintessential *Islamic* thought cannot afford to overlook the area of *fiqh,* though I know of no one who has really exploited it thoroughly. Professor Joseph Schacht, my own revered mentor, could have done it, but, unfortunately, he died before reaching his full potential and productivity.

31 Ghazālī's greatest work was undoubtedly his *Iḥyā*ʾ *ʿUlūm al-Dīn* [The Revivification, or Quickening, of the Sciences of Religion—i.e. of the learning closely related to the religion of Islam]. This is a truly monumental work which alone would place Ghazālī among the great writers and thinkers and deeply spiritual men of mankind. It consists of four "Quarters," each of which contains ten books. The First Quarter begins with two introductory books on knowledge and on the bases of orthodox beliefs. The remaining books deal with ritual purity, the prescribed acts of worship, or the so-called "Five Pillars of Islam"—the canonical Prayer, almsgiving, fasting and the pilgrimage (the first "Pillar," the profession of faith, was dealt with in the second book of this Quarter) —and certain other practices.

32 The Second Quarter discusses what are called *ʿādāt* [usages, ways of acting or of comporting oneself]. These include the etiquette, or decorum, to be observed in the use of food, the proper use of marriage, the practice of friendship, and so on. The Third Quarter has for its subject *al-muhlikāt* [the things which lead to perdition]. It begins with a psychological masterpiece on the explanation of the "mysteries of the heart"" [cf. Appendix V]. The second book deals with the mortification of oneself and the acquisition of good moral qualities and the cure of the heart's maladies. The remaining books are concerned with the overcoming of the appetites, especially those connected with the misuse of food and drink and sex, and of the various other vices.

33 The Fourth Quarter, in which Ghazālī rises to spiritual heights, is the Quarter of *al-munjiyāt* [the things which lead to final salvation]. Among its subjects are repentance, patience, gratitude, fear, hope, poverty, love, familiarity with God, intention, spiritual watchfulness over oneself, the examen of conscience, meditation [or: reflection], and, as a fitting conclusion, death and the afterlife. For a much more detailed synopsis the reader is referred to Bousquet's book mentioned in the Annotated Bibliography.

34 But no synopsis, however detailed, can replace actual contact with the text of the *Iḥyā*ʾ. Several of its books have been translated into various modern languages. But even these fail to convey the indescribable "savor" of the original text. There we find not only a remarkably flexible and beguiling Arabic, but also a clarity of thought and a felicity of example and anecdote combined with deep psychological insights and a grasp

of what I can only call "the divine." A sympathetic global reading makes it easy to understand why one old author affirmed that the *Iḥyāʾ* would supply for all Islamic literature if the latter were to be lost. And he said "Islamic," not "Arabic." For this master work of Ghazālī does, I think, convey all that is best and most appealing in Islam as a religion and a "revelation" of God's love for man and the heights attainable by man's love for God.

35 One of Ghazālī's major concerns was the threat posed to Islam by Bāṭinism. His own protector and patron, Niẓām al-Mulk, was assassinated by a Bāṭinite, as were several other outstanding men of the time. And it has even been suggested that Ghazālī's abrupt departure from Baghdad was motivated by a personal fear for his own safety—though I find this somewhat exaggerated. At any rate he addressed himself to polemic against the Bāṭinites in more than one of his works. Indeed, in some of this polemic he loses his customary academic serenity and becomes almost shrill in his denunciations. However, I need not dwell here on this aspect of his writing, since the reader will find ample evidence of it in Appendixes II and III.

36 Philosophy was another field which occupied Ghazālī's mind and pen. He was certainly a master of the Aristotelian logic and wrote brilliantly on it. He was also preoccupied with the ancient physics and metaphysics, especially as interpreted and taught by the Islamic philosophers such as al-Fārābī and Ibn Sīnā [Avicenna]. With keen perception he saw the dangers inherent in certain doctrines of the latter. This resulted in his writing two important works. The first was *Maqāṣid al-Falāsifa* [The Aims of the Philosophers—Intentiones Philosophorum], a lucid and well-organized exposition of the logic, physics, and metaphysics of the ancients as presented by the "modern" Islamic philosophers. This was followed by the intellectual bombshell entitied *Tahāfut al-Falāsifa* [The Incoherence of the Philosophers—Destructio Philosophorum]. According to some this sounded the death knell of philosophy in Islam—an opinion with which I cannot entirely agree. For many decades it awaited a reply by Ibn Rushd [Averroes], a reply the adequacy of which is debatable [cf. Annotated Bibliography under van den Bergh: his book presents both texts with valuable notes].

37 The only work of Ghazālī which deals explicitly with *kalām* is his *al-Iqtiṣād fī l-Iʿtiqād* [The Golden Mean in Belief]. It addresses the great theological questions succinctly and, in my view, more competently than most of the works of the professed *mutakallimūn.* It has been quite adequately translated by the great Spanish orientalist M. Asin Palacios [cf.

Annotated Bibliography]. It is clear from some of Ghazālī's prefatory remarks, and from other writings of his, that Ghazālī had no very high regard for *kalām.* He recognized its essential character of a defensive apologetic and countenanced its use in certain limited cases as a possible remedy for those beset with doubts about the faith. Interestingly enough his very last work, completed a few days before his death, was *Iljām al-ᶜAwāmm ᶜan al-Khawḍ fī ᶜIlm al-Kalām* [Curbing the Masses from Engaging in the Science of Kalām].

38 Ghazālī authored many other works. I merely call the reader's attention here to the two books which are the subjects of Appendixes I and IV. The first throws considerable light on Ghazālī's theological serenity and liberality. The second is a fine example of his gift for drawing spiritual treasures out of usages which were always in danger of becoming mechanical and ill-informed by the true spirit of Islam. I shall not try to settle any of the vexed questions about certain works which are considered by many to be falsely attributed to Ghazālī. The interested reader will find discussions of these in some of the materials indicated in the Annotated Bibliography. And none of them creates any real problem concerning our primary interest in this book.

The Munqidh

39 I now turn to the work which is unique among all of Ghazālī's books, and, indeed, unique in all of the classical Arabic literature. Whether it was the first of its kind is not altogether clear. Some have referred to the *Munqidh* as "The Confessions of al-Ghazālī" and this led to the inevitable comparison with Augustine's famous work. It has also been called Ghazālī's "Apologia pro vita sua," with a Newman resonance, though Frick more perspicaciously referred to it as "Apologia pro doctrina sua." I still think, however, that the *Munqidh* possesses its own "uniqueness" for reasons which should become apparent to the reader's own appreciation of the book.

40 The title of the book occurs in two readings. One is *Al-Munqidh min al-Ḍalāl wa l-mufṣiḥ ᶜan al-Aḥwāl* [What Saves from Error and Manifests (Makes Plain) the States (the mystical states of the soul)]. The second is *Al-Munqidh min al-Ḍalāl wa l-Muwaṣṣil* [or: *al-Mūṣil*] *ilā Dhī l-ᶜIzza wa l-Jalāl* [What Saves from Error and Unites with the Possessor of Power and Glory]. From this it will be seen that possible translations include: Freedom and Fulfillment; Liberation and Illumination; Salvation and Consummation; Preservation and Perfection. I have chosen *Freedom and Fulfillment,* since it seems to apply to both readings.

41 There are many manuscripts of the *Munqidh.* But there is no real critical edition of the text. In his third chapter Father Poggi discusses the history of the text and of its translations. I have been able to use all the translations except those in Dutch and Turkish. As for the English translations, we have those of Field and of Watt. Father Poggi considers Watt's translation to be the best. Why, then, you may ask, have I undertaken to translate the *Munqidh* again? There are several reasons. First of all, it is obvious that no two translators from Arabic to English—*a fortiori* from English to Arabic!—are ever in perfect agreement on a translation. Then, over several pleasant years, it was part of my duty to teach the *Munqidh* to fine groups of students at Oxford. In the course of repeated readings of the text I made my own personal translation which, understandably, I personally preferred to others. But the chief reason for this new translation is that, thanks to my good friend Father Poggi, I obtained photographs of the manuscript of the *Munqidh* contained in No. 1712 of the Sehid Ali Pasa of Istanbul [Constantinople]. This manuscript is dated 509 A.H. [1115–1116 A.D.—see frontispiece], i.e. five years after Ghazālī's death and so about ten years after the composition of the *Munqidh.* It is an almost perfect manuscript. In hundreds of places it differs from the text edited by Drs. Jamīl Ṣalībā and Kāmil ᶜAyyād, which was used by Watt, and which is printed along with Jabre's translation in the UNESCO edition. It is true that most of the differences are very minor. But in several places the difficulties found in the printed text are cleared up by the manuscript readings. So my translation is based on the precious manuscript, and in my notes I have called attention to several of its different readings. As a final reason I may observe that acknowledged classics deserve to be translated over and over for the sake of new generations and to benefit by the constantly growing body of knowledge about distant times and authors.

42 No doubt seems ever to have been expressed about the authenticity of the *Munqidh.* But some aspersions have been cast on the sincerity of its author, as we shall see. As for its literary genre, it is clearly not a straightforward biographical account. Ghazālī sets forth, in a rather contrived fashion, the stages of his intellectual and spiritual evolution. But he does have an axe to grind. Clearly this is his intention to promote Sufism—and in fact he has been credited with making Sufism "respectable" in the Islamic milieu of his time and after. But quite another view of the *Munqidh* has been taken by an Egyptian author named Dr. ᶜAbd al-Dāᵓim al-Baqarī in his book entitled *Iᵓtirāfāt al-Ghazālī* [The Confessions of al-Ghazālī], Cairo, 1943.

43 To put it bluntly, Dr. al-Baqarī thinks that the account of the *Munqidh* is neither true nor sincere. As Father Abd-El Jalil puts it: "By the sub-title *'Kayfa arrakha al-Ghazālī linafsihi'* [How Ghazālī drafted his own history] the author [al-Baqarī] already orientates his own position. For him the account of the *Munqidh* is neither veridical nor sincere. There would be no question there of an *Apologia pro vita sua,* and still less of an Autobiography, but rather of a sort of novel with a proposition (*roman à thèse*) of which the hero would be Ghazālī himself. The great Muslim thinker would have sought, very consciously and often very judiciously, to leave to posterity a fictional image of his personality and to give an interpretation of his life which give him an unrivalled place in all the domains of thought and of the life of the Muslims of his time, including especially the knowledge and practice of *taṣawwuf* [Sufism]. And that thanks to a wise dosage of avowals and insinuations—in which he sometimes betrays himself—a wise dosage which, without being totally false, would not correspond to the historical reality." Father Abd-El-Jalil goes on to discuss the book at considerable length, and the details of his discussion need not detain us much longer.

44 Father Abd-El-Jalil points out that the control level of all the machinery mounted by al-Baqarī against the *Munqidh* is found in the text where Ghazālī declares that up to the moment of his realization of the necessity of the practices of Sufism his intentions had not been pure; even in his best activity, that of teaching, "it was not directed purely to God, but rather was instigated and motivated by the quest for fame and widespread prestige" [Trans. Para 85]. Al-Baqarī makes this avowal the explicative principle of the whole life of Ghazālī. "of all his actions, movements, reposes and intentions, not only before his withdrawal but even after." So the steps of his intellectual and spiritual evolution, as he describes them in the *Munqidh,* have no real existence: they are imagined by Ghazālī at the moment that he writes his account. The pretended trial of doubt is only the ruse of a rhetorician who wants to make himself pass for a free inquirer among a crowd of the slaves of "conformism" [*taqlīd*]. The alleged mystical experience, of which Ghazālī assumed some external appearances, was aimed at adding, to the prestige and renown of the incomparable jurisprudent and the unrivaled conqueror of the philosophers and the Taᶜlīmites, the aureole of sanctity. Really it was all part of Ghazālī's clever and careful progress toward his goal.

45 "What he wishes is to have ascribed to himself the prestige and the renown unattained, in extension and comprehension, by any other prestige and renown. For that he wishes, by the description of the different

steps of his life as he has imagined them, to inculcate a precise conception of the role which he wanted to be acknowledged in the history of Islam: that of the initiator of a religious reform, of a renewer of religion at the dawn of the beginning century, of a man raised up by God to revivify Islam by leading it to the sole source of certitude, the prophetic light, to which the way of *taṣawwuf* conduces. So the *Munqidh* is found to be stripped of all historical value; it is an account woven from certain lived realities mixed with 'realities of desire' [*mutamannayyāt*], or with symbolic realities [*mithāliy-yāt*]."

46 Al-Baqarī admits that Ghazālī was a great Muslim and that his reputation extends to the non-Muslim world. So he endeavors to find some excuse for his "trickery" in the *Munqidh.* The excuse, curiously enough, he finds in Ghazālī's doctrine on lying as set forth in the *Iḥyā'* [Book XXIV (Fourth of the Third Quarter), On the Defects of the Tongue: the 14th Defect]. Ghazālī agreed with other Muslim doctors that lying is not intrinsically wrong, and that, in certain cases, it is licit and sometimes even obligatory. For language is a means to attain ends. If a praiseworthy end can be attained without lying, then veracity is obligatory and lying is absolutely forbidden. But if such an end can be attained only by lying, then lying is obligatory if the end is necessary, and permissible if the end is permissible, but always within certain limits. For lying is an evil which ought to be avoided and to which men are inclined by egoism and cupidity.

47 Father Abd-El-Jalil points out that al-Baqarī uses this teaching of Ghazālī, but unfortunately with certain lacunae which seem intentional and which permit him to insinuate as a general principle what Ghazālī did not really claim as such. He also makes the term *īṣlāḥ,* which is used by Ghazālī in the sense of "reconciliation," possess the wider sense [which the word may have] of "reform." Hence [Abd-El-Jalil] the thesis: Ghazālī wishes to leave behind him the renown most envied in the Muslim world, that of a reformer who revivifies religion. He constructs the *Munqidh* by directing it toward that end and invents wholly, or nearly so, the account of a spiritual evolution which led him, through theoretical study and practical experimentation, from the doubt of the sophists to the certitude of the mystics. In forging this history he harms no one, or at most only himself. Moreover he has a good intention. So even if he does not invent it to try to justify himself, he does thereby induce believers to reform themselves and presents them with a model, one of their contemporaries, one of the greatest, himself, who was able to preserve himself from all the assaults of error and to verify loyally the ways which presented themselves to lead to certitude, and of which only *taṣawwuf* [Sufism] is sure because it leads to "the light of prophecy."

48 The weakness of such a construction—that of al-Baqarī's—seems evident to Father Abd-El-Jalil because of its apriorism, its contrived [systematique] character, its aggressiveness, its "lacunae," its paralogisms, and "the geometric spirit" of its author. So I have no hesitation in agreeing with Father Abd-El-Jalil's conclusion: "Nothing of that authorizes a doubt about Ghazālī's sincerity. The human, intellectual and spiritual value of the *Munqidh* remains firm, though it cannot *of itself alone* serve as an historical source." Ghazālī's primary purpose in writing seems to have been didactic, not to give a detailed and precise historical account of himself. Some contrivance and some suppression were involved, but not, I believe, any lying. As for al-Baqarī's somewhat strange book, it is not necessarily the kind of "cheap shot" not unknown in history, viz. creating an impression and achieving a certain "fame" by an attack on a figure habitually revered and admired. We need not be uncharitable because another may have been, or may not have been, uncharitable.

49 I now wish to raise a question which is not unrelated to the problem of Ghazālī's sincerity and truthfulness. The question is this: Why did Ghazālī, at the apex of his public career, suddenly give it all up and go off to live, for about ten years, the life of a wandering Sufi? His own account of the affair will be found in my translation, Paras. 84 ff. These are surely the most moving pages of the *Munqidh.* I see no reason why they should not be accepted literally, despite al-Baqarī and, as we shall see, Father Jabre. In other words, I am convinced that Ghazālī, in his second and far greater crisis, underwent a true *conversion,* a real *tawba* [turning to God], a genuine *metanoia* [change of mind and heart], which set him on the path of spiritual perfection. To support this view I feel justified in citing rather largely from Father Poggi, and also, on the other side, from Father Jabre—especially since their works may not be easily available to the general reader.

50 This citation from Father Poggi is from the eighth chapter of his book. This chapter is entitled "Il Sufismo nel Munqiḏ," and my citation begins on p. 187. "But it is only in these last pages of the *Munqidh* . . . that the enthusiasm for Sufism is tempered with reserves concerning the abuses of a degenerate Sufism. On the contrary, in the chapter which is entitled 'The Ways of Sufism (*sic*!)' Ghazālī is not stingy with expressions of praise and his unconditioned approval. Only à propos of the terms with which is designated the apex of contact with God in mystical ecstasy does Ghazālī manifest his aversion for every term which could engender the suspicion of any form whatever of pantheism. But in the *Munqidh* it is not said that such dangerous terminology was in use among the Sufis themselves nor does Ghazālī reproach any of them with it.

51 "Moreover the chapter 'The Ways of the Sufis' occupies a most important place in the structure of the *Munqidh,* not only because the encounter with the Muslim mysticism of his time was decisive for the development of Ghazālī's religious thought as well as because for our author a certain dose of Sufism would seem necessary to revive religious practice and to gain the battle against error, but also because the 'second crisis' of Ghazālī is described precisely in this chapter and is found entirely inserted in a Sufi context. If indeed the first crisis had rescued Ghazālī from the slavery of pure *taqlīd* [conformism] and caused him to find out that one cannot go beyond the first principles and that it is impossible to build on them a science apodeictic and of irrefutable religious convictions, this second crisis of which he speaks in the chapter on 'The Ways of Sufism' is rather a moral crisis and, better than the preceding, could be called 'conversion.' Relating it he describes the passage from the intense and most respected life of the master in the Niẓāmiyya school of Baghdad to the life of the wandering sufi which imposes as an iron rule of conduct the renouncement of the world and of everything which could separate from God. Speaking of Sufism as the spiritual doctrine which insists not only on theory but on practice and which cannot be understood save directly through taste [*dhawq*], i.e. direct experience, Ghazālī affirms his arrival at the conviction that there must be for him a clean break with the past if he does not wish to renounce as of now the hope of eternal life. . . .

52 "Now the battle is engaged within himself between the desire to continue the honored life led up to now and the interior call, impelling and implacable, to a more perfect life of abnegation and renouncement. This is one of the most human pages of the *Munqidh* and it may justly be compared with the 'partim velle, partim nolle' of the *Confessions* of Augustine—VIII, 21. . . .

53 "Here, however, it was not a question of passing from a sinful life to the life of the just, but of abandoning an exterior justice sufficient for being considered a true believer in the eyes of others, yet completely insufficient for responding to the exigences of spiritual perfection. Ghazālī, who had confessed to finding until then theory easier than practice, discovered in the conduct of the Sufis the necessary compenetration of these two aspects, of thought and of action, in personal religious behavior. Indeed his statement that 'theory was easier for me than practice' follows his acquired knowledge that 'the Sufi Way is essentially made up of knowledge and of action.' Of this discovery Ghazālī declares himself an enthusiastic champion . . . [Para. 82].

54 "So one cannot be satisfied with 'knowing.' One must 'do.' And Ghazālī begins coherently with an examen of conscience on the state of soul in which he found himself at that moment [Para. 85].

55 "As we have already said à propos of the truthfulness of the *Munqidh,* this confession which Ghazālī makes publicly has all the criteria of sincerity. . . . The consequence which Ghazālī deduces from this pitiless examination of conscience is fear of the divine chastisements—'So I became certain that I was on the brink of a crumbling bank and already on the verge of falling into the Fire, unless I set about mending my ways' [Para. 85].

56 "In such fashion the interior battle of Ghazālī began. The Author even fixes its chronological extremes and describes it with an extraordinary effectiveness and a noteworthy psychological profundity. Perhaps none of the autobiographical elements of the *Munqidh* is so revelatory of Ghazālī's personality as this page is. 'I therefore reflected unceasingly on this for some time, while I still had freedom of choice' [Para. 86]. And the choice for men like Ghazālī, strongly emotional and introspective but much less inclined to action, becomes precisely a tormenting fury with its steps ahead and its sudden withdrawals, doubts and uncertainties and above all the affective coloration, with more and more painful soul states and a physiological repercussion on the whole humoral condition . . . [Paras. 86–88].

57 "This time too, as in the case of the epistemological crisis, the tension and anguish reach the climax before giving way to the sudden solution which Ghazālī attributes only to the divine mercy [Para. 89]. By now he is so decided on leaving Baghdad that he even devises a stratagem directed at gutting the danger that the authorities might impede him for reasons of public utility from giving up teaching [Para. 89]. His proposing a pilgrimage to Mecca while he had in mind a definitive departure for Syria scandalized Zwemer . . . because its first steps were taken in the sign of falsity and subterfuge. But it seems to us that this overly severe accusation ought to be refuted. The pilgrimage to Mecca was in fact accomplished two years later. The milieu of the time really manifested the greatest obtuseness regarding the reasons which pushed Ghazālī to leave. He had, then, foreseen this hostile incomprehension and had forearmed himself with that innocent pretext of the pilgrimage. We can also even deduce from such a particular that Ghazālī had reached the irrefragable decision to emerge from a state of uncertainty which was consuming body and spirit. The very tone of the narrative now becomes peaceful and serene [Para. 92].

58 "His life in this period is very different from that of the famous imam venerated by students and consulted by princes. He even asserts with a certain pride that he had perdured for ten years far from teaching and that, in this phase, he had reached the loftiest summits of spirituality [Para. 94]. From this point he enters into his unconditioned panegyric of the Sufi life [Paras. 95 ff.].

59 "The fact that the Sufis 'attain to the lamp of the prophetic revelation' is undoubtedly a reason for Ghazālī's sympathy for them, for him who was preoccupied with the indifference of his contemporaries regarding the divine Revelation mediated through the Prophets. But the principal cause of Ghazālī's making himself a propagandist of the 'way of the Sufis' is more profound. They recognize indeed the necessity of purifying the heart and work conformably to such a conviction. In a word it would be a question of a confirmation of what Father Jabre calls 'the great theory of Ghazālī,' or the necessity of purification of the heart to attain the essence of reality." [this notion Father Poggi does not entirely accept: cf. his long note 47, p. 201.]

60 "Simplifying for reasons of clarity one might thus sum up the position of Ghazālī: Sufism is not to be studied, but should be lived. The first condition for entrance into its 'way' is precisely the purification of the heart from all that is not God. In such fashion is theory blended with practice, as is particularly characteristic of Sufism. Thus before the seeker of the truth is opened that new form of knowledge which has as instrument *dhawq,* taste or direct experience.

61 "Such a new form of intuitive and concrete apprehension of reality is essential, for Ghazālī, to grasp the reality of the prophetic revelation and the necessity of an unconditioned and coherent faith in the revealed datum communicated to us from God by means of an authentic Prophet. In such case, seeing the *Munqidh* in its true apologetic aspect as van Leeuwen justly wished, the importance of Ghazālī's encounter with Sufism and the propaganda for that conception of life acquire, it seems to us, all their perspicuous plausibility. Most times error arises from a failure to control the passions and the instinctive tendencies. Speaking of philosophy Ghazālī had said that men can remain attached to a false conception of reality suffered passively at the beginning without remaining convinced by apodeictic contrary arguments because they are slaves 'of vain passion and of love of appearing to be clever' [Para. 40] persisting in a given judgment. Now Sufism, by striking out along the way of ascetism and the purification of the heart liberates man from this most frequent negative factor, one of the main causes of error.

62 "The 'conversion' of Ghazālī, that described precisely in the chapter on Sufism, is only liberation, not so much from actual and proper error, as from this constant danger of falling into it in which Ghazālī found himself when he was intent on diffusing a knowledge promising in return only worldly splendor and honor [Para. 139]. The practice of the purification of the heart and of the control of one's own states of soul, learned in the school of the Sufis carried with it the experience of that form of apprehension through contact which among them was another principal distinctive sign.

63 "Briefly, it is in this perspective, rather than in that of an acclaimed subjectivism (we have in mind the essay of Obermann) that the Ghazālī of the *Munqidh* is to be considered. At most, paradoxically it would have to be said that Ghazālī becomes subjective through a scruple of objectivity. Ghazālī falls back on himself to remove the interior obstacle to the objective vision of reality. Convinced, as we ourselves are, that the religious solution of the problem of reality is a solution postulated by the facts and especially by the discovery of our own limits, Ghazālī seeks a valid and incontestable foundation for sincere religiousness. Augustine had discovered that God is *'intimius intimo meo,'* i.e. He is found above all by reentering into ourselves and listening to the dialogue of our own conscience with Him. On his own part Ghazālī discovers in the school of the Sufis that man enters into conscious contact with God, i.e. fully confronts the religious problem, with all of himself without excluding his emotivity and action. Thus for him, as for the mystics of the Meccan and Baghdad school, *ᶜilm, ḥāl,* and *ᶜamal* are *pleno iure* essential constituents of religiousness.

64 "How much of the Sufi 'way' Ghazālī had covered can be deduced from the pages of the *Munqidh.* He speaks of successive and gradual stages of mystical ascent. 'From the very start of the Way revelations and visions begin. . . . Then their state [*ḥāl*] ascends from the vision of forms and likenesses to stages beyond the narrow range of words' [Para. 96]. Everything leads one to believe that Ghazālī has traversed these different stages, from the purgative askesis to the incessant recital of the name of God [*dhikr*], to the unitive stage of *fanāʾ* [becoming completely lost in God, annihilation: cf. Note 180]. It is true that at a certain point he complains of the preoccupation with his children and the hindrance that cares of a material and economic character constituted for his desire of withdrawal and of solitude. Notwithstanding that, Ghazālī asserts that he sometimes achieved ecstasy and had the revelation of things which could neither be numbered nor expressed [Paras. 9394]. Certainly from the

words of Ghazālī it appears clear that the Author would wish to share with his reader the enthusiasm for similar experiences and for the courageous and heroic undertaking of the Sufi 'way.'

65 "On the contrary it seems to us that Ghazālī would offer to everyone, even to him who would today be called the man in the street, a teaching to draw into contact with Sufism. Certainly the *Munqidh* does not quite encourage the representation of an esoteric Ghazālī determined to reserve for 'the happy few' a spiritual benefit which can turn, according to the various receptive capacities, to the profit of all [Para. 98].

66 "Certainly the royal way to draw fruit from Sufism is actually the way of practice, that precisely which conduces to 'taste it' through the typical form of apprehension which Ghazālī calls *dhawq* [taste, geusis, direct experience]. But, apart from this ideal introduction into the Sufi world, there can be another accessible on a wider scale: that of frequenting the Sufis themselves, of observing them and of listening to them when they narrate their experiences or give counsels of the spiritual life. It is a question in effect of people whose company cannot do other than good. Finally, if not even this entry into contact with them could be realized, an ultimate way would still remain open to the condescension of Ghazālī for those who would at least have the integrity to believe in the existence of this remarkable mystical world. 'But whoever is not favored with their company . . .' [Para. 98].

67 "Ghazālī, on his return from the period of hiding to the public life of Master at Nīsābūr, conscious of a mission which had been reserved to him for the benefit of his co-religionists who were lax in religious practice and hard pressed by the succession of tragic events [Para. 70—'Surely it was to be feared . . .'], then launched to all his calls to inwardness and placed within reach of everyone the fruit of his long sufistic practice." [End of citation from Father Poggi.]

68 I make no excuse for setting this long citation before my reader. It gives what I think is the correct answer to the question asked at the beginning of Para. 49 above. More than that, it emphasizes and interprets the central position played by Sufism in Ghazālī's own life and in his *Munqidh,* and that in a most perceptive way. But now it is only fair to turn to another at least partial answer to that question. This answer is found in two places in the writings of Father Jabre. Since these are not likely to be readily available to the general reader, I shall again have recourse to citations to avoid any appearance of distortion of Father Jabre's view. The first citation is from the Introduction to his translation of the *Munqidh.* He mentions, in abridged form, al-Fārisī's text [Para. 17 above], and then goes on:

69 "What is clearly intended here is the definitive conversion of Ghazālī to sufism. It took place, surely, at the beginning of the year 486/1093–1094. . . . Now one knows from elsewhere that in 484/1091 Ghazālī had arrived in Baghdad with entirely different dispositions. On his own confession he was then seeking 'glory and honors' [Para. 139]. Not that he had lost the faith; he affirms that he had always had a very solid belief in what concerned the three essential dogmas of Islam (the Existence of God, the Last Day and Prophethood) [Para. 83], and there is no reason to doubt his sincerity on this point. But his state of soul vis-à-vis the reasoning built, in his view, on the 'equipollence of proofs,' did not allow him to find on this terrain a valid certitude regarding the three great truths in question. The science of *fiqh* [jurisprudence] does not have as its aim to justify them; it presupposes them as point of departure. Ghazālī, then, could unreservedly give himself up to them and could experience the comforting feeling of touching the real. The concrete object of this discipline [*fiqh*] and the practical results of its deductions were able to give him at least the illusion of the solid, an illusion all the less sensible since he was able to claim to be doing something useful in seconding, on the intellectual level, the effort that Niẓām al-Mulk was supplying to protect the existence of sunnism [roughly: orthodoxy] seriously threatened by the Shiᶜite *Bāṭinism* in its new form, *taᶜlīmism.* So Ghazālī devoted himself to this science of *fiqh* and knew in it success, a success which he appreciated all the more because his profound attachment to his sunnite dogma seemed to him in no wise incompatible with a no less profound attachment to the affairs of this world and their glitter.

70 "What took place between 484/1091 and 486/1093 so that there was in him this total reversal signalized by all the chroniclers and of which [Abū Bakr] Ibn al-ᶜArabī gives the precise date? Why was he thus diverted from the 'Here Below' and its preoccupations to turn himself towards the 'Hereafter' and the 'Science of the hidden aspects of religion' (to resume his own terminology)? Is this 'conversion' due only to factors of an intimate order, spiritual and religious? Their reality certainly must not be denied; but it really seems that these factors were themselves provoked by external causes and that they owe their origin to some historical circumstances which weighed on the life of Ghazālī. Here precise and positive pieces of information are totally lacking, but it is not forbidden, to supply for them, to have recourse to data the cross-checking of which can lead to a certitude, if not convincing, at least quasi-moral.

71 This is that on the 10th of Ramaḍān, 485/1092, Niẓām al-Mulk fell beneath the blows of a young Bāṭinite. It has been said [in another article of Father Jabre] how this event and the upheavals which followed

it, and this in Baghdad itself, must have affected Ghazālī, the protégé and friend of the great Seljuq minister. The death of the latter represented for the Master [Ghazālī] the collapse of a dream of a humano-divine earthly power which together they had long cherished. Is it, then, so rash to affirm that these circumstances led Ghazālī to take no further interest in the 'things of this life' and to turn himself towards the spiritual and religious problems of 'the Hereafter'? In any case it is to this 'conversion' that Ibn al-^{c}Arabī alludes when he declares that from the beginnings of 486/1093 (i.e. several months after the death of Niẓām al-Mulk) Ghazālī pledged himself to sufism and there cleared a way of his own.

72 "But Ibn al-^{c}Arabī was then speaking of a Ghazālī as he had known him in 490/1097 when he met him in Baghdad, which the Master had regained after having left it in 488/1095. Until this date, and despite his engagement in the 'way,' the Master had not believed it necessary to renounce either the intellectual burden of studies or that of teaching. He documents himself on the doctrine of the *falāsifa* [the philosophers] by reading their works; and he still feels himself moved by the 'desire of prestige and a wide renown.' It is only at the last date cited that he feels himself irrevocably pushed to leave all, both the capital of the Caliphs and the 'honorable situation' in which he found himself. And still he does it, following long hesitations, only after he has entrusted his [professorial] chair to his brother and assured the livelihood of his family. Furthermore, he makes it believed that he was going to Mecca when in reality his formal intention was to gain Syria. Whence a whole series of questions: Why does the kind of life which he had been leading since 486/1093 cease to be conformed to the pressing appeals of the Hereafter? Why, in 488/1095, this haste and this decision 'strong and irrefragable' to flee? Why this solicitude to take the precautions necessary so that all hope of recovering his chair at Baghdad be not lost? Why especially conceal his design to betake himself to Damascus and indicate the Holy Places as the goal of his voyage? At bottom, all the while he affirmed that he was giving up all, Ghazālī renounces nothing: not his goods, not his family, nor his chair at Baghdad, neither study nor teaching.

73 "It is certainly impermissible to affirm that the influence of the contemporary events is exclusive of a true authentic spiritual evolution. In a Muslim climate, especially in the case of a *faqīh* borne by conviction and by temperament to action, that might not present itself with the exigencies of an absolute which one would quite naturally expect to find elsewhere. But everything prompts the belief that Ghazālī certainly suppresses here the political circumstances which weighed on his decisions

and options. And if one refers to what has been said elsewhere about the violent death of Niẓām al-Mulk and its repercussions on the life of the Master, and recalls especially that in 488/1095 there was yet no trace of Bāṭinite emissaries at Damascus, it would not appear improbable that what has been elsewhere advanced on the subject of this crucial period of Ghazālī's life constantly retains its value as a highly probable explanatory hypothesis, viz. that it would have been through fear of an immediate danger coming from the Bāṭinites and directly threatening his life that the Master would have decided to leave Baghdad for Damascus after having entrusted his chair to his brother and made everyone believe that he was going to withdraw to Mecca."

74 The second citation from Father Jabre is to be found in his excellent article on the biography and works of Ghazālī in MIDEO [cf. annotated Bibliography]. This citation will be found in pp. 92–94. It sheds more light on the reasons which could have given rise to fear in Ghazālī.

75 "After the death of Niẓām al-Mulk and of Malikshāh disorder reigned in the whole Seljuq empire. . . . Thanks to these troubles the Bāṭinites were quite easily able to infiltrate everywhere accompanied by 'assassins' ready to effect the disappearance of anyone who might oppose himself to their activities. Naturally those most aimed at were on the one hand the influential political men and on the other 'the flower of the Sunnite savants,' especially those who were fighting Batinism on the doctrinal terrain. . . .

76 "Now Ghazālī was certainly the savant most in the public eye of his time (he was officially called 'the Honor of Religion') and, since 486/1093–1094, he had spoken of it [religion] at length against the Bāṭinites. In the *Miʿyār* and the *Miḥakk* he had defended against them the intellect's capacity regarding the first principles of knowledge. In the *Tahāfut,* finished the 2nd of Muḥarram, 488/Jan. 12, 1095, he had done his best to show that reason, strong with its evidence, could not be satisfied with the hypotheses which they had in common with the philosophers. Finally, in the *Mustaẓhirī,* he had expounded and attacked, with his customary clarity, the central point of their doctrine, viz. the necessity of having recourse to an infallible Imam. This work was finished towards the end of 487/1094–1095, and from Muḥarram to Rajab 488/January to July 1095 it had had time to spread. Had Ghazālī had wind of some precise threat? In any case he knew that his life was seriously in danger. This would fit in well with the feeling of fear which underlies his whole doctrinal synthesis, the drafting of which was begun at this time. One would also have the explanation of this 'door of fear'

which he mentions in his confessions to Fārisī [Para. 22 above] as the starting point of his definitive return to religious practice. Finally, these considerations allow an easy understanding of the terror which seized him starting in Rajab 488/July 1095, and which the *Munqidh* describes with such forceful expression.

77 "Our hypothesis is confirmed by the fact that Ghazālī chose Damascus as his place of retirement, all the while concealing this choice and trying to put the authorities as well as his acquaintances on a false scent. Indeed, if one consults the chronicles of the time, one is struck by the verification that Syria-Palestine was then the sole country sheltered from the Bāṭinite terror. The first text signalizing the sect's presence there relates to the year 490/1097; the king of Aleppo is then urged by the 'Master of Egypt' to enter into the Bāṭinite obedience: he complies, then retracts. The first political murder in these regions took place in 496/1102–1103; but, as we shall soon see, Ghazālī leaves Syria before 492/1098–1099.

78 "It is, then, probably through fear of the Bāṭinites that Ghazālī decided to leave Baghdad for Damascus, entrusting his chair to his brother and leading everyone to believe that he was going to withdraw to Mecca. In Syria he would be able to reflect at his ease and to carry on in all security the composition of the *Iḥyāʾ*." [End of citation.]

79 I do not deny that Father Jabre has a point when he mentions Ghazālī's personal fear as a motive for his withdrawal from his eminent teaching post and from Baghdad. However, I do think that he overemphasizes it and finds too much significance in it. Anyone in Ghazālī's position might have felt a certain trepidation about his personal safety. To fear is human and not uncommon. But to experience and carry through the kind of "conversion" which I believe took place in the case of Ghazālī is rather superhuman—not inhuman, but superhuman—and certainly not common. Furthermore, Ghazālī *did* write at length and most strongly against the Bāṭinites and their insidious doctrine which really did threaten the essence and life of Islam. I might also mention that Ghazālī had just as good, or even better, reason to fear for his safety after his resumption of teaching at Nīsābūr: his patron, Fakhr al-Mulk, was murdered by a Bāṭinite in 500. Yet Ghazālī did not give up teaching in Nīsābūr until about three years later.

80 As for the "door of fear" which Ghazālī himself mentioned to al-Fārisī, I think the phrase has a very relevant and extremely profound significance. The "fear" mentioned here may include our ordinary notion of fear; but surely it goes much further and means primarily the fear

which is biblically and proverbially known as "the beginning of wisdom" —*Rās al-ḥikma makhāfat Allāh* [The beginning of wisdom is the fear of God—still heard, in its Arabic version, in the streets and homes of Baghdad]. This is what theologians and spiritual writers call "a salutary fear." In Book XXXIII of the *Iḥyā*ʾ [the third book of the Fourth Quarter] Ghazālī treats of fear and hope [*al-khawf wa l-rajā*ʾ]. It may be helpful to present some of his observations.

81 Ghazālī begins by declaring that hope and fear are the two wings by which the elect fly to heaven and the two mounts on which they traverse the paths to the Hereafter. After discussing the meaning of hope, its merits, and how it is to be made to dominate one's life, Ghazālī turns to fear. He defines what is meant by fear in general; then he discusses, in a religious context, its different manifestations in relation to what one fears, such as death before repentance, or insufficient performance of ritual obligations, or the agony of the punishment of the grave, or coming to a bad end, or the last judgment, and so on. Then Ghazālī expounds the merits of fear and what urges to it. It will be enough for my purpose here to cite the following passage:

82 "A thing's excellence is commensurate with its usefulness in leading to the beatitude of meeting God Most High in the Hereafter. For there is no [real] aim save beatitude, and there is no beatitude for a man save in the meeting with his Lord and nearness to Him. So whatever helps to this possesses excellence, and its excellence is commensurate with its end [cf. the "Principle and Foundation" of the *Spiritual Exercises* of St. Ignatius of Loyola] . It is indeed evident that the attainment of the beatitude of meeting God in the Hereafter can be only by the acquisition of love of Him and intimacy with Him in this life. But love is acquired only by knowledge, and knowledge only by continual reflection [*bi dawām al-fikr*]. And intimacy is acquired only by love and continual remembrance [*dawām al-dhikr*]. And persistence in remembrance and reflection is facilitated only by lopping off the love of this world from the heart, and that is not lopped off save by renouncing the pleasures and appetites of this world. But the renouncement of such desires is impossible save by bridling the passions, and by nothing is passion bridled as it is by the fire of fear, for fear is the fire which burns the appetites [passions]: so its excellence is commensurate with the appetites it consumes and also commensurate with the sins it prevents and the acts of obedience it incites, and that differs in accordance with the differing degrees of fear, as has been said. How can fear not possess excellence when by it one acquires purity [abstinence, temperance, integrity] and liness and piety and self-conquest, i.e. the virtuous acts which bring one very near to God!"

83 I believe, therefore, that the opening of "a door of fear" was Ghazālī's moment of truth, the starting point from which he mounted, so to speak, in reverse order the steps indicated above: from fear to the mastery of passions to the renouncement of desires to the renouncement of the pleasures and appetites of this world to the lopping off of the love of the world from the heart to continual remembrance of God to continual reflection to knowledge to love to intimacy with God and the assurance of the beatitude of meeting God in the Hereafter. It is his program of spiritual awakening and realization leading, I am convinced, to what I can only denominate by a word so little understood by so many: his sanctity [personal holiness, his being a *walī,* or friend of God], i.e. his definitive "freedom," or "fulfillment," or "salvation," not only in the negative sense of escape from error, but much more in the ineffably positive sense of union with God and utter absorption in Him. No amount of technical knowledge and grand theorizing could equal his *dhawq* [tasting] of God and of the things of God. As he himself rather piquantly remarks, there is a world of difference between knowing the definition of drunkenness and actually being drunk! [Para. 82]. I may add that I believe my interpretation of Ghazālī's "door of fear" is corroborated by a reading between the lines of Ghazālī's own words in Paras. 84 and 85.

84 A few points remain to be mentioned. One of these is the question of the possible influence of the *Munqidh* in the Middle Ages. This is discussed by Father Poggi at some length in the second part of his book, Chapters IV, V, and VI. He begins by remarking that it is not easy to adapt oneself to the idea that the *Munqidh* remained absolutely unknown in the West until the nineteenth century, a notion seemingly affirmed by those who speak of the discovery of the *Munqidh* in 1842 with the publication of the work of Schmölders. We know that the author of the *Maqāṣid al-Falāsifa* [*Intentiones Philosophorum*] was known to the Scholastics from the second half of the twelfth century. The Spanish scholar Father Alonso, in his article on the fortunes of Ghazālī in the medieval West, cites some forty-five names of Christian writers, mostly ecclesiastical, who mention the name and one or more works of Ghazālī. And Assemani, in his Florentine catalogue, mentions sixty works attributed to Ghazālī, among which the *Munqidh* occupies an honorable third place.

85 Father Poggi then devotes more than twenty pages to a consideration of the relationship between the *Munqidh* and the Catalan Ramon Martí's *Pugio Fidei adversus Mauros et Judaeos* [The Poniard of the Faith against Moors and Jews]. In this work, finished in 1278, there are certainly many passages seemingly derived from Ghazālī, and even some

citations. Martí also mentions the *Munqidh* several times: "ut ait Algazel in libro qui dicitur Almonkid min Addalel" [as Algazel says in the book which is called . . .]; "ut ait Algazel in libro, Qui eripit ab errore," and so on. Many more details are given by Father Poggi.

86 The second instance of the *Munqidh's* influence, discussed by Father Poggi at some length [twenty-three pages], is that found in the work by the Archdeacon of Segovia, later a collaborator of Juan Hispano [Joannes Hispanus—Ibn Dāwūd, or Avendeuth (?)] in the School of Toledo founded by Archbishop Raymond. The Archdeacon is known as Domenico Gundisalvi [Domenicus Gundissalinus, or Gundisalvo]. To him are attributed various translations from the Arabic of works by al-Kindī, al-Fārābī, al-Ghazālī, Avicenna, and so on. The work of Gundisalvi which interests us here is the *Tractatus de Anima* [Treatise on the Soul], composed, it seems, between 1160–1166, i.e. about fifty years after the death of Ghazālī. Its authenticity has been questioned, but not, according to Father Poggi, very convincingly—and in any case it makes little difference in our present context whether Gundisalvi or Juan Hispano was its author. Jacob Teicher, in a polemic with Gilson, sought to show that the author of the *De Anima,* far from being original, derived from Muslim mysticism what seem to the layman to be his personal conceptions. Teicher mentions Gundisalvi's insistence on exclusively symbolizing the act of mystical knowledge by the sensation of *taste,* Arabic *dhawq,* a term which occurs ten times in the *Munqidh,* once only in its literal meaning, and six times in the sense of a mystical cognitive contact. Gundisalvi also mentions *altior oculus animae* [a higher eye of the soul], which is reminiscent of Ghazālī's "another eye is opened" [cf. Paras. 108 and 124]. For other parallels and a cautious conclusion the reader may consult Father Poggi.

87 Father Poggi next explores the possible influence of the *Munqidh* on Maimonides's [1135-1204] *Dalālat al-Ḥāʾirīn* [The Guide of the Perplexed; also known as *Møreh Nebūkīm,* translation into Hebrew by Samuel Ibn Tibbon]. Maimonides composed the work in Arabic about 1190, almost eighty years after Ghazālī's death. The very title might suggest a relationship to the *Munqidh,* at least in Munk's translation *Guide des Egarés,* though "Perplexed" seems a more exact rendering. From the external standpoint of laymen one might be tempted to regard the *Munqidh* as an "Apology" for Islam and the *Dalāla* as an "Apology" for the Jewish religion, i.e. that Maimonides would have wished to render to the religion of his people the precious service which Ghazālī had rendered to Islam.

88 In the learned introductory essay to S. Pines's translation of the *Dalāla,* by Leo Strauss, the latter remarks: "To the extent to which

the *Guide* is a whole, or one work, it is addressed neither to the vulgar nor to the elite. To whom then is it addressed? How legitimate and important this question is appears from Maimonides' remark that the chief purpose of the *Guide* is to explain as far as possible the Account of the Beginning and the Account of the Chariot "with a view to him for whom (the book) has been composed" (III beginning) . Maimonides answers our question both explicitly and implicitly. He answers it explicitly in two ways; he says on the one hand that the *Guide* is addressed to believing Jews who are perfect in their religion and in their character, have studied the sciences of the philosophers, and are perplexed by the literal meaning of the Law; he says on the other hand that the book is addressed to such perfect human beings as are Law students and perplexed. He answers our question more simply by dedicating the book to his disciple Joseph and by stating that it has been composed for Joseph and his like." Further on Strauss writes: "The readers of the *Guide* were told at the beginning that the first purpose of the book is the explanation of biblical terms. . . . The critical reader, however, will find many reasons for becoming amazed. To say nothing of other considerations, he will wonder why almost the only terms explained are those suggesting corporeality. . . ."

89 If we consider the judgment of *kalām* made by Ghazālī and Maimonides, we are struck by the singular agreement of the two texts. In the *Dalāla* we read: "Thus there arose among them [Greek and Syrian Christians] this science of kalām. They started to establish premises that would be useful to them with regard to their belief and to refute those opinions that ruined the foundations of their Law. When thereupon the community of Islam arrived and the books of the philosophers were transmitted to it, then there were also transmitted to it those refutations composed against the books of the philosophers [p. 177—compare this with what Ghazālī says in Para. 22]. Both authors bring out the essentially "preserving" nature of the Muslim scholasticism. And both make no secret of their dissatisfaction with *kalām.* Maimonides: "When I studied the books of these Mutakallimūn, as far as I had the opportunity—and I have likewise studied the books of the philosophers, as far as my capacity went—I found that the method of all of the Mutakallimūn was one and the same in kind, though the subdivisions differed from one another. For the foundation of everything is that no consideration is due to how that which exists is, for it is merely a custom; and from the point of view of the intellect, it could well be different. Furthermore, in many places they follow the imagination and call it intellect. . . . Now when I considered this method of thought, my soul felt a very strong aversion to it, and had

every right to do so" [pp. 179–80]. And Ghazālī: "So *kalām* was not sufficient in my case, nor was it a remedy for the malady of which I was complaining" [Para. 23]. Both also seek to temper their severity toward *kalām* by protesting that they do not wish to scold those who find satisfaction in *kalām*.

90 Other similarities might be mentioned. In general it may be said that if the *Dalāla* does not furnish sure indications of its author's knowledge of the *Munqidh,* this is not a demonstrative argument for denying that Maimonides knew the *Munqidh.* Father Poggi also mentions that one fruit of his comparative study is the conclusion that the *Munqidh,* unlike the *Dalāla,* is not directed to a real, historical person, but has an impersonal and fictitious addressee. This he considers a new and modest contribution of the comparison instituted between the *Munqidh* and the *Dalāla.*

91 In her book *Al-Ghazālī the Mystic* Margaret Smith mentions the influence which the Toledo translations of Muslim authors, among them Ghazālī, undoubtedly had on Christian writers. She goes on to say: "The greatest of these Christian writers who was influenced by al-Ghazālī was St. Thomas Aquinas (1225–1274), who made a study of the Arabic writers and admitted his indebtedness to them. He studied at the University of Naples, where the influence of Arabic literature and culture was predominant at the time" [p. 220]. It is interesting to note that in one place St. Thomas seems to use the very words of Ghazālī. "Again, in dealing with the spiritual aspiration of the human soul, St. Thomas states that the ultimate perfection of the rational creature is to be found in that which is the principle of its being, since a thing is perfect in so far as it attains to that principle. God is the greatest of all goods and He alone is true perfection, and St. Thomas holds that He is the end towards which all things move, in order to achieve the perfection which can be given by Him alone, which is to become like Him. Man . . . was not created simply for sensual satisfaction, for this is common to both man and the brutes, nor for the pursuit of material ends, for man shares the nature of the angels as well as [of] the brutes. This argument is set forth by al-Ghazālī, in almost the same terms, in his *Kīmiyā al-Saʿāda* [The Alchemy of Happiness] and elsewhere" [pp. 220–21].

92 I am not convinced, however, that Margaret Smith is right when she says that "it is in his teaching on the Beatific Vision and the gnosis which leads to it that St. Thomas seems to have derived most from the teaching of the Muslim mystics and especially al-Ghazālī" [p. 221]. That the Beatific Vision is made possible by the *lumen gloriae* [the light of glory] is certainly the teaching of the Angelic Doctor [cf. *Contra Gentiles,* III, 53]. But to equate this with the *nūr Allāh* [light of God] of Ghazālī

seems to go too far and to base too much on verbal resemblance. From the many scriptural references involving "light" which St. Thomas cites it seems to me quite clear that he had no need to learn about *lumen gloriae* from Ghazālī or from "the teaching of the Muslim mystics"—and one may legitimately question how familiar he was with the latter, since the primary interest of the Scholastics was in the "philosophical" works of the Muslim writers.

93 "A much later writer in whom the influence of al-Ghazālī has been found was the French mystic Blaise Pascal (1623–1662) and his knowledge of the Muslim mystic's teaching no doubt came to him through his study of Raymond Martin's *Pugio Fidei* which came into his hands in a French edition, towards the end of his life, when he was writing his *Pensées"* [M. Smith, p. 225]. However, I am inclined to question her finding a dependence of Pascal on Ghazālī simply because "[Pascal's] faith in intuition recalls al-Ghazālī's belief in the superiority of gnosis to reason": it may "recall" it, but this is far from establishing a dependence.

94 "Pascal's famous wager for and against belief in God [*Pensées,* 233] contains teaching and arguments which are also to be found in al-Ghazālī" [M. Smith, pp. 225–26]. It also, I believe, contains a great deal more—and again I am not prepared to admit that we possess convincing proof of dependence: a surface similarity or verbal likeness [not clear in this case] can lead to unsound and sometimes dangerous conclusions. The pertinent passage occurs in Ghazālī's *Kitāb al-Arbaᶜīn* [The Book of the Forty (Chapters)], a kind of epitome of his *Iḥyāʾ,* toward the end of Part Three. The main point is brought out by Ghazālī in his citation of two verses by an unnamed poet, of whose intellectual ability Ghazālī does not seem to have had a high opinion:

> The astrologer and the physician, both of them, alleged:
> The dead are not raised. I said: Look to yourselves!
> If your allegation be true, I am not a loser;
> If mine be true, the loss is yours!

95 I am in full accord with M. Smith's concluding remark that "al-Ghazālī, therefore, himself indebted to Christianity and the West for not a little of his own inspiration, was able to repay the debt in kind and to give to the thinkers of the West as well as the East and to Christian mystics as well as those of his own faith, much that was inspiring and helpful to them as they also sought to tread the path which he had trodden before them" [p. 226]. I shall have more to say about this later. But

here I would like to call the reader's attention to something else which may be useful to him in helping to deepen his appreciation of the author of the *Munqidh.*

96 In Part Three of his excellent book Father Poggi discusses in three chapters [vii, viii, ix] the point of departure, Sufism in the *Munqidh,* and *Munqidh* and apologetic method. Under the title "The Point of Departure" he mentions several points. The most important of these concern Ghazālī's attitude toward *al-taqlīd* [servile conformism: cf. my Notes 4, 21, 24, 26], his confrontation with "the critical problem" [i.e. the problem of knowledge], and whether or not Ghazālī's "epistemological crisis" was a real, or a methodical, doubt. I have said enough about my personal opinion elsewhere [Note 43]. What Father Poggi has to say involves some important questions.

97 On Father Poggi's discussion of "Sufism in the *Munqidh"* I need not dwell here. Its importance is indicated by the fact that he devotes thirty-five pages to it. But its importance should be very clear to one who reads the text carefully. It will perhaps be more useful here to dwell a little on Father Poggi's final chapter, *Munqidh* e metodo apologetico" [*Munqidh* and Apologetic Method] . He begins by remarking that he several times asked himself the cause of the special interest in Ghazālī shown by Christian ecclesiastics, both Protestant and Catholic. And in fact Bouyges, Allard, Chelhot, Chidiac, Farid Jabre, Asin Palacios, Anawati and Gardet, and Poggi were, and those living still are, Catholic priests [as I also am]. Macdonald, Zwemer, Gairdner, and W. Montgomery Watt were Protestant clergymen. And Frick and van Leeuwen both received doctorates in theology from Protestant faculties. Father Poggi continues: "It is not, therefore, a question of a simple coincidence, but of something real which draws to Ghazālī the attention of those who, though not belonging to his religion, have however at heart the defense of the rights of God and have confidence in a religious renovation of humanity" [p. 214].

98 Speaking for himself Father Poggi declares that as a Catholic interested in the study of the Islamic religion he was attracted to the study of the *Munqidh* by the profound impression which the simple reading of the work awakened in him. "And we think the cause of this singular attraction resides above all in the fundamental honesty of the apologetic method and in the remarkable penetration of the religious problem in general." First of all, then, one must admire the honesty with which Ghazālī the apologist deals with adversaries and with those who do not agree with him. A striking instance of this is the careful study which Ghazālī made of the Bāṭinites [Taᶜlīmites] and their doctrines before he

set about refuting them, a study so detailed that it drew some criticism from Ghazālī's own orthodox coreligionists [Paras. 61 ff.].

99 Another example is Ghazālī's approach to his polemic against the Philosophers [Para. 27]. He was certainly not the type of "integrist" who would shut the adversary's mouth by denying his freedom to speak on the pretext that error has no rights. Ghazālī was also up in arms against the mania of peremptory denials and impulsive answers leaving no place for necessary distinctions and subdistinctions. And his book *Fayṣal al-Tafriqa* [cf. Appendix I] displays his remarkable openmindedness regarding those of other faiths and his detestation of the lavish use of cheap accusations of "heresy."

100 À propos of Ghazālī's respect for the truth the finest phrases of the *Munqidh* are undoubtedly those which centuries ago attracted the attention of Ramon Martī. Ghazālī protests the tendency to identify the truth, all of it, with one party and error, all of it, with another. This seems to be the sense of the words attributed to 'Alī, of which Ghazālī emphatically approves: "Do not know the truth by men, but rather, know the truth and you will know its adherents" [Paras. 53 and 57]. A golden rule indeed!

101 Honesty and the effort to be impartial are key elements of the apologetic method employed in the *Munqidh.* Ghazālī also made a clear distinction between the mathematical sense, or "esprit géométrique," and the religious sense. Mathematics occupies a domain which has nothing in common with religion. "An evident observation, if one wishes, but not as useless as it may seem at first sight if only one thinks of what history relates of mathematicians' forays into the domain of theology and of theologians' ventures into that of the exact sciences. The case of Galileo is only one example" [p. 228]. I am also reminded of Bertrand Russell. And Ghazālī loyally points out the dangers resulting from a too great infatuation with mathematics and from an intemperate zeal for religion.

102 What Ghazālī said of the philosophers and men of science of his time could very well be applied in our own day. "Philosophers, experimentalists, lawyers, in their several ways, have commonly the reputation of being, at least on moral and religious subjects, hard of belief; because, proceeding in the necessary investigation by the analytical method of verbal influence, they find within its limits no sufficient resources for attaining a conclusion" [Newman: *Grammar of Assent,* Burns and Oates, London, 1870, p. 285]. Indeed, Father Poggi believes that a study of the possible parallels between Ghazālī's thought and that of Newman, regarding certainty in religious matters and cognoscitive doctrine might yield the key of an interpretation of Ghazālī's thought more faithful and more coherent than that of Obermann.

103 Ghazālī's balance and impartiality in giving to the theologian what belongs to theology and to the scientist what belongs to science also made him sympathetic to those who cultivated logic [Para. 43]. But students of logic may also run a risk [Para. 44]. Briefly, Ghazālī speaks with respect of science and philosophy so long as they stay within their own areas. Duncan Black Macdonald recognized this merit of Ghazālī when he wrote: "[Ghazālī] never speaks disrespectfully of philosophy and science in their own sphere; his continual exhortation is that he who would understand them and refute their errors must first study them; that to do otherwise, to abuse what we do not know, brings only contempt on ourselves and on the cause which we champion" [article *The Life of Ghazzālī,* p. 85]. Father Poggi also agrees with this judgment of Macdonald: "Dr. Malter's description (p. xii) of al-Ghazzālī as a man who tried to keep on good terms with all parties, though based on Ibn Rushd, is singularly opposed to the facts of the case. Rather, he got himself into trouble with all parties. He had a combative nature, especially in his earlier life, and later it took much grace and discipline to keep it down" [loco cit., p. 132].

104 On another important point Father Poggi takes issue with Macdonald. This is the question of the very important argument, also in Catholic apologetics, of the miracle. Macdonald wrote: "There is a curious parallelism in al-Ghazzālī's attitude here to the latest phase in Christian apologetics. The argument from miracles seems now to be practically thrown aside; the doctrine rather must prove the miracle. The unique fact of the life and person of Christ is emphasized; it is shown how it appeals immediately to the human consciousness, and on that the proof of the truth of His mission is built up. Logically this position is faulty; and practically it proves whatever you wish. Al-Ghazzālī uses it to prove the truth of the mission of Muḥammad. Miracles are difficult, almost impossible to prove—here we have again his attitude of historical agnosticism; but if any one will read the record of Muḥammad's life, he will receive a general impression that will assure him of the truth of the mission. The personality of Muḥammad will be its own proof" [art. cit., p. 96, Note 1]. This view, Father Poggi thinks, is notably nuanced even in the *Munqidh* alone [cf. Para. 72]. And elsewhere Ghazālī recommends a more efficacious way to attain a conviction of Muḥammad's divine mission [Paras. 116–19]. Father Poggi asks: "Would it, then, be really a question, as van Leeuwen would have it, of an attempt 'to anchor theology in subjective experience rather than in objective revelation'? But then, as the same author confesses, this would be to make of Ghazālī an enigma; and enigmas, according to the good rules of the philological method, are to be

avoided as far as possible" [p. 242]. In the quest for a deeply-rooted, sincere personal conviction, Ghazālī clearly prefers "a 'global' conviction in which it is impossible to discern what the single components are and where certainty, become fully conscious, is not attributable to this or that argument in particular" [p. 244].

105 Ghazālī had enemies in times past, and even within the pale of Islam. In modern times he is also subject to misunderstandings. "The genuine and objective penetration of his thought can in fact be prejudiced by two opposed causes always operative: the lack of a personal openness to the religious problem, or an excessive zealotry in favor of one's own religion. In the first case one exposes oneself to misunderstanding totally the true religiousness of Ghazālī through making use of the deformed and aprioristic image of religion in general which one has made for oneself. Of this sort we would be tempted to consider the famous essay of Obermann. . . . On the other hand the second danger is characteristic of one who has strong, deep-seated religious convictions and would therefore seem better prepared to comprehend the religious feeling of others. But he is blinded by his preoccupation with seeking out every defective side in the other's attitude to such an extent as to expose himself constantly to falsifying the true perspectives of that thought which should first be studied and exposed apart from every polemical or self-defensive preoccupation" [Poggi, pp. 247–48].

106 Father Poggi notes that Ghazālī "still has a word to say to the men of today" [p. 214]. This is the subject which I now wish to address. Doctor Lichtenstadter remarks in her preface that the works in this series "should—and can—be read for their own sake. This series differs from previously offered translations in that it will, wherever applicable, emphasize the relevance of the thought contained in these ancient writings for our own culture and times." The question is: Has the *Munqidh* anything to offer to the men and women of today?—or—Does Ghazālī, across the gulf of nearly ten centuries, have anything to say to us?

107 Let me begin by citing the almost classical summary of Ghazālī's works by Duncan Black Macdonald [*Development,* pp. 238–40]. "[Ghazālī's] work and influence in Islam may be summed up briefly as follows: *First,* he led men back from scholastic labors upon theological dogmas to living contact with, study and exegesis of, the Word and the traditions. What happened in Europe when the yoke of mediaeval scholasticism was broken, what is happening with us now [1903], happened in Islam under his leadership. He could be a scholastic with scholastics, but to state and develop theological doctrine on a Scriptural basis was emphatically his method. We should now call him a biblical theologian.

108 *"Second,* in his teaching and moral exhortations he reintroduced the element of fear. In the *Munqidh* and elsewhere he lays stress on the need of such a striking of terror into the minds of the people. His was no time, he held, for smooth, hopeful preaching; no time for optimism either as to this world or the next. The horrors of hell must be kept before men; he had felt them himself. We have seen how otherworldly was his own attitude, and how the fear of the Fire had been the supreme motive in his conversion; and so he treated others.

"Third, it was by his influence that Sufism attained a firm and assured position in the Church of Islam.

109 *"Fourth,* he brought philosophy and philosophical theology within the range of the ordinary mind. Before his time they had been surrounded, more or less, with mystery. The language used was strange; its vocabulary and technical terms had to be specially learned. No mere reader of the Arabic of the street or the mosque or the school could understand at once a philosophical tractate. Greek ideas and expressions, passing through a Syriac version into Arabic, had strained to the uttermost the resources of even that most flexible tongue. A long training had been thought necessary before the elaborate and formal method of argumentation could be followed. All this al-Ghazzālī changed, or at least tried to change. His *Tahāfut* is not addressed to scholars only; he seeks with it a wider circle of readers, and contends that the views, the arguments, and the fallacies of the philosophers should be perfectly intelligible to the general public.

110 "Of these four phases of al-Ghazzālī's work, the first and the third are undoubtedly the most important. He made his mark by leading Islam back to its fundamental and historical facts, and by giving a place in its system to the emotional religious life. But it will have been noticed that in none of the four phases was he a pioneer. He was not a scholar who struck out a new path, but a man of intense personality who entered on a path already blazed and made it the common highway. We have here his character. Other men may have been keener logicians, more learned theologians, more gifted saints; but he, through his personal experiences, had attained so overpowering a sense of the divine realities that the force of his character—once combative and restless, now narrow and intense—swept all before it, and the Church of Islam entered on a new era of its existence.

111 "So much space it has been necessary to give to this great man. Islam has never outgrown him, has never fully understood him. In the renaissance of Islam which is now rising to view his time will come and the new life will proceed from a renewed study of his works" [End of citation from Macdonald].

112 Macdonald's words sum up Ghazālī's importance in the Islam of yesterday and today. But he also has a relevance for us who are outside Islam. Samuel Zwemer has some words on this: "By striving to understand Al-Ghazālī we may at least better fit ourselves to help those who, like him, are earnest seekers after God amid the twilight shadows of Islam. His life also has a lesson for us all in its devoted Theism and in its call to the practice of the Presence of God" [*A Moslem Seeker,* p. 13].

Zwemer, himself an ardent missionary, sees Ghazālī as a help to those working to bring Christ to those of our contemporaries who, like Ghazālī, are sincere seekers of God among the Muslims. But he also points out the lesson which Ghazālī's life can have for us all.

113 Professor Watt, in his *Muslim Intellectual* [pp. 179–80], has this to say: "Finally, there is the question to what extent [Ghazālī] influenced the life of the Islamic community as a whole. Although he produced no tidy theory and did not reform the official intellectual class, he seems to have had a wide influence. By largely removing the tension between ṣūfism and the 'Islamic sciences' he brought the community much nearer to accepting a modified ideation suited to the situation in which it found itself. This modified ideation was implicit in his thinking rather than explicit. It was a new conception of the function of religion in the life of a society. Religion was no longer to be the guide of statesmen in their more far-reaching political decisions, as it had been in the earliest days, and as some religious intellectuals hoped it might be again. It was instead to be the spiritual aspect of the life of the individual in his social relations. Al-Ghazālī seems to have assumed that not merely political decisions but all the outward forms of social life were beyond the ability of a man to control—this fixity of social forms was doubtless the result of the stabilization of the Traditions some two centuries before his time. Up to about 850 the religious aspirations of Muslims may be said to have been largely directed towards the Islamization of society. When this had been achieved in externals, there appeared as a new goal for religious aspirations the cultivation of greater beauty of character. Al-Ghazālī was not an innovator here, for many ordinary men were already looking in this direction, but he gave such men intellectual grounds for thinking their aspirations were sound.

114 "Al-Ghazālī thought himself called to be the 'renewer' of religion for the sixth Islamic century, and many, perhaps most, later Muslims have considered that he was indeed the 'renewer' of this age. Some have even spoken of him as the greatest Muslim after Muḥammad. As his achievement is reviewed, it becomes clear that he was more of a prophet

than a systematizer. Yet he is not simply a prophet, but is best described as a prophetic intellectual. He spoke to his fellows in terms of the highest thought of his time. Above all he made the individualistic aspect of religion intellectually respectable. It is probably his emphasis on the individualistic outlook that has appealed to the endemic individualism of Western scholars and gained him excessive praise; but he was far from being a sheer individualist. In his theorizing he sometimes fails to make explicit allowance for the communalism of the Sharīᶜa, but he always presupposes it, and in his practice he effects a genuine integration of individualism and communalism. This is part of his title to greatness and of his achievement in 'renewing' Islam.

"In the background of the life of al-Ghazālī we see that much real piety continues to exist in the hearts of ordinary men despite the failure and corruption of their intellectual leaders. In his own life we see how the revivals or reforms, which frequently but unpredictably occur in the great religions, have their origin in the heart of a single man.

115 In his *The Faith and Practice of al-Ghazālī* [pp. 14–15] Professor Watt writes: "Al-Ghazālī has sometimes been acclaimed in both East and West as the greatest Muslim after Muhammad, and he is by no means unworthy of that dignity. His greatness rests above all on two things: (1) He was the leader in Islam's supreme encounter with Greek philosophy—that encounter from which Islamic theology emerged victorious and enriched, and in which Arabic Neoplatonism received a blow from which it did not recover. (2) He brought orthodoxy and mysticism into closer contact; the orthodox theologians still went their own way, and so did the mystics, but the theologians became more ready to accept the mystics as respectable, while the mystics were more careful to remain within the bounds of orthodoxy.

"Yet perhaps the greatest thing about al-Ghazālī was his personality, and it may yet again be a source of inspiration. Islam is now wrestling with Western thought as it once wrestled ith Greek philosophy, and is as much in need as it was then of a 'revival of the religious sciences.' Deep study of al-Ghazālī may suggest to Muslims steps to be taken if they are to deal successfully with the contemporary situation. Christians, too, now that the world is in a cultural melting-pot, must be prepared to learn from Islam, and are unlikely to find a more sympathetic guide than al-Ghazālī."

116 The great Hungarian orientalist Ignaz Goldziher wrote in his *Vorlesungen uber den Islam* [*Le dogme etc.*] that Ghazālī was well aware of the danger incarnate in two elements of theological activity which were, in his view, the worst enemies of interior religion: the

subtleties of the dogmatic dialectic and the refinements of religious casuistry [i.e. *kalām* and *fiqh*]. "In the place of the dialectical and casuistical manner of the dogmatists and ritualists Ghazālī demands that one cultivate religion as an experience of an intimate order. It is in the elevation of oneself to the intuitive life of the soul and to the sentiment of man's dependence that he finds the center of the religious life. *The love of God* must operate there as central motive. As he analyzes, in general with great mastery, the moral sentiments, he has given, in his system, a profound monograph on this motive and this goal of religion and has pointed out the way by which one must tend to it."

117 Has Ghazālī anything to say to us? I can now give *my* answer to this in a particular sense, a general sense, and a personal sense. And since it is *my* answer, it must be the result not only of academic and human influence processes, but also of my profoundest personal convictions as a modest Catholic, theoretical and practical. The particular sense concerns my four to five hundred million Muslim brothers. I believe, as has been indicated in some of the above citations, that Ghazālī has a very great relevance for them as sincere Muslims who wish to deepen and spiritualize their Islamic belief and practice. The *Iḥyāʾ* of Ghazālī, as well as others of his books, are still read by many Arabic-speaking Muslims in their original form, and by others in translations. This is attested by the fact that reprints and new editions are continually being brought out and bought out. It is perhaps not too much to say that Ghazālī is still on the all-time "best-seller" list of Arabic literature.

118 My answer in a general sense has been indicated by the Editors of the series "Ethical and Religious Classics of East and West" in their *General Introduction.* They write: "As a result of two Wars that have devastated the World men and women everywhere feel a twofold need. We need a deeper understanding and appreciation of other peoples and their civilizations, especially their moral and spiritual achievements. And we need a wider vision of the Universe, a clearer insight into the fundamentals of ethics and religion. How ought men to behave? How ought nations? Does God exist? What is His Nature? How is He related to His creation? Especially, how can man approach Him? In other words, there is a general desire to know what the greatest minds, whether of East or West, have thought and said about the Truth of God and of the beings who (as most of them hold) have sprung from Him, live by Him, and return to Him. . . .

119 "Mankind is hungry, but the feast is there, though it is locked up and hidden away. . . . No doubt the great religions differ in fundamental

respects. But they are not nearly so far from one another as they seem. We think they are further off than they are largely because we so often misunderstand and misrepresent them. Those whose own religion is dogmatic have often been as ready to learn from other teachings as those who are liberals in religion. Above all, there is an enormous amount of common ground in the great religions, concerning, too, the most fundamental matters. There is frequent agreement on the Divine Nature; God is the One, Self-subsisting Reality, knowing Himself, and therefore loving and rejoicing in Himself. Nature and finite spirits are in some way subordinate kinds of Being, or merely appearances of the Divine, the One. The three stages of the way of man's approach or return to God are in essence the same in Christian and non-Christian teaching: an ethical stage, then one of knowledge and love, leading to the mystical union of the soul with God."

120 In this sense I certainly believe that Ghazālī, in almost all of his writings, has something to offer to all the "hungry" men and women of today. Few, perhaps, can read the *Iḥyā'*, the completest and most spiritual of Ghazālī's books. But all, I think, can profit from a reading of the *Munqidh*. Ghazālī, so to speak, touches all the bases, or at least the truly relevant ones. He makes a complete disjunction in Para. 18. Those who seek the truth can do so whether through Theology [the Mutakallimūn], or through Philosophy [and Science], or through the following of a charismatic, infallible Leader, or through the "Way" of the Ṣūfīs. As it turns out, the four ways are not necessarily exclusive for Ghazālī. Despite his strictures on *kalām*, he found it useful to a certain extent. And he certainly benefited from his study of philosophy. He also followed a charismatic, infallible Leader—Muḥammad, the Prophet and Apostle of God. But for him the "Way" par excellence was that of the Ṣūfīs—the men who *"tasted* and saw how sweet the Lord is."

121 And the "Way" of the Ṣūfīs is not an esoteric way reserved only for the elite. The number who actually follow it may indeed be small, but this is due to many factors including the difficulty of following it sincerely and wholeheartedly. I think that Ghazālī would agree with the evangelical dictum that "one thing is necessary," and also with the declaration that "many are called, but few are chosen." I also agree with the opinion commonly held by Catholic theologians that the mystical life is the "natural," or ordinary, fulfillment and flowering of the graces offered by God to all men of good will. For, as Gerson said, "Theologia mystica est experimentalis cognitio habita de Deo per amoris unitivi complexum" [Mystical theology is knowledge of God by experience, arrived at through the embrace of unifying love]. This is something possible for

all in varying degrees, but the "unitive way" must normally be preceded by the arduous "purgative way" and the difficult and often lengthy "illuminative way." And at the heart of the matter it is God and God's free gift of supernatural grace which are prevenient, accompanying and fulfilling. Yet "facienti quod est in se Deus non denegat gratiam" [God does not deny grace to one who does all that lies in his power].

122 Finally, with some reluctance, I offer my personal answer. It can be put briefly. My reading of Ghazālī has made me, or at least has incited me to be, a better practicing Catholic in the fullest sense of the term. It has not moved me, despite my real admiration, and even veneration, for Ghazālī to embrace Islam. Rather it has made me more aware of the great spiritual riches at hand in my own Catholic tradition. My experience has been, though on a lesser level, somewhat like that of Louis Massignon and Harvey Cox.

123 Massignon, through the impression made upon him by certain Muslim friends and acquaintances and their devout practice of their Faith, was led back to the fervent practice of the Catholic religion of his youth. [One is also reminded of Charles de Foucauld.] And Harvey Cox tells us: "I have not seen Harry, Denise or Michael since the day they knocked at my door. I do not know if they still belong to the Hare Krishna group. They may not. In any case, I am grateful to them and I hope that wherever they now are in their pilgrimages, things are going well for them. They helped start me along a path which took a totally unexpected course. The journey I made, while helping me to appreciate more deeply what the East has to teach us today, also made me in some ways more Christian than I had been at the beginning. My guess is that the same thing, or something very similar, will happen to a lot of us before many more years go by" [*Turning East,* p. 21]. Harvey Cox's "turning East" led him to such diverse modern "gurus" as Dietrich Bonhoeffer, Simone Weil, Dorothy Day, Father Camilo Torres-Restrepo, and Martin Luther King. Above all, it led him to "an authentic contemporary form of spirituality" for which he felt compelled to look in "the primal sources and to the Christians nearest us" [p. 157].

124 To sum it all up, I have to some extent found, and I believe others can find, in the words and example of Ghazālī a true *iḥyāʾ* [quickening, revivification, bringing back to life, causing to live]—an *iḥyāʾ* from the dark, dead coldness of atheism, or, more accurately, "without-Godness"; an *iḥyāʾ* from enervating, debilitating, and crippling sinfulness; an *iḥyāʾ* from lifeless and spiritless intellectualism; an *iḥyāʾ* from the tepidity and listlessness and uncaring of social and moral mediocrity.

125 Someday, be it close or distant, I hope to sit down with Ghazālī in a quiet corner of heaven. We shall have many things to talk about, if indeed in heaven one can be "distracted" from the Vision of God. I shall want to thank him—him and so many others of his co-religionists, such as Rābiᶜa and al-Bisṭāmī and al-Ḥallāj. I cited in the beginning of this Introduction the words of Macdonald: "With the time came the man." Let me conclude by saying: The time is gone; but the man remains, and will remain, for you, for me, and for all men.

126 I must mention a few pedestrian details. The basis of my translation has been the precious manuscript which I have already mentioned. In the "Notes to the Translation" I have tried to avoid the extremes of an irritating minimum and a maddening maximum. I can only hope that the general reader will find them informative and helpful. I have added an "Annotated Bibliography," since I feel that some of my readers may wish to further their acquaintance with Ghazālī. Translations of verses of the Qurʾān are sometimes those of Arberry, sometimes my own. And of course I am very grateful to ever so many persons who have helped me in ever so many ways! To paraphrase Peguy: One man is no man. My undertaking has been a labor of love—and not, I trust, a love's labor lost!

DELIVERANCE FROM ERROR

In the Name of God
Most Gracious and Merciful

I trust in the Living, Who dieth not![1]

1 The most eminent and ascetic Master, the Ornament of Religion and the Proof of Islam, Abū Ḥāimid Muḥammad, son of Muḥammad, son of Muḥammad, al-Ghazālī, said:

Praise be to God, Whose praise should preface every writing and discourse! And God's blessing be upon Muḥammad the Elect, divinely gifted with prophethood and apostleship, and upon his kin and companions, who guided men away from error![2]

2 *Now then:* You have asked me, my brother in religion,[3] to communicate to you the aim and secrets of the sciences and the dangerous and intricate depths of the different doctrines and views. You want me to give you an account of my travail in disengaging the truth from amid the welter of the sects, despite the polarity of their means and methods. You also want to hear about my daring in mounting from the lowland of servile conformism[4] to the highland of independent investigation:[5] and first of all what profit I derived from the science of *kalām;*[6] secondly, what I found loathsome among the methods of the devotees of *taᶜlīm,*[7] who restrict the attainment of truth to uncritical acceptance of the Imam's pronouncements; thirdly, the methods of philosophizing[8] which I scouted; and finally, what pleased me in the way pursued by the practice of sufism.[9] You also wish to know the quintessential truth disclosed to me in the tortuous

course of my inquiry into the views expressed by various men; and what led me to quit teaching in Baghdad, though I had many students there; and what induced me to resume teaching in Nishapur much later.

3 Convinced of the sincerity of your desire, I am losing no time in answering your request. Invoking God's help, and placing my trust in Him, and imploring His favor, and having recourse to Him, I say:

4 You should first of all know—God give you good guidance and gently lead you to the truth!—that the diversity of men in religions and creeds, plus the disagreement of the Community of Islam[10] about doctrines, given the multiplicity of sects and the divergency of methods, is a deep sea in which most men founder and from which few only are saved. Each group alleges that it is the one saved, and "each faction is happy about its own beliefs."[11] This is the state of affairs which the truthful and most trustworthy Chief of God's envoys—God bless him!—ominously promised us when he said: "My Community will split into seventy-odd sects, of which one will be saved."[12] And what he promised has indeed come to pass![13]

5 In the bloom of my youth and the prime of my life, from the time I reached puberty before I was twenty until now, when I am over fifty, I have constantly been diving daringly into the depths of this profound sea and wading into its deep water like a bold man, not like a cautious coward. I would penetrate far into every murky mystery, pounce upon every problem, and dash into every mazy difficulty. I would scrutinize the creed of every sect and seek to lay bare the secrets of each faction's teaching with the aim of discriminating between the proponent of truth and the advocate of error, and between the faithful follower of tradition and the heterodox innovator.[14] I would never take leave of an interiorist[15] without wanting to learn about his interiorism, or of a literalist[16] without wanting to know the substance of his literalism, or of a philosopher without seeking to become acquainted with the essence of his philosophy, or of a *mutakallim*[17] without endeavoring to discover the aim of his discussion and polemic, or of a sufi without eagerly trying to obtain knowledge of the secret of his serenity,[18] or of a devout worshiper[19] without looking into the source and substance of his piety, or of an irreligious nihilist[20] without attempting to find out his background and motivation in order to become aware of the reasons for his bold profession of nihilism and irreligion.

6 The thirst for grasping the real meaning of things was indeed my habit and wont from my early years and in the prime of my life. It was an instinctive, natural disposition placed in my makeup by God Most

High, not something due to my own choosing and contriving. As a result, the fetters of servile conformism[21] fell away from me, and inherited beliefs lost their hold on me, when I was still quite young. For I saw that the children of Christians always grew up embracing Christianity, and the children of Jews always grew up adhering to Judaism, and the children of Muslims always grew up following the religion of Islam. I also heard the tradition related from the Apostle of God—God's blessing and peace be upon him!—in which he said: "Every infant is born endowed with the *fiṭra:*[22] then his parents make him Jew or Christian or Magian."[23] Consequently I felt an inner urge to seek the true meaning of the original *fiṭra,* and the true meaning of the beliefs arising through slavish aping[24] of parents and teachers. I wanted to sift out these uncritical beliefs, the beginnings of which are suggestions imposed from without,[25] since there are differences of opinion in the discernment of those that are true from those that are false.[26]

7 So I began by saying to myself: "What I seek is knowledge of the true meaning of things. Of necessity, therefore, I must inquire into just what the true meaning of knowledge is." Then it became clear to me that sure and certain knowledge is that in which the thing known is made so manifest that no doubt clings to it, nor is it accompanied by the possibility of error and deception, nor can the mind even suppose such a possibility.[27] Furthermore, safety from error must accompany the certainty to such a degree that, if someone proposed to show it to be false—for example, a man who would turn a stone into gold and a stick into a snake—his feat would not induce any doubt or denial. For if I know that ten is more than three, and then someone were to say: "No, on the contrary, three is more than ten, as is proved by my turning this stick into a snake—and if he were to do just that and I were to see him do it, I would not doubt my knowledge because of his feat. The only effect it would have on me would be to make me wonder how he could do such a thing. But there would be no doubt at all about what I knew!

8 I realized, then, that whatever I did not know in this way and was not certain of with this kind of certainty was unreliable and unsure knowledge, and that every knowledge unaccompanied by safety from error is not sure and certain knowledge.[28]

The Avenues to Sophistry and Skepticism[29]

9 I then scrutinized all my cognitions and found myself devoid of any knowledge answering the previous description except in the case of

sense-data[30] and the self-evident truths.[31] So I said: "Now that despair has befallen me, the only hope I have of acquiring an insight into obscure matters is to start from things that are perfectly clear,[32] namely sense-data and the self-evident truths. Hence I must first study these thoroughly in order to reach a sure answer to these questions: Is my reliance on sense-data and my safety from error in the case of self-evident truths of the same kind as that which I formerly had regarding the dicta of authority,[33] and of the same kind as that which most men have regarding speculative matters?[34] Or is it a verifiable safety containing no deception or danger?"

10 With great earnestness, therefore, I began to reflect on my sense-data to see if I could make myself doubt them. This protracted effort to induce doubt[35] finally brought me to the point where my soul would not allow me to admit safety from error even in the case of my sense-data. Rather it began to be open to doubt about them and to say: "Whence comes your reliance on sense-data? The strongest of the senses is the sense of sight. Now this looks at a shadow and sees it standing still and motionless and judges that motion must be denied. Then, due to experience and observation an hour later it knows that the shadow is moving, and that it did not move in a sudden spurt, but so gradually and imperceptibly that it was never completely at rest. Sight also looks at a star and sees it as something small, the size of a dinar;[36] then geometrical proofs demonstrate that it surpasses the earth in size. In the case of this and of similar instances of sense-data the sense-judge makes its judgments, but the reason-judge refutes it and repeatedly gives it the lie in an incontrovertible fashion."

11 Then I said: "My reliance on sense-data has also become untenable. Perhaps, therefore, I can rely only on those rational data which belong to the category of primary truths, such as our asserting that 'Ten is more than three,' and 'One and the same thing cannot be simultaneously affirmed and denied,' and 'One and the same thing cannot be incipient[37] and eternal, existent and nonexistent, necessary and impossible.' "[38]

12 Then sense-data spoke up: "What assurance have you that your reliance on rational data is not like your reliance on sense-data? Indeed, you used to have confidence in me. Then the reason-judge came along and gave me the lie. But were it not for the reason-judge, you would still accept me as true. So there may be, beyond the perception of reason, another judge. And if the latter revealed itself, it would give the lie to the judgments of reason, just as the reason-judge revealed itself and gave the lie to the judgments of sense. The mere fact of the nonappearance of that further perception does not prove the impossibility of its existence."

13 For a brief space my soul hesitated about the answer to that objection, and sense-data reinforced their difficulty by an appeal to dreaming, saying: "Don't you see that when you are asleep you believe certain things and imagine certain circumstances and believe they are fixed and lasting and entertain no doubts about that being their status? Then you wake up and know that all your imaginings and beliefs were groundless and unsubstantial. So while everything you believe through sensation or intellection in your waking state may be true in relation to that state, what assurance have you that you may not suddenly experience a state which would have the same relation to your waking state as the latter has to your dreaming, and your waking state would be dreaming in relation to that new and further state?[39] If you found yourself in such a state, you would be sure that all your rational beliefs were unsubstantial fancies.

14 It may be that this state beyond reason is that which the sufis claim is theirs. For they allege that, in the states they experience when they concentrate inwardly and suspend sensation, they see phenomena which are not in accord with the normal data of reason. Or it may be that this state is death. For the Apostle of God—God's blessing and peace be upon him!—said: 'Men are asleep: then after they die they awake.'[40] So perhaps this present life is a sleep[41] compared to the afterlife. Consequently, when a man dies, things will appear to him differently from the way he now sees them, and thereupon he will be told: 'But We have removed from you your veil and today your sight is keen' (50.21/22)."

15 When these thoughts occurred to me they penetrated my soul,[42] and so I tried to deal with that objection. However, my effort was unsuccessful, since the objection could be refuted only by proof. But the only way to put together a proof was to combine primary cognitions. So if, as in my case, these were inadmissible, it was impossible to construct the proof. This malady was mysterious and it lasted for nearly two months. During that time I was a skeptic in fact, but not in utterance and doctrine. At length God Most High cured me of that sickness. My soul regained its health and equilibrium and once again I accepted the self-evident data of reason and relied on them with safety and certainty.[43] But that was not achieved by constructing a proof or putting together an argument. On the contrary, it was the effect of a light which God Most High cast into my breast. And that light is the key to most knowledge.[44]

16 Therefore, whoever thinks that the unveiling of truth depends on precisely formulated proofs has indeed straitened the broad mercy of God. When the Apostle of God—God's blessing and peace be upon him!—was asked about "the dilation" in the Most High's utterance: "So

he whom God wishes to guide aright, He dilates his breast for submission to Himself (i.e. to embrace Islam)" (6.125), he said: "It is a light which God casts into the heart." Then someone said: "And what is the sign of it?" He replied: "Withdrawal from the mansion of delusion and turning to the mansion of immortality."[45] And it is this of which the Apostle—God's blessing and peace be upon him!—said: "God Most High created men in darkness, then sprinkled on them some of His light."[46] From that light, then, the unveiling of truth must be sought. Moreover, that light gushes forth from the divine liberality at certain times, and one must be on the watch for it according to the saying of the Apostle—Peace be upon him!—"Your Lord, in the days of your lifetime, sends forth gusts of grace: do you then put yourselves in the way of them!"[47]

17 The aim of this account is to emphasize that one should be most diligent in seeking the truth until he finally comes to seeking the unseekable. For primary truths are unseekable, because they are present in the mind; and when what is present is sought, it is lost and hides itself. But one who seeks the unseekable cannot subsequently be accused of negligence in seeking what is seekable.[48]

The Categories of Those Who Seek the Truth

18 When God Most High, of His kindness and abundant generosity, had cured me of this sickness, I was of the view that the categories of those seeking the truth were limited to four groups:

1. *The Mutakallimūn,*[49] who allege that they are men of independent judgment and reasoning.
2. The *Bāṭinites,*[50] who claim to be the unique possessors of *al-ta*ᶜ*līrn*[51] and the privileged recipients of knowledge acquired ftom the Infallible Imam.
3. The Philosophers,[52] who maintain that they are the men of logic and apodeictic demonstration.[53]
4. The sufis,[54] who claim to be the familiars of the Divine Presence and the men of mystic vision and illumination.[55]

19 I then said to myself: "The truth cannot transcend these four categories, for these are the men who are following the paths of the quest for truth. Hence, if the truth eludes them, there remains no hope of ever attaining it. For there can be no desire to return to servile conformism once it has been abandoned, since a prerequisite for being a servile conformist is that one does not know himself to be such. But when a man recognizes

that, the glass of his servile conformism is shattered—an irreparable fragmentation and a mess which cannot be mended by patching and piecing together: it can only be melted by fire and newly reshaped.

20 I therefore lost no time in following these different ways and making a thorough study of the views of these groups. I applied myself first to the science of *kalām,* secondly to the way of philosophy, thirdly to the teachings[56] of the Bāṭinites, and fourthly to the Way[57] of the sufis.

The Aim and Purport of the Science of Kalām

21 I began, then, with the science of *kalām,* which I summarized in the form of notes.[58] I carefully studied the works of the most meticulous *mutakallimūn,* and I wrote on the subject what I had a mind to write. Subsequently, however, I found it a science adequate for its own aim, but inadequate for mine. For its aim is simply to conserve the creed of the orthodox for the orthodox and to guard it from the confusion introduced by the innovators.[59]

22 In the past God Most High and Praiseworthy communicated to His servants, by the tongue of His Apostle, a creed which is the truth, inasmuch as it is, for their religious and secular life, the sound basis as articulated in detail in the Qur᾽ān and the Traditions.[60] Then Satan, through the sinister suggestions of the innovators,[61] injected notions opposed to orthodoxy, with the result that the innovators became passionately addicted to these errors and all but ruined the true creed for its adherents. So God Most High raised up the group of the *mutakallimūn* and motivated them to champion orthodoxy by a systematic discussion designed to disclose the deceptions introduced by the contriving innovators contrary to the traditional orthodoxy. This gave rise to the science of *kalām* and its practitioners.[62]

23 A group of the *mutakallimūn* did indeed perform the task assigned to them by God. They ably protected orthodoxy and defended the creed which had been readily accepted from the prophetic preaching and boldly counteracted[63] the heretical innovations. But in so doing they relied on premises which they took over from their adversaries, being compelled to admit them either by uncritical acceptance, or because of the Community's consensus, or by simple acceptance deriving from the Qur᾽ān and the Traditions.[64] Most of their polemic was devoted to bringing out the inconsistencies of their adversaries and criticizing them for the logically absurd consequences of what they conceded. This, however, is

of little use in the case of one who admits nothing at all except the primary and self-evident truths. So *kalām* was not sufficient in my case, nor was it a remedy for the malady of which I was complaining.[65]

24 To be sure, when the discipline of *kalām* acquired some status and had been much engaged in for some length of time, the *mutakallimūn* showed an earnest desire for attempting to defend orthodoxy by the study of the true natures of things. They plunged into the study of substances and accidents and their principles.[66] But since that was not the aim of their own science, their discussion of the subject was not thoroughgoing; therefore it did not provide an effective means of dispelling entirely the darkness due to the bewilderment about the differences dividing men. I do not regard it as improbable that such may have been the result in the case of others. I do not even doubt that it has actually been the experience of a limited group of men, but in a way vitiated by servile conformism in some matters which are not among the primary truths. In any event, my present purpose is to tell the story of my own case, not to express disapproval of anyone who sought a cure in *kalām*. For healing remedies differ as the sickness differs, and many a remedy helps one sick man and harms another.

PHILOSOPHY

On the gist of philosophy: what is blameworthy in it, and what blameless; what doctrine lays its proponent open to the charge of unbelief, and what doctrine lays him open to the charge, not of unbelief, but of innovation; and an exposé of what the philosophers have stolen from the sayings of the men of truth and mingled with their own affirmations to promote the circulation of their own errors together with those truths; and how souls come to feel an antipathy for those truths; and how to extract the unadulterated truth from amid the counterfeit and spurious views found in the aggregate of the philosophers' teaching.[67]

25 After finishing with the science of *kalām*, I then started on philosophy. I knew for sure that one cannot recognize what is unsound in any of the sciences unless he has such a grasp of the farthest reaches of that science that he is the equal of the most learned of those versed in the principles of that science; then he must even excel him and attain even greater eminence so that he becomes cognizant of the intricate profundities which have remained beyond the ken of the acknowledged master of the science. Then, and then only, will it be possible that the unsoundness he alleges will be seen as really such.[68]

26 I noted, however, that not a single Muslim divine had directed his attention and endeavor to that end. What the *mutakallimūn* had to say in their books, where they were engaged in refuting the philosophers, was nothing but abstruse, scattered remarks, patently inconsistent and false, which could not conceivably hoodwink an ordinary intelligent person, to say nothing of one familiar with the subleties of the philosophical sciences.

27 I knew, of course, that undertaking to refute their doctrine before comprehending it and knowing it in depth would be a shot in the dark.[69] So I girded myself for the task of learning that science by the mere perusal of their writings without seeking the help of a master and teacher. I devoted myself to that in the moments I had free from writing and lecturing on the legal sciences[70]—and I was then burdened with the teaching and instruction of three hundred students in Baghdad. As it turned out, through mere reading in those embezzled moments, God Most High gave me an insight into the farthest reaches of the philosophers' sciences in less than two years. Then, having understood their doctrine, I continued to reflect assiduously on it for nearly a year, coming back to it constantly and repeatedly reexamining its intricacies and profundities. Finally I became so familiar with the measure of its deceit and deception, and its precision and delusion,[71] that I had no doubt about my thorough grasp of it.

28 So hear now my account of the philosophers[72] and my report of the substance of their sciences. For I observed that they fell into several categories and noted that their sciences included several divisions. But to all of them, despite the multiplicity of their categories, cleaves the stigma of unbelief and godlessness.[73] Yet there is a marked difference between the older and the oldest of them and the more recent and the earlier[74] in their distance from and closeness to the truth.

The Categories of the Philosophers and the Fact That the Stigma of Unbelief Is Common to All of Them

29 Know that the philosophers, notwithstanding the multiplicity of their groups and the diversity of their doctrines, can be divided into three main divisions: Materialists, Naturalists, and Theists.[75]

30 *The first category,* the Materialists, were a group of the most ancient philosophers who denied the existence of the omniscient and omnipotent Creator-Ruler.[76] They alleged that the world has existed from eternity as it is, of itself and not by reason of a Maker. Animals have unceasingly come from seed, and seed from animals: thus it was, and thus it ever will be. These are the godless[77] in the full sense of the term.

31 *The second category,* the Naturalists, were men who devoted much study to the world of nature and the marvels found in animals and plants; they also were much taken up with the dissection of animal organs. In these they saw such marvels of God Most High's making and such wonders of His wisdom that they were compelled, with that in mind, to acknowledge the existence of a wise Creator cognizant of the aims and purposes of all things. Indeed, no one can study the science of anatomy and the marvelous uses of the organs without acquiring this compelling knowledge of the perfect governance of Him Who shaped the structure of animals, and especially that of man.[78]

32 However, it appeared to these philosophers, because they had studied nature so much, that the equilibrium of the mixture of humors[79] had a great effect on the resulting constitution of the animal's powers. Hence they thought that man's rational power was also dependent on the mixture of his humors and that its corruption would follow the corruption of the mixture of his humors, and so that power would cease to exist. Once it ceased to exist, they alleged that bringing back the nonexistent would be unintelligible. So they adopted the view that the soul dies, never to return. Consequently they denied the afterlife and rejected the Garden and the Fire, the Assembly and the Recall, and the Resurrection and the Reckoning.[80] So in their view there would be no future reward for obedience, and no punishment for disobedience. Therefore they lost all restraint and abandoned themselves to their passions like beasts. These were also godless men, because basic faith is belief in God and the Last Day—and these men denied the Last Day, even though they believed in God and His Attributes.

33 *The Third category,* the Theists, were the later philosophers, such as Socrates, the master of Plato, and Plato, the master of Aristotle. It was Aristotle who systematized logic for the philosophers and refined the philosophical sciences, accurately formulating previously imprecise statements and bringing to maturity the crudities of their sciences. Taken altogether, these refuted the first two categories of the Materialists and the Naturalists. Indeed, by the arguments they advanced to lay bare the enormities of the latter, they relieved others of that task: "And God spared the believers from fighting (the unbelievers)" (33.25) by reason of the unbelievers' own infighting.[81]

34 Then Aristotle refuted Plato and Socrates and the Theists who had preceded him in such thorough fashion that he disassociated himself from them all. Yet he, too, retained remnants of their vicious unbelief and innovation which he was unsuccessful in avoiding. So they all must be

taxed with unbelief, as must their partisans among the Muslim philosophers, such as Ibn Sīnā[82] and al-Fārābī[83] and their likes.[84] None, however, of the Muslim philosophers engaged so much in transmitting Aristotle's lore as did the two men just mentioned. What others transmitted is not free from disorder and confusion and in studying it one's mind becomes so muddled that he fails to understand it—and how can the incomprehensible be rejected or accepted?

35 The sum of what we regard as the authentic philosophy of Aristotle, as transmitted by al-Fārābī and Ibn Sīnā, can be reduced to three parts: a part which must be branded as unbelief; a part which must be stigmatized as innovation; and a part which need not be repudiated at all.[85] Let us now set this forth in detail.

The Divisions of the Philosophical Sciences

36 Know that the sciences of the philosophers, with reference to the aim we have in mind, include six divisions: mathematical, logical, physical, metaphysical, political, and moral.[86]

37 *The mathematical sciences* deal with arithmetic, geometry, and astronomy. But nothing in them entails denial or affirmation of religious matters. On the contrary, they concern rigorously demonstrated facts[87] which can in no wise be denied once they are known and understood. From them, however, two evils have been engendered.

38 *One of these* is that whoever takes up these mathematical sciences marvels at the fine precision of their details and the clarity of their proofs. Because of that, he forms a high opinion of the philosophers and assumes that all their sciences have the same lucidity and apodeictic solidity as this science of mathematics. Moreover, he will have heard the talk of the town about their unbelief, their negative attitude,[87a] and their disdain for the Law. Therefore he ceases to believe out of pure conformism,[88] asserting: "If religion were true, this would not have been unknown to these philosophers, given their precision in this science of mathematics." Thus, when he learns through hearsay of their unbelief and rejection of religion, he concludes that it is right to reject and disavow religion. How many a man have I seen who strayed from the path of truth on this pretext and for no other reason!

39 One may say to such a man: "A person skilled in one field is not necessarily skilled in every field. Thus a man skilled in jurisprudence and *kalām* is not necessarily skilled in medicine, nor is a man who is ignorant of the speculative and rational sciences necessarily ignorant of the sci-

ence of syntax. On the contrary, in each field there are men who have reached in it a certain degree of skill and preeminence, although they may be quite stupid and ignorant about other things. What the ancients[89] had to say about mathematical topics was apodeictic, whereas their views on metaphysical questions were conjectural. But this is known only to an experienced man who has made a thorough study of the matter."

40 When such an argument is urged against one who has become an unbeliever out of mere conformism, he finds it unacceptable. Rather, caprice's sway,[90] vain passion,[91] and love of appearing to be clever prompt him to persist in his high opinion of the philosophers with regard to all their sciences. This, then, is a very serious evil, and because of it one should warn off anyone who would embark upon the study of those mathematical sciences. For even though they do not pertain to the domain of religion, yet, since they are among the primary elements of the philosophers' sciences, the student of mathematics will be insidiously affected by the sinister mischief of the philosophers. Rare, therefore, are those who study mathematics without losing their religion and throwing off the restraint of piety.[92]

41 *The second evil* likely to follow from the study of the mathematical sciences derives from the case of an ignorant friend of Islam who supposes that our religion must be championed by the rejection of every science ascribed to the philosophers. So he rejects all their sciences, claiming that they display ignorance and folly in them all. He even denies their statements about eclipses of the sun and the moon and asserts that their views are contrary to the revealed Law.[93] When such an assertion reaches the ears of someone who knows those things through apodeictic demonstration, he does not doubt the validity of his proof, but rather believes that Islam is built on ignorance and the denial of apodeictic demonstration. So he becomes all the more enamored of philosophy and envenomed against Islam. Great indeed is the crime against religion committed by anyone who supposes that Islam is to be championed by the denial of these mathematical sciences. For the revealed Law nowhere undertakes[94] to deny or affirm these sciences, and the latter nowhere address themselves to religious matters.

42 The saying of Muḥammad—God's blessing and peace be upon him! —"The sun and moon are two of the signs of God Most High: they are not eclipsed for the death or life of any man; so when you see an eclipse, fly in fear to the mention of God Most High,"[95] contains nothing demanding the denial of the science of calculation[96] which apprises us of the course of the sun and the moon and their conjunction and their opposition in a specific way. As for his (alleged) saying—Peace be upon

him!—"But when God manifests Himself to a thing, it humbles itself before Him," this addition is not found at all in sound tradition.[97] This, then, is the judgment to be made on the character of mathematics and its evil consequences.

43 Nothing in *the logical sciences* has anything to do with religion by way of negation and affirmation. On the contrary, they are the study of the methods of proofs, of syllogisms, of the conditions governing the premises of apodeictic demonstration, of how these premises are to be combined, of the requisites for a sound definition, and of how the latter is to be drawn up. Knowledge is either a concept, and the way to know it is the definition, or it is an assent,[97a] and the way to know it is the apodeictic demonstration. There is nothing in this which must be rejected. On the contrary, it is the sort of thing mentioned by the *mutakallimūn* and the partisans of reasoning[98] in connection with the proofs they use. The philosophers differ from them only in modes of expression and technical terms and in a greater refinement in definitions and subdivisions. Their manner of discoursing on such things is exemplified by their saying: "If it is certain that every A is B, then it necessarily follows that some B is A"—for instance: If it is certain that every man is an animal, then it follows necessarily that some animal is a man. This they express by saying that a universal affirmative proposition is convertible to a particular affirmative proposition.[99]

44 What has this to do with the important truths of our religion, that it should call for rejection and denial? When it is rejected, the only effect of such a rejection in the minds of logicians is a low opinion of the rejecter's intelligence, and, what is worse, of his religion, which, he claims, rests on such rejection. To be sure, the philosophers themselves are guilty of a kind of injustice in the case of this science of logic. This is that in logic they bring together, for apodeictic demonstration, conditions known to lead undoubtedly to sure and certain knowledge. But when, in metaphysics, they finally come to discuss questions touching on religion, they cannot satisfy those conditions, but rather are extremely slipshod in applying them. Moreover, logic may be studied by one who will think it a fine thing and regard it is very clear. Consequently he will think that the instances of unbelief related of the philosophers are backed up by demonstrations such as those set forth in logic. Therefore he will rush into unbelief even before reaching the metaphysical sciences. Hence this evil may also befall the student of logic.[100]

45 *The physical sciences* are a study of the world of the heavens and their stars and of the sublunar world's simple bodies, such is water,

air, earth, and fire, and composite bodies, such as animals, plants, and minerals. They also study the causes of their changing and being transformed and being mixed. That is like medicine's study of the human body and its principal and subsidiary organs and the causes of the alteration of the mixtures of its humors. And just as religion does not require the repudiation of the science of medicine, so also it does not require the repudiation of the science of physics, except for certain specific questions which we have mentioned in our book *The Incoherence of the Philosophers.*[101] Apart from these, it will be clear upon reflection that any other points on which the physicists must be opposed are subsumed in those we have alluded to. The basic point regarding all of them is for you to know that nature is totally subject to God Most High: it does not act of itself but is used as an instrument by its Creator. The sun, moon, stars, and the elements are subject to God's command: none of them effects any act by and of itself.[102]

46 It is in *the metaphysical sciences* that most of the philosophers' errors are found. Owing to the fact that they could not carry out apodeictic demonstration according to the conditions they had postulated in logic, they differed a great deal about metaphysical questions. Aristotle's doctrine on these matters, as transmitted by al-Fārābī and Ibn Sīnā, approximates the teachings of the Islamic philosophers. But the sum of their errors comes down to twenty heads, in three of which they must be taxed with unbelief, and in seventeen with innovation.[103] It was to refute their doctrine on these twenty questions that we composed our book *The Incoherence.*

47 In the three questions first mentioned they were opposed to (the belief of) all Muslims, viz. in their affirming

1) that men's bodies will not be assembled[104] on the Last Day, but only disembodied spirits will be rewarded and punished, and the rewards and punishments will be spiritual, not corporal. They were indeed right in affirming the spiritual rewards and punishments, for these also are certain; but they falsely denied the corporal rewards and punishments and blasphemed the revealed Law in their stated views.

2) The second question is their declaration: "God Most High knows universals, but not particulars." This also is out-and-out unbelief. On the contrary, the truth is that "there does not escape Him the weight of an atom in the heavens or in the earth" (34.3; cf. 10.62/61).[105]

3) The third question is their maintaining the eternity of the world, past and future.[106]

No Muslim has ever professed any of their views on these questions.[107]

48 On other matters—such as the denial of the divine attributes, and their assertion that God is knowing by His essence, not by a knowledge superadded to His essence, and similar views of theirs—their doctrine is close to that of the Muᶜtazilites.[108] But there is no need to tax the Muᶜtazilites with unbelief because of such views. We have already mentioned that[109] in our book *The Clear Criterion for Distinguishing between Islam and Godlessness,* as well as what shows the error of anyone who precipitously brands as unbelief everything that clashes with his own doctrine.[110]

49 In *the political sciences* all that the philosophers have to say comes down to administrative maxims concerned with secular affairs and the government of rulers. They simply took these over from the scriptures revealed to the prophets by God Most High and from the maxims handed down from the predecessors of the prophets.[111]

50 All they have to say about *the moral sciences* comes down to listing the qualities and habits of the soul, and recording their generic and specific kinds, and the way to cultivate the good ones and combat the bad. This they simply took over from the sayings of the sufis.[112] These were godly men who applied themselves assiduously to invoking God,[113] resisting passion, and following the way leading to God Most High by shunning worldly pleasures. In the course of their spiritual combat the good habits of the soul and its shortcomings had been disclosed to them and also the defects that vitiate its actions. All this they set forth plainly. Then the philosophers took over these ideas and mixed them with their own doctrines, using the lustre afforded by them to promote the circulation of their own false teaching. There was indeed in their age, nay but there is in every age, a group of godly men of whom God Most High never leaves the world destitute. For they are the pillars of the earth,[114] and by their blessings the divine mercy descends upon earthdwellers as is declared in the tradition from Muḥammad—God's blessing and peace be upon him!—in which he says: "Because of them you receive rain, and thanks to them you receive sustenance, and among them were the Companions of the Cave."[115] Such godly men existed in ancient times, as the Qurʾān declares (cf. Sura 18).

51 From the Islamic philosophers' mixing the prophetic utterances and the sayings of the sufis with their own writings two evils have sprung: one in the case of the man who accepts their ethical teaching, the other in the case of the man who rejects it.

52 The evil in the case of the man who rejects their ethical teaching is very serious. For some dim-witted persons suppose, since that bor-

rowed prophetic and sufi doctrine has been set down in the philosophers' writings and mixed with their false doctrine, that this doctrine must be eschewed and never cited and even disavowed whenever anyone cites it. This is their attitude because they have heard that doctrine in the first place only from the philosophers. So their weak minds straightway judge it to be erroneous because the one who voices it is in error on other matters. This is like the case of a man who hears a Christian say: "There is no God but God; Jesus is the Apostle of God," and then denies it, saying: "This is what the Christians say." Such a man does not defer judgment while he ponders whether the Christian is an unbeliever because of that statement, or because of his denial of Muḥammad's prophethood—God's blessing and peace be upon him! Hence, if he is an unbeliever only because of his denial of the latter, he should not be contradicted in matters other than what he disbelieves—I mean something which is true in itself, even though the Christian also holds it to be true.[116]

53 This is the practice of those dim-witted men who know the truth by men, and not men by the truth. The intelligent man, on the contrary, follows the advice of the Master of the Intelligent, ᶜAlī—God be pleased with him!—where he says: "Do not know the truth by men, but rather, know the truth and you will know its adherents."[117] The intelligent man, therefore, first knows the truth, then he considers what is actually said by someone. If it is true, he accepts it, whether the speaker be wrong or right in other matters. Indeed, such a man will often be intent on extracting what is true from the involved utterances of the erring, since he is aware that gold is usually found mixed with dirt. The money-changer suffers no harm if he puts his hand into the sack of the trickster[118] and pulls out the genuine pure gold from among the false and counterfeit coins, so long as he can rely on his professional acumen. It is not the expert money-changer, but rather the inexperienced bumpkin who must be restrained from dealing with the trickster. Likewise, a clumsy and stupid person must be kept away from the seashore, not the proficient swimmer; and a child must be prevented from handling a snake, not the skilled snake charmer.

54 It is certainly true, since most men have an overweening opinion of their own competence and cleverness and think they are perfectly equipped intellectually to discern truth from error, that the door must be blocked to prevent the generality of men, as far as possible, from perusing the works of those addicted to error. For they will by no means be safe from the second evil which we shall presently mention, even if they do manage to escape the evil which we have just noted.

55 Some of the remarks found here and there in our works on the mysteries of the religious sciences were objected to by a group of men whose minds were not thoroughly grounded in those sciences and whose mental vision was not open to the ultimate aims of our teachings. They alleged that those remarks were taken from things said by the early philosophers. As a matter of fact, some of them were my own original ideas—and it is not farfetched that ideas should coincide, just as a horse's hoof may fall on the print left by another; and some are found in the scriptures; and the sense of most is found in the writings of the sufis.

56 However, assuming that they are found only in the writings of the philosophers, if what is said is reasonable in itself and corroborated by apodeictic proof and not contrary to the Qur'ān and the Sunna, then why should it be shunned and rejected? If we were to open this door and aim at forgoing every truth which had been first formulated by the mind of one in error, we would have to forgo much of what is true. We would also have to give up a lot of the verses of the Qur'ān and the traditions of the Apostle and the recitals of our pious forebears and the sayings of the sages and the sufis. For the author of the book of "The Brethren of Purity"[119] cites these in his own work, appealing to their authority and thereby enticing the minds of stupid men to embrace his false doctrine. That would be an Invitation to those in error to wrest the truth from our hands by putting it into their own books.

57 The lowest level attained by an intelligent man is to be so different from the gullible man in the street that he feels no aversion to honey, even though he finds it in a cupper's glass, but realizes that the cupping glass does not alter the nature of the honey. For the natural distaste for such honey is based on a popular misconception arising from the fact that the cupping glass is made for blood deemed impure.[120] Consequently the man in the street supposes the blood is deemed impure because it is in the cupping glass and does not realize that it is deemed impure because of a property found in the blood itself. Hence, since this property does not exist in the honey, its being found in such a vessel does not impart to it that property nor does it necessitate its being deemed impure. This is an empty fancy, yet it is prevalent among most men. Thus, whenever you trace back a statement and attribute it to a speaker of whom they have a good opinion, they accept it, even though it be false; but whenever you attribute it to someone of whom they have a bad opinion, they reject it, even though it be true. Thus they always know the truth by men, not men by the truth—which is the ne plus ultra of error! This, then, is the evil due to total rejection of the philosophers' ethical teaching.

58 *The second evil* is that due to total acceptance of their ethical teaching. For one who studies their books, such as that of "The Brethren of Purity" and others, and sees the prophetic maxims and sufi sayings they interspersed with their own utterances, often approves of their writings and accepts them and forms a good opinion of them. Thereupon he may readily accept their errors mixed up with those borrowed truths because of a good opinion acquired about what he has seen and approved. That is a way of luring men into error.

59 Because of this evil the perusal of the philosophers' books must be prevented on the score of the deceit and danger they contain. Just as an unskilled swimmer must be kept away from slippery river banks, so men must be kept from perusing those books. And just as children must be kept from handling snakes, so the ears of men must be protected from the farrago of those sayings. And just as the snake charmer must not handle a snake in the presence of his little boy, since he knows that the boy will imitate him thinking he is like his father, but rather must caution his boy against that by being cautious himself in the boy's presence, so also the man of deep learning must comport himself. Furthermore, when a skilled snake charmer takes a snake and separates the antidote from the poison and draws forth the antidote and renders the poison harmless, he is not free to withhold the antidote from anyone in need of it. So, too, when the money changer skilled in picking out coins puts his hand in the trickster's sack and takes out the genuine pure gold and discards the spurious and counterfeit coins, he is not free to withhold the good and acceptable coins from anyone who needs them. The same holds good for the true scholar.

60 Moreover, a man in need of the antidote whose soul feels a great loathing for it, because he knows that it has been extracted from the snake which is the seat of the poison, must be properly instructed. Likewise, when a poor man in dire need of money is averse to accepting gold drawn from the trickster's sack he must be reminded that his aversion is pure ignorance which will cause him to be deprived of the benefit he seeks. He certainly ought to be informed that the proximity of the counterfeit to the genuine coins does not make the genuine coins counterfeit, just as it does not make the counterfeit coins genuine. In precisely the same way, therefore, the close proximity of the true to the false does not make the true false, as it does not make the false true.

This, then, is as much as we wish to say about the evil and mischief of philosophy.

The Doctrine of Ta^clīmism and Its Danger

61 When I had finished with the science of philosophy—having mastered and understood it and pinpointed its errors—I knew that philosophy also was inadequate to satisfy my aim fully. I also realized that reason alone is incapable of fully grasping all problems or of getting to the heart of all difficulties. Meanwhile the Taᶜlīmites had come into prominence and their talk of an arcane knowledge of the meaning of things derived from the infallible Imam, Master of the Truth, had been bruited about. It occurred to me that I ought to inquire into their views to find out exactly what their position was.[121] Then it happened that a peremptory order reached me from His Highness the Caliph to write a book which would reveal the true meaning of their doctrine.[122] I could not contravene that order, and it became an external incentive added to my original interior motive. So I began to seek out their writings and to collect their views. I had already been struck by some of their novel utterances, the brainchildren of our own contemporaries, views which were not consonant with the program handed down from their predecessors.

62 I therefore collected and marshalled those utterances, combining thoroughness and accuracy, and answered them at great length. The result was that one of the Sunnites[123] found fault with me for overstating their argument. He said: "This is an effort on their behalf. For they would have been unable to defend their doctrine by such specious arguments had it not been for your pinpointing and marshalling them." This criticism is justified in a way. Long ago Aḥmad ibn Ḥanbal found fault with al-Ḥārith al-Muḥāsibī[124]—God have mercy on them both!—for his writing books in refutation of the Muᶜtazilites. Al-Ḥārith said: "Refuting innovation is a duty." Ahmad replied: "Yes, but you have first reported their specious argument and then answered it. What assurance have you that a man may not read the specious argument and it will stick in his mind, but he will pay no attention to the answer, or he will study the answer without understanding its real import?"

63 Aḥmad ibn Ḥanbal's remark is true. But it concerned a specious argument that had not become widespread and notorious. However, once such an argument becomes widespread, replying to it becomes imperative: and replying is possible only after setting the argument forth. To be sure, one should not burden oneself with a difficulty with which they have not bothered.[125] Nor did I do that. On the contrary, I had heard such argument from one of my associates who frequented my company after he had affiliated himself with them and professed their doctrine. He told me they

used to laugh at the works of those who wrote in refutation of them, since those writers had still not grasped their argument. He then cited that argument, relating it in their own words. So I could not personally be content with having it thought that I was unaware of their basic argument, and for that reason I presented it; nor did I want it thought of me that, even though I had heard the argument, I had not grasped it, and for that reason I reported it systematically. My aim was to give the fullest account possible of their specious argumentation and then to prove its error to the hilt.

64 To put it briefly: there is no substance to their views and no force in their argument. Indeed, had it not been for the maladroit defense put forward by the ignorant friend of truth, that innovation, given its weakness, would never have attained its present position. But intense fanaticism led the defenders of the truth to prolong the debate with them over the premises of their argument and to contradict them in everything they said. Thus they fought the Ta^c^līmites over their claim that there must be authoritative teaching and an authoritative teacher, and also in their claim that not every teacher is suitable, but that there must be an infallible teacher. Their argument showing the need of authoritative teaching and an authoritative teacher was loud and clear, whereas the counter-argument of their opponents was weak. Because of that many were seduced into thinking that it was due to the strength of the Ta^c^līmites' doctrine and the weakness of their opponents doctrine, not understanding that it was really due to the dim-wittedness of the defender of the truth and his ignorance of how to go about it. In fact, the right way to proceed is to acknowledge the need for an authoritative teacher who must also be infallible. But our infallible teacher is Muḥammad—God's blessing and peace be upon him! If they say: "He is dead!" we say: "And your teacher is absent!" And when they say: "Our teacher has indeed taught his emissaries and scattered them throughout the countries, and he expects them to return to consult him if they disagree on some point or encounter some difficulty," we say: "Our teacher has taught his emissaries and scattered them throughout the countries, and he has perfected this teaching, since God Most High said: 'Today I have perfected for you your religion and have accorded you My full favor' (5.5/3). And once the teaching has been perfected, the death of the teacher works no harm, just as his absence works no harm."[126]

65 There remains their argument: "How do you judge about a case you have not heard of? By the text? But you have not heard it. Or by personal effort and forming your own opinion?[127] But this is the most likely place for disagreement!" We reply: "We do as Mu^c^ādh did when the Apostle of God—Peace be upon him!—dispatched him to Yemen, viz. we judge by

the text, if the text exists, and by personal effort in its absence."[128] In fact we do as their emissaries do when they are in lands farthest away from the Imam. For they cannot judge by the text, since limited texts cannot exhaust unlimited cases; nor can they return to the Imam's town in each individual case, for by the time they would have covered the distance and returned, the petitioner might well have died and their return would be useless.

66 A man, then, who has a problem about the *qibla*[129] has no recourse but to perform his Prayer in accordance with his personal judgment. For if he were to journey to the Imam's town to learn about the *qibla,* the time for the Prayer would elapse. Hence the Prayer performed facing a direction other than the *qibla is* lawful when based on conjecture. It is said: "The man who errs in personal judgment will receive one reward, and the man who is right will receive a double reward."[130] So it is in all cases involving personal effort. It is also true in the case of paying the legal alms to a poor man.[131] For by his personal judgment one may judge the man to be poor, whereas he is really rich, but not outwardly because he hides his wealth. A man so judging will not be blamed for it, even though he has erred, because he is blameworthy only for what gives rise to his personal opinion. If our opponent says: "His adversary's opinion is as good as his," we reply: "He is commanded to follow his own personal opinion, just as the man exercising personal judgment about the *qibla* must follow his own opinion, even though others disagree with him." He may then say: "The servile conformist follows the opinion of Abū Ḥanīfa[132] or al-Shāfiʿī[133]—God's mercy on both of them!—or of someone else." I reply: "How should a servile conformist who is confused about the *qibla* act when those exercising personal judgment disagree about it?" He will then say: "It is up to him to exercise personal judgment in finding the man best qualified and most knowledgeable about the indications of the *qibla,* and then he must follow that personal judgment." The same is true regarding the various schools.[134]

67 The prophets and religious leaders referred men to the exercise of personal judgment, and necessarily so, despite their knowledge that men might err. The Apostle of God—God's blessing and peace be upon him!—even said: "I judge by externals, but God undertakes to judge the hearts of men."[135] This means: "I judge according to the most probable opinion resulting from the witnesses' statements, but they may err about the matter. The prophets had no way to be safe from error in such cases involving personal judgment; how, then, can anyone else aspire to such safety?

68 At this point the Taʿlīmites raise two difficulties. *One of them* is their statement: "Even though what you say may be true in cases of *fiqh*

[law] involving personal judgment, it is not true regarding the basic articles of belief.[136] For one who errs in these is inexcusable. How, then, can one find a way to safety from error in these matters?" I reply: "The basic articles of belief are contained in the Book and the Sunna, and what is beyond that is a matter of detail. Anyone engaged in dispute about a further matter of detail will find the truth about it by weighing it in "the correct balance," viz. the scales mentioned by God Most High in His Book. These are the five which I have mentioned in *The Book of the Correct Balance.*[137]

69 The adversary may say: "Your opponents disagree with you about that balance." I reply: "It is inconceivable that anyone understand that balance and then disagree about it. For the Taᶜlīmites will not disagree about it, because I have deduced it from the Qurʾān and learned it therefrom.[138] Nor will the logicians disagree about it, because it accords with the conditions they lay down in logic without clashing with them. Nor will the *mutakallim* disagree about it, because it agrees with his statements on the proofs of speculative matters by which the truth in Kalām questions becomes known."

70 My adversary may say: "If you have such a balance at your disposal, then why do you not remove the disagreement existing among men?" I reply: "Were they to hearken to me, I would remove the disagreement among them! Moreover, I have mentioned the way to remove disagreement in *The Book of the Correct Balance:* so study it that you may know that it is true and would definitely abolish disagreement if only men would hearken! But they—all of them!—will not hearken! Or rather, some did hearken to me, and I did remove the disagreement existing among them. Furthermore, your Imam[139] wants to banish disagreement from among them, despite their failure to hearken: why, then, has he not done this up to now? And why did ᶜAlī—God be pleased with him!—not do that, since he was the first and greatest of the Imams? Does the Imam indeed claim that he can forcibly induce men to hearken? If so, then why has he not done that up to now? And to what day has he deferred it? And has anything resulted among men from the Imam's claim but increasing disagreement and the growing number of men at variance? Surely it was to be feared that disagreement would result in a kind of hurt that would finally end in bloodshed, devastation of towns, orphaning of children, brigandage, and plundering of property. And indeed, as a result of the "blessings" of your doing away with disagreement, there has happened in the world a disagreement the like of which has never been known!"[140]

71 He may say: "You have claimed that you can remove the disagreement existing among men. But he who stands perplexed between

conflicting views and opposing differences is not b rather than to your adversary. Most of the adversar and there is no difference between you and them *difficulty,* and I reply: "First of all this objection may you. For when *you* invite the perplexed person to listen to you, say: 'Why are you any better than those who oppose you—and most scholars disagree with you!?' I wonder how you would answer! Would you answer by saying: 'My Imam has been explicitly designated'?[141] But who will believe you in your claim of explicit designation, since he has not heard the explicit designation from the Apostle? All he hears is your claim, accompanied as it is by the scholars' agreement on your forgery and lying.

72 "But grant that he concedes to you the explicit designation of your Imam. If he is then perplexed about the basis[142] of prophethood and says: 'Admitted that your Imam adduces the miracle of Jesus—Peace be upon him!' and avers: 'The proof of my veracity is that I shall bring back to life your dead father. Then he actually does so and declares to me that he is in the right. Yet how do I know his veracity? For not all men recognized the veracity of Jesus—Peace be upon him!—by virtue of this miracle.[143] On the contrary, the matter was beset with certain difficulties which could be answered only by subtle intellectual reasoning. But in your view intellectual reasoning is not to be trusted. Moreover, one cannot know that a miracle proves a prophet's veracity unless he also knows magic and how to distinguish between it and a miracle,[144] and unless he knows that God is not leading His servants astray—and the problem of "leading astray and the difficulty of formulating an accurate answer to it are notorious.'[145] How, then, would you refuse all that, since your Imam is no worthier of being followed than his opponent?"

73 Then he will go back to the rational proofs of which he disapproves, and his adversary will adduce similar, and even clearer, proofs. And thus this difficulty has indeed been retorted against them in such a powerful way that, were they to unite, from first to last,[146] to give some answer to it, they would be unable to do so.

74 This trouble has arisen simply from a group of ineffectual men who disputed with them, not by using the method of retort, but by attempting to give a direct answer. The latter calls for lengthy discussion and does not quickly reach minds,[147] nor is it suitable for silencing adversaries.

75 Some may say: "This is the argument by retort: but is there a reasoned answer to their claim?" I reply: "Certainly! The answer to it is that, were the perplexed person to say that he is perplexed, without specifying

problem about which he is perplexed, one should say to him: 'You are like a sick man who says that he is sick, but does not specify his illness, and yet requests a remedy for it.'" He should be told that there exists no cure for sickness in general, but only for a specific sickness such as a headache or an attack of diarrhea or something else. Likewise, then, the perplexed person must specify what perplexes him. If he specifies the problem, you then inform him of the truth about it by weighing the matter with the five scales. No one understands these without also acknowledging that this is the true balance and that one can have confidence in whatever is weighed in it. So let this balance be understood, then one will also understand the soundness of weighing with it, just as the student of arithmetic understands arithmetic itself as well as the fact that his arithmetic teacher knows arithmetic and teaches it correctly. I have already explained all that in *The Book of the Correct Balance* in the compass of twenty folia: so let it be studied there.

76 My present aim is not to show the wrongness of their doctrine, for I have already done that: (1) in my book *al Mustaẓhirī*[148] (2) in my book *The Proof of the Truth,*[149] an answer to some of their arguments proposed to me in Baghdad; (3) in my book *The Detailed Exposition of the Disagreement,*[150] which contains twelve sections, and is a reply to arguments proposed to me in Hamadhān; (4) in my book *al-Drj al-marqūm bil~jadāwil,*[151] which deals with some feeble arguments of theirs proposed to me in Ṭūs; (5) in my book *The Correct Balance,* an independent work aimed at explaining the scale for weighing knowledge and showing that he who fully understands it has no need of an infallible Imam.

77 Rather, my main point here is that the Ta^{c}līmites have no cure which saves anyone from the darknesses of conflicting opinions. On the contrary, despite their inability to establish a sound proof of the designation of the Imam, for some time we went along with them and assented to their assertion of the need for authoritative teaching and an infallible teacher, and we agreed that he was the one specified. Then we questioned them about the lore they had learned from this infallible one and proposed to them some problems. These they did not understand, to say nothing of attempting to solve them! Then, when they were unable to do so, they referred to the hidden Imam and said: "There is no alternative to making the journey to him." The amazing thing is that they waste their life in seeking the authoritative teacher and in boasting of having found him, yet they have learned nothing at all from him! They are like a man smeared with filth who wearies himself looking for water: then, when he finds it, he does not use it, but remains smeared with foulness!

78 Among them was one who claimed to know some of their lore. But the substance of what he mentioned was a bit of the feeble philosophy of Pythagoras.[152] The latter was one of the early ancients, and his doctrine is the feeblest of all philosophical doctrines. Aristotle had already refuted him and had even regarded his teaching as weak and contemptible. Yet this is what is followed in the book of the Brethren of Purity, and it is really the refuse of philosophy. One can only marvel at a man who spends a weary lifetime in the quest for knowledge and then is content with such flaccid and thin stuff! Yet he thinks he has attained the utmost reaches of knowledge!

79 These also we have tested thoroughly and probed inside and out. The substance of their doctrine comes down to deceiving the common folk and the dim-witted by showing the need for the authoritative teacher, and to disputing men's denial of the need for authoritative teaching by strong and effective argument. So it goes until someone tries to help them about the need for the authoritative teacher by saying: "Give us some of his lore and acquaint us with some of his teaching!" Then the disputant pauses and says: "Now that you have conceded to me that much, do you seek him for yourself![153] For my aim was to tell you only this much." For he knows that, were he to add anything more, he would be put to shame and would be unable to solve the simplest problem. Nay, but he would be unable to understand it, let alone give an answer to it!

This, then, is the true nature of their situation. So try them, and you will hate them![154] Thus, when we had had experience of them, we also washed our hands of them!

Discussion of the Ways of the Sufis

80 When I had finished with all those kinds of lore, I brought my mind to bear on the way of the sufis. I knew that their particular Way[155] is consummated [realized] only by knowledge and by activity [by the union of theory and practice]. The aim of their knowledge[156] is to lop off the obstacles present in the soul and to rid oneself of its reprehensible habits and vicious qualities in order to attain thereby a heart empty of all save God and adorned with the constant remembrance of God.

81 Theory was easier for me than practice. Therefore I began to learn their lore from the perusal of their books, such as *The Food of Hearts* by Abū Ṭālib al-Makkī[157] (God's mercy be upon him!) and the writings of al-Ḥārith al-Muḥāsibī,[158] and the miscellaneous items handed down from al-Junayd[159] and al-Shiblī[160] and Abū Yazīd al-Bisṭāmī[161] (God hallow their spirits!) and others of their masters. As a result I came to know

the core of their theoretical aims and I learned all that could be learned of their way by study and hearing.

82 Then it became clear to me that their most distinctive characteristic is something that can be attained, not by study, but rather by fruitional experience[162] and the state of ecstasy[163] and "the exchange of qualities."[164] How great a difference there is between your *knowing* the definitions and causes and conditions of health and satiety and your *being* healthy and sated! And how great a difference there is between your knowing the definition of drunkenness—viz. that it is a term denoting a state resulting from the predominance of vapors which rise from the stomach to the centers of thought—and your actually being drunk! Indeed, a drunken man, while he is drunk, does not know the definition and concept of drunkenness and has no knowledge of it.[165] But a physician[166] knows the definition and the elements of drunkenness, though he is experiencing no actual drunkenness. So also, when a physician is ill, he knows the definition and causes of health and the remedies which procure it, though he is then actually bereft of health. Similarly, too, there is a difference between your knowing the true nature and conditions and causes of asceticism and your actually practicing asceticism and personally shunning the things of this world.

83 I knew with certainty that the sufis were masters of states, not purveyors of words,[167] and that I had learned all I could by way of theory. There remained, then, only what was attainable, not by hearing and study, but by fruitional experience and actually engaging in the way. From the sciences which I had practiced and the methods which I had followed in my inquiry into the two kinds of knowledge, revealed and rational, I had already acquired a sure and certain faith in God Most High, in the prophetic mediation of revelation, and in the Last Day. These three fundamentals of our Faith had become deeply rooted in my soul, not because of any specific, precisely formulated proofs, but because of reasons and circumstances and experiences too many to list in detail.[168]

84 It had already become clear to me that my only hope of attaining beatitude in the afterlife lay in piety and restraining my soul from passion. The beginning of all that, I knew, was to sever my heart's attachment to the world by withdrawing from this abode of delusion and turning to the mansion of immortality and devoting myself with total ardor to God Most High. That, I knew, could be achieved only by shunning fame and fortune and fleeing from my preoccupations and attachments.

85 Next I attentively considered my circumstances, and I saw that I was immersed in attachments which had encompassed me from all sides.

I also considered my activities—the best of them being public and private instruction—and saw that in them I was applying myself to sciences unimportant and useless in this pilgrimage to the hereafter.[169] Then I reflected on my intention in my public teaching, and I saw that it was not directed purely to God, but rather was instigated and motivated by the quest for fame and widespread prestige.[170] So I became certain that I was on the brink of a crumbling bank and already on the verge of falling into the Fire, unless I set about mending my ways.

86 I therefore reflected unceasingly on this for some time, while I still had freedom of choice. One day I would firmly resolve to leave Baghdad and disengage myself from those circumstances, and another day I would revoke my resolution. I would put one foot forward, and the other backward. In the morning I would have a sincere desire to seek the things of the afterlife; but by evening the hosts of passion would assail it and render it lukewarm. Mundane desires began tugging me with their chains to remain as I was, while the herald of faith was crying out: "Away! Up and away! Only a little is left of your life, and a long journey lies before you! All the theory and practice in which you are engrossed is eyeservice and fakery![171] If you do not prepare now for the afterlife, when will you do so? And if you do not sever these attachments now, then when will you sever them?"

87 At such thoughts the call would reassert itself and I would make an irrevocable decision to run off and escape. Then Satan would return to the attack and say: "This is a passing state: beware, then, of yielding to it! For it will quickly vanish. Once you have given in to it and given up your present renown and splendid position free from vexation and renounced your secure situation untroubled by the contention of your adversaries, your soul might again look longingly at all that—but it would not be easy to return to it!"

88 Thus I incessantly vacillated between the contending pull of worldly desires and the appeals of the afterlife for about six months, starting with Rajab of the year 488 (July, 1095 A.D.). In this month the matter passed from choice to compulsion. For God put a lock upon my tongue so that I was impeded from public teaching. I struggled with myself to teach for a single day, to gratify the hearts of the students who were frequenting my lectures, but my tongue would not utter a single word: I was completely unable to say anything. As a result that impediment of my speech caused a sadness in my heart accompanied by an inability to digest; food and drink became unpalatable to me so that I could neither swallow broth easily nor digest a mouthful of solid food. That led to such

a weakening of my powers that the physicians lost hope of treating me and said: "This is something which has settled in his heart and crept from it into his humors; there is no way to treat it unless his heart be eased of the anxiety which has visited it."[172]

89 Then, when I perceived my powerlessness, and when my capacity to make a choice had completely collapsed, I had recourse to God Most High as does a hard pressed man who has no way out of his difficulty. And I was answered by Him Who "answers the needy man when he calls on Him" (27.63/62), and He made it easy for my heart to turn away from fame and fortune, family, children, and associates. I announced that I had resolved to leave for Mecca, all the while planning secretly to travel to Syria. This I did as a precaution, lest the Caliph and the group of my associates might learn of my resolve to settle in Damascus. Therefore I made clever use of subtle stratagems about leaving Baghdad, while firmly resolved never to return to it. I was much talked about by the religious leaders of the Iraqis, since none among them could allow that giving up my career had a religious motive. For they thought that my post was the highest dignity in our religion—and "that was the farthest limit they had attained in learning!" (53.31/30).

90 Thereupon people got involved in devising explanations of my conduct. Those at some distance from Iraq thought I was acting so because I was afraid of the authorities. But those close to the authorities, who saw their attachment and devotion to me, and how I shunned them and paid no attention to what they said, were saying: "This is something supernal: its only cause is an evil eye which has afflicted Muslims and the coterie of the learned!"[173]

91 I departed from Baghdad after I had distributed what wealth I had, laying by only the amount needed for my support and the sustenance of my children. My excuse for that was that the money of Iraq was earmarked for the welfare of the people, because it was a pious bequest in favor of Muslims. Nowhere in the world have I seen a more beneficial arrangement regarding money which the scholar can use for his family.

92 Then I entered Damascus and resided there for nearly two years. My only occupation was seclusion and solitude and spiritual exercise and combat with a view to devoting myself to the purification of my soul and the cultivation of virtues and cleansing my heart for the remembrance of God Most High, in the way I had learned from the writings of the sufis. I used to pray in seclusion for a time in the Mosque, mounting to its minaret for the whole day and shutting myself in.[174] Then I traveled from Damascus to Jerusalem, where I would go daily into the Dome of the

Rock and shut myself in.[175] Then I was inwardly moved by an urge to perform the duty of the pilgrimage and to draw succor from the blessings of Mecca and Medina and the visit to the tomb of the Apostle of God—God's blessing and peace be upon him!—after finishing my visit to the Friend of God[176]—God's blessings and peace be upon him! So I traveled to the Ḥijāz.[177]

93 Then certain concerns and the appeals of my children drew me to my native land; so I came back to it after being the person most unlikely to return to it. There I also chose seclusion out of a desire for solitude and the purification of my heart for the remembrance of God. But current events and important family matters and gaining the necessities for daily living had an effect on the way to realize my desire and troubled the serenity of my solitude, and the pure state of ecstasy occurred only intermittently. But nonetheless I did not cease to aspire to it. Obstacles would keep me away from it, but I would return to it.

94 For ten years I remained in that condition. In the course of those periods of solitude things impossible to enumerate or detail in depth were disclosed to me. This much I shall mention, that profit may be derived from it: I knew with certainty that the sufis are those who uniquely follow the way to God Most High, their mode of life is the best of all, their way the most direct of ways, and their ethic the purest. Indeed, were one to combine the insight of the intellectuals, the wisdom of the wise, and the lore of scholars versed in the mysteries of revelation in order to change a single item of sufi conduct and ethic and to replace it with something better, no way to do so would be found! For all their motions and quiescences, exterior and interior, are learned from the light of the niche of prophecy. And beyond the light of prophecy there is no light on earth from which illumination can be obtained.[178]

95 In general, how can men describe such a way as this? Its purity—the first of its requirements—is the total purificationof the heart from everything other than God Most High. Its key, which is analogous to the beginning of the Prayer,[179] is the utter absorption of the heart in the remembrance of God. Its end is being completely lost in God.[180] But the latter is its end with reference to its initial stages which just barely fall under the power of choice and personal acquisition.[181] But these are really the beginning of the Way, and everything prior to it[182] is like an antechamber for him who follows the path to it.

96 From the very start of the Way revelations and visions begin,[183] so that, even when awake, the sufis see the angels and the spirits of the prophets and hear voices coming from them and learn useful things from

them. Then their "state" ascends from the vision of forms and likenesses to stages beyond the narrow range of words: so if anyone tries to express them, his words contain evident error against which he cannot guard himself. But speaking in general, the matter comes ultimately to a closeness to God which one group almost conceives of as "indwelling,"[184] and another as "union,"[185] and another as "reaching":[186] but all that is wrong. We have already shown why it is wrong in our book *The Noblest Aim.*[187] But really one intimately possessed by that state ought not to go beyond saying:

> There was what was of what I do not mention:
> So think well of it, and ask for no account![188]

97 Generally speaking, anyone who is granted nothing of that through fruitional experience grasps, of the reality of prophecy, only the name. The charisms of the "saints"[189] are in reality the first stages passed through by the prophets. Such was the initial state of the Apostle of God—God's blessing and peace be upon him!—when he went to Mount Ḥirāʾ,[190] where he would be alone with his Lord and perform acts of worship, so that the Arabs of the desert said: "Muḥammad indeed passionately loves his Lord!"[191]

98 This is a state which one following the way leading to it will verify by fruitional experience. But one to whom such experience is not granted can acquire certain knowledge of that state through experience of others and hearsay, if he frequents the company of the sufis so as to have a sure understanding of that from observing the circumstances accompanying their ecstatic states. Whoever associates with them will derive this faith from them, for they are the men whose associate is never wretched.[192] But whoever is not favored with their company must learn the certain possibility of such mystical states through the evidence of apodeictic demonstration in the way we have mentioned in "The Book of the Marvels of the Heart," one of the books of *The Revivification of the Religious Sciences.*[193]

99 Ascertainment by apodeictic proof leads to *knowledge.* Intimate experience of that very state is *fruitional experience.* Favorable acceptance of it based on hearsay and experience of others is *faith.* These, then, are three degrees, or levels, of knowledge—"God raises in degrees those of you who believe and those to whom knowledge is given" (58.12/11).[194]

100 In addition to the men with such levels of knowledge there are a number of ignorant men who deny its very foundation and are astonished

at such words. They listen and scoff, saying: "Extraordinary! How they rave!" Of such as these God Most High said: "And among them (infidels) are those who listen to you, then, when they have left you, they say to those who have been given knowledge: 'What did he just say?' Those are men whose hearts God has sealed and who follow their own vain desires" (47.18/16)—so God renders them deaf and blinds their eyes.

101 What became clear to me of necessity from practicing their Way was the true nature and special character of prophecy.[195] So attention must be called to its basis because of the urgent need for it.

The True Nature of Prophecy
and the Need All Men Have for It

102 Know that man's essence, in his original condition, is created in blank simplicity without any information about the "worlds" of God Most High.[196] These "worlds" are so many that only God Most High can number them, as He has said: "No one knows the hosts of your Lord but He" (74.34/31). Man gets his information about the "worlds" by means of perception. Each one of his kinds of perception is created in order that man may get to know thereby a "world" of the existents—and by "worlds" we mean the categories of existing things.

103 The first thing created in man is the sense of touch: by this he perceives certain classes of existents such as heat and cold, wetness and dryness, smoothness and roughness, etc. But touch is definitely unable to perceive colors and sounds; indeed, these are, as it were, nonexistent with respect to touch.

104 Next the sense of sight is created for man, by which he perceives colors and shapes: this is the most extensive of the "worlds" of the sensibles.

105 Then the sense of hearing is opened,[197] so that man hears sounds and tones.[198]

106 Next the sense of taste is created for man; and so on until he passes beyond the "world" of the sensibles. Then, when he is about seven years old, *discernment* is created for him. This is another of the stages of man's existence; in it he perceives things beyond the "world" of the sensibles, none of which are found in the "world" of sensation.

107 Then man ascends to another stage, and *intellect* is created for him, so that he perceives the necessary, the possible, the impossible, and things not found in the previous stages.[199]

108 Beyond the stage of intellect there is another stage.[200] In this another eye is opened, by which man sees the hidden, and what will take

place in the future, and other things, from which the intellect is as far removed as the power of discernment is from the perception of intelligibles and the power of sensation is from things perceived by discernment. And just as one able only to discern, if presented with the things perceptible to the intellect, would reject them and consider them outlandish, so some men endowed with intellect have rejected the things perceptible to the prophetic power and considered them wildly improbable. That is the very essence of ignorance! For such a man has no supporting reason except that it is a stage he himself has not attained and for him it does not exist: so he supposes that it does not exist in itself.

109 Now if a man born blind did not know about colors and shapes from constant report and hearsay, and were to be told about them abruptly, he would neither understand them nor acknowledge their existence. But God Most High has brought the matter within the purview of His creatures by giving them a sample of the special character of the prophetic power: sleeping.[201] For the sleeper perceives the unknown that will take place, either plainly, or in the guise of an image the meaning of which is disclosed by interpretation.

110 If a man had had no personal experience of dreaming and someone were to tell him: "There are some men who fall down unconscious as though they were dead,[202] and their perception, hearing, and sight leave them, and they then perceive what is 'hidden,'" he would deny it and give apodeictic proof of its impossibility by saying: "The sensory powers are the causes of perception. Therefore one who does not perceive such things when his powers are present and functioning a fortiori will not perceive them when his powers are suspended."

111 This is a kind of analogy which is belied by factual experience and observation. Just as the intellect is one of man's stages in which he receives an "eye" by which he "sees" various species of intelligibles from which the senses are far removed, the prophetic power is an expression signifying a stage in which man receives an "eye" possessed of a light, and in its light the unknown and other phenomena not normally perceived by the intellect become visible.[203]

112 Doubt about prophecy touches either its possibility, or its actual existence, or its belonging to a specific individual.

113 The proof of its *possibility* is its existence. And the proof of its *existence* is the existence in the world of knowledge which could not conceivably be obtained by the intellect alone—such as the knowledge of medicine and of astronomy.[204] For whoever examines such knowledge knows of necessity that it can be obtained only by a divine inspiration and

a special help from God Most High, and that there is no empirical way to it. Thus among astronomical phenomena there is a phenomenon which occurs only once every thousand years. How, then, could knowledge of that be obtained empirically? The same is true of the properties of medicaments.

114 From this proof it is clearly within the bounds of possibility that a way exists to grasp these things which the intellect does not normally grasp. This is what is meant by prophecy. Not that prophecy signifies such knowledge only. Rather, the perception of this kind of thing which is outside the things normally perceived by the intellect is one of the properties of prophecy. It also has many other properties; what we have mentioned is a drop from its sea. We have mentioned it only because you have in your own experience an example of it, viz. the things you perceive while asleep. You also have knowledge of the same sort in medicine and astronomy. These, too, belong to the category of the prophets' apologetic miracles—the blessing and peace of God be upon them! But men endowed with intellect have no way at all of attaining such knowledge by intellectual resources alone.[205]

115 The properties of prophecy beyond those just mentioned can be perceived only by fruitional experience as a result of following the way of sufism. For you have understood that only because of an example you have been given, viz. sleep; were it not for this, you would not assent to that. If, then, the prophet has a special quality of which you have no example and which you in no wise understand, how can you find it credible? Assent comes only after understanding. But the example needed occurs in the first stages of the way of sufism. Then, through this example, one obtains a kind of fruitional experience commensurate with the progress made plus a kind of assent to what has not been attained based on analogy with what has been attained.[206] So this single property we have mentioned is enough ground for you to believe in the basis of prophecy.

116 If it occurs to you to doubt whether a particular individual is a prophet or not, certainty will be gained only by becoming acquainted with his circumstances, either through personal observation or from impeccable tradition and hearsay. For when you are familiar with medicine and jurisprudence, you can recognize jurisprudents and physicians by observing their circumstances,[207] and also by hearing their dicta, even if you have not seen them yourself. Moreover, you are quite capable of knowing that al-Shāfiᶜī[208] (God's mercy be upon him!) was a jurisprudent and that Galen[209] was a physician—and that with a knowledge based on fact, not on uncritical acceptance of someone's say-so—by your learning something about jurisprudence and medicine and then perusing their writings and works: thus you will acquire a necessary knowledge of their scientific status.

117 Likewise, when you understand the meaning of prophecy and devote much study to the Qurʾān and the traditions, you will acquire the necessary knowledge of the fact that Muḥammad—God's blessing and peace be upon him!—had attained the loftiest level of prophecy. Then back that up by sampling what he said about the acts of worship and their effect on the purification of hearts. Consider, for example, how right he was—God's blessing and peace be upon him!—in his saying: "Whoever acts according to what he knows, God will make him heir to what he does not know";[210] and how right he was in his saying: "Whoever aids an unjust man, God gives the latter dominion over him";[211] and how right he was in his saying: "Whoever reaches the point where all his cares are a single care, God Most High will save him from all cares in this life and the next."[212] When you have had that experience in a thousand, two thousand, and many thousands of instances, you will have acquired a necessary knowledge which will be indisputable.

118 Therefore, seek sure and certain knowledge of prophecy in this way, not from the changing of the staff into a serpent and the splitting of the moon.[213] For if you consider that sort of thing alone, without adding the many, indeed innumerable, circumstances accompanying it, you might think it was a case of magic and deception, and that it was a "leading astray" coming from God Most High, because "He leads astray whom He will and rightly guides whom He will" (16.95/93), and the problems connected with apologetic miracles would confront you.[214]

119 Furthermore, if your faith were based on a carefully ordered argument about the way the apologetic miracle affords proof of prophecy, your faith would be broken by an equally well-ordered argument showing how difficulty and doubt may affect that mode of proof. Therefore, let such preternatural events be one of the proofs and concomitants that make up your total reflection on the matter.[215] As a result, you will acquire such necessary knowledge that you will be unable to cite its specific basis. It would be like the case of a man to whom many men report an unimpeachable tradition. He cannot aver that his sure and certain knowledge is derived from the statement of one specific individual. Rather, he does not know whence it comes: but it is neither outside the group testimony, nor is it due to pinpointing individuals. This, then, is the strong belief based on knowledge. Fruitional experience, on the other hand, is comparable to actual seeing and handling: this is found only in the way of the sufis.

120 This much, then, of the real meaning of prophecy is sufficient for my present purpose. Now I shall mention the reason why it is needed.

The Reason for Resuming Teaching After Having Given It Up

A. *Doctors of Hearts*[216]

121 For nearly ten years I assiduously cultivated seclusion and solitude. During that time several points became clear to me of necessity for reasons I cannot enumerate—at one time by fruitional experience, at another time by knowledge based on apodeictic proof, and again by acceptance founded on faith. These points were: that man is formed of a body and a heart—and by the "heart" I mean the essence of man's spirit which is the seat of the knowledge of God, not the flesh which man has in common with corpse and beast;[217] that his body may have a health which will result in its happiness, and a malady in which lies its ruin; that his heart, likewise, may have a health and soundness—and only he will be saved "who comes to God with a sound heart" (26.89), and it may have a malady which will lead to his everlasting perdition in the next life, as God Most High has said: "In their hearts is a malady" (2.9/10); that ignorance of God is the heart's deadly poison, disobedience to God its incapacitating malady, knowledge of God Most High its quickening antidote, and obedience to Him by resisting passion its healing remedy; that the only way to treat the heart by removing its malady and regaining its health lies in the use of remedies, just as that is the only way to treat the body.[218]

122 Remedies for the body effectively procure health because of a property in them which men endowed with intellect cannot perceive by virtue of their intellectual resources, but rather it must be the object of blind obedience to the physicians who learned it from the prophets, who, because of the special attribute of prophecy, came to know the special properties of things. In a similar fashion it became necessarily evident to me that the reason for the effectiveness of the remedies of the acts of worship, with their prescriptions and determined quantities ordained by the prophets, cannot be perceived by means of the intellectual resources of men endowed with intellect. On the contrary, they must be the object of blind obedience to the prophets who perceived those qualities by the light of prophecy, not by intellectual resources.

123 Moreover, just as medicaments are composed of mixtures of elements differing in kind and quantity, some of them being double others in weight and quantity, and just as the difference of their quantities is not without a profound significance pertaining to the kind of the properties, so, likewise, the acts of worship, which are the remedies of hearts, are composed of actions differing in kind and quantity, so that a prostration is the double of a bowing, and the morning prayer is half as long as the afternoon prayer.[219] This difference is not without a profound significance which pertains to the kind of the properties knowable only by the light of the prophecy. Very stupid and ignorant would be the man who would wish to discover in them a wisdom by means of reason, or who would suppose that they had been mentioned by chance, and not because of a profound divine significance in them which requires them to be such because of the special property in them. And just as in medicaments there are basic elements which are their chief ingredients and additional substances which are their complements, each of them having a special effect on the workings[220] of their basic elements, so, likewise, supererogatory prayers and customary practices[221] are complements for perfecting the effects of the principal elements of the acts of worship.

124 In general, then, the prophets (Peace be upon them!) are the physicians for treating the maladies of hearts. By its activity reason is useful simply to acquaint us with this fact, to bear witness to prophecy by giving assent to its reality, to certify its own blindness[222] to perceiving what the "eye" of prophecy perceives, and to take us by our hands and turn us over to the prophets as blind men are handed over to guides and as troubled sick men are handed over to sympathetic physicians. To this point reason can proceed and advance, but it is far removed from anything beyond that except for understanding what the physician prescribes.[223] These, then, are the insights we gained with a necessity analogous to direct vision during the period of our solitude and seclusion.

B. *The Slackness of Faith*

125 Then we saw the lukewarmness of men's beliefs in the basis of prophecy, and consequently, in the reality of prophecy and in action in accord with the data of prophecy. We also ascertained that this was widespread among men. I then reflected on the reasons for men's lukewarmness and the weakness of their faith, and found them to be four in number:

1. A reason stemming from those engrossed in the science of philosophy.

2. A reason stemming from those absorbed in the way of sufism.

3. A reason stemming from those attached to the claim of authoritative teaching.

4. A reason stemming from the behavior of those popularly regarded as preeminent in learning.[224]

126 For a period of time I next addressed myself successively to individuals, questioning those who were remiss in fulfilling the Law. I would ask a man about his specious reason for that and inquire into his belief and his inner convictions, asking him: "Why are you so remiss? If you believe in the afterlife, but do not prepare yourself for it and barter it for this life—why, this is stupidity! You would not ordinarily barter two things for one. How, then, can you barter what is unending for a limited number of days? And if you do not believe, then you are an infidel! So act wisely in the quest for faith and look into the cause of your hidden unbelief! For this is your real inner conviction and the cause of your outward boldness, even though you do not openly express it, because you want to bedeck yourself with the trappings of faith and to be respected for paying lip service to the law!"

127 One man would reply: "If this were a matter one was bound to observe, then the learned[225] would be those most properly bound to do it. But of those most renowned among the learned,[226] so-and-so does not perform the prescribed Prayer, and such a one drinks wine,[227] and another devours the assets of religious endowments[228] and the property of orphans, and another feathers his nest with the lavish largesse of the Sultan without being wary of what is illicit,[229] and another accepts bribes for judgment and testimony, and so on in many similar instances!"

128 A second man would claim to be an adept in the science of sufism and allege that he had attained a degree beyond the need for formal worship. And a third would offer as his excuse one of the specious reasons advanced by the licentious. These are the erring who profess the way of sufism.[230]

129 A fourth respondent would have had contact with the Taᶜlīmites. So he would declare: "The truth is doubtful, the way to it hard, there is much disagreement about it, and no one view is preferable to any other. Moreover, rational proofs contradict one another so that no reliance can be placed on the opinion of independent thinkers. But the advocate of authoritative teaching makes categorical pronouncements without needing any proof. How, then, can we give up the certain because of the uncertain?"[231]

130 A fifth man would say: "I do not do this out of servile conformism, but I have studied the science of philosophy and I have grasped the

real meaning of prophecy. I know that it comes down to what is wise and beneficial and that the aim of its religious prescriptions is to control the common people and to curb them from internecine strife and contention and from unrestrained indulgence in their passions. Hence I am not one of the ignorant masses and therefore subject to commandment.[232] Rather, I am one of the wise, following the way of wisdom and well versed in it, and in my wisdom I can get along without servile conformism!" This is the limit reached by the faith of those who have studied the philosophy of the theistic philosophers: that is known from the books of Ibn Sīnā and Abū Naṣr al-Fārābī.

131 These are the men who bedeck themselves with the trappings of Islam. Often you may see one of them reciting the Qur'ān and attending the assemblies and public prayers and paying great lip service to the Sharīᶜa.[233] But despite that he does not give up his winebibbing and various kinds of depravity and debauchery. If he is asked: "If prophecy is not authentic, why do you pray?" he may reply: "It is an askesis of the body and the custom of the local people and a way to preserve fortune and family."[234] And he may say: "The Sharīᶜa is authentic and prophecy is genuine." Then one should say: "Why, then, do you drink wine?" And he may say: "Wine was prohibited simply because it causes enmity and hatred.[235] But I, by my wisdom, can guard against that. My only aim in drinking is to stimulate my mind."

132 Indeed, Ibn Sīnā went so far as to write in a testament of his[236] that he made a pact with God to do certain things, and that he would extol the ordinances of the Law and would not be remiss in performing the religious acts of worship, nor would he drink for pleasure, but only for medicinal purposes and to promote his health. So the furthest he got respecting purity of faith and the obligation of acts of worship was to make an exception for winebibbing on the score of promoting his health! Such is the faith of those philosophers who pretend to have faith! Many, indeed, have been deceived by them, and their deception has been intensified by the weak arguments of those who opposed the philosophers. For their opposition was to repudiate the sciences of geometry and logic and others which, for the philosophers, are true of necessity, according to the reasoned explanation we have set forth previously.

C. *My Return to Teaching*

133 I saw, then, that for such reasons as these the faith of the various classes of men had become so weak. Also, I considered myself so

skilled a practitioner in exposing such sophistries that exposing them was easier for me than downing a mouthful of water, because I had studied deeply their sciences and methods—I mean the methods of the sufis and the philosophers and the Taᶜlīmites and the distinguished ulema. It then flashed into my mind that engaging in that activity was a matter destined and inevitable at such a time: "What will solitude and seclusion avail you when the disease has become endemic, the physicians are sick, and men are on the brink of perdition?" Then I said to myself: "When will you devote yourself completely to laying bare this affliction and to battling against this dreadful darkness? It is a time of tepidity and an era of error. But even if you were to engage in calling men from their evil ways to the truth, all the men of this age would be hostile to you: how, then, would you stand up against them? And how could you put up with them? For that could be done only at a favorable time and under a godly and irresistible Sultan.

134 Thus I sought a compromise between myself and God Most High which would permit me to remain in seclusion, alleging as an excuse my inability to expound the truth with competent argument. But God Most High determined to move the Sultan of the time to act on his own, and not because of any external instigation. He peremptorily ordered me to hasten to Nīshāpūr to face the threat of this tepidity. Indeed, so peremptory was his order that, had I persisted in refusing to comply, it would have ended in my disgrace.[237]

135 Then it occurred to me that "the reason for excusing yourself has lost its force. Hence your motive for clinging to seclusion ought not to be laziness and ease and self-aggrandizement and protecting yourself from the harm caused by men. Why, indeed, should you try to find license for such conduct in the difficulty of struggling against men? For God—praised and exalted He! says: 'A. L. M. Do men think they will be left to say "We believe" without being subject to tribulation? Indeed We have already tried those who were before them (and assuredly God knows those who speak truly, and assuredly He knows the liars)' (29.1–2/1–3). He also says—Mighty and Glorious He!—to His Apostle, who is the dearest of His creatures: 'Apostles before you have already been given the lie, and they endured the false charge and the injury done them until Our help came to them. Now there is no one who can change the words of God, and there has already reached you some report about those We sent'" (6.34).

136 "The Mighty and Glorious also says: 'In the name of the merciful Lord of mercy: Y. S. By the wise Qurʾān, you are indeed of those We

have sent on a straight way, sent down by the sending of the Mighty, the Merciful, to warn a people whose fathers were not warned, so that they are heedless. True indeed what has been said against most of them, for they do not believe. Assuredly We have placed on their necks iron collars, chin high, so that their heads are held up. We have also put a barrier before them and a barrier behind them, and We have blinded them so that they do not see. All the same to you whether you warn them or do not warn them—they will not believe. You warn only him who follows the Remembrance and fears the Lord of mercy in the unseen' (36.1–10/1–11)."[238]

137 Subsequently I consulted on that matter a number of those skilled in discerning hearts and visions and they were of one mind in advising me to abandon my seclusion and to emerge from my religious retirement. In addition to that, certain godly men had many recurrent dreams attesting that this move of mine would be a source of good and a right procedure, and that it had been decreed by God—Praised be He!—for the beginning of this century. For God—Praised be He!—has indeed promised to revivify His religion at the beginning of each century.[239] So my hope was strengthened and I became quite optimistic because of these testimonies.[240]

138 God Most High facilitated my move to Nīshāpūr to undertake this serious task in the month of Dhuʾl-Qaʿda, 499 (July, 1106 A.D.). My departure from Baghdad had been in Dhuʾl-Qaʿda, 488 (November, 1095 A.D.). So the period of my seclusion amounted to eleven years. This move to Nīshāpūr was decreed by God Most High, and it was one of the marvels of His foreordinations, not a glimmer of which was in my mind during that period of seclusion, just as the possibility of my leaving Baghdad and giving up my position there had never occurred to my mind. But God Most High is the changer of minds and states, and "the heart of the believer is between two of the fingers of the Lord of mercy."[241]

139 I know well that, even though I have returned to teaching, I have not really returned. For returning is coming back to what was. Formerly I used to impart the knowledge by which glory is gained for glory's sake, and to invite men to it by my words and deeds, and *that* was my aim and my intention. But now I invite men to the knowledge by which glory is renounced and its lowly rank recognized. This is now my intention, my aim, my desire. God knows that to be true of me. I now earnestly desire to reform myself and others, but I do not know whether I shall attain my desire or be cut off by death short of my goal. Yet I believe with a faith as certain as direct vision that there is no might for me and no power save in God, the Sublime, the Mighty; and that it was not I who moved, but He

moved me; and that I did not act, but He acted through me. I ask Him, then, to reform me first, then to use me as an instrument of reform; to guide me, then to use me as an instrument of guidance; to show me the true as true, and to grant me the grace to follow it; and to show me the false as false, and to grant me the grace to eschew it![242]

D. *Remedies for the Tepid*

140 Now we return to the reasons we have mentioned for the weakness of some men's faith. We shall mention the way to guide them aright and to deliver them from their mortal perils.

(1) The treatment for those who claim to be perplexed because of what they have heard from the Taᶜlīmites is what we have mentioned in our book *The Correct Balance.* We shall not unduly prolong the discussion by mentioning it in this epistle.

(2) As for the flights of fancy of the licentious libertines, we have listed their specious arguments in seven categories and laid them bare in our book *The Alchemy of Happiness.*[243]

(3) For the man whose faith has become corrupt through philosophy to the point that he rejects the very principle of prophecy we have already mentioned the true nature of prophecy and its existence of necessity, adducing the proof drawn from the existence of the knowledge of the special properties of medicaments and of the knowledge about the stars, etc. Indeed, we presented that prefatory discussion precisely for that reason. Moreover, we set forth the proof drawn from the special properties of medicine and the stars simply because that pertains to the philosophers' own science. For to each man versed in a particular science[244]—e.g. astronomy, medicine, physics, magic, talismans—we expound the proof of prophecy drawn from his own science.

141 He who pays lip service to the existence of prophecy, but equates the prescriptions of revelation with human wisdom, really disbelieves in prophecy. He believes only in a sage with a special star of destiny whose ascendancy demands that he be followed. This has nothing at all to do with prophecy. On the contrary, faith in prophecy is to acknowledge the affirmation of a stage beyond reason: in it an eye is opened by which a special perception of certain perceptibles is had; from the perception of these reason is excluded, just as hearing is from the perception of colors, and sight from the perception of sounds, and all the senses from the perception of intelligibles. If the man in question does not allow the possibility of this, well we have already given apodeictic proof, not only of its

possibility, but also of its actual existence. But if he does allow it, then he has indeed affirmed that there really are things called properties which in no wise fall within the gambit of reason's activity; on the contrary, reason would almost certainly deny them and judge them to be impossible.

142 Thus, for example, a daniq's[245] weight of opium is a lethal poison, since it congeals the blood in the veins because of its excessive coldness. Now the man claiming to know physics asserts that compounds which congeal do so only because of the two elements of water and earth—for these are the two cold elements. It is also well known that the internal congealing power of several kilos of water and earth is not as great as that of the opium mentioned. So if a physicist were to be told of this, without having experienced it himself, he would say: "Such a thing is absurd! The proof of its absurdity is that opium contains fiery and airy components, and the fiery and the airy do not intensify it with respect to coldness. Even if we suppose that opium were all water and earth, this would not necessitate such excessive congealing power. Therefore, if two hot elements are joined to it, a fortiori it will not necessitate that effect."

143 And he supposes this to be an apodeictic proof! But most of the philosophers' "apodeictic proofs" concerning matters physical and metaphysical are built on this sort of argument. For they conceived things to be in accord with their own experience and comprehension, while presuming the impossibility of what was unfamiliar to them. Indeed, were it not for the familiar fact of true vision in dreams, the claim of anyone asserting that he knew the unseen while his senses were dormant would be rejected by men with such minds.

144 Furthermore, suppose one were to say to such a man: "Can there exist in this world a thing the size of a grain, which, if put in a town, would devour that town in its entirety, and then would devour itself, so that nothing would be left of the town and its contents, nor would this thing itself be left?" He would surely answer: "Such a thing is absurd and belongs to the realm of fairy tales!" Yet this is the case with fire, which anyone who had never seen fire would deny if he heard about it. Most denials of the wonders of the afterlife belong to this category.[246]

145 So we would say to the natural philosopher: "You have already been compelled to say that opium has a special property of congealing which is inconsistent with what is understood in physics. Why, then, can there not be in the revealed ordinances certain properties of healing and purifying hearts, which are beyond the grasp of wisdom based on reason, nay more, that can be discerned only by the eye of prophecy?" Why they even acknowledge properties more marvelous than this in the things they

cite in their books. Such are the wonderful properties experienced in the treatment of a pregnant woman for whom parturition is difficult by using this figure:

4	9	2	D	Ṭ	B
8	5	7	J	H	Z
8	1	6	Ḥ	A	W

This is written on two pieces of cloth never touched by water. The pregnant woman keeps her eye fixed on them and puts them under her feet, and forthwith the child hastens to come out. They have indeed acknowledged this to be possible and have cited it in their work on *The Marvels of Special Properties.*[247] This figure contains nine squares with specific numbers written in them in such a way that the sum of the numbers in any one line, read straight or diagonally, is fifteen [248]

146 How in the world, then, can a man who believes such a thing be too narrow-minded to believe that the prescription of two rakʿas[249] for the morning prayer, and of four for the noon prayer, and of three for the sunset prayer, is because of special properties, unknowable by philosophical reasoning, which have their cause in the difference of the times involved. These properties are perceived only by the light of prophecy.

147 Astonishingly enough, were we to change the mode of expression to that of the astrologers, the natural philosophers would readily understand the difference of these times. Thus we would say: "Does not the judgment concerning the star of destiny differ because of the sun's being at its zenith, or ascending, or descending, so that the astrologers base on this their forecasts of diversity of treatment and disparity in life spans and times of death?"[250] Yet there is no real difference between the sun's setting and its being at its zenith, or between sunset and the sun's being in its descendancy. So what reason can there be for believing such things except that a man hears them put in the jargon of an astrologer whose false forecasts he may have experienced a hundred times? Yet again and again he believes him, so much so that, were the astrologer to tell him: "When the sun is at its zenith, and a certain star is in opposition to it, and such and such a constellation is in the ascendancy, if you put on a new garment at that time, you will be slain in that garment," he then would not put on the garment at that time, even though he might then suffer intense cold, and even though he might have heard it from an astrologer whose false forecasts he had known many times!

148 When one is broad-minded enough to accept such marvels and is compelled to admit that they are special properties, the knowledge of

which is an apologetic miracle for some prophets,[251] how in the world can he deny that the same is true of what he hears said by a truthful prophet, confirmed by miracles, who has never been known to lie? For if a philosopher denies the possibility of such special properties in the numbers of rak^{c}as, the throwing of the stones, the number of the principal ceremonies of the pilgrimage,[252] and the other prescriptions of revelation, he will not find any difference at all between these and the special properties of the medicaments and the stars.

149 He may say: "I have already had some experience of the stars and of medicine, and I have found some of that to be true. Hence belief in it has become firmly fixed in my mind and I have ceased to regard it as improbable and to shy away from it. But I have had no experience of what you have mentioned: how, then, can I know that it exists and is verifiable, even though I admit its possibility?" I would answer: "You do not limit yourself to believing what you have experienced. On the contrary, you have listened to the reports of experienced men and have unquestioningly accepted their statements. Listen, therefore, to the utterances of the prophets: for they have indeed experienced and seen what is true in all that revelation has brought us. Follow in their path, and you will perceive some of that by direct vision."

150 Furthermore I would say: "Even if you have had no such experience, your reason peremptorily judges it necessary to believe and follow the experienced. Let us suppose the case of a man of mature mind who has never experienced sickness, and then he falls sick. He has a sympathetic father skilled in medicine, whose claim to be versed in medicine the sick man has been hearing ever since he reached the age of reason. His father compounds a remedy for him and says: 'This is good for your sickness and it will heal you of your malady.' What, then, does the sick man's reason require, if the remedy be bitter and foul-tasting? That he should take it? Or that he should disbelieve and say: 'I do not understand this medicine's suitability for obtaining a cure, since I have had no experience of it'? Undoubtedly you would regard him as stupid if he acted thus.

151 "So, too, men of insight regard you as stupid in your hesitation to believe. If you then say: 'How can I know the compassion of the Prophet—God's blessing and peace be upon him!—and his knowledge of this spiritual medicine?' I would say: 'And how did you know the compassion of your father, seeing that it is not something perceptible to the senses? Rather, through the indications of his various attitudes and the evidences of his actions in his daily comings and goings you came to know it with a necessary and unquestionable knowledge.'"

152 Anyone who reflects on the sayings of the Apostle—God's blessing and peace be upon him!—and on the reports that have come down about his concern for guiding men rightly and his subtlety and delicacy in drawing people by the various forms of gentleness and kindness to the improvement of their morals and the patching up of discord and, in general, to whatever is best for their religious and temporal affairs, obtains a necessary knowledge of the fact that the compassion of the Apostle for his Community was greater than a father's compassion for his son.

153 Moreover, when one considers the marvelous deeds manifested at his hands, and the wonders of the unseen reported in the Qurʾān and the traditions, and what he mentioned about the distant future—which in the event turned out just as he had said—he knows with necessary knowledge that the Apostle had reached the stage which is beyond reason and that the eye had been opened for him to which are unveiled the unseen and the special properties and things which reason does not perceive. This, then, is the way to acquire the necessary knowledge of giving credence to the Prophet—God's blessing and peace be upon him! So try it yourself and meditate on the Qurʾān and study the traditions—then you will know that by seeing with your own eyes.[253]

154 What we have said is enough to warn the devotees of philosophy. We have mentioned it because of the urgent need for it at this time.

155 (4) As for the fourth reason, viz. the weakness of faith due to the scandalous conduct of the learned, there are three remedies for this sickness. One of them is for you to say: "The learned man who, you allege, devours what is illicit, knows that such illicit things are forbidden just as well as you know that wine and pork and usury—to say nothing of backbiting, lying, and slander—are forbidden. Now you know that, yet you do such things, not because of the lack of your belief that it is disobedience, but rather because of your desire which gets the better of you. Well his desire is like yours, and it has indeed got the better of him. So his technical knowledge of subtle questions beyond this prohibition, by which he is distinguished from you, does not necessarily involve a more severe warning against this or that specific illicit action. How many a man who believes in medicine cannot abstain from fruit and cold water, even though he has been warned against them by his physician! But that does not prove that they are not injurious, or that faith in medicine is unsound. This, therefore, is the way to construe the faults of the learned."

156 The second remedy is that the man in the street be told: "You ought to believe that the learned man has acquired his learning as a provision for himself in the afterlife and supposes that his learning will

save him and will be an intercessor for him. So in view of that he may be negligent in his actions because of the merit of his learning. And though it be possible that his learning will be additional evidence against him, yet he thinks it possible that it will procure him a higher rank in heaven. This may be the case, for, even though he has given up good works, he can adduce his learning in his favor. But you, common man that you are, if you pattern yourself on him and give up good works without having any learning, you will perish because of your evildoing, and there will be no intercessor for you!"

157 The third remedy, and this is the real one, is that the true man of learning commits a sin only by way of a slip, but will in no wise stubbornly persist in his sins. For true learning is that which leads to the knowledge that sin is a deadly poison and that the afterlife is better than this life. And anyone who knows that will not barter the better for something inferior. This knowledge is not the fruit of the various types of knowledge with which most men busy themselves. Hence the knowledge they acquire only makes them bolder in disobeying God Most High. True knowledge, on the other hand, increases its possessor's reverence, fear, and hope, and this stands between him and the commission of sins, save for those slips from which, in moments of weakness, no man is free. But this is not a sign of weak faith, for the believer is tried but continually repentant, and he is far from stubborn impenitence.

158 This is what I wanted to mention concerning the criticism of philosophy and talimism and their shortcomings and of the failings of those who reject them in an unsuitable way. We beg almighty God to count us among the men of His predilection and choice whom He directs to the truth and guides, whom He so inspires with remembrance of Him that they never forget Him, whom He so preserves from their own evil that they prefer none to Him, and whom He so attaches to Himself (12.54) that they serve none but Him alone![254]

And God's blessing be upon Muḥammad, best of men, and upon his Community, best of communities!

Notes to the Translation

Note: The following abbreviations are used in my Notes. The number *after* each abbreviation refers to the Annotated Bibliography.

AGth 3
Alonso
BM 17
EI (1) and (2)
F
Gh—Ghazālī
J—Jabre's translation and other material 62
Ja—Jabre's Arabic text
Jadaane 60
JC 63
JM 64
Kemali 65
M 74
Poggi 86
Sch 117
VDB 103
VR 104
W 110
WConc 113
Wensinck: *Handbook* 114
WPK 116
WPT 108

1. This invocation and the first part of Para. 1 are from M.

2. It was customary for Muslim authors to begin a treatise or book or discourse with praise of God and a blessing on the Prophet and his family, known technically as the *khuṭba.* Sometimes it is long and elaborate, with ingeniously contrived rhyming phrases containing allusions to the subject matter of the work, as in Gh's *Mustaẓhirī* (App. II). The real beginning is after the standard phrase *ʾammā baʿd* (Now then). This *khuṭba* is simple and direct as befits a relatively short treatise containing a simple account of a comparatively uncomplicated, though partly contrived, story.

3. This "brother" may have been a definite individual to whose idenity we have no clue; or, as seems more likely to me, the use of the phrase a literary device. It then implies that Gh is addressing himself to all his Muslim brothers capable of following what he has to say.

4. *Al-taqlīd:* an important concept in the *Munqidh* and in the thought of Gh. The word contains the basic notion of putting a rope on an animal's neck; then, to put on a necklace; then, to copy, imitate, ape; then, to follow someone blindly and to accept a thing without hesitation or question. I usually translate it by "servile conformism." J: conformisme; W: naive and second-hand belief; VR: conformismo; F: traditional belief; Sch: la foi la plus absolue à l'autorité; BM: la croyance routinière. We shall note the further occurrences of this term and the possible shades of meaning it may have in other contexts. Cf. Poggi 139–40; *taqlīd* contrasted with *ijtihād.*

5. *Istibṣār:* J: observation; W: direct vision; VR: l'indagine personale; F: assurance; Sch: spéculations abstractives; BM: la certitude. The verb means: observe attentively, investigate a hidden thing, be able to see, be endowed with reason. Here it is obviously intended as the contrary of *taqlīd:* hence my translation implying "seeing for oneself."

6. *ᶜIlm al-kalām:* often translated by "Islamic, or Muslim, Theology," or "Scholastic Theology." I think (with AGth) that it is more accurately translated by "defensive apologetic." The word *kalām* means: speech or discourse, and, in this context, speech about God and His attributes of essence and action (ad extra). It is not *fides quaerens intellectum,* but rather, *defensio fidei.* It will be discussed at some length by Gh in Paras. 21–24 of this translation. So I prefer to keep the term in transliteration, since our "theology" does not render it exactly and might even be misleading at times. Cf. AGth, WPT, and WPK.

7. *Al-taᶜlīm:* lit, teaching, or instruction; here, as the author indicates, it is the charismatic teaching of the infallible and impeccable Imam. The followers of this doctrine are the Bāṭinites (Interiorists), or Taᶜlīmites: cf. Note 15 and Paras. 61–79 of my translation. The word *Imām* is from a root meaning "to lead the way, be an example to"; it was used early to designate the leader of the canonical Prayer. It later came to be used to designate the charismatic leader of the Shiᶜites and the Bāṭinites, and also such leaders as the "founders" of the schools of Law, distinguished *mutakallimūn* (practitioners of *kalām,* the "loquentes in lege Maurorum" of St. Thomas Aquinas), etc. It is the word translated by "Master" in Para. 1 of this translation. J: les partisans de l'"Enseignement"; W: the party of *taᶜlīm* (authoritative instruction); VR: i partigiani deli' insegnamento di autorità (*taᶜlīm*)*;* F: the Ta'limites; Seb: Ia secte des Talîmîtes; BM: les Ta'limites. Other possible translations which have occurred to me: the Authoritarians, the Infallibilists, the Doctrinaires, the Dogmatists.

8. *Al-tafalsuf:* Cf. Paras. 25–60, where the nature of the philosophizing which concerned Gh is discussed and annotated. Here I call attention to three works in English which will help anyone seeking further enlightenment on philosophy in Islam. WPT (Cf. my Annotated Bibliography); Dr. T. J. Boer: *The History of Philosophy in Islam* (trans. E. R. Jones), 1st ed. 1903, reprinted London, 1970; Majid Fakhry: *A History of Islamic Philosophy,* New York, 1970. Some interesting problems and subjects are discussed in: G. C. Anawati: *Études de Philosophie Musulmane,* Paris, 1974.and precious material will be found in R. Walzer: *Greek into Arabic: Essays on Islamic Philosophy,* Oxford, 1962.

9. *Al-taṣawwuf:* this word is much used in Arabic for what we know as Sufism. The Arabic word means: to embrace the way of Sufism: lit, to put on wool (an allusion to the very probable origin of the name "Sufi": the wearing of a white woolen garment). There is an abundant literature on Sufism; it is enough here to refer the reader to the recently published authoritative work of Annemarie Schimmel: *Mystical Dimensions of Islam,* Chapel Hill, N. C., 1975, which contains a splendid bibliography, pp. 437–67, and to A. J. Arberry's *Sufism,* London, 1956, a good brief account.

10. Ja has *al-a^ʾimma:* the leaders of sects, etc., plural of Imam. M has *al-umma:* the Community, i.e. of Islam, a word commonly used to designate the "body politic and religious" of Islam.

11. Qurʾān 23.55/53; 30.31/32. Hereafter references to chapters and verses of the Qurʾān are included in the text of the translation. I remind the reader that in references like 55/53 and 31/32 the first number is that of the verse in Flügel's edition, still widely used in the West, and the second number is that of the verse in the more or less standard text published in Cairo in 1923 A.D./1342 A.H. (the year of the Hijra, or Emigration, of Muḥammad from Mecca to Medina—622 A.D.—the beginning of the Muslim era).

12. This tradition is found in Wensinck: *Handbook,* p. 47 s.v. Community. It is used as a basis for one or more heresiographies: cf. ᶜAbd al-Qāhir al-Baghdādi: ed. M. Muḥyī l-Dīn ᶜabd al-Ḥamīd, Cairo, n.d., pp. 3–11; K. C. Seelye: *Moslem Schisms and Sects,* Part I, New York, 1920—a translation of the first part of ᶜAbd al-Qāhir's book; for the rest (in a much better translation): A. S. Halkin: *Moslem Schisms and Sects,* Part II, Tel-Aviv, 1935.

13. Ja: *fa qad kāda;* M: *wa qad kāna.*

14. *Mutasannin:* one who follows the *sunna* (custom), especially that of Prophet Muḥammad. The "orthodox" Muslims are commonly considered to be the "Sunnites" (*ahl al-sunna*), as opposed to the Shiᶜites (*shīᶜa:* the faction of ᶜAlī and his descendants). Hence: a faithful, or orthodox, follower of tradition.

Mubtadiᶜ: the exact opposite of the preceding: one who introduces or embraces a *bidᶜa,* innovation or novelty. My translation brings out both the notions implicit in the term. Often the expression *ahl al-bidᶜa* (the people of innovation) is translated by "heretics" or "the heterodox": the reason they are such is that their doctrine is an innovation and therefore anathema to all who follow the traditional *sunna* of the Prophet and the early Community. (One is reminded of the use of the Latin term *Novatores* [Innovators] to designate the early Protestants.)

15. *Bāṭinī:* from *bāṭin* (interior, inner): in general one who finds an "inner," or esoteric, or allegorical, meaning beneath the obvious, literal, or outer (*ẓāhir*) meaning of the text. Cf. EI (2) and my App. II. J: Intérioriste; W: one of the Bāṭinīyah; VR: un bāṭinita; F: one who maintained the hidden meaning of the Koran; Sch: un partisan des Allégoristes; BM: un disciple du sens allégorique (and in No. 18: Les Mystiques ou *ta'limites*). The "interiorism" chiefly envisaged by Gh is that of the *Taᶜlīmites;* ef. Paras. 61 ff. of this translation, and also Note 7.

16. *Ẓāhirī:* from *ẓāhir* (outer, external, exterior, evident): one who holds to the literal and immediate sense of the revealed text. J: Extérioriste; W: one of the Zāhirīyah; VR: un ẓāhirita; F: a partisan of its (the Koran's) exterior sense; Sch: on Formaliste; BM: un partisan du sens extérieure.

17. *Mutakallim:* one who engages in the science of *kalām.* Cf. Note 6. I prefer to keep the Arabic term in transliteration to avoid misconceptions.

18. "His serenity": *ṣafwatihi.* I was tempted to change the reading of Ja to *ṣūfiyyatihi* (his Suflsm)—and actually Sch has "son çoûfisme" and *ṣūfiyyatihi;* but M clearly reads *ṣafwatihi* (his serenity). One of the derivations given for the term *ṣūfi* is *ṣafwa*—cf. Massignon, *Lexique,* 153–55. The use of *ṣafwa* here might be regarded (tentiously[?]) as support for this derivation.

19. "A devout worshiper": *mutaᶜabbid.* J: le dévot; W: an ascetic; VR: persona dedita a pratiche pie; F: the devout adorer of Deity; Sch: un Orthodoxe; BM: le pieux adorateur de Dieu.

20. *Zindīqan muʿaṭṭilan: zindīq* seems to have been used as a general term for any freethinker or heretic or atheist, though its earliest use seems to have been to designate a dualist (Manichean, Magian, etc.). J says it is a transposition of the Persian *zendegar.* Ibn Manẓūr, in the famous dictionary *Lisān al-ʿArab* (The Language of the Arabs), says it is an Arabic form of the Persian *zandikirāy,* and that when the Arabs want to express the notion they say *mulḥid* (atheist) and *dahrī* (materialist—cf. my Note 75). Cf. EI(1), and AGth p. 45, Note 7, and the article of F. Gabrieli: *La "Zandaqa" au Ier Siècle Abbasside* in *L'Élaboration de l'Islam,* Paris, 1961, pp. 23–38. *Muʿaṭṭil* is from the verb *ʿaṭṭala,* here in the particular sense of making void or empty, stripping, divesting, depriving. The theological point involved is the denial of the divine attributes, a very large question in the science of *kalām.* The Muʿtazilites were called *muʿattila* (strippers, divesters) by their "orthodox" adversaries because of their insistence that God has no attributes distinct from His essence. Cf. AGth and WPT and WPK.

J: le matérialiste négateur; W: one of the Zanādiqah or Muʿaṭṭilah; VR: un eretico negatore di Dio; F: the atheist; Sch: on Hérétique ou un Moâttil; BM: le *zendiq* et l'athée. "irreligious nihilist" is an effort to convey the sense. One might even say: godless unitarian, or atheistic essentialist, or freethinking kenotist, or kenotic freethinker—but these and other possibilities might be misunderstood.

21. *Taqlīd* again—cf. Note 4. J: les liens traditionels; W: mere authority; VR: i legami della cieca soggezione alle idee altrui; F: tradition; Sch: l'autorité; BM; la routine. Here the term used in Para. 2 has the more specific sense of the conformism, or unquestioning acceptance of authority, found in the young vis-à-vis their parents and first teachers. A somewhat pejorative sense is given by the coupling of *taqīd* with *rābiṭa* (bonds, fetters, shackles).

22. *Fiṭra:* an interesting term about which there has been considerable discussion within Islam and outside of it. Cf. EI(2), 931–32 s.v. *fiṭra.* The word is from a root meaning to cleave or split and to create (God). So *fiṭra* means: creation, nature, natural disposition, constitution, temperament, etc., i.e. what is in a man at his creation. J: la nature saine; W: a sound nature; VR: la religione naturale; F: the germ of Islam; Sch: le même besoin religieux; BM: le germe de l'islam. I prefer to keep the Arabic word in transliteration.

23. This tradition: Bu 23.80 and 93; 65: sūra 30; 82.3. Mu 46.22–25. And Quʾrān 30.29/30.

24. *Taqlīd* again: the sense is that indicated in Note 21. J: conformisme; W: authority; VR: la cieca soggezione; F: authority; Sch and BM: l'autorité.

25. I think my translation of this sentence is correct. Watt's version turns on a different interpretation of *talqīnāt,* which, I think, should be understood as "things inculcated or dictated" or "suggestions imposed from without." J: ces traditions dont les prémisses sont passivement reçues; VR: La distinzione fra questi conformismi, come anche gli inizi loro, avviene per suggerimenti; F: I was moved by a keen desire to learn what was this innate disposition in the child, the nature of the accidental belief imposed on him by the authority of his parents and his masters, and finally the unreasoned convictions which he derives from their instructions; Sch: has different reading in his Arabic text, which, I think, is incorrect; BM: et enfin cette conviction aveugle qu'il doit leurs leçons; W: The attempt to distinguish between these authority-based opinions and their principles developed the mind.

26. Note that Gh is not condemning all *taqlīdāt* (traditional beliefs) out of hand. And he himself, even in his crises, seems always to have had the "sure and certain faith"

which he mentions in Para. 83. Now he is about to embark on a very interesting epistemological discussion involving what we may call his "crisis of skepticism" as opposed to his later and much profounder crisis of conscience, or, of the spirit. These two crises must not be confused.

27. This definition of "sure and certain knowledge" (*al-ᶜilm al-yaqīnī*) is basic for the ensuing discussion. With it we may compare al-Bāqillānī's definition of what the *mutakallimūn,* in their philosophical prolegomena, called *al-ᶜilm al-ḍarūrī* (necessary knowledge): "[a knowledge] which imposes such compulsion on the creature's soul that the creature, once it is had, cannot escape it, or be separated from it, or entertain any doubt or suspicion about its term of reference" (*Tamhīd,* my ed., Para. 9). Whether such knowledge exists or is even possible has, of course, been the subject of lengthy debate among philosophers. Many observations on certitude and knowledge will be found in JM and JC, particularly in the latter work (references s.v. *yaqīn*).

28. This statement of Gh might be questioned by some. The certainty of what he calls "sure and certain knowledge" seems to be that which some philosophers call "metaphysical certainty or certitude" (as opposed to "physical" and "moral" certainty). There do seem to be degrees of certainty. Indeed, for some thinkers and theologians, the very highest certainty is the totally "irrational" (but not unreasonable) certainty of faith. The latter, however, is outside the domain of the "natural," since it involves divine prevenience and divine grace. Gh seems to be moving within the confines of the "natural," though we may later find reasons for questioning this. He is about to deal with a problem and a crisis which, I believe, are not so very unusual at a certain stage in the development of many individuals. Here, perhaps, we are in the area mentioned by Professor Starbuck—cf. W. James: *The Varieties of Religious Experience* (Mentor Cd.), p. 164.

29. M: *al-qawl fī madākhil at-safsaṭa wa jaḥd al-ᶜulūm.* J: Les Sophistes et le problème radical de la connaissance; W: Preliminaries: Scepticism and the Denial of All Knowledge; VR: Preambolo sofistico e Negazione del sapere; F: The Subterfuges of the Sophists; Sch: Sur les subterfuges des sophistes et sur la négation de toutes les connaissances; BM: Sur les subterfuges des Sophistes et sur la négation des connaissances en général. I believe that the correct literal translation is: Discussion of the entrances (ways of entry) of sophistry and the denial of (all) knowledge (or: of all cognitions held to be certain). The Arabic *ᶜulūm* is often neatly translated in French by "connaissances"; in English "cognitions" seems best here, but the nuance of "cognitions held to be certain" seems present, especially in view of what follows.

30. *Al-ḥissiyyāt:* i.e. sensations, or things having to do with sensation (*ḥiss*). In Paras. 102–106 Gh details the classic division of the external senses and their objects.

31. *Al-ḍarūriyyāt:* i.e. the things that are necessary (*ḍarūrī*) in the sense mentioned in Note 27. "Self-evident truths" seems to be a fair translation, since, as will be seen, Gh has in mind analytic propositions which the normal mind, once it has understood them, must accept as patently true.

32. *Al-jaliyyāt:* things that are *jalī* (clear, evident, manifest).

33. *Al-taqlīdiyyāt:* i.e. the things that are the object of *taqlīd* (servile conformism, or unquestioning acceptance of authority).

34. *Al-naẓariyyāt:* i.e. things related to *al-naẓar* (reflection, thought, speculation, reasoning). Here there is a little more than a hint of the almost contempt for the rational capacity of ordinary men which Gh seems to have sometimes shared with the Islamic philosophers and the other "intellectuals" of his day.

35. Ja has *al-tashakkuk,* M has *al-tashkīk,* which seems much better in the context.

36. The "dinar" of Gh's time was a relatively small gold coin.

37. *Ḥādithan:* the root indicates newness, novelty, beginning.

38. Here Gh exemplifies what is meant by "primary *truths*"—*awwaliyyāt:* things that are *awwalī* (first, primary, basic). They are, as I mentioned in Note 31, analytic propositions.

39. The sentence is somewhat involved, even in the Arabic, but the sense seems clear. In the Arabic the apparent confusion is due to the *ilayhā* (to it) with which the sentence ends. I have clarified the reference of the pronominal suffix by explicitating it—"to that new and further state." But M reads *ilayhi;* here the reading of Ja seems better. The form *ḥāl* may be masculine or feminine; but the form used here is *ḥāla,* which is feminine.

40. This tradition is not in WConc, but it is a tradition which Gh seems to have been fond of.

41. Ja has *nawm* (sleep), but it is not in M. Ja's reading seems better.

42. J: Quand ces pensées me vinrent à l'esprit, elles me rongèrent; W: had occurred to me and penetrated my being (the "and" of Ja is not in M, but there is an "and" in M, and not in Ja, before *ḥāwaltu* (I tried); VR: Quando tali pensieri mi venno alla mente e mi penetrarono nell'animo; F: Such thoughts as these threatened to shake my reason; Sch: Ces pensées m'étant venues et ayant frappé mon âme; BM: Lorsque ces pensées eurent envahi mon esprit.

43. Thus this crisis is solved. But what exactly was the crisis, and how was it solved? Gh answers the second question in his further remarks. Here I would like to offer my tentative and somewhat timid answer to the first question. Apparently this crisis of skepticism took place when Gh was still in his early teens. What I suggest is that his experience may have been one not uncommon to bright and sensitive young men of that age group. Speaking personally (and I beg indulgence for including myself among the "bright and sensitive"—*si mihi, a fortiori aliis*), I can remember going through a minor version of Gh's experience when I was a seventeen year old freshman in college. And some of my peers had a similar experience. I suddenly began to doubt whether anything was true and real, even including my own existence. This state of mind lasted at most for a few days, and not, like Gh's, for nearly two months. As I reflect on what might have triggered such an experience, several points occur to me. At that age one is young and is making the great step, or steps, from adolescence to maturity—i.e. one is growing up, but not yet grown up, mentally and morally as well as physically. One becomes conscious of new and untried mental powers, but is still aware of one's lack of knowledge and experience and of one's still being subject to adult authority which may not always be gentle, understanding and sympathetic. One wants to try one's wings, to step into a somewhat alien, and perhaps hostile, adult world with assurance and confidence. One wants to be be noticed, to do something which will attract attention, and often enough the first thing to suggest itself is some sort of act or posture which protests against and defies the "establishment," be the latter mental, moral, religious, or whatever. One way to do this is to pose as a more or less fierce young skeptic who questions everyone and everything. Happily enough it usually is only a pose, only a quickly passing phase which ends on the first rung of the ladder of maturity and mental equilibrium, for thoroughgoing skepticism is indeed theoretically absurd and practically impossible in sane and balanced human living. I suggest, therefore, that it is something like this which offers some explanation of Gh's first and youthful crisis of skepticism. But ahead of him lies a much greater crisis in which (and perhaps even

in this first crisis) deadIly and subtle powers of evil are involved. For a very interesting discussion of the view which regards the youthful skepticism of Gh as *methodical* rather than *real* ef. Poggi 171 ff.

44. For nearly two months Gh was "a skeptic in fact, but not in utterance and doctrine." He was not a philosophical skeptic, nor a heretic, nor a real unbeliever, but simply, as I think, a troubled young man. Then, as he tells us, God cured him of his sickness—and note that he calls it a "sickness." We might be tempted to say that he regained his balance or came to his senses. But Gh, as we shall see, was a dedicated occasionalist, and for him God was the only effective agent. And how did God cure him? By means of a "light" which He "cast" into the young skeptic's "breast."J: au moyen d'une Lumière que Dieu a projeté dans ma poitrine; W: same as mine; VR: per una luce che Dio mi proiettò nel petto; F: the light which God caused to penetrate into my heart; Sch: par on éclat de lumière que Dien me jeta dans le coeur; BM: mais à la lumière que Dieu fit pénétrer dans mon coeur.

These are the words which we must try to understand: light—cast—breast. "Breast" presents no great difficulty, since it is surely the principal organ in the breast which is intended, i.e. the heart *(qalb),* which, for Gh, is the seat of intelligence and intellect, and is closely related to soul *(nafs),* spirit *(rūḥ),* and reason or intellect (*ᶜaql*). He explains this at some length in the first chapter of Book XXI of his major work, *The Revivification of the Religious Sciences,* i.e. "The Book of the Marvels of the Heart"—cf. Appendix XXI.

But what is the "light" to which Gh here refers? In his *Mishkāt al-Anwār* (The Niche of Lights—cf. Ann. Bibliog.) Gh affirms that the only *real* light is God. But the word is also used in other senses: 1) the ordinary sense, e.g. the light of the sun etc.; 2) the eye, or sight; 8) the intelligence, or intellect, and this more truly deserves the name "light." This is as far as we need go for the moment. At first sight, then, it would seem possible that Gh means in our present text to indicate nothing more than sound intellect or intelligence or reason. But the word "cast" gives us pause, in conjunction with what follows in our text. For if, as Gh says, God cast, or threw, or sent down, this light, then the latter would seem to have been some sort of special intervention on God's part. This notion is reinforced by the traditions which Gh proceeds to cite, and especially by the last sentence of Para. 16. I must confess that I am puzzled by the sentence, and at least part of my puzzlement seems due to the possibility that Gh himself in this paragraph confuses, or combines, several notions and views which are expressed individually and clearly in some of his other works. In fine, I incline to think that he principally intends the "light" of intellect or intelligence, while not excluding some indefinable sort of "gust of grace."

45. Tradition: not in WConc.

46. Tradition: not in WConc, but cf. Tir. *īmān* 18, and Aḥ. b. Ḥ. 2.176, 197 *khalaqa khalqahu fī ẓulma* (He created His creatures in a darkness). BM has a note citing Zamakhsharī's *Kashshāf* (Commentary on the Qurʾān): "God, after having created the thinking beings, men and jinn, in the darknesses of the corporeal nature and of the evil passions, cast into their soul the light of true knowledge and of salvation."

47. Tradition: not in WConc, but cf. *Iḥyāʾ,* III.9.3, where it is attributed to Abū Hurayra and Abū Saᶜīd.

48. Para. 17 may sound a little odd at first, but I think the meaning is quite clear. W and VR obscure the meaning by overlooking (?) the negative in the last sentence; F and Sch and BM are adequate.

49. *Mutakallimūn:* plural of *mutakallim*—cf. Notes 6 and 17.

50. *Bāṭinites:* cf. Notes 7 and 15.

51. Cf. Note 7.

52. *Al-falāsifa:* plural of *faylasūf* (from the Greek). The practitioners of *falsafa,* or *tafalsuf*—cf. Note 8. They would have claimed to be much more than logicians.

53. *Al-burhān:* this is demonstration, or proof, in its strict and absolute sense, which leads to certainty as opposed to dialectical and rhetorical arguments which lead only to probability. Gh discusses it at length in the first section of his *Maqāṣid al-falāsifa* (The Intentions, or Aims, of the Philosophers) and in his *Mi*ᶜ*yār al-*ᶜ*ilm* (The Norm, or Standard, or Gauge, of Knowledge).

54. *Al-ṣūfiyya:* cf. Note 9.

55. *Al-mushāhada* and *al-mukāshafa:* J: la Vision et la Révélation; W: vision and intuitive understanding; VR: la Visione e la Rivelazione; F: intuition and knowledge of the truth by means of ecstasy; Sch: être favorisés d'une intuition immédiate et assister comme témoins oculaires à la manifestation des vérités; BM: possesseurs de l'intuition et de la connaissance du vrai (par l'extase). These are two terms of the sufi vocabulary, of which I have given the basic meaning. The notions involved will come in for more attention later in the section on the Way of the Sufis.

56. Ja has *bita*ᶜ*līm,* singular; M has *bita*ᶜ*līmāt,* plural, in the sense of "teachings" or "doctrines."

57. *Ṭarīq:* method, way, road. Usually I have reserved the capitalized "Way" for the Arabic *ṭarīqa,* a more particularized "way," and also a sufi "order" (Cf. Ann. Bibliog. under Trimingham).

58. M has ᶜ*allaqtu:* ᶜ*allaqa* (annotate, gloss, make an extract from). The other translations seem to follow the reading ᶜ*aqaltuhu:* ᶜ*aqala* (comprehend, understand).

59. *Ahl al-bid*ᶜ*a:* cf. Note 14.

60. *Al-akhbār:* plural of *khabar* (information, news, report), often used as an equivalent of *ḥadīth* (talk, report and esp. an account of some saying or action of the Prophet). Ja has ᶜ*alā mā fīhi;* M has ᶜ*alā mā hiya,* the *"hiya"* referring to ᶜ*aqīda* (creed). And for the *bima*ᶜ*rifatihi* of Ja M seems to have *bimufarraqātihi* (details, detailed things).

61. *Wasāwis,* plural of the onomatopoetic *waswasa* (whispering, suggestion temptation of Satan). In Book XXI of the *Iḥyā,* Bayān (Chapter) 11, Gh has a fascinating, and lengthy, discussion of Satan's *wasāwis*—cf. Appendix V.

62. In Note 6 I have indicated that *kalām* is really a defensive apologetic. This is borne out by all the well-known manuals of *kalām,* in which we find, not so much a systematic exposition of dogma, as attacks on non Islamic religions and replies to arguments advanced by non-Muslims and by heterodox Muslims. Ibn Khaldūn's definition of *kalām* lays primary stress on its defensive nature—cf. AGth 121–24; in his famous *Prolegomena* he says: (Kalām) is a science which contains the demonstrations of the articles of faith by means of rational proofs and the refutation of the innovators who deviated in their beliefs from the doctrines of the pious forbears and the adherents of the *sunna* (*ahl al-sunna*—cf. Note 14). Gh himself did not have a very high regard for *kalām,* but rather almost regarded it as a necessary evil. This is evident from various remarks he makes in different works of his. In the first three of four Preambles to his own famous work on *kalām, al-Iqtiṣād fi*ʾ*l-I*ᶜ*tiqād* (The Golden Mean in Belief), he discusses: 1) the importance of *kalām* for religion (Islam); 2) why, though *kalām* is important, it is more important for some men not to engage in it; 3) engaging in *kalām* is a collective, or Community, duty (*farḍ kifāya*), not an individual duty (*farḍ* ᶜ*ayn*)—i.e. there must be some experts in *kalām* to defend religion, but not everyone needs to be, or can be, an expert. He also has interesting

remarks on the relative importance of *fiqh* (jurisprudence) and *kalām:* the former is much more important and necessary, since it enters intimately into the daily life of the Muslim in his earthly pilgrimage to the afterlife.

63. Ja has *waʾl-taghyīr;* M has *waʾl-taghbīr* (a difference of only one dot). J: (ils ont) lutté contre les innovations religieuses; W: rectified heretical innovations; VR; rettificò le innovasioni che erano stato suscitate; F: by proving . . . the falsity of heretical innovations; Sch: en corrigeant sur-le-champs tout ce qui s'y était glissé d'altérations hérétiques; BM: en démontrant la fausseté des innovations hérétiques. The verb *ghabbara* coupled with the phrase *fī wajh* (as it is here) has the sense of surpass, outdo, be superior to—hence my translation.

64. This sentence may sound a bit strange at first. But we must remember that the "adversaries" mentioned were of two kinds: non-Muslims and Muslims (such as the Muʿtazilites). It is the latter who particularly made use of Traditions and Qurʾānic texts. A double criticism is implied: of a too-ready acceptance of *ijmāʿ* (consensus) and of a noncritical acceptance of what is presumed to be the meaning of a Tradition or a sacred text.

65. What was this "malady"? At the beginning of Para. 18 he seems to have been cured of his "sickness" of skepticism. There is a connection, however, since his main concern was the possibility of acquiring sure and certain knowledge, or, in other words, what he calls "the truth." With this section on *kalām* he considers the first of the four ways to acquire "the truth," viz. *kalām,* or "theology," since the *mutakallimūn* may conceivably have found the way to "the truth." Incidentally, as I have suggested in my introductory remarks, we need not think that Gh proceeded as schematically as the structure of the *Munqidh* might suggest. He had studied *kalām* as a comparatively young man under the Imām al-Ḥaramayn.

66. How much of a "study" they made is questionable. But as one peruses the manuals of *kalām,* from the earliest to the latest, the introductory sections devoted to epistemological and ontological questions become longer and longer. However, one feels obliged to agree with Gh's criticism. Much interesting information will be found in WPK (Wolfson's *The Philosophy of the Kalam*).

67. Ja has the simple title: Philosophy. The long title given here is from M.

68. Gh certainly sets a high ideal. It is an insight into his own apologetic method. No facile apriorism would suit him. The lesson is still valuable.

69. Lit. a throwing in blindness, i.e. a random shot.

70. We must not forget that Gh was primarily a *faqīh* (jurisprudent, expert in religious law) and that the main subject taught at the Nizāmiyya was *fiqh.*

71. *Takhyīl:* J: imaginaire (contenu d'hérésies et d'illusions); W: representation of reality; VR: suggerimento di fantasticherie; F: illusion; Sch: chimérique; BM: de chimères. In two other places (Ja 37.1 and 44.3) W has "delusion" and "deception"; almost: its fact and its fiction.

72. Ja: *ḥikāyatahum* (account of them, i.e. the philosophers); M has *ḥikāyatahu:* account of it (referring to philosophy, and particularly to the word *muntahā* in the preceding paragraph).

73. *Al-kufr waʾl-ilḥād: kufr* means unbelief, and of course would remove the *kāfir* (unbeliever) from the Islamic Community. *Ilḥād* is deviating from the true religion (Islam), becoming a heretic or an apostate; it is also used for godlessness and atheism.

74. The Arabic is a bit confusing, but the sense is quite clear.

75. *Al-dahriyyūn* (Materialists). Cf. El (2)—Dahr (Watt) and Dahriyya (Goldziher-Goichon). The notion of *dahr* is that of endless time and (blind) fate or destiny; hence a thoroughgoing materialism as Gh himself describes it.

Al-ṭabīʿiyyūn (Naturalists): from *ṭabīʿa* (nature). This word can also mean "element," and many of the *mutakallimūn* (and seemingly the Muʿtazilites) wrote polemics against *aṣḥāb al-ṭabāʾiʿ* (The Naturalists, or Elementalists). But it is not clear that the latter are the same as those Gh has in mind here.

Al-ilāhiyyūn (Theists): from *ilāh* (god). Allāh (God) is a contraction of *al-ilāh* (*The* god).

76. *Al-ṣāniʿ al-mudabbir al-ʿālim al-qādir:* the notions of creation and providence were dear to the *mutakallimūn.* But all the major Islamic philosophers (with the exception of al-Kindī) held the eternity of the world by necessary emanation from the First (God). This will be a major point later on (Paras. 46–47). The philosophers meant by Gh are those we call the pre-Socratics.

77. *Al-zanādiqa:* plural of *zindīq*—cf. Note 20. The Arabic phrase is very emphatic: the godless par excellence, or, to the nth degree.

78. The argument from design also found its place in Islamic thought.

79. *Iʿtidāl al-mizāj: mizāj* (mixture) here refers to the old theory of the humors. A very good translation would be "complexion," i.e. the combination of the hot, cold, moist, and dry qualities held in medieval physiology to determine the quality of a body; but in this sense "complexion" is somewhat archaic and obsolete. J: l'équilibre du tempérament; W: the equal balance of the temperament; VR: l'equilibrio degli umori; F: the proper equilibrium of its organism; Sch: la juste proportion de la composition élémentaire; BM: le juste équilibre de l'organisme.

80. All these terms are much used in Islamic eschatology. The "Garden" and the "Fire," from the Qurʾān onward, are commonly used to designate heaven and hell. The "Assembly," "Recall," and "Resurrection" (*al-ḥashr waʾl-nashr waʾl-qiyāma*) refer to the reunion of souls with bodies and their rising on the Last Day. The "Reckoning" is the Judgment in which God squares all accounts. On Islamic eschatology cf. Lammens: *L'Islam croyances et institutions,* 3rd ed., Beyruth, 1943, 68–71—trans. of 1st ed. by Sir E. D. Ross: *Islam, Beliefs and Institutions,* London, 1929.

81. "By reason of the unbelievers' own infighting (or fighting among themselves)" is not, as Ja would lead one to think, in the Qurʾānic text; it is a traditional explanation of the text.

82. Ibn Sīnā: the Avicenna of the medieval schoolmen; one of the greatest, and perhaps the greatest, of the Muslim philosophers, physicians, and thinkers. Cf. the excellent article in EI(2). The reader can easily find many other articles and accounts, of which he is the subject, in encyclopedias and histories of philosophy. Cf. the references given in Note 8.

83. Another of the great names of Islamic philosophy, also well known to the medieval schoolmen.

84. For example: al-Kindī and al-Rāzī (Rhazes). What Gh goes on to say is quite true. AI-Fārābī received the honorific title of *al-muʿallim al thānī* (The Second Teacher; the First was Aristotle himself), and Ibn Sīnā was commonly referred to as *al-shaykh al-raʾīs* (The Principal, or Leading Master, or, the Master of Masters).

85. Accepting what is worthy of *takfīr* (branding as unbelief) would excommunicate one from the Community of Islam; the acceptance of what is worthy of *tabdīʿ* (stig-

matizing as innovation) would render one a "heretic," but not a non-Muslim. We shall see more about this a little later. And cf. Note 110.

86. These are the six classical divisions of philosophy. For an example of an Islamic classification of the sciences cf. that of al-Fārābī in AGth, 106.

87. Umūr *burhāniyya:* the second word might be translated by demonstrated, or demonstrable, or the result of apodeictic demonstration (*burhān*)—cf. Note 53.

87a. *Taᶜṭīlihim:* i.e. their denial of the divine attributes.

88. He goes from one *taqlīd* to another. Such behavior is not unknown in our own days.

89. *Al-awāʾil:* the early, or ancient, philosophers. Watt takes the word in another sense ("elementary matters"), but I think it is better taken, with J, VR, F, Sch, and BM, as I have translated it. Cf. Poggi 231, and his long Note 34 with its interesting observations on the word *takhmīnī* ("conjectural"), which he translates by "estimativa."

90. M has *taḥmiluhu ᶜalayhi;* Ja has *taḥmiluhu ghalabatu.* (In this case Ja seems preferable.)

91. Ja has *al-shahwatu ᶜl-bāṭila* (vain passion); M has *shahwatu ᶜl-bāṭila* (the passion, or love, for what is vain). Perhaps M's reading is slightly better.

92. Today we do not think of mathematics as a part of philosophy proper, though it does play a part in some forms of logic. But the old philosophers regarded it as a kind of propaedeutic to the study of philosophy. Indeed al-Kindī, in one of his treatises, lays down the study of mathematics as an essential precondition for the study of philosophy. (Cf. M. Guidi, R. Walzer: *Studi su al-Kindi* I. *Uno scritto introduttivo allo studio di Aristotele,* Rome, 1940; Abū Rīdah: *Rasāʾil al-Kindī,* I, 363 ff., and esp. 376 ff.—VII of Guidi, Walzer). It may surprise us a little to find Gh so strict on the study of mathematics. But in his day, if not in ours, it did often lead to the study of philosophy proper, and his argument is not without a certain psychological value and finesse. Many will remember the case of a very famous modern mathematician whose dicta on moral and theological topics were received with a kind of reverential awe, principally, it seemed, because he was such an outstanding "mathematician"—and I do not mean Einstein.

93. *Al-sharᶜ:* I translate this term, and also *al-sharīᶜa,* by "revealed Law." Schacht translates it by "the sacred Law of Islam" and defines it as "an all-embracing body of religious duties, the totality of Allah's commands that regulate the life of every Muslim in all its aspects" (*Introduction to Islamic Law,* p. 1). *Fiqh* (jurisprudence, Islamic Law) is the science of the *sharīᶜa.* It is, as Schacht remarks, "the epitome of Islamic thought, the most typical manifestation of the Islamic way of life, the core and kernel of Islam itself." And let us remember that Gh was primarily a *faqīh* (a specialist in *fiqh,* jurisprudent, a kind of combination of canon lawyer and moral theologian).

94. "Undertakes" (or: addresses itself to) seems a more correct translation of *taᶜarruḍ* than W's "opposed," though the latter has a certain possibility.

95. Tradition: Bu *libās* 2, *kusūf* 1, 2, 4–6, 9, 13, 15, 16; Mus *kusūf* 1, 3. It is related that the Prophet, about a year before his death, lost a young son, Ibrāhīm, the fruit of his marriage with Mary the Copt, and that the sun was eclipsed on the day the child died. The Arabs saw a connection between the two events, and Muḥammad wanted, by this dictum, to put an end to their ignorant supposition. Cf. *Prairies d'or,* IV, 160.

96. *ᶜIlm al-ḥisāb:* the science of arithmetic. J: l'arithmétique; W: the science of arithmetic; VR: l'aritmetica; F: the astronomical calculations; Sch: des sciences de calcul; BM: des calculs astronomiques.

97. Addition—Gh's statement seems to be correct; it is not found in Bukhārī's famous collection of traditions.

97a. "Concept"—*taṣawwur;* "assent" or "judgment"—*taṣdīq:* the two basic notions which include all human cognitions. Cf. *Maqāṣid,* Intro, to the first part on Logic; Alonso 8 ff.; VDB II, 1, Note I; Jadaane 106 ff. Gh himself also dealt with the science of logic in his *Miᶜyār al-ᶜilm* and his *Miḥakk al-naẓar* (The Norm, or Measure of Knowledge, and The Touchstone of Reasoning, or Speculation).

98. *Ahl al-naẓar:* or, those who engage in speculation, such as the Muᶜtazilites and the Ashᶜarites, and perhaps certain jurisprudents.

99. Cf. Jadaane, 117 ff.

100. I have taken the *ilayhi* to refer to the one who engages in the study of logic; the "also" recalls the student of mathematics. J avoids the reference by a very free translation. W and VR refer the *ilayhi* to "unbelief"; F and Sch and BM seem to refer it to "logic" itself, which is also possible.

101. This is the famous *Kifāb tahāfut al-falāsifa.* I translate *tahāfut* by "incoherence," as many others do. The medieval Latin translation was "destructio." The word also has the meanings: collapse, inconsistency, effondrement, chute. Cf. BM's Note 1, p. 32; and my Annot. Bibliog. under Kemali and VDB.

102. As a faithful Ashᶜarite Gh is a thoroughgoing occasionalist. The only real agent is God. The reader who wishes to know more should consult Majid Fakhry's *Islamic Occasionalism,* esp. 56–78.

103. It is perhaps worth listing these twenty heads, as given by Gh in the *Tahāfut,* since the reader may not have easy access to Kemali or VDB. They are as follows:

1. The refutation of their doctrine on the preeternity (*azaliyya*) of the world.
2. The refutation of their doctrine on the posteternity (*abadiyya*) of the world.
3. Exposé of their deception in their affirming that God is the Maker of the world, and that the world is of His making.
4. On showing their inability to prove the existence of the Maker.
5. On showing their inability to establish proof of the impossibility of [the existence of] two Gods (i.e. to prove the unicity of God).
6. On the refutation of their doctrines on the denial of [God's] Attributes.
7. On the refutation of their affirmation that the essence of the First is not divisible into genus and specific difference.
8. On the refutation of their affirmation that the First is a simple being without a quiddity.
9. On showing their powerlessness to demonstrate that the First is not a body.
10. On showing that they are logically bound to hold the eternal existence of the world (*dahr*) and to deny the existence of the Maker.
11. On showing their inability to affirm that the First knows anything other than Himself.
12. On showing their inability to affirm that He knows Himself.
13. On the refutation of their affirmation that the First does not know particulars.

14. On their affirmation that the heaven is an animal (*ḥayawān:* living being) which moves voluntarily.

15. On the refutation of what they mentioned of the aim (purpose) which moves the heaven.

16. On the refutation of their affirmation that the souls of the heavens know all the particulars.

17. On the refutation of their affirmation of the impossibility of violation of customs (*kharq al-ᶜādāt*).

18. On their affirmation that the soul of man is a substance subsisting in itself and neither a body nor an accident.

19. On their affirmation of the impossibility of ceasing-to-be (annihilation) for human souls.

20. On the refutation of their denial of the resurrection of bodies with consequent pleasure and pain in the Garden and the Fire by reason of bodily pleasures and pains.

104. The word "assembled" (*tuḥshar*) is a term for the resurrection, i.e. the raising up of men's bodies on the Last Day. The major Islamic philosophers seem certainly to have denied this fundamental dogma of orthodox Islam. Or perhaps it would be better to say that they interpreted it in such a way as to deprive it of its literal meaning. Cf. VDB 859 ff.

105. The difficulty here involves God's omniscience and immutability. He must know everything, but there can be no change in His knowledge such as would be consequent on His knowing an event as future, then present, then past. Cf. VDB 275–85.

106. This question seems to occupy a disproportionately lengthy part of the *Tahāfut*. But a very fundamental doctrine of Islam is involved: that of God's creation of the world *ex nihilo sui et subiecti* (as put by one of he *mutakallimūn*: "God was and the world was not; God was and the world was"). The problem is an old one. It also concerned St. Thomas Aquinas who, reasonably enough it seems, decided that the question of the preeternity of the world could not be solved by reason, and that holding it to be eternal would not matter, provided that it was held to have been entirely dependent on God's will and power—his opusculum: *De aeternitate mundi.* An acquaintance of mine who was part of NASA recently informed me that the scientists now have hard scientific proof that the universe had a beginning—this would have pleased Gh, though he is doubtless occupied now with more important matters.

107. The conclusion clearly is that the Islamic philosophers who held the three views mentioned (or any one of them) were not really Muslims. This is a strong, but logical enough, view for Gh who, as we know, severely criticized those who were swift to hurl accusations of unbelief and heresy at their adversaries. Cf. Note 110.

108. *Al-muᶜtazila:* The Muᶜtazilites have been called—incorrectly, I believe—the "freethinkers" and "rationalists" of Islam. In their *kalām* they made some use of notions and methods derived from Greek philosophy. After ruling the theological roost for many years they were finally vanquished, as much by their own intransigence and illiberalism as by the polemic efforts of al-Ashᶜarī and his "school." There is a classic article by Nyberg—Muᶜtazila—in EI(1). Cf. also WPT and WFP and WPK.

109. My translation is of M, which reads: *wa qad dhakarnā dhālikā fī . . . wa mā yatabayyanu.*

110. This is Gh's book: *Fayṣal al-tafriqa bayn al-islām wa'l-zandaqa.* On *zandaqa* cf. Note 20. This book is very interesting both because of its contents and because of the light it throws on Gh's own character as an enlightened and liberal defender of the faith. The reader will find that it forms the subject of my Appendix I.

111. On political philosophy cf. E. I. J. Rosenthal, *Studia Semitica,* Vol. II, Cambridge, 1971, and the same author's *Political Thought in Medieval Islam,* 3rd ed., Cambridge, 1968.

"The predecessors of the prophets"—J: des Prophbtes anciens; W: (reads *al-awliyā'* instead of *al-an biyh'*) the saints of old; VR: antichi profeti; F: ancient sages; Sch: des premiers califes; BM: des sages de l'antiquité. The translation "the ancient prophets" may be better.

112. This does not seem to be quite true. The Muslim philosophers were certainly influenced by the ancient Greeks in their ethical writings. Cf. also F. Jadaane, pp. 177–237. Gh's own *Mizān al-ᶜamal* (French trans. *Critère de l'action* by Hikmat Hachem, Paris, 1945) shows that his own "Ethics" was not derived solely from Sufi sources.

113. *Dhikr Allāh: dhikr* means: remembrance, mentioning, invoking God. It is used to designate a well-known practice of the Sufis which consists in the constant repetition of the name of God, or of certain formulas or verses. A very interesting account will be found in G. Anawati and L. Gardet: *Mystique Musulmane,* Paris, 1961, pp. 187–234.

114. *Awtād al-arḍ: watad* means: tent peg, stake, pole. The plural was applied to a group of apotropaic "saints" in the hierarchy which was beaded by the *quṭb* (Pole), the Saint who, in each age, mysteriously supports and directs the world.

115. Tradition not in WConc. The story of the Companions of the Cave is found in Sura 18 of the Qur'ān, a borrowing from the legend of the Seven Sleepers of Ephesus.

116. This sentence is rather involved in the Arabic, but the sense seems quite clear.

117. I have not succeeded in finding a reference to this saying attributed to ᶜAlī. Of course many dicta were attributed to him as the legend about him grew.

118. *Al-qallāb:* J: faux-monnayeur; W: counterfeiter; VR: falsario; F: coiner of false money; Sch: changeur; BM: faux-monnaycur. Despite the apparent consensus, I am not sure that they are right; it seems to me we have to deal with a "trickster," or even a "confidence man" who handles, but is not necessarily the maker of, counterfeit coins.

119. Ikhwāin al-Ṣafā: Cf. M. Fakhry: *A History of Islamic Philosophy,* New York and London, 1970, pp. 184–204, for an account of this group and its views; also the article in EI(2), III, 1071–76.

120. "Deemed impure": *al-mustaqdhar,* i.e. it is deemed impure in a legal sense. One can understand the natural repugnance for honey found in a cupping glass. But Gh's point is that, just as it is perfectly good honey, so also, the ethical teaching of the philosophers may contain things that are perfectly good and acceptable.

121. W uses the reading: *mā fī kutubihim* (what is in their books). M and Ja have: *mā fī kinānatihim* (what is in their quiver), i.e. what intellectual arms and weapons they have. Following the latter reading: "what their strength was (strong points were)."

122. This is the book called by Gh *Fadā'iḥ al-Bāṭiniyya wa Fadā'iḥ al-Mustaẓhiriyya* (The Infamies of the Bāṭinites and the Virtues of the Mustaẓhirites). It forms the subject of my Appendix II.

123. We do not know who this was.

124. Aḥmad (164/780–241/855) was one of the famous champions of orthodoxy and the eponym of the very rigid and traditionalist Ḥanbalite school of *fiqh* (Law). Cf. H.

Laoust's excellent article in EI(2), pp. 272–77, and W. M. Patton's *Aḥmad ibn Ḥanbal and the Miḥna,* Leiden, 1897.

Al-Ḥārith (d. 243/857) was an ascetic who wrote several ascetical works which are referred to by Gh in Para. 81 of this work. Cf. J. van Ess:*Die Gedankenwelt des Ḥādriṯ al-Muḥāsibī,* Bonn, 1961.

125. Ja adds [*yatakallafūhā*]*;* M has *yutakallaf* (M: *naᶜam yanbaghī an lā natakallafa* [?] *shubhatan lam yutakallaf*).

126. This argument about Muḥammad being *the* Infallible Imam is given in a more developed form in the *Mustaẓhirī*—cf. Appendix II.

127. *Al-ijtihād wa 1-raʾy: "ijtihād"* means "effort"; it is a legal term and denotes the personal effort made when the answer to a problem is not clear from the Qurʾān or Tradition of Consensus. *"raʾy"* is individual reasoning. In early usage the two terms are practically synonymous—cf. J. Schacht: *An Introduction to Islamic Law,* Oxford, 1964, pp. 37 ff.

128. The Prophet sent Muᶜādh b. Jabal to Yemen to exercise the functions of a *qāḍī* (judge). When asked how he would perform his duties, he replied that he would base his judgments on Qurʾānic texts, if available, then on the *sunna* (custom) of the Prophet. If both of these were unavailable, he would exercise his own personal judgment.

129. The *qibla* is the direction to be faced when one is performing the Prayer, i.e. the direction of Mecca and the Kaᶜba.

130. Cf. Bukhārī *iᶜtiṣām* 13, 20, 21.

131. "Legal alms": i.e. the obligation of the *zakāt,* one of the "Five Pillars of Islam" (Cf. Lammens: *L'Islam,* 74 ff.). Gh himself devoted a whole book of his *Iḥyāʾ* to the subject, I, Book 5; it has been translated into English by N. A. Faris: *The Mysteries of Almsgiving,* Beirut, 1966.

132. Abū Ḥanīfa: (80/696–150/767)—founder of the Ḥanafite school of *fiqh.* Cf. Schacht's art. in EI(2).

133. Al-Shāfiᶜī: (150/767–204/820)—founder of the Shāfiᶜite school of *fiqh.* Gh was a Shāfiᶜite. The reader may find further material on al-Shāfiᶜī in Majid Khadduri: *Islamic Jurisprudence,* Shāfiᶜīʾs *Risāla* (English translation), Baltimore, 1961; also: J. Schacht: *The Origins of Muhammadan Jurisprudence,* Oxford, 1959, and *An Introduction to Islamic Law,* Oxford, 1964, and N. J. Coulson: *A History of Islamic Law,* Edinburgh, 1964.

134. *Al-madhāhib:* I take it as a reference to the "schools" of *fiqh;* the word can also mean "doctrines."

135. Tradition not in WConc.

136. *Qawāᶜid al-ᶜaqāʾid:* this is also the title of Book 2 of the *Iḥyāʾ* of Gh. English translation—N. A. Fans: *The Foundations of the Articles of Faith,* Lahore, 1963.

137. On this curious work of Gh cf. my Appendix III.

138. This is not strictly true. The five "balances" are the five forms of the syllogism, which Gh undoubtedly learned from the logicians. But they are exemplified in texts from the Qurʾān.

139. The Fatimid Caliph in Egypt.

140. A true picture of the times? Cf. Amedroz and Margoliouth: *The Eclipse of the Abbassid Caliphate,* Oxford-London, 1920–1921, and G. Makdisi: *Ibn 'Aqīl et la résurgence de l'Islam traditionaliste au XIe siècle,* Damas, 1963, and H. Laoust: *La politique de Gazālī,* Paris, 1970, pp. 34 ff. and 107 ff.

141. *Manṣuṣ ʿalayhi:* i.e. there is a *naṣṣ* (text) in which the Prophet explicitly designated him. The opposite of this is *ikhtiyār,* choice or election, as held by the Sunnites.

142. *Aṣl al-nubuwwa:* i.e. what the claim of prophethood is based *upon,* as appears from the following.

143. This raises the interesting question of Gh's attitude towards the apologetic miracle. Cf. Poggi, 239 ff. It does seem that Gh had what Poggi calls "a minimist apologetic attitude." But this should not lead us to think, as van Leauwen does, that there is really an attempt to anchor theology, not in objective revelation, but in subjective experience.

144. Cf. R. J. McCarthy: *Miracle and Magic,* Beyrouth, 1958. This is an edition of al.Bāqillānī's *Kitāb al-Bayān,* a treatise on the nature of the apologetic miracle and its differentiation from charisms, trickery, divination, magic, and spells. There is an Analytical Summary in English, pp. 13–27.

145. The problem of "leading astray" (*iḍlāl*) arises from the fact that in the Qurʾān God is often said to "lead astray" whomever He wills—e.g. 16.95/93: "If God had willed, He would have made you one nation; but He leads astray whom He will, and guides whom He will." One can understand how such texts would create difficulties, and various ingenious answers were excogitated. Gh himself, as is clear from other places in his writings, is entirely for what Wensinek called "la prédestination sans aucune mitigation."

146. J: du premier au dernier; W: the older and younger members of the sect; VR: dal primo all'ultimo; Sch: soit les premiers, soit les derniers d'entre eux; BM: tous leurs docteurs.

147. One can read *al-afhām* (minds) with VR, or *al-ifhām* (make to understand) with W (?).

148. *Al-Mustaẓhirī:* cf. Note 122 and Appendix II.

149. *Ḥujjat al-ḥaqq:* cf. Bouyges: *Essai,* p. 32, no. 23. We know of no manuscript of this work.

150. *Mufaṣṣil al-khilāf:* cf. Bouyges: *Essai,* p. 45, no. 31.

151. Instead of *kitāb* (book) M has *jawāb* (reply). Cf. Bouyges: *Essai,* p. 56 no. 41. *Drj* may be *Durj* (W, VR, BM, Bouyges) or *Doraj* or *Darj.* The exact sense is not clear. J: *Al-Darj,* disposé en tableaux; W: the book of the *Durj* drawn up in tabular form; VR: *ad-Durj* ("Lo stipetto—small cabinet), libro disposte in tavole; Sch. la Tablette reglée; BM: *Kitāb al-Dourj,* ouvrage divisé en tableaux.

152. Cf. references in Note 119. We do not know who the informant was.

153. I think J and BM are more accurate here than W, VR, and Sch, in reading *fa ṭlubhu* (i.e. an imperative).

154. This is still a popular proverb in Baghdad.

155. Cf. Note 57. Here *ṭarīqa;* in the preceding sentence, *ṭarīq.*

156. W and VR read *ʿamalihim* (their practice). This does seem better fitted to the context, but M clearly has *ʿilmihim* (their knowledge), and from another viewpoint this is better.

157. He died in 386/996. His book is a Sufi "classic." Cf. Schimmel: *Mystical Dimensions of Islam,* p. 85.

158. Cf. Note 124; and Schimmel, p. 54.

159. Cf. Schimmel, pp. 57–59.

160. Cf. Schimmel, pp. 77–80.

161. Cf. Schimmel, pp. 47–51, and Ritter's article in EI(2), pp. 162–63.

162. *Al-dhawq:* literally "taste" or "tasting." J: le "goût"; W: immediate experience; VR: "il gusto": F: transport; Sch and BM: le transport. Cf. EI(2), II, p. 221 (F. Rahman):

"dhawķ has . . . qualitative overtones of enjoyment and 'intoxication' (*sukr*) besides the noetic element which it shares with the term 'sight.' Thus Rūmī says 'you cannot appreciate the intoxication of this wine unless you taste it.'" For this reason I use "fruitional (or: fruitive) experience" (in the same sense that Louis Gardet defines mysticism its general as "'l'expérience fruitive d'un absolu"). In Watt, *Muslim Intellectual,* pp. 164–65, Gh is said to hold a doctrine of three possible intellectual or cognitive conditions in which a man may be: 1) *taqlīd:* faith based on servile conformism; 2) *ᶜilm:* knowledge or science, where a man can give reasons for what he believes; 3) *dhawq:* insight or immediate experience—the highest degree. On this, and on Watt's use of the *dhawq*-criterion, cf. Poggi, 8–9, 88–89, 202–206. *Dhawq* immediately reminded me of Ps. 34,8 "Gustate et videte quoniam suavis est Dominus"—RSV: "O taste and see that the Lord is good"—perhaps more accurately in The Anchor Bible, Psalms I, M. Dahood's translation: "Taste and drink deeply, for Yahweh is sweet." The Hebrew verb is *ṭaᶜamū* (taste, relish, savor)—like the Arabic *ṭaᶜima.* I think, then, that *dhawq* is not simply a kind of cognition, but an immediate experience accompanied by savoring, or relishing, and enjoyment, i.e. what I like to call a fruitional (fruitive) experience.

163. *Al-ḥāl:* literally "state," "condition," "circumstance." It is used as a term for a mystic ecstatic state in Sufi writings. Cf. L. Gardet's article in EI(2), III, pp. 83–85.

164. *Tabaddul al-ṣifāt:* the change, or mutation, or exchange, of qualities. This refers to a moral change, i.e. the acquiring of virtues. VR explains in a note: "Man must strive to take on the qualities indicated by the divine attributes, as far as possible, modifying his own nature—I 13, n. 5. This subject plays a large part in Gh's *al Maqṣad al-asnā* (The Noblest Aim); The Fourth Chapter of Section One is entitled: On Showing that the servant's perfection and happiness lie in his putting on the moral qualities of God Most High and his being adorned with the meanings (ideas, notions) of His Attributes and His Names to the extent that this is conceivable in the servant's regard. Cf. my Appendix IV.

165. The Arabic text is, at first glance, a bit confusing. I think my translation does no violence to the text and agrees substantially with W and VR, though it differs somewhat from J, F, Sch, and BM. A possible suggestion: read *wa mā maᶜahu min al-ṣaḥwi* (sobriety, lucidity) *shayʾ,* to parallel the expression in the following line: *wa mā maᶜahu min al-sukri shayʾ.*

166. Ja has *wa l-ṣāḥī* (But the sober man); M has *wa l-ṭabīb* (But the physician).

167. "States": cf. Note 163. It was also a fact that many Sufis were very reluctant, and even refused, to write anything about their experiences, which they regarded as truly "ineffable."

168. This passage seems to me significant. Gh always had an unshakable belief in the "three fundamentals"—even, it would seem, during his earlier crisis of skepticism, which was not properly a *religious,* but rather a *psychological* and *epistemological* crisis. Cf. Note 26. This may also help to explain what follows. For here we begin the important account of the great crisis of Gh. This is a *religious* crisis, a crisis of the spirit, not of the intellect alone: to be or not to be a true and wholly committed follower of the way logically consequent on a profound and living faith in the "three fundamentals."

169. This seems a little exaggerated. Gh's chief task was teaching *fiqh* (jurisprudence). And in the preamble to his *al-Iqtiṣād fī l-iᶜtiqād* (The Golden Mean in Belief) he calls *fiqh* "the most important of the sciences" and stresses its necessity and value as opposed to *kalām* and medicine.

170. A candid confession by Gh. But it is used rather unfairly by Dr. al-Baqarī—cf. Abd-El-Jalil: *Autour de la sincérité d'al-Gazzālī,* in *Mélanges Louis Massignon,* Damascus, 1956, I, 61 ff. And ef. the beginning of Para. 139 of this translation.

171. "Fakery"—Arabic *takhyīl*: literally to make (one) believe, suggest—almost "play-acting" or "make-believe." Cf. Note 71. J: faux-semblant; W: delusion; VR: illusione; F: fantasy; Sch: vain; BM: chimères.

172. Paras. 84–88 are a moving account of a religious crisis of a classic kind ending in a true "conversion." I do not think that Gh's "flight" from Baghdad and from his professorship and his family is adequately explained by a fear of falling a victim to a Bāṭinite dagger as proposed by Jabre (in his French Introduction to Ja and in his article *La biographie et l'oeuvre de Ghazālī reconsiderées à la lumière du Ṭabaqāt de Sobkī,* MIDEO I [1954] 73–102). It may have been a factor, but not, I think, the major one. I prefer to believe Gh's account and to take it quite literally. To me it is a case of his generous response to an Islamic, and no less divine, equivalent of "If thou wouldst be perfect . . ." and "Be ye perfect. . . ." I believe, from what follows, that he did answer the "call" with a large measure of heroism and with an even larger measure of fidelity. William James, in his *The Varieties of Religious Experience* (Mentor ed., 1958, 309–11), cites this and further passages (trans. from Schmölders) as a Mohammedan example of the "incommunicableness of the (mystical) transport (which) is the keynote of all mysticism." This is not the place for theological polemic. I can only say that the only way Gh makes sense to me is that he received a divine grace which was at once a call and a help to personal holiness, and that he accepted the grace and really became a holy man.

173. Supernal: *samāwī*—heavenly, coming from on high, unearthly, abnormal, beyond nature, preternatural; "supernatural" might be ambiguous. And on this whole "conversion" passage I strongly recommend the remarks of Poggi, pp. 187 ff.

174. This was the Umayyad Mosque. This minaret is now called the Minaret of al-Ghazālī—cf. M. Smith: *ol-Ghazālī the Mystic,* London, 1944, p. 27

175. The Dome of the Rock: i.e. the great Mosque in Jerusalem, still regarded by Muslims as a very holy place, since they believe that from its location Muḥammad began his famous *Miᶜrāj,* or Ascension to the seven heavens.

176. *Al-khalīl:* i.e. Abraham. The "visit" would have been to his tomb in Hebron.

177. The Ḥijāz in Arabia where the holy cities of Mecca and Medina are located. Mecca was the birthplace of Muḥammad and his home until his *hijra* (emigration, hegira) to Medina (Yathrib at the time, later known as Medīnat al-Nabī: the City of the Prophet) in 622 A.D. At Medina he organized Islam and laid the ground for its future conquests and expansion. There he died in 632 A.D., and there he is buried. The focal points of the pilgrimage are the Kaᶜba in Mecca (which contains the Black Stone) and Muḥammad's tomb in Medina.

178. The reference to the "niche of prophecy" in connection with "light" evokes two things. The first is the Qurʾānic verse 24.35, "God is the Light of the heavens and the earth; the likeness of His Light is as a niche wherein is a lamp, etc." The second is Gh's own book *Mishkāt al-Anwār* (The Niche for Lights), published in an English translation by W. H. T. Gairdner, London, 1924; reprinted Lahore, 1952. We shall have more to say about this "light" later on. And cf. Note 44.

179. *Al-taḥrīm:* the opening formula of the Prayer (*Allāhu akbar:* God is greater, i.e. greater than all else).

180. *Al-fanā*ʾ*:* literally "annihilation." Cf. Anawati and Gardet: *Mystique Musulmane,* Paris, 1961, pp. 104–106; and Jabre: *L'Extase de Plotin et le Fanā' de Ghazālī,* in *Studio islamica,* fasc. IV, Paris, 1956, pp. 101 ff.

181. *Al-ikhtiyār wa l-kasb:* for Gh, supposedly a convinced Ashᶜarite, a kind of straddling phrase. Cf. Gardet's article in EI(2), IV, 692–94.

182. "To it": As the text reads, the "it" seems to be *al-fanā*ʾ. So W. VR: ad essa (i.e. la Via), which seems wrong. F: not clear; Sch and BM also seem to mean "the Way." And note that where Ja has *qabla dhālika* (prior to it), M has *baᶜda dhālikā* (after it). A possible explanation of the latter reading would be that "to it" be understood as "to Him," i.e. to God. But I prefer Ja's reading, though the passage still remains somewhat unclear.

183. *Al-mukāshafāt wa l-mushāhadāt:* Cf: Note 55. And cf. Anawati and Gardet: *Mystique Musulmane,* p. 47 and p. 227, n. 44.

184. *Al-ḥlulūl:* literally "dismounting," "alighting," "taking up residence," "descending." J: l'Inhérence; W: inherence; VR: discesa di Dio in loro; F: intermixture of being; Sch: être amalgamés Dieu; BM: la fusion de l'être. "In-dwelling" or "inhabitation," despite their Christian connotations, seem to be good translations. But see Appendix IV.

185. *Al-ittiḥād:* J: l'Union; W: union; VR: unione con Lui; F: identification; Sch: lui être identifiés; BM: l'identification.

186. *Al-wuṣūl:* J: La Connexion; W: connection; VR: raggiungimento (and cf. their note); F: (intimate union); Sch: lui être associés; BM: l'union intime.

187. Gh's *al-Maqṣad al-asnā*—the relevant passage will be found in Appendix IV.

188. The verse is by the poet Ibn al-Muᶜtazz (d. 908 A.D.).

189. *Karāmāt al-awliyā*ʾ*:* The "orthodox" view was that there is no substantive difference between *muᶜjizāt* (the apologetic miracles of prophets) and *karāmāt.* The latter, however, were denied by the Muᶜtazilites. Cf. ᶜAbd al-Qāhir al-Baghdādi's *Kitāb uṣūl al-dīn,* Stamboul, 1928, 174–75, 184–85. The word I translate by "saints," *awliyā*ʾ, sing. *walī,* means: friends, close associates, and then: men close to God. And cf. Note 144.

190. This is a hill a few kilometers from Mecca. Cf. the *Sīra* (A. Guillaume: *The Life of Muhammad,* Oxford, 1955, p. 105).

191. The verb used here is *ᶜashiqa,* to love passionately, not *aḥabba,* which is the more general verb for "love" in its ordinary senses. *ᶜAshiqa* is preferred by, and better indicates the love of, the mystics (Sufis). Cf. Watt: *Muhammad at Mecca,* p. 40, B (*taḥannuth:* performance of works of devotion and piety).

192. *Yashqā* (is wretched) occurs only once in the Qurʾān (20.122). The saying here may he proverbial or poetic or traditional—or simply an observation of Gh.

193. The book referred to here is Book XXI, i.e. the first Book of the Third Quarter of the *Iḥyā*ʾ. Cf. Appendix V

194. The verse refers to behavior in the Council of the Prophet, or in meetings in general, according to the reading adopted. Just as there are higher and lower places in meetings, so there is a hierarchy of those "who believe and those to whom knowledge is given." The tripartite division is interesting—*ᶜilm, dhawq* and *īmān.* Is this an ascending order in which the primacy is given to "faith?" Or is it a descending order of these three kinds of *maᶜrifa* (knowledge in general)? Is the "faith" mentioned here the same as "faith" in the generally accepted sense of belief in God, etc.? In reply to the last question, the "faith" mentioned here seems to be no more than credence, or belief, in human testimony, and not religious faith. The other two questions should not, perhaps, be insisted upon too much. We are in the context of mystics and their "states," or experiences. JC and JM contain many interesting observations, especially. in this case, JC 138 ff.

195. Or "the reality (*ḥaqīqa*) and special character, or property, of prophecy." J: la réalité de la Prophétie et de sea particularités; W: the true nature and special characteristics of prophetic revelation; VR: la verità e la proprietà della profezia; F: the true nature of inspiration; Sch: la véritable nature et les qualités distinctives du prophétisme; BM: du véritable caractére de la prophétie. Note the phrase "of necessity": this seems to indicate a very close similarity between the knowledge of the sufi and that of the prophet. I refer the reader again to JM, which contains many remarks and references on *ma^c rifa* (knowledge) in Gh.

196. Gh here seems to say that the mind of the newborn is a *tabula rasa.* The phrase "in his original condition" (*fī aṣl al-fiṭra*) contains the word *fiṭra*—cf. Note 22. There is at least the appearance of a contradiction between what Gh says here and the tradition which indicates that every man is a "born Muslim," i.e. he is born with a mind somehow inclined to Islam. On the other hand, Gh gives here the normal (in his time) description of the growth and development of man. Cf. JC 180 ff.

197. Ja has *yunfakhu fīhi* (there is breathed into him); M has *yanfatiḥ* (there is opened), and no *fīhi* (in him).

198. *Al-aṣwāt wa l-naghamāt:* or, voices and melodies. J: les sons et les mélodies; W: sounds of various kinds; VR: suoni e canti; F: has only "the sense of hearing succeeds"; Sch: les sons et les tons; BM: les bruits at les sons.

199. "The necessary"—*al-wājibāt;* "the possible"—*al-jā^c izāt;* "the impossible"—*al-mustaḥīlāt.* A general classification of beings which also provides a schema for some theological works. For a philosophical view of the development of a unique individual ef. L. E. Goodman's *Hayy Ibn Yaqẓān,* 1972 (the first volume of this series).

200. This stage is that of *nubuwwa* (prophecy, or prophethood). It is here described as "another eye," i.e. a kind of "vision" superior to the normal process of intellection. Gh does not really explain it further, nor does he offer a strict (apodeictic) proof of its existence. In some of the Islamic philosophers *nubuwwa* is related to the activity of the Active Intellect (*al-^c aql al-fa"āl,* intellectus agens). Cf. JC 255 ff. In a footnote to his French translation of this passage (J 104) he invites comparison of this passage with texts in other works of Gh and then goes on to say: "Il n'y a pas ici affirmation d'une faculté supra-rationnelle chez le Prophète, mais il s'agit de la raison instinct qui chez lui atteint son plain développement normal."' For a contrary position regarding the passage in the *Mishkāt* cf. Watt: *The Authenticity of the Works Attributed to al-Ghazālī,* in JRAS, April 1952, 26–27, and *A Forgery in Al-Ghazālī's Mishkāt,* in JRAS, April 1949, p. 9 f.

201. "Sleeping"—text has *al-nawm.* Really Gh means dreaming. The topic introduced here has from time immemorial exercised a powerful fascination as is attested by Aristotle's *De somno et divinatione* (and he probably had predecessors) and the latest pamphlets on the interpretation of dreams. The argument may seem to some rather strange, but it is not surprising in the setting of Gh and would perhaps find a sympathetic hearing among some modern psychologists.

202. This does not sound so much like a description of sleeping as it does of someone in a kind of fit or trance. But perhaps we need not press this point.

203. The eye cannot see if there is no light. So the new "eye" of prophecy needs a special "light" for its functioning. Cf. JC 180 ff. and JM 28 ff. And cf. Note 44. Is revelation involved necessarily? The Islamic philosophers or many of them, speak of the reception of "species" (impressions, the Scholastic "species impressae") from the Active Intellect.

204. W: The proof of the possibility of there being prophecy and the proof that there has been prophecy is that there is knowledge in the world etc. This seems to be a mistranslation. J and VR translate as I do. F, Sch and BM also seem to mistranslate. Gh is simply arguing from the principle expressed by the Scholastics in the formula "ab esse valet illatlo ad posse" (From the fact that a thing exists it can be inferred that it is possible for it to be). He avoids a long theoretical discussion of the possibility of prophecy by showing that knowledge similar to that involved in prophecy actually exists.

The argument from the knowledge found in medicine and astronomy may seem strange. A similar argument with regard to nutriments and medicaments is developed by al-Bāqillānī in his *Tamhīd,* Paras. 222–26 of my ed., in the course of a polemic against the denial of prophecy by the "Barāhima" (Brahmans). The probative force of such an argument may be questioned, yet it is also used by Ibn Ḥazm—cf. VDB I, 125 and II, 125.2; and JC 255 ff., asp. 271–75.

205. From this paragraph it seems that prophecy is regarded by Gh as a way of perceiving things which the intellect normally cannot perceive. But this is said to be only one of the properties, or special qualities, of prophecy. Gh does not tall us what the many other properties are, since they are perceptible only to one who follows the way of Sufism.

206. This sentence is somewhat obscure, as is the entire Para. 115, and none of the translations is of much help in dispelling the obscurity. However, the main point seems clear enough. The knowledge obtained through prophecy is somehow of the same nature as that obtained through the practice of Sufism. But I am not sure what Gh means by his statement that "the example [needed] occurs in the first stages of the way of Sufism." I think, from what he goes on to say, that any mystical experience is enough to enable one to appreciate what the prophet may experience in much more profound and intense ways.

207. *Li mushāhadati aḥwālihim:* the phrase may sound a bit awkward in English; it obviously means actually seeing them performing their peculiar functions.

208. Cf. Note 133.

209. Galen had a tremendous influence on Arab medicine. Sea, for example, *The Legacy of Islam* (2d ed.), 425–60.

210. Not in WConc. Cf. *Iḥyāʾ,* 111.13: related by Abū Naʿīm in *al-Ḥilya* as from a tradition of Anas. And a fuller form in *Iḥyāʾ,* III.23.

211. Not in WConc.

212. Cf. Ibn Mājah: Muqaddima 23, Zuhd 2. "A single care," i.e. care about God and the things of God. More literally: Whoever makes all his cares a single care . . .

213. The miracle of the staff is that of Moses, mentioned in the Qurʾān, e.g. 20.72–73/69–70; 26.44/45, etc. The splitting of the moon is a miracle attributed to Muḥammad on the basis of Qurʾān 54.1.

214. On the problem of the apologetic miracle, i.e. the miracle worked by a prophet to prove his prophetic claim, cf. my *Miracle and Magic,* Beyrouth, 1958, esp. pp. 13–27 (English summary of the Arabic text); cf. Note 144.

Also: I read *wa taridu asʾilatu l-muʿjizāt,* and make this the end of Para. 118, and not, as in Ja, the beginning of Para. 119. J is ambiguous; W reads *turaddu:* thus the topic of miracles will be thrown back upon you; VR: Domande ti saranno poste sui miracoli; F: we shall find ourselves involved in all the difficulties which the question of miracles raises; Sch: et las questions sur les miracles te seront toujours difficiles à résoudre; BM: Alors les difficultés que soulève Ia question des miracles se retournent contre toi.

215. At this point we may raise the question of what Macdonald calls Ghazālī's "attitude of historical agnosticism" (ef. Poggi, 239–45). Macdonald writes: "There is a curious parallelism in al-Ghazzālī's attitude here to the latest phase in Christian apologetics. The argument from miracles seems now to be practically thrown aside; the doctrine rather must prove the miracle. The unique fact of the life and person of Christ is emphasized; it is shown how it appeals immediately to the human consciousness, and on that the proof of the truth of His mission is built up. Logically this position is faulty; and practically it proves whatever you wish. Al-Ghazzālī uses it to prove the truth of the mission of Muḥammad. Miracles are difficult, almost impossible to prove—here we have again his attitude of historical agnosticism; but if any one will read the record of Muḥammad's life, he will receive a general impression that will assure him of the truth of the mission. The personality of Muḥammad will be its own proof." JAOS, XX (1899) 96, Note 1. Father Poggi thinks that Macdonald's judgement of Gh's "historical agnosticism," even if only the *Munqidh* be considered, must be notably "nuanced." Traditional Islamic thought does not deny the probative force of the miraculous event itself. But some deny that the genuinity of the miracle can be known easily. Indeed, some do not see how one can exclude the possibility that God may be using, so to speak. a "false" miracle to lead men astray—cf. Paras. 118 and 72. Gh certainly seems to have a "minimist" apologetic attitude. And, as the *Munqidh* makes clear, he recommends that one base one's faith in the prophecy of Muḥammad on a study of the data provided by the Qur'ān and the Traditions. We may ask, with Father Poggi: "Is it, then, really a question—as van Leauwen would have it—of an attempt to anchor theology in subjective experience rather than in objective revelation?" This, as van Leauwen confesses, would be to make of Gh an enigma—and enigmas are to be avoided, if possible. Van Leauwen finds it impossible to harmonize the defense of revelation against the heretical conclusions of the philosophers, found in the *Tahāfut,* with Gh's insistence, in the *Munqidh,* on the interior personal conviction of the believer. Father Poggi does not agree with van Leauwen, but finds the latter guilty of an unjust apriorism (p. 243, Note 51). "We are always," writes Father Poggi, "as we said à propos of liberation from pure *taqlīd* (conformism), in search of a profoundly rooted and sincere personal conviction, but which is referred precisely to the objective revealed datum"—and he then cites the text (Paras. 116 and 117 of this translation).

The second-last sentence of Para. 119, "This, then, is the strong, etc."—*fa hādhā huwa l-īmān al-qawī l-ʿilmī.* J: (italics) *C'est cela, Ia foi solide et scientifiqua;* W: This is strong, intellectual faith; VR: Questa è fede forte, scientifica; F: Such are the characteristics of scientific certitude; Sch: Telle est la foi farina, la foi fondée sur la science; BM: Tels sont les caractères de la certitude scientifique. I prefer my own translation because it retains a certain ambiguity with respect to *īmān* and *ʿilmī.*

216. The titles preceded by the capital letters A, B, C, and D are not in the text. I have borrowed them from Jabre's translation as a help to the reader.

217. Cf. Appendix V.

218. The Arabic seems a bit awkward here. I refer especially to the *biʾizālatihi.* Or perhaps I should translate: "and that remedies are the only way to treat the heart, by removing its malady and obtaining its health." If we were to change *biʾizālatihi* to *liʾizālatihi* I think the awkwardness would vanish.

219. M has *ṣalāt al-ẓuhr:* the noon prayer. Cf. Calverley: *Worship in Islam.* The *ṣalāt al-ṣubḥ* (or *al-fajr*) has two *rakʿas* (series of formulas and postures), whereas the *ṣalāt al-ẓhur* and the *ṣalāt al-ʿaṣr* have four *rakʿas.*

220. The Arabic is *ʾʿmāl* which can be read *ʾaʿmāl* (workings, actions) or *ʾiʿmāl* (activation, making work). J is rather free; W: the efficacy; VR: servono a perfezionare gli effetti; F: omits; Seb and BM: l'action.

221. *Al-sunan:* pl. of *sunna.* This usually means "custom" or "usage," and especially the customary way the Prophet acted. Here, as VR points out, it has rather the sense of something recommended which it is meritorious to do. On *nawāfila* (supererogatory works, usually prayers) ef. EI(1) or *The Shorter Encyclopaedia of Islam,* s.v. *nāfila.*

222. M has *bil-ʿamā* (blindness): Ja has *bil-ʿajz* (inability). And "to the prophets" is not in M. The *ilayhā* is supplied in Ja, and is not in M; presumably it refers to "prophecy." The addition does not seem to be really necessary.

223. Arabic: *yulqīhi* (lays down, proposes). This Para. is interesting for the limitations it places on the role of reason in Gh's view.

224. We are back to the four major divisions of "the seekers after truth," but this time from the angle of religious attitudes and behavior. The fourth class mentioned here is called *al-mawsūmīn bi l-ʿilm,* lit. those characterized by (the possession of) knowledge. Clearly he means the *ʿulamāʾ* and *fuqahāʾ,* the theologians and jurisprudents. those whom Watt calls "the scholar jurists." Al-Kindī has a somewhat similar phrase: *al-muttasimīn bi l-naẓar,* but, as Dr. Ivry indicates. he seems to mean the Muʿtazilites—A. Ivry: *Al-Kindī's Metaphysics,* Albany, 1974. p. 129, Note 103.13.

225. Arabic: *al-ʿulamāʾ*—cf. the preceding Note. The order is not the same as that in Para. 125.

226. Arabic: *al-fuḍalāʾ*—plural of *faḍīl* and *fāḍil* (eminent, outstanding, learned, etc.); an honorific equivalent of *ʿulamlāʾ*

227. Arabic: *al-khamr.* For an account of the prohibition of *khamr* cf. EI(1) or *Shorter Encyclopaedia of Islam,* s.v. *khamr.*

228. Arabic: *al-awqāf*—plural of *waqf* (a pious foundation or mortinain). Cf. references of preceding Note, s.v. *waḳf.*

229. Arabic: *al-ḥarām*—what is legally forbidden.

230. Perhaps it would be more exact to translate, "These are those who have strayed from the (true) way of Sufism." M has *min tarīq al-tasawwuf,* and Ja: *ʿan al-taṣawwuf.* The latter reading also conveys the nuance: have gone astray through (a misuse of) Sufism. My translation implies that the erring in this case claim to be Sufis. "The licentious": *ahl al-ibāḥa,* the men of permissiveness; the nuance is that of licentiousness, libertinism, anti nomianism, latitudinarianism; cf. EI(2), II, 662–63, art. Ibāḥa.

231. "Makes categorical pronouncements": *mutaḥakkim*—from a verb meaning: to pass judgment, judge arbitrarily; the nuance here is indicated by the following phrase *lā ḥujjata lahu* (having, or needing, no proof at all). The sense is that the Taʿlimite alone possesses certainty and therefore his certain view is not to be given up for the uncertainties of the others mentioned. Ja: *àdaʿu* (can I give up), but M: *nadaʿu* (can we give up).

232. This reflects justly the intellectual arrogance that seems to have marked most of the Islamic philosophers and their scorn for the "ignorant" masses. This was also a reason why many of them recommended a certain asoterism, or elitism.

233. The revealed Law—cf. Note 93.

234. That is, by seeming to be a practicing Muslim: the abandonment of Islam would make him an unbeliever (*kāfir*) whose life and property would be forfeit.

235. There is a measure of truth in this—cf. the references in Note 227.

236. Cf. Arberry: *Avicenna on Theology,* pp. 9–24.

237. The Sultan was Fakhr al-Mulk, the son of Gh's great patron. Niẓām al-Mulk. "In my disgrace": *ilā ḥadd al-waḥsha.* The latter word means: loneliness, coldness (of relations), estrangement.

238. The point of the texts cited from the Qur'ān is that apostles and reformers must expect opposition and even tribulation; but they must carry out their task, even though their efforts are unsuccessful as far as results are concerned.

239. This tradition is found in Abū Dā'ūd 36 (Malāḥim—Battles) 1. Cf. my *Theology of Al-Ashᶜarī,* p. 157. "The reformers for the first two centuries were the Caliph ᶜUmar b. ᶜAbd al-ᶜAzīz and the great jurisprudent, al-Shāfī'ī. For the third century there is mention of Aḥmad b. Ḥanbal, al-Ashᶜarī, Abū Naᶜīm al-Astarābādi, and Abū l-'Abbās Aḥmad b. ᶜUmar b. Surayj. Al-Bāqillānī and Abū l-Ṭayyib Sahl al-Ṣuᶜlukī have been suggested for the fourth century, and for the fifth al-Ghazālī and al-Mustarshid Billāh. In my opinion (Ibn ᶜAsākir) the list should read: ᶜUmar, al-Shāfi'ī, al-Ashᶜarī, al-Bāqillānī, and al-Ghazālī." (The previous is an extract from Ibn ᶜAsākir: *Tabyīn kadhib al-muftarī,* etc., a work of the famous historian of Damascus devoted to the vindication and glorification of al-Ashᶜarī.)

240. In M *fa staḥkama . . . al-shahādāt* is after *ᶜalā ra'si kulli mi'a.*

241. Cf. Tir. *qadar* 7 and *daᶜawāt* 89; Mus. *qadar* 17; Ibn Mājah *muqaddima* 13; Aḥ. b. Ḥanbal 2.168, 173 and 6.182, 251, 302, 315. It is explained by Gh in *Iḥyā',* III, 27, 11. 20 ff. In this explanation Gh says that the "two fingers" are an angel and a devil, and the heart of a man is "changed" by reason of his following the good suggestions of the angel or the bad suggestions of the devil.

242. This rather touching prayer seems to ma to be an added indication of Gh's sincerity.

243. H. A. Homes: *The Alchemy of Happiness* (trans. from the Turkish), Albany, 1873, pp. 57 ff. has seven classes; Field: *The Alchemy of Happiness* (trans. from the Hindustani), Lahore, 1964, reprinted 1971, has only six classes. And in connection with these cf. O. Pretzl: *Die Sfreitschrift des Ġazālī gegen die Ibāḥīja,* Munich, 1933 (Sitzungsberichte der Bayerischen Akademie der Wissensehaften, Philosophisch-historische Abteilung, Jahrgang 1933, Heft 7), which contains the Persian text and a German translation. And cf. Bouyges: *Essai,* p. 60, n. (1).

244. "Science": here in a rather broad sense, almost like "field, or area, of knowledge."

245. *Dāniq:* Hava: weight of two carob-grains; Wehr: an ancient coin, one-sixth of a dirham, a small coin; Steingass: the sixth part of a dram, or two carats; also a small silver coin; Watt: about eight grains; Sch: Ia sixième partie d'une drachme; BM: Un sixième d'once; VR: Otto grani.

246. W: The rejection of the strange features of the world to come usually belong to this class. Sch: La refus de croire aux merveilles de l'autre monde est ordinairement du même genre. This need not be simply an esehatological reference, but may include anything beyond ordinary experience and especially what forms the object of the "eye" of prophecy.

247. It is not clear that this is a specific book or treatise. All that the Arabic has is *fī ᶜajā'ibi l-khawāṣṣ.* I have added "in their works." J, W and VR regard it as the title of a book, but Sch and BM do not.

248. Here we have the *budūḥ,* a magic square which has been called "the threefold talisman, or seal, or table, of Ghazālī." Cf. the article *Budfūḥ* in EI(1), I, 770–71 by

Macdonald; and the article Djadwal in EI(2) II, 370; and Zwemer, *A Moslem Seeker after God,* 1920, 165–67; and Ibn Khaldūn: *Muqaddima,* VI, 27 and 28 (V. Montail's French trans., III, 1087–1153); and BM, 85, Note 1. In a note to me Dr. Ilse Lichtenstadter asks: "Why 15? Is it possible there is a reminiscence of (or influence by) the Jewish shunning of the letters yōdh and hē (לה) that represent Yah (God—Yahweh); yōdh: 10 and hē: 5. The Arabic letters, too, have the same numerical equivalents as the Jewish letters. God's help may be invoked symbolically by this talisman."

249. Cf. Note 219.

250. Arabic: *al-a*^{c}*mār wa l-ājāl.* The *ajal* (one's "term," or appointed time of death) was discussed by the theologians in connection with the vexed questions of divine predestination and human liberty—see, for example, al-Bāqillānī's *Tamhīd* (my ed.), pp. 332–34.

Sch's text: *ḥattā thabatū* ^{c}*alā hādhā fī tasyīrātihim ikhtilāf al-hīlāj wa tafāwut. . . .* BM, 86–87, has a long note on the word *al-hīlāj;* but the reading *al-*^{c}*ilāj* seems much better.

251. "The knowledge of which, etc"—The phrase is a little puzzling at first sight. But it seems to be a kind of parenthetical remark.

252. The pilgrimage (*ḥajj*) is one of the "Five Pillars" of Islam. Cf. EI(2) s.v. *ḥadjdj,* for a complete account of this very significant Islamic institution.

253. On the "apotheosis" which Muḥammad underwent in the history of Islam cf. F. M. Pareja: *Islamologie,* Beyrouth, 1964, pp. 790–813 (Ch. XVI, Mahomet dans l'Islam).

254. This final prayer of Gh does not seem to me to be a stereotyped collection of phrases, but rather another point in favor of his sincerity.

APPENDIX I

Fayṣal al-Tafriqa bayn al-Islām wa l-Zandaqa

THIS is the book mentioned by Ghazālī in the *Munqidh,* Para. 48. I have translated the title there as *The Clear Criterion for Distinguishing between Islam and Godlessness.* The word *fayṣal* means: a sharp, or cutting, sword; thence a clear, or decisive, criterion. On *zandaqa* cf. Note 20 to my translation. The title might also be translated: *The Sharp Sword of Cleavage between Islam and Godlessness.* The chief point at issue is *takfīr,* i.e. stigmatizing or branding with, or imputing or accusing of, *kufr* (unbelief, infidelity). This is closely bound up, as will be evident, with *taʾwīl:* the interpretation of a text. The translation presents no great difficulties. The text I have used is that edited by Doctor Sulaymān Dunyā, Cairo, 1961. The paragraphing is mine, as are any words in parentheses in the titles. I have indicated the page references to the Arabic edition. Alternate translations and some remarks are enclosed in brackets. I have been able to control my translation to a certain extent by the long passage translated by Father Jabre: *La notion de certitude selon Ghazali,* Annexe III, pp: 406–85. He had the advantage of an excellent text which was not available to me at the time I made my translation. This, I believe, is the first complete English translation of this work of Ghazālī, a work which gives us further insights into the mind of this great thinker.

IN THE NAME OF GOD
THE MERCIFUL THE BENEFICENT

The learned and virtuous Master, Abū Ḥāmid, Muḥammad, son of Muḥammad, son of Muḥammad, al-Ghazālī—God's mercy be upon him!—said:

[*Khuṭba*]

1 I praise God Most High, submitting to His might, begging the fullness of His favor, seeking the benefit of His succor and His support, and of obedience to Him, beseeching preservation from being forsaken by Him and from disobeying Him, and imploring His abundant favors! And I ask His blessings on Muḥammad, His servant and His Apostle and the best of His creatures—to show my humble submission to his prophetic office, to attract his intercession, to pay what is due to his apostolic status, and to hold fast to the benediction of his heart and his soul. I also (ask blessings) on his Family and his Companions and his Kinsfolk!

[INTRODUCTION]

2 *Now then:* O sympathetic brother and ardently devoted friend, I see you boiling with rage and mentally distraught because you have chanced to hear some calumnious remarks directed by a group of envious persons against some of our books written about the mysteries of the practice of (our) religion. These persons pretended that these books contain matter contrary to the teaching of the masters of old and the leading *mutakallimūn* [polemic theologians]. They also claimed that deviating from the doctrine of al-Ashᶜarī by even so much as a palm's width is unbelief (*kufr*), and that differing from him in even a trivial matter is error and perdition (or: error leading to perdition).

3 Compose yourself, O sympathetic and ardently devoted brother, and be not distressed by that. Dampen your impetuosity a little, and bear calmly what they say, and disassociate yourself from them courteously. Disdain him who is neither envied nor slandered, and think little of him who is not "known" for unbelief and error.

4 What summoner (to Truth) was more perfect and saner than the chief of God's envoys?—God's blessing and peace be upon him! Yet they said: 'Truly he is a used man (cf. 15.6; 26.26; 44:13; 51.89, 52; 68.51)!" And what speech was loftier and truer than the speech of the Lord of the Worlds? Yet they said: "Truly it is the fables of the ancients (cf. 6.25; 8.31; 16.26; 23.85; 25.6; 27.70; 46.16; 68.15; 83.13)!" Beware, then, of devoting yourself to wrangling with them and of striving to silence them, for you would then be striving for the unattainable and crying to deaf ears!

5 Surely you have heard the saying:

All enmities allow hope of peaceful settlement
Save the enmity of him who is your enemy out of envy.

Had there been any hope of it in any man among men, the verses of despair [hopelessness] would not have been recited to the most illustrious of men. Surely you have heard the Most High's utterance: "And if their turning away is distressful for thee, why, if thou canst seek out a hole in the earth, or a ladder in heaven, to bring them some sign—but had God willed, He would have gathered them to the guidance; so be not thou one of the ignorant" (6.35); and the Most High's utterance: "Though We opened to them a gate in heaven, and still they mounted through it, yet would they say: Our eyes have been dazzled; nay we are a people bewitched!" (15.14–15); and the Most High's utterance: "Had We sent down on thee a Book on parchment and so they touched it with their hands, yet the unbelievers would have said: This is naught but manifest sorcery" (6.7); and the Most High's utterance: "Though We had sent down angels to them, and the dead had spoken with them, had We mustered against them every thing, face to face, yet they would not have been the ones to believe, unless God willed; but most of them are ignorant" (6.111).

6 Know that the true meaning and the real definition of unbelief and of faith, and the true meaning and the profound [inner] secret [sense] of truth and of error, are not disclosed to hearts defiled by the pursuit and love of fame and fortune. [p. 129] On the contrary, that is unveiled only to hearts which (1) have been purified from the dirt of the world's filth, then (2) have been refined [burnished, polished] by integral [perfect] askesis (*al-riyāḍa*), then (3) have been enlightened by serene recollection (*al-dhikr*), then (4) have been nourished by right thinking (*al-fikr al-ṣāʾib*), then (5) have been adorned by

adherence to the prescriptions of the Law to such a degree that the light from the niche of prophecy has inundated them and they have taken on the likeness of a polished mirror, and the light [lamp] of faith has become in the glass of the believer's heart an orient of lights with its oil all but illuminant, though untouched by any fire.

7 How could the mysteries of the Kingdom [*al-malakūt:* Jabre: le monde intelligible; the spiritual world; cf. EI(2) s.v. *ᶜālam*] be revealed to people whose God is their own caprice [passion: *hawāhum*], whose object of worship is their rulers, whose *qibla* [direction faced in Prayer] is their dirhams and their dinars, whose Law (*sharīᶜa*) is their frivolity, whose volition [will, desire, motive force] is their fame and their lusts [appetites], whose worship is their service of their wealthy [patrons, masters], whose recollection (*dhikr*) is their wicked thoughts [inspired by Satan], whose treasure is their grooms [? stablemen, leaders—*suwwās*], whose thought [meditation, reflection, contemplation: *fikr*] is devising stratagems for what is demanded by their external show [keeping up appearances, entourage, household: *ḥashma*].

8 Whence, for such as these, can the darkness of unbelief be discerned from the brightness of faith? By a divine inspiration (*ilhām*)? But they have not emptied their hearts of the impurities of the world so as to receive such things. Or by reason of some perfection of knowledge? But their wares, as far as learning goes, are simply the question of legal impurity and saffron water and the likes [an indication that Gh has in mind the ulema, the *fuqahāʾ*, or "scholar jurists"]. Preposterous! Preposterous! This objective is too precious and too dear to be attained by desires or obtained with ease. So busy yourself with your own affairs and don't waste your remaining time on them! "So turn thou from him who turns away from Our Remembrance and desires only the present life. That is their attainment of knowledge. Surely thy Lord knows very well those who have gone astray from His way, and He knows very well those who are guided" (53.50/29–31/30).

[p. 131]

CHAPTER [ONE]

9 Now if you wish to pluck out this thorn [i.e. enmity, according to the Editor's note] from your own breast and from that of him who is in the same state as you are and who is one not moved by the seduction of the envious and not fettered by the blindness of servile conformism, but rather has a thirst for independent investigation because of his hatred for a difficulty provoked by some consideration and stimulated by some reflection [or: reasoning], then speak to yourself and to your fellow and demand of him the definition of unbelief.

10 If he claims that the definition of unbelief is: That which is contrary to the doctrine of the Ashᶜarite, or that of the Muᶜtazilite, or that of the Ḥanbalite, or that of others—then know that he is a gullible [or: inexperienced] and stupid man fettered by servile conformism and one of the blind: so don't waste any time in trying to set him right. And let it suffice you as a proof to silence him to oppose his claim with that of his adversaries: for he will find no difference or distinction between himself and all the servile conformists who are opposed to him.

11 Perhaps his fellow has a leaning, from among all the systems, toward the Ashᶜarite and alleges that opposition to it in any detail at all [lit, in any coming to and return from water] is flagrant unbelief. Ask him, then, whence comes his unshakable conviction that the truth is so much his special endowment that he judges al-Bāqillānī guilty of unbelief because he opposed al-Ashᶜarī on God Most High's attribute of duration [*al-baqāʾ*]

and claimed that it is not a quality of God Most High superadded to His Essence. [p. 132] And why is al-Bāqillānī more deserving of being charged with unbelief by reason of his opposition to al-Ashᶜarī than al-Ashᶜarī is by reason of his opposition to al-Bāqillānī? And why is the truth the special endowment of one of them rather than of the other? Was that because of precedence in time? But al-Ashᶜarī was preceded by others of the Muᶜtazilites so let the truth belong to him who preceded him! Or was it because of difference in merit and learning? But by what scale and measure has he estimated the degrees of merit so that it has become clear to him that there exists no one more meritorious than the one he follows and blindly accepts?

12 If he gives leave to al-Bāqillānī to oppose al-Ashᶜarī, why does he deny it to others? What is the difference between al-Bāqillānī and al-Karābīsī and al-Qalānisī and others? And what is the point of particularizing this leave? If he claims that al-Bāqillānī's opposition comes down to a word needing no further inquiry, as is arbitrarily affected by some of the fanatics, alleging that both of them agree on the perpetuity of God's existence, and [if he also claims] that the dispute over whether that goes back to the Essence, or to a quality superadded to the Essence, is a simple difference which necessitates no severity, then why is it that he speaks so severely against the Muᶜtazilite about the latter's denial of the attributes, since he does acknowledge that God Most High is knowing, encompassing all the knowables, and powerful over all the possibles, and he opposes al-Ashᶜarī simply regarding whether He is knowing and powerful by His Essence or by a superadded attribute?

13 What, then, is the difference between the two oppositions? And what problem is loftier and more important than the Attributes of the True—Praised be He and Exalted!—with regard to speculation (*al-naẓar*) on denying them and affirming them? He may say: "I tax the Muᶜtazilite with unbelief simply because he claims that from one and the same Essence proceeds the effect (*fāʾida*) of knowledge and power and life. But these are attributes differing in definition and reality, and differing realities cannot be qualified by union (*al-ittiḥād*), nor can one and the same Essence stand in their stead [be interchangeable with them]."

14 [p. 133] Why is it, then, that he does not deem farfetched on al-Ashᶜari's part the latter's affirmation: "Speech is a superadded attribute subsisting in God Most High's Essence: but despite its being one, it is Torah, Gospel, Psalms and Qurʾān, and it is command andI prohibition, and enunciation and question?" For these are different meanings—and how could it be otherwise, since the definition of enunciation is "That which is susceptible of assent and denial," which is not the case with command and prohibition? How, then, can one and the same meaning be susceptible of assent and denial and not susceptible of them? And how could denial and affirmation be united regarding one and the same thing?

15 If he hems and haws over the answer to this, or is incapable of making it clear, know that he is not a practitioner of reasoning, but is simply a servile conformist. And the condition attached to the servile conformist is that he neither speak nor be spoken to, since he is incapable of following the path of argument: for if he were fit for it, he would be one followed, not a follower, and a leader, not one led. So if the servile conformist plunges into debate, that is officiousness on his part, and one who busies himself with him is like a man hammering on cold iron and a man seeking the soundness of what has gone bad—and can the perfumer restore what time has corrupted?

16 Perhaps, if you are just, you will recognize that one who makes truth the special endowment of one particular reasoner is very close to unbelief and to contradiction.

To unbelief: because he puts that reasoner in the place of the Prophet preserved from any slip, to agree with whom alone makes faith fast and to oppose whom alone makes unbelief imperative. And to contradiction: this lies in the fact that every one of the reasoners enjoins reasoning and that "your view in your reasoning be my view, and every view of mine be a proof" [i.e. that the conclusion of your reasoning be the same as mine, and that my conclusion constitute a proof]. Now what difference is there between one who says: "Follow me blindly in my doctrine" and one who says: "Follow me blindly in both my doctrine and my proof?" Is this latter anything but contradiction? [i.e. even though the reasoner enjoins reasoning and investigation, this one enjoins slavish acceptance of *his* reasoning and of the doctrine which such reasoning is supposed to establish].

[p. 134] CHAPTER [TWO]

17 Perhaps you very much desire to know the [true] definition of unbelief after having experienced the contradiction of the definitions advanced by the different types of servile conformists. Know, however, that the explanation of that is lengthy and its meaning abstruse. But I shall give you an authentic sign (*ᶜalāma*) so that you can follow it and convert it [i.e. "Unbelief is A" and "A is unbelief"] and adopt it as the goal [*maṭmah:* almost "norm" or "ultimate ground"] of your reasoning and desist, because of it, from taxing the sects with unbelief and letting your tongue go about the adherents of Islam, even though their paths [ways] differ, so long as they hold fast to the declaration: "There is no god at all save God; Muḥammad is the Apostle of God," sincere in [uttering] it and not opposing it.

18 I say, then: Unbelief is taxing the Apostle—Blessings and peace be upon him!—with lying with reference to anything of that which he brought. And belief (*al-īmān*) is believing him with reference to everything which he brought. So the Jew and the Christian are unbelievers because they tax the Apostle—Blessings and peace be upon him!—with lying. And the Brahman is an unbeliever in the first way [i.e. with all the more reason], because he denies, along with our Apostle, all the other Envoys. And the Materialist [Atheist: *dahrī*] is an unbeliever with greater reason, because he denies, along with our Apostle, [God's] Envoy, all the other Apostles. This is because unbelief is a legal category [qualification; *ḥukm sharᶜī*], like slavery and liberty for example, since it means declaring blood licit and the sentence of eternity in the Fire. Its meaning is legal and is perceived [*yadrak:* or, attained, realized] either by an explicit text or by an analogy with something explicitated by a text. Explicit texts have come to us in the case of the Jews and the Christians, and attached to them with greater reason are [p. 135] the Brahmans, the Dualists, the Zendiks, and the Materialists [*al-dahriyya*][1] [p. 174], all of whom are polytheists, because they tax the Apostles with lying. So every unbeliever is one who taxes the Apostles with lying; and every one who taxes the Apostles with lying is an unbeliever. This, then, is the sign which is to be followed and which is convertible.

[p. 175] CHAPTER [THREE]

19 Know that what we have mentioned, although it is clear, yet it has beneath it something involved, indeed, something extremely involved. For each sect taxes with

1. The editor of the Arabic text inserts here a lengthy footnote. Gh's text continues on p. 174.

unbelief him who opposes it and accuses him of taxing the Apostle—Blessings and peace be upon him!—with lying. Thus the Ḥanbalite taxes the Ashᶜarite with unbelief, claiming that the latter taxes the Apostle with lying regardling the affirmation of "above" of God Most High and "the being firmly settled on the Throne." And the Ashᶜarite taxes the Ḥanbalite with unbelief, claiming that the latter is an anthropomorphist and that he taxes the Apostle with lying regarding the fact that "there is nothing at all like Him" (42.9/11). Moreover, the Ashᶜarite taxes the Muᶜtazilite with unbelief, claiming that the latter taxes the Apostle with lying anent the "possibility of the ocular vision of God Most High" and "the affirmation that God possesses knowledge and power and the other Attributes." And the Muᶜtazilite taxes the Ashᶜarite with unbelief, claiming that the affirmation of the Attributes is a multiplication of "eternals" and a taxing of the Apostle with lying about the proclamation of the divine unity (*al-tawḥīd*).

20 The only thing which will save you from this muddle is to know the definition and real meaning of "giving the lie to" (*al-takdhīb*) and "giving assent to" (*al-taṣdīq*) regarding the Apostle [Ar. *fīhi*—the Editor's view that the pronoun refers to "Islam" seems wrong to me], so that there will be clear to you the excess and extravagance of the sects in taxing one another with unbelief. So I say: "Giving assent to" applies only to the enunciation (*al-khabar*), or rather, to the enunciator (*al-mukhbir*). Its real meaning is: confession of the existence of that of which the Apostle—God bless him and grant him peace!—enunciated the existence.

21 However, existence has five grades [ranks, degrees: *marātib*], and because of inattention to these, each sect taxes its adversary with *takdhīb* [i.e. giving the lie to the Apostle]. For existence is (1) essential (*dhātī*), (2) sensible (*ḥissī*), (3) imaginary [representational, imaginative—*khayālī*], (4) mental [intellectual—*ᶜaqlī*], and (5) analogous [*shabahī* or *shibhī*: similar, metaphorical, analogical; Asin Palacios: semejante; Jabre: métaphorique]. [p. 176] So one who confesses the existence, in one of these five ways, of that of which the Apostle—Blessings and peace be upon him!—enunciated the existence, is absolutely not one who gives the lie to the Apostle. Let us, then, explain these five categories and cite an example of them with respect to interpretations (*al-taʾwīlāt*).

22 (1) *Essential existence* is real and stable [*thābit:* or, certain] existence outside of sensation and intellection [extrasensory and extramental]. But sensation and intellection take from it an image [*ṣūra:* representation, species, form], and this "taking" is called "perception." An example of this is the existence of the heavens and the earth and the animals and the plants. This is the obvious, indeed, the well known, which is the only meaning of existence known to most men.

23 (2) *Sensible existence* is that which is imaged [represented—*yatamaththal*] in the visual power of the eye and which has no [such] existence outside the eye. Thus it is existent in the sensing [sensation], and it is peculiar to the man sensing and unshared by any other. An example of that is what the dreamer sees, or even what the waking sick man sees. For there may be represented to him a form [an image] which has no existence outside his sensing in such fashion that he sees it just as he sees all the other things existing outside his sensing. Nay more, there may be represented to the Prophets and the saints, in wakefulness and health, a beautiful form [image] imitating the essence of the angels, by means of which there comes to them revelation and inspiration (*al-waḥy waʾl-ilhām*) so that they learn of the invisible world in their wakefulness what others learn in their dreaming. That is because of the intense purity of their interior. It is as the Most High said: "that presented himself to her a man without fault" (19.17). And it was thus that the Apostle—

Blessings and peace be upon him!—often saw Gabriel—Peace be upon him! But he saw him in his own form only twice, and he used to see him in different forms in which he would represent himself. [p. 177] [The Editor takes exception, perhaps with reason, and for obvious reasons, with Gh's example of Gabriel's appearance to the Prophet. The example certainly raises some interesting questions.] Thus, too, the Apostle of God—God's blessings and peace be upon him!—is seen in dreams. Indeed, he said: "Who sees me in sleep has seen me truly, for Satan cannot represent himself in my image." But seeing him is not in the sense of the transfer of his person from the Garden of Medina to the place of the sleeper: rather it is by way of the existence of his image [form] in the sensing of the sleeper, and that only.

24 The cause of that and its underlying reason [*sirr:* secret, mystery] is a lengthy matter which we have already explained in one of our books. If you do not believe it, then believe your own eye. For if you take from a fire a live coal like a single point, then you move it rapidly with a straight motion, you see it as a line of fire; and if you move it with a circular motion you see it as a circle of fire. The circle and the line are seen and are existing in your sensing, not outside of your sensing, because what exists outside is at every moment a point. It becomes a line only in points of time succeeding one another. So the line is not existing at one moment, yet in your vision it is stationary at one moment.

25 (3) *Imaginative existence* is the image [form] of such sensible objects when the latter are absent from [not present to] your sensing. For you can originate in your imagination an image of an elephant and of a horse, even though you have your eyes shut, so that you see it and it exists with the perfection of its form in your brain, not outside. [p. 178]

26 (4) *Mental existence* consists in the thing's having a "spirit" (*rūḥ*) and a reality (*ḥaqīqa:* essence) and a meaning: then the intellect acquires its abstract meaning without its image remaining in imagination or sensing or outside, as, for example, 'the hand." For the latter has a sensible and imaginable form, and it also has a meaning which is its reality, viz. "the power to strike"—and "the power to strike" is the mental [intellectual, intelligible] hand. The pen also has an image [form], hut its reality is "that by which cognitions are written," and it is this which the mind receives without its being linked with a form of cane and wood and other imaginative and sensible forms.

27 (5) *Analogical existence* is had when the thing itself does not exist in its form, or in its essential meaning, or outside, or in sensing, or in the imagination, or in the mind; but that which exists is something else which resembles [is similar or analogous to] it in one of its properties and one of its qualities. This you will understand when I cite for you the example of it in the matter of interpretations.

These, then are the grades of the existence of things.

[p. 179]

CHAPTER [FOUR]

28 Hear, now, the examples of these grades with reference to interpretations.

Essential existence needs no example, for it is that which is to be taken according to what is obvious and which is not subject to interpretation. This is absolute and real [actual] existence. This is like the report of the Apostle—God's blessings and peace be upon him!—ahout the Throne and the Chair [Seat] and the seven heavens. For it is to be taken according to its obvious meaning and it is not subject to interpretation, since these are bodies existing in themselves, be they perceived or not perceived by sensation and imagination.

29 As for *sensible existence,* there are many examples of it in the matter of interpreta-

tions: here I shall be content with two examples of them. *One of these* is the statement of the Apostle of God—God's blessings and peace be upon him!—"On the Day of the Resurrection death will be brought in the form of a black and white ram, and it will be slaughtered between the Garden and the Fire." Now one who has apodeictic proof that death is an accident, or the privation of an accident, and that the changing of an accident into a body is impossible and not an object of any power will take this enunciation in the sense that the men of the Resurrection will see that [ram] and will believe that it is death, and that will exist in their sensation, not outside, and that will be a cause of acquiring certainty that there can be no expectation of death thereafter—since what is slaughtered is despaired of [lost, irretrievably gone]. But one who has no such apodeictic proof may believe that death itself will in its essence be changed into a ram and will be slaughtered.

30 *The second example* is the utterance of the Apostle of God—God's blessings and peace be upon him!—"The Garden was shown to me in the breadth [on the side] of this wall." He who has apodeictic proof that bodies cannot compenetrate and that the small cannot contain the large takes that to mean that the Garden itself did not move to the wall, but that its image [form] was represented to sensation on the wall so that it was as though he were seeing it. [p. 180] It is not impossible for the likeness of a large thing to be seen in a small body, just as the heaven is seen in a small mirror. But that is a seeing different from the simple imagining of the image of the Garden, since you perceive the difference between your seeing the image of the heaven in the mirror and your closing your eyes and perceiving the image of the heaven in the mirror by way of imagining.

31 An example of *imaginative existence* is the saying of the Apostle—God's blessings and peace be upon him!—"It was as though I were looking at Yūnus the son of Mattā, wearing two cotton [*quṭwāniyyatān*—?] abas [cloaks, or, wraps], answering and the mountains replying to him, and God Most High saying to him: Here I am [at your service—*labbayka*] O Yūnus!" The literal meaning is that this is a notification of the representation of the image in his [Muḥammad's] imagination, because the existence of this circumstance was prior to the existence of the Apostle of God—God's blessings and peace be upon him!—and it had already ceased to be and was not existing at the moment [of the Apostle's vision]. And it is not farfetched to say also: This was represented in his sensation so that he came to see it as the sleeper sees images. However, his saying "as though I were looking" makes one feel that it was not the reality of looking, but rather like looking. But my aim is to make you understand by the example and nor this particular image. And in general everything which is represented in the locus of the imagination can conceivably be represented in the locus of sight—and the latter would be seeing. But rarely can there be distinct apodeictic proof of the impossibility of seeing what can conceivably be represented imaginatively.

32 Of *mental existence* there are many examples: I shall be content with two. *One of these* is the utterance of the Apostle—God's blessings and peace be upon him!—"He who is brought forth from the Fire [or: excluded from the Fire—?] will be given a portion of the Garden equivalent to ten times this world." The literal meaning of this points to its being ten times it in length and breadth and surface, and this is sensible and imaginative difference. Then one may be astonished and say: "The Garden is in the heaven, as the literal meanings of Traditions have indicated: [p. 181] how then can the heaven be broad enough to contain ten times the world when the heaven also is part of the world?" [The Arabic editor takes exception to this in his Note (1), p. 181.] The interpreter may surmount this astonishment and say: "What is meant is an abstract and mental difference, not that

which is sensible and imaginative." It is, for example, like saying: This jewel is many times a horse—i.e. in the sense and meaning of financial worth which is perceived mentally, not in its [physical] size [lit, area or surface] which is grasped by sensation and imagining.

33 *The second example* is the saying of the Apostle—God's blessings and peace be upon him!—"God Most High leavened [*khammara:* here equivalent of "kneaded"—?] the clay of Adam with His hand for forty mornings." Thus he indeed affirmed of God Most High a hand. [p. 182] Now he who has solid apodeictic proof of the impossibility of God Most High's having a hand which is a sensible or imaginable member affirms that God—Praised be He!—has a spiritual and mental hand. I mean that he affirms the meaning and essence spirit of the hand, not its [physical] form. The spirit and meaning of the hand is "that by which one strikes [or: snatches or seizes] and effects and gives and holds back"; and God Most High gives and holds back by means of His Angels, as Muḥammad—Blessings and peace be upon him!—said: "The first thing God created was *al-ᶜaql* [the Intellect]: then He said: By you I give, and by you I hold back." Now it cannot be that what was meant by that "Intellect" was an accident, as the *mutakallimūn* believe, since it is impossible for an accident to be the first thing created. Rather it is a designation of the essence of one of the Angels named ᶜAqi because he understands [intellects] things by his substance and essence without any need of a learning process. He may also be called Pen [*Qalam*] in view of the fact that through him the truths [realities: *ḥaqāʾiq*] of cognitions are written on the tablets of the hearts of the Prophets and the Saints and the other Angels as revelation and inspiration. For there has come to us in another Tradition that "The first thing God Most High created was the Pen."

34 For if that does not refer to the "Intellect," the two Traditions contradict one another. Besides, it is possible for one and the same thing to have many names under different respects. Thus he would be called "Intellect" with respect to that; and "Angel" with respect to his relation to God Most High in his being an intermediary between Him and His creatures; and "Pen" with respect to his relation to what proceeds from him in the way of "writing" cognitions by inspiration and revelation. It is like Gabriel's being called "Spirit" with respect to his essence, and "Faithful" [or: "Trusty"] with respect to the mysteries entrusted to him, and "Terrible in power" with respect to his power, and "Very Strong" with respect to the perfection of his strength, and "With the Lord of the Throne Secure" with respect to the closeness of his position [to God], and "Obeyed" with respect to his being followed on the part of some of the Angels. [p. 183] Now this affirmer will have already affirmed a pen and a hand mentally, nor sensibly and imaginatively. This is also the case with him who adopts the view that the hand is a designation for an attribute belonging to God Most High, either power or something else, as the *mutakallimūn* have differed on the subject.

35 The example of *analogical existence* is anger and yearning and joy and patience and other such things in what has reached us regarding God Most High. For the real meaning of anger, for example, is that it is the ebullition of the blood of the heart due to the desire of revenge. But this is not free from imperfection and pain. So one who has solid apodeictic proof of the impossibility of real anger's abiding in God Most High essentially and sensibly and imaginatively and mentally [the Arabic editor questions the "mentally," Note (2), p. 183] reduces it to the abiding of another attribute [or: quality—*ṣifa*] from which proceeds what proceeds from anger, like the will to punish. But the will does not correspond to anger in the reality of its essence, but in one of the qualities which goes with it and one of the effects which proceeds from it, viz. the infliction of pain.

These, then, are the degrees of interpretations.

[p. 184] CHAPTER [FIVE]

36 Know that anyone who reduces some utterance of the trustee of the Law to one of these degrees is of the number of those who believe [assent to, find credible] [the Apostle]. Imputing lying is simply that one deny all these meanings and allege that what the Apostle said is meaningless and is simply a sheer lie and that his purpose in what he said was to deceive and to obtain worldly advantage. That is downright unbelief and godlessness [*zandaqa*]. Unbelief need not necessarily be affirmed of interpreters so long as they continue to adhere to the law of interpretation as we shall point it out. How could it be necessary to affirm unbelief because of interpretation when there is not a group of the people of Islam save that it is compelled to use it?

37 The man most remote from interpretation was Ahmad ibn Hanbal—God's mercy be upon him! And the most bizarre of interpretations and that farthest removed from reality [*al-ḥaqīqa*] is that you make the thing said a trope [*majāzan:* figure of speech] or a metaphor [*isti*ᶜ*āra:* borrowing], this being mental existence and analogical existence. But even the Ḥanbalite is compelled to it and professes it. I have indeed heard certain trustworthy Ḥanbalite leaders of Baghdad say that Aḥmad ibn Ḥanbal—God have mercy on him!—was explicit about the interpretation of only three traditions.

38 One of them is the saying of Muḥammad—God's blessings and peace be upon him!—"The Black Stone is the right hand of God upon the earth." The second is his saying—God's blessings and peace be upon him!—"The Believer's heart is between two of the fingers of the Merciful." The third is his saying—God's blessings and peace be upon him!—"I shall surely find the Merciful Himself from the direction of Yemen." See now how he interpreted this, since he accepted the apodeictic proof of the impossibility of its literal meaning. He says: The right hand is kissed in customary fashion to bring oneself closer to its possessor. And the Black Stone is kissed to bring oneself closer to God Most High. [p. 185] So it is like the right hand, not in itself, and not in the qualities of its essence, but in one of its nonessentials [i.e. one of the things which befall it], and therefore it is called a right hand. This existence is that which we have called analogical existence, and it is the remotest of the ways of interpretation. See, then, how the man farthest removed from interpretation was compelled to use it.

39 Similarly he thought impossible the existence of the two fingers belonging to God Most High in a sensible fashion, since one who searches his breast does not see therein two fingers. So he interpreted it in the sense of the spirit of two fingers, i.e. the mental and spiritual finger—I mean that the spirit of the finger is "that by which it is easy to upset [alter, turn over] things." The heart of man is between the angel's touch and the devil's touch, and by means of the two of them God upsets hearts: so they were alluded to by "the two fingers." [Ahmad's interpretation of the third Tradition is not mentioned.] Aḥmad ibn Ḥanbal—God be pleased with him!—confined himself simply to the interpretation of these three Traditions because impossibility was clear to him only to this extent. For he did not apply himself assiduously to rational speculation: had he done so, that would have been clear to him regarding specification by the direction of "above" and other matters which he did not interpret.

40 The Ashᶜarite and the Muᶜtazilite, because of their greater preoccupation with [rational] research, went far beyond to the interpretation of many literal texts. Those closest to the Ḥanbalites regarding matters connected with the afterlife were the Ashᶜarites—God

favor them! For they affirm, regarding these matters, all but a few of the literal texts. The Muᶜtazilites, however, are much more vigorous than the Ashᶜarites in going deeply into interpretations. But in spite of this they—I mean the Ashᶜarites—also are compelled to interpret certain matters, such as the Apostle's saying which we have mentioned, "Death will be brought in the form of a black and white ram," and like what has reached us concerning the weighing of actions in the Balance.

41 For the Ashᶜarites interpreted the weighing of actions and said: The leaves of the actions are weighed and God creates in them weights commensurate with the degrees of the actions. [p. 186] This is a reducing to the remote analogical existence. For leaves are bodies on which are written symbols which designate by convention actions which are accidents. What is weighed, therefore, is not the action, but the place of a writing which by convention designates the action. The Muᶜtazilite interprets the Balance itself and makes it a figurative allusion to a cause by which is disclosed to each one the amount of his action. This is farther removed from the arbitrariness in the interpretation by the weighing of the leaves.

42 But our aim is not to justify one of the two interpretations. Rather it is that you may know that every faction, even though it goes far in holding fast to literal meanings, is compelled to use interpretation—unless one exceeds the bounds in stupidity and ignorance and affirms that the Black Stone is actually a right hand, and that death, even though it is an accident, is transformed and changed into a ram by way of alteration, and that actions, even though they are accidents and have ceased to exist, are transported to the Balance and there come to be in them accidents which are a weight. Now anyone who reaches this degree of ignorance has been stripped of the noose [has lost the bridle] of reason!

[p. 187] CHAPTER [SIX]

43 Hear now the law of interpretation. You already know the agreement of the sects on these five degrees concerning interpretation, and that nothing of that falls within the area of charging with lying. They also agree that the allowability of that rests on solid apodeictic proof of the impossibility of the literal sense. The first literal meaning is that of essential existence. If this is sure, it guarantees what comes after it [i.e., with Asín Palácios: it is guaranteed against all the others]. But if it be impossible, then sensible existence: for if this is sure, it is guaranteed against what comes after it. And if it be impossible, then imaginative or mental existence. And if this be impossible, then analogical and figurative existence.

44 Now it is not permissible to turn from one degree to what is beneath it except because of the necessity deriving from the apodeictic demonstration. So the disagreement really comes down to the matter of apodeictic proofs. For the Ḥanbalite affirms that there is no apodeictic proof of the impossibility of the Creator's being specified by the direction of "above." And the Ashᶜarite avers that there is no apodeictic proof of the impossibility of the ocular vision of God. Each one, as it were, disapproves of what his adversary says and does not consider it a decisive proof.

45 However it may be, each faction ought not to tax its adversary with unbelief on the ground that he considers him mistaken in the apodeictic proof. To be sure it is permissible for him to call him one astray or an innovator. "One astray," because in his view he has strayed from the path of truth. "An innovator," because he has introduced an affirmation no clear statement of which is known from our pious forebears: for the accepted

view among the latter was that God Most High will be seen—so the affirmation of him who says He will not be seen is an innovation, and his open sanctioning of the interpretation of "the vision" is an innovation. Nay more, if it be clear in his view that the meaning of that "vision" is the "seeing of the heart [mind]," then he ought not to divulge it or mention it, because our forbears did not mention it. But at this point the Ḥanbalite says: Affirming "above" of God Most High was accepted among our forbears, and none of them mentioned that the Creator of the world is neither united to the world, nor separated from it, not inside it, nor outside it, [p. 188] and that the six directions are free of Him, and that the relation of the direction of "above" to Him is like the relation of the direction of "below": so this is a novel affirmation, since "innovation" is an expression for originating a view not handed down from our forebears.

46 At this point it is clear to you that here we have two positions. *One of them* is the position of the masses of men. In this the right thing is to follow [the literal, or common, view] and to refrain entirely from changing literal meanings, and to be wary of introducing the sanctioning of an interpretation that was not sanctioned by the companions [of the Prophet], and to shut immediately the door to questioning, and to restrain men from engaging in discussion and inquiry and following what is ambiguous in the Book and the Sunna. This is like what has been related about ᶜUmar—God be pleased with him!—that someone asked him about the conflicting verses of the Qurᵓān, and he struck him with a whip. It is also like what has been reported of Mālik—God have mercy on him!—that he was asked about "the being firmly seated" [*al-istiwāᵓ*: i.e. on the Throne], and he replied: "The being firmly seated is something well known, and faith in it is obligatory, and the modality is unknown, and inquiry about it is an innovation."

47 *The second position* [is that found] among the men of speculation whose traditional beliefs have been troubled. Their inquiry ought to be as much as necessity requires and they should forsake the literal meaning because of the necessity imposed by decisive apodeictic proof. But one ought not to tax another with unbelief on the ground that he considers him to be mistaken regarding what he thinks to be an apodeictic proof, for that is not something simple and easily grasped. So let there be among them an agreed rule for apodeictic proof acknowledged by them all. For if they do not agree about the balance, they cannot do away with difference over the weighing. Now we have already mentioned the five scales in the *Book of the Correct Balance.* They are those about which dispute is absolutely inconceivable once they have been understood. Nay more, every one who understands them acknowledges that they are the channels of sure and certain knowledge in a decisive fashion. For those who have learned them it is easy to be fair and equitable and to uncover the truth and to eliminate dispute.

48 But disagreement on their part is also not impossible—(1) because of the inability of some of them to grasp completely its [the Balance's] conditions; or (2) in connection with their resorting in their speculation to simple innate bent and nature [common sense?] divorced from weighing with the Balance, as in the ease of one who, after learning perfectly [the use of] prosody in poetry, goes back to [natural] taste [sensitivity—*dhawq*] because he finds it burdensome to submit every poem to [the rules of] prosody—so it is not unlikely that he will err; [p. 189] or (3) because they differ about the cognitions which serve as the premises of the apodeictic proofs: for among the cognitions which form the bases of such proofs some are empirical, some based on impeccable transmission, and some other kinds: and men differ about experience and impeccable transmission so that one may consider as impeccable transmission what another does not; or (4)

because of mixing up judgments of the imagination with those of reason; or (5) because of mistaking sayings which are accepted and esteemed for analytical judgments and primary truths, as we have detailed that in our book *The Touchstone of Reasoning.* But in general, when they learn those scales and verify them they can—when they forego obstinacy—easily come to know the places of error.

[*p.* 190] CHAPTER [SEVEN]

49 Among men is the man who rushes into interpretation because of probable conjectures without any decisive apodeictic proof. But one ought not to be equally hasty in assuming his unbelief in every situation. Rather one ought to look into the matter. And if his interpretation concerns something which has nothing to do with fundamental and important beliefs, we do not tax him with unbelief. Such a case is the declaration of one of the Sufis that what is meant by the Friend's [Abraham]—Peace upon him!—seeing of the star and the moon and the sun and his saying "This is my Lord" [6.76–78] is not its apparent meaning: rather they are luminous angelic substances, and their luminosity is mental, not sensible, and they have degrees in perfection; and the relation of the difference between them is like the relation of the star and the moon and the sun.

50 He concludes to this on the ground that the Friend—Peace upon him!—was too great to believe of a body that it was a god, so that he would need to witness its setting. Do you suppose that, had it not set, he would have taken it for a god—even had he not known the impossibility of its divinity because of its being a quantified body? He also argued from this: How could the first thing he saw have been the star, when the sun is plainest and is the first thing seen? And he argued from the fact that God Most High first said: "So We were showing Abraham the kingdom of the heavens and earth" [6.75], then He related this utterance [of Abraham: 6.76–78]: how, then, could he have supposed that after the revelation of the kingdom to him?

51 These are conjectural indications, not apodeictic proofs. In reply to his assertion that Abraham was too great for that it has been said that he was a child when that happened to him. It is not farfetched that such a thought might occur, in his childhood, to one who was to be a Prophet, but he would soon outgrow it. Nor is it improbable that the setting's proof of incipience [*al-ḥudūth*] would in his view be clearer than the proof of quantification and corporality. As for seeing the star first, why it has been reported that Abraham, in his childhood, was kept in a cave and emerged from it only at night. And as for the Most High's first saying: [p. 191] "So We were showing Abraham the kingdom of the heavens and earth" [6.75], it is possible that God Most High may have already mentioned the state of his ending and then He returned to the mention of his beginning [i.e. to the state of Abraham before his prophetic call—?]. Thus these and similar assertions are conjectures which are thought to be apodeictic proofs by him who is not familiar with the real nature and condition of apodeictic proof.

52 Such is the sort of their interpretation. Indeed, they have interpreted "the staff" and "the two shoes" in the Most High's utterance: "Put off thy shoes" [20.12] and "Cast down what is in thy right hand" [20.72/69]. Perhaps conjecture in such matters as these which have no connection with basic beliefs is analogous to apodeictic proof regarding basic beliefs: so let there be no taxing with unbelief or innovation in this matter. To be sure, if the opening of this door were to lead to confusing the minds of the masses, one should particularly tax its author with innovation in everything of which no mention has

come down from our pious forebears. Close to it is the assertion of one of the Bāṭinites that the "calf" of the Samaritan [20.87/85 ff.] is to be interpreted, for how could many men be devoid of an intelligent man who would know that what is made of gold cannot be a god? This also is a conjecture, for it is not impossible that a group of men would go so far as that, as did the worshipers of idols. Its being a rare occurrence does not engender sure and certain knowledge [of its nonoccurrence].

53 However, in the case of this sort [of interpretation] which touches on the important basic beliefs, one must tax with unbelief anyone who changes the literal meaning without a decisive apodeictic proof. Such would be one who would deny the Assembly of bodies and would deny sensible punishments in the afterlife on the grounds of conjectures and fancies and improbabilities without any decisive apodeictic proof. So he absolutely must be taxed with unbelief, since there is no apodeictic proof of returning [the disembodied] spirits to [their] bodies. Mentioning such a thing would severely harm religion. So everyone who is attached to such a view must be taxed with unbelief. This [the view about the Assembly and sensible punishments] is the doctrine of most of the Philosophers.

54 Similarly, too, one must tax with unbelief those of them who hold [p. 192] that God Most High knows only Himself, or knows only the universals, but does not know the particular matters pertaining to individuals—because [holding] that is positively to charge the Apostle—God's blessings and peace be upon him!—with lying and it does not belong to the kind of degrees we have mentioned regarding interpretation. For the proofs of the Qurʾān and the Traditions in support of making understood the Assembly of bodies and the detailed connection of God Most High's knowledge with everything which happens to individuals are [a fact] surpassing a limit [level] which admits of no interpretation.

55 And they themselves acknowledge that this [view of theirs], is not a matter concerned with interpretation. But they assert: Since it is beneficial for men to believe in the Assembly of bodies—owing to their mental inability to grasp the intellectual afterlife—and since it is beneficial for them to believe that God Most High is aware of what happens to them and watchful over them, so that that may engender desire and fear in their hearts, it was permissible for the Apostle—Peace be upon him!—to make them understand that: and one who acts for the good of others [or: but one who consults the advantage of others] and says what benefits them is not lying, even though the matter is not as he declares it to be.

56 This assertion is absolutely false, because it is a clear affirmation of charging with lying and then a seeking an excuse in [the claim] that the one so charged did not lie. The office of prophecy must be deemed too lofty for this vice, and in veracity and improving men thereby there is an alternative to lying. Moreover, this is the first of the degrees of godlessness [*al-zandaqa*] and it is a station between Muᶜtazilism [*al-iᶜtizāl*] and absolute godlessness. For the method of the Muᶜtazilites is close to that of the Philosophers except in this one matter, viz. the Muᶜtazilite does not allow that lying is permissible for the Apostle—Peace upon him!—on the score of such an excuse, but rather he interprets the literal meaning, whenever its contrary [seems] plain to him by apodeictic proof. But the philosopher does not limit himself, in his going beyond the literal meaning, to what is susceptible of interpretation either proximately or remotely.

57 [p. 193] As for absolute godlessness, it is that you deny the basis of the afterlife rationally and sensibly, and that you deny the Maker of the world totally and directly. But affirming the afterlife in an intellectual way while denying sensible pains and pleasures, and affirming the Maker while denying His detailed knowledge of cognitions, is godless-

ness limited by a kind of acknowledgment of the veracity of the Prophets. And the clear thing in my view—and the [real] knowledge is with God!—is that these are the ones meant by the statement of the Apostle—Blessings and peace be upon him!—"My Community will split into seventy-odd sects, all of which will be in the Garden except the zendiks," and they are a sect. [The Arab editor has a long note on this Tradition—p. 193, Note (1).] This is the wording of the Tradition in one of the transmissions. [Cf. Paras. 87, 92, 93 below.]

58 [p. 194] The obvious meaning of the Tradition indicates that he meant thereby "the zendiks" of this Community, since he said "My Community will split": but one who does not profess his prophethood does not belong to his Community. Those, however, who deny the fundamental dogma of the afterlife and that of [the existence of] the Maker do not acknowledge his prophethood. For they allege that death is pure nonexistence, and that the world has never ceased to exist as it is of itself without a Maker, and they believe neither in God nor in the Last Day, and they impute deception to the Prophets: so they cannot be ascribed to the Community. Therefore "the zendiks of this Community" cannot mean anything except what we have mentioned.

[p. 195] CHAPTER [EIGHT]

59 Know that the explanation of what gives grounds for taxing with unbelief, and what does not, calls for a wealth of details which would necessitate citing all the views and doctrines, and mentioning the specious argument and proof of each individual, and the way he is remote from the literal meaning and the mode of his interpretation. Many tomes would not contain that, nor would my time be ample enough to explain it. So I am content now with one directive [*wasiyya:* counsel, recommendation, injunction] and one rule [*qānūn*].

60 *The directive* is that you restrain your tongue from [criticism of] the People of the Qibla [the direction faced in Prayer—hence: the Muslims] so far as you can as long as they continue to affirm "There is no divinity but God: Muḥammad is the Apostle of God" and do not contradict this word of witness. Contradiction would be their allowing that the Apostle of God—God's blessings and peace be upon him!—could lie, with a pretext or without a pretext. For taxing with unbelief contains a danger: but silence contains no danger.

61 *The rule* is that you recognize that speculative matters are of two sorts: one which touches on the roots of beliefs [basic beliefs], and one which touches on the branches [*al-furūᶜ:* ramifications, secondary matters]. Now the roots of the Faith are three: belief in God, and in His Apostle, and in the Last Day: all other things are branches. Know, too, that there can in no wise be any taxing with unbelief regarding the branches save in one matter, viz. that one deny a basic religious tenet which is known [to derive] from the Apostle—God's blessings and peace be upon him!—by impeccable transmission. But in some cases there is room for taxing with error, as in juridical matters; and in some cases there is room for taxing with innovation, as in the case of error concerning the Imamate and circumstances involving the Companions [of the Prophet].

62 Know also that error about the principle of the Imamate, and its specification and its requisites, and what is connected with that principle, in no case necessitates taxing with unbelief. Thus Ibn Kaisān denied the principle of the necessity of the Imamate, but it is not necessary to tax him with unbelief. And no heed should be paid to a group who

make much of the matter of the Imamate and put faith in the Imam on a par with faith in God and in His Apostle, nor to their adversaries who tax them with unbelief simply because of their doctrine on the Imamate. [p. 196] All that is exaggeration, since in neither of the two views is there any imputation at all of lying to the Apostle—God's blessings and peace be upon him!—but whenever there is any such imputation, taxing with unbelief is obligatory, even though it be regarding branches.

63 Thus, for example, if one were to assert that the House which is in Mecca is not the Kaᶜba to which God Most High commanded pilgrimage, this would be unbelief. For the contrary is sure by reason of impeccable transmission from the Apostle of God—God's blessings and peace be upon him! And were he to deny the witness of the Apostle—God's blessings and peace be upon him!—to that house that it is the Kaᶜba, his denial would not avail him. On the contrary it would be known for certain that he was pigheaded in his denial—unless he were a recent convert to Islam and that was not known to him by impeccable transmission. So also one who would impute adultery to ᶜĀᵓisha—God be pleased with her!—after the Qurᵓān has indeed revealed her innocence, would be an unbeliever. For this and its likes would be impossible save by charging the Apostle with lying or by denying impeccable transmission.

64 A man may deny impeccable transmission with his tongue, but he cannot be ignorant of it in his heart. Of course, if he were to deny something established by the reports of individuals, unbelief would not thereby cleave to him. And if he were to deny something established by consensus, this would be open to speculation. For knowing consensus to be a decisive proof is a matter involving a certain abstruseness well known to those who have acquired the science of the principles of jurisprudence [*ᶜilm uṣūl al-fiqh*]. Al-Naẓẓām [a famous Muᶜtazilite of Baṣra and Baghdad, d. 836 or 845] denied that consensus is in any wise a proof: so [the question of] consensus being a proof became a disputed question. This, then, is the status of [or: judgement regarding] the branches.

65 As for the three basic dogmas, and everything which in itself cannot bear interpretation and has been transmitted impeccably and for the contrary of which apodeictic proof is inconceivable—why contradicting that would be pure charging with lying. An example of this is what we have mentioned regarding the Assembly of bodies, and the Garden and the Fire, and God Most High's knowledge encompassing the details of things. As for what is open to the possibility of interpretation, even in a remote figurative way, we look regarding it to the apodeictic proof. If the latter be decisive, one must affirm it. But if bringing it to light with the masses would involve harm because of the defectiveness of their understanding, then bringing it to light would be innovation.

66 On the other hand, if the proof be not decisive but leads to a more probable conjecture, and along with that it is not known to be of any harm [p. 197] to religion—like the Muᶜtazilites' denial of the ocular vision of God Most High—this is innovation, not unbelief. But that which seems to involve some harm falls within the scope of personal effort and speculation, and it is possible for it to be branded as unbelief, and it is possible for it not to be so branded.

67 Of this sort is the claim of one who allegedly follows the path of Sufism that he has attained a state of intimacy with God Most High which dispenses him from the canonical Prayer and permits him to drink wine and to commit sins and to accept the largesse of the Sultan. Such a one is undoubtedly one who ought to be killed, even though his status regarding eternity in the Fire may be debatable. Killing such a one is better than killing a hundred unbelievers, since the harm he does religion is greater and thereby a door

to licentiousness is opened which cannot be shut. Moreover, the harm wrought by such a man surpasses that of him who holds for licentiousness absolutely, because the obvious unbelief of the latter prevents men from hearkening to him. But the former tears down the Law by using the Law itself. He alleges that he has perpetrated regarding the Law only a particularization of something general, since he has restricted the generality of obligations to him who does not have the same rank in religion that he himself has. He may also allege that he takes on and commits sins with his exterior, but in his interior he is innocent of them. Now this would lead to every sinner's claiming such a state as his and the restraining strap of religion would be loosed.

68 It must not be thought that taxing with unbelief and its rejection ought to be perceived for certain in every situation. On the contrary, taxing with unbelief is a legal qualification which comes down to declaring the licitness of [the confiscation of] goods and the shedding of blood and the sentence of eternity in the Fire. Its source is like that of all other legal qualifications. So sometimes it is perceived with certitude; and sometimes with a more probable conjecture; and sometimes there is doubt about it. Whenever doubt occurs, it is preferable in such a case to suspend taxing with unbelief therein, for rushing to tax with unbelief prevails only over those who are dominated by ignorance.

69 One must also call attention to another principle [*qā*ᶜ*ida*]. This is: The contradictor [p. 198] may contradict a text based on impeccable transmission and claim that it is to be interpreted. But there is not the faintest indication of the mention of its interpretation in language either remotely or proximately. So that is unbelief, and its champion is one who charges [the Apostle] with lying, though he claims that he is an interpreter. An example of this is what I have seen in the words of one of the Bāṭinites: "God Most High is One in the sense that He bestows oneness and creates it, and Knowing in the sense that He bestows knowledge on others and creates it, and Existent in the sense that He brings others into existence. But as for His being One in Himself, and Existent and Knowing in the sense of His being qualified [i.e. having the attributes of existence and knowledge]—no!" This is out and out unbelief! For understanding "the one" as "the production of oneness" in no way pertains to interpretations and it is in no wise supported by the language of the Arabs. If the Creator of oneness were to be called "One" because of His creating oneness, He would be called "Three" and "Four," because He also created the numbers. So such assertions as these are cases of charging [the Apostle] with lying which are falsely designated as "interpretations."

[p. 199] CHAPTER [NINE]

70 You have understood from these instances of taxing with unbelief that the consideration of taxing with unbelief depends on several factors. *One of them* is whether the revealed [*al-shar*ᶜ*ī*] text, the literal meaning of which is abandoned, is susceptible of interpretation or not. If it is, is it a proximate or a remote interpretation? Now the knowledge of what is and what is not susceptible of interpretation is not an easy matter. On the contrary, the only one who really possesses it is the main expert and well versed in the science of the [Arabic] language, who is familiar with the principles [*uṣūl*] of the language and also with the usage of the Arabs in the employment of their metaphors and allowances and their method in coining similes.

71 *The second* concerns the text abandoned: Was it established by impeccable transmission? Or by the report of individuals? Or by consensus alone? If it was established

by impeccable transmission, were the conditions of impeccable transmission fulfilled or not? For what is widespread may be thought to be based on impeccable transmission. But the definition of impeccable transmission is: that which cannot admit any doubt, such as the knowledge of the existence of the Prophets, and the existence of the well known countries, and other such things. And was there impeccable transmission in all the ages, age after age, back to the time of the prophetic mission? And is it conceivable that the number [required for] impeccable transmission was deficient in one of the ages?

72 Now it is the condition of impeccable transmission that such a thing be impossible, as in the case of the Qur^əān. But apart from the Qurʾān the perception of that is very difficult, and the only ones who really possess it are the students of the history books and of the circumstances of past centuries and of the collections of Traditions and of the conditions of men and their aims in the transmission of views [or: utterances—*maqālāt*]. For the number requisite for impeccable transmission may exist in every age and yet not result in sure knowledge. For it is conceivable that a numerous group may have a common bond regarding agreement, especially after the incidence of fanaticism [or: partisanship] among those who hold the views. That is why you see the Rāfiḍites claiming the specific textual designation of ʿAli ibn Abī Ṭālib—God be pleased with him!—in the case of the Imamate, because, in their view, it is based on impeccable transmission. But in the view of their adversaries there is impeccable transmission of many things contrary to what the Rāfiḍites hold to be based on impeccable transmission because of the solid agreement of the Rāfiḍites on the establishment of their lies and following them [or: of the Rāfiḍites and their followers . . .; or: of their lies and inducing men to follow them].

73 [p. 200] In the case of what is based on consensus the perception of that [its validity, or sureness] is one of the most difficult of things. For its condition is that the authorities [lit, the masters of loosing and binding] should be united without distinction [or: on an equal footing, or, common basis] and agree completely on one and the same thing in plain words, and should also continuously adhere to it, at one time according to some, and to the final conclusion of the age according to others. Or it is required that an Imam in one of the countries of the earth should correspond with those authorities and receive their *fatwas* [formal legal opinions] at the same time in such fashion that their affirmations agree unequivocally so that it would be impossible to revoke or contradict that agreement at a later time. Then one must consider if one who contradicts later on is to be taxed with unbelief. For there are those who say that if it was allowable at that time for them to disagree, then their mutual conformity can be referred to a [prior] agreement [on their part], and it would not have been impossible for one of them to revoke his agreement thereafter—and this also is an obscure matter.

74 *The third* is to consider whether, in the view of the proponent of the view [i.e. the opposing view] the report was based on impeccable transmission, or whether the consensus reached him. For everyone who is born is not equipped with a knowledge of things based on impeccable transmission, nor, for him, are the subjects of consensus distinguishable from the subjects of disagreement, but he perceives that only little by little and becomes aware of it only from reading the books written about difference and consensus by his predecessors [or: of the difference and the consensus of the pious forebears]. Moreover, sure knowledge of that does not result from the perusal of one or two works, since that does not result in impeccable transmission of the consensus. Indeed, Abū Bakr al-Fārisī—God have mercy upon him!—wrote a book on the problems of consensus, and much of what he wrote was rejected [censured] and he was opposed on some of those problems. Therefore, one who

contradicts the consensus when it has not yet been established in his view is ignorant and in error, but he is not one who charges [the Apostle] with lying, so it is impossible to tax him with unbelief. But real possession of accurate knowledge about this is not an easy thing.

75 *The fourth* is to consider the opposer's proof which induced him to oppose the literal sense: Doees it fulfill the condition of apodeictic proof, or not? It would be possible to explain knowledge of the condition of apodeictic proof only in several volumes: but what we have mentioned in the book of [p. 201] *The Correct Balance* and the book of *The Touchstone of Reasoning* is a specimen of it. But the natural disposition of the jurisprudents of our time is too dull to compass the detailed presentation of the condition of apodeictic proof. Yet the knowledge of that is indispensable, for apodeictic proof, if it be decisive, sanctions interpretation, even though it be remote. And if it be not decisive, it sanctions only a proximate interpretation occurring spontaneously to the mind.

76 *The fifth* is whether or not the mention of that [opposing] view would augment its harm to religion. For the matter is much easier in the case of what does no great harm to religion, even though the utterance be repulsive and patently false. An instance is the assertion of the Expectant Imamites and that the Imam is hidden in a subterranean vault and that his emergence is expected [awaited]. For this is a lying assertion, patently false and very repulsive. But it contains no harm in religion—rather it harms only the stupid man who believes that, since he leaves his town daily to welcome the Imam until night falls and he returns home disappointed. This is an example, but our aim is that one ought not to stigmatize as unbelief every wild assertion, even though it he patently false.

77 If then, you understand that consideration of taxing with unbelief depends on all these steps which, individually, are not mastered by the outstanding scholars, you know that one who precipitously taxes with unbelief him who contradicts al-Ashʿarī or others is a reckless fool. How, indeed, would a jurisprudent, by jurisprudence alone, completely master this vast matter? And in what area of jurisprudence would he encounter all this lore? So when you see a jurisprudent whose equipment is simple jurisprudence wading into taxing with unbelief and error, shun him and do not occupy your mind or tongue with him. For vying in [the claim to] learning is something innate in human nature which fools cannot refrain from. Because of it disagreement has multiplied among men, and if no attention were to be paid to those who do not know, there would surely be less disagreement among men.

[p. 202]

CHAPTER [TEN]

78 The most violently immoderate and intemperate of men are a group of the *mutakallimūn* who have taxed the masses of the Muslims with unbelief, alleging that he who does not know Kalām "as we know it" and does not know the legal proofs "by our proofs which we have precisely formulated" is an unbeliever. These have straitened the broad mercy of God to His servants, in the first place. And they have made the Garden a mortmain of a small group of the *mutakallimūn* and have ignored what has been impeccably transmitted of the Sunna, in the second place. For it was plain to them that in the age of the Apostle of God—God's blessings and peace be upon him!—and in that of the Companions, that these had judged [favorably] the Islam [submission] of groups of the rude desert Arabs who had been preoccupied with idol worship and had not busied themselves with the science of proof—and even if they had busied themselves with it, they would not have understood it.

79 One who supposes that the way to attain faith is Kalām and bare proofs and orderly divisions is indeed guilty of innovation. On the contrary, faith is a light which God casts into the hearts of His servants, a gift and present from Him. Sometimes [faith comes] through an evidence from within [the interior of] a man which he cannot express. And sometimes because of a vision in one's sleep. And sometimes through seeing the state of a godly person and the emanation of the latter's light into the observer when he associates and keeps company with the godly one. And sometimes it is due to the conjunction of a circumstance. Thus a desert Arab had come to the Prophet—God's blessings and peace be upon him!—rejecting and disavowing him. And when his eye fell on [the Prophet's] radiant aspect which God had augmented in dignity and nobility, and he saw shining from it the lights of prophethood, he said: "By God this is not the face of a liar!" And he asked him to set forth Islam to him and then embraced Islam. And another came to him—Blessing and peace on him!—and said: "I adjure you by God—has God sent you as a Prophet?" He answered him—Blessing and peace on him!—"Yes, by God! He has sent me as a Prophet!" And the Arab believed him because of his oath and embraced Islam.

80 These and similar examples are too numerous to be numbered. Now not one of those Arabs had busied himself with Kalām and schooling in proofs. Rather the light of faith would appear in their hearts in such circumstances in a white flash—then it would go on increasing in radiance through witnessing those memorable circumstances, and reciting the Qur᾽ān and purifying their hearts. I would like to know when it was ever reported of the Apostle of God—God's blessings and peace be upon him!—or from the Companions—God be pleased with them!—that he summoned a desert Arab who had embraced Islam and said to him: "The proof that the world is an incipient [p. 203] is that it is not free from accidents: but what is not free from incipients is itself incipient. And: God Most High is knowing by a knowledge and powerful by a power superadded to His Essence: but they are not He, nor are they other than He." And so for the other formalities of the *mutakallimūn.*

81 I do not say that these terms did not occur, or that the equivalents of these terms did not occur. But a battle would not end without a group of the rude Arabs embracing Islam under the shadows of the swords and a group of captives embracing Islam one by one after a long time or short. And once they had uttered the Word of Witness [*kalimat al-shahāda*] they would be instructed in the Prayer and in almsgiving and would be sent back to their occupation such as tending sheep, etc.

82 Of course I do not deny that citing the proofs of the *mutakallimūn* may be one of the causes of faith in the case of some men. But that is not confined to it, and also it is rare. Indeed, what is most useful is the "kalām" which takes place in the form of preaching according to what the Qur᾽ān contains. But the "kalām" precisely formulated according to the prescription of the *mutakallimūn* makes the souls of the listeners feel that it contains a contrived dialectic designed to paralyze the powers of the common man, and not because of its being true in itself: and that may be a cause of obduracy becoming deeply rooted in the heart. Hence it is that you do not see a discussion session of *mutakallimūn,* or of jurisprudents, ending in a single person's changing from Muᶜtazilism or from an innovation to something else, or from the school of al-Shāfiᶜī to that of Abū Ḥanīfa, or vice versa. Such changes come about through other causes, even in battling with the sword. For that reason it was not the custom of our forebears to appeal by means of such debates, but rather they spoke severely against anyone who engaged in Kalām and busied himself with investigation and inquiry.

83 If we set aside flattery and human respect, we declare plainly that engaging in Kalām is a thing unlawful, because of the great hurt it involves, except for one of two persons. One is a man who has experienced a doubt [*shubha*] which cannot be removed from his heart by ordinary homiletic "kalām," nor by a traditional report from an Apostle. It is possible, then, that ordered kalām argument would dispel his doubt and be a remedy for his sickness. [p. 204] So it should be employed in his case, but the well man in whom such sickness is not found should be safeguarded from hearing that [kalām]. For it might well be that it would stir up a difficulty in his soul and would pose for him a doubt which would make him sick and cause him to forego his settled and sound belief.

84 *The second* is a person of mature intellect, with his foot firmly rooted in our religion, and unwavering in his belief in the lights of sure and certain knowledge, who wants to acquire this skill to use it as a medicine for a sick man when the latter experiences a doubt, and to silence with it any innovator if the latter should appear, and to protect thereby his belief if any innovator should aim at seducing him. So learning that with this intention belongs to the category of general [or: community] obligations, and learning an amount by which doubt may be removed and sophism averted in the case of a problem is an individual obligation, if it be impossible to restore one's settled belief by any other way.

85 The plain truth is that whoever believes absolutely in what was brought by the Apostle—Blessings and peace be upon him!—and is contained in the Qur᾽ān is a believer, even though he does not know the proofs of it. On the contrary, faith which derives from kalām proof is very weak and prone to vanish at the incidence of any specious argument. But deep-rooted faith is the faith of ordinary men. It comes to be in their hearts in childhood by repeated hearing, or it comes to be after puberty through conjunctions of circumstances which cannot be put into words.

86 Its full confirmation must be accompanied by worship and remembrance [*al-dhikr*]. For in the case of one in whom worship persists until the achievement of genuine piety and the cleansing of the interior from the impurities of this world and the incessant practice of the remembrance of God Most High, there are revealed to him the lights of knowledge and for him the things which he had accepted through servile conformism become like [objects of] seeing and direct vision. That is the real meaning of the knowledge [*al-maʿrifa*] which comes to be only after the resolution of the knot of dogmas [beliefs] and the expansion of the breast by the Light of God Most High. "Whomsoever God desires to guide, He expands his breast to Islam" [6.125] "so he walks in a light from his Lord" [39.23/22]. It is as when Muḥammad—God's blessings and peace be upon him!—was asked about the meaning of "the expanding of the breast," and he replied: "A light which is cast into the heart of the believer." And someone said: "And what is the sign of it?" He replied: "Turning away from the mansion of delusion and turning to the mansion of immortality." From this it is known that the Mutakallim who applies himself to [the vanity of] this life and goes all out for it does not perceive the real meaning of knowledge: were he to do so, he would turn away from the mansion of delusion once and for all.

[p. 205]

CHAPTER [ELEVEN]

87 You may say: You take [understand, derive] "taxing with unbelief" from "imputing falsehood to the revealed texts": but the one who brought the Law—God's blessings be upon him!—is the one who straitened the mercy [of God] toward men, not the *mutakallimūn*. For he said—Peace upon him!—"God Most High will say to Adam—

Peace upon him!—on the Day of the Resurrection: O Adam, I shall send from your progeny the delegation [i.e. those destined for] of the Fire. And Adam will say: O Lord, from how many? And [God] will reply: From every thousand nine hundred and ninety-nine." He also said—Blessing and peace upon him!—"My Community will split into seventy-odd sects, one of which will be saved." [Cf. Para. 57 above.]

88 *The answer* is that the first Tradition is sound, but it does not mean that they are unbelievers condemned forever to the Fire, but rather that they will enter the Fire and be exposed to it and be left in it according to the number of their sins. However, the sinless in [every] tbousand will be only one. Similarly God Most High said: "Not one of you there is, but he shall go down to it [Gehenna]" [19.72/71]. Moreover, "the delegation of the Fire" is an expression signifying him who deserves the Fire because of his misdeeds. But it is possible that such men may be turned away from the path to Gehenna by the intercession [of the Prophet], as the Traditions have brought down [to us]—and many Traditions witness to this and indicate the amplitude of God Most High's mercy—and these are Traditions too numerous to be enumerated.

89 Among such Traditions is what has been reported from ᶜĀᵓisha—God be pleased with her!—namely that she said: "One night I missed the Prophet—God's blessings and peace be upon him!"—so I sought him out, and there he was praying in an upper chamber, and I saw on his head three lights. When he finished his prayer he said: Who is it? I said: I, ᶜĀᵓisha, O Apostle of God. He said: There came to me one from my Lord and he brought me the good tidings that God Most High will introduce into the Garden seventy thousand of my Community without reckoning or punishment. Then there came to me in the second light one from my Lord and he brought me the good tidings that God Most High will introduce into the Garden for each one of the seventy thousand seventy thousand [others] of my Community without reckoning or punishment. [p. 206] Then in the third light there came to me one from my Lord and he brought me the good tidings that God Most High will introduce into the Garden for each one of the multiplied seventy thousand seventy thousand [others] of my Community without reckoning or punishment. Then I said: O Apostle of God, your Community does not amount to so many. He said: They will be completed for you from among the desert Arabs who fast not and pray not." This and its likes among the Traditions showing the amplitude of the mercy of God Most High are numerous.

90 The above concerns the Community of Muḥammad—God's blessings and peace be upon him!—in a special way. But I go on to say: The divine mercy will embrace many of the bygone nations, even though most of them will be exposed to the Fire either slightly, even for a moment or for an hour, or for a period of time, so that one may apply to them the expression "the delegation of the Fire." Nay more, I would say: Most of the Christians among the Byzantines [Greeks] and Turks in this time of ours will be embraced by the [same] mercy, if God Most High wills. I mean those who are among the remotest Byzantines and Turks whom the call [to Islam] has not reached.

91 These [Christians] are three classes. *One* is the class of those whom the name of Muḥammad—God's blessings and peace be upon him!—has never reached at all: these are excusable. *The second* is the class of those to whose ears his name and description have come, and also the miracles manifested in his regard: these are persons neighboring the Islamic countries and having intercourse with the Muslims—they are the godless unbelievers. *The third* is the class of those in between the other two. The name of Muḥammad—God's blessings and peace be upon him!—has reached their ears, but not

his description and qualification. Rather, they have also heard from childhood that a deceitful liar named Muḥammad claimed the prophetic office, as our children have heard that a liar named Muqaffa[c] claimed that God had sent him and falsely arrogated to himself the prophetic office. In my opinion these are the same as the first class, for, though they have heard Muḥammad's name, they have heard the contrary of his qualities, and this would not stimulate any motive for considering the search [for him: i.e. investigating him].

92 As for the other Tradition—viz. "one of which will be saved—the transmission differs regarding it. It has indeed been transmitted as "of which one will be lost"—but the best known transmission is that which we have mentioned. [p. 207] And the meaning of *al-nājiya* [the one saved] is "that which will not be exposed to the Fire and will not need the intercession [of the Prophet]." But he to whom the *zabāniya* [angels who thrust the damned into the Fire] cling to drag him to the Fire is absolutely not saved, even though he be snatched from their clutches by the intercession [of the Prophet]. And another transmission has "All of them will be in the Garden except the zendiks"—and these are a sect. [Cf. Para. 57 above.]

93 It may be that all the transmissions are sound. Thus the sect lost will be one, viz. that condemned eternally to the Fire. In this case "the lost" would be an expression for him whose goodness [*ṣalāḥ:* probity] is despaired of—because there is no hope of any good for the lost after he is lost. And "the sect saved" would be one, viz. that which will enter the Garden without reckoning or intercession: for one from whom the reckoning is exacted has been purified and therefore is not "one saved," and one who has been exposed to intercession has been exposed to humiliation [lowliness] and likewise is not "one saved" absolutely speaking.

94 These are two ways [*ṭarīqāni*] and they are an expression of the evil and the goodness of men. And all the remaining sects are between these two degrees. So among them is he who is punished by the reckoning alone. And among them is he who is brought close [or: draws near] to the Fire, then is turned away [from it] by the intercession. And among them are those who enter the Fire and are then brought forth [from it] according to the number of their errors in their beliefs and their innovation, and in accordance with the multiplicity and the paucity of their sins. But among these sects the one lost and condemned forever to the Fire is a single sect, viz. that which charged [the Apostle] with lying and declared lying permissible for the Apostle of God—God's blessings and peace be upon him!—on the ground of some advantage.

95 As for the other nations, he who imputes lying [to the Prophet] after he has heard the impeccable transmission of his appearance and his quality and his miracles which violated custom—such as the splitting of the moon and the praise of the pebbles and the welling up of water from between his fingers and the miraculous Qur'ān which he challenged the eloquent to rival and they could not—if that has reached his ears and he shuns it and turns his back and does not consider it and reflect on it and does not hasten to believe it, then such a one is a lying [*kādhib:* the Arab Ed. prefers *mukadhdhib:* charging with lying] disbeliever and he is the infidel; [p. 208] but there do not enter into this [category] most of the Greeks and Turks whose countries are remote from those of the Muslims.

96 Nay more, I say: Inevitably there would be roused in the mind of one whose ears this had reached a motive for inquiring [or: seeking] so that he might know the truth of the matter, if he were of the men of religion and not one of those who prefer this life to the afterlife. And if such a motive were not roused, that would be because of his reliance on this life and his freedom from fear and the gravity of the matter of religion—and that

would be unbelief. And if the motive were roused, and he then failed in the quest, this would also be unbelief. Nay but among the followers of every religion one possessed of faith in God and in the Last Day cannot be remiss in the search after [he has seen] the appearance of signs due to causes which violate custom. So if he busies himself with reflection and searching and does not flag, and death overtakes him before the completion of his inquiry, he also will be pardoned and will then receive the ample mercy [of God].

97 Have, then, a broad view of God's ample mercy and do not weigh divine things with limited conventional [or: official] scales. And know that the afterlife is close to this life, for "Your creation and your upraising are but as a single soul" [31.27/28]. Just as most of the men of this world who are enjoying ease and security or a state which makes this life delightful, if they were to be given a choice between it and killing and destruction [with nuance of: mortification and impoverishment] for example, they would choose it [their present life], but the tormented one who desires death is rare, so also those condemned eternally to the Fire in comparison with the saved and with those brought forth from the Fire in the afterlife will be rare: for the attribute of the divine mercy does not change because of the diversity of our circumstances [states]—and "this life" and "the afterlife" are simply two expressions designating the diversity of your circumstances. Were it not for this, there would be no meaning to the saying of the Apostle—Blessing and peace be upon him!—when he declared: "The first thing indited by God in the first Book was: I am God. There is no god but Me! My mercy takes precedence over My wrath: so he who witnesses that there is no god but God and that Muḥammad is His servant and His Apostle, for him will the Garden be."

98 Know also that men of insight have already had disclosed to them the prevenience of [God's] mercy and its comprehensiveness through causes and revelations other than what they had of Traditions and reports—but the mention of that would be lengthy. So I give you the good tidings of God's mercy and of absolute salvation if you combine faith and good works, and of absolute perdition if you are devoid of both together. [p. 209] But if you possess certainty regarding basic belief, but are in error regarding some interpretation, or [if you have] a doubt about both, or possess a mixture of [good and bad] works, then do not hope for absolute salvation, but know that you stand between being punished for a time and then released on the one hand, and on the other of being interceded for by him whose veracity in all that he brought you have known for certain or by some one else. Work hard, then, that God by His bounty may dispense you from the intercession of the intercessors, for the matter regarding that is perilous.

[p. 210] CHAPTER [TWELVE]

99 Some men have indeed thought that the source of taxing with unbelief is reason, not the Law, and that he who knows not God is an unbeliever and he who knows Him is a believer. So one should say to such a one: The determination of licitness of blood and eternity in the Fire is a legal determination which had no meaning before the coming of the Law. If he means by it that what is understood from the legislator is that "he who knows not God" is equivalent to "the unbeliever," such restriction is impossible, because he who knows not the Apostle and the Last Day is also an unbeliever. Moreover, if he restricts that to ignorance of the Essence of God Most High by rejecting His existence or His oneness, but does not hold the same regarding the [divine] attributes, he may find some support.

100 But if he also believes that he who errs regarding the attributes is an ignorant man or an unbeliever, then he is bound to tax with unbelief him who denies the attribute of perdurance and the attribute of preeternity, and him who denies that speech is a quality superadded to knowledge, and him who denies that hearing and seeing are superadded to knowledge, and him who denies the possibility of the ocular vision [of God], and him who affirms direction [of God], and him who affirms a will incipient neither in God's Essence nor in a substrate [locus—*maḥall*], and [he must] tax with unbelief those who are opposed regarding it. In short, he is bound to tax with unbelief in every question related to the attributes of God Most High—and that is a determination [*ḥukm*] entirely groundless.

101 And if he restricts that to one of the attributes rather than another, he will find for that no [supporting] distinction or reason, and there will be no way [of acting] for him save to hold fast to charging with lying, so that it will be common to him who denies the Apostle and the afterlife [i.e. the doctrine of the afterlife], while the interpreter will escape it. Moreover, it is not unlikely that doubt and reflection may occur regarding one of the questions from the totality of interpretation or charging with lying, with the result that the interpretation would be remote and decided on by conjecture or by what is demanded by personal effort: and you already know that this is the problem of personal effort [*ijtihād*].

[p. 211]

CHAPTER [THIRTEEN]

102 Among men there is one who says: "I tax with unbelief any of the sects who taxes me with unbelief, but anyone who does not tax me with unbelief I do not so tax." There is no source for this. If anyone says that ᶜAlī—God be pleased with him!—was worthier of the Imamate, if he be not an unbeliever, then, by the fact that the holder of this view errs and he thinks [read: *wa yaẓunnu*] that one opposed on this matter is an unbeliever, he does not become an unbeliever, but it is simply an error about legal question. Similarly the Ḥanbalite, if he be not taxed with unbelief because of the affirmation of direction [of God], he is not taxed with unbelief because he errs or thinks that the man who denies direction [of God] is one who charges with lying and is not an interpreter.

103 As for the saying of the Apostle of God—God's blessings and peace be upon him!— If any Muslim accuses his fellow Muslim of unbelief, then it [unbelief] is indeed attributed to one of the two [i.e. one of them is really an unbeliever—the one accused, if the accuser is right, or the accuser, if his accusation is false]," it means that he taxes him with unbelief because of his knowledge of what he has. So when one knows of another that he is a believer in the Apostle of God—God's blessings and peace be upon him!— and then taxes him with unbelief, the one who taxes with unbelief will be an unbeliever. But if he taxes him with unbelief because he thinks he has charged the Apostle with lying, this is an error on his part regarding the status of a single individual: since it may be thought of him that he is an unbeliever who charges [the Apostle] with lying, when he is not such—and this would not be unbelief.

104 By these repetitions [or: preventions, warnings] we have acquainted you with an alert about the very great depths [intricacies] involved in this principle [*qāᶜida*] and have called your attention to the rule which ought to be followed in this matter. So be content with it, and peace to you!

The book is finished.

APPENDIX II

Faḍā᾿iḥ al-Bāṭiniyya wa Faḍā᾿il al-Mustaẓhiriyya

THIS is the book to which Ghazālī refers in the *Munqidh,* Para. 61 (Note 122). I translate its title as *The Infamies (Enormities) of the Bātinites and the Virtues (Merits) of the Mustaẓhirites.* By the Mustaẓhirites Ghazālī means the reigning Caliph, al-Mustaẓhir Billāh, and his family. He was Caliph from 478/1094 to 512/1118. The book was partially edited and translated by Goldziher in his *Streitschrift des Ġazālī gegen die Bāṭinijja-Sekte,* Leiden, 1916. He used a manuscript of the British Museum. The complete text (which is the basis of my translation) was edited hy Dr. ᶜAbdurraḥmān Badawī, Cairo, 1964, who used the British Museum manuscript and another of the Qarawiyīn Mosque in Fez (Morocco). Goldziher's book contains a good deal of useful and interesting information.

My translation is fairly literal, without, I hope, being too barbarous. Some parts are summaries of certain sections completely translated in Goldziher's splendid book. I have added certain explanations, references, and alternate translations in square brackets. For more complete details on Ghazālī's "politics" I refer the reader to: H. Laoust: *La politique de Gazālī,* Paris, 1970.

Laudatory Preface [*Khuṭba*]

1 Praise he to God, the Living the Subsistent, the essence of Whose Subsistence cannot be mastered by the description of a describer; the Glorious, the quality of Whose Glory cannot be encompassed by the knowledge of a knower; the Mighty—and there is no mighty one save that he clings to the threshold of His Might with the foot of infants; the Splendid—and there is no monarch save that he circumambulates the pavillions of His Splendor; the Coercer [Omnipotent, Compeller]—and there is no ruler save that he hopes for the gusts of His pardon and fears the outbursts of His wrath; The Imperious [Proud, Great]—and there is no holy one [*walī:* master, governor, proprietor, holy one] save that his heart is the mortmain of His Love and his soul stands ready for His service; the Compassionate [All-merciful]—and there is no thing save that it would mount the back of danger in terrifying situations, were it not for its expectation of His Mercy by reason of His prevenient and previous promises; the Gracious [Beneficent, Benefactor]—if He wish good for you, nothing can repel or turn away His favor; the Avenger—if He afflict you with harm, none but He can remove it; sublime His Majesty and hallowed His Names, unbeguiled by any intimate, and unharmed by any adversary; mighty His power, unduped by any covert trickster and unopposed by any overt enemy!

2 He created men parties and quantities [different factions and descents ?], and ordered them, with respect to the vanities of the world, as base and noble; and brought them into proximity, with respect to the truths of religion, as attached and deviate, ignorant and learned; and divided them, with respect to the bases of belief [fundamental dogmas], into sects and classes [categories] agreeing with each other harmoniously and separating from each other in disagreement, so that they were divided regarding dogmas by denial and confession, arbitrariness and fairness, moderation and excess. They likewise differed in origin and qualities. This one is a wealthy man whose riches multiply daily and who receives wholesale [on a large scale] and spends wholesale. This other is a weak man who has to support frail offspring and who lacks a day's supply of food so that he has been reduced to importuning people. Another finds a ready welcome in men's hearts and in his need meets only with compliance and aid. But another is hated by men and his claims are unjustly treated with inequity and unfairness. This one is godly and aided by God and grows daily in his piety and godliness in boundlessness and loftiness. But this other is forsaken [by God] and grows with the passage of the days [p. 2] in his transgression and wickedness in excess and deviation. That is the ordaining of your Lord [cf. Qur. 6.95–96], the Powerful, the Wise, from Whose domination no sultan can turn away, the Irresistible, the Omniscient, Whose decision no one can withstand, despite the Bāṭinite unbelievers who deny that God appoints disagreement among the People of the Truth, for they know not that mercy follows disagreement among the Community just as admonition [warning, example] follows their differing in ranks and qualities.

3 Thanks be to God Who has aided us to profess His religion publicly and privately [openly and secretly], and Who has guided us to submit to His rule [authority] outwardly and inwardly. He has not made us of the number of the erring Bāṭinites who make outward confession with their tongues while they harbor in their hearts persistence and willfulness [in their error]. They bear heavy loads of misdeeds, and manifest regarding religion piety and gravity, and store up [fill their saddle-bags with] burdens of iniquities, because they do not hope for forbearance from God [do not ask gravity of deportment of God, or, do not show grave deportment toward God]. And were the summoners to Truth to address them night and day, their appeal would only make them flee the more [from the Truth]. When the sword of the People of the Truth dominates them they quickly choose the Truth, but when its shadow lifts from them they persist in their arrogance. So we ask God not to leave any of their dwellings on the face of the earth. And we ask God's blessings upon His Elect Apostle and his family and his orthodox Caliphs who came after him—blessings as numerous as the drops of the clouds which pour forth abundant showers, which will continually increase with the passage of the days and will be renewed as the years succeed uninterruptedly and repeatedly!

[*Introduction*]

4 *Now then:* During the length of my stay in the City of Peace [Baghdad] I never ceased longing to serve the sacred, prophetic, caliphal, Mustaẓhirite positions [stands, policies, attitudes, positions]—may God multiply their glory and extend their shadow [protection, patronage] over all the strata [classes] of men—by composing a book about the science [or: *biʿalam*—the star, luminary, eminent person—i.e. the Caliph?] of our religion, by which I would pay my debt of gratitude for his kindness and fulfill my obligation to serve, and, by the trouble I would take, reap the fruits of approval and closeness [to

him]. However, I tended to temporize because of my perplexity about specifying the area of learning which I would aim at in my composition and particularizing the discipline which would meet with the approval of the [Caliph's] noble and prophetic opinion. This perplexity was surpassing my intent and preventing my natural disposition from compliance and submission until the noble, sacred, prophetic, Mustaẓhirite orders came with an instruction [suggestion, intimation, command] to the servant to compose a book on the refutation of the Bāṭinites which would contain the exposure of their innovations and their errors, and of the kinds of their cunning and artfulness, and of the way they allure common and ignorant men. It would also make plain the hidden dangers in their deception and their dupery, and their slipping out of the noose of Islam and their abandoning and being stripped of it [Islam]. And it would bring out their infamies and their abominations by what would result in rending their veils and revealing their depths. Thus the [Caliph's] precedence in employing me in this weighty matter was, in appearance, a favor which answered before the request and responded before the appeal, although in reality it was a goal which I was seeking and a wish at which I was aiming.

5 So I considered obedience a duty and hurrying to comply a firm obligation. And how could I not hasten to do that?! For if I considered it from the standpoint of the commander, I found it to be a command forwarded by the Leader of our Community and the Glory of our Religion and originating [p. 4] in the Delight of the Nations, the Commander of the Faithful, obedience to whom is enjoined by the Creator of Creatures and the Lord of the Worlds—for God Most High has said: "Obey God, and obey the Apostle and the Rulers among you" [4.62/59]. And if I considered the command, it was to defend the plain truth and to stand up for the Proof of our Religion and to eradicate the godless. And if I consulted myself—and I, among all creatures, had been honored with a message about it—I saw that hastening to submit and comply was, on my part, a personal duty. For rare in the world is the man who, in the matter of the fundamental dogmas, can independently [undertake to] establish proof and demonstration in such fashion that he raises it from the lowlands of conjecture and reckoning to the highlands of positiveness and certainty. For it is a momentous concern and a weighty matter to the essentials of which the resources of the jurists are not equal and with the basic elements of which only he is conversant who has devoted all his attention to this problem become devilish ["hairy"] because of the capricious tendencies regarding the fundamentals of religions which have appeared and become intermingled with the method of the early philosophers and sages. For it is from the depths of the latter's error that these Bāṭinites seek provision, since they vacillate between the doctrines of the dualists and the philosophers and buzz around the limits of logic in their wranglings. I had indeed long sought the like of its [Bāṭinism's] antagonist [opposition], when it was appointed for me to subdue and overcome it. In a similar case the poet has said:

I got to know evil, not
For evil's sake, but to guard against it:
And he who knows not the evil
Of men falls into it.

6 [p. 5] The reasons of obligation and necessity made common cause against me and I welcomed the inevitable with the embrace of one duty bound. I hurried to obey and comply and applied myself to composing this book built on ten chapters, begging from God—Praised be He!—help to pursue the right course. I have called it *The Infamies of the*

Bāṭinites and the Virtues [Merits] of fhe Mustaẓhirites. And God Most High is He Who gives help for the fulfillment of this intention!

7 Here is the list of the chapters:

Chapter One: The clear statement of the method I have chosen to follow in the course of this book.

Chapter Two: Explanation of their appellations and disclosure of the reason which moved them to institute this misleading propaganda.

Chapter Three: Explanation of the degrees of their artifices in deceiving and disclosure of the reason for men's being misled by their artifices despite their patent wrongness.

Chapter Four: Account of their doctrine in general and in detail.

Chapter Five: On their interpretations of the literal meanings of the Qurʾān and their arguing from numerical matters. It contains two sections:

Section 1—On their interpretation of the literal meanings.

Section 2—On their arguments from numbers and letters.

Chapter Six: Presentation of their rational proofs in defense of their teaching and disclosure [p. 6] of their argument which they embellished with their allegation in the form of apodeictic proof of the invalidation of intellectual reasoning.

Chapter Seven: Refutation of their argument from textual designation to the appointment of the infallible Imam.

Chapter Eight: On the necessity of the legal opinion about them with respect to taxing with unbelief and charging with error and the shedding of blood.

Chapter Nine: Establishment of the canonical and legal proof that the true Imam in this age of ours is the Caliph al-Mustaẓhir Billāh—God preserve his sovereignty!

Chapter Ten: On the religious duties by persistence in which the Imamate [Caliphate] is continuously merited.

8 This is the account of the chapters. It is suggested to the noble, prophetic view [of the Caliph] that he read the book as a whole, then single out Chapters Nine and Ten for him who wishes to make a close study. Thus he will learn from Chapter Nine the extent of the Most High's favor to him, and perceive, from Chapter Ten, how to render thanks for that favor, and he may also know that if God Most High is not content to have a servant of His on the face of the earth higher in dignity than the Commander of the Faithful, then the Commander of the Faithful will not be Content that God should have on the face of the earth a servant more devoted and more grateful than he himself. We beg God Most High to supply him with His succor and to guide him to His own right path. This is the sum total of the book—and God is the resort for help in following the thoroughfare of the Truth and in treading the road of sincerity!

CHAPTER ONE

The Clear Statement of the Method I Have Chosen to Follow in the Course of This Book

9 [p. 7] You should know that the method of discoursing in books differs (1) with regard to meaning, in profundity and precision as against carelessness and meretriciousness, and (2) with regard to expression, in prolixity and elaborateness as against

brevity and conciseness, and (3) with regard to intention [aim, purpose], in multiplying and prolonging as against restricting and reducing. These, then, are three standpoints [aspects, approaches], and each of these divisions has its advantage and its disadvantage.

[The First Standpoint]

10 As for the first standpoint, its purpose—in profundity and precision and plumbing the mysteries and meanings to their farthest limits—is to guard against the ridicule of experts and the reproach of specialists. For if they look attentively at this book and do not find it in conformity and agreement with what thinkers [speculators] regard as the rules of dialectic and the prescriptions of logic, they will find the author's performance feeble and his discourse nauseating [Or, from another root: scrawny, weak, thin] and will think him unacquainted with the goal of inquiry [investigation] and one affiliated with the masses.

11 But this has a disadvantage, viz. its small benefit and utility with respect to most men. For if the discourse be to the taste of disputation and dialectic, and not to the point of persuasive speech, [p. 8] only the experts will be able to understand it and only skilled researchers will know how to fathom its abstruse meanings. As for following the way of indulgence [simplicity, ease] and restricting oneself to a kind of discourse which is deemed nice in addresses to others, this has the advantage of being pleasing to men's ears and most natures are not too dull to understand it and to grasp its aims, and it induces conviction in everyone who has brains and intelligence, even though he has not delved deeply into the sciences. This kind of discourse is a cause of praise and commendation—on the part of the superficial; its disadvantage is that it is a motive for contempt on the part of experts. So I have thought it best to follow the via media [middle way] between the two extremes. I shall not leave my book devoid of matters apodeictical which the skilled researchers will understand, nor of rhetorical remarks from which those who proceed by conjecture will derive profit. For the need for this book is general, with respect to both the elite and the common folk, and embraces all the strata of the adherents of Islam, and this procedure is the closest to the straight path. How often has it been said:

Each of the two extremes of seeking things is reprehensible.

The Second Standpoint
On Prolixity and Conciseness in Expressing the Aims

12 The advantage of prolixity is explanation and clarification which spare one the trouble of thought and long reflection; but its disadvantage is being boring. The advantage of conciseness is uniting and compacting intentions and conveying them to minds quickly; but its disadvantage is the need for intense scrutiny and reflection to deduce the subtle meanings from the concise and elegant expressions. The best procedure in this standpoint is to adopt a middle course between remissness and excess, for prolixity is inseparable from boring, while conciseness [p. 9] is not free from harm. So it is preferable to lean toward brevity—and many an utterance is brief and to the point while not boring.

The Third Standpoint
On Reducing and Multiplying

13 I have already read the books written about this subject and I have found them filled

with two kinds of discourse. One concerns histories of accounts of them and their circumstances from the beginning of their affair until the appearance of their error, and naming every one of their propagandists in each and every region, and enumerating their events in bygone times. This is a kind [of writing] engaging in which I consider a preoccupation with long talks more suitable for historians and chroniclers. But the discourse of those learned in the Law should be restricted to the important religious matters and to establishing apodeictic proof of what is the clear truth. For each job there are men.

14 The second kind [of discourse] is concerned with refuting doctrines of theirs which are beliefs they have taken from the dualists and the philosophers, and which they have twisted from their places and changed their terms with the aim of obscuring and deceiving. I also do not think it worth occupying myself with this [kind of discourse], because argument against such things and laying bare their falseness is not the concern of the group which constitutes their present generation. So the duty designated is to strip down one's intent to reporting their peculiar doctrines which they alone believe in contradistinction to all the other sects. Hence a writer should direct himself in his book only to the intention which he seeks to attain and the aspect which he desires to pursue. For it belongs to the excellence of a man's Islam that he leave aside what does not concern him—and that is something which does not concern him in this standpoint. And even though [p. 10] engaging in it is, in general, a defense of Islam, yet each piece of writing has its own standpoint. So in this book of ours let us confine ourself to the amount which will make known the peculiar features of their doctrine and call attention to the ways of their artifices. Then we shall disclose the falseness of their specious objections in such fashion that the attentive observer [intelligent man] will have no doubt about it and the muddiness of misrepresentation will be removed from the face of the truth.

15 Then we shall close [our] book with that which is [its] heart and essence [underlying reason and core], viz. the establishment of the legal apodeictic demonstrations of the validity of the holy, prophetic, Mustaẓhirite positions on the basis of rational and juristic proofs, as its [the book's] contents were clearly stated in the account of the chapters.

CHAPTER TWO

Explanation of Their Appellations and Disclosure of the Reason Which Moved Them to Institute This Propaganda: It Contains Two Sections

Section One

16 On their appellations [designations, nicknames, agnomens] which have been current on men's tongues in different ages and times. These are ten appellations: (1) the Bāṭinites [*al-Bāṭiniyya*]; (2) The Qarāmiṭa [*al-Qarāmiṭa*]; (3) the Qarmaṭiyya [*al-Qarmaṭiyya*]; (4) the Khurramites [*al-Khurramiyya*]; (5) the Khurramdīnites [*al-Khurramdīniyya*]; (6) the Ismailis [*al-Ismāʿīliyya*]; (7) the Seveners [*al-Sabʿiyya*]; (8) the Bābakites [*al-Bābakiyya*]; (9) The Muḥammara, or, Muḥammira [*al-Muḥammara, al-Muḥammira*]; (10) the Taʿlīmites [*al-Taʿlīmiyya*]. And there is a reason for each appellation.

17 (1) al-Bāṭiniyya: They were thus named simply because of their claim that the literal texts [*ẓawāhir*, pl. of *ẓāhir:* outward, exterior] of the Qurʾān and the Traditions have inner meanings [*bawāṭin*, pl. of *bāṭin:* inward, interior] analogous, with respect to the literal meanings, to the kernel with respect to the shell, and that the literal meanings

by their forms [representations] instill in the ignorant and foolish clear forms, but in the view of the intelligent and discerning they are symbols and indications [signs] of specific [or: spiritual, reading *maᶜnawiyya*] truths [realities]. [They also claim] that he whose mind is unequal to delving deeply into hidden things and mysteries and inner meanings and depths and who is content with their literal meanings as he hastens to be deluded, is in bonds and fetters and tormented by heavy loads and burdens. By "fetters" they mean the prescriptions [p. 12] of the Law. For he who rises to the knowledge of the inner meaning is relieved of prescription and freed from its encumbrances, these are the ones meant by the Most High's saying: "and who removes [1. *yaḍaᶜu*] from them their burden and the fetters which were upon them" [7.156/157]; and often they falsify their witness against him [or: for their doctrine] by asserting that the ignorant men who deny the inner meaning are those who were meant by the Most High's saying: "And a wall shall be set up between them having a door in the interior [*bāṭinuhu*] of which is Mercy, and facing its exterior [*ẓāhiruhu*] Torment" [57.13]. Their ultimate goal is to destroy revealed Laws [religions]. For if they tear away from creeds the exigency of the literal meanings, they will be able to impose the claim of the inner meaning in accordance with what will necessitate the abandonment of the bases of religion, since confidence [trust] in the binding force of plain expressions will fall away and thus there will remain for the Law no resort and support.

18 (2) and (3) al-Qarāmiṭa and al-Qarmaṭiyya: from a man named Ḥamdān

19 Qarmaṭ [cf. EI(2)], one of their early propagandists. The story of Ḥamdān. . . .

20 (4) and (5) al-Khurramiyya and al.Khurramdīniyya [Bāsqillāni: *Tamhīd,* 190.6 has al-Khurramdāniyya]—so called from the substance and essence of their teaching which comes down to libertinism *"khurram,"* a Persian word for something pleasurable and delightful. Was also a name for the Mazdakiyya. The Khurramdīniyya differ on some nonessential points from the Khurramiyya.

21 (6) al-Bābakiyya—a group who swore allegiance to a man named Bābak al-Khurramī, who emerged in the mountains near Adharbaijān in the days of al-Muᶜtaṣim Billāh. A group of them has survived [cf. Laoust: *Les schismes dans l'Islam,* p. 95].

23 (7) al-Ismāᶜīliyya—from Muḥammad bin Ismāᶜīl bin Jaᶜfar. They claim that the stages of the Imāmate ended with him, since he was the seventh from Muḥammad, and in their view the stages of the Imāmate are seven by seven. . . .

24 (8) al-Sabᶜiyya—so called (1) because of their belief that the stages of the Imāmate are seven, and (2) because of their view that regulation of the lowest [sublunary] world belongs to the seven planets: the highest Saturn, then Jupiter, Mars, the Sun, Venus, Mercury, the Moon—a doctrine filched from the godless astronomers [*al-munajjimīn*] and turned to the teachings of the dualists about the mixture of light and darkness in these seven planets.

25 (9) al-Muḥammira—so called because they dyed their clothes red in the days of Bābak. Also said that it was because they judged their adversaries to be *ḥamīr* [donkeys]. The first explanation is more correct.

26 (10) al-Taᶜlīmiyya—so called because the basis of their doctrine is the invalidation of individual reasoning [*al-raʾy*] and the invalidation of the exercise of intellects and the call to men to instruction issuing from the infallible Imam and the affirmation that the only way to acquire knowledge(s) is instruction [teaching]. They say at the beginning of their disputation: "Truth must be known either by individual reasoning or by [authoritative] instruction; but reliance on individual reasoning is useless because of the mutual con-

tradiction of individual reasonings and the mutual opposition of the passions [*al-ahwā'*] and the disagreement of the results of the speculation of the intelligent: so recourse to [authoritative] instruction and learning [from an Imam] is obligatory. This name is the most appropriate for the Bāṭinites of this era, because their greatest reliance is on summoning to [authoritative] instruction and invalidating individual reasoning and imposing the following of the infallible Imam and putting him—with regard to the necessity of believing him and following him—on a par with the Apostle of God—God's blessings and peace be upon him!

Section Two: Explanation of the Reason Which Led Them to Institute This Propaganda and to Elaborate This Innovation

27 All the transmitters of views agreed that this propaganda was not initiated by anyone belonging to a religion or believing in a creed and supported by a prophetic mission, because its course is being gently pulled from religion as the hair is gently pulled from the dough [?]. Rather a group of the Zoroastrians and the Mazdakites and a gang [party] of the godless dualists and a large hand of the godless early [?] philosophers deliberated and actively devoted their individual reasoning to finding [devising, contriving] a measure [plan] which would relieve them from what had befallen them of the domination of men of religion and give them a respite from the distress which had come over them from the power of the Muslims. So they gagged [held] their tongues from speaking of what their belief was—viz. denying the Maker and branding the Apostle with lying [or: calling the Apostle a liar] and rejecting the Assembling and the Resurrection and the return to God at the end of the affair.

28 They alleged: "After we have come to know that all the Prophets are swindlers and cheats, because they enslave men by what they make them believe through different sorts of legerdemain and shrewd analysis [cf. Dozy under *Zaraq*—Sab^ciyya usage]—and the matter of Muḥammad has become grave and his call has spread in (all countries, quarters) and his rule has become widespread and his means and might are well organized. As a result they [Muslims] have possessed the property of our forebears and abandoned themselves to a life of luxury in their governments [administrative districts], disdaining our minds. Indeed they have covered the face of the earth in its length and its breadth. There is no hope of opposing them by a fight. The only way to make them forego what they have made up their minds about is by cunning and guile. Were we to address to them a call to our doctrine, they would rage against us and be unable to listen to us. So our way is to take over the creed of a group from their sects [a group] who are the feeblest in minds and the most fatuous in individual reasoning and the most pliable in disposition to accept absurdities and the most compliant in believing embellished lies—and these are the Rāfiḍites.

29 "We shall strengthen our position by affiliating with them and by tracing our descent to the people of the [Prophet's] house to avoid their evil [i.e. their being against us], and we shall ingratiate ourselves with them by that which suits their character, viz. the mention of the great injustice and terrible humiliation effected against their forbears. We shall pretend to weep with them over what befell the family of Muḥammad—God's blessings and peace be upon him!—and thereby we shall succeed in denigrating the leaders of their forbears who are their model and pattern. The result will he that, once we have made the circumstances of their [forbears] repulsive in their eyes, and also what their 'Law' transmits to them by the transmission and report of those [forbears] the door of recourse to the

Law will he closed [or: hard] for them and it will be easy for us to entice them into being stripped of [forfeiting, losing] religion. If there then remains among them anyone holding fast to the literal meanings of the Qur'ān and unimpeachable Traditions, we shall suggest among them that those literal texts contain secrets and inner meanings, and that the mark of the stupid man is being deceived by their literal meanings and the sign of acumen [intelligence] is believing their inner meanings. Then we shall communicate to them our beliefs, alleging that they are what is meant by the literal meanings of the Qur'ān. Then when we have duped [read: *makarnā*] these, it will he easy for us to entice the rest of the sects after joining [siding with] these [Rāfiḍites] and pretending that they support us.

30 Then they said: "Our method will be to choose such a man as will help us in our doctrine. We shall claim that he belongs to the 'People of the House' [Muḥammad's family], and that all men must swear allegiance to him and are bound to obey him, for he is the Caliph of the Apostle of God and preserved from error and slip by help from God Most High. [p. 20] Moreover we shall not make this propaganda known near to the vicinity of the Caliph whom we have characterized with infallibility, because the proximity of his abode might rip apart these veils. But if the distance be remote and far away, then when will the one who responds to the propaganda he able to investigate his condition and to get to know the reality of his real situation?"

31 Now their aim in all that was power and domination and making free with the wealth and women of the Muslims, and revenging themselves on them for what they believed about them and for what they had over taken them of pillage and bloodshed and had poured upon them of various kinds of misfortune. This, then, is their ultimate aim and the fundamental principle of their affair. The confirmation of that will become clear to you through our clear exposure of the evils of their teaching and the infamies of their creed.

CHAPTER THREE

On the Degrees of their Artifices and the Reason Why Men are Seduced by Them Despite their Patent Falsity— It Contains Two Sections

Section One: On the Degrees of their Artifices

32 They have arranged [classified] their artifices according to nine ordered degrees, and each has a name. The first is shrewd analysis [discernment] and scrutiny [detection of qualities—cf. Dozy], then (2) putting at case, (3) inducing doubt, (4) suspending, (5) binding, (6) swindling [cheating], (7) duping [making unclear, confusing], (8) stripping [denuding], (9) skinning [flaying]. Let us now explain in detail each of these degrees, for in becoming aware of these artifices there are numerous advantages for the masses of the Community.

33 (1) *Discernment and scrutiny:* This consists in their saying: "The propagandist [emissary] must be astute, intelligent [sharp-witted] correct in surmising, true in discerning, understanding the inner [qualities] by looking at the characteristics [?] and exterior [signs, qualities]. Let him be able to do three things: (a) the first and most important—to discern one regarding whom it can be hoped to entice him and one can rely on the pliability of his disposition to accept what is presented to him contrary to his belief. For many a man is inflexible about what he has heard (and) it is impossible to wrest from

his mind what is firmly rooted therein. So let not the emissary waste his speech with such a one. Let him cut off any hope regarding him and let him seek out one who is passive and is influenced by what is said to him. Such are those characterized by the qualities which we shall mention in Section Two, which follows this Section. In any case, we must be wary of scattering seed in salty soil and of entering a house in where there is a lamp [light]. By this is meant warning away from summoning the ᶜAbbāsids—may God prolong their dynasty in defiance of its enemies!—because that [propaganda] will never become implanted in their minds, just as seeds will not take root in the salty marsh, as they allege. They also warn against propagandizing the intelligent among eminent men and those who possess insight into dialectic [argument] and the ambuscades of trickery—this is what they mean by warning away from a house which contains a lamp.

34 (b) [He must also] be on fire with intuition and [be] clever minded in interpreting the literal texts and reducing them to the inner meanings, either by [linguistic] derivation from their wording, or by learning [?] from their number, or by likening them to what resembles [?] them. In general, if the responsive man will not accept from him denial of the Qurᵓān and the Sunna, he ought to draw forth from his heart its meaning, which he has understood, leaving with him the wording reduced to a meaning which is conformed to this innovation—for were he to speak directly of the denial to him, it would not be accepted from him.

35 (c) The third element of discernment and scrutiny is that he should not invite each one to one and the same way [course of action]. [p. 23] Rather he should first inquire into his belief and what he inclines to in his nature [character] and his belief. As for his character, if he sees him inclined to asceticism and mortification and piety and purification, he calls him to obedience and submission and following the command issuing from the [one to be] obeyed, and warns him away from following [his] passions, and charges him with the duties of the religious observances and the execution of the things he is entrusted with, viz. veracity [sincerity] and right behavior [conduct] and good morals and the lessening of trouble [?] for those in need and holding fast to commanding the good and forbidding the evil. But if he is naturally inclined to buffoonery and wantonness he fixes it in his mind that worship is foolishness and piety stupidity and that those afflicted by the injunctions of the Law are like asses tormented by heavy loads; but intelligence is simply in following passion [desire] and procuring pleasure and getting what one wants out of this moribund life for the delights of which there will be no way to make up once one days are ended.

36 As for the state of the one called with reference to orientation, if he be of the Shiᶜites, then we begin by telling him that the whole matter lies in hating the Banū Tamīm and the Banū ᶜAdiyy and the Banū Umayya and the Banū ᶜAbbāss and their factions and in having nothing to do with them and their followers and in being partisans of the Good Imāms and in waiting for the emergence of the Mahdī. And if the one called be a Nāsibite [dissenter violently hating ᶜAlī], he mentions to him that the Community agreed only on Abū Bakr and ᶜUmar, and precedence is to be given only to him to whom the Community gives it. Finally, when his mind tranquilly accepts it the emissary thereafter begins to communicate the mysteries [secrets] according to the way of enticement which will be mentioned later. Similarly, if the one responding be a Jew or a Zoroastrian or a Christian, the emissary will discuss with him what corresponds to [resembles] their doctrine from his own beliefs—because the creed of the emissaries is gleaned from various kinds [p. 24] of innovations and unbelief, so that there is no species of innovation but that

they have adopted some of it that thereby it might be easy for them to address these sects, as we shall relate of their doctrine.

37 As for the artifice of *putting at ease* [cultivating togetherness or intimacy], it is that he conform to [harmonize with] him who pays attention to his summons [propaganda] in actions which he undertakes with him whose mind inclines to him, and the first thing by which intimacy is effected is by observing what in his own Law [? the *dāʿī*?] accords with the belief of the one called. They prescribed for the emissaries and the licensed [*maʾdhūnīn*] to pass the night at the home of one of the responders [*mustajībīn*] and to strive to take along one who had a good voice for reciting the Qurʾān to recite for them for a time. Then the emissary should have all that followed by some tactful discourse and bits of fine sermons which captivate hearts. Then he should complement that by defaming the authorities [Sultans] and the ulema of the time and the ignorant masses and mention that relief from all that is awaited by the benediction of the People of the House of the Apostle of God—God's blessing and peace be upon him!—and during that he should weep at times and sigh deeply. And when he mentions a verse of the Qurʾān or a Tradition he should mention that God has a secret meaning in its [His] words which is made known only to him whom God has chosen from His creatures and favored with a superabundance of His bounty [*lutf*]. And if he is able to watch the night, praying and weeping, in the absence of the master of the house, so that the latter will get to know about him, and he then perceive that he has come to know about him, let him return to his lodging and lie down like one who intends to keep secret his worship—and all that so that his intimacy with him [the one called] will take deep root and [the latter's] heart will incline to hearkening to what he has to say. This, then, is the degree of *taʾnīs* [cultivating intimacy].

38 [p. 25] As for the artifice of *inducing doubt,* it means that the propagandist, after *al-taʾnīs,* must strive to change the belief of the respondent [prospect, candidate] by shaking his conviction regarding what he firmly holds. The way to achieve this is to approach him first by questioning the wisdom in the things laid down by the [revealed] laws [*al-shariʾāʿ*] and in obscure problems [questions] and about the ambiguous verses [of the Qurʾān] and about what does not immediately yield a rational sense. Thus he should say about the sense of the ambiguous [verses]: "What is the meaning of the 'R,' and of 'KHY'S,' and of 'Ḥāʾ Mīm ʿAyn Sīn Qāf' [ḤMʿSQ], and of the likes in the beginnings of the sūras [chapters of the Qurʾān]? And one should say: 'Do you think the assignment of these letters took place in accord with the outstripping [anticipation] of the tongue, or that their specification was intended because of mysteries depicted under them and not found elsewhere? I do not think that could be in jest or in vain and useless [meaningless]." And he should induce doubt regarding the legal ordinances: "Why should the menstruating woman be free from the fast, but not the prayer? [And] why is a major ritual ablution obligatory with respect to pure semen and not obligatory regarding unclean urine?"

39 And he should induce doubt regarding the reports of the Qurʾān and say: "Why are the gates of the Garden eight, and the gates of the Fire seven? And what is the meaning of God's utterance 'And upon that day eight shall carry above them the Throne of the Lord' [fi9.17]? And of His utterance—Exalted He!—'over it [*Saqar,* "Fire"] are nineteen' [74.30]? Do you suppose (think) that the rhyme (the 'r') was too confined [cramped, narrow?] and therefore the [number] twenty was not completed? Or did that take place in accord with the force of the outstripping [?] of the tongue? Or was this restriction intended to give the impression that there is a mystery beneath it, and that in itself [it] is a mystery knowable only to the Prophets and the Imams 'rooted in knowledge'? I do not think

that that is devoid of a mystery and without a secret sense: and the amazing thing is that men ignore it and do not strenuously seek it out!"

40 Then he should induce doubt about the constitution of the world and the human body and say: "Why are the heavens seven rather than six or eight? And why are the planets [p. 26] seven and the stations of the zodiac [*burūj*] twelve? And why are there seven holes in man's head—the eyes, ears, nostrils and mouth—and only two holes in his body? And why is man's head made in the shape of a *mīm,* and his hands—when he extends them—in the shape of a *ḥāʾ*, and his rump in the shape of a *mīm,* and his legs in the shape of a *dāl,* so that when the whole is combined it is shaped in the form of MḤMD (Muḥammad)? Do you therefore think that it contains a simile and a symbol? How great are these wonders! And how great is man's indifference to them!" And he should keep on presenting to him this sort of thing until he makes him doubt and he has a glimmering [a sudden flash] that beneath these literal texts [senses] there are mysteries barred to him and his fellows and there springs up in him a desire [longing] to seek that out.

41 As for the artifice of *suspending* (*al-taʿlīq*), it consists in concealing from him the aspects of these doubts if he inquires of him about them and in not reassuring him at all, but leaving him in suspense and making the matter seem terrible to him and making it seem great in his mind and saying to him: "Don't be in a rush! For religion is too serious to he toyed [played] with or to be put in the wrong place and to be revealed [disclosed] to those unworthy of [unfitted for] it—absolutely not!"

> The two of you have come to me to learn the secret of my
> happiness!
> You find me stingy [niggardly] with the secret of
> my happiness!

Then he will say to him: "Don't be in a hurry! If good fortune favors you we shall divulge to you the secret of that. Have you not heard the utterance of the Master of the Law: 'This religion is strong [solid]; so penetrate [apply yourself to] it gently, for the one cut off [from it?] has not traversed the land nor left behind a rear part [1. *ẓahr^{an}—or walā ẓahr^{an} baqiya* —nor has remained behind ?].'"

42 Thus he will not cease driving [urging] him, then resisting him, until, if he sees him turning from him and despising [p. 27] him and saying: "What have I to do with this meddling?" and the vehemence of these doubts does not leave a mark on his interior, he will give up any hope of [winning] him [over]. But if he sees him yearning [thirsty] for him he will make an appointment with him and will bid him to offer fasting and prayer and penance before it, and he will make much of this hidden mystery. Then, when the appointed time comes, he will say to him: "These mysteries are hidden; they will not be entrusted save to a fortified [pure] heart. So fortify [purify] your sanctuary and strengthen its entrances so that I may entrust this matter [mystery] to it." And the prospect will say: "And what is the way to do this?" And he will reply: "That I exact the pact and covenant of God on concealing this mystery and keeping it from being dissipated, for it is the precious pearl and the priceless treasure. The least degree of the one coveting it is to guard it from being dissipated. And God entrusted these mysteries to His prophets only after exacting their pact and covenant: and he will recite the Most High's utterance: 'And when We took the compact from the Prophets, and from thee, and from Noah, and Abraham, Moses, and Jesus, Mary's son; We took from them a solemn compact' [33.7]; and the Most High said:

'Among the believers are men who were true to their covenant with God' [33.23]; and the Most High said: 'and break not the oaths after they have been confirmed' [16.93/91].

43 The Prophet—God's blessing and peace be upon him!—divulged it only after exacting the pact of the caliphs [successors] and exacting fealty from the Helpers beneath the tree. So if you covet (it), swear to me to hide it, and thereafter you will be of the elite [or: well-off, blessed], and if you are divinely helped to grasp its reality [truth], you will be extremely happy. But if your soul recoils from it, small wonder, for every one is facilitated for that for which he was created. And we shall presume that it is as though you have neither heard nor sworn and no harm will come to you regarding a true oath." So if he refuses to swear, he should leave him; but if he is graciously disposed and complies, he should direct the oath to him and exact it fully.

44 [p. 28] As for the artifice of *binding,* it is that he bind his [the prospect's] tongue by sacred oaths and confirmed pacts which he will in no circumstance dare to break. This is the text of the pact:

"The propagandist [emissary] will say to the prospect: 'You impose on yourself the pact of God and His covenant and the compact of His Apostle—Peace upon him!—and the pact and covenant which God exacted from the Prophets, that you will keep secret what you have heard and will hear from me, and what you have learned and will learn about me and about the representative, resident in this country, of the Master of the Truth, the Rightly guided Imam, and about his brethren and his fellows and his children and the members of his household, and about those who obey him according to this religion, and the sincere following of the Rightly guided One and sincerity toward his faction, men and women, young and old; and you will not disclose of that little or much by which you would show [indicate] it [him?], except for what I permit you to speak of or [what] you are permitted by the "Master" residing in this country or in another; and then you will do just so much as we prescribe for you and not go beyond it. You have obliged yourself to carry out what I have mentioned to you and you have obligated yourself to it in the state of desire and of fear, of anger and of satisfaction, and you have bound yourself by God's pact and covenant to follow me and everyone I shall name to you and disclose to you of what you will keep yourself from, and to be very sincere to us and to the Imam, the Friend of God, outwardly and inwardly, and not to betray [be disloyal to] God or His Friend or anyone of his brothers and his friends and anyone who is related to him and to us by any reason such as kinship and property and favor; and that is our view [*raʾy*] and no promise [pact] will you accept against this pact which would render it vain.

45 [p. 29] "If, then, you do anything of that, knowing that you have contravened it, you will be quit of God and His Apostles, early and recent, and His favored Angels, and all of His Books revealed to His preceding Prophets, and you will be outside of every religion, and outside of God's party and that of His Saints, and you will be included in Satan's party and that of his friends; and may God forsake you most patently [in a way that] will quickly bring upon you vengeance and punishment if you violate anything of what I have made you swear to, with an interpretation or with no interpretation. And if you violate any of that you will owe God thirty pilgrimages, as of binding vow, on foot and unshod. And if you violate that, then all you possess at the time you go back on your words will be alms [to be given to] the poor and destitute unconnected with you by any kinship. And every slave you possess on the day you violate it will be free. And every woman you have or marry in the future will be triply and irrevocably divorced if you violate any of that. And if you intend or secretly harbor, regarding this oath of mine, the contrary of what you have

[outwardly] purposed, this oath, from its first to its last, will be binding on you. God is the witness of the sincerity of your intention and the bond [contract, document] of your conscience [innermost mind]—and He is the best of witnesses between me and you!—Say 'Yes'!' and he will say: 'Yes!'" This is [the artifice of] *binding.*

46 As for the artifice of *swindling* [cheating, falsifying], it is that after the oath and the confirmation of the pact it is not allowed to divulge [p. 30] the mysteries [secrets] to him all at once, but that is done gradually and with regard for several things. *The first* is that at the beginning one confine oneself to mentioning the [prime] fundament of the doctrine and say: "The lighthouse of ignorance is men's making judges of their defective minds and their clashing views and their turning away from 'following' [compliance] and receiving [taking, learning] from God's best friends and His Imams and the tent pegs [poles, sustainers] of His earth and those who are the Vicegerents of His Apostles after him. Among them are those to whom God has consigned His hidden mystery and His secret religion. He has revealed to them the inner meanings of these literal expressions and the secrets of these allegories. Right guidance and salvation from error are by returning [resorting] to the Qur'ān and the People of [the Prophet's] household. That is why he said—Peace be upon him!—when someone asked: "Whence will the truth be known after you?" he replied: "Have I not left among you the Qur'ān and my family [kin]?" By this he means his progeny—and it is they who are familiar with [aware of] the meaning of the Qur'ān. He will confine himself at first to this much and will not clearly state the detail of what the Imam says.

47 *The second* is that he use artful means [stratagems] to nullify the second way of the ways of attaining the truth, viz. the literal meanings of the Qur'ān. For the seeker of truth either takes refuge in thought and reflection and consideration of the sources of the intelligible [?] as God Most Praiseworthy has commanded: and the reflection of the mind is spoiled for him by the imposition of the obligation of learning and following; or he takes refuge in the literal meanings of the Qur'ān and the Sunna. If one were to state openly to him that it is deception and a contrived thing, he would not be listened to. So let him concede to him the formal expression, but let him snatch from his mind its meaning by saying: "This literal text has an interior [meaning] which is the quintessence [core, pith], and the exterior is a skin in relation to it which contents the man beset by inability to grasp the real meanings [of things]"—so that there will remain for him no intellectual support or traditional help.

48 *The third* is that he give no personal indication that he is opposed to the whole Community and that he has cast off the Religion and the Creed, for hearts would shun him. Rather he should ascribe himself to the sect farthest from the right way and readiest to accept fables. He should hide behind them and adorn himself with affection for the people of the [Prophet's] family, i.e. the Rawāfiḍ [cf. Laoust, p. 35].

49 [p. 31] *The fourth* is that he place at the head of what he says that the false is evident and clear, but the truth is so subtle that, were most men to hear it, they would reject it and shun it; and that the seekers of truth and those who profess it are, among the seekers of ignorance, single persons and individuals, so that he will make it easy for him to be distinguished from the masses regarding the denial of intellectual speculation and the literal traditional texts.

50 *The fifth* is that, if he sees him shunning being singular among the masses, he says to him: "I shall divulge to you a secret, and you must keep it." And if he says "Yes!" he will say: "Such a one and such a one believe in this doctrine, but they keep it a secret"—and he will mention some distinguished person who is believed by the prospect to possess

acumen and astuteness. But let the one mentioned be far from his country so that it will not be easy for the prospect to have recourse to him—just as they make their propaganda far from the abode and country of their Imam. For if they were to manifest it in his vicinity they would be exposed by the impeccable report of his views and his circumstances.

51 *The sixth* is that he awaken his desire [raise his hopes] for [by?] the appearance of the power of this sect and the spread of their affair and the loftiness of their view and the victory of its supporters over their enemies and the vastness of their wealth and [the fact that] every one of them attains his desire so that there will be combined for them the happiness of this life and the afterlife; and let some of that be attributed to [p. 32] the stars, and some of it to the [true] vision in sleep—if he can make up some dreams that will reach the prospect on the tongue of another.

52 *The seventh* is that the emissary prolong not his stay in one and the same country, for his affair might become known and his blood shed. So he must be careful about that, and deceive people about himself and make himself known to each group of people by a different name [lit. by one name and another]. At times, let him change his appearance and dress for fear of hurt so that that may be a more effective means of precaution.

Then, after these premises, gradually and little by little he will make known the detail of the doctrine to the prospect and mention it to him according to what we shall report of his belief.

53 As for the artifice of *duping* [confusing, making unclear] it is that he agree with the prospect on premises which he will accept from him, outwardly acceptable and well known and widespread among men, and he will implant that in his mind for a time. Then he will lure him from them by false consequences, e.g. his saying: "Those engaged in speculation hold contrary views, though the circumstances [read *wa l-aḥwāl*] are the same—and 'each faction is happy about its own beliefs'" [23.55/53; 30.31/32]. The one perfectly cognizant of the substance [essence] is God. And it cannot be that God hides the truth, and there is no one—[gap of two words]—all the matter to men: they fumble about it like a nyctalopic she-camel and plunge into it in blind ignorance [folly]—and other such premises—[gap containing four or five words] [deemed] baffling [puzzling].

54 As for the artifice of *stripping* [denuding] and [that of] *skinning* [flaying], they are in accord and differ only in that *denuding* has to do with action—so if they lead the prospect to give up the precepts and ordinances of the Law, they say: I have reached the degree of denuding. As for *skinning,* it has to do with belief—which is the denuding [stripping off] of religion. So if they pluck that from his heart they call that *skinning* [flaying]. And this rank [stage] is called "the ne plus ultra" [the ultimate attainment]. This, then, is the detailing of their step by step ensnaring of men: so let the observer consider it and let him ask God's forgiveness for erring about His Religion.

[p. 33] *Section Two:*

Explanation of the Reason for the Ready Circulation [Marketability] of Their Trickery and the Spread of Their Propaganda [Call] Despite the Weakness of Their Argument [Proof] and the Wickedness of their Creed

55 Someone may say: "It is inconceivable that the enormities you have disclosed be hidden from an intelligent man. But we have indeed seen many men and a large number of people who follow them in their belief and have followed them in their religion. So

perhaps you have wronged them by transmitting these opinions from them contrary to what they [really] believe! And this is likely and possible. For if they had divulged these secrets hearts would have eschewed them and minds would have known their cunning [trickery]. <But they divulge them> only after pacts and covenants and they guard them save from one agreeing with them in belief—so whence has it happened to you to become cognizant of them, since they hide their religion and strive to keep their beliefs secret?"

56 I reply: As for becoming cognizant of that, we came across it simply through many men who had professed their religion and responded to their propaganda, then they became aware of their error and returned from their seduction to the plain truth and [then] reported the views those men had proposed to them. As for the cause of men's submission to them in some countries of the earth, they divulge this matter only to some of those who answer their call, and they advise the propagandist and say to him: "Beware of following the same way with all: for not everyone who can accept these doctrines can put up with 'stripping' and 'skinning,' nor can everyone who can stand 'stripping' stand 'skinning'; so let the propagandist speak to men in accordance with the capacity of their minds." This, then, is the reason for the attachment and [ready] circulation of these artifices.

57 *If it be said:* "This also, despite the secrecy [concealment], is patently false: how, then, could an intelligent man be deceived by the likes of this?"

We say: The only ones deceived by it are those who deviate from a state of equilibrium and soundness of opinion. And for the intelligent there are impediments which make them blind to the ways to what is right and condemn them to being deceived by the shimmering of the mirage—and they are eight classes [kinds]:

58 *The first class* is a group of men with weak minds [p. 34] and little insight [intelligence] and with silly ideas about religious matters because of their ingrained stupidity and silliness—like the masses and the rude Arabs and the Kurds and the uncouth foreigners [Persians?] and silly youngsters—and perhaps this class is the largest in number. And how can their acceptance of that be considered farfetched when we see a group in one of the towns near Basra who worship men, claiming that they have inherited divinity from their fathers, who are known as the Shabāsiyya. And a group believed about ʿAlī—God be pleased with him!—that he is the God of the heavens and the earth, the Lord of the Worlds; and they are numerous men unrestricted by a number and uncontained by a country. So wonder at man's ignorance ought not to increase when Satan gets mastery over him and abandonment [by God] overwhelms him.

59 *The second class* is a group of men whose forebears' power [dynasty, empire, rule] was cut off by the power [rule] of Islam—like the descendants [scions, sons] of the Khosraws [Persian kings] and the [Persian] grandees and the children of the arrogant Zoroastrians. These are wronged persons [wronged by the murder of a relative but still denied blood vengeance] in whose hearts rancor is hidden like a secret malady: then, when the suggestions of the liars stimulate it, its fires flare up in their hearts and they submit to the acceptance of every absurdity out of a longing to attain their vengeance and to redress their affairs.

60 *The third class* is a group of men who have ambitions directed toward the exalted [heights] and are bent on mastery [influence, authority] and domination. However, the time does not help them, but rather misfortunes [the current calamities] make them lag behind their contemporaries [comrades] and peers. So when these are promised the attainment of their aspirations [desires, longings] and are enticed by victory over enemies, they hurry to accept what they think will lead to their aims and be a path [way] to their desires

and demands. And how often it has been said: "Your love for a thing blinds and deafens." And there shares in this everyone whom a master from the class of Islam overcomes, and he can find a way to triumph [p. 35] and taking vengeance only by seeking the help [backing] of these gullible dolts, so he has many motives for accepting that in which he sees his desire.

61 *The fourth class* is a group of men with a natural propensity for love of being distinguished from the masses and of being marked off from them because they deem themselves above resemblance to them and claim the honor of siding with a special class which claims that it possesses the cognizance of realities [truths], and that the people in their ignorance are like frightened asses and wandering [forlorn] beasts. This is the chronic disease which overcomes the intelligent, to say nothing of the ignorant [and] stupid. And that is a love for the rare [and] the unusual and an aversion for the common and the ordinary. This is a natural trait of some men, as is witnessed to by experience and indicated by observation.

62 *The fifth class* is a group of men who have followed the ways [methods] of reasoning, but they have not fully attained the degree of independence [competence] [in their reasoning], although they have indeed risen above the rank of the ignorant. So they are always craving [longing for] [a show of] indolence and indifference and the manifestation of intelligence to attain things which the masses imagine to be remote and shun, especially if the thing be ascribed to someone renowned for superiority, so that the longing to be like him takes possession of [their] nature. How many groups of men have I seen believe in pure unbelief [in downright infidelity] out of servile conformism to Plato and Aristotle and a group of philosophers who had become noted for superiority! Their motive for that servile conformism was the desire to be like the philosophers and to side with [be numbered among] their crowd [*ghumārihim*] and against whoever is believed to be inferior to them in intelligence and excellence. So they are drawn [*yustajarrūna*] to this innovation by attributing it to someone of whom the respondent has a good opinion and so [then] he rushes to accept it, seeking to be like him who is reported to be one of its followers.

63 [p. 36] *The sixth class* is a group of men who happened to grow up among the Shīᶜites and the Rawāfiḍ [Rāfiḍites] and who believed in the profession [of their creed] because of association. They saw this sect helping them to that [?], and so their minds inclined to help them and to be friendly with them, and they were drawn with them [the Bāṭinites] to what was beyond that, viz. the special features of their doctrine.

64 *The seventh class* is a group of the godless philosophers and dualists and those baffled about religion who believe that revealed Laws are compiled laws [rules, codes], and that apologetic miracles are elaborate tricks. So when they see these [Bāṭinites] honoring those affiliated with themselves and pouring out the treasures of [their] wealth upon them, they stand ready to aid them, seeking the vanities of the world and disdaining the outcome of the matter. This group of men are those who have contrived [fabricated] for them [Bāṭinites] specious arguments and adorned for them, by way of misrepresentation, proofs, and arranged them, with respect to the exterior, according to the requisites of dialectic and the prescriptions of logic, and covered [concealed] the hidden places of deception and deceit in them beneath compendious words and general and vague expressions, of which the weak reasoner is rarely rightly guided to untying their intricacy and removing the veil from the hidden place of their deceit, as we shall present their fabrication [falsification] and call attention to the way and path [method] they have followed and pursued and reveal its viciousness [wrongness] from a number of aspects.

65 *The eighth class* is a group of men who have been mastered by passions and lured by the pursuit of pleasure and for whom the threats of the Law have become unbearable and its injunctions burdensome; so their life is not happy, since they are loathed because of [their] sinfulness and depravity and are threatened by a bad end in the abode of the afterlife. So when they encounter one who opens the door to them and removes from them restraint and barrier and depicts to them as desirable [good] what they themselves deem good by [their] nature, they rush to believe passionately and spontaneously—and every man gives credence to what accords with his inclination [passion, craving, caprice, pleasure] and suits his purpose and desires. These, and those who follow the same course, are they who are deprived of [divine] assistance [guidance] and are deceived by these tricks and swerve from the straight path and the borders [limits] of verification [i.e. of what is true].

[p. 57]

CHAPTER FOUR

On the Report of their Doctrine, Summarily and in Detail

66 As for the summary, it is that it is a doctrine, the exterior of which is *rafḍ* [rejection, i.e. of first three Caliphs], and its interior out-and-out infidelity [unbelief]; and its beginning is the restricting of the ways to attain knowledge [sure cognitions] to the utterance of the Infallible Imam, and the removal [isolating] of minds [intellects] from being [able to] perceive [grasp] the truth because of the doubts which befall them and the disagreements to which reasoners are open, and imposing, for the seeking of the truth, the way of instruction and learning, and the judgment that the Infallible Imam is *the* seer [the only one able to see], and that he is informed—from the part of God—of all the secrets of the revealed Laws: he guides to the truth and explains problems [difficulties], and that every age must have an Infallible Imam to whom recourse is to be had concerning any ambiguities in religious matters.

67 This is the beginning [basis, starting point] of their propaganda. Then, in the end they present [produce] what contradicts the Law. And it is as though this is their ultimate aim. For the manner of their propaganda is not fixed in one way, but rather they address each group with that which accords with its opinion, after they have obtained from them submission to themselves and friendship for their Imam: thus they agree with Jews and Christians and Zoroastrians on the sum of their beliefs and they confirm [*?*] them in them [their beliefs]. This, then, is the sum of their doctrine.

68 As for its detail, it is concerned with matters pertaining to God, and prophetic missions, and the Imamate, and the Gathering and the Resurrection [eschatology]: and these are four areas. And I shall limit myself, in each area, to a small part of the account of [p. 38] their doctrine, for the report from them differs [disagrees]. Most of what is related from them, when it is presented to them, they disown, and when those who have answered their summons are consulted about it, they deny it. And what we have premised about the sum of their doctrine undoubtedly requires that the report from them be different and disordered, since they do not address men in one and the same way, but rather their aim is to seduce and to dupe: therefore their words disagree and the transmission of the doctrine from them differs. For they bring forth what is related from them about "stripping" and "skinning" only with him who has reached the ultimate stage: nay, but they may speak of "stripping" to one with whom they would deny "skinning." Let us then return to the exposé of the areas of [their] doctrine.

69 [*The First Area*] On their belief about matters pertaining to God. The statements of the transmitters of views [*maqālāt*] are unhesitatingly agreed that they profess two preeternal Gods, whose existence had no beginning with respect to time: however, one of them is the cause of the existence of the other. The name of the cause is *al-sābiq* [The Preceder], and the name of the caused is *al-tālī* [the Follower]. [They hold] that the Preceder created the world by the intermediary of the Follower, not by Himself. The first may also be called *ʿaql* [Intellect], and the second *nafs* [Soul]. And they claim that the first is the perfect in act, and the second, in comparison with Him is imperfect, since He is His effect. And they sometimes confuse the masses by concluding to that from certain verses of the Qurʾān, like the Most High's saying: "Surely We have sent down" [15.9 and 76.23] and "We have divided" [43.31/32]. They claim that these [i.e. verses] are an allusion to a plural [*jamʿ*—combination] which does not proceed from one: and therefore He said: "Glorify the Name of Thy Lord the Most High" [87.1], alluding to the Preceder of the two Gods, for He is the Most High—and were it not that there is with Him another God Who also possesses "highness," it would not be correct to apply the expression "the Most High." And sometimes [p. 39] they say: The Law calls the two of them by the name *al-Qalam* [the Pen] and *al-Lawḥ* [the Tablet]. The first is the Pen, for the pen benefits and influences and the tablet derives benefit and is influenced—and what benefits is superior to what derives benefit. And sometimes they say: the name *"al-tālī"* is *"qadar"* [divine foreordaining] in the language of revelation, and it is this by which God created the world, where He said: "Surely We have created everything in measure [Blachère: selon on decret]" [54.49] [Pickthall: by measure; Rodwell: after a fixed decree; Dawood: according to a fixed decree; Yusuf Ali: in proportion and measure; M. Zafrulla Khan: in due measure].

70 Then they say: *al-Sābiq* is described [qualified] neither by existence, nor by nonexistence, because nonexistence is a negation and existence is its cause: so He is neither existent nor nonexistent; nor is He known [knowable] nor unknown [unknowable]; nor is he qualified nor unqualified. They claim that all the Names are to be denied of Him—and it seems that, in general, they have in mind denying the Maker. For if they were to affirm that He is nonexistent, it would not be accepted from them. Rather, they prevent people from calling Him existent—and this is the very same denial with a change of expression; but they are clever and call this denial deanthropomorphism, and they call its contrary anthropomorphism, so that minds may incline to accepting it. Then they say: The world is preeternal, i.e., its existence is not preceded by a temporal nonexistence, but rather it had its inception from *al-Sābiq-al-Tālī*—and He is a first producer. And from the first producer the universal soul had its inception whose particulars are diffused [spread] in these composite bodies. From the motion of the soul hotness was engendered, and from its quiescence coldness; then wetness and dryness were engendered from both of them. Then, from these qualities were engendered the four elements, viz. fire and air and water and earth. Then, when they were mingled in an imperfect equilibrium the minerals were engendered from them. Then, when their proximity to equilibrium increased and the activity of mutual contrariness destroyed from them, plants were engendered from them; and when it increased, animals were engendered; and when it increased in proximity, man was engendered—and he is the ultimate in equilibrium.

71 [p. 40] This, then, is what is related of their doctrine, along with other matters more monstrous than what we have mentioned. We did not think it well to blacken the white [paper] by transmitting them or by explaining how to refute them, for two reasons. One of them is that those deceived by their deceit and falsehood and those dangling by the rope of

their deception in this age of ours have not heard this from them, [and] so they would deny all that if it were reported of their doctrine and they would say in themselves that these [adversaries] are opposed simply because they do not possess the true nature of our doctrine: and were they to know it, they would concur with me about it. So we think it best to busy ourselves with refuting them in what they agree on—viz. invalidating reasoning and summoning to learning from the Infallible Imam. For this is the main point of their belief and the essence [fresh butter] of their churning—so let us turn our attention to it. What is beyond that is divided into patently false drivel and unbelief filched from the dualists and Zoroastrians about the profession of the two gods, with the change of the expression "the Light and the Darkness" into *"al-Sābiq* and *al-Tālī,"* and error taken from the discourse of the Philosopher, in their saying that the First Principle is a cause of the existence of the Intellect [Intelligence] by way of necessary following from it, not by way of purpose and choice, and that it comes to be of itself, without any intermediary distinct from it. Yes indeed! They affirm preeternal existents, necessarily following one from another, and they call them "intellects" [" intelligences"]. And they assign the existence of each sphere to an intellect of those intellects—in a long mishmash of theirs. We have already gone deeply into the way to refute them on that in the discipline [science] of *kalām,* and in this book we are devoting ourselves only to what is peculiar to this sect, viz. the invalidation of *raʾy* [reasoning] and the affirmation of *taʿlīm* [authoritative teaching].

72 [*The Second Area*] On the Explanation of their belief about matters concerning the Prophetic Missions.

What has been transmitted from them is close to the doctrine of the Philosophers, viz. that "the Prophet" is an expression for an individual [a person] upon whom there emanates from the *Sābiq,* by means of the *Tālī,* a pure, holy power disposed [prepared], when united to the Universal Soul, to have impressed in it what the latter contains of particulars, just as that may happen to certain pure souls [p. 41] in sleep so that they see one of the courses of events [*?*] in the future, either clearly and as it is, or embodied in an example [image] which bears some resemblance to it, so that there is a need regarding it for an interpretation. However, the Prophet is he who is disposed for that while awake. Therefore, the Prophet perceives [the] intellectual universals at the shining of that light and the clarity of the prophetic power, just as the likeness of the sensibles is imprinted in the eye's visual power at the shining of the sun's light on the surfaces of the sublunary bodies [or: polished bodies].

73 They also pretend that "Jibrīl" is a designation of the Intellect emanating upon him [Prophet] and a symbol of it, and not that he is a materialized individual composed of a body, subtle or dense, compatible with a locus so that he can move from high to low. As for the Qurʾān, in their view it is Muḥammad's interpretation [expression] of the cognitions [information, lore] which emanated upon him from the Intellect, which is what is meant by the name "Jibrīl." It is called "the speech of God Most High" figuratively, for its ordering [arrangement] is from Him. But what emanates upon him [the Prophet] from God through the intermediary of Jibrīl is simple, without any composition in it; it is also interior, without having any exterior [external manifestation]. But the speech of the Prophet and his interpretation of it is external without possessing any "interiorness." They also pretend that this holy power emanating on the Prophet is not perfected at the beginning of its descent, just as the sperm descending into the womb is not perfected save after nine months. So it is with this power: its perfection lies in its being transferred [conveyed] from the speaking Prophet to the silent *asās* [foundation]. And thus it is transferred to [p. 42] individuals one after another, and becomes perfect in the seventh—as we shall relate the meaning of their doctrine about *al-nāṭiq* and *al-asās* and *al-ṣāmit.*

74 These doctrines are also extracted [drawn] from the doctrines of the Philosophers on Prophetic Missions, with some alteration and change. But we shall not plunge into the refuting of them concerning it. For some of it can he interpreted in a way we do not reject, and the amount which we reject we have already gone deeply into the way to refute the Philosophers regarding it. In this book we aim only at the refutation of what is currently prominent regarding the doctrine of theirs which is unique to them as opposed to others, viz. the enjoining of *taᶜlīm* and the invalidation of *raʾy* [personal reasoning].

75 [*The Third Area*]*:* Exposé of their belief about the Imamate.

They are indeed agreed that there must be, in every age, an Infallible Imam, practicing in charge of the truth, to whom recourse is to be had regarding the interpretation of the literal meanings and the solution of difficulties in the Qurʾān and the Traditions and rational matters [intelligibles, objects of thought or reasoning]. They are [also] agreed that he is the one who undertakes this matter, and that that goes on among their lineage uninterruptedly and forever, and it cannot be interrupted, because in that would be the neglect [dereliction] of the Truth, and the concealment of it from men, and the falsifying of the Prophet's statement—Peace be upon him!—"Every relationship and lineage will be interrupted [cut off] except my relationship and my lineage," and his utterance "Have I not left among you the Qurʾān and my family [relations]?" And they are agreed that the Imam equals the Prophet in infallibility-impeccability and in knowledge of the realities of the truth in all matters, except that revelation [*al-waḥy*] is not sent down to him, but he simply receives that from the Prophet, for he is his vicar [deputy, successor] and of comparable status. And it is inconceivable that there be two Imams in one and the same age, just as it is inconceivable that there be two Prophets with different [religious] Laws.

76 To be sure the Imam seeks help from *al-ḥujaj* and *al-maʾdhūnūn* and *al-ajniḥa* [proofs—authorized—wings]. The *ḥujaj* [Proofs] are the summoners [propagandists]. They affirmed that the Imam in every period must have twelve "Proofs" who are assigned among countries and scattered among cities. And four of the total of twelve must be constantly in his presence and not leave him. And each "Proof" must have his helpers in his business, for he is not of himself the sole possessor of the summons [call, propaganda]. And among them the name of the helper is *"al-maʾāhūn"* ["authorized"?]. And the propagandists must have messengers to the Imam who will carry the circumstances to him and proceed from him to them. And the name of the messenger is "the wing" (*al-janāḥ*). [p. 43] And the propagandist must be extensive in knowledge. The *maʾdhūn*, though he be inferior to the former, yet there is no objection to his being learned in general, and so also the *janāḥ*.

77 Then they asserted that each Prophet's Law has a certain duration [limited period]. So when one's period is finished God sends another Prophet to abrogate his Law. The period of the Law of each Prophet is seven lifetimes, i.e. seven generations. The first of them is the "speaking Prophet," and the meaning of "the speaking" is that his Law abrogates what preceded it. The meaning of "silent" [*al-ṣāmit*] is that he keep [preserve, look after] what was established [founded] by another. Then there arise, after his death, six Imams: Imam after Imam. Then when their lifetimes are terminated God sends another Prophet to abrogate the preceding Law. And they claim that the affair of Adam proceeded according to this pattern, and he was the first Prophet sent by God at the opening of the door [category, field] of bodily things and the termination of the stage [phase, period] of spiritual things.

78 And every Prophet has a *sūs* [? spokesman, mouthpiece, representative lit.: root]. The *sūs* is the door to the Prophet's knowledge during the latter's lifetime and the executor

[curator, authorized agent, trustee] after his death, and the Imam for his contemporaries, as the Prophet—Peace be upon him!—said: "I am the City of Knowledge and ᶜAlī is its Gate." They allege that Adam's *sūs* was Seth, and he was the second, and [each one] after him is called "Finisher" [*mutimm*] and "Appended" [*lāḥiq:* attached, subsequent] and "Imam." The completion of the period of Adam was seven, because the completion of the turn [rotation] of the Upper World is by seven of the stars. And when Adam's stage was finished, God sent Noah to abrogate his Law, and Noah's *sūs* was Sām [Shem]. And when his stage was finished by the passing of six others and seven including him, God sent Abraham to abrogate his Law, and his *sūs* was Isaac; and among them are those who say: No, but rather Ishmael.

79 And when his [Isaac's] stage was finished by the seventh, including him, God sent Moses to abrogate his Law, and his *sūs* was Aaron: and Aaron died in Moses' lifetime, then Joshua son of Nūn became his *sūs*. And when his stage was finished [p. 44] by the seventh, including him, God sent Jesus to abrogate his Law, and his *sūs* [was] Simon. And when his stage was finished by the seventh God sent Muḥammad—God bless him!—and his *sūs* [was] ᶜAlī—Peace be upon him! And his stage finished with Jaᶜfar son of Muḥammad. For the second of the Imams was al-Ḥasan son of ᶜAlī, and the third al-Ḥusain son of ᶜAlī, and the fourth ᶜAlī son of al-Ḥusain, and the fifth Muḥammad son of ᶜAlī, and the sixth Jaᶜfar son of Muḥammad—Peace be upon him!—and were finished seven including him [Muḥammad] and his Law became abrogative [*nāsikha*]. And thus the matter goes on perpetually.

This is what has been transmitted from them, along with a lot of nonsense which we have left out to spare the white [papers] from being blackened by it.

80 [*The Fourth Area:*] Exposé of their Doctrine on the Resurrection and the Return [to God].

They have agreed completely on the denial of the Resurrection [of the body], and that this order [situation, regularity] seen in this world, viz. the succession of night and day, and man's coming to be from sperm and sperm from man, and the generation of plants, and the generation of animals, will never, never finish; and that the nonexistence of the bodies of the heavens and the earth is inconceivable. They interpreted the Resurrection and declared: it is a symbol of the emergence of the Imam and the rising of the Head of the Age [Master of the Time] i.e. the seventh who abrogates the Law and changes the ordinance. Sometimes some of them say: The celestial sphere has universal rotations, [and] the circumstances of the world change completely by reason of a universal flood or some cause. So the meaning of the Resurrection is the finishing of our stage in which we are.

81 As for the Hereafter [afterlife, Return], they deny what the Prophets have brought, and affirm neither the gathering and resurrection for [of] bodies nor the Garden and the Fire. Rather they say: the meaning of the Hereafter is the return of everything to its origin [principle]. Man is composed of [something from] the spiritual and the corporeal world. And the corporeal part of him, i.e. his body, is composed of the four humors: the yellow bile, the black bile, the phlegm and the blood. Then the body is resolved [disintegrates] and each humor returns to the higher [high] nature [element]: [p. 45] the yellow bile becomes fire, the black bile earth, and the blood air, and the phlegm water—and that is the *maᶜād* [hereafter] of the body.

82 As for the spiritual [part], i.e. the perceptive rational soul of man, if it be purified by the assiduous performance of the acts of worship, and cleansed [rendered sinless] by the shunning of caprice and the passions [appetites], and nourished with the food of learn-

ing and lore received from the Imam-Guides, when it leaves the body it is united to the spiritual world from which it was separated [detached], and it is made happy by the return to its original homeland. Therefore it is called "a return," and it has been said: "(O soul at peace), return unto thy Lord, well-pleased, well-pleasing!" [89.27–28]—and this is the Garden. The symbol of it occurred in the story of Adam and his being in the Garden, then his separation from it and his descent to the lower [base] world, then his return to it in the end.

83 They also claim that the perfection of the soul is realized by its death, because thereby it is freed from the straitness [confinement] of the body and of the corporeal world—just as the perfection of the sperm is in freedom from the darknesses of the womb and emergence into the space of the world. Man is like the sperm, and the world is like the womb, and knowledge is like nourishment, and when the latter is effective [operative] in him it [soul] truly becomes perfect and is freed [delivered]. So when the soul is disposed for the emanation [outpouring] of spiritual cognitions [lore], by the acquisition of cognitions from the Imams and following their [the cognitions'] ways, profitable by their [Imams'] guidance, it is perfected when it leaves the body and there appears to it what had not appeared.

84 Therefore the Prophet—Peace be upon him!—said: "Men are asleep: then, when they die, they awake." And the more remote the soul becomes from the world of sensible things, the more disposed it is for spiritual cognitions [lore]. Similarly, when the senses are still [suspended?] in sleep, the soul becomes aware of the invisible world and becomes conscious of what will appear in the future, either as it is, and then it needs no interpreter, or by a likeness [example], and then there is need of interpretation. So sleep is the brother of death, and in it becomes evident the knowledge of what did not exist in wakefulness: and thus, by death, things are revealed which did not occur to a man's mind in [his] lifetime. This [will be] for the souls hallowed by practical and theoretical askesis.

85 But the inverted [upside-down, topsy-turvy] souls which were immersed in the natural world [p. 46] and turned away from their right guidance [received] from the Infallible Imams will remain forever and ever in the Fire in the sense that they will remain in the material world, transmigrating [into] bodies in which they will ceaselessly be subjected [exposed] to pain and sickness, and will not leave one body but that another will receive them. Therefore the Most High said: "as often as their skins are wholly burned, We shall give them in exchange other skins, that they may taste the chastisement" [4.59/56]. This, then, is their doctrine of the Philosophers.

86 And it spread among them simply when a group of the Dualists and the Philosophers devoted themselves to the support of their doctine. And each one supported their doctrine out of greed [covetousness] for their possessions and their robes of honor and to seek the backing of their followers for what he had become familiar with in his own doctrine. So most of their doctrine came to agree with the Dualists and the Philosophers interiorly, and with the Rāfiḍites and Shiʿites exteriorly. Their aim, by these interpretations was to wrest exterior [literal] beliefs from the souls of men that desire and fear might thereby come to naught [be abolished, become void]. Furthermore, their deceptive drivel is not understandable in itself, nor does it effect any awakening of desire or any incitement to fear. We shall indicate a concise discussion on refuting them in this field, and information about it at the end of the chapter.

87 [*The Fifth Area*]: On their belief concerning legal prescriptions [injunctions].

What is transmitted from them is absolute licentiousness [libertinism, license], and the lifting of the barrier, and the deeming forbidden things lawful and licit, and the rejection of the [religious] Laws. However, they will all of them deny that when it is ascribed to them. What is authentic of their belief about it is simply that they say: There must be obedience [submission] to the Law regarding its ordinances [injunctions] according to the detail set forth by the Imam, without following al-Shāfiᶜī and Abū Ḥanīfa and others. That is incumbent on men and those who respond [to the propaganda] until they obtain the rank of perfection in the sciences. Then, when they comprehend through the Imam the real natures [realities] of things and become aware [informed] [p. 47] of the "interiors" [inner meanings] of these "exteriors" [literal texts] these fetters are loosed from them and the action-oriented injunctions fall away from them. For the aim of the acts of the members is to alert the mind that it may undertake the quest for knowledge. So when one has obtained it, he is ready for the maximum happiness, and the enjoining of the members drops from him. Indeed, the enjoining of the members is with respect to him who, by his ignorance, is analogous to asses which can be trained only by hard labors.

88 But the intelligent and those who perceive [grasp] realities are higher in rank than that. This is a kind of seduction [enticement] very effective with the intelligent. Their purpose is to destroy the precepts of the Law. But they try to deceive each weak man by a way [method] which allures him and suits him. This is a weak [inane] kind of leading astray, and it is equivalent to giving an example: like one's saying that abstaining from harmful foods is obligatory only on one whose temperament [mixture of humors, physical constitution] is impaired: but let him who has acquired a well-balanced complexion [constitution] persist in eating what he wants when he wants. For the man who hears this error will lose no time in overindulging in harmful comestibles until they vie in bringing about his ruin!

89 *Someone may say:* You have reported their doctrines, but you have not mentioned how to refute them: what is the reason for this?

We say: What we have reported from them is divided into matters which can be explained in a way we do not reject and into what the Law enjoins is to be rejected. And what is to be rejected is the doctrine of the Dualists and the Philosophers. Refuting them on that would be a lengthy affair. But that is not one of the things peculiar to their doctrine so that we should busy ourselves with it. But we shall refute them simply regarding what is peculiar to their doctrine, viz. the invalidation of reasoning [*raʾy*], and the affirmation of *taᶜlīm* [instruction] by the Infallible Imam. However, along with that, we shall mention one way which is really a mortal blow [to them], we mean regarding the refutation of their doctrine on all that we shall report, and have reported, from them.

90 This is that, regarding all their claims by which they are distinguished from us—such as the denial of the Resurrection, and the preeternity of the world, and the denial of the resurrection of bodies [p. 48] and the denial of the Garden and the Fire according to what the Qurʾān has indicated [regarding those beliefs] with the fullest explanation in deseription of them, we say to them: Whence do you know what you have mentioned? From necessity? Or from reasoning? Or from transmission from the Infallible Imam and aurally [by hearing]? If you have learned it by necessity [necessarily], then how is it that men with sound minds have contradicted you on it? For the meaning of a thing's being necessary and in no need of reflection is that all intelligent men share in perceiving [grasping] it. And if it were allowable for a man to talk wildly about the claim of necessity regarding anything he fancied, then it would be allowable for their adversaries to claim necessity regarding the contrary of what they claimed. And at that [point] they find no escape in any way at all!

91 And if they allege: We have known that by reasoning, this is false from two standpoints. *One* of *them.* is that, in their view, reasoning is invalid, for it is making use of the mind, not of *taᶜlīm* [being guided in behavior by reason, not by *taᶜlīm*]. But the propositions [?] of [men's] intellects are mutually contradictory and untrustworthy. Therefore, they [reject *raʾy* completely] regard *raʾy* as completely futile. [and (but) we have not composed this work with a view to refuting this doctrine, so how can that be possible on their part?!]—[Badawi thinks these words, in the brackets, are to be omitted]. *The second* is to say to the Philosophers and those who acknowledge the ways of reasoning: How did you learn the Maker's inability to create the Garden and the Fire and to raise bodies as has come down in the Law? Have you anything but a pure thinking [it] unlikely [farfetched] which, if its like were presentetl to one who had not seen the first creation, he would have thought it unlikely [farfetched] and that denial would have occurred to him? So the refutation of them is by the argument hidden beneath the saying of God Most High: "Say: He shall quicken them, who originated them the first time" [36.79]. One who reflects on the wonders of workmanship [design] in the creation of a man from a dirty drop [unclean sperm] will not think anything remote from the power of God and will know that the bringing back [restoration] is easier than the beginning [cf. 36.79].

92 [p. 49] *If one says:* The bringing back is unintelligible, but the beginning is intelligible, since, once a thing has ceased to exist, how can it return? *We say:* Let us understand "the beginning" so that we may build on it the bringing back. The view of the *mutakallimūn* regarding it is that the beginning is by the creation of life in a body—although life is an accident which is renewed hour after hour by the creation of God Most High. So it is not impossible, according to their principle, for [God] to refrain from the creation of life in the body for a period, then to return to creating the life, just as it is not impossible [for Him] to create motion after quiescence and black after white. And the view of the Philosophers is that the foundation [basis] of life is the disposition [readiness] of a particular body—by a kind of equilibrium—to be acted upon by the soul, which is a substance subsisting in itself, not occupying a space [locus], and not embodied, and not imprinted in a body, and with no relation between it [masc. refers to *jawhar*] and the body save by acting upon it, and no relation between the body and it save being acted upon by it. And the meaning of death is the cutting off [interruption, cessation] of this act-relation by the stopping of the disposition of the body. For the body is disposed to be acted upon only when it possesses a certain specific mixture of humors, just as iron is disposed to receive in it the impression of a sensible form or for the reflection of rays from it only when it possesses a certain specific form: so if that form does not exist, the iron will not be acted upon by the form opposite it and no imprint will be made in it.

93 If this, then, is their doctrine, how can the one able to produce the relation between a soul—which is not embodied, and not localized, and not describable as united to the body or separate from it—and the body to which [the soul] is not similar in its essence and to which it is not united sensibly, be unable to bring back [restore] that relation?! The surprising thing is that most of them allow the affirmation of that relation with another body by way of metempsychosis [transmigration]: why, then, is it not allowable for the soul to return to its own body?! For it is more unlikely that, in the case of a body of which its mixture of humors has corrupted, its mixture will be repaired and that relation will be restored to it. That, then, is what is meant by the bringing back [restoration], and it resembles waking up after sleep, for it [the latter] restores the motion [activity] of the senses and the remembrance of bygone things.

94 [p. 50] *If one says:* Once the mixture of humors has corrupted it will return to equilibrium only through the resolution of the body's parts into the elements, then their being combined a second time, then its becoming a living being, then its becoming sperm; for this equilibrium belongs to the sperm particularly. *We say:* And whence do you know that it is not in God's power to repair the rupture which has occurred in any way except the way mentioned?. And whence do you know that this which you have mentioned is a way? And do you have any support [for that] other than the observation of [actual] status [circumstances]? And have you, for the refutation of other ways, any support other than the absence of observation? Had you not observed the creation of man from sperm [a sperm drop] your minds would shrink from believing in it. And among the causes which change the status of bodies are marvels which would be rejected by one who does not observe them.

95 One man will reject peculiar properties, and another will reject magic, and another the apologetic miracle, and another information about the invisible [prediction of the future]. And each relies, in his affirmation, on the amount of his observation, not on a rational method in establishing impossibility. Then [moreover?] one who has not observed it and known it for certain, announces that his natural shrinking from belief is due to the absence of observation. Among the things God can do are marvels which no man has come to know. So it is not impossible that the bringing back of those bodies and the restoration of their mixture of humors would be due to a cause with God which He alone knows. When He brings it [the body] back, the soul again becomes active in it as was the case, by their claim, during life. One is astonished that a man who claims expertise in rational matters, and then sees the marvels and signs in the world, has, nevertheless, too narrow a craw to accept that regarding God's power. But when what he has not observed is referred to what he has observed, he does not see anything more wonderful than it!

96 To be sure, *if someone were* to *say:* This is a matter which the intellect does not prove to be impossible, but it also does not prove [p. 51] its possibility: rather it refrains from pronouncing on it—for there may be something there unknown to it which makes it impossible or something unknown to it which makes it possible, *this* man would be closer [to the truth] than the first, and by his judgment it would be necessary to believe the Prophet—God bless him!—if it was reported from him. For he would report about something the existence of which is not impossible in reason.

97 In general [in short] the utterance of God Most High has indeed embraced the stages and ranks of creation: "We created man of an extraction of clay, [then We set him, a drop, in a receptacle secure, then We created of the drop a clot, then We created of the clot a tissue, then We created of the tissue bones, then We garmented the bones in flesh; thereafter We produced him as another creature. So blessed be God, the fairest of creators! Then after that you shall surely die, then on the Day of Resurrection you shall surely] be raised up" [23.12–16]. Thus He encompassed creatures with belief by the totality of the premises, except for raising, because they had seen all that except raising. Had they never seen a death, they would have denied the possibility of death. And had they not seen the creation of a man from sperm [a drop] they would have denied its possibility. So the raising is in unison [uniform] with what is prior to it in the balance of the intellect: let us, therefore, believe the Prophets regarding what they brought, for it is not impossible. All of this is a discussion with the Philosophers who employ reasoning. But the Bāṭinites who reject reasoning cannot hold on to reasoning.

98 Of course, *if a Bāṭinite were to say:* The Infallible Imam informed me that the raising is impossible, so I believe him—one *would say to him:* And what has called you to believe the Imam, who is infallible by your pretension, when he has no apologetic miracle, and has turned you away from believing Muḥammad, the son of ᶜAbdallāh, with his apologetic miracles, [p. 52] and the Qur᾽ān from its beginning to its end proves the possibility and the actuality of that? And have you any obstacle save that his [Muḥammad's] infallibility is known by his apologetic miracle, whereas the infallibility of him whom you claim is known by your senseless jabber [mania, delirium] and your passion [by your passionate drivel]?!

99 *If he says:* What is in the Qur᾽ān are literal expressions which are symbols of inner meanings which they [men] did not understand, but the Infallible Imam *has* understood them and we have learned [them] from him. *We say:* You have learned from him by actually seeing that in his mind [heart] with [your] eye, or by hearing from his utterance [words]. There can be no claim of seeing, so it must be a question of reliance on hearing his words. *[Then] we say:* And what assures you that his words do not have an inner meaning which you have not come to know [you are not aware of], so that you cannot rely on what you have understood from the literal expression of his speech? *If you then claim* that he has spoken clearly with you and said: What I have mentioned is a literal expression containing no symbol, and what is meant is its literal meaning. *We say:* And how do you know that this utterance of his—viz. that it is a literal expression containing no symbol—is not also a literal expression containing a symbol of what you are not aware of?

100 *Then he will* continue affirming his utterance, and *we will say:* We are not in the category of one who is misled by literal expressions, so perhaps there is an underlying symbol. *And if he denies* the inner meaning, *we say:* Underlying his denial there is a symbol. Even if he swears by the [formula of] triple divorce [repudiation] that he means only the literal meaning, *we say:* In his "divorce" there is a symbol, and he is simply manifesting one thing and concealing another. *If you say:* That would lead to shutting the door of communication. *We say:* It is you who have shut, for the Apostle, the door of communication. For two-thirds of the Qur᾽ān is about the description of the Garden and the Fire and of the Assembling and the Resurrection, [all] confirmed by swearing and oaths. Yet you say: Perhaps there is a symbol underlying that, and you say: What difference is there between delaying in understanding matters such as that known regarding the Qur᾽ān and the Traditions, and your saying: I mean only the literal meaning? [*We say* (?)]*:* If it was allowable for him to communicate the literal expression while his meaning was other than that which he positively knew would reach the understandings of men, and he would [thus] be lying in all he said for the sake of some advantage and secret in that, then it would be allowable for your Imam—the infallible by your claim—to conceal, in your regard, the opposite of what he manifests [declares] and the contrary of what he communicates and the contradictory [antithesis] of what he knows for certain is what reaches your understandings, and for him to corroborate that by binding [mighty] oaths for some advantage of his own and some secret in that. And to this there will never, never be an answer.

101 And at this point a man ought to recognize that the rank of this sect is lower [viler, baser] than that of any of the erring sects, [p. 53] since we do not find any sect whose doctrine is invalidated by that doctrine itself save this sect. For its doctrine is the invalidation of [the use of] reason and changing words from their [agreed upon] meanings by the claim of symbols. But everything they can conceivably give tongue to is either reasoning or transmission. But they have invalidated reasoning, and as for utterance [transmission], it is

declared allowable [by them] that one intend by the utterance something different than its [agreed upon] meaning. Hence there remains for them nothing to cling to.

102 *If it be said:* This can be retorted against you! For you also allow the interpretation of literal texts, such as your interpreting the verse of "the being firmly seated" and the Tradition of [God's] descent, and others. *We reply:* How wide off the mark this retort is! For we have a norm for interpretation, viz. when reasoning and its proof show the falsity of the literal meaning of a text we know of necessity that what is intended is something different, provided that the utterance be in conformity with it by way of figure and metaphor. And proof has indeed shown that falsity of "the being firmly seated" and "the descent [of God]," for that belongs to the qualities [attributes] of incipients—so it is interpreted as [taken to mean] "mastery [domination]," and this agrees with linguistic usage.

103 But the mind [intellect] has no proof of the falsity of the Assembling and the Resurrection and the Garden and the Fire; nor is there any agreement between the expressions which have come down regarding that and the meaning in which they interpret it so that it can be said that the latter was intended. On the contrary, interpretation in this case is out-and-out imputation of lying [to the Prophet]. What agreement is there between God's words: "therein a running fountain, therein uplifted couches and goblets set forth and cushions arrayed and carpets outspread" [88.12–16], 'mid thornless lote-trees and serried acacias, [and spreading shade and outpoured waters, and fruits abounding unfailing]" [56.27–32/28–33], and what they believe, viz. the union of spritual substances with [p. 54] spiritual intellectual things in which there is no entry for sensible things?!

104 If it is allowable for the possessor of an apologetic miracle to be branded as a liar by these interpretations which [have] never occurred to the mind of him who hears them, why, then, is it not allowable to brand as a liar your infallible one, who has no apologetic miracle, by reason of his interpretation of things which do not occur to men's minds, for the sake of some advantage or some pressing need? For the purpose of his utterance is to speak plainly and to swear, and these expressions in the Qur'ān are plain and are corroborated by swearing. But they pretend that that is mentioned [cited] for some advantage and that what is meant is different from what spontaneously occurs to understandings from [hearing] them [expressions]. There is also no escape from this [argument].

[p. 55]

CHAPTER FIVE

Refutation of Their Interpretations of the Clear Literal Texts and of Their Arguments from Number-related Matters It Contains Two Sections

The First Section On Their Interpretations of the Literal Texts

105 A concise [summary] statement about this is that, since [when] they are unable to turn men away from the Qur'ān and the Sunna, they turn men from their meaning to trickery [*mahhārīq*] they have elaborated, and they seek, by what, on their own part, they have wrested from the exigency [requirement] of words [expressions], the invalidation of the meanings of the Law, and, by the interpretations they have elaborated, to effect men's submission to allegiance and friendship. But if they were to declare openly plain denial and naked imputation of lying, they would not gain the friendship of friends but would be the first to be sought out and killed.

106 We shall relate a small part of their interpretations that we may infer from them their infamies. They have asserted that all the literal texts which have come down regarding injunctions [precepts], and the Assembling and the Resurrection, and divine matters, are allegories [images] and symbols of inner meanings. As for legal matters, they hold that *al-janāba* [major ritual impurity] means a "respondent's" embarking on divulging a secret to him [i.e. to someone else] before he attains the stage of deserving it [or: having a right to do that?]. And the meaning of *al-ghusl* [major ritual ablution] is the renewing of [p. 56] the pact with one who has done that. And they hold that *mujāmaᶜat al-bahīma* [bestiality] means the treatment of one who has no pact and who has paid nothing of the *ṣadaqat al-najwā* [alms of confidentiality]—and this, according to them is 119 dirhams. And therefore the Law imposes killing on the one doing it [bestiality] and the one to which it is done—and otherwise the beast—when is killing obligatory regarding it? and adultery [fornication] is casting the sperm of inner knowledge into the soul of him who has not previously been bound by the pact. And pollution [lit. attaining puberty, wet dream] is that one's tongue spontaneously divulges the secret out of its proper place—then he is bound to *al-ghusl,* i.e. the renewal of the pact.

107 *Al-ṭuhūr* [ritual purity] is being free and clean from believing any doctrine except allegiance to the Imam, *Al-ṣiyām* [fasting] is refraining from divulging the secret. The Kaᶜba is the Prophet, and the Bāb ᶜAlī, al-Ṣafā is the Prophet and al-Marwa ᶜAlī. And the *mīqāt* [rendezvous of the pilgrims] is *al-asās.* And the *talbiya* [response—the *labbayka* "at your service! here am I!" of the pilgrims when they reach Mecca] is the response to the propagandist. And the *ṭawāf* of the House seven times [circumambulation of the Kaᶜba] is making the rounds of Muḥammad to the completion of the seven Imams. And the five canonical Prayers are the indication of the four fundaments and of the Imam: the Dawn Prayer is the indicator of the *Sābiq,* and the Noon Prayer is the indicator of the *Tālī,* and the Afternoon Prayer of the *Asās,* and the *Sunset Prayer* is the indicator of the *Nāṭiq,* and the Evening Prayer is the indicator of the Imam. Likewise they claim that the forbidden things [*al-muḥarramāt*] are an expression for those men who are evil, and that we have been enjoined to shun them, just as the acts of worship [*al-ᶜibādāt*] are an expression for the innocent, good [men] whom we have been commanded to follow.

108 [p. 57] As for the Hereafter [*al-Maᶜād*], some of them claim that the Fire and the fetters are an expression for the commands which are the [legal] precepts. For they are imposed on those who are ignorant of the science of the "inner meaning," and so long as they remain [bound] by them they are [being] punished [tormented, afflicted]. Then, when they acquire the science of "the inner meaning," the fetters of the precepts are removed from them and they are made happy by freedom from them.

109 Moreover, they undertake to interpret every expression that has come in the Qurʾān and the Sunna. Thus they say: "rivers of milk" [47.16/15], i.e. the mines [sources] of religion: the inner knowledge, by which the one worthy of them [the rivers] is suckled and by which he is nourished in a way by which his subtle life continues, for the nourishment of the subtle spirit is by being suckled on the knowledge from the teacher, just as the life of the dense body is by being suckled on the milk from the mother's breast. And "rivers of wine" [47.16/15] are "exterior" knowledge, and "rivers of honey purified" [47.17/15] are the science of "the interior" received from the "Proofs" and the Imams.

110 As for the apologetic miracles, they interpreted all of them and said: The meaning of the Flood is the flood of knowledge by which were drowned those clinging to the Sunna; and the ship [is] the refuge [sanctuary] of him who responds to the "call" by which

he is fortified. And the "fire of Abraham" is an expression for the anger of Nimrod, not for real fire. And the "sacrifice of Isaac" means imposing the pact on him. The staff of Moses [cf. 20.72/69] is his proof which swallowed their lying sophisms, not the wood. The splitting of the sea is the separation [division] of Moses' knowledge among them according to divisions [parts]. And the sea is the world. And the cloud[s] which overshadowed them mean the Imam whom Moses appointed to guide them aright and to pour forth knowledge upon them. The locusts and the ants [ticks, winged insects—gnats] and the frogs are the questions [demands] of Moses and his injunctions which were imposed on them. And the manna and quail are a knowledge which came down from heaven to a certain propagandist [emissary] who is the one intended by the quail.

111 The praising of the mountains [cf. 21.79 and 34.10] means the praising of men strong in religion [and] deeply rooted in [p. 58] sure and certain knowledge. The jinn whom Solomon son of David mastered were the Bāṭinites of that time, and the devils were the Literalists on whom the hard labors were imposed. Jesus had a father, with respect to the exterior—and he meant by "the father" simply the Imam, since he had no Imam but derived knowledge from God without an intermediary [i.e. God was his "Father" in the sense that He was his Imam]; and they claimed—God curse them!—that his father was Joseph the carpenter. His speech in the cradle was his coming to know in the cradle of the mould [i.e. the body?] before becoming free from it what others come to know after death and freedom from the mould [body]. The quickening of the dead on the part of Jesus means quickening by the life of knowledge from the death of ignorance of "the interior." And his healing the blind man means from the blindness of error and the leprosy of unbelief by the understanding of [insight into] the plain truth. Iblīs and Adam are a designation of Abū Bakr and ᶜAlī, because Abū Bakr was commanded to prostrate himself to ᶜAlī and to obey him and he refused and was proud [arrogant]. They pretend that Antichrist [*al-dajjāl*] is Abū Bakr, and he was one-eyed because he saw only with the eye of the exterior and not with the eye of the interior. And Yaᵓjūj and Maᵓjūj [Gog and Magog] are the devotees of the exterior.

112 This is some of their drivel [insane babbling] about interpretations. We have related it to be laughed at [ridiculed, mocked, derided]. We take refuge in God from the felling [i.e. being felled in a wrestling match because of negligence] of the negligent and the stumble of the ignorant. In refuting them we follow only three ways: [direct] refutation, confrontation [contradiction, objection], and verification [substantiation].

113 [*The first way*] [Direct] refutation [invalidation, proving false] consists in saying: How do you know that what is meant by these expressions [p. 59] is what you have cited? If you have gotten it from the reasoning of the intellect [mind]—why, in your view, this is futile [useless, invalid]. And if you have heard it from the utterance of the Infallible Imam—why his utterance is not stronger in clarity than these expressions which you have interpreted: so perhaps its [his] meaning is something else of even greater "interiority" than the "interior" [inner meaning] which you have mentioned. But he goes a step beyond the literal meaning to such an extent that he claims that by "the mountains" is meant "the men": what, then, is meant by "the men"? Perhaps something else is meant by that expression. And the meaning of "the devils" is "the literalists"—and what [is the meaning of] "the literalists"? And by "milk" is meant "knowledge"—and what is the meaning of "knowledge"?

114 *If* you *say:* "knowledge" and "the men" and "the literalists" are plain [obvious] regarding what they require by linguistic convention—you are looking with one eye at one of the two sides, and so you are the Antichrist—since he is one-eyed—because you

see with one of the two eyes, for "the men" is exterior [literal], but you are blind in the other eye which is looking at "the mountains," for they also are something exterior—[literal]. *If you say:* It is possible to allude by "the mountains" to "the men." *we say:* And it is possible to allude by "the men" to something else, as the poet expressed [designated] by the two men of whom one was a tailor and the other a weaver [certain] astronomical matters and celestial causes, and said:

Two men: a tailor and another a weaver
confronting one another in Spica Virginis
One unceasingly weaving a cloak of one going
and his companion sewing the garment of the one coming.

[Spica Virginis: *al-simāk al-aᶜzal* (unarmed): One of two stars in constellation Virgo; it is so called because it has nothing before it, unlike the other, *al-simāk al-rāmiḥ* (Arcturus: "the lance-throwing") which has before it a small star known as "its banner and lance."]

115 And so [it is] in every case [branch of knowledge]. And if "the praising of the mountains" stands for "the praising of the men," then let the meaning of "the men" in the Most High's utterance: men whom neither commerce nor trafficking diverts from the remembrance of God" [24.37] stand for "the mountains," for the fitness [aptness] exists on both sides. Then, if "the mountains" is made equivalent to "the men," and "the men" is made equivalent to something else, it would be possible to make that third inner meaning equivalent to [p. 60] a fourth and there would be a continuous sequence to a degree which would destroy mutual understanding and communication, and it would be impossible to decide that the one having the second rank is inferior to the third, or that the third is inferior to the fourth.

116 *The second way* is the confrontation of the false with the false. This consists in taking all the traditions in [a sense] opposed to their doctrine. For example, one would say: The Prophet's statement "the angels will not enter a house containing an image" means: Reason will not enter a brain containing belief in the Infallible [Imam]. And his utterance "If a dog licks [laps] in a dish of one of you, let him wash it seven times" means: If a Bāṭinite marries the daughter of one of you, let him wash her from the filth of the association with the water of knowledge and the purity of action after her having been begrimed by the dust of degradation. Or a speaker says: Marriage is not contracted without witnesses and a guardian. As for the Prophet's saying: "Every marriage not attended by four" is fornication—it means that every belief not attested to by the four caliphs—Abū Bakr and ᶜUmar and ᶜUthmān and ᶜAlī is false. And his statement: "There can be no marriage save with a guardian and two just witnesses" means: There can be no intercourse save by a male and two females—and other such farces ["humbuggery"—lies].

117 My intention in mentioning this much is the confrontation of the false with the false and the communication of the way to open this door. Then, when you have been guided to it, you will not be unable to make every expression from Book or Sunna mean the opposite of their belief. *If they claim* that you have made "the image" mean "the Infallible [Imam]" in the Prophet's utterance "Angels will not enter a house containing an image—and what agreement is there between the two? *I say:* And you have made "the serpent" mean "the demonstration," and the Father—with respect to Jesus—the Imam," and "the milk" "the knowledge" in the case of the rivers of milk in the Garden, and "the Jinn" the Bāṭinites, and "the devils" "the Literalists," and "the mountains" "the men—and what is the agreement

[fitness]? *If you say:* The demonstration crunches specious arguments as the serpent crunches another [something else], and the Imam gives scientific [knowledgeable] existence as the Father gives personal [individual?] existence, and milk nourishes the individual as [p. 61] knowledge nourishes the spirit, and the Jinn are interior [hidden] like the Bāṭinites.

118 *Then* one *would say* to *them:* If, then, you are content with this amount of sharing, why God has never created [any] two things without there being between them a sharing in some quality! For we made the image mean the Imam, because the image is a likeness [figure] [and] contains no spirit, just as the Imam, in your view, is infallible but has no apologetic miracle; and the brain is the abode of the intellect, as the house is the abode of the intelligent; and the angel is a spiritual thing just as the intellect is such. So it is certain that the meaning of his utterance The angels will not enter a house containing an image" is: The intellect will not enter a brain containing the belief in the infallibility of the Imam.

119 So if you have learned this, then take any expression they mention, and take also whatever you wish, and seek their sharing in some aspect, and then interpret it in that sense and it will be a proof by the exigency of what they affirm, as I have informed you about the sharing between angel and intellect, and brain and house, and image and Imam. When the door is opened to you, you will become aware of the way of their stratagems in deception by extracting the necessities of the expressions and supposing wild fancies in place of them as a means of destroying [invalidating] the Law. This amount is enough to show the falsity of their interpretation.

120 *The third way* is verification [substantiation]. It consists in *your saying:* These inner meanings and interpretations which you have cited, were we to be indulgent with you and admit that they are correct [authentic], what is their status in the Law? Should they be concealed, or should they be divulged? *If you say:* They should be divulged to every one. *We say:* Then why did Muḥammad—God bless him and grant him peace!—conceal them and not mention anything of that to the Companions and to the masses so that that age passed without anyone's having a report of this sort? [p. 62] And how could he have deemed it permissible to conceal the religion of God, when God Most High had said: "You shall make it clear with the people, and nor conceal it" [8.184/187], to give notice [warn, call attention to the fact] that it is not lawful [licit] to conceal [our] Religion.

121 But if they claim that it ought to be concealed, *we say:* What it was made incumbent on the Apostle of God—God bless him and grant him peace!—to conceal of the mystery [secret] of [our] Religion, how is it licit for you to divulge it? The crime regarding a secret by its being divulged by one who has come to know it is among the greatest of crimes. So were it not that the trustee of the Law [i.e. Muḥammad] knew a great secret and a universal advantage in concealing these [such] secrets, he would not have concealed them, and he would not have repeated these literal meanings to the ears of men and there would not have been reiterated in the words of the Qurʾān the description of the Garden and the Fire in plain terms—because he would have known that men would understand from that the contrary of its inner meaning, which is [the] true [one], and would believe these literal expressions which would have no truth.

122 And if you ascribe to him ignorance of what men understood from him, this is to accuse [him] of ignorance of the meaning of speech, for the Prophet—God bless him and grant him peacel—knew positively that men would understand from God's utterance "and spreading shade and outpoured waters, and fruits abounding" [56.29–31/30–32] only what is understood from it in the language [linguistic usage]—and so [of] the other

expressions. Furthermore, despite his knowledge of that, he used to corroborate it for them by repetition and swearing, and he did not divulge to them the inner meaning which you have mentioned, because he knew it to be the hidden secret of God—why, then, have you divulged this secret and rent this veil? Is this anything but a departure from [our] Religion, and an opposing of the trustee of the Law, and a wrecking of all he founded?!—if it be granted to you for the sake of argument that the inner meaning you have mentioned is true in God's view. They have no way to escape from this!

123 *If it be said:* This is a secret which it is not permissible to divulge to the masses of men, and for this reason the Apostle of God—God bless him and grant him peace!—did not divulge it. But the Prophet had the right to divulge it to his *sūs,* who was to be his trustee and vicar after him. And he did divulge it to ᶜAlī and not to anyone else. *We say:* And ᶜAlī—did he divulge it to anyone other than his *sūs* and vicar, or not? [p. 63] And if he divulged it only to his *sūs,* and so the *sūs* of his *sūs* and the vicar of his vicar down to the present—then how did it finally come to these ignorant men among the masses so that they bandy it about, and books are loaded with the account of it, and it is the talk of the town? *It must be replied:* One of the vicars disobeyed and divulged the secret to those for whom it was not intended, and so it spread—but in their view they are impeccable and cannot conceivably disobey!

124 *If it be said:* The *sūs* mentions it only in the company of him with whom he has made a pact about it. *We say:* And what was it that prevented the Apostle from making a pact and mentioning it, if it was allowable to divulge it with a pact? *If it be said:* Perhaps he did make a pact and mention [it], but it was not transmitted because of the pact which he exacted from him to whom he divulged [it]. *We say:* And why did that spread among you, since your Imams disclose that only in the company of him from whom a pact has been exacted? And what was it that preserved the pact of those but not the pact of these? Moreover, *it should be said:* If it is allowable to divulge this secret with a pact, and it is conceivable that the pact be violated, is it conceivable that he divulge it to one who the Infallible Imam *knows* will not violate it, or is it sufficient that he suppose this by reason of his intuitive knowledge of human nature and his personal judgment and what he infers from the signs?

125 *If you say:* It is permissible [to divulge it] only to him who the Infallible Imam knows will not violate it by a notification received from God, then how did these secrets spread to all men, since they could spread only from him who had heard [them]? So either the informer violated the pact, or no pact was made at all. In one of these [alternatives] there is an ascription of ignorance to the Infallible, and in [p. 64] the other an ascription of disobedience [sin]. But according to them there is no way to either one. *And if you claim* that it is licit to divulge with a pact when discernment testifies about the one with whom the pact is made that he will not violate it by inference from the signs, then in this is the destruction of the basic principle of their doctrine. For they pretend that it is not permissible to follow the proofs of reason and its speculation, because the intellectuals [because men of reason] disagree about speculation [reasoning] and in it is the danger of error—how, then, can they judge by intuition and sign in which error is more prevalent than the right, when that involves divulging the secret of religion, which is the most dangerous of things? They have indeed forbidden adherence to supposition and personal reasoning in juridical matters which are a judgment among men by way of mediation in disputes, but then reduced the divulging of the secret of religion to the realm of fantasy and intuition.

126 This is a strong [solid] way [to argue], understood by the intelligent man and gloried in by the one engaged in the legal sciences, because he knows positively that the speaker is two kinds: *One is* he who holds that these literal expressions have no inner meaning and admit of no interpretation—hence interpretation is absolutely false [futile]. *The other* is he to whom it occurs [?] that that may possibly be allusions to inner meanings, [and] God did not permit the Apostle of God—God bless him and grant him peace!—to declare plainly the inner meanings, but obligated him to utter the literal meanings—so speaking of the inner meaning became an illicit falsehood and a forbidden iniquity and a hostile break with the Lawgiver—this is a principle agreed upon [by convention]. And the men of our age—given their remoteness from the trustee of the Law, and the spread of corruption and the domination of the passions over men and the turning away of all from religious matters—are not more submissive to truth and more disposed for [receptive of] the secret and more trustworthy keepers of it and better suited to understand it and profit from it than the men of the time of the Apostle of God—God bless him and grant him peace!

127 These secrets and interpretations, if they have any reality, [p. 65] he [the Apostle] closed their hearings against them and bridled [curbed] the mouths of speakers from speaking [constantly] of them. Now we have in the Apostle of God a splendid model in his speech and his action. So we say only what he said, and manifest only what he manifested, and are silent about what he passed over in silence. And in actions we observe the acts of worship, and even the vigils [night-watching] and supererogatory prayers [practices] and the different kinds of strivings [against self-mortifications]. We also know that what the trustee of the Law did not dispense with, we cannot dispense with it. Nor are we taken in by the assertion of the stupid that when our souls become pure through knowledge of the inner meaning we can dispense with external acts.

128 Rather do we contemn this deluded speaker and say to him: Poor man! Do you think your soul is purer and cleaner than the soul of the Apostle of God—God bless him and grant him peace!? Yet he used to rise at night to pray until his feet became swollen! Or is it thinkable that he [Muḥammad] used to practice deception on ᶜĀᵓisha to make her think that [his] religion was true, while he knew it to be false? If you think the former, how stupid you are—and we can't add to it! And if you think the latter—how godless and unbelieving you are—and we are not going to argue with you about it!

129 But we say: If we assume the worst of circumstances, and our rational proofs [?], for example, fail to overtake your error and your ignorance and to grasp the veracity of the Apostle of God—God bless him and grant him peace!—we see the fundamental principles [truths] of our minds judging that "loss" [i.e. being a loser] in the group of Muḥammad—God bless him and grant him peace!—and conformity to him and contentment with what he wanted for himself, is better than victory [i.e. being a Winner] with you, O abandoned and ignorant man—nay more—demented and [p. 66] deranged man! So let the fair-minded [equitable] man now consider the last of this and its first: its last convinces the masses—and even old women; and its first provides true apodeictic proof to every inquirer familiar with the legal sciences. And let it suffice you to know a discourse [argument] which is profitable to all men despite the difference of their categories regarding knowledge and ignorance.

The Second Section

On Their Argument from Numbers and Letters

130 This is a kind of folly [ignorance, stupidity] peculiar to this sect from among all the sects. For the erring groups, despite the ramification of their discourse [*kalām*] and the spread of their methods in organizing specious arguments, never was one of them soiled by this kind [of stupidity], but men found it feeble and the masses and the ignorant knew of necessity its falsity and detested it. But these [Bāṭinites] adhered to it—and small wonder, since the drowning man clings to anything and the dolt [numbskull, ignoramus] is shaken and doubts because of every deception. We shall mention a small part of it that the man considering it may thank his Lord for integrity of mind and equilibrium of the mixture of humors and soundness of constitution, because being deceived [taken in] by the like of that can proceed only from idiocy and disorder in the mind.

131 They have asserted that the holes [apertures] in the head of man are seven, and the heavens are seven, [p. 67] and the regions are seven, and the stars are seven—I mean the planets—and the days of the week are seven. This, then, shows that the stage of the Imams is completed in [by] seven. They also pretend that the elements are four, and that the seasons of the year are four—and this shows that the principles fundaments] are four: the *sābiq* and the *tālī,* the two divinities, and the *nāṭiq* and the *asās,* the two Imams. Moreover, they claim that the stations of the zodiac are twelve, and [this] indicates the twelve proofs, as we have reported concerning their doctrine [cf. Para. 76].

132 And often they elicit from the form of the animals indications. Thus they assert that man is in the shape of the letters of "Muḥammad." For his head is like a *mīm,* and his two arms are outstretched like the *ḥāʾ*, and his rump is like the *mīm,* and his two legs are like the *dāl.* And in such fashion they discourse about the form of the birds and the beasts.

133 And often they make interpretations from letters and numbers. Thus they say: The Prophet—God bless him and grant him peace!—said: "I have been commanded to fight men until they say: There is no god save God: and when they say it they safeguard [immunize] from me their lives and their property except for what is due [owed] of them." It was said: And what is due of them? He said: "The knowledge of their limits." [p. 68] And they pretend that "their limits" [the pronominal suffix seems, from the following, to refer to the phrase *lā ilāha illa llāh*] are the knowledge of the secrets [mysteries] of their letters, viz. that *lā ilāha illa llāh* consists of four words, and seven divisions [syllables], viz.

1 234 56 7

the parts [divisions: *qiṭa*^{c}] of *lā ilāha illa llāh,* and three substances [*jawāhir*], because *lā* is a particle, and there remain *ilāha* and *illa* and *allāh,* and these are three substances, and the total is twelve letters [lām—alif—alif—lām—hāʾ—alif—lām—alif—alif—lām—lām—hāʾ].

134 They claim that the four words indicate the two supernal governors: *al-sābiq* and *al-tālī,* and the two lower governors: *al-nāṭiq* and *al-asās.* This is its indication of the spirituals. But it also indicates the corporeals, because they are the four elements. As for the three substances, they indicate Jibrīl and Mīkāʾīl and Isrāfīl from among the spirituals, and from the corporeals they indicate length and breadth and depth, since by these bodies they are seen [visible]. And the seven syllables indicate from the spirituals the seven Prophets, and from the corporeals the seven stars: because, were it not for the seven Prophets, the religious Laws would not differ; and were it not for the seven stars the times [seasons] would not differ. And the twelve letters indicate the twelve Proofs, and among the corporeals the twelve stations of the zodiac.

135 Similarly they arbitrarily explain what was said by Muḥammad the Apostle of God, and the letters, and the beginnings of the Suras, and present varieties of silliness which would make madmen laugh, to say nothing of reasonable men. Let this suffice to show you the ignominy of a group which argues in this way! We are not going to prolong the account of this kind of argument of theirs, being content with this amount to make known their infamies. This is a kind [of argument] the falsity of which is known by logical necessity, [p. 69] and so it requires no refutation. However, we shall inform you of two ways to silence those of them who are stupid and obstinate: demanding [*muṭālaba:* importuning], and objecting [confronting—*muʿāraḍa*].

136 As *for demanding,* it consists in saying: And whence do you know these indications? Were a man to pass judgment on them, he would pronounce against himself that that was from a bad mixture of his humors which had stirred up his blend of humors against him and produced confused dreams [nightmares]—and God had indeed led them [text—you] astray to such a point that they [read: you?] are not ashamed of them. Do you know their authenticity [correctness] by logical necessity, or a reasoning or a hearing from your Infallible Imam? If you claim necessity you flabbergast [slander] your minds and are guilty of forgery, and then you are not safe from an objector who would claim that he knows the falsity of that by necessity, and then his position vis-à-vis the mutual opposition of the true by the false would be the position of him who opposes the false by the false.

137 And if you know [that] by the reasoning of the mind, why you hold reasoning of the mind to be futile [false] because of the disagreement of the intelligent in their reasoning. But if you believe it, then apprise me of the mode and process of reasoning and from what one infers these stupidities. And if you know that from the words of the Infallible Imam, then show that the one who reports from him is infallible, or that the transmitters from him reach the degree of impeccable transmission; then establish as true that the Infallible Imam cannot err; then show that he cannot communicate what he knows to be false—for perhaps he has deceived you by these stupidities, and he knows them to be false, as you claim that the Prophet—God bless him and grant him peace!—deceived men by the description of the Garden and the Fire, and by what is related of [p. 70] the Prophets such as the quickening of the dead and the changing of the staff into a serpent, and [that] he [Muḥammad] lied in all those things and mentioned them despite his knowledge that none of those things existed, and that men would definitely understand from them their literal meanings, and that he intended [purposed] the communication of the literal meanings while knowing that they would understand the literal meanings he communicated to them, though this was the contrary of the truth—but he saw in that some advantage.

138 Perhaps, then, your Infallible Imam saw some advantage in condemning your intelligences and laughing at you [leading you round by the nose]—so he tossed to you these hoaxes to show his absolute mastery and enslavement of you and to vaunt his supreme cunning and cleverness in deceiving you. I would like to know how you can be sure he is not lying for some advantage he saw, when you have plainly stated that about the Prophet—God bless him and grant him peace!! Is there any difference between them? Except that the Prophet—God bless him and grant him peace!—was corroborated by the apologetic miracle proving his veracity, whereas he upon whom you rely has no apologetic miracle save your stupidity! This is the way of demanding [importuning].

139 *As for objecting* [confronting], we do not propose to specify [all] the forms, but we shall teach you a method which embraces [p. 71] all the forms [shapes] and letters there are in the world. For every existent is undoubtedly from one to ten or more. So

whenever you see one thing, Then argue from it to Muḥammad—God bless him and grant him peace! And if you see two, then say that it is an indication of the two Shaykhs, Abū Bakr and ᶜUmar. And if it be three, then Muḥammad—God bless him and grant him peace!—and Abū Bakr and ᶜUmar. And if it be four, then the [first] Four Caliphs. And if it be five, then [an indication] of Muḥammad with the Four Caliphs. And say: Do you not know the secret [of the fact] that the holes in man's head [face] are five? What is one, i.e. the mouth, indicates the Prophet Muḥammad, for he is one; and the two eyes and two nostrils indicate the Four Caliphs. *And we say:* Do you not know what the secret is in the name of Muḥammad and its being four letters [i.e. *mīm, ḥāʾ, mīm, dāl*—as written]? *If they say:* No! *We say:* It is the secret known only to an angel brought near [an Angel of the Throne or Presence], for he builds it on the fact that the name of his vicar is four letters and he is old [mature], nor ᶜAlī whose name is three letters.

140 And if you find [a] seven, argue therefrom to seven of the Caliphs of the Umayyads to emphasize contempt [hatred] for them and to exalt the ᶜAbbāsids above comparison with them. And say: The number of the seven heavens and of the stars and of [the days of] the week indicates Muᶜāwiya and Yazīd, then Marwān, then ᶜAbd al-Malik, then al-Walīd, then ᶜUmar son of ᶜAbd al-ᵓAzīz, then Hishām, [8 here! leave out Muᶜāwiya?] then the seventh the Awaited—and this is the one called al-Sufyānī, and this is the doctrine of the Umayyad Imamites. Or confront them with the doctrine of the Rāwandiyya and say: It indicates al-ᵓAbbās, then ᶜAbdallāh son of al-ᵓAbbās, then ᶜAlī son of ᶜAbdallāh, then Muḥammad son of ᶜAlī, then [p. 72] Ibrāhīm, then Abū ᵓl-ᶜAbbās al-Saffāḥ then al-Mansūr. And likewise what you find of ten or twelve, reckon the same number of the ᶜAbbāsid Caliphs, and see whether you find any difference between the two utterances. By this the falsity of their *kalām* [of what they say] is clear [evident] as is their being exposed and constrained by their own [way of] argument [inference]. This kind of *kalām,* it is not fit for its collector to expatiate on it: so let us turn from it to something else.

[p. 73]

CHAPTER SIX

On the Disclosure of the Deceptions Which They Bedecked with Their Claim in the Form of Apodeictic Proof of the Invalidation of Intellectual Reasoning and of the Affirmation of the Necessity of Learning from the Infallible Imam

141 Our method will be to put in order their specious arguments to the limit of our ability and then to disclose where deception is hidden in them.

Their ultimate claim is that he who knows the realities of things is the one occupying the post of Caliph in Egypt, and that it is incumbent on all creatures to obey him and to learn from him that they may obtain through him [or: thereby] happiness in this life and the next.

142 Their proof of it is their assertion that

(1) Everything which can conceivably be negatively and affirmatively enunciated has true and false in it; and the true is one, and the false is what confronts it, for all is not true, nor all false: and this is a premise.

(2) Then, the true must be distinguished from the false, and this is a matter of obligation which no one can dispense with in the matter of his best religious and secular interests: and this is a second premise.

(3) Then, the attainment of the truth must be known to man either through himself, from his intellect by his reasoning, and not by a learning process, or he knows it from another by a learning proceess: and this is a third premise.

143 (4) And if knowledge of it [the true] cannot be by the way of independent reasoning and making minds [the] judge of it, learning from another is imperative; moreover, the teacher [p. 74] must either be stipulated to he safeguarded from error and slip, and uniquely qualified by this property, or it is allowable to learn from anyone. And if learning from anyone—whoever he be—is untenable, because of the multiplicity of the speakers and teachers and the mutual contratliction of their utterances, it is certain that the learning must be from a person who among all men is the unique possessor of infallibility: and this is a fourth premise.

144 (5) Then, it must either be possible for the world to he devoid of that infallible one, or be impossible for it to be devoid [of him]. But allowing it to be devoid is impossible, because, since it has been established that he is the means of attaining the truth, allowing the world to be devoid of him would involve a concealing [eclipse] of the truth and a closing down of the way to perceive [attain] it—and in this would be the ruin of men's religious and secular affairs. But this would be injustice itself, opposed to wisdom—and that is impossible on the part of God—Praised be He!—since He is the Wise and the far removed from injustice and shameful deeds: and this is a fifth premise.

145 (6) Then, that infallible one, who must exist in the world, must either be allowed to conceal himself and not [to] appear or [to] call men to the truth, or he must publicly declare himself. But it is false that he can legitimately conceal [himself], for this would be a concealment of the truth, and it would be an injustice opposed to inerrancy: and this is a sixth premise.

146 (7) Now it is indeed certain that there is in the world an infallible one who openly makes this claim, and it remains to consider his specification. If, then, there are in the world two claimants, it would he complicated for us to distinguish the right one from the wrong one. But if there is only one claimant, in the place of complication that one is [p. 75] definitely the infallible one, and there is no need of any proof and any apologetic miracle. The likeness of that would be: If it be known that in a room in the house there is a man who is an *ᶜālim* [scholar jurist]; then we see in a room a man; and if the house contains another room, we have a lingering doubt about the one whom we have seen, whether he is that *ᶜālim* or someone else is. So if we know that there is no room in the house except this room, we know of necessity that he is the *ᶜālim.* So it is to be said of the Infallible Imam: and this is a seventh premise.

147 (8) It is known decisively that the only one in God's world claiming that he is the true Imam and the knower of God's secrets regarding all problems [and] the deputy of the Apostle of God concerning all rational and religious matters [and] the one who knows the revelation and the interpretation with a peremptory, not a conjectural, knowledge is the one who occupies himself with the matter [or: the Imamate] in Egypt: and this is an eighth premise.

148 Therefore, he is the Infallible Imam from whom it is incumbent on all men to learn the realities of the truth and to become acquainted with the meanings of the Law—and this is the conclusion we were seeking.

149 At this point they say: It is indeed a mercy of God and of His way of acting with creatures that He allows no one among creatures to claim infallibility save the true Imam. For if another claimant were to appear it would be difficult to distinguish the right one from

the wrong one, and creatures would err in the matter. So for this reason we never see an antagonist of the Imam, but rather we see a disavower [repudiator] of him: just as the Prophet—God bless him and grant him peace!—never had an antagonist. The antagonist is he who says: You are not a Prophet, but I am the Prophet; and the repudiator is he who does not claim [it] for himself, but simply denies his prophethood. This, then, is the case with the Imam.

150 *They say:* As for the ᶜAbbāsids—although the time has not been free from opposition to them—there was no one among them who claimed for himself infallibility and coming to know, from God Most High, the realities of things and the secrets of the Law, and dispensing with reasoning and the independent exercise of [personal] opinion. And it is this property which is sought. The sole ones to make this claim were the family of the Apostle [p. 76] of God—God bless him and grant him peace!—and his progeny. And God turned men's motives away from opposing them in the claim of the like of that, that the truth might firmly abide in its proper place and that doubt might be dislodged from the hearts of the Believers, [as] a mercy and favor from God. As a result, if one assume a person who would claim that for himself, he would mention it only in the form of jesting or argument: but that he would persist in believing that, or act on the strength of it—certainly not!

151 These are clear premises; of their sum total we have omitted only the proof of the invalidation of the mind's [intellect's] reasoning when we said: Either a man knows the truth by himself through his [own] mind [intellect], or he learns it from another. We shall now prove the invalidity of the mind's [intellect's] reasoning by rational and Law-based proofs. These are five:

152 (1) *The first* is a rational proof. He who follows what reason [the intellect] requires and assents to it, unconsciously has in his assent to it disbelief of [denial of] it. For there is no speculative question which he believes by his intellectual reasoning, but that he has regarding it an adversary who believes by the reasoning of the intellect its contrary. So if [your] intellect is a truthful judge, why the intellect of your adversary is also truthful. *If you say:* My adversary is not truthful, *what you say* involves a contradiction, since you believe one intellect and disbelieve its like. And *if you say:* My adversary is truthful—your *adversary says:* You are lying and wrong. And if you pretend that "My adversary has no intellect, but I only have it"—this is also the claim of your adversary. So by what are you distinguished from him? By length of beard? Or whiteness of face? Or by frequency of coughing? Or by vehemence in claiming?!! At this point they loose the language of mockery and disdain, believing that by what they say they have the upper hand which is unanswerable.

153 [p. 77] (2) [*The Second Proof*] is their saying: When a judge seeking guidance is doubtful about a legal or rational problem and claims he is unable to get to know its indication [proof—i.e. the way to solve it], what do you say to him? Do you refer him to his intellect—and perhaps he is a rude common man who is unacquainted with rational proofs, or he is an intelligent man who has shot the arrows of *raʾy* [personal judgment or opinion] to the best of his ability, but the problem has not been disclosed to him and he remains doubtful? Do you, then refer him to his intellect the deficiency of which he acknowledges? This is absurd. Or do you say to him: Learn the way of reasoning and the guide to the problem from me? If you say that, you have contradicted your affirmation of the invalidation of *tāᶜlīm:* for you have enjoined *tāᶜlīm* and made it a way [method]—but it is *our* doctrine. Unless, indeed, you refuse for yourselves the office of *tāᶜlīm,* and are not ashamed of your adversary who opposes you and who, in his intellect, is like you in yours.

154 This learner will say: Your adversary has invited me to learn from him, but indeed I am also perplexed about the designation [specification; selection] of the teacher. No one of you claims infallibility for himself, nor has he an apologetic miracle which marks him out, nor is he the sole possessor of anything by which he differs from others. So I do not know whether to follow the Philosopher, or the Ash^{c}arite, or the Mu^{c}tazilite—since their assertions are mutually contradictory though their intellects are like one another. I do not find in myself a preference because of length of beard and whiteness of faces, nor do I see any difference save in that, if it occurs. As for the intellect and the claim and the delusion of each about himself that he is the one right and his fellow is the one wrong which is like the delusion of his fellow—how intense is the contradiction of this way of talking in the view of him who is familiar with it!

155 (3) [*The third proof*] is their saying: oneness is the indication of the true, and multiplicity is the indication of the false. For when we say: How much is five and five? the true is one, viz. that one say: Ten. But the false is multiple [and] boundless, viz. everything other than ten, which is above or below it. And oneness is an inherent property of the doctrine of *ta^{c}līm,* for a thousand thousand are agreed on this belief and all say the same thing, and disagreement among them is inconceivable. But to men of *ra^{ɔ}y* [personal reasoning] there continually attaches disagreement and multiplicity. So this shows that the truth is in the sect to the word of which oneness cleaves. This was shown by the Most High's utterance: "If it had been from other than God surely they would have found in it much inconsistency" [4.84/82].

156 [p. 78] (4) [*The Fourth Proof*] is their saying: If the reasoner does not perceive the similarity between himself and his adversary, and has a good opinion of himself and a bad opinion of his adversary, it is no wonder, then, that this delusion is one of the things which dominates men, viz. their infatuation with their own opinions and the excellence of their own intellects—even though that is one of the indications of folly [stupidity]. The astonishing thing is simply that he does not perceive the similarity between his two states. How many times he has seen himself in one state, and his state has changed and he believes a thing for a while and judges it to be the truth imposed by the reliable [truthful] intellect, then there suddenly occurs to him a thought and he believes its contrary and claims that he now has become aware of the truth, and that what he formerly believed was a fancy [imagination] by which he was deceived: he sees himself possessed of a decisive belief, in his second state, which is equivalent to his preceding belief, for it was decisive with the like of his present decisiveness! I would like to know whence he is safe against being deceived and sure that he will not become aware of something by which it will become clear that what he now believes is false. There is no reasoner but that he often believes the like, then he ceaselessly glories finally in his belief which is like the other beliefs of his which he abandoned and came to know their falsity after deciding on them and holding them positively.

157 (5) [*The Fifth Proof*], and it is Law-based, is their saying: The Apostle of God—God bless him and his family and grant them peace!—said: "My Community will split into seventy-odd sects of which one will be saved." And it was said: "Who are they?" He said: "The people of *al-sunna* [the custom] and *al-jamā^{c}a* [the consensus]." It was said: "And what is the custom and the consensus?" He said: "What I and my Companions are now doing [saying and doing]." They say: And what they were doing [p. 79] was only following the *ta^{c}līm* regarding what happened among them [their disputes] and constituting the Apostle—Peace upon him!—judge regarding that, and not following their own

personal opinion and their intellects. So this proves that truth is in following, not in the reasoning of intellects.

158 This is the accurate formulation of their proofs in the strongest mode of presentation —and perhaps most of them would be unable to attain such a degree of perfection in precisely formulating them. So we say—and in God is succor—the argument against that is [by way of] two methods: general [summary] and detailed.

The First Method, viz. the General [Summary]

159 This is that we say: This belief which you have deduced from putting together these premises and ordering them by way of reasoning and reflection—if you claim to know it of necessity you are obstinate [pigheaded], and your adversaries are not unable to claim necessity in their knowledge of the falsity of your doctrine. And if they claim that, they would, in the view of a fair man, have a sounder claim. And if you claim to perceive it by consideration of the combining of these premises and ordering them in the form of valid syllogisms, then you acknowledge the validity of intellectual reasoning—and its falseness is claimed [by you]! This argument will silence him and disclose his vileness [ignominy].

160 Or one should say to him: Do you know the falsity of reasoning of necessity or by reasoning? And there is no way to claim necessity, because the necessary is that the knowledge of which is common to [shared by] the possessors of sound intellects [minds]—like our saying: The whole is greater than the part, and, Two is more than one, and, One and the same thing cannot be eternal and incipient, and, One and the same thing cannot be in two places [simultaneously]. And if he claims to perceive the falsity of reasoning by reasoning, his words involve a contradiction. And there will never, never be a way out of this! And this [argument] comes against every Bāṭinite who claims knowledge of something peculiar to himself. For he must claim either necessity or reasoning or hearing from a truthful infallible one, whose veracity and infallibility he also claims to know either of necessity or by reasoning. But there is no way to claim [p. 80] necessity; and in the claim of reasoning is the refutation of the very doctrine itself! Marvel, then, at this evident contradiction and the disregard of it by these deluded men!

161 *If some denier of reasoning says:* This can be retorted against you, because one can say to you: And how do you know the validity of reasoning? If you claim necessity, you rush into what you have deemed farfetched, and you are embroiled in precisely what you have rejected. But if you claim: We have perceived it by reasoning, then how do you know the validity of the reasoning by which you have perceived that, since there is a dispute about it? If you then claim to know that by a third reasoning, the same difficulty is inevitable regarding a fourth and a fifth and so on *ad infinitum. We say:* To be sure, this argument could be retorted if intelligibles [the objects of *ᶜaql*] were obtained by [due to] verbal comparisons [counterbalancings, weighings], but that is not the case. Consider, then, the subtlety of the difference: For we say that we know intellectual reasoning to be a guide to knowledge of the object of reasoning by following the path of reasoning and arriving at it. So he who follows it, arrives; and he who arrives knows that what he followed is the way [path]. But he who doubts before following should he told: The way to remove this doubt is to follow [the path].

162 And an example of this is: When we are asked about the way to the Kaᶜba and we indicate a specific way, and it is said to us: Whence do you know it to be a way? *We*

say: We know it by following [it]—because we have followed it and reached the Ka^{c}ba, and so we know it to be a way. And a second example of this is that when it is said to us: How do you know that reasoning on arithmetical matters, such as geometry and geodesy [surveying] and others, is a way to knowing what is not known of necessity? *We say:* Following the way of arithmetic [reckoning], since we have followed it and it has given us a knowledge of the object of the reasoning, so we know that reasoning of the intellect is a proof [guide] in arithmetic. And so regarding intellectual matters: we have followed the way of reasoning and arrived at the knowledge of intelligibles; so we know that reasoning is a way; [p. 81] and there is no contradiction in this.

163 *If it be said:* And how do you know that what you have reached is a knowledge concerning the cognoscible as it is—and not rather an ignorance you have assumed to be a knowledge? We *say:* If someone were to deny arithmetical cognitions, what should be said to him? Is he not to be called mentally incompetent and to be told: This proves the slightness of your understanding of arithmetical matters. For the reasoner on geometry, when he brings together the premises and arranges them according to their requirements, acquires knowledge of the conclusion necessarily in a way that cannot be doubted. Thus, also, we answer regarding the intelligibles. For if the speculative premises be arranged according to their conditions, they afford knowledge of the conclusion in a way that cannot be doubted, and the knowledge derived from the premises, once they exist, will he necessary like the knowledge of the necessary premises which produce it.

164 And if we wish to disclose that to him who has scanty resources of scientific knowledge, we give him a geometric example, and then give him an intellectual example, so that the veil may be lifted for him and hiddenness removed from his belief. The geometric example is that Euclid draws [traces] in his work regarding the first figure, from the first treatise, a triangle, and claims that it is equilateral. Now that is not known by an intuition of the intellect. But he claims that it is known by apodeictic proof through reasoning. And his apodeictic proof is by premises. *The first* is that straight lines proceeding from the center of a circle to the circumference are equal in every respect; and his premise is necessary, because the circle is drawn by the compass [dividers] opened in one way, and the straight line from the center to the circle [i.e. the circumference] is simply the opening of the compass, and this is one and the same in [all] directions.

165 [*The* second *premise*]*:* When two circles are equal by straight lines from their center to their circumference, the lines are also equal—and this also is necessary. [*The third premise*] is that the equal to the equal is equal—and this is also necessary. Then, let us now occupy ourselves with the triangle and point to two lines from it and we say: They are equal because they are two straight lines proceeding from the center of the circle to its circumference. And the third line is like one of them because it also [p. 82] proceeds from the center of the circle to its circumference along with that line. And if it is equal to one of the two lines, it is equal to the other, because the equal to the equal is equal. So after this reasoning we know decisively the mutual equality of the sides of the posited triangle, as the other premises are known, such as our saying: Straight lines from the center of the circle to the circumference are similar, and others of these premises.

166 The metaphysical [lit, divine] intellectual example is: When we wish to prove the [existence of the] necessarily existent being, subsistent in itself, independent of any others, from whom every existent derives its existence, we do not perceive the existence of a being necessarily existent and independent of any other of necessity, but by reasoning. And the meaning of reasoning is that we say: 'There is no doubt about the principle

[fundament] of existence, and that it is certain. For he who asserts that there is no existent at all in the world has staggered necessity and sensation. So our affirming that there is no doubt about the principle [fundament] of existence is a necessary premise. Then we say: The existence acknowledged by all is either necessary or possible. This is also a necessary premise because it is restrictive between negation and affirmation, like our saying: The existent is either external or incipient—so its truth will be necessary; and so of every every division revolving [turning] between negation and affirmation. Its meaning is that the existents either are independent or they are not independent. Independence of a cause is what is meant by "necessity" [*al-wujūb*], and the lack of independence is what is meant by "possibility" [*al-jawāz*]. This, then, is a third premise.

167 Then we say: If this acknowledged existent is necessary, then a Necessary Being exists; but if it is possible, every possible needs a Necessary Being. The meaning of its possibility is that it can not-exist and exist indifferently. But what has this quality [is of this description], its existence is distinguished from its non-existence only by a specifier—and this also is necessary: so by these necessary premises a Necessary Being certainly exists, and [p. 85] the knowledge, after its coming to be becomes necessary and cannot be doubted.

168 *If it be said:* There is room in it for doubt, since he may say the acknowledged is possible and say: Your assertion that every possible needs a necessary is inadmissible; rather it needs a cause, then that cause may be possible of existence. *We say:* In those premises is what contains potentially [?] the removal of this. For everything which certainly possesses possibility, its need for a cause is necessary. Then, if the cause is taken to be possible, it enters into the totality which we call "a whole." And we know of necessity that all the possibles need a cause.

169 So if you assume the cause to be possible, then assume it to enter into the totality and seek its cause, since it is impossible for another possible to support that, and so on *ad infinitum.* For in that case all the causes and the caused would be a possible totality and the attribute [description] of possibility would apply to its individuals and to its whole, and so the whole would require a cause outside the attribute of possibility to bring it forth [be. make it—the whole—emerge into existence]: and therein of necessity is the affirmation of a Necessary Being. And after that we would discourse about His quality and show that a Necessary Being cannot be a body, or impressed in a body, or changeable, or localized—and so on of all that follows that, and each one of those affirmations would be certain by premises not open to doubt, and the conclusion, after its advent [resulting, coming to be] from the premises, would be in clarity [obviousness] commensurate with the immediate perception [*dhawq:* experience] of the premises.

170 *Someone may say:* Arithmetical cognitions are acknowledged because they are necessary, and therefore there has been no disagreement about them. But intellectual matters involving reasoning, if their premises are such, why has disagreement about them taken place? For the occurrence of disagreement about them cuts off safety [from error]. *We say:* This is false in two ways: (*One of them*) is that there has been disagreement about arithmetical cognitions in detail and in general in two ways: *One of them* is that the ancients disagreed about many of the forms of the celestial sphere [*al-falak*] and the knowledge of their quantities, and these are based on arithmetical premises. But [p. 84] when there is an increasing concatenation of the premises, the mind is too weak to retain them, and perhaps one slips from the mind and so it errs regarding the conclusion. But the possibility of that does not make us doubt about the method. True enough, disagreement about arithmetical

premises is rarer because they are clearer [more evident], and in intellectual matters it is more frequent, because they are more hidden and veiled. But among matters involving reasoning [there are some] that are clear, and on which they have agreed, viz. that the eternal cannot not-exist. This is a question involving reasoning and no one has ever been opposed regarding it: so there is no difference between the arithmetical and the intellectual.

171 *The second* [way of disagreement about arithmetical cognitions] is that one may restrict the avenues of cognitions to the senses and deny cognitions involving reasoning *in toto,* the arithmetical and the non-arithmetical: but does the opposition of men like that make us doubt our knowledge that arithmetical cognitions are true and real? *If you say:* Yes!, your inclination to be unfair is clear. *And if you say:* No!—then why has the opposition regarding it occurred? *If you say:* His opposition does not make us doubt the premises, so why should it make us doubt the conclusion? So likewise the opposition of him who opposes us regarding the detail of what we know of the proof of the existence of a Necessary Being does not make us doubt the premises of the proof: why, then, should it make us doubt the conclusion?

172 *The second way* [first way was begun in Para. 170] to reply is that the Sophists deny "necessaries" and are opposed regarding them and claim that they are figments of the mind without any foundation. They argue to this from the fact that the clearest of them are the sensibles, and there is no reliance on a man's being positive about his sensation. The more he sees a man and speaks to him, the more positively he affirms his presence and his speech: and this is an error. For perhaps he sees him in sleep [a dream]. How many a dream does a man see and is certain of it [thinks it certain] and has no personal doubt of its reality: then he wakes suddenly and it is clear that it has no [real] existence. He may even see in a dream his own hand cut off and his head severed and think it certain, yet what he thinks certain has no existence. Moreover, the opposition of these does not make us doubt the necessaries, and so also the matters involving reasoning, for since the latter come to be from the premises they remain necessary [and] no doubt is had about them, as in the case of arithmetical matters.

173 All of this is an argument [polemic] against him who denies reasoning in toto. But the Taᶜlīmites are unable to [p. 85] hold peremptorily the invalidation of reasoning in toto, because they propound the proofs and demonstrations of the affirmation of *taᶜlīm,* and they organize the premises as we have related. How, then, can they reject that? And hereupon *they say:* The reasoning of the intellect is false. Then *one should say:* And how do you know its falsity and the existence of *taᶜlīm?* By a reasoning or by a necessity? And the answer must be: By a reasoning. And whenever one argues from the opposition [disagreement] about matters involving reasoning to the wrongness of such matters, confront him with the disagreement [opposition] on the part of the Sophists regarding "necessaries." There is no difference between the two positions.

174 *If they say:* And how are you safe from error? How many times have you believed something through reasoning, then its contrary became evident! *Then one should say to him:* And how do you know you are present in this place in which you are, and how many times your soul has believed and seen itself to be in another place in which it was not—so how do you distinguish between sleep [dreaming] and wakefulness? How can you be safe from yourself—for perhaps now in this polemic you are sleeping! *If he claims:* I perceive the difference of necessity. *One should say:* And I have also perceived the difference between that in the premises about which there can be error, and that about which there cannot be, of necessity: and there is no difference. Similarly, how often does a man err in

arithmetic, then he becomes aware [of it]. And when he becomes aware, he knows [perceives] of necessity the dlifference between the state of being right and that of being wrong.

175 If a Bāṭinite speaker says: We reject reasoning in toto. But what you have mentioned has nothing to do with matters involving reasoning, but they are necessary, peremptory premises which we have organized [arranged]. *We say:* Then you now do not understand the meaning of the reasoning which we hold. For we do not hold other than the like of the necessary true premises which you have set in order, as we shall show. For every syllogism which is not [constructed] by the ordering of necessary premises, or by the ordering of premises deduced from "necessaries," contains no proof [*ḥujja*]. This is the intelligible [rational] syllogism. It is always composed simply from two premises: either absolute or "divisional" [disjunctive], and they may be called categorical and conditional. The "absolute" is like our saying: The world is incipient; but every incipient has a cause. These two are two premises the first a fact of sensation, and the second an intellectual "necessary." The conclusion of it is: That the incipients [or: incipience] of the world have a cause [rather: Therefore the world has a cause. ?].

176 [p. 86] The "divisional" is that we say: If it is certain that the incipients of the world have a cause, the postulated cause is either incipient or eternal. And if it is false that it is incipient, it is certain that it is eternal. Then we invalidate [show the falsity of] its being incipient by such syllogisms as these, and so finally it is certain that the existence of the world has an eternal cause. This, then, is the reasoning professed [by us]. So if you are doubtful about its validity, then how do you deny him who refrains from accepting your premises which you have set in order and says: I am doubtful about their validity? If you ascribe to him the denial of necessity, we ascribe the like to you regarding what we claim to know by reasoning—and there is no difference.

177 This is the general [summary] method of refuting them, if they declare invalid the reasoning of intellects. And it is the decisive way necessary to silence them. So we ought not wade with them into detail and should confine ourselves to saying to them: All that you know of your doctrine, viz. the veracity and infallibility of the Imam, and the falsehood of *ra*ʾ*y* [personal reasoning], and the necessity of *ta*ᶜ*līm*—how do you know it? The claim of necessity is impossible: so there remains reasoning and hearing. And the veracity of "hearing" also is not known of necessity: so there remains reasoning. There is no way out of this!

178 *Someone may say:* It is unthinkable that an intelligent man would claim a doctrine that is not necessary, and then reject reasoning. So perhaps they acknowledge reasoning, but hold that learning the method of reasoning is obligatory, because a man cannot be independent regarding matters involving reasoning. If you deny that, you have spontaneously [instinctively] denied intellects. For instructors and teachers are trained [nominated] only to teach: why, then, do they undertake it, when they can be dispensed with? If you acknowledge that, you have acknowledged the necessity of a reacher, and that intellects are not of themselves alone sufficient: So it remains that you allow *ta*ᶜ*līm* on the part of anyone, and they enjoin learning from an infallible one, because the views of teachers differ and contradict one another and one is not preferable to another.

179 [p. 87] *We say:* This question also is unsound, for we do not deny the need for learning [in another reading: *ta*ᶜ*līm*-teaching]. On the contrary, cognitions are divided into three divisions. *A division* which can be acquired only by hearing and learning, like information about bygone events and the apologetic miracles of the Prophets and what will happen on [the Day of] the Resurrection and the circumstances of the Garden and the Fire. This is knowable only by hearing from the infallible Prophet, or by impeccable transmission

from him. So if it is heard from the report of individuals it results in a knowledge that is conjectural, not sure and certain. This is one division.

180 The *second division* comprises the intellectual, speculative cognitions. In the natural constitution [of man] there is not anything to guide to the proofs regarding it, but for it there must be learning, not that one may blindlly follow the teacher on that, but that the teacher may call attention to the way to it; then the intelligent man returns regarding it to himself and perceives [grasps] it by his own reasoning. At this point let the teacher be who he will, even the most sinful and untruthful of men. For we do not follow him blindlly but become aware by his pointing out, and so we do not need for that an infallible man. It is like the arithmetical and geometrical cognitions: they are not known by [one's] natural constitution and need a teacher. But we have no need of an infallible teacher, but rather the method of demonstration is learned and the learner is equal to the teacher after reasoning about intellectual matters in our view, and arithmetical matters in theirs. How many a person errs in arithmetical matters, then becomes aware finally after a time: but that does not induce doubt about the arithmetical proofs and demonstrations, nor does it entail [imply?] a need, for them, of an infallible teacher.

181 *The third division* comprises religious and juridical cognitions, i.e. knowledge of the licit and the illicit, and the obligatory and the recommended. The basis of this knowledge is hearing from the trustee of the Law. Hearing from him engenders knowledge. However, the acquisition of peremptory knowledge of this is not possible absolutely with regard to every person and every case. Rather one must be satisfied with conjecture [probability] about it necessarily in two ways: One of them concerns the hearers. For men in the Prophet's era—God bless him and grant him peace!—were divided into those who saw and heard and verified and knew [p. 88] and those who were absent and then heard from the informers and individual leaders and rulers and derived a probability from the utterance of the individuals. But it was obligatory on them to act according to the probability because of [the] necessity. For the Prophet—God bless him and grant him peace!—was unable to make each one hear personally without an intermediary, and it was not a condition that there he an impeccable transmission from him of every word about every incident, because of the impossibility of this. Knowledge results from one of these two ways, and it is definitely impossible [impracticable] [i.e. to have *tawātur* in every case?].

182 [And the second way, or part] [*al-ṭaraf:* should it be *al-ṭarīq*—or 1.21 of p. 87 should have *ṭarafayn*—p. 89, 1.2 has *al-ṭarafayn*] concerns the juridical form [model, formula] itself and the actual incidents. Therefore there is no case [incident] save that there is a precept regarding it. But the cases are unlimited, nay, in possibility, infinite. The texts cannot be assumedl to be other than limited and finite and what is finite can never compass what is infinite. The aim of the trustee of the Law, for example, was [not] to designate textually [?] the legal status of every form [model, formula] contained in the work of the writers on *fiqh* [jurisprudence] down to this age of ours. But had he done that exhaustively, the possible cases outside of the works would be more numerous than those written down in them—nay, there would be no proportion of the former to the latter! For those written down are limited, and those possible are unlimited. How, then, could he exhaust textually what is infinite!

183 So of necessity opinion must be made to judge the relationship to the former of the generalities, even though it is probable that they have been expressed out of a desire for the particular, for with this [desire] most of the generalities [are concerned ?]. Therefore, when the Apostle of God—God bless him and grant him peace!—sent Muᶜādh

to al-Yemen, and said to him: "By what will you judge?" Muᶜādh said: "By the Book of God." The Apostle said: "And if you do not find [anything there]?" Muᶜādh replied: 'Then by the custom [*sunna*] of the Apostle of God." The Apostle said: "And if you do not find [anything there]?" Muᶜādh replied: "I shall exercise my personal reasoning." Then he [the Apostle] said—God bless him and grant him peace!—"Praise be to God Who has guided [helped] the apostle of His Apostle to what His Apostle approves." So he permitted him to exercise personal judgment simply because it was necessarily impossible for specific texts to contain all the cases.

184 This is the explanation of this division, and for it there is no need of an Infallible Imam, nay but [p. 89] the Infallible Imam is of no use at all! For he adds nothing to the Trustee of the Law, and the latter was not of use in both of the parts [i.e. in reaching all men personally (*al-ᶜulūm al-dīniyya*) and in textually settling every case possible (*al-ᶜulūm al-sharᶜiyya*)]; for there is [he has] no power to include all the forms in the texts, nor can he speak to all men or enjoin them to stipulate impeccable transmission in everything which is transmitted from him—Peace be upon him! Then I would like to know [of] what use your infallible teacher is in these two parts. Do all men know the texts of his utter ances, and they are in the Far East and the Far West, by the utterance of these individual propagandists—and these have no infallibility so that they should be relied on—or is it stipulated that there be impeccable transmission from him regarding every word, when he in his own person is concealed and is met only by individuals and isolated persons? This—even though it were conceded that he knows the truth by revelation regarding every case, as did the Trustee of the Law. How, then, when the situation is as we know it and as his leading followers know it who surround him in his town and his province! [add. in ms. Q: viz. stupidity, and little understanding, and ignorance, and silliness, and foolishness, and bad stumbling [?], and scarcity of religion, and multiplicity of treason (betrayal) and invalidation of the religious Laws, and commanding the evil and forbidding the good, and claiming divinity].

185 It has indeed become clear from this polemic that they are deceitful and say: If you say there is no need for *taᶜlīm,* you have indeed denied what is customary; but if you acknowledge [it], then you have indeed agreed with us in the affirmation of *taᶜlīm.* Thus they take *al-taᶜlīm* as a general admitted expression, then they detail [particularize] it as containing the acknowledgment of the necessity of learning from the Infallible [Imam]. You have understood what knowledge needs no teacher, and what knowledge needs a teacher. And if there is need of a teacher, what is obtained from him is his method, and he is not blindly followed in his own person—so there is no need of his infallibility. But when he is to be blindly followed in himself, then there is need of his infallibility.

186 And [you know] that that Infallible [Imam, teacher] is the Prophet—God bless him and grant him peace! And [you know] how what is received from him is divided into what is known to be certain [lit. by verification] and what is a matter of probability, and [p. 90] how all men are forced to be content with probability regarding the veracity of him who passes on the information from the Trustee of the Law, and regarding the attachment of what is not textually specified to [specific] texts. If you know this rule for certain, you have mastered the disclosing of all their deceptions. For it is always their wont to lay down unpointed [i.e. ambiguous] premises on which they build a false conclusion—like their saying: You, when you acknowledge the need for *taᶜlīm* have indeed acknowledged our doctrine. So we say: our acknowledgment of learning [or: teaching *?*] in the case of matters involving reasoning is like your acknowledgment of it in the case of arithmetical matters.

This is the general method of the polemic against them.

The Second Method in Refuting Them in Detail

187 Our method will be to speak of each premise of the eight premises which we set in order. So we say: (*The first premise* [ef. Para. 142]) This is your assertion that everything which can be stated negatively and affirmatively contains true and false, and the true is one and the false is what confronts it. This is a true premise, about which we do not think there is any dispute: but it is not right on your part to use it. *For we say:* Among men is he who denies the realities of things, and claims that there is neither any true nor any false, and that things follow beliefs: so what is believed to have existence exists with respect to that believer, and what is believed not to exist is nonexistent with respect to the believer. This is the thesis of one of the sects of the Sophists.

188 And perhaps *they will say:* Things have no reality and they will liken things sensed to dreams, the reality of which is definitely believed, though their contents have no reality. *We say:* Is this premise a premise they hold for certain? You see things in sleep and they have no reality—so how are you safe from error about them? How often you have seen yourselves in sleep holding something for certain which had no reality! And what has assured you that your adversaries are not right and you wrong? And we would continue to bring up to them what they bring up to the partisans of reasoning to induce doubt about it [reasoning]—and they will find no distinction.

189 *If they claim* that: We know of necessity the error of the [p. 91] Sophists who oppose us, and we know of necessity the truth of this premise—*One should say to them:* How, then, do you repudiate the partisans of reasoning when they claim that about their own doctrine, and about their distinguishing between that in which they err and that in which they do not err, and about their making a distinction between themselves and their adversaries?

190 *If they claim* that that requires reflection, whereas what concerns us is something intuitive. *We say:* And in arithmetical matters there is need of the subtlest reflection. So if in an arithmetical question with which you are familiar a man errs whose reasoning is inadequate or whose intelligence is feeble, does that make you doubt that the arithmetical cognitions are true? If you say: No!—one should say: That is exactly like the state of the meticulous reasoners when adversaries oppose them. And this ought to be [urgedl] against them regarding every position, because they flaunt so much the disagreement of reasoners and [hold] that that ought to do away with safety [from error]. But our disagreeing with them has not done away with their safety from error about their premises which they set in order, then wanted, along with that, to do away with our safety from error about matters involving reasoning by the disagreement of him who disagrees about them. This is an inane desire and feeble assumption by the like of which no intelligent man would be deceived.

191 (*The second premise* [ef. Para. 142]) is their assertion: If it is certain that there is in every case [a] true and [a] false, then the true in it must be known.

This is a fallacious premise, since they take it generally, and in it there is a particularization. But this is their wont in deceiving—so let not the knowledgeable man be heedless of it. *So we say:* One's saying: "The true must be known" is like one's saying "The question must be known," or 'The questions must be known." It should, then, be said: This is an error. On the contrary, "the question" is a common noun which includes what must be known and what need not be known—so there must be a particularization. Similarly also [p. 92] the true: we can dispense with it in most matters.

192 For the totality of the chronicles and the annals [of events] which have been and shall be until the end of the world or are today taking place in the world—all this can be stated negatively and affirmatively. And the true is one—but we do not need to know it. This is like one's saying: Is the King of the Byzantines existing now or not? The true is undoubtedly one of them. And the earth beneath my feet, after going beyond five cubits, is it dirt or stone? And are there worms in it or not? The true is undoubtedly one of them. And the quantity of the sphere of the sun or of Saturn and their distance—is it a hundred parasangs or not? The truth is one of them. And so also the areas of the mountains and the countries, and the number of the animals on the land and in the sea, and the number of [the grains of] sand. In all these there is a true and a false—but there is no need to know these things. Nay, but the well-known sciences such as syntax and poetry and medicine and philosophy and *kalām,* etc., contain true and false—but we do not need [to know] most of what is said in them.

193 Rather, what we admit must be known comprises two questions: the existence of the Maker Most High, and the veracity of the Apostle—God bless him and grant him peace! This is a must! Then, once the Apostle's veracity is established, the rest is connected with it by unquestioning acceptance, or by knowleilge of report of impeccable transmission, or by supposition based on the report of an individual. That much knowledge is enough for this life and the next, and anything else can be dispensed with. As for the Maker's existence and the Apostle's veracity, the way to know it is reasoning on [consideration of] creation [creatures] to deduce from it [them] the [existence of the] Creator, and [consideration] of the apologetic miracle to deduce from it the veracity of the Apostle.

194 And regarding these two there is no need for an infallible teacher. For men, regarding this, are two divisions. *One division* is of those who have believed that by unquestioning acceptance and hearing from their parents and they resolutely accepted it, positively affirming it and giving voice to it by their saying: There is no god save God; Muḥammad is the Apostle of God—God bless him and grant him peace!—without any inquiry into the demonstrative methods—and these, these are truly the Muslims. That belief suffices them, and they are not obliged [p. 93] to seek out the methods of apodeictic proofs. We have come to know that for certain from the Trustee of the Law. For he used to be repaired to by the rude Arabs and by the gullible common folk: in sum, by a group who, had they been cut to pieces, would not have grasped anything of the rational demonstrations—nay, they can clearly be distinguished from the beasts only by speech. He used to propose to them the word of the two witnesses, then judge them to have the faith and to be content with that on their part, and he enjoined on them the acts of worship. So it is known positively that resolute belief is sufficient, even though it be not the result of an apodeictic demonstration but rather of an unquestioning acceptance. Often a desert Arab would come to him [Muḥammad] and make him swear that he was the Apostle of God and that he was truthful in what he said—and he would swear to him, and the latter would believe him, and he would judge him to have accepted Islam. So these—I mean the unquestioning accepters—do not need the Infallible Imam.

195 (*The second division*) includes him whose unquestioning acceptance has been unsettled [disturbed] either by reflection, or by another's inducing him to doubt, or by his considering that error is possible regarding his views. This man can be saved only by the positive apodeictic demonstration proving the existence of the Maker, viz. reasoning on [His] creation, and [proving] the veracity of the Apostle, viz. reasoning on the apologetic miracle. And I would like to know what use their Infallible Imam is to them [such men]!

Would he say to such a one: Believe that the world has a Maker and that Muḥammad—God bless him and grant him peace!—is truthful out of servile conformism to me, without any proof, since I am the Infallible Imam? Or would he cite to him a proof and call his attention to how it proves? And if his inclination is servile conformism, then how can he believe him, nay more, whence can he know his infallibility, when he does not know the infallibility of his fellow, who claims that he is his vicar, after many steps [stages]?!

196 And if he cites the proof, does the one seeking guidance need to consider the proof and to reflect on its composition and the mode of its proving, or not? If he does not reflect, then how can he grasp [it] without reasoning and reflection, since these cognitions are not necessary? But if he reflects and perceives [grasps] how the necessary, valid premises sought by his reflection lead to a conclusion, and thereby is outside the limit of servile conformism to him, then what is the difference between the one who calls his attention to the mode of the proof and the arrangement of the premises being [p. 94] the infallible one alluded to, or a propagandist or some other one of the ulema [learned men] of the time? For each one does not call him to blind following of himself, but leads him simply to what the proof necessitates, and the latter is perceived only by reflection. So if he reflects and perceives, he is not a blind follower of his teacher, but he is like the learner of arithmetical proofs. And in that there is no difference between the most sinful of men and the most godly—just as the teacher of arithmetic is not required to possess godliness, to say nothing of infallibility, because he is not the object of servile conformism, but it is simply the proof which is followed. Therefore men do not go beyond these two divisions: the first does not need the infallible [one], and the second gets no benefit at all from the infallible [one]. So two premises are already false [invalid]: one of them that every truth [everything true] must be known, and the other that the true can be known only from an infallible one [this seems to involve three premises: cf. Paras. 142–43].

197 *If it be said:* The knowledge of God Most High and of His Apostle is not sufficient, but there must also be knowledge of God's Attributes and knowledge of the prescriptions of the Law. *We say:* The Attributes of God Most High are two divisions: One [The second division is not discussed: presumably it includes other attributes, for which revelation suffices.] is such that knowledge of the Apostle's veracity and mission can be had only after it is known—e.g. God's being knowing and able to send envoys. This is known, in our view, by intellectual proofs, as we have mentioned; but the infallible one is of no use, because the one who believes it by servile conformism or hearing from his parents has no need of the teacher—as has preceded. And of what use is the infallible one to one who hesitates about it?! Would he say to him: Follow me blindly in the matter of God Most High's being able and knowing. Then he would say to him: How can I follow you blindly, when my soul will not allow me to follow blindly Muḥammad son of ᶜAbdallāh—God bless him and grant him peace!—although he is the possessor of an apologetic miracle?! But if he cites to him the modality of the proof, discussion of it comes back to what has preceded about the foundation [principle] of the existence of the Maker and the veracity of tbe Apostle—without any difference.

198 As for the prescriptions of the Law, everyone must know what he needs concerning his duties. These are two divisions: (*The first division*) is that which can be known for certain, and this is what is included in the text of the Qurʾān and [that] on which there is an impeccable tradition from the Trustee of the Law: e.g., the number of *rakᶜas* in the five prayers, and the amounts of the *nuṣub* [minimum amounts of property liable to the alms tax] with respect to the *Zakāt* [alms taxes], and the regulations of the acts of worship,

and the pillars [chief elements] of the Pilgrimage, or that on which there is a consensus of the Community. For this division there is no need whatever of an Infallible Imam.

199 (*The second division*) is that which cannot be known for certain, but it is open to doubt [conjecture]. This is *either* a text the transmission of which is open to uncertainty because it is transmitted by individuals: so it must be believed tentatively, as it was obligatory on men in other countries in the time of the Apostle of God—God bless him and grant him peace!, *or* a case about which there is no explicit text, and so it needs to be compared with what is textually specified and to be approximated to the latter by the exercise of personal judgment: this is that of which Muᶜādh said: "I shall exercise my personal opinion." The fact that this is an object of probability is necessary regarding both sides together, because one cannot stipulate impeccable transmission for everything, and all cases cannot be exhausted by specific textual designation.

200 So in this the infallible one is of no use. For he cannot make what an individual transmits *mutawātir* [an impeccable transmission]—nay, even if he were certain of it he would not speak of it to all men, nor could he enjoin it on their hearing it from him by impeccable transmission, so that his partisans would blindly follow the propagandists of the infallible one, when they are not infallible, but rather can err and lie. We unquestioningly follow the ulema of the Law, who are the emissaries of Muḥammad—God bless him and grant him peace!—who was confirmed by dazzling apologetic miracles. So what need is there of the infallible one in this regard? As for the case which is not the object of an explicit text, let personal judgment be exercised about it, since the infallible one is of no use in it.

201 For either he must acknowledge that he [the infallible one] also is a "conjecturer—and error is possible for everyone who has a conjecture, and that is not different in individuals—so what is it that distinguishes his conjecture from that of others, when he allows error of himself?! *Or* he claims knowledge of it: Does he claim it from a revelation, or from hearing an explicit text about it, or from a rational proof? If he claims the impeccable transmission of revelation to him [p. 96] in every case, then he is a claimant of prophethood and needs an apologetic miracle. How [could it be otherwise] when the assumption of the apologetic miracle is inconceivable, since it is clear to us that Muḥammad—God bless him and grant him peace!—is the Seal of the Prophets? So if we allow of Muḥammad lying in his statement: "I am the Seal of the Prophets," despite the establishment of the apologetic miracle, how can we be secure against the lying of this infallible one, even though he establish an apologetic miracle?!

202 And if he claims to know it from a specific text which has reached him, how can he not be ashamed of claiming a specific text of the Trustee of the Law on cases which cannot conceivably be limited or numbered: nay, but even though a man were granted a life as long as that of Noah, and were to apply himself only to counting the cases and the explicit texts about them, he would not exhaust a hundredth of them, So in what lifetime did the Apostle—God bless and grant him peace!—exhaust all the cases with textual explicitness! And if he claims such knowledge by a rational proof, how ignorant he is of both juridical and rational matters! For juridical matters are positive, conventional [technical] matters which differ with the circumstances [conventions, usages] of the Prophets and of ages and nations, as we see religious Laws to be different: how, then, is it possible to have decisive rational proofs of them? And if he claims it from a rational proof helpful for reasoning—why all the jurisprudents possess this rank!

203 So it is clear that what they mention is a deception far removed from verification, and that the common man deceived by it is extremely stupid. For they dupe the common

folk into following conjecture. and conjecture is of no help at all to truth. But in juridical matters one must follow conjecture, and this is [something] necessary—as in commercial and political matters and in deciding disputes for the general advantage—for all matters touching the general advantage are built on conjecture. And how can the infallible one dispense from [be a substitute for] this conjecture when the Trustee of the Law did not dispense from it, and was unable to, but rather permitted the exercise of personal judgment and reliance on the utterance of individuals reporting from him and on holding fast to general [or broad] principles [statements of principle] and all that is conjecture which was a basis for action in the Apostle's time and while he existed—so how can that be disapproved of after his death?!

204 [p. 97] *Someone may* say: And when those exercising personal judgment differ because of the different ways conjectures are arrived at, what is your opinion? If you say: "Everyone exercising personal judgment is right," what you say involves a contradiction, because your adversaries, however much [?] they are right in their belief, assert that you have erred [are wrong]. So you are not right therefore—and how [could you be] when among the sects is that which deems the shedding of your blood licit [lawful]? So if they also are right, then we are right in shedding your blood and plundering your possessions: so why do you censure us? And *if you say:* The one right is one—then how do we discern the right one from the wrong one? And how can we be free from the danger of error and conjecture?

205 *We say:* There are two views regarding it. If we say: "Everyone exercising personal judgment is right," we are not involved in a contradiction, because we mean by it that he attains [is right regarding] the prescription of God regarding him and those who unquestioningly follow him, because God has prescribed for him that he follow what he thinks more probable in every case, and he has done this. And this is [also] God's prescription for his adversary. And their assertion that he is therefore right regarding the shedding of blood is the utterance of one ignorant of juridical matters. For what the sects have differed about of that in which the shedding of blood is deemed proper are definite intellectual problems [questions] in which the one right is [only] one. But the juridical conjectural questions on which there is disagreement between al-Shāfiᶜī and Abū Ḥanīfa and Mālik do not lead to fighting one another and the shedding of blood, but rather each group believes in respecting the other group to such a point that it judges that its judgment is not to be opposed if sentence is given for it [or: based on it] and that it [p. 98] is incumbent on the opponent to follow [it]. To be sure, they disagree about whether or not one should apply the name of error [mistake] to the other sect in other than a denial and objection.

206 And [regarding] their saying: Your adversary says "You are wrong"—and if he is right, then you are wrong—*we say:* If my adversary says "You are wrong,'' i.e. I think you are wrong, he is truthful; and I also am truthful in my saying "I am right—and there is no contradiction. But if he says: "I know for certain that you are wrong," then he is not right in this assertion: rather, the falsity of the assertion of him who is certain of error in matters of personal judgment is not an object of conjecture, but is an object of certainty in the sum total of the decisive questions touching on the *uṣūl* [the bases of Islamic Law, or, here dogmatic beliefs, i.e. *uṣūl al-dīn*]. So the assertion "Of two exercising personal judgment the one right is both of them or one of them" is an *uṣūl* problem [question] involving certainty, not conjecture—but for them *uṣūl* matters have become mixed up with *fiqh* matters which are conjectural. But whenever the veil is removed, the discussion does not involve a contradiction.

207 Someone *may say:* If you consider everyone to be right, then let it be permissible for the one exercising personal judgment to accept his adversary's declaration and to act on it because the latter is right, and let it be permissible for the servile conformist to follow whom he will of the Imams who exercise personal judgment. *We say:* As for the one who exercises personal judgment following another—it is an error, For God prescribes for him that he follow his own conjecture—and this is certain. So if he follows another's conjecture, be errs in a decisive *uṣūl* question, and that is known by decisive consensus.

208 But the matter of those blindly following the Imams—some have held it [this opinion], but it seems preferable to us that he ought to follow blindly him whom he thinks to be the best and most knowledgeable of the people. The support of his belief is either aural conformism from his parents, or general inquiry about his circumstances, or what has got around on the tongues of jurists: in general he comes [p. 99] to have a more probable conjecture from these supports, and so he must follow his own conjecture, just as the one exercising personal judgment must follow his own conjecture. But this is not universal regarding the Law, because the Law contains a particular benefit in each question, and a universal benefit in the totality. The particular is that of which is known the proof [indication?] and rationale of every precept. But the universal benefit is that everyone obligated to be under a specific law [rule?] of the precepts of the Law regarding all his movements and his utterances and his beliefs, so that he is not like the freed beast which does as it pleases, so that he schools himself by the bridle of piety and the discipline and division of the Law into what it gives him free rein in, and what it forbids him: so he is bold when the Law gives him free rein and abstains where it forbids, and does not take as his god his caprice [cf. 25.45/43] and follow therein his desires.

209 And whenever we inform the servile conformists about the views of the Imams that one may take from them the best in his view, those speaking about it are confused and there remains for him no recourse save his caprice regarding the choice, and this is opposed to the general aim. So we think it best to confine him to [one] mold and to control him by [one] rule, viz. the opinion of one person on this matter. Because of this the laws of the Prophets in the [various] ages have differed in relation to detail, but they have not differed regarding the basic principle of imposing obligation and calling men from following caprice to obedience to the rule of the Law. This is what we consider preferable regarding invididual servile conformists. This is one of the two views, viz. that everyone exercising personal judgment is right.

210 And he who thinks that the one right is [only] one—there is also no contradiction in what he says. And [regarding] his utterance: "How are you [text: he] safe from the possibility of error?"—*We say:* First their clash [mutual opposition]. He whose dwelling was remote from the Apostle of God—God bless him and grant him peace!—and was relying on the statement of an individual, and so also he whose dwelling is remote from your infallible one, and he is divided from him by obstructing seas and perilous deserts—how can he be safe from error on the part of the informant, when the latter is not infallible? *They will say:* He judges by conjecture and is not bound [p. 100] to more than that. Then this is our reply!

211 *If you say:* He does have a way to escape conjecture. This is that he go to see the Prophet—God bless him and grant him peace!—for directing oneself to him is one of the possibles: and likewise, one should go to see the Infallible Imam in every age. *We say:* Is it obligatory to purpose that when[ever] he allows the possibility of error? If you say 'No," then what profit is there in its possibility, when it is allowable for him to plunge

[rush, hurtle] into the roadway [surface, the very midst] of danger regarding that about which he allows the possibility of error? So if that be allowable, there is no harm in the passing of the possibility. How [could it be otherwise] when every penniless sick man flat on his back is unable to traverse a thousand parasangs to ask about an actual legal problem [question]? And how, even if he did make that trip, how would his suspicion [conjecture] about your Infallible Imam pass away, even though he were to speak to him directly about it, since he has no apologetic miracle attesting his veracity? So in what way could he trust in what he says? And how could his suspicion of him abate?

212 *Then he says:* There is no escape for him from the possibility of error: but it does him no harm, since the farthest one can go on this subject is that attaining what is right contains an excellent [or: increased?] advantage. In all matters connected with [his] worldly [material] advantage a man speaks according to conjectures and cannot escape the possibility of his being in error: but it does him no harm. Nay more, were he clearly to err about a legal problem, it would do him no harm. On the contrary, error on details of legal matters is legally excused by reason of his declaration—God bless him and grant him peace!—"He who exercises personal judgment and is right will have two rewards; and he who exercises personal judgment and errs will have one reward."

213 So the danger of error about which they make a great fuss is disdained in itself among those men of religion who are knowledgeable and the matter is thereby magnified only for the masses [common people] who are unaware [heedless] of the secrets [mysteries] of Revelation [the Law]. Error in legal matters is not [p. 101] one of the causes of perdition in the afterlife. Nay more, the commission of a grave sin does not necessitate the eternity of the punishment or require it in a way not susceptible of forgiveness [pardon]. As for mattters involving personal effort, no sin is imputed to him who errs therein. The Ḥanafite declares: The traveler prays [should pray] two *rakᶜas,* and the Shāfiᶜite declares: He prays [should pray] four [*rakᶜas*]. However he acts, the difference is slight, and even if it were rated as an error in him, it would be forgiven him. The acts of worship are simply endeavors [strivings] and exercises which bestow on souls purity and assure an honored place in the afterlife, just as the repetition of profit [*manfaᶜa*—cf. Wehr—term of Islamic Law] for what one learns makes one the *faqīh* [expert] of the soul and brings him to the rank of the ulema. And his advantage [benefit] differs because of the multiplicity of the repetition and its paucity, and his raising his voice therein and lowering it.

214 If, then, he errs in limiting himself to repeating one lesson twice, when three [times] would make a greater impression on his soul in God Most High's knowledge, or if he errs in [limitation to] three, when limiting himself to two would be more effective in safeguarding him from dulling boredom, or if he errs in lowering his voice, when raising it would be better suited to his nature and to altering [rousing] his soul, or lowering it would be more conducive to reflection on its [the lesson's] essential meaning—the error in anything of that one night or several nights would not cause despair of [attaining] the Imamate [rank of Imam] and procuring *fiqh* of the soul. And he, in all that he conjectures [projects] and arranges [determines, fixes] regarding the amounts of repetition with respect to quantity and quality and time, would be therein one exercising personal effort and a conjecturer and one travelling to the way of achieving [accomplishing, gaining] his goal so long as he continues to apply himself steadily to the fundamental thing, even though he is certain to err at time in the details [particular points].

215 The danger lies simply in attributing error [or: neglect?] and being opposed and being misled by native intelligence on the supposition that the latter makes one able to dis-

pense with personal effort, as a group of the Bāṭinites supposed that their souls were pure [and] well exercised [trained] [and] in no need of the exercises of the legal acts of worship, and so they neglected them and because of that they ran the risk of the grievous punishment in the abode of the afterlife. So let the seeker of guidance believe that the leading of the legal strivings to the honored, sublime stations in the abode of the afterlife is like the leading of personal effort in mastering sciences and applying oneself assiduously to them to the station [rank] of the Imams. And at this [point] [or: in view of this] we disdain what the Bāṭinites have made a great to-do about [p. 102], viz. the danger of error for those exercising personal effort regarding raising one's voice in the *Basmala* [saying: *Bismillāh al-raḥmān al-raḥīm*] and repeating [doubling] the performance [of the Prayer] and the likes. Difference in this, after applying oneself assiduously to the well-known basic elements is like difference regarding raising or lowering the voice in the repetition [of lessons] without any difference. And how [could it be otherwise] when the Law has called attention to the facilitation of the excuse of him who errs therein, just as there has been unimpeachable report 'of that from the Trustee of the Law. This is the complete argument [polemic] against the second premise.

216 *The third premise* [cf. Para. 142] is their assertion: If the obligation of knowing the true be certain, then a man must either know it of [through] himself or from another, This is a true and undisputed premise. To be sure, the argument against it by what will silence the Bāṭinites and prevent *them* from using it is like what we have mentioned regarding the first premise—and it applies to every true premise.

217 *The fourth premise* [ef. Para. 143] is their assertion: If it be false that a man know the true of himself by the way [method] of reasoning, then the obligation of learning from another is certain. This [premise] is true on the supposition that reasoning is futile and granting the obligation of knowing the true. But we do not grant the futility of reasoning, as has been said previously and as we shall mention in showing the falseness of their embellished [tinselly] specious arguments in support of the invalidation of reasoning; nor do we concede the obligation of knowing the true, since the totality of the latter contains what is left to our choice, and what is [really] needed is the knowledge of the Maker and of the Apostle's veracity. This knowledge men have believed in firmly by hearing and by blindly following their parents: in that is what suffices them so that there is no need for them to recommence learning from an infallible teacher. And if they are content with instruction [received] from [their] parents, [why] we concede that children in their early growth [development] have need of that and we do not deny it. But there is no solace for them [Bāṭinites] in this concession.

218 Belonging to [a part of] this premise is their assertion: If the need for the teacher is certain, then let the teacher be infallible. This [p. 103] is a subject of dispute. For if the teacher gives his teaching [instruction] and mentions along with it the rational proof and calls attention to the way it proves that, the learner [disciple] may reflect on it with the intellectual power he has, and he can have confidence in [rely upon] what his intellect requires after the teacher has called attention; then let the teacher be the most sinful of creatures—and why is there any need of his infallibility, since the learner [disciple] does not get from him the blind following of what he gets? Rather it is like arithmetic, of which one must know the truth regarding it for the advantages [sought] in transactions. A man does not know this of himself, but needs a teacher. However, there is no need of his infallibility, since arithmetic is not a rote science but one based on demonstration.

219 If you claim that the learner does not learn by demonstration and proof, because he attains that by the reasoning of his intellect—and there is no confidence in his intellect, given the weakness of men's intellects and their disparity: therefore he needs an infallible [teacher]—then this is now stupidity! For he knows his infallibility either of necessity or by servile conformism—and there is no way to claiming anything of that. So he must know it by reasoning, since there is no person in the world whose infallibility is known of necessity or whose assertion "I am infallible" can be relied upon, however much he urges it. And if his infallibility be not known, how can he blindly follow him?! And if he does not trust in his reasoning, how can he know his infallibility?! So if the matter be as you have mentioned it, then men would stray from [i.e. give up] learning the truth and that would become one of the impossible things.

220 *If they say:* There must be learning of the truth [but] not by way of reasoning—it is like one's saying: There must be union of white and black. For if he learns from another by reflecting on the proof of the question [problem] which he learns, he is a reasoner rushing into the danger of error, But if he blindly follows him because he is infallible, he is a perceiver of his infallibility by reasoning about the proof of infallibility. And if he does not believe in infallibility and is taught by anyone, then the matter finally comes down to what they have disqualified [considered farfetched], viz. learning from one whose infallibility is not known—and among these there is a multiplicity and their statements contradict one another, as they have mentioned. And they will never never find an escape from this!

221 *The fifth premise* [cf. Para. 144] is their assertion: The world is either not devoid of containing that Infallible [one] who must be had, or is devoid of him. But there is no way to suppose [assume] that the world is devoid [p. 104] of him, because that would lead to the concealing [eclipse] of the truth—and this would be an injustice unbefitting the wisdom [of God]. This also is an unsound premise. For if we conceded the other premises, and conceded men's need of an Infallible Teacher, we would then say: It is not impossible for the world to be devoid of him. On the contrary, in our view it is possible for the world to be unendingly devoid of a Prophet. It is even possible for God to torment all His creatures and to compel them to [enter] the Fire. For in all that He can act without restriction in His realm according to His will, and there can be no opposition to the Sovereign on the part of reason regarding His behavior [free actions]. Injustice would be simply in putting some thing in other than its [proper] place and acting freely in something other than what the free agent is entitled to. But this is inconceivable on the part of God. So perhaps the world is devoid of him [the Infallible one] in the sense that God has not created him.

222 *Someone may say:* So long as God is able to guide men to the path of salvation and the attainment of happiness by sending Apostles and setting up [appointing] Imams, and yet does not do that, this would be to do injury to men while denying of God Most High any benefit resulting from this injury—and this would be most shameful and contrary to the perfect qualities of His Wisdom and His Justice—and that does not befit the divine attributes, *We say:* This argument is faulty and it is a "cover" by which the simple man is deceived, but which is despised [scorned] by experts in the sciences. Indeed, some groups of the Muᶜtazilites were deceived by it. Exhaustive treatment of the way to refute them is found in the discipline of Kalām. I shall now limit myself to a single example which will show decisively that God Most High is not bound, in the qualities of His perfection, to consult [have a regard for] the advantage of His creatures.

223 This is that we suppose three children one of whom died as an infant, and one attained puberty as a Muslim, and the other reached maturity and embraced unbelief, then died. Then God requites each according to his merits, and He will execute justice. So He will lodge the one who matured and embraced unbelief in the depths of hell, and the one who matured and embraced Islam in the ranks of the blessed [lit. the ascending steps of exaltedness] [p. 105] and the one who died an infant without embracing Islam and sustaining an act of worship after puberty in a rank inferior to that of him who reached maturity and embraced Islam. Then the one who died as an infant will say: O Lord! Why have you put me behind my brother the Muslim who reached maturity and died? Only justice is worthy of Your magnanimity, yet You have indeed denied me the prerogatives of that rank. But had You favored me with them I would have benefited from them; they would not have harmed You. How, then, does that befit [Your] justice? And God will tell him, according to the pretension of him who claims "Wisdom," that [the other] reached maturity and embraced Islam and toiled and endured the hardships of the acts of worship—So how does justice demand putting you and him on an equal footing [on the same level]?"

224 Then the infant will say: O Lord! You are the one who caused me to live and caused me to die. And You ought to have prolonged my life and caused me to reach the stage of independence and guided me to Islam as You guided him. So putting me off from it [or: making me second to him] in life was a swerving from justice. Then God will say to him—according to the pretension of him who claims "Wisdom—It was to your advantage to cause you to die in your childhood: for had you reached maturity, you would have embraced unbelief and deserved the Fire. Whereupon the unbeliever who dies after he had reached maturity will cry out from the depths of hell and say: "O Lord, You knew of me that if I reached maturity, I would embrace unbelief. Could You not, then, have caused me to die in my childhood? For I would be satisfied with the lower rank in which You have lodged the child who yearns for the sublime ranks." At this point it remains for him who claims "Wisdom" only to stop replying and venturing [any farther]!

225 By this disparity [in the three cases] it is clear that the matter is more sublime than what they suppose. For the attributes of Lordship [Divinity] are not weighed in the scales of conjectures [suppositions], and God does what He will "and is not answerable for what He does, but they [p. 106] are answerable" [21.23]. And by this it is clear that there is no obligation to send a Prophet or to set up [appoint] an Imam. So their assertion that the world must contain him is indeed false.

226 *The sixth premise* [ef. Para. 145] is their assertion: If it be certain that the Imam is existing in the world, then he either must openly declare the claim [to be the Imam] and claim infallibility, or he must hide it. But hiding it is false, because it is obligatory on him and concealment is [would be] a sin contrary to infallibility [impeccability]—so he must openly declare it. This premise is unsound, because it is not unlikely that he should not openly declare that because of his being encompassed by enemies, conscious [of that] in his soul and fearful for his spirit [i.e. his life], so he conceals that through dissimulation [prudence]—and that is something on the possibility [permissibility] of which they are agreed. This was the view of the Imamites, all of them. They alleged that the Imam is living, in office, existing, and that he possesses infallibility, but he is waiting for the end of the rule of the false and the extinction of the strength [power] of [his] enemies. Now he is simply protected [fortified] by the garment of concealment, guarding himself from destruction to preserve the secret from disclosure until his time comes and the Imam of the false and his time pass away.

227 What, then, is the answer of these Bāṭinites to this view [doctrine, belief] of the Imamites? And what prevents the likelihood of that? For they [Imamites] support them on all their [Bāṭinites] premises except this premise. And that because of what they saw of the defective state of him whom these [Batinites] characterized with infallibility, and [what] they ascertained of reasons contrary to godliness and respectability. So they were ashamed to claim infallibility [impeccability] for one from whose circumstances they saw its contrary [opposite]. So they alleged that the Infallible [one] is concealed and that we await his appearance at his [proper] time. And at [p. 107] this point we say: By what do the Bāṭinites know the falseness of the view of the Imamites regarding this question? If they know it of necessity, then how has disagreement arisen regarding necessary truths? And if they know it by reasoning, then what has necessitated the soundness of their reasoning as against their adversaries' reasoning, and the announcement of the credibility of their intellects as against that of the intellects of their adversaries? Is that known by the length of beards or the whiteness of faces—and so on, to the same path they have followed? From this there is no escape in any circumstance whatsoever!

228 *The seventh premise* [cf. Para. 146] is their assertion: If it is certain that the Infallible [one] must declare [himself] openly, and if there is in the world only one who declares [himself] openly, then he is that Infallible [one], since he has no adversary, nor has he a second to himself in the claim so that distinguishing would be difficult. This is unsound in two ways [from two aspects]. *One of them* is: By what do they know that there is no claimant of infallibility and no one declaring openly in the countries of the world save one person [individual]? Perhaps in farthest China or in the extremities of the Maghrib there is one who claims something of that: and the negation of that is something known neither of necessity nor by reasoning.

229 *Someone may* say: That is known of necessity. For if there were [such a one], it [knowledge] would be widespread, because there are many motives [reasons] for transmitting such a thing as this. *We say:* It is possible that this was, but it did not spread to our country, given the great distance, because the claimant of that could not [cannot] mention it save in the company of his *sūs* and the possessor of his [its] secret, and about him was a party of his enemies, so he feared the exposure and disclosure of his secret and thought it best to conceal it. Or he disclosed it, but those who heard him were prevented from spreading in [other] countries and informing men of it because they were beleaguered by enemies and compelled to stay in [their] native country out of fear of the harm [that might be inflicted] by those who had overwhelmed them. What, then, annuls this possibility, when [since] it is a fact, be it supposed likely [near] or farfetched [or far], and is something possible which does not belong to the category of the impossibles? Yet you claim to be positive about what you adduce: how, then, is such positiveness undisturbed by [free from] this possibility?

230 *The second way* to upset this premise is that you suppose [have supposed] that no one claims [p. 108] infallibility in the world save one person [individual]—and this is an error. For by unimpeachable report we hear from others of [several] claimants. One of them is in Jīlān [south of the Caspian Sea?]. For that country is never without a man who gives himself the honorific title of Nāṣir al-Ḥaqq [Champion of the Truth] and claims infallibility for himself and that he occupies the place of the Apostle and he so enthralls the stupid among the inhabitants of that region that he allots to them the parts [sections] of the Garden by surface reckoning and is so severe on a man that the latter [or: is so severe among them that *he*] will not sell a cubit [rod] of the Garden—no, not for a hundred

dinars. And they carry to him the treasures of their wealth [possessions] and buy from him dwellings in the Garden. This, then, is one of the claimants [summoners?]. By what, then, have you known that he is wrong? And since the claimant is [may be] indeed multiple, and no one is preferable, since there is no apologetic miracle, do not think that stupidity is restricted to you, and that the tongue of no other does not utter this word. Rather astonishment at your thinking that this stupidity is at present restricted to you is greater than astonishment regarding the basis [principle] of this stupidity!

231 The second claimant is a man in the islands" [peninsula? delta?] of Baṣra who claims Divinity and who has prescribed a religion and put together a "Qur᾽ān" and appointed a man who is called ᶜAlī son of Kaḥlā, and alleged that he [himself] is in the position of Muḥammad—God bless him and grant him peace!—and that he [ᶜAlī b. Kaḥlā] is his Apostle to creatures. And indeed there surrounded him a group of simpletons [fools], roughly ten thousand souls—and perhaps their number exceeds yours—and he claims for himself infallibility and what surpasses it. And what is your answer to a man of the Shābāsites who cites these premises up to this premise, then [p. 109] says: If there must be an infallible teacher, and the infallible one has no apologetic miracle but is known simply by the claim [to infallibility], and the Master of the Bāṭinites does not claim Divinity—how could he when the Master of the Shābāsites claims Divinity—then following him [the latter] is preferable. *If you say:* When one claims Divinity the falseness of his assertion is known of necessity—the answer is in two ways. *One of them* is that he claims that simply by way of indwelling [*at-ḥulūl*] and alleges that it is an inheritance in their genealogy [family or ancestral line], and that has continued in their family for a long period, and that the grandfather of the present claim and claimed that. And "indwelling" has been the belief of many groups.

232 The falseness of the belief of the "Indwellers" [partisans of *al-huhūl*] is not a necessary [truth]. And how could it be necessary when there is regarding it such well-known disagreement as can scarcely be hidden. [This disagreement was such] that a large group of Sūfī inquirers and a great many Philosophers inclined to [had a propensity for] that. To this al-Ḥusayn son of Manṣūr al-Ḥallāj who was crucified in Baghdad alluded where [when] he used to say "Anā l-ḥaqq, anā l-ḥaqq [I am the True—i.e. God]," and he was reciting at the time of [his] crucifixion "But they did not kill him nor crucify him, but he was likened to them" [4.156/157]. And Abū Yazīd al-Bisṭāmī alluded to it in his utterance: "Praise to me, praise to me! How great is my dignity!" And I have indeed heard one of the Sūfī Masters who was most highly regarded and a cynosure regarding solidarity [strength] of religion and abundance of learning, relate to me of his own Master highly regarded for religion and piety [godliness] that the latter said: "What you hear of the Most Beautiful Names of God, which are ninety-nine, all of them become a description of the Sūfī proceeding by his way to God while he [p. 110] is still of the totality of those in via to God and not of the group of the 'attainers' [reachers, those who have arrived]."

233 And how can this ["indwelling"] be rejected [denied] when it is the belief of the Christians regarding the union of the Divinity with the humanity of ᶜĪsā [Jesus]—peace upon him!—so that some of them call him "a God," and some "The Son of God," and some assert: He is a demigod [the half of God]. And they are agreed that he was slain, his humanity was slain, not his divinity. How [can this "indwelling" be rejected (denied)] when a group of the Rāfiḍites imagined that in [the case of] ᶜAlī—God be pleased with him!—and alleged that he was God! And that happened in his own time, so that he commanded their being burned by fire. They did not recant, but said: By this is shown [clear]

our veracity in our assertion that he is God, because the Apostle of God—God bless him and grant him peace!—said: "Only its Lord punishes by fire." By this, then, it is plain [evident] that the falseness of this belief is not necessary [i.e. known of necessity], but it is a kind of stupidity and its falseness is known by intellectual reasoning, as the falseness of their [Bāṭinites] doctrine is known. Hence their assertion "No one claims infallibility save our Master" is indeed false—on the contrary, there has indeed appeared he who claims infallibility and more.

234 *The second way* [goes back to Para. 231] to answer their assertion "The falseness of their [Indwellers] doctrine is known of necessity": There is no difference between the falseness of something being known of necessity and its falseness being known [p. 111] by seeing or by unimpeachable transmission. Now the nonexistence of infallibility-impeccability in him whose infallibility you have claimed is known by seeing what is contrary to the Law in several ways. The first of these is collecting property [wealth] land the taking of taxes and petty levies and claiming [demanding] obsolete land taxes—and this is something impeccably transmitted in all regions; then luxury in life style and augmenting rich ornaments and extravagance [prodigality] in the kinds of self-adornment and the use of sumptuous garments of silk, etc.; and honesty [probity] of testifying would be prohibited by a tenth of a tenth of that—how, then, infallibility!

235 If they deny these circumstances, they deny what many people of those regions have seen and what their tongues have impeccably transmitted to the other countries. That is why you do not see a single one of the inhabitants of those countries misled or deluded by these deceptions—because they have seen what contradicts them. And among their artifices is the fact that they disseminate [their] propaganda only in far away [distant, remote] regions where the prospect would need to traverse an enormous distance if there occurred to him a doubt about it so that the obstacles may repel him from undertaking the journey. For if they were to see [with their own eyes], there would be disclosed to them the defect of those elaborate deceptions and contrived artifices.

236 *The eighth premise* [cf. Para. 147—put a bit differently here] is their assertion: If it is clear [evident] that so long as the claimant of infallibility is one there is no need to infer [seek proof] that he is infallible; and our Master, then, is alone the claimant of infallibility; therefore he is the Infallible Imam. This is a premise regarding which we give them the lie. And we do not concede that their Master claims infallibility for himself. For we have never heard him [it] at all, nor has it come to us in impeccable transmission on the tongue of one who heard it from him. On the contrary that has been heard simply from their individual propagandists, and these are not infallible, nor do they attain the level of impeccable transmission.

237 And even if they did attain the level of impeccable transmission sure knowledge would not be obtainable by their declaration and their report for two reasons. *One of them* is that those directly speaking [uttering] this propaganda on the part of their Master are few [in number], for he is concealed and appears only [p. 112] to the elite, and moreover he speaks directly only to the elite of the elite, and furthermore he discloses this propaganda [call] only in the company of one of the elite of the elite. So those who hear [directly] from him do not attain the number [required for] impeccable transmission. If they did attain it and were all spread out, there would be only one of them in a district. And also most places are devoid of their individuals.

238 *The second reason* is that even if they attained the level of impeccable transmission, the condition of the latter would be lacking in their report. For the condition of that

report is that it be not related to an event collusion on which might spread from a large group for some advantage uniting them, as [such as something] what is related to policies [politics, political or adminstrative matters?]. For a single purpose might unite the men [people] of one camp so that, by agreement, they would relate the same thing, and that would not engender [sure] knowledge. But one or two might report a thing, and it would he known that some purpose did not unite them, and that would result in [sure] knowledge. Perhaps these propagandists were in collusion on this invention that by it they might succeed in seducing the common folk and appropriating their property, and by the latter they would attain their hopes.

239 In general, then, [their?] good opinion [high regard for] of their Master requires [us] to give them the lie. For if they reported that from a sick man in the hospital we would believe that a lie on his part. However it would be thought madness in that sick man since no intelligent man would claim immunity from interdicted things and accepting forbidden things when men of learning were seeing his acceptance of them and his pursuing [pursuit, practice of] them. One of the least signs [marks, effects] of intelligence [intellect] is being ashamed of the degradation [humiliation, ignominy, disgrace] of boldness. And when one bedecks himself with something other than what is in him, and that is plain and clear to him who reflects on it, it may be inferred thereby that his intelligence is defective. Therefore their veracity in attributing this claim to their Master is not clear to us—and this is their last premise.

240 If *may he said:* Had men in distant parts of the world in the time of God's Apostle—God bless him and grant him peace!—denied the veracity of the emissaries of the Apostle of God and said: We do not believe you in your assertion that Muḥammad claims the [apostolic] mission—nay, but such a thing is not to be supposed of his intelligence: what would have been said to them? *We say:* How evil is your likening (the) angels to blacksmiths! For there is no equality, since he—God bless [p. 113] him and grant him peace!—used to appear personally with his followers, manifestly engaging in battle, coming and going in regions, explaining the call to a crowd of men, not hidden or concealed, and, moreover, manifesting apologetic miracles which violated custom. So his call spread because of the spread of his going forth and his fighting and the diffusion of (the fact of) his existence. But that is not the case now regarding your Master. To be sure, there is impeccable report of his existence and of his being a candidate, along with his forbears, for the Caliphate, and their claim that they are worthier of it than others.

241 But his claim, and that of those of his forbears who preceded, of immunity from sin and from error and slip and negligence [inadvertence], and of the knowledge of the truth regarding all rational and legal secrets—that is not manifest to us. Nay, but there is in no wise manifest his claim of knowledge of any of the disciplines such as jurisprudence or kalām or philosophy in the manner in which individual ulema in [different] regions claim it. How, then, could there be a manifest claim of his to know the secrets of prophecy and to be familiar with the lore of this life and the next?! This is something fabricated by collusion in order to entice and deceive the prospect.

242 This is the complete and detailed refutation of them regarding their premises, although in the first way comprising the general refutation of them there is a convincing sufficiency. It remains only to speak of the refutation [upsetting] of their proofs, already mentioned, of the invalidation of reasoning.

243 *The first proof* [cf. Para. 152] is their assertion: He who believes his intellect gives it the lie: for he believes his adversary's intellect, and his adversary explicitly states

that he gives him the lie, *We say:* This is an empty [a vain] show [deception, put-on] for several reasons [from several aspects]. The first is opposing it by the like. This is that we say: We believe intellects regarding their speculative matters and you believe them regarding their necessary matters; but your sophist adversaries give you the lie regarding them. So if that required having to acknowledge the falseness of the necessary knowledges [cognitions], we would have to acknowledge, as a result of your opposition, the falseness of speculative knowledges. For if the intellect believes [p. 114] in necessary matters, then why is it that the intellect of the sophists disbelieves? And what is the difference between your intellect and their intellect? Do you say that that on their part is stupidity and a bad complexion [mixture of humors]?

244 *We say:* Just so is your state regarding the denial of speculative matters, and it is like him who denies arithmetical cognitions. For he does not make us doubt about the arithmetical demonstrations, even though the dull-witted person does not understand [lacks comprehension]. One who rejects reasoning *in toto* denies it. But our way of proceeding with him is to present to him the premises, which are necessary. Then, if he grasps them, he grasps the conclusion. Thus, too, if our adversary gives us the lie [disbelieves us] in one of the problems [questions], such as the denial of the existence of a Necessary Being, we lay before him the premises of the syllogism proving it and say: Do you contest our statement "There is no doubt about the principle of existence"? Or our statement "Every existent is either possible or necessary"? Or our statement 'If it is necessary, then a Necessary Being is established"? Or our statement "If it is possible, then undoubtedly every possible is founded ultimately on a Necessary Being"?

245 If he is unable to doubt about the premises, he cannot doubt about the conclusion. Men do disagree about it simply because their natural [native] temperament [ability] is not sufficient to determine [explain] the organization of these premises, but they must be learned from the learned. And such a learned man must have learned most of them [from another] or must have succeeded in discovering some of them by himself. Thus the matter finally ends in an infallible teacher who is a prophet to whom revelation from God Most High has come. Such is the case with all cognitions [scientific lore ?]. If they then claim that you have acknowledged the need of a teacher, and he who does not acknowledge it offers stubborn resistance to ocular witness—so the need for him is acknowledged.

246 But this need is like the need for a teacher in the science of arithmetic. For one does not need therein an infallible [teacher], since there is no servile conformism in it. But one needs an arithmetican who will call attention to the method of reasoning. Then, when the learner is alerted he is the equal of the teacher in the necessary knowledge derived from the premises, one after [upon] the other. And there is no doubt that the teacher of arithmetic also learned [from another] most of what he teaches, though he may independently have discovered how to put together some [of that]. The same is to he said of the teacher's teacher and so on until the origin [beginning, start] of the science of arithmetic ends finally in one of the prophets confirmed by revelation and an apologetic miracle. But after God sent down the science of arithmetic among men, there was no need, for learning it, of an infallible teacher. So, too, speculative intellectual cognitions—with no difference.

247 [p. 115] *The second* objection [goes back to Para. 243] is that one say to them: You have denied, on the part of your adversaries, giving credence to the intellect in its reasoning and have chosen to give it the lie. By what, then, do you know the true and distinguish between it and the false? By the necessity of the intellect?—but there is no way to

claim it. Or by its reasoning?—and then you would be forced to return to reasoning—and you would have given it credence after giving it the lie: so what you say would contain a contradiction. *If you say:* We accept it from the Infallible Imam. *We* say: And by what do you know his veracity? *If you say:* Because he is infallible. *We say:* And by what do you know his infallibility? *If you say:* By the necessity of the intellect—you are well aware of your shame [ignominy] and you know in the interior of your souls the contrary of what you proclaim. For the infallibility of God's Apostle—God bless him and grant him peace!—accompanied by his apologetic miracle, was not known by the necessity of the intellect. Consequently some groups denied his apostolic mission: nay more, all the Brahmins denied the sending of the Apostles. And most Muslims deny the impeccability of the Prophets, arguing from God Most High's utterance "And Adam disobeyed his Lord and went astray" [20.119/121] and other accounts contained in the Qurʾān about the circumstances of the Prophets. So if the infallibility of the possessor of the apologetic miracle was not known of necessity, then how can the infallibility of your Master be known of necessity?

248 *It may be said:* We know it by reasoning—but the reasoning was learned from him. And reasoning is divided into sound and unsound, and distinguishing the sound from the unsound is impossible for all men save the true Imam. This is the scale [norm] which makes clear the difference between the specious argument and the demonstration. So we indeed know the soundness of the reasoning which we have learned from him and our souls are sure of [have confidence in] it by reason of his attestation and his instruction. *We say:* And the reasoning which he has taught you: to understand it, did you have need of reflection, or was it grasped intuitively? If you claim intuition, how intense your ignorance [folly] is, since the purport of this comes down to the knowledge of his infallibility being known intuitively—and this is a downright lie!

249 But if you needed reflection, then was that reflection known [recognized] by the intellect or not? *And one must answer:* By the intellect. *Then we say:* And if, upon reflection, the intellect decided something, was it veracious or not? If they say it was not—then why did they give it credence? And if they say it was veracious—then they have indeed invalidated the principle [basis] of their doctrine: viz. their assertion that there is no way to give credence to intellects. *If it be said:* [p. 116] The Imam knows certain things about the profound secrets of God, and if he mentions them, the learner, when he hears them, gets an intuitive necessary knowledge of his veracity and thereby has no need of subtle reasoning and reflection. *We say:* And the Apostle of God—God bless him and grant him peace!—did he know that [i.e. those things] or not? If you say "No," you have preferred the successor to the original. But if you say "Yes," then why did he conceal those things, and why did he not manifest and disclose them so that intellects would have been compelled intuitively to remember them and would have rushed to believe him in his claims? And why did he leave groups of men forced to dive into specious arguments, tripping over the tails [hems] of errors, fighting with their possessions and their lives to champion empty fancies?

250 How [could that be?]—And when you had learned that from your Imam and were able to mention it so that his veracity would be known intuitively why was that particular hidden and to what day was it deferred—when the concealing of religion is one of the greatest of the grave sins?! Furthermore, how were the hearers of the varieties of your error divided into one giving ear and one rejecting and one mistaken and one alerted [mindful]—and [why] were not all inserted into the noose of belief and submission? In general, the claim of such polemic indicates only impudence [insolence] and lack of

shame—otherwise we would know of necessity that you have not perceived intuitively the veracity and infallibility of your Imam, but perhaps you are forced, to promote deception, to cast off the garment of shame—thus does God do to the masters of error and caprices. So we take refuge with God from the tumble [error] of the foolish. This lie issuing from you is not a remark to be uttered or a false step to be advocated or a deception to be reached beforehand by the ignorant, to say nothing of learned men!

251 *The third objection* is that we say to one seeking guidance, for example, if he doubts about the soundness of reasoning and argues from the general disagreement: You must specify [particularize] the question [problem] about which you doubt. For questions are divided into what cannot be known by the reasoning of the intellect, and what can be known with conjectural knowledge, and what can be known with sure and certain knowledge. But there is no meaning to accepting a general question: [p. 117] rather one must specify the question in which the difficulty occurs so that the veil may be removed from it and the questioner informed that the one opposed therein has failed to understand the way to put together the premises which lead to its conclusion. We now claim knowledge of only two questions: one of them is the existence of the Maker, the necessarily existent, in no need of maker and manager [governor]; and the second is the veracity of the Apostle. And regarding the remaining questions it suffices us to learn them by blind acceptance from the Apostle—God bless him and grant him peace! This is the amount [the absolute minimum] which must be had regarding religion.

252 There is no obligation to acquire the other knowledges—rather men can do without them, even though that be possible, e.g. arithmetical, medical, astronomical, and philosophical lore. Those two questions we know for certain—the existence of a Necessary Being by the premises which we have known, and the veracity of the Apostle by premises which are like them. One who comprehends them does not doubt about them, but knows the error of him who opposes them as one knows the error of the arithmetician in arithmetic. And our adversaries are also forced [impelled] to know these two questions by reasoning: otherwise the Prophet's utterance is of no avail regarding them—how, then, is the utterance of the infallible one of any avail regarding them?!

253 *If it be said:* The knowledge of God's attributes and the knowledge of the revealed Laws and the knowledge of the Assembling and the Resurrection are all necessary: whence, then, is it known? *We say:* It is learned from the Prophet—God bless him and grant him peace!—infallible and confirmed by the apologetic miracle, and we believe him in what he reports as you blindly follow your Master who has neither infallibility nor apologetic miracle. *Then if it be said:* And by what do you understand what he says? *We say:* By that by which we understand this speech of yours in your questions and you understand our speech in our answers, viz. the knowledge of the language and of the conventional meaning of words—as you understand from him who in your view is infallible.

254 *If it be said:* In the discourse of the Apostle and in the Qur᾿ān there are difficulties and generalities, such as the letters of the beginnings of the sūras, and what is ambiguous [obscure, unclear], such as the matter of the resurrection. Who, then, acquaints you with its interpretation, since the intellect does not show [indicate] it? *We say:* The words [expressions] of the revealed Law have three divisions. [*The first comprises*] plain words not open to probability, so for them there is no need of a teacher. Rather, we understand them as you understand the speech of the Infallible Imam. For if the plain speech of the Legislator needed a teacher and interpreter, then the [p. 118] plain speech of the infallible teacher would need another interpreter and teacher and there would be a processus ad infinitum.

255 *The second* [*division*] comprises general and ambiguous words [expressions], such as the letters of the beginnings of the sūras. Their meanings cannot be grasped by the intellect, for languages are known by convention and there was no prior convention on the part of men regarding the letters of the alphabet. And the "*rāʾ*" and "*ḥāʾ-mīm*," "*ᶜ-s-q*" are an expression of what? So the infallible one also does not understand it, but that is under stood simply from God Most High if [when] He explains what is meant by it on the tongue of His Apostle—and that is understood by hearing. And that must either have *not* been mentioned by the Apostle, because there was no need to know it and it was not enjoined on men. So the infallible one shares in not knowing it, since he has not heard it from the Apostle. And if he knew it and mentioned it, then he has indeed mentioned what men were not obligated to know, because it will never be [or: it was not] enjoined on them. But if the Apostle mentioned it, then knowledge of it is shared by whomever the report reached—by impeccable transmission or through individuals—and there is a transmission regarding it from Ibn ᶜAbbās and a group of the commentators. If it be impeccable transmission, it affords [sure] knowledge, otherwise it affords conjecture. And conjecture is sufficient regarding it—nay, but there is no need to know it since there is no prescription regarding it.

256 As for the time of the Resurrection, God Most High did not mention it, nor did His Apostle—Peace be upon him! It is obligatory simply to believe in the fundament [i.e. the basic dogma] of the Resurrection, but it is not obligatory to know its time—rather the advantage of men lies in concealing it from them, and therefore it has been hidden from them. So whence has the infallible one known that utterance since neither God nor His Apostle mentioned it, and there is no scope for the necessity of the intellect or its reasoning to pinpoint the time?! Furthermore, let us suppose that he knew that and claimed that he—God bless him and grant him peace!—mentioned it secretly [privately] in the company of ᶜAlī bin Abī Ṭālib—God be pleased with him!—and every Imam mentioned it in the company of his *sūs;* then what advantage is there for men in it, since it is a secret which can be mentioned only in the company of the Imams? So if your Infallible [Imam] were to mention and disclose this secret which God Most High commanded to conceal—since the Most High said: "I would [am about to, intend to] conceal it" [20.15]—he would oppose God and His Apostle; but if he does not divulge it, then how can one learn from him what cannot be taught? So it shows [proves] that intellectual matters [p. 119] need teaching. However, if the teacher calls attention to the method of the reasoning about it, his infallibility is not required. But if he be blindly followed, without [affording] any proof, then his infallibility must be known by an apologetic miracle. And this is the Prophet: let him suffice you as teacher, then there is no need of anyone else!

257 *The third division* comprises the words [expressions] which are neither general nor explicit, but they are evident, for they cause [give rise to] a conjecture—and conjecture is enough in that kind and sort [of thing]. And it is all the same whether that concern legal affairs or the matters of the afterlife or God's attributes. So men are bound only to believe in [the proclaiming of] God's unity—and the expressions are explicit regarding it—and to believe that He is powerful, knowing, hearing, seeing, there is nothing like Him [42.9/11], and the Qurʾān contains all of that and explicitly declares it. As for speculation on the modality and real nature of these attributes and whether they are equivalent to our power and knowledge and right or not—His utterance "there is nothing like Him" [42.9/11] indicates the negation of likeness to all [other] existents. With this men may be content, so they have no need of an infallible [teacher, Imam].

258 To be sure, one who reasons about it and argues to it from rational proofs may reach certainty [sure and certain knowledge] in [on] part of what he reasons about and conjecture regarding other points. That will differ according to the difference of acumen and intelligence and the difference of obstacles and motives and the aid of [divine?] help in reasoning. But the "knower" [*al-ᶜārif*—gnostic] "tastes" [*yadhūq*—has an experimental (direct) knowledge of] the certain, and when he is certain he does not doubt about it nor is he made to doubt by the inability of others to grasp [what he knows]. Perhaps his [?] soul may be weak and he will be made to doubt by the opposition of others. But all that contains no harm [for him], because he is not commanded that; and the infallible one would be of no avail, were he to follow him, because pure servile conformism is not enough for him. And if the matter of the proof is mentioned, it makes no difference whether it issues from an infallible one or from another, as we have previously declared.

259 *The second proof* [cf. Para. 153] is their assertion: If a perplexed man seeking guidance comes to you and asks about religious knowledges, do you refer him to his intellect that he may reason independently—and he is incapable [of that] [p. 120] or do you command him to follow you in your doctrine—and you are challenged by the Muᶜtazilite and the Philosopher, and so of the other sects? So by what is one doctrine distinguished from another, and one sect from another? *The answer* is in two ways. *One of them* is that we say to them: If one perplexed about the basis of the existence of the Maker and the veracity of the Prophets were to come to you, this difficulty would be turned [retorted] against you—so what would you say? If you cited a rational proof we would not trust his reasoning, and if you referred him to his intellect, the same would be true. Perhaps, then, you would quench his thirst by referral to the Infallible [Imam]? How cold [inane—stupid] this quenching would be! For he would say: Suppose me to have come in quest of guidance in the time of Muḥammad Ibn ᶜAbdallāh accompanied [as he was] by his apologetic miracle—but your Infallible [Imam] cannot [adduce] an apologetic miracle! Or suppose that I were to see your Infallible [Imam] turn a staff into a serpent, or quicken the dead, or cure the born blind and the leper while I saw it, yet his veracity would not be clear to me by the necessity of the intellect, nor do I trust reasoning. How many kinds of men saw that and rejected it! Some of them ascribed it to magic and trickery, and others to something else.

260 Perhaps, then, you would satisfy his hunger [need] by saying to him: Blindly follow the Infallible Imam and ask not about the reason. *Then he should say:* And why should I not follow those opposed to you in rejecting prophethood and infallibility? Is there between the two any difference in length of beard or whiteness of face or other such things as they rave about? This is a retort which, were they to unite from their first to their last in escaping from it without commanding reflection and reasoning about the proof, they would find no way to do so.

261 (*The second answer*) is verification [pinpointing, precise determination, substantiation]. This is that *we say* to the one seeking guidance: What do you seek? For if you seek all cognitions [lore, knowledges], how intense is your curiosity, and how great your concern, and how large your expectation! So busy yourselves with those cognitions which concern you. *If he says:* I want what concerns me. *We say:* The only important [serious] thing is knowledge of God and of His Apostle. This is the meaning of His utterance: "There is no god [divinity] save God; Muḥammad is the Apostle of God." It is easy for us to teach you these two questions. And thereupon [p. 121] should be mentioned to him the necessary premises which we have mentioned in establishing the existence of a Necessary

Being, then the like of them in the apologetic miracle's proof of the veracity of the Apostle. *If he then alleges:* The opposition of the adversaries is what makes me doubt about this knowledge: shall I, then, follow you or follow your adversaries? We *say to him:* do not follow us, and do not follow our adversaries, for learning the way of servile conformism is allowed: but servile conformism regarding the conclusion is not to be trusted. Your doubt, then, concerns which of our premises? Is it about our assertion: The basis of existence is acknowledged [i.e. that there must be a reason for the existence of a thing]? If that be so, then your treatment should be in the hospital, for this is due to a bad mixture of the humors. For one who doubts about the basis of existence has indeed doubted first of all about his own existence.

262 *If you say:* I do not doubt about this, contrary to the Sophists. *We say:* Then you are indeed certain of one premise. So do you doubt about the second, viz. our assertion: If this existence be necessary, then there exists a Necessary Being? We say this is also something necessary. [Then] we say: So do you doubt about our assertion: If it be possible, one of the two extremes of the possibility is not particularized respecting the extreme like it save by a "particularizer." This also is a necessary premise in the view of him who grasps the meaning of the expression [wording], and if there is any hesitation in him it is hesitation about grasping what the speaker means by his words. *If he says:* Yes—I do not doubt about it. *We say:* And if that needed "particularizer" be possible, then the statement about that is like the statement about it [the former] and so it requires a "particularizer" which is not "possible—and this is what is meant by a Necessary Being. So what do you doubt about?

263 *If he says:* I still have a doubt—one knows thereby his stupidity and misunderstanding, and there is no hope of his being sensible. He is not the first stupid man who fails to grasp truths—so we leave him alone. He is like one who seeks knowledge of arithmetic and we mention to him the obscure premises of arithmetic dealing with form [sector] [p. 122] which comes at the end of Euclid's book and he does not understand it because of his stupidity. Nay more, even regarding the first figure, which contains the establishing of demonstrations concerning the equilateral triangle, he does not grasp it. [So] we know that his temperament is not capable of this subtle science [knowledge]. Not every nature is capable of the sciences, or even of the arts and crafts. So this does not prove the unsoundness of this principle [basis].

264 *If the seeker of guidance says:* I do not doubt about these premises nor about the conclusion. But why are you opposed by him who opposes you? *We say:* Because he does not know how to put together these premises, or because of his obstinacy [pigheadedness], or because of his stupidity. The veil is removed by our directly addressing one of them inclined to be fair and our asking [consulting] him about these premises so that it may be clear to you that either he understands and is fair and acknowledges, or he does not understand because his stupidity, or fanaticism [partisanship] and servile conformism prevent him from giving it a fair hearing and so he does not understand it—and there upon his error is known [revealed]. So one should do with him regarding each question, and one should consider in him what his circumstance can tolerate and his acumen and intelligence accept, and not impose on him what he cannot stand, but rather he may be convinced by what is bequeathed to [effected for] him by determined [resolute] belief regarding the truth. For with that the Law is content on the part of most of the common folk. And the modality of the demonstrations should not be disclosed to him, for he might not understand them.

265 *The third proof* [cf. Para. 155] is their assertion: Oneness is the proof [indication, sign] of the true and multiplicity is the proof of the false. And oneness is the property of [cleaves to] the doctrine of *al-ta*ᶜ*līm* [authoritative teaching], whereas multiplicity is the property of your doctrine. For the disagreement of the group opposed to *al-ta*ᶜ*līm* constantly multiplies, whereas the way of the group accepting *al-ta*ᶜ*līm* is ceaselessly united. *The answer* is in several ways. One of them is objecting [confrontation], another refutation, and the third verification. *Objecting* [confrontation] is that you say: Those who hold the need for an infallible teacher have disagreed about that infallible one. The Imamites hold that he is not visible and not known individually [and his identity is not known], but he has concealed himself out of prudence. Others hold that he is not existing, but his existence is awaited, and he will exist when the time can bear the manifesting of the truth, and if [p. 123] the time did bear its manifesting, he would exist—for there is no advantage in his existing when it is impossible to show [himself] because of prudent fear. And others said of one [? some ?] of the Caliphs who have died that they are alive and will appear at its [the proper] time [Wehr: = at the right time]. And they disagreed about pinpointing him so that one group believed that the one called al-Ḥākim [al-Ḥākim bi Amr Allāh—EI(2)] is still alive. And others held that of another—to a long kind of disorder [random claims].

266 *If it be said:* These are a crowd of simpletons not to be numbered in our group. If you join them to us and combine us and them multiplicity would attach to us: why, then, do you add to us him who opposes us as he opposes you? On the contrary fairness [demands] that you look at us alone—and there is no disagreement at all in what we say. *We say:* And we also, if we are considered by ourselves, do not oppose ourselves. This objection may undoubtedly be warded off by one who believes on all questions a doctrine which does not oppose itself [and] who has with him a group of men who agree with him on his belief regarding all [the questions]. So if you regard him with his group, and do not join to them one who opposes them, then you will find their "word" united by silliness and stupidity and inadequate reasoning: so it does not prove that the truth is among them. *If you then say:* And by what do you know the folly of your opponents?—that is turned against you regarding your opposition to those who hold the necessity of *al-ta*ᶜ*līm* from the Infallible [Imam]. And if you allege that those holding that reasoning is sound are one sect, although they disagree about the details of the doctrine, *We say:* And those who hold that there must be an Infallible Imam are one sect, even though they disagree about the detail. And there will never, never be any escape from this!

267 *The second answer* is that we say: Your assertion that oneness is the sign of the true and multiplicity is the sign of the false is false in both parts: for many a one is false,and many a multiple [p. 124] is not devoid of the true. For if we say: The world is incipient or preeternal, and the incipient is one and the preeternal is one; so they indeed share in the property of oneness, but they are divided into the true and the false. And if we say: Are five and five ten or not? Then our saying "No" is one negation, as our saying "Ten" is one affirmation: then they differ, so one of them is true and the other false.

268 *If you say:* Your saying "Ten" you cannot divide or separate save by one; and your saying is not separable by nine and seven and the other numbers—so there is multiplicity in it. *We say:* And the necessity of multiplicity in the like of this separating does not indicate falseness. For if we apply ourselves to two bodies approximating each other, we say: Are they equal or not? Our saying "Equal" is one but it is false, and it cannot be separated [divided] save by one. And our saying "No," if we say "Different" is true, and it is one, and it is susceptible of separation [division] by what is divided into the true and the false,

since one can say: This body is different from that body, i.e. it is larger, or it is explained by its being smaller, and the true is one of the two and the false faces it in its being one and in its sharing in being included under one expression. This is something true which shows that what they have mentioned is a deception.

269 *The third answer* to their assertion that multiplicity is the sign of the false [is that] our doctrine is one and contains no multiplicity. But the multiplicity is simply in the individuals who are united on one question, then divided on some questions. Why, then, have they confronted this with a multiplicity in answer to the question, viz. about our saying: How many are five and five? Rather is his view of [from; regarding ?] the doctrine that he give a legal opinion about one question by many contradictory legal opinions. Thereupon it can be said: Multiplicity is an indication of the false. But we give a legal opinion on each question only by one: for we say: God is one, and Muḥammad—God bless him and grant him peace!—is His Apostle, and he is veracious and confirmed by the apologetic miracle, so this is one legal opinion: let it, then, be true. But if it be false, it agrees with their doctrine.

270 And our assertion that the reasoning of the intellect is a way which brings [one] to grasp what is not grasped of necessity is one doctrine containing no multiplicity—so let it be true, just as our assertion that arithmetical cognitions [knowledges] are true knowledges is one assertion and is true. One must marvel at their going so far in deception, since they take the word "multiplicity" which is [p. 125] an annexed, shared [common] word by which at one time is meant multiplicity in the answers to a single question, such as the answer to five and five, and seven and six, and others, and at another time it is used in the sense of the multiplicity of individuals agreeing on a doctrine and disagreeing about it. Then they see the separation of the false [to be] due to the multiplicity annexed to the number of answers regarding a single question and infer from it the falseness of a single assertion regarding a single question on which a numerous group agree whose utterance disagrees regarding questions other than that difficulty.

271 But although this is a deception unlikely [to influence] a knowledgeable person, the intention of its author is to deceive the masses, and the [ready] circulation is something to be expected [anticipated]. So the artifice against the masses to seduce them is not impossible for a group of the stupid who claim Lordship [divinity]: how, then, could it be too difficult for others? As for the Most High's utterance: "If it [Apostle's Preaching] were from another than God, they would find in it much disagreement" [4.84/82], [the use of] it is of this kind in deceiving. For what is meant by it is the contradiction of the words in the single speaker: if his speech is contradictory, it is unsound. But the speech of one of us regarding a question is not contradictory. Rather, a group have agreed on a question, viz. the affirmation of reasoning, just as a group have agreed on *al-ta^{c}līm* and its affirmation: then they have disagreed about other questions. What, then, has this to do with the disagreement of one and the same speech?!

272 *If it be said:* If the learners [disciples] agree on *al-ta^{c}līm* and on one teacher, and all hearken to [heed] him, there is no opposition among them, even if they are a thousand thousand. *We say:* And those who reason, if they agree on the reasoning on the proof and on specifying one proof for each question and stop at [learn, understand] the latter, opposition among them is inconceivable. *If you say:* And how many a reasoner on that very proof has opposed! *We say:* And how many a listener to your Teacher has indeed opposed! *If you say:* Because he did not believe him to be infallible. *We say:* And because the reasoner did not know the mode of the proving of the proof. *If you say:* Perhaps he

knows the mode of the proving, then denies [it]. *We say:* This is inconceivable save out of pigheadedness, just as [when] one believes the existence of the Infallible Imam to be true, then opposes him, that is only because of pigheadedness. There is no difference between the two procedures.

273 *The fourth proof* [ef. Para. 156] is their assertion: If the reasoner does not perceive the equality [p. 126] between him and his adversary in the matter of belief, then why does he perceive the equality between his two states [or: then he does not perceive, etc.]? How many a question he has believed through a reasoning, then his belief changed. So by what does he know that the second is not like the first? *We say:* He knows that by a necessary knowledge about which he does not doubt. This is also your belief [as exemplified ?] in two examples—and no polemic is stronger [more effective] than retort and opposition [objection, confrontation] in such discourses as these. For they are wont to extend the hand of adherence [preservation] to difficulties which are not peculiar to the doctrine of [any] group, and thereby they perplex the minds of the masses and lead [them] to think it is peculiar to the doctrine of their opponents. And when will the poor common man advert to that's being turned [retorted] against him regarding his doctrine?!

274 So *we say:* Did this speaker believe the doctrine of *al-taᶜlīm* and the invalidation of reasoning out of servile conformism because he heard it from his parents, or did he hear a doctrine from his parents and then after that advert to its falseness? *if he says:* I believed it because of hearing [it] from my parents. *We say:* Now the children of the Christians and the Jews and the Zoroastrians and the children of those who oppose you on the question of reasoning happened to grow up in the opposite of your belief—so by what do you distinguish between yourselves and them? By length of beards, or blackness of faces, or some other reason, when the servile conformism is universal?

275 *And if you say:* We believed your doctrine, then we abandoned servile conformism and became aware of the soundness of the doctrine of *al-taᶜlīm, We say:* Did you become aware of the falseness of our doctrine intuitively or by reasoning of the intellect? If it happened intuitively, then how was the object of the intuition concealed from you in the beginning of your affair, and from your forefathers [parents], and from us, who are [among the] intelligent and have indeed covered the face of the earth far and wide? And if you know that by your reasoning, then why did you trust in reasoning when perhaps your subsequent state was like the prior state—so what is the difference [distinguishing factor]? *If you say:* We knew it from the Teacher. *We say:* If it was servile conformism, then what is the difference between servile conformism to the last and servile conformism to the first, and between your servile conformism and that of the groups of [your] opponents from among the Jews and the Christians and the Zoroastrians and the Muslims? And if you understood [it] by reasoning, then what is the difference between you and other reasoners? There is no answer to this save to say: Of necessity we perceive the difference between what is known for certain and about which there can be no error and that [about which] there can be [error]. Just so is our answer.

276 *The second example* [cf. Paras. 273–74]: One who errs in an arithmetical question and then adverts to it—is it conceivable that his doubt passes away after his being alerted? *We reply:* He knows that he is not wrong and that error is not possible [p. 127] for him, and that the error in the past was because of a premise which eluded him. If you say "No," you have indeed denied ocular witness. And if you say "Yes," then by what do you perceive the difference if not by necessity? And the very same difficulty is turned against [you]. And how can you deny that when you have certainly seen one who claims

acumen and intelligence in the science of arithmetic judge that going to the right regarding the *qibla* [direction faced in Prayer] is obligatory in the city of Nishapur, and that one must incline to the right from its agreed upon *miḥrāb,* [prayer niche]. He inferred that from an admitted premise, viz. that the sun stands in the middle of the heaven at the zenith in Mecca at the longer [part] of the day at noontime. Then he said: At the longer [part] of the day at noontime in Nishapur you see the sun inclining a little to the right of one facing its *miḥrāb,* so one knows that it is directly over the head of one standing in Mecca, and that Mecca inclines to the right.

277 So a group of arithmeticians followed him in that and believed that to be obligatory by reason of this proof, until they adverted to the place of the error in it and their violating [infringing] of another premise, viz. that it binds one only if noontime in Nishapur is noontime in Mecca. But such is not the case, but rather it falls an hour later and the sun will have begun [to decline ?] in the direction of the west to the right side [?], so one sees noontime inclining from the *qibla* of Nishapur, because noontime and setting [time] are not in agreement [do not coincide] in all places. And that is known by the ascension [elevation] and declension [sinking] of the two poles, nay, more by their occultation and their being revealed in the different regions. So this error and its likes [occur] in arithmetic. Does that, then, show that reasoning in arithmetic is not a way leading to the knowledge of the truth? Or the one alerted thereafter will doubt and say: Perhaps [p. 128] another premise has eluded me and I am unaware of it as in the first case. This, if its door be opened, is pure sophistry, and that would lead to the invalidity [falsity] of all knowledges and beliefs: How, then, could there remain along with it the necessity of learning [from an infallible one] and knowledge of infallibility and knowledge of the invalidation of reasoning!

278 *The fifth proof* [ef. Para. 157] is their assertion: The Trustee of the Law—God bless him and grant him peace!—said: "The one saved from among the sects will be one [sect], viz. the people of the custom and the consensus." Then he said: "What I and my Companions are now holding. This belongs to the "amazing" [wonderful, astonishing, remarkable, odd] inferences [proofs]. For they deny [reject] reasoning about rational proofs because of the possibility of error in it, and begin holding fast to the reports of individuals and the noncanonical additions in them. The origin of the report belongs to the class of [reports of] individuals, and this addition is noncanonical: so it is conjecture upon [added to] conjecture. Moreover it is an expression susceptible of innumerable ways of interpretation. For what he and his Companions were holding, if it all be stipulated regarding words and actions and movements [policies, undertakings, procedures, impulses] and skills [? crafts?], is impossible. And if some of it be taken [adopted, accepted], then who is to specify and determine [evaluate] that "some"? And how is its accuracy to be grasped? Is that conceivable save by a weak conjecture the like of which would not be approved in *fiqh* matters despite their triviality: how then could it be the basis of arguing to [basic] positive matters?

279 However, *we say:* They were [engaged] in following a Prophet confirmed by an apologetic miracle. You, therefore, do not belong to the sect which will be saved, for you follow one who is neither a prophet nor confirmed by an apologetic miracle. *Then they will say:* It is not necessary to be equal to him [lege: them] in every respect. *We say:* We are equal to them in every respect: for we enjoin following the Book and the Sunna and exercising personal effort when it is impossible to hold fast to them, as he commanded Muᶜādh, and as the Companions continued to do after his death, viz. consultation and the exercise of personal effort about things. So the tradition determines [appoints]

salvation for us and perdition for you, because you have deviated from following the infallible Prophet to another.

280 *If it be said:* And the meanings of the Book and the Sunna: [p. 129] how do you understand them? *We say:* We have already explained that they are three divisions: explicit, apparent and general [cf. Paras. 254ff.]. And we have shown that our knowledge of them is like the knowledge of all the Companions, and like the knowledge of him for whom you claim infallibility, without any difference. *If it be said:* But you call for the reasoning of the intellect, and this was not the wont [habit] of the Companions. *We say:* Far from it! For we call for following and for believing the Apostle of God—God bless him and grant him peace!—in the utterance of "There is no divinity save God: Muḥammad is the Apostle of God." Whoever believes in that spontaneously without contention and disputation we are content [with that] on his part as the Apostle of God—God bless him and grant him peace!—[was] content with it on the part of the rude [desert] Arabs.

281 Men are three divisions. *One* [comprises] the blindly accepting masses brought up in belief of the truth through hearing [it] from their elders: and the soundness of their Islam is acknowledged. *The second* [division] comprises the unbelievers brought up on the contrary of the truth through hearing from their elders and servile conformism. These, in our view, are called to follow blindly the infallible Prophet confirmed by the apologetic miracle and to follow his Sunna and his Book: but you call him to your Infallible [one]. I would like to know which of us resembles more the Companions of the Apostle of God—God bless him and grant him peace!—he who summons to the Prophet confirmed by the apologetic miracle, or he who summons to him who claims infallibility of his own wish [craving, passion] without an apologetic miracle!

282 *The third division* comprises the man who has left the position of the servile conformists and knows that in servile conformism there is danger of error, so that he has become dissatisfied with it. We invite him to consideration of the creation of the heavens and the earth that be may know thereby the Maker and to reflection on the apologetic miracles of the Prophet—God bless him and grant him peace!—that he may know thereby his veracity. But you call him to blind following of the Infallible [one] and you deny and denigrate the reasoning of the intellect. I would like to know which of the two calls is more in accord with the call of the Companions of the Apostle of God—God bless him and grant him peace! So when they say to the seeker of guidance who is in doubt: Be wary of the reasoning of the intellect and reflecting on it, for in it is the danger of error and therefore reasoners have disagreed; [p. 130] rather you must blindly accept what you hear from us without understanding or reflection—this, were it to issue from a madman, would be laughed at.

283 And one should say to him: Why should we follow you blindly and not follow blindly him who gives you the lie? So if the carpet of the proof which distinguishes by way of reasoning between you and your adversary be rolled up, and it is impossible to grasp a discerning [differentiating] of necessity, then by what are you distinguishable from your opponent who gives [you] the lie?! I would like to know whether he who opens the door to reasoning which leads to the knowledge of the truth, following therein what the Qur'ān contains of urging consideration and reflection on the verses [signs?] in the Qur'ān and [on] the inability of men to produce its like and his [the Apostle's] arguing therefrom, [whether he] is closer to agreement with the Companions and the people of the Sunna and the Consensus, or he who makes men despair of reasoning on the proofs by [his] imputing of falsehood [disbelief, denial] so that there remains to religion no strap

[thong, support] to cling to save claims which contradict one another?! Is this other than the doing of him who wishes to extinguish the light of God and to eclipse [cover over] the Law of the Apostle of God—God bless him and grant him peace!—by stopping up his way leading to Him?

284 *If it be said:* So we see you inclining at one time to following and at another to reasoning. *I say:* So you should believe it—but concerning two [types of] individuals. Those who have the good fortune to be born among the Muslims and have accepted the truth by unquestioning acceptance have no need of reasoning. The same is true of unbelievers if it be made easy for them to believe the Apostle of God—God bless him and grant him peace!—by unquestioning acceptance, as it was made easy for the rude [desert] Arabs. But one who doubts and knows the risk of servile conformism, must know our veracity in our saying "There is no divinity save God: Muḥammad is the Apostle of God."

285 Then after this he will be in a position to follow the Apostle of God—God bless him and grant him peace!—but he will not know the proclamation of God's unity and the prophetic mission save by reasoning about the proof which the Companions indicated and by which the Apostle called men. For he did not call them by pure arbitrariness and naked force, but rather by disclosing the ways of the proofs. So this is the way to speak with every doubter. Otherwise let the Bāṭinite expose his belief respecting him [or: this] and how he escapes from his doubt if the door of reflection and reasoning be closed to him!

286 [p. 131] This, then, is the solution of these specious arguments [doubts, sophistries]. In the view of a knowledgeable man they are too feeble to require for their solution all this prolixity. But some men's being deceived by them and the conspicuousness [show, visibility] of deception in this time demand this disclosure and elucidation [clarification]. God Most High will aid us to knowledge and action and [to] right conduct and right guiding by His favor and His kindness!

[p. 132]

CHAPTER SEVEN

Refutation of Their Holding Fast to Textual Designation Concerning the Establishment of the Imamate and of Infallibility

It Contains Two Sections

Section One

On Their Holding Fast to the Textual Designation of the Imamate

287 A group of them turned [from the use of reasoning] to the method of the Imamites, i.e. the claim of textual designation of the Imam, ᶜAlī, and the designation by each father of his son.

288 This they cannot do because it would involve them in reports of individuals. So they are forced to claim an unimpeachable report about it from the Trustee of the Law [Muḥammad]. This is impossible, as it was impossible for the Imāmites.

289 For it would require unimpeachable report in each age regarding each individual [Imam].

290 This cannot be, for in each case four things would be required. (1) That he actually died leaving a son. (2) That he actually designated his son before he died.

291 (3) That there also be unimpeachable transmission that the Prophet put the designation of all his children on the same level as his [own] designation regarding the necessity of obedience, etc., so that error in specifying would be inconceivable in any one of them, (4) That there also be transmission of the perdurance of infallibility and fitness for the Imamate from the time of the designation to the death of the designator. [132.6–134.17]

292 If there were really *tawātur* [unimpeachable transmission] about these things, they would be known as are other subjects of *tawātur.* But men do not share in such knowledge of their *tawātur*—quite the contrary! It cannot be established.

293 They themselves even disagree about details regarding this or that Imam. . . . They are hopeless, and in leaving reasoning for textual designation are like one who plunges into the sea to avoid getting wet! [134.19–135.9]

294 *Objection:* You press them in many ways; but really they need only one report, viz. that the Apostle of God said: "The Imamate, after me, goes to ᶜAlī, and after him to his children; it will not go outside of my lineage, and my lineage will never be cut off; and no one of them will die before charging his son with the commission—this is enough for them.

295 *Answer:* Certainly—if any error can be contrived and reported unimpeachably! But this is not true of their claim. And it could be matched by an opponent.

296 *Objection:* These claims may not work for these Bāṭinites: but do they work for the Imamites concerning ᶜAlī? *Answer:* No! they can claim only probable words transmitted by individuals, e.g. "He whose Master I am, ᶜAlī is his Master" and "You are to me in the position of Aaron to Moses," etc. Such texts are dealt with in Kalām works [cf. al Bāqillānī: *Tamhīd,* ed. Khuḍayrī and Abū Rīdab, pp. 164 ff.]. This is not our aim now, but we mention its impossibility by two ways. [135.10–136.18]

297 *One way:* If such texts were unimpeachable, we would not doubt about them; for the Apostle's statements about designation would be of such importance as not to be passed over in silence.

298 This is a decisive proof of the falseness of their claim. Their assertion is no different from that of the Bakriyya regarding the designation of Abū Bakr or of the Rāwandiyya regarding that of Al-ᶜAbbās. [136.18–137.12]

299 *The second way:* The partisans of ᶜAlī against Abū Bakr clung to the probable expressions transmitted by individuals. How could they be silent about an unimpeachable text? They were egged on by godless opponents of religion who inspired the Jews to report utterances of Moses.

300 Our way to refute such men is that they used every artifice to discredit Muḥammad and his Law: why, then, did they refrain from transmitting explicit texts from Moses?

301 *Objection:* Perhaps they did, but the transmission has been lost. *Answer:* There has been transmitted the contention of the Anṣār [Helpers] about the Imamate—and there were more motives for transmitting textual designation. To open this door would be to allow every godless man to claim that the Qurᵓān was rivaled but that was not transmitted and Muslims concealed it,

302 *Objection:* You are compelled to know this *tawātur* report, but you stubbornly conceal it out of fanaticism. *Answer:* Why do you deny him who retorts this against you and claims that you are obstinate in inventing? How are you differentiated from the Bakriyya and the Rāwandiyya in their claiming that about the textual designation of Abū Bakr and al-ᶜAbbās?

303 *Objection:* You claim among the Apostles' apologetic miracles the splitting of the moon and the speech of the wolf and the yearning of the [palm] trunk and the multi-

plication of a little food, etc—all denied by all unbelievers and by groups of the Muslims; yet their opposition has not prevented you from claiming *tawātur. Answer:* We claim the *tawātur* which imposes necessary knowledge only regarding the Qur'ān. As for the other miracles, they were transmitted by a group less than that needed for *tawātur* whose veracity is known by different speculative proofs and inference from circumstances and others' refraining from denial, etc. which lead to knowledge through scrutiny and subtle thought—and one who turns from the latter will not have knowledge. But you cannot do so, because you invalidate the ways of reasoning.

304 *Objection:* The splitting of the moon is a heavenly sign; how could it be peculiar to a number less than that needed for *tawātur*? If the number were that needed for *tawātur,* how could there be any hesitation or denial?

305 As for a small number seeing it, the ulema declare it took place at night when people were asleep or indoors, and many might not advert to it, as in the case of those who do not see a falling star; and the splitting did not last long and may have been seen only by those around the Apostle. And some say that God restricted seeing it to those with whom the Apostle was contending with at the time for a good reason.

306 So it was the Prophet's miracle in two ways violating custom: (1) showing it to those; (2) concealing it from others. Such things mentioned by the ulema. One said that the splitting of the moon is certain from God's saying: "The Hour is nigh and the moon is split" [54.1]. Discussion of it would be lengthy. In any case, what reaches the level of *tawātur* cannot conceivably be doubted: this is a known rule [*qāʿida*] on which are built all the rules of religion. Prolixity is not in accord with our purposes, so I think concinnity best. [137.13–141.18]

Section Two
Refutation of Their Claim That the Imam Must Be Preserved [*Immune*] *from Error and Slip and from Sins Great and Small*

307 We say to them: By what do you know the correctness of the Imam's being infallible and the existence of his infallibility? By a necessity of the intellect, or by a reasoning, or by hearing a *tawātur* report from the Apostle which gives rise to necessary knowledge? There is no way to claim necessity or a *tawātur* report, because all men would share in knowing that. Not even the fact of the Imam's existence is known of necessity: how, then, his infallibility? And reasoning, in your view, is futile. The Imam's say-so is not enough until his infallibility be proved.

308 However, we say: What reasoning has made known to you the necessity of the Imam's infallibility? *If it be said:* The proof is the necessity of agreement that the Prophet must be infallible, since we learn the truth by means of him: otherwise there can be no reliance on what he says. So also the Imam since we have recourse to him about difficulties:otherwise there can be no reliance on him.

309 *We say:* The cause of your error is your supposing that we need the Imam to acquire knowledge from him: not so! Cognitions [knowledges] are rational and traditional [*samʿiyya*]*:* the former decisive and probable, each with its own way and proof, which can be learned from anyone and involve no *taqlīd* [servile conformism].

310 The traditional rest on hearing of *tawātur* reports or reports of individuals—and the Imam is not needed here.

311 *Objection:* Why, then, do we need the Imam, if he can be dispensed with? *Answer:* And why is there need of a qāḍī [judge] in every town? Does the need of him prove that he must be infallible? *They say:* He is needed for practical reasons such as warding off disputes, effecting harmony, etc. And the totality of the world regarding the Imam is like one town regarding the qāḍī.

312 [We say:] Just as the qāḍī need not be infallible, but his office [function] is needed, so the Imam need not be infallible, but he is necessary for general administrative reasons such as defending Islam, etc.

313 For such reasons an Imam is needed, and he must possess justice, knowledge. intrepidity, competence, and the other requisites which we shall mention in Chapter Nine: but he need not possess infallibility, If they insist on the infallibility of qāḍīs and governors and every least officeholder—as the Imamites believe—

314 we take refuge in God from a belief which forces its upholder to deny what he sees and perceives by intuition and necessity. The wrong done to the classes of men is seen from the circumstances of their Imam's appointees. When an adversary denies necessity one can only let him alone and limit oneself to offering condolences for the blow his mind has suffered!

CHAPTER EIGHT

Disclosure of the Legal Opinion Regarding Them with Reference to Imputing Unbelief and the Shedding of [Their] Blood

The contents of this chapter are jurisprudential decisions. We limit its aim to four sections,

Section One
On Imputing Unbelief to Them, or Declaring Them Astray, or Imputing Error to Them

315 Whenever we are asked about one of them or a group of them "Do you pronounce on their unbelief [find them guilty of unbelief]," we do not hasten to impute unbelief save after inquiring about their belief and doctrine, consulting the one judged or appealing to trustworthy witnesses, and then we judge accordingly.

316 Their doctrine has two grades [degrees]: one necessitates charging with error and straying [deviation] and innovation; the other necessitates charging with unbelief and washing one's hands of them ["excommunication"].

The first grade—which necessitates charging with error and deviation and innovation—is that we meet a common man who believes that entitlement to the Imamate is on the principle of the House [i.e. Muḥammad's family], and that the one now entitled to it is the one of them who undertakes the office and that in the first age it was ᶜAlī. He also claims that the Imam is preserved from error and slip [is infallible and impeccable] and must be so. But he does not declare licit the shedding of our blood or believe that we are unbelievers, but thinks we are men of injustice whose minds erroneously fail to attain the truth out of obstinacy and misfortune.

317 Such a man's blood is not licit, nor is he to be charged with *kufr* [unbelief] because of such views, but with error and innovation, and he is to be warned away from his

error and innovation. This because he does not believe in what we have related of their doctrine on divine and eschatological matters [Paras. 69–71 and 80–86], but in this believes as we do.

318 *Question:* Would you not charge them with unbelief for holding that ᶜAlī should have been Imam rather than Abū Bakr and ᶜUmar and ᶜUthmān? In that is a contravention of Consensus. *Answer:* Granted the contravention; and so we ascend from *takhṭīʾa* [charging with error] to *taḍlīl* [charging with deviation] and *tafsīq* [charging with sinfulness] and *tabdīᶜ* [charging with innovation], but not to *takfīr* [charging with unbelief]. It is not clear to us that the contravener of Consensus is a *kāfir* [unbeliever]. . . .

319 *Q:* Would you not charge them with unbelief for holding that the Imam is *maᶜṣūm* [infallible-impeccable]—a quality proper to the prophetic mission? *A:* This does not necessitate unbelief: what does that is affirming the prophetic mission of one after Muḥammad, or affirming of another the function of abrogating Muḥammad's Law. *ᶜIṣma* [preservation, immunity, from error and sin] is not a property of prophethood.

320 Some of our associates hold that immunity from venial sins is not certain of a Prophet; they infer this from 20,119/121 and some stories of the Prophets. A matter of error, not of unbelief.

321 *Q:* If one were to believe in the sinfulness of Abū Bakr, ᶜUmar and others of the Companions, but not in their unbelief, would you judge this to be unbelief? *A:* No, but we would judge it to be sinfulness, error and opposition to the Consensus of the Community. God ordained only eighty stripes [lashes] for one falsely accusing a chaste person of adultery—and this prescription extends to all persons thus accused, even Abū Bakr and ᶜUmar, had they been so accused.

322 *Q:* If one were to explicitly declare the unbelief of Abū Bakr and ᶜUmar, should he be assigned the same position as that of one who declares the unbelief of another Muslim person or judge or Imam? *A:* So we hold. So, declaring the unbelief of the former differs from declaring the unbelief of other Muslims only in two things: (1) opposition to and contravention of Consensus; (2) contradicting reports about the former being promised the Garden and praise of them, etc—so, one accusing them of unbelief is himself guilty of unbelief, not because he charges them with unbelief, but because he gives the lie to the Apostle of God.

323 *Q:* What do you hold about him who charges a Muslim with unbelief —*is* he an unbeliever or not? *A:* If he knows that the Muslim believes in the Oneness of God and in the Apostle etc. and charges him with unbelief in such things, then he is an unbeliever. But if he thinks the Muslim believes false doctrines and charges him with unbelief, then he is mistaken in his supposition, but truthful in charging with unbelief one he thinks holds such doctrines.

324 But "thinking" unbelief of a Muslim is not unbelief. Such thoughts may be right or wrong—but no one is bound to know the Islam of every Muslim and the unbelief of every unbeliever. A person might believe in God and His Apostle without ever hearing of Abū Bakr or ᶜUmar, and would die a Muslim. Faith in them is not a pillar of religion.

325 Here we must rein in our discussion, for plunging into this would lead to problems and stir up fanaticisms. Not all minds are ready to accept truth supported by demonstrations because of deeply-rooted beliefs. In fine, it would take a volume to treat even summarily what necessitates unbelief and "excommunication"—so let us restrict ourselves in this book to what is important.

The Second Grade
Doctrines Entailing Charging with Kufr

326 This grade is that one believe what we have mentioned, and more, and believe in our unbelief and the licitness of our property and our blood. This undoubtedly entails charging with *kufr* [unbelief]. For they know that we believe in sound doctrines . . . which are the pivot of authentic religion: so one who thinks them unbelief is undoubtedly an unbeliever. If there be added to that any of their dualistic, eschatological errors, the latter certainly entail charging with unbelief.

327 *Question:* What if one were to believe basic doctrines, but were to engage in interpretation [*taʾwil*] of certain eschatological matters? viz. that beatitude is something spiritual, not corporeal, and that [eternal] misery is failing to attain that beatitude;

328 and that the Qurʾān uses the parable of material pleasures for common men who cannot grasp that spiritual beatitude. For this reason the Prophet used pleasures they could understand—the houris, etc.—but really God has prepared for His servants what "eye bath not seen, nor ear heard. . . ."

329 And that advantage in representing such things in familiar images is like that in expressions indicating *tashbīh* [anthropomorphism] regarding God's Attributes. If one were to tell men that "the Creator of the world is an existent, neither substance nor accident nor body, neither united with the world nor distinct from it, etc.," they would forthwith deny His existence because their minds could not believe in something beyond sense and image. So representation is used to anchor in them belief and obedience.

330 *We say:* Holding two Gods is downright unbelief. As for the other matters, one might hesitate and say: If they hold the basics, dispute about details does not entail charging with unbelief. What we opt for and hold positively is the charging with unbelief of anyone who holds any of that, because it is plainly giving the lie to the Trustee of the Law [Muḥammad] and to all the words of the Qurʾān from their first to their last. Descriptions of the Garden and the Fire are in plain terms plainly intended—so what such a person holds is *takdhīb* [charging with lying], not *taʾwīl* [interpretation].

331 In the days of the Companions such a one would have been slain. *Objection:* Perhaps they so acted and exaggerated for the advantage of the common people, because the latter were incapable of understanding mental pleasures and their simple faith had to be protected.

332 *Answer:* You acknowledge by the consensus of the Companions that such a one is an unbeliever and is to be killed, which is all we say. There remains your assertion that the reason for declaring their unbelief was regard for the welfare of the common people. This is pure fancy and supposition. We know positively that they [the Companions] believed that to be giving the lie to God and to His Apostle and rejection of that which the Law brought and which was not contradicted by reason.

333 *Objection:* Did you not follow such a way regarding the similes [*al-tamthīlāt*] about God's attributes, such as the verse of "the being firmly seated [on the Throne]" and the tradition about [God's] "descent" [to the lower heaven] and other reports [numbering] perhaps more than a thousand? Yet you know that our pious forbears did not interpret these literal texts. Then you have not charged with *kufr* [unbelief] the one who rejects literal meanings and interprets them—but rather you believe in and openly declare the interpretation.

334 *We say:* How [p. 155] can this comparison be established when the Qurʾān explicitly states that "there is nothing like Him" [42.9/11] and the reports indicating it are too many to be enumerated? If anyone had explicitly declared among the Companions that

God is not contained by a place or bounded by a time . . . and other such things denying anthropomorphic attributes, they would have considered that to be of the essence of *tawḥīd* [proclamation of God's Unity] and *tanzīl* [revelation; or perhaps *tanzīh:* deanthropomorphization ?] But had he denied the houris, etc., that would have been regarded as a kind of lie and denial—and there is no equality between the two degrees.

335 Moreover we have already called attention to the difference in the chapter on refuting their doctrine [Chap. 5, Sect. 1] in two other ways. *One of them* is that the expressions which have come down [revealed] on the Assembly, Resurrection, Garden and Fire are explicit, without any *taʾwīl* [interpretation] or way of turning except neutralizing and denial; but the expressions on *istiwāʾ* [being firmly seatedl] and *al-ṣūra* [the form], etc., are allusions and verbal extensions which admit *taʾwīl* [interpretation] in description of God. *The other* is that rational demonstrations repel belief in anthropomorphism, "descent," "motion," and "occupying a place" by a proving which cannot be doubted; but no rational proof precludes the possibility of what is promised in the afterlife regarding the Garden and the Fire; on the contrary, the eternal power comprehends them and they are things possible in themselves, and the eternal power is not incapable of what is possible—how, then, can this be likened to what concerns God's attributes?!

336 The course of this discussion would require the unfolding of a mass of the mysteries of religion, were we to start treating it exhaustively. But since it occurs as an objection in the context of our discussion, let us be content with saying this much and occupy ourselves with the more important aims of this book. In this section we have indeed shown who of them is to be charged with unbelief, and who not, and who strays [errs, deviates], and who does not.

Section Two
On the Legal Status of
Those of Them Guilty of Unbelief

337 Briefly, they are to be dealt with like apostates with regard to [the shedding of their] blood, property, marriage, sacrifice, the execution of judgments, and the performance of acts of worship. As for "spirits" [*i.e.* souls, lives], they are not to be treated like the original *kāfir* [unbeliever] with respect to whom the Imam has the option of (1) boon [favor], (2) ransom, (3) enslavement, and (4) killing. But with the apostate his only option is killing him and riddling the world of him. This is the legal status of Bāṭinites guilty of *kūfr* [unbelief].

338 The allowability of killing them is not peculiar to the state of their fighting [i.e. when they actually engage in combat], but we even assassinate them and shed their blood. For if they engage in fighting, they can be killed; and if they be of the first group not judged guilty of unbelief, but in battle they attach themselves to the unjust—why the unjust *is* to be killed even if he is a Muslim—but not to be pursued if he flees, nor, if wounded, is he to be killed; but if we judge him guilty of unbelief, then there is no hesitation about killing him.

339 *Question:* Are their children and wives to be killed? *Answer:* Their women, yes, so long as they are guilty of unbelief. To be sure, the Imam can exercise his own personal effort, and if he follows Abū Ḥanīfa's opinion, he can refrain from killing the women. When their children grow up we propose [p. 157] Islam to them. If they accept, fine; if they persist in their unbelief, they are treated like apostates.

340 As for *property,* theirs has the status of that of apostates. . . .

341 If they die, no bequest or inheritance is valid. . . .

342 Their women cannot be married. . . . Other points on the validity of their marriages [p. 158] and on the use of property.

343 Their sacrifices [animals for slaughter: ef. EI(2), 213] are not licit, like those of a Zoroastrian or a Zendīq—but those of Jews and Christians are. Their judgments inoperative and their testimony rejected. So, too, their fasting, prayer, pilgrimage and poor tax. If they repent, they must perform all the duties omitted or performed in the state of unbelief, as in the case of the apostate.

344 This is as much as we wish to call attention to of their *aḥkām* [legal statuses]. *Question:* [p. 159] Why do you judge them to be attached to the apostates? The latter once held to the true religion, but the former never did. So why not equate them with the original *kāfir* [unbeliever]? *Answer:* What we said is clear about those who embrace their religion after believing its opposite, or not belonging to it. Those who are raised in it are the children of the apostates, for their forbears embraced it. It is not like the belief of Jews and Christians based on Prophets and Scripture, but an innovation introduced by the godless and zendīqs in recent times.

345 And the status of the zendīq is like that of the apostate. It remains only to consider the children of the apostates. One view is that they are followers in apostasy like the children of unbelievers, in war, and of *dhimmis* [protected ones who pay a tax]. Another view is that they are like original unbelievers. Another view is that they are judged to have Islam, unless they grow up and manifest unbelief.

346 The latter view in our view is preferable regarding the children of Bāṭinites. Muḥammad said: "Every one is born in the *fiṭra* [cf. Note 22 to my translation] and his parents make him a Jew or a Christian or a Zoroastrian." So the children have Islam, and as soon as they are of age the truth is to be disclosed to them: if they accept it, fine; otherwise they are to be treated as apostates.

Section Three
On the Acceptance and Rejection of Their Repentance

347 We have annexed them to the apostates, and from an apostate repentance must be accepted. It is even preferable not to kill him before urging him to repent. But the repentance of a Bāṭinite and of any zendīq who harbors unbelief and considers *taqiyya* [dissimulation] a religious practice and believes in hypocrisy when he is filled with fear is a matter on which the ulema differ. Some hold that the repentance of such is to be accepted because of the Apostle's saying: "I am commanded to fight men until they say 'There is no divinity save God.' If they say this, they preserve from me their life and property except for what is due [owed, for some other reason]"; and because the Law has built religion only on the external, and so we judge only by the external, and God takes care of hearts.

348 The proof of it is that if one coerced embraces Islam at sword's point while he is fearful for his life, [and] we know by some circumstances that he conceals something other than what he manifests, we judge him to have embraced Islam and ignore what is known from circumstances about his heart [interior]. It is also proved by the Prophet's displeasure with Usāma who slew an unbeliever after the latter had pronounced the *shahāda* [the word of witnessing: There is no god etc.]. Usāma said: [p. 161] "He did that only to escape the sword." The Prophet said: "Surely you split open his heart," calling attention to the fact that creatures are not informed about interiors and that the place [*manāṭ:* place

to which something is attached] of *al-taklīf* [imposing obligation] is external things. And it is also proved by the fact that this sort of unbelievers, and all other sorts, must not be cut off from the way to repentance and return to the truth. So also in the present case.

349 And some hold that his repentance is not to be accepted. They allege that if this door were opened it would be impossible to overcome their danger [harm]. For part of their inmost belief is *taqiyya* [dissimulation] and concealing unbelief when they feel fear. This they could always do when pressed. The report mentioned concerned unbelievers whose religion did not allow them to declare anything opposed to their religion. Therefore you see them cut to ribbons rather than agree with Muslims in a word. So how can one who believes otherwise repent and give up his religion?

350 We have exhaustively treated this disagreement in our *Shifāʾ al-ʿalīl* [The Cure of the Ailing—cf. Bonyges, p. 18, Note 4]; here we limit ourselves to what we opt for regarding them. We say: The one who repents of this error [may be in one of] several states. *The first* is that he hastens to manifest repentance without any fighting or pressure or compulsion, but by preference [p. 162] and choice, voluntarily and without any fear. This one's repentance positively must be accepted. For we must believe what he says and think it more probable that his interior agrees with that, since there is no motive for *taqiyya.* And the way of guidance cannot be closed to him. Such is the case of many an ordinary man, deceived for a time.

351 *The second state:* One who embraces Islam at sword's point, but belongs to their ordinary and ignorant men, not to their propagandists and erring. His repentance is also to be accepted. For his harm is limited to himself; and the ignorant common man is easily deluded in religious matters; but his interior agrees with his exterior.

352 Therefore you see captive slaves and bondwomen from lands of unbelief transported to the House of Islam [Islamic territory] readily and gratefully adopting Islam. If asked the reason, they know no reason save agreement with their masters for the advantage of their state, and this influences their interior beliefs. If it is known that the common man changes quickly, then we believe him in his change to the truth as we do in his turning from it . . . for we are between condoning a secret unbeliever and not killing him, and killing a Muslim, if such a one holds interiorly what he manifests. Condoning the unbelief of an unbeliever who is no threat is not a big deal [a big prohibited thing]. How many unbelievers have we treated kindly and overlooked because of the spending [offering] of a dinar [reference to the tax ?]. But risking killing one who is Muslim outwardly, and may very well be so inwardly, is prohibited.

353 *The third state:* One of their propagandists who is known to think their doctrine false, but embraces it as a means to power and worldly vanities—such a man's evil is to be feared. The case of such a man depends on the *raʾy* [personal opinion] of the Imam who examines the circumstances and seeks signs to determine his sincerity or his hypocrisy and *taqiyya* [dissimulation] and acts accordingly: if he has any doubt, he charges some one to observe him carefully and acts according to what thus becomes clear to him.

[p. 164]

Section Four
On the Artifices [Legal Devices]
of Getting Out of Their Oaths and Pacts
If They Have Concluded Them with the Prospect

354 *Question:* What is your view regarding their covenants and pacts and oaths—are they valid [in force]? It is allowable to break them? Or is breaking them obligatory or prohibited? And if the one swearing breaks [them], is he thereby bound by a sin and an expiation [atonement, amends] or not? How many a person has been the subject of a pact and been confirmed by an oath and accepted that through being seduced by their delusion, then, when their error was disclosed to him, he desired to expose them and lay bare their weaknesses, but was prevented by the binding oaths imposed on him: so there is an urgent need to teach the legal device for getting out of those oaths. *Answer:* Escape from those oaths is possible, and it has ways which differ according to the difference of states [conditions] and expressions.

355 *The first* is that the swearer was aware of the gravity of the oath and the possibility of its containing deception and deceit: so he mentioned to himself following that the "exception," i.e. his saying "If God Will—so the oath is not valid and be can violate it. And if he violates it he is not bound by any legal determination at all. This is the legal status of any oath followed by the phrase of exception, such as one's saying "By God I shall do thus, if God will," and "If I do such and such, my wife is divorced, if God will," and the like.

356 *The second* is that he convey in his oath a thing and intend the contrary of what he manifests, and the interior holding be in a way borne by the expression so that he concert between himself and God. Then he can violate his external words and follow therein the dictate of his conscience and his intention, *Objection:* In an oath the dependence is on the intention of the exactor, for if one were to rely on the intention of the swearer and his "exception," oaths in judgment meetings [assemblies, sittings, of judges] would be null and the one sworn could conceal [harbor] an intention and "exception" which would lead to the nullification [ruin, frustration] of rights [*al-ḥuqūq*].

357 *Answer:* The analogy [*qiyās:* norm] is that one rely on the intention and "exception" of the swearer—and the one making to swear presents the oath to him, but it is a status about [or: a judgment about] following the intention of the exactor of the oath out of concern for and protection of rights in virtue of the necessity calling for that, and that concerns one in the right in exacting [an oath] which is conformed to the Law and the data of *tawqīf* [positive data] about it: but as for one unjustly coerced and one aggressively [hostilely] duped—no. And one must consider the affair of the swearer along with that [?] in the analogous law regarding consideration of the side of the swearer, because the reason for turning to the consideration of the side of the exactor is the intensity of the need. And what need have we to make injustice rule over imposing [*?*] an oath on weak Muslims by varieties of deceit and deception?! So one must return regarding it to the law [*al-qānūn*]. [This Para. is rather involved. It seems to say that normally one considers the intention etc. of the one exacting the oath; but in this case, i.e. of a Bāṭinite unjustly exacting an oath from a prospect, it is the latter's intention which is paramount.]

358 *The third* is that one look at the wording of the oath. If he said: "God's covenant and pact upon you, and what covenants were exacted of the Prophets and the just; and if you disclose the secret, you are quit of Islam and the Muslims," or, "an unbeliever in God,

Lord of the Worlds," or, "all your goods are an alms—no oath at all is concluded by these words. For if he said: "If I do such and such, I am quit of Islam and of God and His Apostle," this would not be an oath because of the saying of Muḥammad—God bless him and grant him peace!—"Whoso swears, let him swear by God or be silent." And swearing by God is that he say *"Tallāhi"* and *"Wallāhi"* [By God] and the like.

359 We have already discussed at length the unambiguous oath in the discipline of jurisprudence, and these expressions are not part of it. So also is his saying "Upon me God's covenant and pact and what God exacted from the Prophets." For if God does not exact their pact and His covenant, it is not concluded by the utterance of another; and God did not exact their pact to conceal the secret of unbelievers and deviants, and this covenant is not like that of God—so nothing is obligatory because of it. Similarly, were a man to say: "If I do such and such a thing, my goods are an alms," nothing would be incumbent on him—unless he says: "God's due from me that I give my property as alms": and this is the oath of anger and obstinacy, and there frees him [from it], according to the preferable opinion, an oath expiation.

360 [p. 166] *The fourth* is to look at what is sworn to. If the swearer's expression regarding it was what we have related [Paras. 44–45], i.e. their saying "You will conceal the secret of the friend of God and champion it and not oppose it"—then let him expose the secret whenever he will, and he will not break his oath, because he swore to conceal the secret of the friend of God, and what he has divulged is the secret of the enemy of God. So also his saying "You will champion his relatives and followers—for that is referred to the friend of God and not to the one meant by the exactor, for he is God's enemy.

361 But if the person was specified by name or indication . . . then one man held that he does not break his oath by divulging the secret, having in view the quality [i.e., friend of God] and turning from the indication. And they have said that it is as though one were to say "I buy from you this ewe," and the thing indicated is a mare—for it is not valid. We opt for the view that the oath is valid; it is not like saying "By God I shall drink the water of this *idwāt* [a small vessel for carrying water]," and there is no water in it.

362 And were he to restrict and say that he will not divulge the secret of *this* person, or of Zayd, it would be valid, even though he refrained from saying that he is the friend of God. But whenever the oath is concluded in this way, he is allowed to, indeed must, disclose the secret, and then is bound to an expiation—enough to feed ten poor men, or, if he is unable, to fast three days. An easy matter requiring no meticulousness in seeking a legal device [p. 167]. And there is no sin in breaking his oath, for the Apostle said: "Whoso swears an oath, then sees something else to be better, let him do what is better and expiate his oath." One who swears to fornicate and not to pray must break his oath and is bound to expiation.

363 *The fifth:* If the swearer left out intention and exception, and the exactor left out the expression of covenant and pact and "friend of God," and produced plain oaths by God and attachment of divorce and manumission and all he would ever possess and obligation of a hundred pilgrimages and fasting a hundred years and praying a million *rakᶜas* and the like—then his way out of oath by God is feeding ten poor people, as we have said. This also releases him from the pilgrimage, fasting, etc., because that is an oath of anger and obstinacy.

364 As for the attachment of future divorce and manumission—it is null and void. So let him break his oath and marry when he will, for there is no divorce before marriage

and no manumission before possession. If he owns a slave and fears manumitting him, let him sell him to a relative or friend, then disclose the secret, then get him back by sale or donation or whatever. Everyone has such a friend. As for his wife, let him divorce her for a dirham [small coin], of hers or of a stranger, then divulge the secret, then remarry her and be safe from any divorce thereafter.

365 *Question:* [p. 168] What if he had previously divorced her twice and had only one divorce left—and in divorce at his wife's insistance is what makes her illicit for him until she marries another? *Answer:* He should say: "Whenever my divorce falls on you, you are divorced before it three times." So whenever he breaks his oath his divorce does not occur. This is the "circular oath" which frees from breaking [the oath] and prevents the incidence of divorce. *Objection:* The ulema disagree about that, and perhaps the cautious man will not be pleased to risk a doubtful divorce. *Answer:* If the asker be a blind follower [*muqallid*], he must blindly follow the muftī [one who gives a legal decision]. And the responsibility is assumed peculiarly by the muftī, not the *muqallid;* and if the mufti exercises *ijtihād* [personal reasoning], he is responsible for what his *ijtihād* necessitates. If his *itjihād* leads to that [?—the incidence of the divorce ?], the incidence of the divorce is not excluded: so he [the asker] has the option of substituting another or of refraining from divulging their secret, but giving up their belief.

366 And in refraining from divulging there is no agreeing with them about religion: rather agreeing lies in believing what they believe and expressing his belief and summoning to it. So if he dismisses their error outwardly and inwardly, he is not bound to speak of what he has heard from them, since there is no specific obligation to recount unbelief from every unbeliever. These, then, are the methods of the legal device to get out of the oath. Some who have studied this branch [discipline] hold that in no case are the oaths issuing from them valid, but this is an utterance proceeding from scanty insight into jurisprudential determinations [statuses, decisions, consequences]. What agrees with the practice of *fiqh* [jurisprudence] and the prescriptions [*aḥkām*] of the Law is simply what we have mentioned. Peace!

CHAPTER NINE

On the Establishment of the Legal Demonstrations That the Imam Charged with the Truth Whom All Men Are Bound to Obey in This Age of Ours Is the Imam al-Mustaẓhir Billāh— God *Guard His Authority!*

367 The aim of this chapter is to prove his Imamate [Caliphate] in accordance with the Law and to show that all the ulema of the time must give the legal decision that men are definitely and positively bound to obey him and to carry out his decisions in the way of the truth [in the true way] and [to acknowledge] the validity of his appointment of governors and investiture of *qāḍīs* [judges], and that he is quit of obligation to his subjects at the turning over to him of God's rights, and that he is God's vicegerent over men, and that obedience to him is a duty incumbent on all men.

368 This chapter, with respect to religion, calls for the turning of attention to ascertaining [verifying] it and establishing the demonstration of the way and path of the truth. For what the discussion of most writers about the Imamate is directed to is that we do not

believe [that there is] a Caliph in this age of ours and in bygone ages who does not unite the requisites for the Imamate and is not qualified by their qualifications so that the Imamate would remain inactive [suspended] without anyone exercising it and the one undertaking [occupying] it would remain in violation of the conditions of the Imamate, unworthy of it and unqualified by them,

369 This is a serious attack on Law-based judgments [*aḥkām:* prescriptions] and an explicit declaration of their inoperativeness and neglect, and it would call for the clear declaration of the invalidity of all administrative posts and the unsoundness of the judging of Qāḍīs [judges] and the ruin of God's rights and prescriptions and the invalidation of [retaliation for] blood and wombs [offspring] and property and the pronouncement of the invalidity of marriages [marriage contracts] issuing from Qāḍīs in [all] the regions of the earth and the remaining of the rights of God Most High in the custody [care] of creatures. For all such things would be legal only if their fulfillment issued from Qāḍīs duly appointed by the Imam—which would be impossible if there were no Imamate. So the exposure of the corruption of a doctrine calling for that is an important task and duty of religion, but not an easy one. With God's help we shall attempt it.

370 We claim that the Imam al-Mustaẓhir Billāh is the true Imam who must be obeyed. Our detailed and convincing argument:

There must be an Imam in every age.
But only he is qualified for the office.
Therefore he is the rightful Imam.

371 What if the first premise be denied? We reply that it is agreed upon by us and by the Bāṭinites and by all the Muslims. The principle is not questioned, but only the specification of an individual—except for the man known as ᶜAbd al-Raḥmān ibn Kaisān.

372 All knowledgeable men agree on the falseness of the latter's doctrine: two things to be pointed out to those seeking guidance on it. . . . (1) The haste of the early Companions, after Muḥammad's death, to set about appointing an Imam...

373 (2) The defense and championing of religion undoubtedly necessary and obligatory. To preserve order there must be someone to keep a watchful eye on men and to nip danger in the bud: otherwise anarchy, etc.

374 The conflict of wills and passions would lead to the neglect of the afterlife and the triumph of vice over virtue, and of the lowly over the learned with the consequent dissolution of religious and secular checks. So it is clear that the Imam is an indispensable necessity of men.

375 *Question:* How do you repudiate one who challenges the second premise, viz. that only al-Mustaẓhir is fit [suited] for the Imamate? For the Bāṭinites summon men to another. How can they make this claim? *Answer:* We do not deny that some claim the Imamate undeservedly. But we say: If the Bāṭinites' claim is false, the Imamate is specified for him who claims it and our aim is achieved. For if, by agreement, there must be an Imam, and if it is certain that the Imamate is not outside of two persons, and if it is certain that the Imamate of one of them is false, then there remains no doubt about its being certain of the other.

376 The ways showing the falseness of the Imamate claimed by the Bāṭinites are innumerable. We confine ourselves to two factual, decisive [irrefutable] proofs, convincing to all and understood by all. *The first* is that the key conditions of the Imamate are

correctness of belief and soundness of religion; and we have related of the doctrine of the Bāṭinites and their Master what at the least entails charging with innovation and deviation, and at the most entails charging with unbelief and excommunication [being quit of them], viz. their affirmation of two preeternal Gods according to what all their sects are agreed upon.

377 *The second* is their rejection, by false interpretations, of many eschatological details revealed in the Qurʾān. How, then, could anyone who holds such things be fit for the Imamate?

378 *The second* [*general*] *way* [of showing the falseness of the Imamate claimed by the Bāṭinites and the preference of what we claim]: Even if we concede, for the sake of argument and gratuitously, that the Master of the Bāṭinites is fit for the Imamate . . . still the Imamate we claim is something agreed upon by all the leaders and ulema of the age and by all the masses of men in farthest East and West, so that obedience and submission to him [Mustaẓhir] are embraced by all save the little gang of Bāṭinites who all together do not equal the number of the followers of the ᶜAbbāsid Imamate in a single township, much less those of a district or province!

379 Could an impartial man doubt that the Bāṭinite extremists do not equal a tenth of a tenth of those who support this conquering State [government of the ᶜAbbāsids]?—If the Imamate is by might [power], and might is by mutual help and the plurality of followers, etc., then this is a most powerful argument for preferring our Imamate!

380 *Objection:* Truth does not follow plurality, but is hidden and is attained only by a minority, whereas error is plain and the majority hasten to submit to it. Your argument uses the false premise of plurality. But the Imamate, according to the Bāṭinites, is valid simply by textual designation, whether the one so designated be acknowledged or not. So how can such an argument from plurality be valid?

381 *Answer:* The mode of that argument is clear to one who understands the source of the Imamate. In Chapter Seven we showed that its source is not textual designation. . . . So if the latter is false, there remains only choice [*ikhtiyār:* election] by the people of Islam and their agreement on submission.

382 Hence it is clear that whenever there is agreement, anyone who ambitions the Imamate for himself is unjust—and the overwhelming majority is for our Imamate—the dissenters are a mere drop in the sea.

383 *Question:* How do you repudiate one who states "The source of the Imamate is either textual designation or choice; so if choice is false, textual designation is certain"? And he proves the falseness of choice by arguing that one must consider in it the consensus of all men, or the consensus of the authorities in all the regions of the earth, or the consensus of the men in the town in which the Imam lives, which may be estimated as the consensus of ten or five—or the allegiance may be that of a single person. Now the consensus of all men is impossible, nor was it imposed in bygone times.

384 And the consensus of authorities is impossible, since it might involve waiting over a period longer than the Imam's life. Then there is the case of Abū Bakr. So also regarding the consensus of the men of a town, etc.: mere arbitrariness. . . .

385 There remains only being content with the allegiance of a single person—in a plurality there is diversity of circumstances, etc., and one is preferable to another only by *ᶜiṣma* [infallibility-impeccability]. So the Master of the agreement is one person, and let him be *maᶜṣūm* [infallible-impeccable], which is our doctrine and belief, and the plurality of dissenters will be of no avail. So your attachment to plurality is of no help.

386 *We say:* To be sure, the only source of the Imamate is either textual designation or choice; and we say that if textual designation is false, then choice is certain. Your argument against choice is really ignorance of the doctrine we choose and prove. We choose to hold that one person can suffice if he is on the side of the multitudes: his agreement is theirs.

387 We also say: When ᶜUmar swore fealty to Abū Bakr, the latter's Imamate was established, but by the succession of those who followed ᶜUmar's lead. Not so had there been a split and factions—for the aim we seek by an Imam is the uniting of views—and one would not be followed unless his authority and influence were recognized and revered. The pivotal point here is *al-shawka* [personal power and influence].

388 If this [choice] is the source of the Imamate, there can be no doubt about al-Mustaẓhir's Imamate. . . .

389 Is is now clear to you how we have ascended from this dark depth and resolved the problem about the number of the men of choice: for we specify no number; one is sufficient, if all follow him—and this is a gracious gift from God.

390 Apparently we have reduced the specification of the Imamate to the choice of a single person; but really we have reduced it to God's choice and appointment. The real justification of the choice is that all follow and obey the Imam—a grace and gift of God, unattainable by any human contriving.

391 The only way the Bāṭinites support their view is by claiming an invention [forgery], viz. that Muḥammad textually designated ᶜAlī, and by claiming that the designation passed from father to son—false claims! Their argument that we designate the Imam by passion and choice is false: since we have shown that God does the choosing.

392 Were ever so many men to unite in trying to turn men from the ᶜAbbāssid, Mustaẓhirite Imamate, their efforts would be completely fruitless.

393 This is the method of establishing the demonstration of the fact that the true Imam is Abū l-ᵓAbbās Aḥmad al-Mustaẓhir Billāh. It remains only to refute the challenge of opponents in their claim that the conditions of the Imamate and qualities of the Imam are lacking in him. We shall do this in the form of question and answer.

394 *If it be said:* Your argument in support of Mustaẓhir is valid only if you show the existence of the conditions of the Imamate and the qualities of the Imam. These are many and the lack of even one precludes the Imamate. So detail the conditions and show their fulfillment. . . .

395 *Answer:* What the ulema of Islam have enumerated of the qualities of Imams and the conditions of the Imamate is limited to ten qualities, six of them innate [inborn, natural, physical] and not acquired, and four of them acquired, or increased by acquisition. The six innate qualities must undoubtedly exist and their existence cannot conceivably be contested. (1) *al-bulūgh:* maturity [afterlife; attainment of puberty]; (2) *al-ᶜaql:* intelligence [Integritat der Vernunft]; (3) *al-ḥurriyya:* freedom;

396 (4) male sex; (5) *nasab Quraysh:* descent from [the tribe] Quraysh;

397 (6) *salāma ḥāssat al-samᶜ wa l-baṣar:* soundness of hearing and sight. It is disputed whether or not there should be freedom from leprosy and elephantiasis and palsy and amputated limbs and other loathsome and repugnant defects. . . .

398 The four acquired qualities: (1) *al-najda:* intrepidity [bravery, courage; Kampfestüchtigkeit—fitness for combat, war, fighting]; (2) *al-kifāya:* competence [Kompetenz zur Regierung]; (3) *al-ᶜilm:* knowledge; (4) *al-waraᶜ:* piety [godliness; fromme, zweifelhafter Dinge sich enthaltende Lebensführung: pious way of life refraining

from doubtful things]. These they are agreed upon. We shall show that the quantity of these requisite for the Imamate exists in al-Mustaẓhir Billāh.

399 *On the first quality:* intrepidity [*al-najda*], i.e. so circumstanced as to be able to handle rebels, unbelievers, insurrections, etc—and through power based on the Turks.

400–404 Answer to an objection.

405 *On the second quality:* competence [*al-kifāya*]. Al-Mustaẓhir's reflection and governance based on his astuteness and intelligence admired by all.

406 He seeks enlightenment from consulting men of insight and experience and choosing an able Wazīr [Minister] . . .

407–408 This is the competence sought. Example of al-Mustaẓhir's competence in dealing with the circumstances which followed the death of al-Muqtadī. . . .

409 *On the third quality:* piety [*al-wara*ᶜ]. This is the fundamental and noblest quality. . . .

410 Praise be to God Who has so abundantly gifted al-Mustaẓhir with piety and godliness from his youth onwards.

411–417 Reply to an objection. Al-Mustaẓhir's use of funds, etc. And *al-*ᶜ*iṣma* [impeccability, sinlessness] is not a requisite for the Imamate.

418 *On the fourth quality:* knowledge [*al-*ᶜ*ilm*]. *If it be said:* The ulema are agreed that the Imamate is only for one who has attained the rank of personal effort [*al-ijtihād*] and giving a [legal] decision [*fatwā*] in the science of the Law. You cannot claim this requisite is present, nor can you deny that it is a requisite. *We say:* If one denied that it is a requisite he would only be departing from past ulema. Requisites for the Imamate must be proved, and proof is either a text from the Trustee of the Law [Muḥammad], or a reasoning about the good [*maṣlaḥa:* advantage] for which the Imamate is sought. The only text is that about descent from Quraysh.

419 The other requisites from necessity and need involved in the purposeof the Imamate. The rank of "personal effort" is not indispensable:piety calling for consultation with the learned would suffice. The Imam can know by his own reasoning or by that of others.

420 Why can he not fulfill the aim of knowledge through the best men of his time, just as the aims of power and competence can be fulfilled through others? Most of the problems of the Imamate are jurisprudential and conjectural and may be solved by following the prevailing opinion.

421 But I do not wish to follow a singular opinion and depart from past ulema. I seek a way borrowed from the argument of the Imams mentioned. Men differed about choosing as Imam an inferior when there was a better man present: most say that such a choice is valid.

422 I start from this and say: In principle one ought to prefer one of independent personal effort to one who follows that of others. But if the latter is chosen, and has the support and the submission of all, and there is no Qurayshite *mujtahid* [one who can exercise personal effort] who has all requisites, the choice is valid.

423 But if there were a qualified Qurayshite, but the deposition of the other would lead to various vexations, insurrections and disturbances, it would not be licit to depose the first and change him. For we know that knowledge lends luster to the Imamate, but that the fruit sought from the Imamate is to extinguish dissensions—and this is not to be sacrificed out of a desire to have more precision in differentiating between reasoning and conformism to the views of others.]

424 But this is a supposition that we have indulgently allowed—i.e. that there is a fully qualified Qurayshite now, and that men can effect a change of Imam; both of these

are impossible in our time, for men cannot be turned from al-Mustaẓhir and the ulema are bound to acknowledge formally the validity and legality of his Imamate.

425 This said, there remain two conditions. *One* is that he not settle any problem except after exploiting the talents of the ulema and seeking their help, and, in doubt, choose to follow the best and most learned—and the City of Peace [Baghdad] will rarely be without such men. *The second* is that he strive to acquire knowledge and gain the rank of independence in the science of the Law—for God has enjoined the acquisition of knowledge. And he is young enough to do that in a short time.

426 If it is clear in this chapter by these proofs that al-Mustaẓhir Billāh is the true Imam, how worthy this grace is of being met with thanks. Gratitude is evidenced by knowledge and by action and by assiduous application to what I have set forth in the last chapter of this book. In general gratitude for this grace is that the Commander of the Faithful be not content that God have on the face of the earth a more faithful and grateful servant than himself, just as God has not been content to have on the face of the earth a servant dearer and nobler than the Prince of the Faithful!

CHAPTER TEN

On the Religious Duties by the Assiduous Performance of Which Worthiness for the Imamate Is Perpetuated

427 The Commander of the Faithful [Imam, Caliph] is religiously bound to read and reflect on this chapter continually; and if God's help aids in striving for the mastery of one of these duties, even though it takes a year, it will be maximum success [ultimate bliss]. Some of these tasks are theoretical pertaining to knowledge]; others are practical [matters of action, or practice]. The former have pride of place, because knowledge is the root [*al-aṣl*] and practice is a branch of it, for cognitions are countless. But we shall mention four basic and fundamental matters.

[Duties Connected with Knowledge (ʿilm)]

428 *The first* is that he knew why man has been created in this world, and to what good directed, and for what quest prepared [nominated, assigned]. It is well known to a man of insight [discernment] that this "house" [world, life] is not a house of abiding but is simply a house of passage, and that in it men are like voyagers. The starting point of their voyage is their mothers' wombs, and the house of the Hereafter is the goal of their voyage. Its distance is the span of life, its years are its [his] stopping-places, its months are its [his] parasangs and its days are its [his] miles [milestones], its steps are his breaths, and men are brought [go] [like] a ship's passage [transit] with its passenger. Each person, with God, has an allotted life without increase or decrease. Therefore Jesus said: "The world [this life] is a bridge: so cross it and do not dwell on it."

429 Creatures are summoned to the meeting [encounter: *apantēsis, apantēma*—Matthew 25:6] with God in the Abode of Peace and the bliss of eternity [10.26/25]. The voyage will not lead to the goal save by a provision [stores] which is piety [*al-taqwā:* godliness (2.193/197)]. He who is not supplied [does not supply himself] with provisions [*viaticum*] in this life of his for his Hereafter by assiduous application to worship will have

taken from him what he was dazzled [seduced] by of his body and his wealth and will sigh [grieve] where sighing will avail him not and will say: "Would that we were returned [to life on earth], and we would not treat as lies the signs of our Lord, and we would be among the believers" [6.27], and, "Have we intercessors to intercede for us, or can we be returned [to life on earth] so that we could do other than we used to do?" [7.51/53], and then "its faith will be of no avail to a soul which did not believe before or did not acquire any good in its faith" [6.159/158].

430 In another way, man is a tiller [*ḥārith*] and his action is his tilling and his "world" [i.e. his life on earth] is his tilth [tillage] and the time of [his] death is his harvest. Therefore Muḥammad said: "This life is the plantation of the next life." The sowing [seed] is the span of life. If a single breath of a man goes by without his worshiping God in it by an act of reverence, he is defrauded because of the loss of that breath, for it will never return. In his life span man is like one who was selling ice in the summer time and who had no other wares; so he used to call out, saying: "Have mercy on [be kind to] one whose capital is melting": man's capital is his span of life which is the time of obedience, and it is constantly melting away. The older he gets the more the remainder of his life diminishes—so a man's increase is really his decrease.

431 So one who does not take advantage of his breaths to bag all the acts of obedience [he can] is defrauded. Hence Muḥammad said: "One whose two days are alike [equal] is defrauded [gulled]; and one whose today is worse than his yesterday is cursed." Whoever directs his life to worldly things is a failure and his work is lost, as God Most High said: "Those who will have desired the present life and its showiness We shall pay them in full for their works . . ." [11.18/15]. But he who works for his Hereafter, his effort succeeds, as God Most High said: "He who desires the next life and strives for it, while being a believer, the striving of such will be thanked [recognized]" [17.20/19]

432 *The second duty* [connected with knowledge] is that whenever he recognizes the fact that the viaticum for his voyage to the afterlife is piety [godliness] he must then know that the seat and source of piety is the heart, because of Muḥammad's saying: "Piety is here" while he pointed to his breast. So diligence ought to be had first of all in the correction [reform, amelioration] of the heart, since that of the members follows on it, because Muḥammad said: "In the body of the son of Adam is a bit [little piece]: if it be sound, all the rest of the body is sound because of it; but if it be corrupt, all the rest of the body is corrupt because of it: of a certainty it is the heart."

433 The condition for ameliorating the heart is first to purify it—and its purity is in its being clean of the love of the world, because of Muḥammad's saying: "And this is the malady which paralyzes [cripples] men." One who thinks he can combine enjoyment of this life and greed for its luxuries with the bliss of the afterlife is deceived, because of the Commander of the Faithful's [ᶜAlī] saying: "This life and the afterlife are two fellow-wives: the more you please one of them, the more you displease the other."

434 To be sure, if a man were to occupy himself with his life for the sake of religion, not for the sake of his own desire, like one who would devote his life to the advantage of men out of sympathy for them, or were to devote some of his time to acquiring nourishment, his intention in that being to have strength for undertaking obedience and piety, this would be of the very essence of religion. This was the attitude of the Prophets and the rightly guided Caliphs toward worldly things. Since, then, the viaticum is piety, and the condition of piety is the heart's being free from the love of this world—then effort must be devoted to freeing it from this love. The way to this is that man recognize the world's

[this life's] flaw [blemish] and defect, and recognize the dignity and beauty of bliss in the afterlife, and know that regard for this despicable life [world] contains the escaping [slipping away] of the momentous [importantj afterlife.

435 The least of this life's [world's] defects, known for certain by every intelligent and ignorant man is that it soon passes away [is soon ended], whereas the afterlife has no end. This is so when this life is free from flaws and annoyances and exempt from painful and disturbing things. But not so! Not so! For no one in this life is free from length and trouble and suffering of miseries [adversities, hardships]. And once one knows [recognizes] the passing of this life and the permanence of bliss in the end, let him reflect [on this]: If a man were so infatuated with, and so doted on, a person that he could not bear parting from him, and were to be offered a choice between having the meeting with him advanced by one night, and being patient apart from him for one night, overcoming himself, then being alone with him for a thousand nights, how would it not be easy for him to be patient for one night in expectation of the pleasure of seeing him for a thousand nights! If he chose the other, he would be considered silly and outside the group of rational men. This life [world] is a beloved, [and] we are enjoined to renounce her for a short time, but we are promised many times these pleasures for a period without end. Giving up a thousand for one is irrational: and the choice of a thousand in the place of one brought forward is not difficult [impossible] for the reasonable man.

436 At this point a man ought to compare the longest period of his abiding in this life, e.g. a hundred years, and the length of his abiding in the afterlife, which is endless. Nay, but were we to seek an example of the length of eternity, we could not find it. However, we say: Were we to suppose that the whole world [*al-dunyā*] to the end of the heavens were filled with tiny particles [*al-dharra:* powder, salt, sand ?], and to suppose that a bird would with his beak take a single grain every thousand years and to keep returning until there did not remain of the tiny particles a single grain—these tiny particles would be finished and there would remain many times more of them. How, then, would an intelligent man, if he verified for himself this matter, be unable to despise the world and to devote himself exclusively to God Most High?!

437 This [is so] were the duration of life supposed to be a hundred years, and the world were supposed to be free of odious things: how, then, when death lies in wait [ambush] at every moment and the world is not free of [all] sorts of toils and trouble! This is something one ought to meditate on at length until it is firmly fixed in his heart and piety arises [springs] from it. So long as the vileness of the world is not evident to a man he will not conceivably strive for the other abode [of the afterlife]. He ought to be helped to the knowledge of that by consideration of the preceding children of the world—how they toiled in it and departed from it with no profit, accompanied only by sorrow and regret [remorse]. That poet spoke truly who said:

The intensest [most violent] distress [grief] is in a joy
The possessor of which is sure that it will go away.

438 *The third duty* [connected with knowledge] is that [he know that] the meaning of being God's vicegerent [Caliph] over men is the betterment of men; and only he will be able to better men of the world who is able to better the people of his town and the people of his household and himself. He who cannot better himself ought to begin with the reform of his heart and the management of his soul. One who does not better himself and

yet is desirous of bettering others is deceived, as God Most High said: "Do you enjoin pious goodness on men and forget yourselves?" [2.41/44]. And it is in a Tradition that God said to Jesus the son of Mary: "Admonish [preach to] your soul, and if it be admonished, then admonish men: otherwise be ashamed to face Me." The likeness of one unable to better himself and desirous of bettering others is the likeness of a blind man when he wishes to guide blind men—it will never go well for him.

439 One is able to better himself only through knowledge of his soul [of himself]. A man's knowledge in his body is like that of a governor in his town [district]; his members and senses and limbs are in the position of artisans and workers, and the Law is to him like a sincere counselor and an efficient minister; and desire [appetite, passion] in him is like an evil servant fetching supplies and food, and his nerves are like a chief of police; and the servant fetching supplies is wicked and wily, representing himself to the man in the form of a sincere counselor, but his counsel is the infiltration [influx—*dabīb*] of succession [reptiles ? of consequence ?], and he opposes the minister in his management, and not for a single hour does he neglect fighting and opposing him. So the governor in his state, when he consults his minister about his regulations, and not this wicked and evil servant, and trains his chief of police and makes him a counselor [adviser, collaborator] of his minister and empowers him over the wicked servant and his followers so that this servant is ruled, not ruling, and managed, not managing—the affairs of his district are in good order.

440 So also the soul. When it seeks the help, in its arrangements [dispositions], of the Law and of reason and so disciplines ardor [passion] and anger [irascibility] that it is aroused [excited, stirred] only at the signal [intimation] of the Law and of reason, and empowers it [the latter] over passion [appetite, concupiscence], its affair is well ordered; otherwise it becomes corrupt and follows vain desire and worldly pleasures, as God Most High said: "[O David] . . . follow not passion . . ." [38.25/26]; and the Most High said: "Have you seen him who has taken his caprice [passion] as his God . . ." [45.22/23]; and He said: "He inclined to the earth and followed his passion and his likeness is that of the dog" [7.175/176]; and the Most High said in praise of those who resist it [passion]: "As for him who feared the standing of [i.e. standing before] his Lord and restrained his soul from passion . . ." [79.40]. In general, the servant all his life long ought to be in combat with his anger and his passion, working hard [briskly] to resist them as he does to resist his enemies, for they are two enemies, as Muḥammad said: "The greatest enemy is your soul which is between your two sides."

441 An example [parable] of one who occupies himself with pleasure at the onslaughts of concupiscence and with vengeance at the onslaught of irascibility is a horseman-hunter who has a horse and a dog heedless of his hunting. He loses his time in trying to train and tame them. Man's passion is like his horse and his anger is like his dog. If the horseman be skillful and the horse trained and the dog disciplined and taught, he will be fit for attaining what he wants of hunting. But when the horseman is, clumsy [stupid] and his horse unruly or refractory and his dog voracious [mordacious], neither will his horse move under him submissively nor will his dog let itself go at his signal obediently, and he will be fit to perish, to say nothing of attaining what he seeks.

442 Whenever a man combats in it [soul] his passion three circumstances are possible for him: (1) that vain desire [passion] overcome him and he follow it and turn away from the Law, as God Most High said: "Have you seen him who has taken his caprice [passion] as his God" [45.22/ 23]; (2) that he combat it and conquer it at one time, and it conquer him at another—and he will have the recompense of those who combat—and this is what

is meant by Muḥammad's saying: "Combat your passion as you combat your foes"; (3) that he overcome his passion, like many of the Prophets and of God's choicest friends—because of Muḥammad's saying: "There is no one but that he has a devil, and God helped me against my devil until I mastered him."

443 In general, Satan holds sway over a man according to the existence of passion in him.

Passion [appetite] is likened to a horse and anger to a dog because, were it not for them, the worship leading to the bliss of the afterlife would be inconceivable. For a man, in his worship, has need of his body, and cannot subsist save by nourishment, and is able to take in nourishment only because of appetite; and man needs to protect himself from perils by repelling them, and repels the harmful only by the motive [incitement] of anger [irascibility]. So the two of them are, as it were, servants for the survival of the body; and the body is the ship [mount] of the soul, and by means of the two of them man comes to worship—and worship is his way to salvation.

444 *The fourth duty* [connected with knowledge] is that he recognize that man is compounded of angelic and bestial qualities and is perplexed [confused] between angel and beast. His likeness to the angel is by knowledge and worship and temperance [*al-ᶜiffa:* also—chastity] and justice and the praiseworthy qualities; and his resemblance to beasts is by passion and anger and rancor and the blameworthy qualities. One who directs his ardor to knowledge and action and worship is worthy to be joined [annexed] to the angels and to be called an angel and "divine" [spiritual, lordly, godly, *rabbānī*], as the Most High said: "This is naught but a noble angel!" [12.31]. But one who directs his ardor to following passions and pleasures, eating like the beasts do, is worthy to be joined to the beasts and to become either gullible like the ox, or greedy like the pig, or weak [submissive] like the dog, or spiteful [malicious] like the camel, or proud like the leopard [tiger], or wily and hypocritical [dissembling] like the fox—or he unites all that and becomes like the rebellious devil. To that alludes the Most High's saying: "and He made of them [objects of His anger] apes [monkeys] and pigs and the idol-worshiper" [5.65/60]. And He said: "like the beasts, nay, they are even more astray" [25.46/44]. And He said: "The worst of beasts in the eyes of God are the deaf and dumb who do not understand [reason]" [8.22].

445 The blameworthy qualities are combined in a human being in this world, and he in the form of a man, so that the quality is interior and the form exterior. But in the afterlife the forms and qualities are united so that each person is represented in [by] the quality which was predominant in him during his life [on earth]. So one dominated by evil [wickedness] is raised in the form of a pig, and one who was dominated by anger is raised in the form of a beast of prey, and one who was dominated by stupidity is raised in the form of an ass, and one who was dominated by pride is raised in the form of a leopard [tiger]—and so on of all the qualities. But one who was dominated by knowledge and action, and by them mastered these [bad] qualities, is raised in the form of the angels "[they are with] the Just, the Witnesses [Martyrs] and the Saints . . . and they are good companions!" [4.71/69].

446 These duties which we have mentioned are connected with knowledge [are theoretical] [and] must be meditated upon until they are represented [take shape] in the heart and are before the eye at every moment [are the cynosure of the eye at every instant]. These cognitions become deeply rooted in the soul only when they are strengthened [confirmed] by action [practice] according to what we shall presently have to say about the duties [tasks] related to action [the action-oriented duties].

On the Duties Connected with Action [al-ᶜamal]

Note: This section is interesting because of the insights it gives into Ghazālī's thought and spirituality and into what might be called a truly Islamic ideal of politics and government. But I can give it here only in a brief outline form lest this Appendix assume too great a length. The reader may consult F. R. C. Bagley: *Ghazālī's Book of Counsel for Kings,* London, 1964, pp. 14 ff. The latter is another work of Ghazālī.

447 (1) In every case he settles he ought to judge himself, and what he would not approve of for himself he should not approve of for another.
448 (2) He should have a great desire for, rejoice at, and be grateful for the counsel of the ulema [the learned].
449 (3) He should respond quickly to those in need and not keep them waiting.
450 (4) He should give up comfort and luxury and finding pleasure in the passions regarding food and raiment.
451 (5) He should know that his office facilitates worship and seize every
454 opportunity to serve God thereby, by humility and justice and sincere counsel to the Muslims and sympathy with them.
455 (6) Kindness in all matters should be more predominant in him than
456 harshness [severity].
457 (7) His most important aim should be to gain the approval and love of men in a way conformed to the Law.
458 (8) He should know that the approval of men can be rightly gained
461 only by conformity to the Law, and that obedience to the Imam is incumbent on men only when he invites them to conformity to the Law.
462 (9) He. should recognize that the Imamate is momentous and perilous:
472 it can lead to bliss and to unsurpassed misery.
473 (10) He should be eager for the counsel of the ulema of religion and
487 profit from the admonitions of the rightly guided Caliphs and peruse the religious elders' admonitions to bygone princes—many examples. . . .
488 (11) As far as lies within his power his prevailing custom should be
498 pardon, clemency, good morals, and restraining his anger. . . .
499 This amount of traditions and accounts and the lives of the Caliphs and rulers is enough for the attentive man concerning the refinement of morals and the knowledge of the duties of the Caliphate.

British Museum Ms.—dated Rabīᶜ II, 665 A.H.
Qarawiyin Ms.—dated Rabīᶜ II, 981 A.H.

APPENDIX III

Al-Qisṭās al-Mustaqīm

THIS is the work Ghazālī refers to in Paras. 68, 69, 70, 75, and 76. I translate the title as *The Correct Balance.* The expression occurs twice in the Qur᾽ān: 17.37/35 and 26.182. Blachère translates "la balance exacte," and Arberry "the straight balance." Ghazālī appropriately took his title from the Qur᾽ān, since this work is a somewhat curious attempt to Islamicize, or "Qurānize," some of the Aristotelian, and Stoic, logic which he expounded more "scientifically" in others of his works. I have used the Arabic text edited by Victor Chelhot, S.J.—*al.Qisṭās al-Mustaqīm,* Beyrouth, 1959, and his French translation Institut Français de Damas, *Bulletin d'Etudes orientales,* Tome XV, annèes 1955–1957, Damas, 1958. "Ar" followed by a number indicates the pagination of the Arabic text, and "Fr" that of the French text. Some discrepancies seem due to the fact that Father Chelhot did his French translation from other texts before he himself edited the Arabic text. I have enclosed in brackets references, transliterations, variant translations, and explanatory notes. No great deal of explanation is needed. The reader unfamiliar with Arabic will no doubt be interested, and perhaps even intrigued, by the light this work throws on the character and thought of its brilliant author.

[CHAPTER ONE]

Introduction [Fr 43–47; Ar 41–46]

1 First I praise God Most High; secondly I invoke His blessings on His Elect Apostle. Then I say: My brethren, is there among you one who will lend me his ears that I may relate to him something [that took place in one] of my conversations? On a certain trip a companion who belonged to the group professing *al-taᶜlīm* [authoritative instruction; a Bāṭinite] unexpectedly questioned me and disputed with me like one sure of his skill and his brilliant argument. *He said:* I see that you claim the perfection of knowledge. By what balance, then, is true knowledge perceived? Is it by the balance of independent reasoning [*al-ra᾽y*] and analogy [*al-qiyās*]? But that is extremely contradictory and ambiguous and is the cause of disagreement among men. Or is it by the balance of authoritative instruction? In this case you would be obliged to follow the infallible Teacher-Imam—but I do not see you desirous of seeking him out.

2 *I replied:* As for the balance of independent reasoning and analogy, God forbid that I should cling to it—for it is the balance of Satan. And I ask God Most High to protect religion from the evil of any of my friends who alleges that it is the balance of know-

ledge, for he is an ignorant friend of religion—and such a one is worse than an intelligent enemy. Had he been gifted with the happiness of [professing] the doctrine of authoritative instruction [Ghazālī is being sarcastic], he would first have learned how to dispute from the Qur᾿ān, where the Most High said: "Call thou to the way of thy Lord with wisdom and good admonition, and dispute with them in the better way" [16.126/125]. God thus taught that some men are called by wisdom [philosophy; Chelhot: connaissance rationelle, as opposed to the vision of faith], and some by admonition [exhortation, preaching], and some by disputation [dialectic].

3 [Fr 44; Ar 42] If those called by admonition [preaching] are fed wisdom [philosophy] it harms them, just as feeding with the meat of fowls harms the suckling child. And if dialectic is used with those called by wisdom [philosophy] they are nauseated by it, just as the robust man's nature is nauseated by being breast-fed with human milk. And one who uses dialectic with those called by dialectic, but not in the better way as he has learned from the Qur᾿ān, is like one who feeds the desert Arab with wheat bread, when the latter is used only to dates, or the townsman with dates, when he is used only to wheat. Would that he had found a good example in Abraham, the Friend of God—God's blessings be upon him!—where he disputed with his adversary [Nimrod] and said: "My Lord is He who gives life and makes to die" [2.260/258]. Then, when he saw that that did not suit Nimrod and was not good in his view, so that the latter said: "I give life, and I make to die" [ibid.], Abraham shifted to what was better suited to his nature and more accessible to his understanding, and he said: "God makes the sun rise from the east; do you, then, make it rise from the west": then the unbeliever was confounded [ibid.]. The Friend [of God]—God's blessings be upon him!—did not stubbornly persist in proving his adversary's inability to quicken the dead, since he knew it would be difficult for him to understand that—for he on his side thought that "slaying" was "making to die." But proving that would not have suited Nimrod's bent or have been in keeping with the limit and level of his intelligence. And the Friend's aim was not to annihilate Nimrod, but to animate him: and feeding with suitable food is an animating, but stubbornness in forcing to what is not suitable is an annihilation. These are subtleties perceived only by the light of [the true] authoritative instruction acquired from the illumination of the world of prophecy. Therefore they have been excluded from understanding, because they have been excluded from the secret of the doctrine of the [true] authoritative teaching [i.e. that brought by the Prophet Muḥammad].

4 *He said:* If you find their [the Ta^{c}līmites'] way rough and their proof weak, with what do you weight your knowledge? *I said:* I weigh it with "the correct balance" [17.37/35 and 26.182] so that its true and its false, its straight and its deviant, may be evident to me. In this I follow God Most High and learn from the Qur᾿ān sent down on the tongue of His truthful Prophet, where He said: "And weigh with the correct balance" [17.37/35]. [Ar 43] He *said:* And what is the correct balance? *I said:* The five scales which God Most High sent down in His Book and with which He taught His Prophets to weigh. He who learns from the Apostle of God and weighs with God's scales is indeed rightly guided. But he who turns from them to independent reasoning and analogy indeed errs and is ruined. *He said:* Where are these scales in the Qur᾿ān—and is this anything but falsehood and untruth [slander]?

5 *I said:* Have you not heard what the Most High said in the Sūra of the Benefactor [All-Merciful]: "The All-Merciful has taught the Qur᾿ān. He created man and He has taught him the Explanation . . . and heaven—He raised it up, and set the Balance

[transgress not in the Balance, and weigh with justice, and skimp not in the Balance] [55.1–3/1–4 and 6/7–8/9]. Have you not heard what He said in the Sūra of Iron: "Indeed, We sent Our Messengers with the clear signs, and We sent down with them the Book and the Balance so that men might uphold justice" [57.25]? Do you think that the Balance joined with the Book is the balance for wheat and barley and gold and silver? Do you imagine the Balance whose setting corresponds to the raising of heaven in His utterance "and heaven—He raised it up, and set the Balance" [55.6/7] is the assay balance [coin balance, "trébuchet"] and the steelyard [*qabbān:* cf. Dozy *Suppi* II, 315; "balance romaine"]? What an improbable reckoning and enormous slander [calumny]! So fear God and do not interpret arbitrarily! Know for sure that this Balance is the Balance of the knowledge of God and of His angels and of His Scriptures and of His Apostles and of His material and spiritual worlds [or: sensible and mental, or, visible and invisible: *mulkihi wa malakūtihi* —cf. Wensinck: *La pensée de Ghazzālī,* pp. 86 ff.], so that you may learn how to weigh with it from His Prophets, as they learned from His angels. God Most High, then, is the first teacher, the second is Gabriel, and the third the Apostle. And all men learn from the Apostles that which they have no other way of knowing [the negative is missing from Chelhot's Arabic text, but is clearly required].

6 *I said:* I also know that by authoritative teaching [*al-ta*ᶜ*līm*]—but from the Imam of the Imams [i.e. the supreme Imam], Muḥammad ibn ᶜAbdallāh ibn ᶜAbd al-Muṭṭalib —God's blessings be upon him! For I, though I do not see him, hear his teaching [*ta*ᶜ*līm*] which [Ar 44] has come to me through impeccable transmission which I cannot doubt. His *ta*ᶜ*līm* is simply the Qurᵓān, and the clearness of the correctness of the Qurᵓān's scales is known from the Qurᵓān itself. *He said:* Then give me your proof, and educe your balance from the Qurᵓān and show me how you understand it and how you understand, from the Qurᵓān itself, its correctness and its soundness.

7 *I said:* Then give me your own proof: tell me how you know the correctness and soundness of the balance for gold and silver. Knowledge of that is a prerequisite of your debt, if you owe something, so that you may settle it completely without any deficiency, or, if someone owes you some thing, that you may receive it justly without any excess. So when you enter a Muslim market and take a balance by which you pay the debt or exact payment of it, how do you know that you are not unjust by paying too little or exacting too much? *He said:* I esteem Muslims, and I say that they would not engage in business except after regulating [equilibrating] the scales. But if a doubt occurred to me about one of the balances, I would take it and raise it and look at the two pans and the tongue [needle, indicator] of the balance. And if the needle was perfectly vertical with no inclination to one of the two sides, and I saw, along with that, the exact equilibrium of the two pans, I would know that it was a sound and correct balance.

8 [Fr 46] *I said:* Granted that the needle is perfectly vertical and that the two pans are at the same level, how do you know that the balance is correct? *He said:* I know that by a necessary knowledge deriving from two premises, one empirical and the other a fact of sensation. The empirical is that I know from experience that a heavy thing sinks downwards, and the heavier it is the more it sinks. So I say: "If one of the two pans were heavier, it would sink more." Now this is a universal empirical premise which I come to have and [it is] necessary. The second premise is: I see that one of the two pans of this very balance does not sink but is on a perfect level with the other. This premise is [Ar 45] a fact of sensation which I have seen with my own eyes. So I doubt neither about the sensible premise, nor about the first which is an empirical premise. In my mind, then, there

necessarily follows from these two premises a peremptory conclusion, viz. the equipoise of the balance. For I say:

> If one of the two [pans] were heavier, it would sink more.
> But it is perceived by sensation that one does not sink more.
> Therefore it is known that it is not heavier.

[This is a conjunctive hypothetical syllogism.]

9 *I said:* But this is independent reasoning and rational analogy! *He said:* Not at all! It is a necessary knowledge following necessarily from certain premises, by which certitude derives from experience and sensation. How, then, could this be independent reasoning and analogy, when analogy is surmise and conjecture not giving serene certitude—and I feel in this serene certitude? *I said:* If you know the soundness of the balance by this proof, by what do you know the [correctness of the] *ṣanja* and the *mithqāl* [weights used as counterpoises]? Perhaps the *mithqāl* is lighter or heavier than the true *mithqāl*. *He said:* If I doubt about this, I take its measure from a *ṣanja* which I know and I compare this with it. If it is equal, I know that the gold, if it is equal to it, is equal to my *ṣanja:* for the equal to the equal is equal.

10 *I said:* And do you know who he was who originally set up the balance? For he was the first originator from whom you learn this [way of] weighing. *He said:* No! And whence have I need of him, since I have already come to know the soundness of the balance by seeing with my own eyes? Nay, but I eat greens without inquiring about the kitchen garden [truck farm]. For the one who sets up the balance is not wanted for his own sake, but he is wanted that one may know from him the soundness of the balance and the manner of weighing. But I have already known it, as I have related and explained. So I can dispense from consulting the one who set up the balance at [Fr 47] every weighing. For that would take a long time and he would not be accessible at every moment—in addition to my not needing him!

11 *I said:* Then if I bring you a balance for knowledge like this [physical] balance, and even sounder than it, and I add to that that I know [Ar 46] its institutor and its teacher and its user—for its institutor is God Most High, and its teacher Gabriel, and its user the Friend [Abraham] and Muḥammad and all the other Prophets—God's blessings be on them all!—and God Most High has born witness to their veracity in that—would you accept that from me and believe it? *He said:* Yes, by God! How could I not believe it, if it is as clear as what I recounted to you [about the physical balance]?

12 *I said:* Now I see in you the good qualities of intelligence and my hope has come true of putting you right and making you understand the real meaning of your doctrine about your *taᶜlīm* [authoritative teaching]. So I shall disclose to you the five balances revealed in the Qurᵓān that by it [the Qurᵓān] you may have no need of any Imam and may surpass the level of the blind. And your Imam will be al-Muṣṭafā [the Elect, Muḥammad] and your leader [chief, director] the Qurᵓān, and your norm [standard, gauge] seeing with your own eyes. So know that the balances of the Qurᵓān are basically three: the balance of equivalence, and the balance of concomitance, and the balance of opposition. But the balance of equivalence is divided into three—the greater, the middle, and the lesser: so the total is five.

[Ar 47]

[CHAPTER TWO]

On the Greater Balance of Equivalence [Fr. 47–53; Ar 47–54] [First Figure of the Categorical Syllogism; *Analytica Priora* I, IV 25b, 26–26b, 34 M–P; S-M; S-P]

13 Then this intelligent companion from the associates of the devotees of *ta^clīm* said: Explain to me in the first place the greater balance of equivalence and explain to me the meanings of these terms, viz. equivalence and concomitance and opposition and the greater and the middle and the lesser: for they are strange terms and doubtless beneath them there are subtle meanings. *I said:* As for the sense of these words, you will understand them only after they have been explained and their meanings understood so that you may, after that, grasp the aptness of their names for their realities.

14 I tell you first of all that this balance [of equivalence] resembles the [physical] balance of which you have given an account in sense [notion, essence, "fond"], not in form. For it is a spiritual [*rūḥānī*] balance [Chelhot: une balance pour la pensée] and so is not equivalent to a physical balance. And why should it be equivalent to it, when physical balances also differ? For the *qarasṭūn* [Chelhot: la balance romaine; cf. Dozy II, 335] is a balance and the assay [coin] balance [Chelhot: le trébuchet] another. [Fr 48] Nay, but the astrolabe is a balance [measure] for the amounts of the movements of the celestial body [orbit of celestial bodies], and the ruler a balance [measure] for the amounts of linear distances, and the plumbline a balance for ascertaining straightness [perpendicularity] and deflection [curvature]. These, though their forms differ, share in common the fact that by them one knows excess from defect. Indeed, prosody is a balance [measure] for poetry by which one knows the metres of poetry so that dragging [or: faulty, i.e. verse] is distinguishable from the correct [straight]. And this is more spiritual than the material [three-dimensional] balances, but it is not devoid of relations to bodies, because it is the balance [measure] for sounds—and a sound is not separable from a body. The most spiritual of [Ar 48] balances [measures] is the balance of the Day of Judgment, since in it will be weighed actions and the beliefs of creatures and their cognitions—and knowledge and belief have no relation at all to bodies. Therefore this balance [measure] is purely spiritual.

15 Similarly the balance [measure] of the Qur^ɔān for knowledge is spiritual. But its definition in the visible world [*^cālam al-shahāda*] is bound up with a wrapper [envelope. covering] which itself has a contact [adhesion] with [to] bodies, though it is not itself a body. For in this world communicating something to another is possible only orally, i.e. by sounds [voices]—and sound is corporeal—or in writing, viz. signs [symbols] which moreover are a writing on the surface of the paper and it is a body. This is the determination [status] of its wrapper in which it occurs. But in itself it is purely spiritual and has no connection at all with bodies. For by it is weighed the knowledge of God which is outside the world of sensation—[for God is] far removed from being involved with directions and districts, to say nothing of bodies themselves. Despite that it [the balance of the Qur^ɔān] has an arm and two pans. The two pans are attached to the arm, and the arm is common to the two pans because of the attachment of each of them to it. This is the balance of equivalence. As for the balance of concomitance, it is more like the steelyard [Chelhot: la balance romaine], for it has one pan; but on the other side there corresponds to it a spherical weight [knob] by which the difference and evaluation become evident.

16 *He said:* A mighty booming, this! But where is the meaning? I hear the clapping of the mill wheel, but I see no flour! *I said to him:* Patience! "And hasten not with the

Qur'ān ere its revelation is accomplished unto thee; and say: O my Lord, increase me in knowledge" [20.113/114]. Know that haste is from the devil and deliberateness [slowness] is from God! [Ar 49]

17 Know that the Greater Balance is that which the Friend [Abraham] used with Nimrod. So from him [Fr 49] we have learned it, but by means of the Qur'ān. Nimrod claimed divinity. And "God," by agreement, is a designation of "the one who can do everything [is omnipotent]." So Abraham said: "God is my God, because He it is who makes to live and causes to die: He can do it and you cannot do it!" Nimrod replied: "I make to live and cause to die," meaning that he makes the semen live by coitus and causes to die by killing. Then Abraham knew that it would be difficult for him to understand his error. So he turned to what would be clearer for Nimrod and said: "God brings the sun from the east: do you bring it from the west"—and he who misbelieved was astonished [2.260/258]. And God Most High praised Abraham, saying: "And that was Our proof which We brought to Abraham against his people" [6.83].

18 From this, then, I knew that the argument and apodeictic proof were in the utterance and balance of Abraham. So I considered how it weighs, as you considered the balance for gold and silver. And I saw in this argument two principles which were coupled, and from them was engendered a conclusion which was the knowledge [cognition], since the Qur'ān is built on ellipsis and concinnity. The full form of the balance is that we say:

> Whoever can make the sun rise is God [one principle].
> But my God can make the sun rise [a second principle].
> [Therefore] my God is God—and not you, Nimrod.

[Darii: A–I-I]

19 Consider now whether one who admits the two principles can then doubt about the conclusion. Or is it even conceivable that anyone can doubt about these two principles? Not at all! For there is no doubt about the statement "God is the one who can make the sun rise," because, for them [Taʿlīmites] and for everyone, "God" is a designation for the omnipotent, and making the sun rise belongs to the totality of those things [which he can do]. This principle is known by convention and agreement. And our statement "The one who can make the sun rise is not you" is known by seeing [ocular vision]—[This is not exactly the premise used, but the text is that of the Ms.]. For the impotence of Nimrod [Ar 50] and of everyone except him who moves the sun is attested by sensation. And by God we mean the mover of the sun and the one who makes it rise. So we are compelled to conclude, from the knowledge of the first principle, known by agreed-upon convention, and of the second principle, known by seeing, that Nimrod is not God, but the "God" is God Most High.

20 So consult yourself: do you think this clearer than the empirical and sensible premise on which you built [based] the soundness of the balance for gold? *He said:* This knowledge follows from it of necessity. And I can doubt neither about the two principles, nor about the entailment of this conclusion from them. But this is useful to me only [Fr 50] in this instance and in the way Abraham—Peace be upon him!—used it, viz. to deny the divinity of Nimrod and to affirm the divinity of the one who alone can make the sun rise. So how can I weigh by it the other cognitions [*ma'ārif:* knowledges] which are a problem for me and in which I need to distinguish the true from the false?

21 *I said:* Whoever weighs gold in a balance can weigh in it silver and all the precious stones. For the balance makes known its quantity, not because it is gold, but because

it is a quantity. Similarly, then, this proof [*al-burhān*] disclosed to us this knowledge, not because of the knowledge itself, but because it is a truth [*ḥaqīqa*] among truths and a meaning [*ma^cnan*] among meanings. So let us ponder why this conclusion necessarily follows from it and take its spirit and divest it of this particular example so that we may profit by it whenever we wish.

22 This necessarily followed simply because "the judgment made regarding the attribute" [*ṣifa*] is of necessity a judgment regarding the subject [*mawṣūf:* "attributized" cf. Chelhot's note on varying terminological usage of grammarians, *mutakallimūn,* jurisprudents and logicians]. The explanation of this is that the abridgment of this argument is:

> My Lord is the one who makes the sun rise.
> And the one who makes the sun rise is a god.
> So it follows from it that my Lord is a god.

[This seems to violate the rule for the First Figure, viz. that the minor must be affirmative and the major universal; also it does not seem to be: M-P; S–M; S-P. ??? Should it rather be: The one who makes the sun rise is a god; and my Lord is the one who makes the sun rise; so it follows from it that my Lord is a god. ?] Thus "the one who makes the sun rise" is an attribute of the Lord. And we have judged regarding "the one who makes the sun ise"—which is an attribute—that he has divinity. So there follows from it the judgment regarding my Lord that He has divinity. And so every case in which I acquire a knowledge of the attribute of a thing, and acquire [Ar 51] another knowledge of the certain existence of a judgment about that attribute, there will he engendered for me necessarily from it a third knowledge of the certain existence of that judgment with reference to the thing qualified [by the attribute].

23 *He said:* Grasping this is almost too subtle for my understanding. If, then, I doubt, what should I do so that the doubt may disappear? I *said:* Rake its measure from the balance-weight which is already known to you, as you did in the case of the balance for gold and silver. *He said.* How shall I take its measure? And where is the balance-weight known regarding this sort of thing? *I said:* The known balance-weight consists of the necessary [Chelhot here cites the *Mustaẓhirī;* "The meaning of a thing's being necessary and in no need of reflection is the sharing of the intelligent in perceiving it"] primary cognitions derived either from sensation, or from experience, or from the nature of the intellect.

24 Reflect, then, on the primary [cognitions]. Can you conceive that a judgment regarding an attribute exists without its being also applicable to the subject [qualified]? For example. if there passes in front of you an animal with a swollen belly, and it is a mule, and someone says: "This animal is pregnant, and you say to him: "Do you know that a mule is sterile and does not bear offspring?" and he says: "Yes, I know this by experience," and you say: "Do you know that this is a mule?" and he looks, then says: "Yes, I know that by sensation and sight," and you say: "Now, then, do you know that it is not [Fr 51] pregnant?"—he will be unable to doubt it after knowing the two principles, one of them empirical and the other a fact of sensation. On the contrary, the knowledge that it is not pregnant will be a necessary knowledge engendered by the two prior knowledges, just as your knowledge about the balance is derived from the empirical knowledge that the heavy sinks and the sensible knowledge that one of the two pans is not sinking with reference to the other.

25 *He said:* I have understood this clearly. But it is not evident to me that the cause of its entailment is that the judgment about the quality [attribute] is a judgment about the qualified [subject]. *I said:* Reflect! For your statement "This is a mule" is a qualifying [description] and the qualification [quality; attribute] is the mule; [Ar 52] and your statement "Every mule is sterile" is a judgment about the mule which is a quality of sterility. So there is entailed the judgment of sterility about the animal which is described as [is qualified by being] a mule.

26 Similarly, if it is evident to you, for example, that every animal is sensitive [*ḥassās*: possessed of sensation, sensing], and then it is evident to you about the worm that it is an animal, it is impossible for you to doubt that it is sensitive. Its method [*minhāj*], then, is that you say:

> Every worm is an animal.
> And every animal is sensitive.
> Therefore, every worm is sensitive.

[Barbara: but better to invert the major and the minor ??] For your statement "Every worm is an animal" is an attribution to the worm of being an animal, and "animal" is its attribute [quality]. So when you judge of the animal that it is sensitive, or is a body, or is something else, the worm undoubtedly falls under it. This is necessary and cannot be doubted. To be sure the condition of this is that the attribute be equal to the subject [the qualified], or more general than it, so that the judgment about the qualified will necessarily include that by which it is qualified.

27 Similarly, whoever admits, in legal reasoning, that every wine is intoxicating, and that everything intoxicating is forbidden, cannot doubt that every wine is prohibited. For "intoxicating" is a qualification of the wine, and so the judgment of its being forbidden includes the wine, since the qualified undoubtedly is included in it. And so for all the areas [classes] of speculative matters.

28 *He said:* I have understood necessarily that effecting the union of the two principles in this way engenders a necessary conclusion, and that the proof of Abraham—Peace be upon him!—is a sound proof and his balance a true balance. I have also learned its definition [*ḥaddahu:* Chelhot—principe de déduction] and its reality [real meaning, essence] and I have known its measure [norm, gauge] from the balance-weights known to me. But I wish to know an example of the use of this balance in the problematic areas of cognitions [or: the sciences]. For these examples are clear in themselves and for them one does not need a balance or a proof.

29 *I said:* Far from it! For some of these examples are not known in themselves, but are engendered from the coupling of the two principles. For only he knows that this animal is sterile who knows through sensation that it is a mule, and knows empirically that a mule does not bear offspring. Only a primary cognition [*al-awwalī:* Chelhot—le premier] is clear in itself. But what is engendered from two principles has a father and a mother: so it is [Fr *52*] not clear in itself but by reason of something else. But that something else, i.e. the two principles, may be clear in some circumstances, viz. after experience and seeing. Similarly, the fact [Ar 53] that wine [*al-nabīdh*] is illicit is not clear in itself, but is known by two principles: one is that it is intoxicating—and this is known empirically; and the second is that everything intoxicating is illicit—and this is known through the report which has come down from the lawgiver.

30 This informs you how to weigh with this balance and how to use it Should you desire an example obscurer than this, why we have unlimited and endless such examples. Indeed, it is by this balance that we come to know most of the obscure cases. But be content with a single example of that.

31 Among the obscure cases is this: Man is either incipient by himself, or he has a cause and a maker. The same is true of the world. Now when we have recourse to this balance we know that man has a maker and that his maker is knowing. For we say:

> Every possible has a cause.
> But the world's, or man's, being characterized by the quantity peculiar to it [him] is something possible.
> Therefore it necessarily follows from this that it [he] has a cause. [Darii]

No one who admits and recognizes the two principles can doubt about this conclusion. But if he doubts about the two principles, then let him deduce the knowledge of them from two other clear principles until he finally reaches the primary cognitions about which there can be no doubt. For the clear primary cognitions are the principles [for knowing] of the obscure and hidden cognitions and they are their seeds. But they are to be exploited by one who is expert in exploiting by cultivation and producing [deduction, inference] in bringing about coupling between them.

32 *If you say:* I doubt about both of the two principles. So why do you affirm that every possible has a cause? And why do you say that man's being characterized by a specific quantity is possible, and not necessary? *I say:* My affirmation "Every possible has a cause" is clear if you understand the meaning of *al-jā'iz* [the possible]. For I mean by "the possible" that which hesitates [wavers: is between] two equal divisions [or: parts]. Now when two things are equal, one of them is not specified [marked, singled out for] by existence and nonexistence of itself—because what is established for [affirmed of] a thing is of necessity established for its like: and this is a primary truth. As for my statement "Man's being characterized by this quantity, for example, is possible and not necessary," it is like my saying that the line written by the writer—and it has a specific quantity—is possible. For the line, qua line, has no single determined quantity, but conceivably may be longer and shorter. The cause of its being characterized by its quantity, as against what is longer or shorter, is undoubtedly the agent—since the relation of the quantities to the line's reception of them is equal [in all cases]: and this is necessary [a necessary truth]. Similarly, the relation of the quantities of man's form and extremities is equal: so its specification must undoubtedly be through an agent.

33 [Ar 54] Then I progress from this and say: Man's agent is knowing, because every well-ordered and well-done action is based on the knowledge of an agent. But the structure [physical constitution] of man is a well-ordered and well-made structured. So undoubtedly [Fr 53] its ordering is based on the knowledge of an agent. Here we have two principles: if we know them, we do not doubt about the conclusion. One of them is that the structure of man is well ordered: this is known through seeing the harmony of man's members and the disposition of each for a special purpose [end], such as the hand for grasping [striking] and the leg for walking; and knowledge of anatomy [the dissection of organs] produces necessary knowledge of this. As for the need of what is well organized and ordered for knowledge, it is also clear. No intelligent man doubts that the well-ordered line of writing proceeds only from one who knows how to write, even though it be by

means of the pen which does not have knowledge; and that a construction suitable for the purpose of sheltering, such as a house and a bath and a mill and so forth, proceeds only from one who knows how to build.

34 If it were possible to doubt about any of this, our procedure would be to progress to what is clearer until we come to the primary truths. To explain that is not our purpose. Rather, our purpose is to show that the coupling of primary truths, in the way the Friend [Abraham] effected it—God's blessings be upon him!—is a true balance which gives knowledge of the truth. No one declares this false, for it would be to declare false God's teaching of His Prophets and to deny what God praised—Glorious and Exalted He!—when He said: "And that was Our proof which We brought to Abraham against his people" [6.83]—and the authoritative teaching [*al-ta*ᶜ*līm:* i.e. brought by Muḥammad] is undoubtedly true, [even] if independent reasoning be not true; and the denial of this involves the denial of both independent reasoning and authoritative teaching—and no one at all holds this.

[Ar 55]

[CHAPTER THREE]

Discussion of the Middle Balance [of Equivalence] [Ar 55–58; Fr 53–55]

[Second Figure of the Categorical Syllogism: Anal. Pr. I, V, 26b, 34–28a, 9]

35 *He said:* I have now understood the Greater Balance and its definition and standard and ordinary use. So explain to me [now] the Middle Balance—what is it, whence came the teaching of it, who instituted it, and who used it?

36 *I said:* The Middle Balance is also the Friend's [Abraham's]—Peace be upon him!—in the place where God Most High said: "I love not the things which set" [6.76]. The full form of this scale is:

> The moon is a thing which sets.
> But God is not a thing which sets.
> Therefore the moon is not a God.

But the Qur'ān is its foundation by way of concinnity and ellipsis. However, knowledge of the denial of divinity of the moon becomes necessary only by knowledge of these two principles, viz. that the moon is a thing which sets and that God is not a thing which sets. When the two principles are known, the knowledge of the denial of the divinity of the moon becomes necessary.

37 [Fr 54] *Then he said:* I do not doubt that the denial of the divinity of the moon is engendered from the two principles, if both are known. However, I know that the moon is a thing which sets—and this is known by sensation; but that God is not a thing which sets I know neither necessarily nor by sensation.

38 *I said:* My aim, in reporting this balance, is not to make you know that the moon is not [Ar 56] a God. Rather it is to apprise you that the balance is accurate [faithful] and that the knowledge stemming from it by this way of weighing is necessary. From it knowledge resulted in the case of the Friend—Peace be upon him!—only because it was known to him that God is not a thing which sets, though that knowledge was not primary for him, but rather was derived from two other principles which give rise to the knowledge

that God is not a thing which changes [a changer]. And every changer is incipient: and setting is changing. So he based the weighing on what was known to him. Do you, then, take the balance and use it where there exists for you knowledge of the two principles.

39 *He said:* I now understand of necessity that this balance is accurate and that this knowledge follows necessarily from the two principles once the latter are known. But I want you to explain to me the definition [logical principle; principe de déduction] of this balance and its real nature [*ḥaqīqatahu:* Chelhot—son véritable mode d'emploi], and then to explain to me its standard with reference to a weight [counterbalance] known to me, and then [to give me] an example of its use in the area of the obscure: for denying divinity of the moon is like what is clear to me.

40 *I said:* Its definition [logical principle] is that any two things, one of which is qualified by a quality which is denied of the other, are different [distinct one from the other]—i.e. one of them is denied of the other and is not qualified by it. And just as the logical principle of the Greater Balance is that the judgment applying to the more general is a judgment applying to the more particular and is undoubtedly included therein, so the logical principle of this balance is that that of which is denied what is affirmed of another is different [distinct] from that other. Now setting is denied of God and affirmed of the moon: so this necessitates difference [distinction] between God and the moon, viz. that the moon is not a God, nor is God a moon.

41 God Most High taught His Prophet Muḥammad—Peace be upon him!—to weigh by this balance in many places in the Qurʾān, to follow the example of his father the Friend—Peace be upon him! Be content with my calling attention to two places and seek the rest in the verses of the Qurʾān.

42 *One of the two* is the Most High's saying to His Prophet: "Say: Why then does He chastise you for your sins? No, you are mortals, of His creating" [5.21/18]. [Ar 57] That was because they claimed to be the sons of God. So God Most High taught him how to expose their error by means of the correct balance. [Fr 55] He said: "Why then does He chastise you for your sins?" The full form of this balance is:

> Sons [of God] are not chastised [by God].
> But you are chastised [by God].
> Therefore you are not sons [of God]. [Festino]

So they are two principles. That sons are not chastised is known by experience; and that you are chastised is known by seeing. From these two necessarily follows the denial of sonship.

43 The second place is the Most High's saying: "Say: You of Jewry, if you assert that you are the friends of God, apart from other men, then desire death, if you speak truly. But they will never desire it" [62.6–7]. That was because they claimed friendship [with God]. Now it is a known fact that the friend desires to meet his friend; and it was also known that they did not desire death, which is the cause of the meeting. So it follows of necessity that they are not the friends of God. The full form of the balance is to say:

> Every friend desires to meet his friend.
> But the Jew does not desire to meet God.
> Therefore [it follows necessarily from this that]
> he is not the friend of God. [Camestres]

[This syllogism seems to me to involve four terms. Would it perhaps be more correct to say: Every friend of God desires to meet his friend God. But the Jew does not long to meet God. Therefore the Jew is not a friend of God. ??]
And its logical principle is that desire is attributed to a friend but denied of the Jew: so the friend and the Jew are different and one of the two is denied of the other—so the friend [of God] is not a Jew, nor is the Jew a friend of God.

44 Its standard with reference to a known weight is not, I think, something you need, in view of its clarity. However, if you want a clarification, then consider this: how it is that, when you know that a stone is inanimate, and then know that man is not inanimate, you necessarily know that man is not a stone. It is because inertness is affirmed of the stone and denied of man: surely, then, man will be denied of stone, and stone will be denied of man—so man is not a stone, nor is a stone man. [In form: All stones are inanimate. No man is inanimate. Therefore, no man is a stone. Camestres.]

45 The place of usage of this balance in obscure cases is frequent. One of the two divisions of knowledge [*al-ma^{c}rifa*: here seems to mean the knowledge (gnosis) of God] is the knowledge of declaring [God] holy [*ma^{c}rifat al al-taqdīs,* i.e. the negative way, or, *via remotionis,* as opposed to the affirmative way, or, *via affirmationis*], i.e. what the Lord [Exalted and Transcendent!] is too holy to be associated with. All knowledges of God are to be weighed in this balance. For the Friend [Abraham]—Peace be upon him!—used this balance in the case of proclaiming God's holiness and taught us how to weigh with it. For by this balance he knew [Ar 58] the denial of corporeity of God Most High. Similarly, God is not a localized substance, because God is not caused; but everything localized is caused by reason of its being specified by the locus peculiar to it; hence it follows necessarily from this that God is not a [localized] substance. [Camestres] We also say: God is not an accident, because an accident is not living and knowing; but God is living and knowing; so He is not an accident. [Festino] Similarly the knowledge of the other areas of declaring God holy follow from the coupling of two principles in this fashion: one of the two is a negative principle, its content [purport] negation, and the second is an affirmative principle, its content [purport] affirmation. And from the two of them results a knowledge by [or: of ?] negation and declaring holy [Chelhot: la connaissance de ce qui est nié (de Dieu) et de sa sainteté].

[CHAPTER FOUR]

Discussion of the Lesser Balance [Ar 59; Fr 56]

[Third Figure of the Categorical Syllogism:
Anal. Pr. I, VI, 28a, 10–29a, 19]

46 *He said:* I have understood this clearly and of necessity. Now explain to me the Lesser Balance along with its definition [logical principle] and standard and its usage in obscure cases.

47 *I said:* The Lesser Balance we have learned from God Most High where He taught it to Muḥammad—Peace be upon him!—in the Qur$^\circ$ān, viz. in the Most High's saying: "They measured not God with His true measure when they said: God has not sent down aught on any mortal. Say: Who sent down the Book that Moses brought as a light and a guidance to men?" [6.91].

48 The way to deal with this [balance] is that we say: Their declaring the denial of the sending down of revelation upon men is a false declaration because of [read: *lil-izdiwāj* ??] the productive coupling of two principles; or: a declaration devoid of the productive coupling of two principles; [Chelhot: leur négation de la révélation fait à l'homme est une proposition qui ne résulte pas de l'union de deux principes.] One of them is that Moses is a man, and the second is that Moses is one upon whom the Book was sent down: so there necessarily follows from this a particular proposition, viz. some man has had sent down upon him the Book [Scripture]—and by this is refuted the general claim that Scripture is not sent down upon any man at all. The first principle, viz. our statement "Moses is a man," is known by sensation. The second, viz. "Moses is one upon whom Scripture was sent down," is known by their own admission—since they used to conceal part of it and manifest part of it, as the Most High said: "You reveal them [parchments] and you hide [Ar 60] much" [6.91]. And He mentioned this only in the form [manner] of disputing by what is better [cf. 16.126/125: "and dispute with them in the better way"]. A particular feature of disputing is that it suffices regarding the subject [?] that the two principles be conceded by the adversary and accepted by him, even though doubt about it be possible for another; for the conclusion binds him if he admits it [the coupling? the principles?]. Most of the proofs [*adilla*] of the Qurʾān proceed in this fashion. So if you encounter in yourself the possibility of doubting about some of their principles and premises, know that their aim is disputing with one who does not doubt about it [the Qurʾān ???]. But the aim in your regard is that you learn from it [the balance ?; or, the Qurʾān ?] how to weigh in the other places. [In form: Moses is a man. Moses is one upon whom Scripture was sent down. Some man has had Scripture sent down upon him.—Darapti—if it is valid; Aristotle reminds us that all the syllogisms of this Figure are imperfect.]

49 The standard [gauge] of this balance is that one who says: "It is in conceivable that an animal walk without a leg" knows that when you say: "The snake is an animal, and the [Fr 57] snake walks [moves along] without a leg," there necessarily follows from this that some animal walks [moves along] without a leg, and [knows also] that the affirmation of him who says: "An animal walks [moves along] only by means of a leg" is a false and nullified affirmation.

50 The obscure cases in which it is used are many. For someone says:"Every lie is evil of itself." Then we say: 'When one sees a friend [of God] who has hidden himself from a tyrant, and the tyrant asks him where he is, and he conceals it [or: keeps him hidden], is what he says a lie?" He says: "Yes." We say: "Is it, then, evil?" He says: "No, but the evil would be veracity leading to his perdition." So we say to him: "Look then to the balance. For we say: His utterance in keeping his place hidden is a lie—this is a known principle; but this utterance is not evil—and this is the second principle; so it follows necessarily from this that every lie is not evil [strictly: that some lie is not evil]. Reflect now: is doubt about this conclusion conceivable after the admission of the two principles? And is this clearer than the empirical and sensible premise which I cited in the knowledge of the balance of proclaiming [God] holy?"

51 The logical principle of this balance is that when any two qualities [attributes] concur [agree] respecting one and the same thing, then some [part, one] [Ar 61] of one of the two qualities must of necessity be qualified by the other, [cf. Anal. Pr. 1, 6, 28a, 10] but it does not necessarily follow that all of it be qualified by it. As for the qualification of all of it, it does not follow in a necessary way; rather it may be so in some cases, and may not be in others—so one cannot rely on it. Don't you see that in man there concurs

the quality of animal and of body—so it follows necessarily from this that some body is an animal [Darapti], but it does not follow from this that every body is an animal? And be not deceived by the possibility of describing every animal as a body! For if the qualification of every attribute by the other be not necessary in every case, the knowledge resulting by it is not necessary.

52 *Then my companian said:* I have now understood these three balances. But why have you specified the first by the name "The Greater," and the second by the name "The Middle," and the third by 'The Lesser"? *I said:* Because the Greater includes [is applicable to] many things, whereas the Lesser is its opposite and the Middle lies between them. The first balance is the broadest [widest] of the balances because by it knowledge can be derived by general affirmation and particular affirmation, and by general negation and particular negation [Anal. Pr. I, 4, 26b, 29]—so it is indeed possible to weigh by this balance four kinds of knowledges. By the second balance one can weigh only negation [Anal. Pr. I, 5, 28a, 8]: but one can weigh by it both general and particular negation. By the third balance one can weigh [Fr 58] only the particular [negation], as I have mentioned. But there follows necessarily from it that a part of one of the two descriptions [attributes] is described by the other because of their concurring regarding one and the same thing. And that which includes only the particular partial judgment is undoubtedly "lesser" [Anal. Pr. I, 6, 29a, 16]. Certainly to weigh the universal [general] judgment thereby is of the balances of Satan. And the adherents of *Ta*^{c}*līm* have indeed weighed thereby some of their knowledges; and Satan cast it into the aspiration of the Friend [Abraham]—Peace be upon him!—in his saying: "This is my Lord: this is greater!" [6.78]—and I shall recite to you his story hereafter.

[Ar 62]

[CHAPTER FIVE]

Discussion of the Balance of Concomitance [Ar 62–64; Fr 58–60]

[The Conjunctive, or Hypothetical, Conditional Syllogism.
Jadaane, 117 ff.]

53 *He said:* Explain to me the balance of concomitance [inseparability] now that I have understood the three balances of equivalence. *I said:* This balance is derived from the Most High's utterance: "Why, were there gods in them [earth and heaven] other than God, they would surely go to ruin" [21.22], and from the Most High's utterance: "If there had been other gods with Him, as they say, in that case assuredly they would have sought a way unto the Lord of the Throne" [17.44/42], and from His utterance: "If those had been gods, they would never have gone down to it [Gehenna]" [21.99].

54 The effectuation of the form of this balance is that you say: If the world has two gods, heaven and earth would have gone to ruin.—This is one principle.

But it is a known fact that they have not gone to ruin.—And this is another principle.

So there follows from these two a necessary conclusion, viz. the denial of the two gods.

And

If there had been with the Lord of the Throne other gods they assuredly would have sought a way to the Lord of the Throne.

But it is a known fact that they did not seek that.

So there follows necessarily the denial of gods other than the Lord of the Throne.

55 The testing of the accuracy of this balance by a known weight is your saying: If the sun has risen, the stars are hidden [invisible, unseen]—and this is known empirically. Then you say: But it is a known fact that the sun has risen—and this is known [Ar 63] by sensation. So it follows necessarily that the stars are hidden. And you also say: If so-and-so has eaten, he is sated—and this is known empirically. Then you say: But it is known that he has eaten—and this is known by sensation. So it follows necessarily from the empirical principle and the sensation principle that he is sated.

56 [Fr 59] The use of this balance in obscure cases is frequent, so much so that the jurisprudent says: "If the sale of an absent thing is valid, it is obligatory by reason of an explicit obligation [obliging]; but it is known that it is not obligatory by reason of an explicit obliging; so it follows necessarily from this that it is not valid." The first principle is known by legal induction which gives probability [conjecture], though it does not give sure knowledge; and the second is known by the concession and aid of the adversary.

57 We also say regarding speculative matters: "If the workmanship [*ṣan*ᶜ*a:* fabrication, making] of the world and the structure [*tarkīb:* composition] of man are well ordered, marvelous, and well done, then the maker of that is knowing—and this is [something] primary in the intellect; but it is known that it is marvelous and well ordered—and this is perceived by ocular vision; hence it follows from this that its Maker is knowing." Then we ascend [progress] and say: "If its Maker is knowing, He is living. But it is known that He is knowing by the preceding balance; hence it follows that He is living" Then we say: "If He is living and knowing, then He is subsisting in Himself and is not an accident; but it is known by the preceding two balances that He is living and knowing; hence it follows from this that He is subsisting in Himself." Thus, then, we ascend from the quality of the composition of man to the attribute of his Maker, viz. knowledge; then we ascend from knowledge to life, then from it to the essence. This is the spiritual ascension, and these balances are the steps [stairs, ladders] of the ascension to heaven, or rather to the Creator of heaven, and these principles are the steps [rungs] of the stairs [ladders]. As for bodily ascension, no power can effect it, but that is peculiar to the power of prophethood [or: the prophetic mission].

58 The logical principle of this balance is that everything which is a necessary concomitant [*lāzim*] of a thing follows it in every circumstance: hence the denial of the conditioning [*al-lāzim*] of necessity entails the denial of the conditioned [*al-malzūm*], and the existence of the conditioned necessarily entails the existence of the conditioning. But the denial of the conditioned and the existence of the conditioning leads to no conclusion: rather they belong to the balances of Satan, and by this one of the devotees of *ta*ᶜ*līm* may weigh his knowledge. [On *lāzim* Chelhot writes: ce qui est nécessaire à une chose et lui est indispensable d'une façon telle qu'il la conditionné; on *malzūm:* ce qui est accompagné et dépend, pour être ce qu'il est, d'un autre au point qu'il en eat conditionné]

59 [Ar 64] Do you not see that the validity of the Prayer must have as a necessary concomitant [*yalzamuhā lā maḥālata*] that the one praying be in a state of ritual purity? Certainly it is correct for you to say: "If Zayd's Prayer is valid, he is in a state of ritual purity; but [Fr 60] it is known that he is not in a state of ritual purity—and this is the denial of the conditioning; hence it follows from this that his Prayer is invalid—and this is the denial of the conditioned. And you say: "But it is known that his Prayer is valid—and this is the existence of the conditioned; hence it follows from this that he is in a state of ritual purity—and this is the existence of the conditioning. But if you say: "But it is known that he is in a state of ritual purity; hence it follows from this that his Prayer is valid," this is

an error, because his Prayer may be invalid for another reason. This is the existence of the conditioning, and it does not denote the existence of the conditioned. Similarly if you say: "But it is known that his Prayer is invalid; hence he is not in a state of ritual purity," this is an error which is not necessary, because it is possible that the nonvalidity is due to the absence of a condition other than that of being in a state of ritual purity. This is the denial of the conditioning and it does not denote the denial of the conditioned. [Chelhot: Mais cela n'est pas nécessairement une erreur, parce qu'il est possible que la non validité découle de l'absence d'une condition autre que celle de la purification. Cela est la négation du conditionné et ne dénote pas celle du conditionnant.]

[CHAPTER SIX]

Discussion of the Balance of Opposition

[The Disjunctive (Conditional) Syllogism]

60 *Then he said:* Explain to me now the Balance of Opposition, and mention its place in the Qurʾān and its gauge and the place of its use. *I said:* Its place in the Qurʾān is the Most High's utterance, in instructing His Prophet—Peace be upon him!—"Say: 'Who provides for you out of the heavens and the earth?' Say: 'God.' Surely, either we or you are upon right guidance or in manifest error" [34.23/24]. For He did not mention His utterance "or you" in the form of equalization or inducement of doubt, but rather it contains the concealment of another principle, viz. We are not in error in Our utterance "Surely God provides for you out of the heaven and the earth." For it is He who provides from the heaven by sending down water and from the earth by causing plants to germinate; therefore you are in error by [your] denial of that. The full form of the balance is: "We or you are in manifest error—and this is one principle. Then we say: "But it is known that We are not in error"—and this is a second principle. So there follows from their coupling a necessary conclusion, viz. that you are in error.

61 Its gauge among the known weights is that if one enters a house which has only two rooms, then we enter one of the two rooms and do not see him, we know with necessary knowledge that he is in the second room. This is because of the coupling of the two [Fr 61] principles, [Ar 66] one of them his saying that he is definitely in one of the two rooms, and the second that he is in no wise in this room: hence it follows from them that he is in the second room. Hence we know that he is in the second room, at one time because we see him in it, and at another because we see the other room empty of him. If we know it [*ᶜalimnāhu*] by our seeing him in it, this is ocular knowledge; but if we know it [*arafnāhu*] by not seeing him in the other room, this is balance-knowledge—and this balance-knowledge is peremptory like the ocular.

62 The logical principle of this balance is that when anything is limited to two divisions, the existence [*thubūt*: certainty] of one of them entails the denial of the other, and from the denial of one of them follows the existence of the other—but on condition that the division be restricted [i.e. a complete disjunction], not diffuse [unrestricted, incomplete disjunction]. Weighing with the unrestricted division is the weighing of Satan. With it certain devotees of *taᶜlīm* have weighed their discourse [*kalāmahum*] in many places which we have mentioned [cited] in *al-Qawāṣim* [The Mortal] Blows] and in the *Jawāb mifṣal al-khilāf* [The Answer to the Detailed Exposition (or: Crux, Decisive Point) of

Disagreement; or: controversy; cf. Bouyges: *Essai,* p. 32, no. 23] and in my book *al-Mustaẓhirī* and in other books [of mine].

63 The place of the use of this balance in obscure cases is limitless, and perhaps most speculative matters revolve around it. Thus when one denies an eternal being, *we say to him:* Beings are either all incipient, or some [one] of them are [is] eternal. This is restrictive [all-embracing] because it revolves between negation and affirmation. *If he says:* And why do you say that all of them are not incipient? *We say:* Because if all of them were incipient, their incipience would be through themselves without a cause, or among them would be an incipient without a cause; but it is false that the incipience of an incipient [takes place] at a particular time without a cause; hence it is false that all of them are incipient, and so it is certain that among them is an eternal being. And similar cases of the use of this balance are unlimited.

64 *Then he said:* I have truly understood the correctness of these five balances. However, I desire to know the significance of their names, and why you have designated the first by "The Balance of Equivalence," and the second by "Concomitance," and the third by "Opposition." [Ar 67] *I said:* I called the first the Balance of Equivalence because in it are two principles in equilibrium as though they were two parallel pans. And I called the second the Balance of Concomitance because one of the two principles contains two parts, one of them a conditioning and the other a conditioned, like your saying: "If there were gods in the two of them [other than God], they would surely go to ruin" [21.22]. For your saying "they would surely go to ruin" is a conditioning [*lāzim*], and the conditioned [*malzūm*] is your saying "If there were gods in the two of them"—and the conclusion necessarily follows from the denial of the conditioning. And I called the third [Fr 62] the Balance of Opposition because it comes down to the restricting of two parts between denial and affirmation [so that] there follows from the existence [*thubūt:* or, certainty] of one of them the denial of the other, and from the denial of one of them the existence of the other: thus between the two divisions there is contradiction and opposition.

65 *Then he said:* Did you invent these names, and are you the only one who has deduced them [from the Qur᾽ān], or were you preceded in that? *I said:* As for these names, I invented them. And as for the balances, I deduced them from the Qur᾽ān, and I do not think that I was preceded by anyone in deducing them from the Qur᾽ān. But I was preceded in the deduction of the principles of the balances. Among their deducers from the later [philosophers] they have names other than those which I have mentioned. And among some of the past nations, prior to the mission of Muḥammad and Jesus—God's blessings on them both!—they had other names which they had learned from the books [*ṣuḥuf*] of Abraham and Moses—Peace be upon them both!

66 But what induced me to change their dress for other names was my knowledge of your weak natural disposition [ability] and your soul's submissiveness to illusions [*awhām:* caprices, delusions, wild fancies]. For I have remarked that you are so deceived by appearances that, were you to be offered red honey [miel rosat, honey of roses] to drink in the glass of a cupper, you would be unable to accept it because of your natural aversion to the cupping-glass, and because your mind is too feeble to apprise you that honey is pure in whatever glass it may be. Nay more, you see a Turk wearing a patched garment and a loose outer garment slit in front and you judge that he is a sufi or a jurisprudent; but if a sufi were to put on a caftan [*qabā᾽*: outer garment with full sleeves] and a high cap, your fancy would judge him to be a Turk. [Ar 68] Thus your fancy always seeks to draw you to regard the cover [outside] of things and not their quintessence [kernal, marrow, pith].

Because of that you do not look at an utterance with reference to its being an utterance, but with reference to the elegance of its formulation or to your good opinion of him who says it. So if its expression is loathed by you or its utterer is in a shameful state in your belief, you reject the utterance, even though in itself it is true. And if someone were to say to you: "Say: There is no god other than God, Jesus is the Apostle of God," your nature would recoil from that and you would say: "This is what the Christians say: how, then, can I say it?" You would not have brains enough to know that this utterance is in itself true, and that the Christian is odious, not because of this utterance, nor because of the others, but rather because of two assertions only. One of the two is his statement: Muḥammad is not an apostle; and the second is his statement: God is the third of three. His other statements, apart from that, are true.

67 So when I saw you and your Taᶜlīmite companions so feeble of mind and deceived by appearances only, I descended to your level and gave you the remedy to drink in a water jug and I led you thereby to the cure, and I was gentle with you as a physician is with his sick patient. But had I told you it was a remedy and presented it to you in a medicine glass your nature would have shrunk from accepting it—and even if you had accepted it you would have gulped it and scarcely have been able to swallow it. This, then, is my excuse for changing those names and inventing these: he will acknowledge this who knows it, and he who is ignorant of it will reject it.

68 [Fr 63] *Then he said:* I have understood all that: but where is what you promised, viz. that the balance has two pans and a single beam from which the pans are suspended? I do not see, in these balances [Chelhot has singular "règle"], the pan and the beam! And where are the balances you mentioned which resemble the steelyard [la balance romaine]?

69 *I said:* Did I not derive these cognitions from two principles? So each principle is a pan, and the part common to the two principles, which enters into the two of them, is a beam [middle term]. I shall give you an example of it from legal matters and perhaps you will more readily understand it. So I say: Our statement "Every intoxicant is illicit" is a pan. And our statement "Every *nabīdh* [a wine made by allowing dates or grapes to ferment in water] is an intoxicant." And the conclusion is that every *nabīdh* is illicit. Now we have here in the two principles only three things: *"nabīdh"* and "intoxicant" and "illicit." *"Nabīdh"* is present in only one of the two principles, and it is a pan. And "illicit" is present in the second principle only, which is the second pan. But "intoxicant" is mentioned in both of the principles, and is repeated in both, common to both: so it is the beam [middle term]. And the two pans are suspended from it, because [Ar 69] one of them is attached to it as the subject [*al-mawṣūf*] is attached to the attribute [*al-ṣifa*], viz. your saying "Every *nabīdh* is an intoxicant—for *nabīdh* is qualified by "intoxicant"; and the other is attached to it as the attribute is attached to the subject, viz. your saying "But every intoxicant is illicit." Reflect on that so that you may know it. So the weakness [*fasād:* incorrectness, falseness] of this balance comes at one time from the pan, and at another from the beam, and at another from the suspension of the pan from the beam, as I shall call your attention to a simple example of that in [the case of] Satan's balance.

70 The balance which resembles the steelyard is the balance of concomitance, for one of its sides is much longer than the other. For you say: "If the sale of an absent thing were valid, it would be binding because of an explicit obliging—and this is a long principle containing two parts: a conditioning and a conditioned. The second is your saying: "It is not binding because of an explicit obliging—and this is another principle shorter than the former: thus it is like the short spherical weight corresponding to the pan of the steelyard.

71 In the balance of equivalence two pans are in equilibrium, and one of the two [sides] is not longer than the other, but each of them contains only an attribute and a subject. So understand this along with what I explained to you, viz. that the spiritual balance is not [exactly] like the material balance, but has a certain correspondence to it. Similarly it can be compared [with it] because of the conclusion's being engendered from the coupling of the two principles. For something of one of the two principles must enter into the other, viz. the "intoxicant" present in the two principles, so that the conclusion may be engendered. For if nothing of one of the two principles enters into the other, no conclusion at all is engendered from your saying "Every intoxicant is illicit" and "Everything despoiled is guaranteed." These two are also two principles, but no marriage and coupling takes place between them, since a part [Fr 64] of one of the two does not enter into the other. The conclusion is engendered only from the common part which enters from one of the two into the other—and it is this which we called the beam of the balance.

72 If there were opened for you the door of the comparison between the sensible and the intelligible, there would be opened for you a great door regarding the knowledge of the comparison between this material and visible world and the invisible and spiritual world. This domain contains great mysteries and he who does not come to know [Ar 70] it is deprived of learning from the lights of the Qur'ān and deriving instruction from it and will have attained only the husks of its lore. And just as in the Qur'ān there are the balances of all the sciences, so also in it are the keys of all the sciences—as I have indicated in [my] book *Jawāhir al-Qur'ān* [The Jewels of the Qur'ān]—so seek it there. The secret of the comparison between this visible world and the invisible [spiritual] world is revealed in dreaming by spiritual realities in imaginative examples—because the [true] vision [in dreams] is a part of prophethood, and in the world of prophethood the material and spiritual worlds are perfectly manifested.

73 An example of it from sleep is that a man saw in his dream as though he had in his hand a seal by which he sealed up the mouths of men and the vulvas of women. Then he related his vision to Ibn Sīrīn. The latter said: "You are a muezzin, and you give your call to prayer in Ramaḍān [the month of fasting] before daybreak." He replied: "That is so." Consider now why his state was made evident to him from the invisible world in this example, and seek the comparison [parallelism] between this example and the call to prayer before daybreak in Ramaḍān [which call was the signal for abstention from eating and from sexual relations]. Perhaps this muezzin sees himself on the Day of Resurrection, and in his hand a seal of fire, and it is said to him: "This is the seal wherewith you used to seal up the mouths of men and the vulvas of women." Then he says: "By God, I did not do this!" And it is said to him: "Yes, you used to do it, but you were ignorant of it—because this is the spirit [profound meaning] of your action." And the real meanings of things and their inner senses are manifest only in the world of spirits. But the spirit [inner meaning] is in an envelope of the image in the world of deception, the world of the imagination. But now "We have removed from thee thy covering, and so thy sight today is piercing" [50.21/221. And in like manner will be known everyone who forsakes one of the prescriptions of the revealed Law [*al-shar*ʿ]. And if you wish a confirmation of it, seek it in the chapter on the real meaning of death in [my] [Ar 71] book *Jawāhir al-Qur'ān* [The Jewels of the Qur'ān] that you may see the wonders therein and prolong [your] reflection on it and there may he opened for you an aperture to the spiritual world through which you may eavesdrop.

74 But I do not see its door being opened to you while you simply await knowledge of the truths [or: realities] from an absent teacher whom you do not see: and if you were

to see him, you would find him much weaker than you in knowledge. So take it from him who has traveled, investigated and become acquainted: for according to the expert it has descended into such [?].

75 *Then he said:* This is now another question and insisting on it would occupy us both for a long time. For this absent teacher, though I have not seen his appearance, I have heard the report of him—like the lion: though I have not seen it, I have seen its trace. And my mother, until she died, and our master, the lord of the stronghold of Alamut [i.e. Ḥasan al-Ṣabbāḥ—cf. EI(2) under Ḥasan-i Ṣabbāḥ, III, 253], used to praise him lavishly, even to saying that he is aware of everything that takes place in the world—even at a distance of a thousand parasangs. Shall I then impute lying to my mother, that chaste and modest old lady, or to our master, that leader of good life and conscience? Certainly not! Rather they are two veracious witnesses. How [could they be otherwise] when there agree with them on that, all of my comrades of the people of Dāmghān and Isfahan, who possess authority and in their control are the inhabitants of the fortresses? Do you think they are deceived, and they are intelligent people, or that they are deceitful, and they are pious folk? Far from it! Far from it! Forsake slander—for our master is undoubtedly aware of what is taking place between us, for "not so much as an atom's weight escapes him" on earth or in heaven [cf. 34.3]. So I am afraid of exposing myself to his hatred by simply listening and hearkening. So roll up the scroll of drivel and return to discussing the balance, and explain to me the balance of Satan.

[Ar 72]

[CHAPTER SEVEN]

Discussion of the Balances of Satan and How the Devotees of Taʿlīm Weigh with Them

76 *Then I said:* Hear now, poor man, the explanation of the balance of your comrades, for you have greatly exaggerated. Know that Satan has, beside each balance I have mentioned of the balances of the Qurʾān, a balance attached to it, which he likens to the true balance so that one may weigh with it and commit an error. But Satan enters only through places where there are gaps. So one who closes the gaps and strengthens them is safe from Satan. Now the places of his gaps are ten in number, and I have collected them and explained them in [my] book *Miḥakk al-naẓar* [The touchstone of Speculation] and in [my] book *Miʿyār al-ʿilm* [The Criterion (Norm, Standard, Gauge) of Knowledge], with other fine points concerning the conditions of the balance which I have not mentioned now because of the inability of your mind to grasp them. But if you want the knotty points of their summaries [their cruces in general] you will find them in the *Miḥakk;* and if you want the explanation of their details you will find them in the *Miʿyār.*

77 But I now offer a single example, that which Satan cast into the mind [thought] of the Friend [Ahraham]—Peace be upon him!—[Fr 66] when God Most High said: "We sent not ever any Messenger or Prophet before thee, but that Satan cast into his fancy, when he was fancying; but God annuls what Satan casts, [then God confirms His signs—surely God is All-knowing, All-wise]"—[22.51 /52]. And that was only regarding his hastening to the sun and his saying: "This is my Lord; this is greater!" [6.78]. Because it is greater he wished to deceive him thereby.

78 [Ar 73] The way to weigh with it is that: God is the greatest—and this is a principle known by agreement; but the sun is the greatest of the stars—and this a second principle known by sensation; so it follows from this that the sun is a god—and this is the

conclusion. Now this is a balance which Satan has attached to the Lesser Balance of the balances of equivalence [i.e. of the Third Figure]. For "the greatest" is an attribute found in God and found in the sun, and so this leads one to suppose that one of the two is qualified by the other. But this is the opposite of the Lesser Balance, since the logical principle of that balance is that two things be present in one thing, not that one thing be present in two things. For if two things are present in one thing, a part of one of them is qualified by the other, as we have mentioned previously [cf. Para. 51]. But when one thing is present in two things, one of the two things is not qualified by the other. See, then how Satan creates confusion by the opposite.

79 The gauge of this false balance is found in a weight which is patently false, viz. color. For this is present in both black and white, but it does not necessarily follow that white is qualified by black, or black by white. On the contrary, were one to say: "White is a color; and black is a color; so it follows from this that black is white," it would be an absurd error. Similarly, then, with his saying: "God is greater [*akbar*]; and the sun is greater; so the sun is a god—this is an error, since two contradictories may be qualified by a single attribute. Thus two things being qualified by a single attribute does not necessitate any union between the two: but a single thing's being qualified by two things does necessitate a union between the two attributes. However, a dim-witted person does not perceive the difference between one thing's having two attributes and two things having one attribute.

80 *Then he said:* The falsity of this balance has become clear to me; but when have the devotees of *ta*ᶜ*līm* weighed what they say [*kalāmahum:* or, their argument, or, discourse] by it? *I said:* They have weighed there with many of their utterances—but I am too stingy with my time to waste it in recounting those instances. However, I shall show you one specimen. You have certainly heard their affirmation: "The true is with oneness and the false is with multiplicity; but the doctrine of individual reasoning [*al-ra*ʾ*y*] leads to multiplicity, and that of *tal*ᶜ*līm* leads to oneness; so it follows necessarily that the true is in the doctrine of *ta*ᶜ*līm."* [Ar 74] *He said:* Yes, I have heard this often and believed it, and I know it to be a decisive apodeictic proof about which I do not doubt. [Fr 67] *I said:* This is the balance of Satan. See how your comrades have relapsed [or: fallen headlong]: they have used the analogy [syllogism] and balance of Satan to nullify [falsify, refute] the balance of the Friend [Abraham]—Peace be upon him!—and the other balances.

81 *He said:* And how can it be brought out [elucidated] against him [Satan]? *I said:* Satan creates confusion regarding the balances only by multiplying speech about it and so muddling it that one cannot know just where it is deceptive. This is a frequent argument the substance of which is that the true is qualified by oneness—and this is a principle; and that the doctrine of *ta*ᶜ*līm* is qualified by oneness—and this is another principle; so he affirms: "So it follows necessarily from this that the doctrine of *ta*ᶜ*līm* is qualified by 'the true.'" For oneness is in one thing, and two things are qualified by it: so one of the two things must he qualified by the other. It is like one's saying: "Color is a single attribute by which both white and black are qualified—so it follows necessarily from this that white is qualified by black." It is also like Satan's saying: "The greatest is a single attribute by which God and the sun are qualified—so it follows necessarily from this that the sun is qualified by God." There is no difference between these balances—I mean the presence of color in black and white, and the presence of "the greatest" in God and the sun, and the presence of oneness in *ta*ᶜ*līm* and the true. Reflect, then, that you may understand that.

82 *Then he said:* I have definitely understood this, but I am not content with a single example. So cite for me another example of the balance of my comrades that my heart may have increased assurance of their being deceived by the balances of Satan. *I said:* Haven't you heard their saying: "The true is known either by pure individual reasoning or by pure *ta*ᶜ*līm,* and if one of the two is false, the other is certain; but it is false that it is known by pure intellectual individual reasoning—because of the mutual opposition of [men's] minds and doctrines; so it is certain that it is known by *ta*ᶜ*līm*"? *Then he said:* Yes, by God, I have often heard that, and it is the key of their propaganda [mission, claim] and their leading argument. *I said:* This is a weighing with the balance of Satan which he has attached to the balance of opposition. For the denial of one [Ar 75] of the two divisions results in the certainty of the other—but on condition that the division be restricted and not incomplete. But Satan confounds the incomplete with the restricted. And this [division] is incomplete, because it does not turn between negation and affirmation; on the contrary, there can be between them a third division, viz. that the true be perceived by reason and *ta*ᶜ*līm* together.

83 Its gauge from among the weights known to be false is the utterance of one saying: "Colors are not perceived by the eye, but rather by the light of the sun." We say: "Why?" He replies: "They must he perceived either by the eye or by the light of the sun; but it is false [Fr 68] that they are perceived by the eye—because it does not perceive them at night; so it is certain that they are perceived by the light of the sun." Then one should say to him: "Poor man! There is a third division between them, viz. that they are perceived by the eye, but in the light of the sun."

84 *Then he said:* I would like you to add to the explanation of the error occurring in the first example, viz. the discussion of the true and oneness, for understanding the place of the error in it is a very subtle matter. *I said:* The way the error occurs is what I have mentioned, viz. the confusion [ambiguity] of one thing's being qualified by two things with two things being qualified by one thing. But the origin of the error is the illusion induced by the reversal; for he who knows that every true [thing] is one may suppose that every one [single thing] is true. But this conversion is not necessary: rather what necessarily follows from it is a particular conversion, viz. that part of the one is true. For your saying "Every man is an animal" does not entail a universal contrary, viz. that every animal is a man: rather what is entailed is that some animal is a man.

85 By his ruses Satan does not overwhelm the feeble more effectively and more often than by inducing supposition of the universal conversion, even to the extent of sensibles. Thus one who sees a long parti-colored rope is frightened by it because of its resemblance to a snake. The reason for this is his knowledge that every snake is long and parti-colored; so his fancy rushes ahead to its universal conversion and he judges that everything long and parti-colored is a snake. What is entailed by it is a particular conversion, viz. that some long and parti-colored thing is a snake—not that all of it is such. In the case of conversion and contradictory there are many fine points which you will understand only from [my] book *Miḥakk al-naẓar* [The Touchstone of Reasoning] and [my] *Mi*ᶜ*yār al-*ᶜ*ilm* [The Norm of Knowledge].

86 [Ar 76] *Then he said:* In every example you cite I find another reassurance of the knowledge of Satan's balances. So do not niggardly withhold from me another example of the balances of Satan. *I said:* The faultiness of the balance sometimes comes from the bad composition [mounting, structure] because the suspension of the two pans from the beam is not a straight suspension, and sometimes it comes from the pan itself and the

weakness of the material from which it is taken. For it is taken either from iron or from copper or from an animal's skin. But if it were taken from snow or cotton, one could not weigh it. A sword may sometimes he defective in shape, by being in the form of a rod [staff] neither flat nor sharp, and sometimes it will be because of the weakness of its substance and matter from which it is made, by reason of its being made from wood or clay.

87 Similarly the falsity of the balance of Satan may be due to the wrongness of [Fr 69] its structure, as I have mentioned in the example of the greatness of the sun and the oneness of the true: for their form is defective and converted, as in the case of one who would put the pans above the beam and would want to weigh with it. And sometimes it is due to the weakness of the material, as in the case of Iblis's saying: "I am better than he; Thou createdst me of fire, and him Thou createdst of clay," in reply to the Most High's utterance: "What prevented thee to bow thyself before that I created with My own hands?" [38.77/76 and 75/74]. And in this Iblis introduced two balances, because he justified the prevention of bowing by his being better, and then confirmed the "betterness" by the fact that he was created from fire. And when one explicitates all the parts of his argument, one finds that his balance is correct in structure, but false in matter. Its full form is that he say: "I am better than he; but the better does not bow; therefore I do not bow." Each of the two principles of this syllogism [analogy: *qiyās*] is to be denied, because it is not known: but hidden knowledge is weighed by clear cognitions. And what he cited is unclear and inadmissible: because we say: "We do not admit that you are better—and this invalidates the first principle; and the other: we do not admit that the better is not obliged to bow—because obligation and merit are by command, not by betterness." But Iblis forsook proving the second principle, viz. that obligation is by command, not by betterness, and busied himself with establishing the proof that "I am better because I was created from fire" —which is the claim of betterness because of relationship [affinity, origin].

88 [Ar 77] The full form of his proof and his balance is that he say: "The related to [originated from] the better is better; but I am related to the better; therefore I am better." And each of these two pans is also unsound [false]. For we do not admit that "The related to the better is better—rather, betterness is because of essential qualities, not because of relationship [origin]. Thus it is possible that iron is better than glass: then there is made from glass by excellent craftsmanship something which is better than what is made from iron. Similarly we say: Abraham—Peace be upon him!—was better than the children of Noah—Peace be upon him! Yet Abraham was created from Azar, an unbeliever, [cf. 6.74] and the children of Noah [were born of] a Prophet. As for his second principle, viz. that "I have been created from something better—because fire is better than clay—this also is inadmissible. On the contrary, clay is from earth and water, and one may say that by their mingling comes about the subsistence of animals and plants, and by reason of them generation and growth come about; but fire spoils and destroys everything. So his assertion that fire is better is false.

89 [Fr 70] So these balances are correct in their forms, but unsound in matter, like the sword made of wood—or rather like the mirage of a woody place [a place full of roots] which the thirsty man reckons to be water until, when he comes to it, he does not find it to be anything—but he finds God there and He gives him his full reckoning. And just so the devotees of *taʿlīm* will see their states on the Day of the Resurrection when the real natures of their balances will be revealed to them. This also is one of the ingresses of Satan—so it must be blocked up.

90 The correct matter which is used in reasoning is any principle decisively known either by sensation, or by experience, or by perfect, uninterrupted transmission, or by primary rational truths, or by inference [deduction] from this ensemble. But what is used in debate and disputation [dialectically] is that which the adversary admits and concedes, even though it be not known in itself: for it [matter ? his argument?] becomes an argument against him. That is the way certain proofs of the Qur'ān proceed—and you must not deny the proofs of the Qur'ān, when [but, though] it is possible for you to doubt about their principles, because they were adduced against groups who admitted them.

[Ar 78]

[CHAPTER EIGHT]

Discussion of One's Being Dispensed by Muḥammad [Peace Be Upon Him!] and by the Ulema of the Community from Any Other Imam; and the Explanation of the Knowledge of the Veracity of Muḥammad [Peace Be Upon Him!] by a Way Clearer and Surer Than the Consideration of Apologetic Miracles, viz. the Way of the Knowers

91 *Then he said:* You have perfected the cure and removed the veil and have skillfully corroborated. But you have built a castle and destroyed a metropolis. For up to now I have been expecting to learn from you how to weigh with the balance and to get along, thanks to you and the Qur'ān, without the infallible Imam. But now that you have mentioned these subtleties about the ingresses of error, I despair of getting along by myself with that. For I would not feel safe from erring were I to busy myself with weighing—and I indeed know now why [Fr 71] men disagree in doctrines. It is because they have not understood these subtleties as you have [Chelhot has "as I have"; the Arabic is ambiguous]: so some have erred, and some have been right. The readiest way for me, therefore, is to rely on the Imam so that I may he saved from these subtleties.

92 *Then I said:* Poor man! Your knowledge of the true Imam is not "necessary." For it is either servile conformism to parents, or it is weighed by one of these balances. For every cognition which is not primary necessarily comes to be in its possessor through the existence of these balances in his soul, even though he is not conscious of it. [Ar 79] For you know the correctness of the balance of assessment [*al-taqdīr:* valuation] because of the order [systematic arrangement] in your mind of the two principles, the empirical and the sensible. It is also so for other persons without their being conscious of it. One who knows that this animal, for example, does not bear offspring because it is a mule, knows [this] by the arrangement of two principles, even though he is not conscious of the source of his knowledge. Similarly every cognition in the world which comes to be in a man is like that. So if you have accepted the belief of infallibility in the true Imam, or even in Muḥammad—Peace be upon him!—from parents and comrades by servile conformism, you are no different from the Jews [Ch adds: and the Christians] and the Magians [Zoroastrians]: for so they have done. But if you have accepted [it] from weighing with one of these balances, you may have erred in one of the fine points, and so you ought not to trust therein.

93 *Then he said:* You're right! But where, then, is the way? For you have blocked up both the ways of the *taʿlīm* and of weighing. *I said:* Far from it! Consult the Qur'ān.

For it has taught you the way, where [the Most High] said: "The godfearing, when a visitation of Satan troubles them, remember, and then see clearly" [7.200/201]. He did not say: "They travel, and then see clearly." You know that cognitions are numerous. So, if you were to begin travelling to the Imam, infallible according to your claim, in every difficulty, your trouble would be long and your knowledge little [you would toil much for little knowledge]. But your way is to learn from me how to weigh and to fulfill its conditions. Then, if something causes difficulty for you, you submit it to the balance and "remember" its conditions with serene mind and full diligence, and "then you will see clearly."

94 It is like when you reckon what you owe the greengrocer or what he owes you, or when you settle a question touching religious obligations, and you doubt about being right or wrong. It would take you too long to travel to the Imam. But you learn arithmetic well [lege: *ᶜilm al-ḥisāb*] and remember it and keep repeating it [the reckoning] until you are absolutely certain that you have not erred in one of its [Fr 72] fine points. This is known by him who is familiar with arithmetic. Like wise one who knows weighing as I do is finally brought by remembrance and reflection and repeating time after time to the necessary certainty [sure knowledge] that he has not erred. But if you do not follow this way you will never, be successful, and you will doubt because of "perhaps" and "it may be." And perhaps you have erred in your servile conformism to your Imam, nay even to the Prophet in whom you have believed—for knowledge of the veracity of the Prophet is not "necessary."

95 [Ar 80] *Then he said:* You have helped me to [understand] that the *taᶜlīm* [of Muḥammad] is true, for the [true] Imam is the Prophet—Peace be upon him! And you [or: I ?] have acknowledged that no one can receive knowledge from the Prophet—Peace be upon him!—without knowing the balance, and that he can know the balance perfectly only through you. So it is as though you claim the Imamate for yourself in particular: what, then, is your apodeictic proof and your apologetic miracle? For my Imam either works an apologetic miracle or argues from successive explicit designation from his forefathers down to himself: where, then, your explicit designation or your apologetic miracle?

96 *Then I said:* Your saying "You claim the Imamate for yourself in particular" is not true. For I allow that another may share this knowledge with me, and it can be known from him just as it can be learned from me: so I do not make *taᶜlīm* my personal monopoly [lit. mortmain, endowment]. As for your saying: "You claim the Imamate for yourself," know that by "the Imam" may be meant he who learns from God by means of Gabriel—and this I do not claim for myself; and there may be meant by it he who learns from God, and not from Gabriel [lege: *walā min Jibrīl*], by means of the Apostle. In this sense ᶜAlī—God pleased with him!—is called an Imam—because he learned from the Apostle, not from Gabriel. In this sense I [also] claim the Imamate for myself.

97 As for my apodeictic proof of this, it is clearer than the explicit designation and than what you believe to be an apologetic miracle. For if three persons were to claim in your presence that they know the Qurᵓānʼ by heart, and you were to say: "What is your apodeictic proof?" and one of them were to say: "My proof is that al-Kisāᵓī, the master of reciters, has authorized me, because he authorized the master of my master, and my master authorized me—so it is as though al-Kisāᵓī authorized me"; and the second were to say: "My proof is that I will change this stick into a snake"—and he changes the stick into a snake; and the third were to say: "My proof is that I shall recite the whole of the Qurᵓān before you without a copy of the Qurᵓān"—and he recites: I would like to know which of these proofs is clearest, and to which of them your mind assents most strongly!

98 *Then he said:* To him who recites the Qur'ān. For this is the ultimate proof, since no doubt about it troubles my mind. But his master's authorizing him, and al-Kisā'ī's authorizing his master, may conceivably be subject to errors, especially when the chain [of authorizers] is long [Ch reads *al-asfār* (voyages) in place of *al-isnād*]. As for his changing the stick into a snake, he may have effected that by a trick of deception; and if it be not [Ar 81] a deception, it is at most a remarkable feat. But whence does it follow that one who can effect a remarkable feat must be a *ḥāfiẓ* [memorizer] of the Qur'ān?

99 [Fr 73] *Then I said:* And my proof also is that just as I have known these balances I made them known and understood and removed from your mind doubt about their [?] correctness. So you are bound to believe in my Imamate. It is like when you learn arithmetic and its science from a master. For when he teaches you arithmetic, you come to have a knowledge of arithmetic and another necessary knowledge that your teacher is an arithmetician versed in arithmetic. Thus you have known from his instruction [*ta*ᶜ*līm*] his knowledge and also the correctness of his claim "I am an arithmetician."

100 Similarly I have believed in the veracity of Muḥammad—Peace be upon him!—and in the veracity of Moses—Peace be upon him!—not by reason of the splitting of the moon and the changing of the staff into a serpent: for that way is open to ambiguity, and one may not rely on it; nay, one who believes in the changing of the staff into a serpent may disbelieve in the lowing of the calf with the disbelief of the Samaritan [or: may disbelieve because of the lowing of the calf; cf. 20.85–97/87–97 and 7.146/148] because there is a very great deal of mutual contradiction regarding the sensible, visible world. But I learned the balances from the Qur'ān, then weighed with them all cognitions about God, and even the circumstances of the afterlife and the punishment of the iniquitous and the reward of the obedient, as I have mentioned in my book *Jawāhir al-Qur'ān* [The Jewels of the Qur'ān]. And I found them all conformed to what is in the Qur'ān and what is in the Traditions. Thus I knew for sure that Muḥammad—Peace be upon him!—was veracious and that the Qur'ān is true. I did as ᶜAlī—God be pleased with him!—said, when he declared: "Do not know [measure] the truth by men: know the truth and you will know its possessors [adherents]."

101 So my knowledge of the veracity of the Prophet was necessary, like your knowledge when you see a stranger [Ch un arabe; he read *ᶜarabiyyan* in place of *gharīban*] disputing about a legal problem and excelling therein and presenting sound and clear legal argument: for you do not doubt about his being a *faqīh* [jurisprudent], and your conviction resulting thereby is clearer than the conviction resulting regarding his *fiqh* [jurisprudence] were he to change a thousand sticks into [Ar 82] snakes, for the latter is open to the possibility of magic and deception and a charm and so forth until it is uncovered—and thereby results a feeble faith which is the faith of the masses and of the *mutakallimūn.* But the faith of those who possess vision and who see from [through] the niche [lamp] of Lordship [divinity], that is the way it comes to be [lit.: comes to be in the *former* manner, i.e. by *seeing*].

102 *Then he said:* I also desire to know the Prophet as you have known him. But you have mentioned that that can be known only by the weighing of all the cognitions of God with this balance, and it is not clear to me that all the religious cognitions can be weighed with these balances. So by what can I know that? *I said:* Far from it! I do not claim to weigh with them the religious cognitions only, but I also weigh with them arithmetical and geometrical and medical and legal and *kalām* cognitions, and every science [cognition] which is true and not positive [conventional, based on authority]—for by these balances I

[Fr 74] distinguish its true from its false. How could it not be so, when it is the Correct Balance and the balance which is the companion of the Book and the Qurʾān in God's utterance: "Indeed, We sent Our Messengers with the clear signs, and We sent down with them the Book and the Balance" [57.25]. But your knowledge of my power to do this will not come through an explicit text, nor because of the changing of a stick into a snake, but by your seeking to discover that through experience and examination [trial, testing]. The veracity of one who claims horsemanship is not disclosed until he mounts a horse and races in the race course. So ask me what you will about the religious cognitions, that I may lift for you the veil from what is true in it one by one, and I may weigh it with this balance in a way that will result for you in a necessary knowledge that the weighing is correct and that the knowledge derived from it is certain. But so long as you do not try it, you will not know.

103 *Then he said:* Can you apprise all people of all the truths and cognitions pertaining to God and thus put an end to the disagreements which have occurred among them? *I said:* Far from it! I cannot do it. And it is as though your infallible Imam up to now has put an end to the disagreement among men and has removed difficulties from [their] minds!! Nay more, when did the Prophets—Peace be upon them!—[Ar 88] put an end to disagreement, and when were they able to do it? On the contrary, the disagreement of men is a necessary and everlasting law: "But they continue in their differences excepting those on whom thy Lord has mercy. To that end He created them" [11.120/118–19]. Shall I, then, claim to contradict the judgment of God which He made in eternity? Or can your Imam claim that? And if he did claim it, why has he saved it until now, and the world is overflowing with disagreements? I would like to know whether the Chief of the Community, ʿAlī bin Abī Ṭālib, was the cause of putting an end to disagreement among men, or [rather] was the cause of the setting up of disagreements which will never, never come to an end!

[Ar 84]

[CHAPTER NINE]
Discussion of the Way to Deliver Men from the Darknesses of Disagreements

104 *Then he said:* How deliver men from these disagreements? *I said:* If they would listen to me, I would put an end to the disagreement among them by means of the Book of God Most High. But there is no artifice to assure their listening. They did not all listen to the Prophets and to your Imam—how, then, will they listen to me, and how will they agree on listening when it has been eternally judged of them that they "continue in their difference. . . . [Fr 75] To that end He created them" [11.120/118–19]? That the existence of disagreement among them is necessary you [will] know from [my] book *Jawāb mifsal* [Ar. text has *mufaṣṣal*] *al-khilāf* [The Answer to the Crux—or: Detailed Exposition—of Disagreement], which contains the twelve chapters [or: with its twelve chapters].

105 *Then he said:* And were they to listen, how would you do [it]? *I said:* I would deal with them by a single verse from the Book of God Most High, where He said: "Indeed . . . We sent down with them the Book and the Balance so that men might practice justice, And We sent down iron, etc." [57.25]. Now He sent down these three simply because people are three classes, and each one—the Book, the iron, and the Balance—is a treatment of a people [group, class]. *He said:* Who, then, are they, and how are they to be treated? [Ar 85] *I said: common people,* who are the safe [sound] people, the dull-

witted, the people of the Garden; and *the elite* [privileged], who are the men of insight and special intelligence; and there is formed between them a group who are *the contentious wranglers*—"they follow the ambiguous part [of the Book], desiring dissension" (3.5/7].

106 As for *the elite,* I would treat them by teaching them the just balances and how to weigh with them, and thus the disagreement among them would be removed in short order. These are people in whom three qualities [traits] are united. One of them is a penetrating natural intelligence [disposition] and a powerful acumen [perspicacity]—and this is an innate, instinctive, natural gift which cannot be acquired. And the second is the freedom of their interior from servile conformism and fanatical enthusiasm for an inherited, orally transmitted doctrine. For the servile conformist does not listen, and the stupid man, even though he listens, does not understand. And the third is that he believes of me that I am a man of discernment in [the use of] the balance—for there is no guidance except after belief, and one who does not believe that you know arithmetic will not be able to learn from you.

107 The second class, *the simple,* are all the common people. These are men who do not have [enough] intelligence to understand realities [truths]. And if they possess natural intelligence, they do not have a motive for seeking [knowledge], but rather their preoccupation is with arts and crafts [or: crafts and trades]. They also have no reason for disputation and for making a show of the skillfulness of those who pretend to be clever in delving into knowledge, in view of their inability to understand it. So these do not disagree, but they choose among the disagreeing Imams. Therefore I would summon these to God by preaching, as I would summon the men of insight by wisdom [*al-ḥikma:* philosophy], and I would summon the wranglers by disputation. Now God has indeed united these three in a single verse, as I have previously recited it to you—and it is the Most High's saying: "Call thou to the way of thy Lord with wisdom and good admonition (and dispute with them in the better way)" [16.126/125].

108 So I would say to them what the Apostle of God—God bless him!—said to the desert Arab who came to him and said "Teach me some of the curiosities [marvels] of knowledge [*al-ᶜilm*]." The Apostle of God—God bless him!—knew that he was not fit for that, so he said: "What have you done regarding the beginning [*raᵓs:* head, main part] of knowledge, viz. faith and piety and preparation for the afterlife? Go and master the beginning of knowledge, [Ar 85] then come back to me that I may teach you some of its curiosities." So I would say to the common man: Delving into the differences [*al-ikhtilāfāt:* i.e. differences in legal and dogmatic views] is not a part of your nest [i.e. not your concern, or business]—so leave [it]. Beware of delving into it or listening to it lest you perish! For if you have spent your life in the craft of goldsmithing, you are not a weaver; but you have spent your life in other than knowledge—how, then, can you be fit to delve into it? Beware, beware of losing your soul! For every grave sin committed by a common man is less important than his delving into knowledge with the result that he misbelieves without knowing how! *If he says:* I must have a religion to believe in and act by so that I may thereby attain pardon: but men are different in religions—so which religion do you command me to adopt? *I say:* Religion has roots [*uṣūl:* primary dogmas, fundamentals] and branches [*furūᶜ:* secondary beliefs, applications]: and disagreement occurs in both of them.

109 As for the roots, you are bound to believe only what is in the Qurᵓān. For God Most High has not hidden from His servants His attributes and names. So you must believe that there is no god but God, and that God is living, knowing, powerful, hearing, seeing, mighty, magnificent, all-holy, "there is nothing like Him" [42.9/11], and so on of all that

has come down in the Qur᾽ān and that the Community is agreed upon: that is sufficient for soundness [authenticity] of religion. And if anything is unclear to you, say: "We believe in God: everything is from our Lord" [cf. 3.5/7], and believe everything which has come down concerning the affirmation and the negation of the attributes with a view to magnifying and sanctifying [God], along with the denial of resemblance and the belief that "there is nothing like Him" [42.9/11]. And after this pay no attention to discussions [*al-qīl wa᾽l-qāl:* lit, the "it was said" and the "he said"], for that is not enjoined on you, nor is it commensurate with your ability.

110 If he begins to feign cleverness and says: "I have indeed known from the Qur᾽ān that God is knowing: but I do not know whether He is knowing by His essence or by a knowledge superadded to Him—and the Ashᶜarites and the Muᶜtazilites have disagreed about this," then by this he goes beyond the level of the simple folk, because [Fr 77] the heart [mind] of the simple man does not advert to such as this unless it be moved by the demon of dialectic [or: the devil of dispute]. For God Most High makes a people perish only by bringing discussion [dialectic] to them: thus it has come down in the Tradition. And if he is attached to the wranglers, why I shall mention their treatment. This is what I preach [exhort to] regarding the roots, viz. to refer to the Book of God. [Ch Fr adds: For God sent down the Book and the Balance and the Iron—and these (i.e. the wranglers) are men of reference to the Book].

111 [Ar 87] As for the branches, I say: Don't busy your heart [mind] with the places of disagreement so long as you have not finished with all that is agreed upon. For the Community is agreed that the provisions [viaticum] for the afterlife are piety and god-fearing, and that illicit gain and forbidden wealth and slander and calumny and adultery and theft and treachery and other prohibited things are illicit, and all religious duties are obligatory. So if you finish with all of these, I shall teach you how disagreement [occurs]. And if he demands [it] of me before finishing with all of that, then he is a wrangler and not a common man: for when would a common man finish with these [to occupy himself] with the places of disagreement? Have you seen your comrades finish with all that, and then the problem of disagreement seized them by the throat? Far from it! Their feeble minds, in this error, are simply like the mind of a sick man who has an illness which has brought him to death's door, and there is for it a treatment agreed upon among the physicians, but he says to the physicians: "Physicians have disagreed about a certain remedy, whether it is hot or cold, and I may have need of it some day: so I shall not have myself treated until I find someone who will teach me how to put an end to the disagreement about it."

112 Certainly, if you were to see a just man who had accomplished all the prescriptions of piety, and he were to say: "Here now I have certain problems: for I do not know if I should perform the ablution because of touching and contact and vomiting and nose-bleed, and make my intention to fast at night in Ramaḍān or in the daytime [cf. Fans: *The Mysteries of Fasting,* pp. 9 and 14], and so in other cases," I would say to him: "If you are seeking safety in the way to the afterlife, then follow the path of precaution and adopt what all agree on. So perform the ablution because of anything which is a subject of disagreement, for he who does not enjoin it deems it recommendable [preferable, desirable], and make your intention at night in Ramaḍān, for he who does not enjoin it deems it preferable."

113 *If he says:* Look here: it is hard for me to observe precaution when I am confronted by problems revolving between negation and affirmation, for I do not know whether

to stand long in prayer in the morning or not, and whether to raise my voice or not in the *tasmiya* [in saying *bismillāh*], [Fr 78] *1 say* to him: Now form an independent judgment for yourself and consider which of the Imams is better in your view and who is more generally right in your mind. It is as though you were sick and there were several physicians in the town. For you would consult one of the physicians by reason of your personal judgment, not by reason of your caprice and natural temper; and the like of that personal effort will suffice you [in religious matters]. So whoever you think it more likely that he is the best, follow him. Then if he is right in God's view in what he says, you and he will have two recompenses; but if he errs in God's view, then he and you will have one recompense.

114 And thus said [the Prophet]—Peace be upon him!—when he declared: "Whoso exercises personal judgment and is right will have two recompenses, and whoso exercises personal judgment [Ar 88] and is wrong will have one recompense." And [God] returned the matter to the practitioners of personal effort, and He said: "those of them whose task it is to investigate would have known the matter" [4.85/83]. And [Muḥammad] approved of personal effort by its practitioners when he said to Muᶜādh: "By what will you judge?" He replied: "By the Book of God." Then Muḥammad said: "If you do not find [a basis in the Qurʾān]?" He replied: "By the *sunna* [custom] of the Apostle of God." Then Muḥammad said: "If you do not find [a basis in the *sunna*]?" He replied: "I shall exercise my individual reasoning." He said that before Muḥammad ordered him to do it and allowed him to do it. Then Muḥammad—Peace be upon him!—said: "Praise be to God Who has graciously guided the apostle of the Apostle of God to what the Apostle of God approves." From that it is understood that it was approved by the Apostle of God—God bless him!—on the part of Muᶜādh and of others. Just as the desert Arab said: "I have perished and caused to perish, because I had intercourse with my wife during the daytime in Ramaḍān!" Then [Muḥammad] said: "Free a slave." And it was understood that a Turk or an Indian, in a similar case, is bound to manumit.

115 This is because men are not enjoined to do what is [de facto] right in God's view—for that is something impossible, and there is no imposition of what cannot be done—but rather they are enjoined to do what they deem to be right. It is just as they are not enjoined to pray in a pure [clean] garment, but rather in a garment they deem to be pure. And if they were to remember its impurity, they would not he bound to perform the Prayer again [i.e. to start over], because the Apostle of God—God bless him and grant him peace—took off his sandal during the Prayer when Gabriel informed him that there was some dirt on it but he did not repeat or recommence the Prayer. Similarly the traveller is not enjoined to pray towards the *qibla* [the direction of Mecca], but rather towards the direction he deems to be the *qibla* by inference from mountains, stars and the sun. If he is right, he will have two recompenses, otherwise he will have one recompense. And men are not enjoined to give the *zakāt* [alms tax] to a poor man, but rather to one they deem to be poor—because the latter's interior cannot be known. And judges are not enjoined, in cases of bloodshed and rape, to seek witnesses whose veracity they know, but rather those they deem to be veracious. Now if it is allowable to shed blood [i.e. to inflict capital punishment] by a supposition which may be wrong, viz. the supposition of the veracity of the witnesses, then why is it not allowable by the supposition of the testimony of the proofs in the exercise of personal judgment? [Ch: pourquoi la prière ne serait-elle permise en se basant sur le témoignage des preuves produites par la réflexion personnelle?—But "la prière" is not in the Arabic text.]

116 [Fr 79] I would like to know what your comrades would have to say about this! Would they say that, if one has a difficulty about the *qibla,* he should put off [Ar 89] the Prayer until he travels to the Imam and asks about it? Or would he [sic] enjoin upon him being right, which is beyond his power? Or would he say: "Exercise personal judgment and follow it" [to] one who cannot exercise personal judgment, because he does not know the proofs of the *qibla* and how to infer from the stars and the mountains and the winds?

117 *He said:* I do not doubt that be would permit him to use personal effort, and then would not impute sin to him if he expended his best effort, even though he were to err and to pray in a direction other than that of Mecca. *I said:* If one who makes the direction of Mecca behind him is excused and recompensed, then it is not farfetched that one who errs in other exercises of personal effort will be excused. So those who exercise personal effort, and those who imitate them, are all excused: some of them attaining what is right in God's view, and some sharing with the attainers in one of the two recompenses. Hence their positions are near one another and they have no reason to stubbornly oppose one another and to form fanatical cliques with one another, especially since the one right is not specified, and every one of them thinks that he is right. It is as though two travellers were to exercise personal effort about the *qibla* and were to differ in personal judgment: each would have the right to pray in the direction he thought most probable, and to refrain from disapproving of and objecting to his companion, because he is enjoined only to follow what his own supposition enjoins. As for facing the precise direction of Mecca [as it is] in God's view, he cannot do it. Similarly, in the Yemen, Muᶜādh used to exercise personal effort, not in the belief that error on his part was inconceivable, but in the belief that, if he erred, he would be excused.

118 This is because, in the positive legal matters about which it is conceivable that religious laws [*al-sharāᵓiᶜ*] may disagree, one thing is close to [approximates] its contrary provided it be an object of supposition in the secret [mystery] of preparation [for the afterlife]. [The passage is not clear; Ch: une chose se rapproche de son contraire après avoir été objet de conjecture dans le secret de la recherche; or: read *al-istibṣār* in place of *al-istiᵓdād* and drop "for the afterlife," giving: in the secret (mystery) of acting reasonably, or, pondering, reflecting.] But there is no disagreement about that on which the religious laws do not differ. And the real nature of this disagreement you will know from *The Secrets of the Followers of the Sunna* [*Asrār atbāᶜ al-sunna*], which I have mentioned in the tenth principle [or: basis, fundament] of external actions [*al-aᶜmāl al-ẓāhira*] of [my] book *Jawāhir al-Qurᵓān* [The Jewels of the Qurᵓān]. [Chelhot reads *Asrār atbāᶜ as-sunna;* It seems to me that it should be: *Asrār ittibāᶜ al-sunna*—The Secrets, or Mysteries, of Following the Sunna.]

119 As for the third class, viz. the wranglers, I would summon them to the truth with gentleness. And I mean [Ar 90] by "gentleness" that I would not be fanatical against them or scold them, but I would be friendly [kind, courteous] and I would "dispute with them in the better way" [cf. 16.126/125]: God Most High enjoined that on His Apostle.

120 The meaning of "disputing in the better way" is that I accept the principles admitted by the wrangler, and I deduce from them [*minhā* seems better than Ch's *minhu*] the truth by means of the verified [or: sure] balance in the way I presented in [my] book *al-Iqtiṣād* [*fīᵓl-iᶜtiqād:* The Golden Mean in Belief] and to that degree [extent]. If that did not convince him because of his desiring, in virtue of his intelligence, an additional clarification, I would raise [promote] him to learning the balances. And if it did not convince him, because of his stupidity and his perseverance [Fr 80] in his fanaticism and his obsti-

nacy and his pigheadedness, I would treat him with the Iron. For God Most High made the Iron and the Balance the associates of the Book to make known thereby that all creatures accomplish justice only by these three: thus the Book is for the simple; and the Balance is for the elite [privileged]; and the Iron, which has a terrible strength [power, harm; cf. 57.25 "wherein is great might"; Blachère: qui contient danger terrible] is for those who follow what is unclear in the Book "desiring dissension and desiring its interpretation" [3.5/7] and who do not know that that is no business of theirs and that its interpretation is known only by God and by those firmly rooted in knowledge [d. 3.5/7], not by the wranglers.

121 And I mean by "the wranglers" a group who possess a certain cleverness by which they have risen above the simple folk: but their cleverness is imperfect—for in their original constitution it was perfect, but in their interior is a malice and a stubbornness and a fanaticism and servile conformism. That prevents them from perceiving the truth, and these qualities are "veils upon their hearts lest they understand" [57.25 and 3.5/7], and only their imperfect cleverness destroys [damns] them. For a faulty constitution and an imperfect cleverness are much worse than simple-mindedness. Moreover, in the Tradition [it is said] that the majority of the denizens of the Garden are the simple-minded and that the uppermost heaven is for the possessors of minds [the intelligent], and excluded from the totality of the two groups are those who wrangle about the signs of God: and they, they are "the followers of the Fire—and God curbs by the power of the Sultan [Ch: par le bras séculier] what He does not curb by the Qur'ān.

122 These must be prevented from wrangling by the sword and the lance, as ʿUmar did when a man asked him about two ambiguous verses in the Qur'ān, and he struck him with a whip; and as Mālik replied when he was asked about God's seating Himself firmly on the Throne: "The being firmly seated is a truth, and faith in it is obligatory, and the manner is unknown, and asking about it is an innovation [*bidʿa:* or, heresy]"—[Ar 91] and by that he cut off the way to [shut the door] wrangling; and thus did all [our] pious forbears. But there is great harm for the servants of God in the opening of the door to wrangling.

123 This, then, is my procedure in summoning men to the truth and bringing them forth from the darknesses of error to the light of the truth. And that is that I summon the elite by wisdom, viz. by teaching the balance, with the result that when one of them learns the just balance he is master, not of one knowledge, but of many knowledges. For one who has with him a balance knows thereby the quantities of substances without limit. Similarly, one who has with him the Correct Balance has with him the wisdom which, whoso is given it is not given one good, but is given much good without limit [cf. 2.272/269]. And were it not for the Qur'ān's containing the balances it would not be correct to call the Qur'ān "Light" [cf. 4.174; 5.18/15], for light is not seen in itself but by it other things are seen, and this is the quality of the balance; nor would God's utterance be true: "not a thing, [Fr 81] fresh or withered, but it is in a Book Manifest" [6.59]: for all knowledges are not present in the Qur'ān explicitly, but they are present in it potentially because of what it contains of the just balances by means of which the doors of limitless wisdom are opened. By this, then, I summon the elite [privileged].

124 And I summon the simple man by "good admonition" [16.126/125] by referring him to the Book and restricting myself to the attributes of God Most High contained therein. And I summon the disputatious by the disputation which is better [cf. 16.126/125]. And if he refuses it I give up talking to him and stop his harm by the power of the Sultan and the Iron revealed with the Balance [cf. 57.25].

125 I would like to know now, my companion, how your Imam treats these three classes! Does he teach the simple folk and enjoin on them what they do not understand—and [thus] contradict the Apostle of God—God bless him!? Or does he expel wrangling from the brain of the wranglers by means of argument—when that could not be done by the Apostle of God—God bless him!—despite God's frequent debate with the unbelievers in the Qurʾān? How great, then, is the power of your Imam, since he has become more powerful than God Most High and His Apostle! Or does he summon men of insight to follow him blindly, when they would not accept the utterance of the Apostle by servile conformism, nor would they be convinced by the changing of a stick into a snake? Rather would they say: "This is an unusual feat—but whence does it follow from it [Ar 92] that its doer [or: claimant] is veracious? Among the marvels of magic and talismans [charms] in the world is that by which men's minds are baffled, and only he can distinguish an apologetic miracle from magic and talisman who is familiar with all of them and with their multiple kinds, so that he can know that the apologetic miracle is outside them, just as [the] magicians [of Pharaoh] recognized the feat of Moses because they were among the masters of magic. And who is capable of that?" Rather they would wish to know his veracity from his words [what he says], as the learner of arithmetic knows, from arithmetic itself, the veracity of his teacher in his saying: "I am an arithmetician."

126 This, then, is the sure and certain knowledge by which the possessors of intelligence and men of insight are convinced, and they are in no wise convinced by anything else. Such men, when they know by the like of this method the veracity of the Apostle and the truth of the Qurʾān, and understand the balances of the Qurʾān, as I have mentioned to you, and take from it the keys of all the sciences along with the balances, as I have mentioned in [my] book *Jawāhir al-Qurʾān* [The Jewels of the Qurʾān]—whence have they any need of your Imam and what could they learn from him? I would like to know what you have learned, up to now, from your infallible Imam, and what religious problems he has solved, and what obscure things he has unveiled! God Most High said: "This is God's creation: now show me what those have created that are apart from Him!" [31.10/11].

127 But this is my method regarding the balances of knowledges—so show me what you have learned of the obscurities of the sciences from your Imam up to now. [Ch adds: and what your friends learn from him. O how I would like to know what you have learned from your infallible Imam! Show me what you have seen. . . . Not in the Arabic.] [Fr 82] The aim of an invitation to a meal is not the bare invitation without eating and taking food from the table! Now I see you invite people to the Imam, then I see that one who accepts the invitation is just as ignorant after it as he was before: the Imam has not loosened any knot for him, but rather has made knotty for him what was untied! And his acceptance of the invitation has brought him no knowledge, but rather he has thereby become more overbearing and more ignorant.

128 *Then he said:* I have had a long association with my comrades: but I have learned from them nothing except that they say: You must follow the doctrine of *taʿlīm;* and beware of personal opinion and analogy [reasoning], for that is contradictory and varying. *I said:* One of the curious things is that they invite to *taʿlīm* but do not busy themselves with *taʿlīm.* So say to them: You have invited me to *taʿlīm,* and I have accepted the invitation—so teach me some of what you possess! [Ar 93] *Then he said:* I do not see them adding anything to this.

129 *I said:* I advocate *taʿlīm* and the Imam, and I hold the futility [falsity] of personal opinion and analogy. But I add for you to this—if you could give up servile con-

formism—the teaching [*taʿlīm*] of the marvels of the sciences and the mysteries of the Qurʾān, and I deduce from it [Qurʾān] for you the keys of all the sciences, as I have deduced from it the balances of all the sciences, according to my indication of the manner of the branching of the sciences from it in [my] book *Jawāhir al-Qurʾān.* But I do not summon to any Imam save Muḥammad—Peace be upon him!—and to any Book save the Qurʾān, and from it I deduce all the secrets of the sciences. My apodeictic proof of that is what I say and my clear explanation. If you doubt, you ought to try me and test me: do you, or do you not, consider me better suited for your learning from me than your comrades?

[Ar 94]

[CHAPTER TEN]
Discussion of the Formation of Analogy and Personal Opinion and the Showing of Their Futility

130 *Then he said:* Breaking with [my] comrades and learning from you might prevent me from what I related to you, viz. the injunction of my mother when she was dying. But I would like you to disclose to me how personal opinion [*al-raʾy*] and analogy [*al-qiyās:* also, syllogism, reasoning] are wrong [weak]. For I think that you deem me weak in mind and you deceive me [make things complicated for me]: thus you call *qiyās* and *raʾy* a "balance," and you recite to me, in accordance with that, a Qurʾān [i.e. a verse of the Qurʾān]—but I think it [the "balance"] is precisely the *qiyās* claimed by your associates. *I said:* Far from it! And now I shall explain to you what I and they mean by *al-ray* and *al-qiyās.*

131 As for *al-raʾy,* an example of it is the assertion of the Muʿtazilites: "God Most High must arrange [contrive, observe] what is best [Fr 83] for His servants." When they are requested to substantiate this, they refer to nothing save that it is an opinion [*raʾy*] of which their minds have approved on the basis of comparing the Creator with creatures, and likening His wisdom to their wisdom. The things approved by men's minds are the *raʾy* which I do not regard as reliable: for it produces conclusions the falseness of which is testified to by the balances of the Qurʾān—like this doctrine [of the Muʿtazilites]. For when I weigh it with the balance of concomitance, I say: "If the best were obligatory on God, He would do it. But it is known that He has not done it; so [that] proves that it is not obligatory—for He does not omit the obligatory." Then if someone says: "We concede that if it were obligatory, He would do it; but we do not concede that He has not done it," I say: "Had He done the 'best,' He would have created them in the Garden and left them there—for this would have been better for them; but it is known that He has not done that; so [that] proves that He has not done the best." This also is a conclusion from the balance of concomitance.

132 Now the adversary [is caught] between [two alternatives]—that he say: He left them in the Garden—and his lie is seen; or that he say: "The best for them was to be expelled into the world, the abode of tribulations, [Ar 95] and [that] He expose them to sins, then say to Adam on the day the hidden things will be disclosed: Bring forth, O Adam, the delegation [to be sent to] the Fire. Then he will say: How many? And God will say: From every thousand nine hundred and ninety-nine—as has come down in the sound Tradition [cf. Bukhāri: VI, 122—*sūrat al-ḥajj*]. And [the adversary] claims that this is better than creating them in the Garden and leaving them there, because their felicity in that case would not be because of their effort and merit, and thus the [divine] favor would have been great [oppressive ?] for them—and [divine] favor is weighty [burdensome]. But if

they hear and obey, what they receive is a recompense and a wage containing no favor. I make it easy for your hearing and my tongue [by refraining] from the report of such discourse and consider them [hearing and tongue] above it [too good for it], to say nothing of replying to it!

133 Consider it, then: do you see the abominations of the conclusion of *raʾy*—[how great] they are?! Now you know that God Most High leaves children, when they die, in a place in the Garden below the places of obedient adults. So if they [children] said: "O our God! You are not stingy with what is better for us: but it is better for us that You make us attain their rank," then according to the Muʿtazilites God would say: "How could I make you attain their rank, when they have grown up, toiled and obeyed, and you have died as children?" Then they would say: "It is You Who caused us to die and deprived us of a long sojourn in this life and of noble ranks in the afterlife. So the best for us was that You not cause us to die—why, then, did You cause us to die?" Then God Most High would say: "I knew that if you grew up you would misbelieve and merit the Fire forever: so I knew that the best for you was to die in childhood."

134 Thereupon the grown up unbelievers would call out from the lowest levels of the Fire, shouting [for help] and saying: "Did You not know that we, if we grew up, would misbelieve? So why did You not cause us to die in childhood? For we would be content with a hundredth part of the ranks of the children!" At this [Fr 96] point there remains for the Muʿtazilite no reply to give on God's part, and so the argument would be in favor of the unbelievers against God—Exalted He above what the liars assert! To be sure the doing of the "best" involves a mystery derived from the knowledge of the secret of God Most High concerning *al-qadar* [the divine decree]. But the Muʿtazilite does not reflect [on it] starting from that principle, for he does not get to know that secret by the resources of Kalām. Consequently he gropes after it at random and opinions are for him confused. This, then, is the example of the false *raʾy* [opinion].

135 The example of the [false] *qiyās* [analogy] is affirming a judgment regarding something by analogy [comparison] with something else, like the assertion of the Corporealizers: [Ar 96] "God is—Exalted God above what they say!—a body." We say: "Why?" They reply: "Because He is an agent-maker: so He is a body, by analogy with all the other artisans and agents." Now this is the false *qiyās,* because we say: "Why do you say that an agent is a body because he is an agent?" That cannot be shown when it is weighed in the balance of the Qurʾān. For its balance is the Greater Balance of the balances of equivalence. The form of weighing it is to say: Every agent is a body; but the Creator is an agent; therefore He is a body. Then we say: We concede that the Creator is agent; but we do not concede the first principle, viz. that every agent is a body. So whence do you know that? At this there remains only resort to induction and extended division [Ch: la division indéterminée]: but neither contains a proof.

136 Induction is that one says: "I have scrutinized the agents, viz. weaver, cupper, shoemaker, tailor, carpenter, etc., etc., and I have found them to be bodies: so I know that every agent is a body." One should say to him: "Have you scrutinized all the agents, or has an agent eluded you?" "I have scrutinized a part of them—there does not follow from that the judgment regarding all. And if he says: "I have scrutinized all—we do not concede [this] to him, for all the agents are not known to him. How? Has he scrutinized in that ensemble the Creator of the heavens and the earth? If he has not, then he has not scrutinized all, but a part; and if he has, did he find Him to be a body? If he says: "Yes," then one should say to him: "If you have found that in the premise of your analogy [syllogism],

how have you made it a principle by which you infer it?" Thus you have made your very feeling the proof of what you felt—and this is an error [i.e. a petitio principii].

137 On the contrary, he in his scrutiny is simply like one who scrutinizes the horse and the camel and the elephant and the insects and the birds, and sees that they walk with a foot [leg], but he has not seen the snake and the worm. So he judges that every animal walks with a foot. And he is like one who scrutinizes the animals and sees that in [Fr 85] masticating they all move the lower jaw: so he judges that every animal in masticating moves the lower jaw; but he has not seen the crocodile, and that it moves the upper jaw. This is because it is possible for a thousand individuals of a single genus to be the object of a judgment and for one to be different from the thousand. So this does not give serene certainty: this, then, is [the example] of the false *qiyās.*

138 [Ar 97] As for his resorting to extended [indeterminate, inadequate] division, it is like his saying: "I have examined the qualities of agents. and they are bodies. So they are bodies either because they are agents, or because they are existent, or because they are such and such." Then he refutes all the divisions, and so it follows from this that they are bodies because they are agents. This is the indeterminate [inadequate] division by which Satan weighs his gauges [criteria, analogies]—and we have already mentioned its falsity [Paras. 76 ff.].

139 *Then he said:* I think that, when the other divisions are false, there is imposed [specified] the division which you want. And I consider this a powerful [apodeictic] proof on which most of the *mutakallimūn* rely regarding their beliefs. For they say regarding the question of the ocular vision [of God]: 'The Creator is visible because the world is visible [read: because He is existent ?]." It is false that it [He ?] be said to be visible because it [?] has whiteness, because black is visible; and it is false that it [*?*] be said to be visible because it is a substance, because an accident is visible; and it is false that it is visible because it is an accident, because a substance is visible. And when the divisions are refuted, it remains that it [He] is visible because it is existent. So I want you to unveil to me the weakness [wrongness] of this balance in a clear way about which I cannot doubt. [This Para. is a bit unclear; cf. my *Theology of Al-Ashᶜarī,* Ch. IV, and my edition of Bāqillāni's *Tamhīd,* 266 ff.]

140 *I said:* I shall present you with a true example deduced from a false analogy [*qiyās*], and I shall remove the veil from it. So I say: Our assertion "The world is incipient" is true. But the assertion of one saying: "It is incipient because it is formed [*muṣawwar:* shaped, molded; Ch: has a form], by analogy with the house and other formed structures" is false and does not give [sure] knowledge of the incipience of the world. For you say: its true balance is that it be said: "Everything formed is incipient; but the world is formed; so it follows that it is incipient—and the second principle is conceded, but your assertion "Everything formed is incipient" is not conceded by the adversary.

141 At this he turns to induction and says: "I have examined every formed thing and found it to be incipient, like the house and the glass and shirt and such and such." Now you already know the falsity of that [i.e. this induction, from the preceding]. He may come back to examining and say: "A house is an incipient: so let us examine its qualities. It is a body, subsisting in itself, existent, and formed. These, then, are four qualities. Now it is certainly false to explain [its being an incipient] by its being a body, and its subsisting in itself, and its being existent: so it is certain that it is explained by its being formed—i.e. the fourth [of its qualities]." [Ar 98] One should say to him: 'This is false in many ways, of which I shall mention four.

142 *The first* is that, if one concedes to you the falsity of the [first] three [qualities], the cause you [Fr 86] seek is not established, for perhaps the judgment [that it is incipient] is explained by a limited cause which is neither general nor transitive [i.e. outside itself], like, for example, its being a house. For if it is certain that something other than a house is an inceptum [*muḥdath*], then perhaps the judgment is explained by a notion limited to what is patently an incipient—since it is possible to suppose a particular quality which unites [includes] all and is not transitive [outside itself, i.e. the house. Chelhot remarks "Ce passage est obscure."].

143 *The second* is that it would be correct only if the examination were effected so exhaustively that it would be inconceivable that any part [division] could escape. But if it is not restrictive, and does not revolve between negation and affirmation, it is conceivable that a part might escape—and restrictive exhaustive examination is not an easy matter. Generally the *mutakallimūn* and the jurisprudents are not concerned about it, but rather they say: "If it contains another part, then show it." And the other may say: "I am not obliged to show it." And they continue in this for a long time. And maybe the "inductor" [Ch: logicien] may seek to prove the analogy and say: "If there were another part, we would know it and you would know it: so the nonexistence of our knowledge roves the negation of another part; for the nonexistence of our seeing an elephant in our gathering proves the negation of the elephant." This poor man does not know that we have never known an elephant to be present which we did not see, and then have seen him. But how many ideas have we seen to be present, which we were all incapable of perceiving, then we became aware of them after a while! So perhaps there is in it part which eludes us, which we are not aware of now—and perhaps we will not be aware of it all our life long.

144 *The third* is that, even if we concede the restriction [i.e. the complete disjunction], the certainty of the fourth does not follow necessarily from the elimination of three. On the contrary, the combinations resulting from four are more than ten and twenty. For it is possible that the cause be the units of these four, or two of them, or three of them; then the two and the three are not specified [determined]. On the contrary, it is conceivable that the cause is its being existent and a body, or existent and subsisting in itself, or existent and house, or house and formed, or house and subsisting in itself, or house and body, or body and formed, or body and subsisting in itself, or body and existent, or subsisting in itself and existent. These are some of the combinations of two—and so for the combinations starting with three. And know that most frequently judgments depend on many causes united. Thus ạ thing is not seen because the seer has an eye—for it is not seen at night; nor because the thing seen is illuminated by the sun—because the blind man does not see; nor because of the two together—because the air [wind] is not seen; but because of the totality of that plus [Ar 99] the fact that the thing seen is colored and other factors. This is the judgment of what exists: but the judgment of the ocular vision [of God] in the afterlife is another judgment.

145 [Fr 87] *The fourth* is that, if the exhaustive examination is conceded, and combination is left aside, then the refutation of three in no wise entails the attachment of the judgment to the fourth, but rather [entails] the judgment's being restricted to the fourth. But the fourth may be divisible into two parts, and the judgment may be linked to one of them. Surely you see that, were one first to divide and to say: "either its being a body, or existent, or subsisting in itself, or formed, for example in a square form, or formed in a

circular form," then were to refute the [first] three divisions, the judgment would absolutely not be attached to the form, but perhaps would be relevant to [have to do with] a particular form.

146 So because of [their] neglect of such fine points as these, the *mutakallimūn* have acted rashly and their contention has multiplied, since they held fast to *ra*ʾ*y* and *qiyās.* But that does not give serene certainty: rather it is suitable for legal, conjectural analogies [syllogisms] and for inclining men's hearts in the direction of the right and the true. For their thought [reasoning] does not extend to remote probabilities, but rather their belief is decided by weak reasons.

147 Surely you see that when somebody says to a simple man who has a headache: "Use rose water, for I, when I have a headache, use it and benefit from it," it is as though he were to say: "This is a headache, so rose water will lessen it by analogy with my headache." So the heart of the sick man inclines to it and he uses it, and he does not say to him: "First establish that rose water is good for every headache, be it due to cold or heat or the vapors of the stomach—for the kinds of headaches are many; and prove that my headache is like yours, and my humors [temperament, complexion] like yours, and my age and occupation and my circumstances like yours—for the treatment will vary because of all that."

148 For the endeavor to verify these things is not the concern of the simple folk, because they do not note these things. Nor is it the concern of the *mutakallimūn,* for they—even though they note them, contrary to the common folk—do not find the ways which produce serene certainty. These are simply the practice of men who have learned them from Aḥmad—God's blessings be upon him!—viz. men who have been guided by the light of God to the brightness of the Qurʾān, and have learned from it the just scale and the Correct Balance, and have become guardians for God of justice [or: energetic executors of justice for God; Ch: ils sont devenus des gens équitables envers Dieu].

149 [Ar 100] *Then he said:* Now indeed the signs and tidings of the truth appear to me from your discourse. Will you, then, permit me to follow you on the condition that you teach me some of what you know to be proper conduct? *I said:* By no means! You will never be able to be patient with me. And how could you be patient with what you have not understood through report [*khabar:* tradition]?

150 *He said:* God willing you will find me patient and I shall not refuse you obedience in anything. [Fr 88] *I said:* Do you think I have forgotten your learning a lesson from the counsel of your companions and your mother and your throbbing conformism [i.e. your deeply ingrained, or, felt conformism]? So you are not suited to be my companion, nor am I suited to be yours. So leave me! This is a parting between us. For I am too busy with correcting myself to correct you, and too preoccupied with instruction [received] from the Qurʾān to instruct you. So you will not see me hereafter, because I shall not see you. I do not have leisure for more than this to reform the evil and to beat the air [take futile steps; lit, to hammer cold iron]. I have indeed "advised you sincerely; but you do not love sincere advisers" [7.77/79].

And praise to God, the Lord of the Worlds!
And God's blessing upon the Prince of Messengers!

[Ar 101] [*Conclusion*]

151 So there you have, my brothers, my story with my companion, which I have recited to you with its obvious and its hidden shortcomings [with all its defects], that you might be full of amazement at it and find profit in the contents of these conversations by the comprehension of things more sublime than the correction of the doctrine of the devotees of *ta^c^līm.* That, then, was not my aim, but: "You I mean [intend], but listen O neighbor!" [A proverb still popular: something is said to A, but is really meant for the listening B.]

152 And I request the sincere to accept my excuse, when they read these conversations, for what I have preferred, regarding the doctrine, of synthesis and analogies, and what I have introduced, regarding names, of change and substitution, and what I have contrived, regarding meanings [notions], of imagery and comparison. For under each one I had a sound aim and a secret plain to men of insight [those with understandings].

153 Beware of changing this order, and of stripping these ideas of this apparel! I have indeed taught you how the "intelligible" is to be weighed [Ar has "adorned," but the reading adopted here is preferable and has manuscript authority] by using the support of the traditional that hearts may be quicker to accept. Beware also of making the "intelligible" a principle and the traditional a consequent and following! For this is abominable and repellent, and God Most High has commanded you to give up the abominable and to dispute in the better way [cf. 16.126/125]. So beware of transgressing this command lest you perish and cause to perish, and go astray and lead astray!

154 But of what use is my injunction when the truth has been obliterated and the flood gates have been broken and turpitude has become widespread [Ar 102] and has taken wing to all countries and has become a subject of pleasantry in all cities? For some people have considered this Qur'ān to be something obsolete [antiquated, uncouth] and they have taken the prophetic directives to be airy nothings. All that comes from the meddling [officiousness] of the ignorant and their claiming, in the defense of religion, the rank of the savants [*al-^c^ārifīn:* the "knowers"]. "But surely many lead astray by their caprices, without any knowledge; thy Lord knows very well the transgressors" [6.119].

APPENDIX IV

Al-Maqṣad al-Asnā fī Sharḥ Maᶜāni Asmāᵓ Allāh al-Ḥusnā

THIS is the work to which Ghazālī refers in Para. 96 of my translation. The title means: *The Noblest of Aims in the Explanation of God's Fairest Names.* I have used the text edited by Professor Fadlou A. Shehādi—cf. Annotated Bibliography.

I present here some selections from this very interesting work, among them the whole of the passage to which Ghazālī refers in the *Munqidh.* I have also included my translation of Ghazālī's comments on a few of the ninety-nine Names. R. C. Stade [cf. Annotated Bibliography] has translated fully Chapter One of Section Two [Shehkdi, pp. 63–171], and the interested reader will find there much that will give him a deeper insight into Ghazālī's religious and spiritual doctrine. A summary of this chapter will be found in Appendix III of *El justo medio* by Asín Palácios, pp. 437–47; in the same work, pp. 458–71, there is a translation of the passage referred to in the *Munqidh.*

[*The Introduction: Khuṭba*]

In the Name of God, Merciful and Kind!

1 Praise be to God, matchless in His majesty and His might, solely sublime and sempiternal, Who clipped the wings of intellects [so as to keep them, restrain them] from the glow of His glory, and Who has made the way to know Him to consist solely in powerlessness to know Him, and Who rendered the tongues of the eloquent incapable of the [due] praise of His majestic high beauty save by the employ of His own praise of Himself and His own enumeration of His Names and His Attributes. And blessings upon Muḥammad, the best of His creatures, and upon his Companions and his family!

2 *Now then:* A brother in God—Mighty and Glorious!—to answer whom it is a religious duty asked me to explain the meanings of God's most beautiful Names. His requests kept coming to me one after another, and on my part I kept putting one foot forward and withdrawing the other, vacillating between complying with his demand so as to fulfill the duty of brotherliness and seeking an excuse from his solicitation so as to take the path of caution [the way of wariness] and to abstain from mounting the back of danger, and because I deemed human power inadequate to accomplish this aim.

3 How could it be otherwise? For there are two things which deter the man of discernment from plunging into such an abyss as this. One of them is that in itself the thing

is an extraordinary desire hard to attain and difficult to comprehend. For in sublimity it is the acme and the most distant goal: minds are baffled [bewildered, perplexed] by it, and the sight [perceptive powers] of intellects falls far short of its beginnings [starting points], to say nothing of its farthest reaches. Whence, then, can human powers [essay to] follow the path of study and investigation of the Attributes of Divinity? [It is like asking] How can the eyes of bats endure the light of the sun?

4 [p. 12] The second deterrent is that in speaking clearly about the essence [true nature, essential being] of the True [the Truth, God] one must almost directly contradict the a priori notions of the masses of men. But weaning men from their habitual usage and familiar beliefs is difficult. And the abode [excellence] of the Truth is far above being a thoroughfare for every comer [a common thoroughfare, or market], and too sublime for men to gaze at save one by one [one after another]. And the greater the thing sought, the fewer the helpers. One who associates with men deserves to be shunned, but it is difficult for one who sees the True to pretend not to see [to shut his eyes]. For one who knows not God—Mighty and Glorious!—silence is imperative, and for one who knows God Most High silence is prescribed. For that reason it has been said: "The tongue of him who knows God is weak [blunted, languid, dull, expressionless]." But the sincerity of the demand, along with its persistence, have outstripped these excuses. So I ask God—Mighty and Glorious!—to make easy [supply, provide] that which is right and to enhance the recompense by His largesse and benevolence and lavish liberality: truly He is the Munificent, the Magnanimous, the Indulgent to His servants!

[p. 13] *The Beginning of the Book*

5 We think it good to divide the discourse in this book into three Sections: the First Section on the Antecedents and the Preambles, the Second Section on the Aims and Goals, the Third Section on the Consequents and Complements. The chapters of the First Section address the Aims by way of preface and introduction; and the chapters of the Third Section are attached to them by way of completion and complement [supplement]. But the quintessential object is what the middle [chapters] contain.

6 The First Section explains (1) the true meaning of what is affirmed about the name and the named and naming, and discloses the error which has befallen such affirmation in the case of most of the sects; (2) whether any name the meaning of which approximates the Name of God Most High, such as *ᶜal-ᶜaẓīm* and *al-jalīl* and *al-kabīr,* is to be predicated univocally, so that such names are synonyms, or [whether] their meanings must differ; (3) whether a single name with two meanings is "common" [shared: *mushtarak*] by [its] relation to the two meanings [and to be] predicated of them as the general is of its particulars [the things it names], or [is to be] predicated particularly of one of the two; (4) that the creature has a share in the meaning of each of the Names of God—Mighty and Glorious!

7 The Second Section explains (1) the meanings of the ninety-nine Names of God; (2) how all of them come down to an Essence and seven Attributes in view of the People of the Sunna; (3) how, according to the doctrine of the Muᶜtazilites and the Philosophers, they come down to a simple Essence containing no multiplicity.

8 [p. 14] The Third Section explains (1) that the Names of God Most High are more than ninety-nine by positive tradition [*tawqīfan*]; (2) the permission to describe God Most High by whatever He is qualified by [can be described by], even though there has

come no positive tradition regarding it, providing it is not [explicitly] prohibited; (3) the advantage of the enumeration and specification by one hundred minus one.

[p. 15]

SECTION ONE

On the Antecedents and Preambles
It Contains Four Chapters

[p. 17]

Chapter One

Explanation of the Meaning of "Name," "Named," "Naming"

9 Many have plunged into the [meaning of] the *name* and the *named,* and have gone different ways. Most of the sects have deviated from the truth. Some say: The *name* is identified with the *named,* but different [distinct] from the *naming.* Another view is that the *name* is different [distinct] from the *named,* but identified with the *naming.* A third group, known for skill in the art of dialectic and polemic, alleges that the *name* may be identified with the *named,* as [in] our saying of God Most High: He is an essence and existent [being]; and it may be distinct from the *named,* as [in] our saying [of God]: He is creating, sustaining—for this indicates sustaining and creating, and these are distinct from Him; and it may be such that one cannot say it is identified with the *named,* or that it is distinct from it, as [in] our saying: Knowing and powerful—for these indicate knowledge and power, and one cannot say of God's Attributes that they are God or that they are other than God.

10 The dispute comes down to two points: one is whether or not the *name* is the *naming,* and the second is whether or not the *name* is the *named.* The truth is that the *name* is other than the *naming* and other than the *named,* and that these three names are different and not synonymous. The only way to lay bare the truth in this matter is to explain individually the meaning of each of these three words [terms], then to explain the meaning of our saying "it is [the same]" and the meaning of our saying "it is distinct [diverse]"—[i.e. of identity and diversity]. This is the method of disclosing realities [truths, facts], and one who deviates from this method will in no wise succeed.

11 Every judgmental [propositional: *taṣdīqī*] cognition [knowledge: *ʿilm*], i.e. one susceptible of being declared true or false, is undoubtedly a proposition containing a subject and a predicate [*mawṣūf wa ṣifa*: something described or qualified, and something describing or qualifying, quality, attribute], and the relation of that predicate to the subject. So it must be preceded by the knowledge of the subject and its definition by way of conceiving [representing; *al-taṣawwur,* also: concept] [p. 18] its definition and its reality [true meaning, essence: *ḥaqīqa*], then by the knowledge of the predicate and its definition by way of conceiving its definition and its reality, then by the consideration of the relation of that predicate to the subject—whether it exists [as] belonging to it or is denied of it. For example, if one wishes to know whether an angel is eternal or incipient, he must first know the meaning of the term [word] "angel," then the meaning of "eternal" and 'incipient," then he must consider the affirmation or denial of one of the two descriptions of the angel. Similarly one must have knowledge of the meaning of "name" and of "named" and knowledge of the meaning of identity [*al-huwiyya*] and "diversity" [*al-ghayriyya*] so that he may conceivably know thereafter whether it [name] is it [named; is identified with it] or different from [other than] it.

12 In explanation of the definition and reality of *name* we say: Things base an existence in individuals [*al-a*ᶜ*yān;* or, essences; individual, or essential, existence], and an existence in the tongue [linguistic, or, verbal existence], and an existence in minds [mental existence]. The existence in individuals is the basic [fundamental], real [actual] existence; and the existence in minds is the cognitional, formal existence; and the existence in the tongue is the verbal, indicative existence. For example, "the heaven" [*al-samā'*] has an existence in its essence and itself; then it has an existence in our minds and our souls, because the representation [form] of the heaven is impressed in our eyes [sights] and then in our imagination [*khayāl*], so that, were the heaven to cease to exist and we were to continue [existing], the representation of the heaven would be present in our imagination. And this representation is what we express by "knowledge" [cognition], and it is the likeness of the cognoscible, for it imitates the cognoscible and corresponds to it, and it is like the form impressed in the mirror, for it imitates the form outside and confronting it.

13 The existence in the tongue is the word composed of sounds divided into three [p. 19] syllables, the first of which is expressed by the *sīn* [s] and the second by the *mīm* [m] and the third by the *alif* [with the *hamza*]—and they are like our saying *samā'*. So this saying is an indication of what is in the mind, and what is in the mind is a representation of what is in [individual] existence and is conformed to it. If there were no existence in individuals, no form [image, representation] would be impressed in minds, and if it were not impressed in the form [image] of the minds and a man were unaware of it, he would not express it by the tongue. So the word and the cognition and the cognoscible are three different things, but they are mutually corresponding and comparable, though they may be confused for a stupid person and one of them may not be distinguished from another.

14 And how can these existents not be different, and how can there not attach to each of them properties [*khawāṣṣ*—special qualities] which do not attach to the other? For a man, for example, insofar as he exists in individuals, there attaches to him that he is asleep and awake, living and dead, standing, walking, and sitting, etc.; and insofar as he exists in minds, there attaches to him that he is an inchoative and a predicate, and general and specific, and universal and particular, and a proposition, etc.; and insofar as he exists in the tongue, there attaches to him that he is Arabic and Persian and Turkish, and having many letters and having few letters, and that he is a noun and verb and particle, etc. This latter existence is something which may differ in [different] ages and be diverse in the usage of [different] countries. But the existence in individuals and in minds in no wise differs in [different] ages and nations.

15 Now that you know this, set aside the existence which is in individuals and in minds and consider [reflect on] verbal [linguistic] existence—for our aim concerns the latter. We say, then: Words are an expression of the separate [syllabified] letters which have been posited by human choice to indicate the individuals [essences] of things. They are divided into what is posited primarily and what is posited secondarily. [The use of "posited," *mawḍū*ᶜ, indicates a "conventional" origin of language.]

16 [p. 20] What is posited primarily is like your saying: heaven, tree, man, etc. As for what is posited secondarily, it is like your saying: noun, verb, particle, command, prohibition and imperfect [aorist]. We say that it is posited secondarily simply because the words posited to indicate things are divided into what indicates a meaning in something else, and it is called a particle, and what indicates a meaning in itself. The latter is divided into what indicates the time of the existence of that meaning, and it is called a verb, e.g. your saying "he struck, he strikes or will strike," and what does not indicate the time,

and it is called a noun, e.g. your saying "heaven, earth." Words were first posited as indications of individuals [essences], and thereafter the noun, verb and particle were posited as indications of the divisions of words, because the words, once they were posited, also became existents in individuals and their forms were impressed in minds, and [so] were also suited to be indicated by the movements of the tongue.

17 Conceivably there are words which have been posited thirdly and fourthly, so that when the noun is divided into [several] divisions, and each division is known by a name, that name is the third rank [degree], as one says, for example: The noun is divided into indefinite and definite, etc. The purpose of all this is that you know that the noun comes down to the word posited secondarily. So if one says to us: "What is the definition of the noun?" we say: It is the word posited for indication; and perhaps we add to that what distinguishes it from the particle and the verb. But the formulation of the definition is not our present purpose; the purpose is simply that what is meant by the name is the meaning which is in the third rank, i.e. which is in the tongue, not what is in individuals and minds.

18 Once you know that by the name is meant simply the word posited for indication, then know [p. 21] that everything posited for indication has a positor and a positing and an object of the positing [that for which it is posited]. The latter is called "the named," i.e. the indicated qua [as] indicated. The positor is called "the namer," and the positing is called "the naming." One says: So-and-so named his son—when he posits a word to indicate him, and his positing is called "naming." The term "naming" may also be applied to the mention of the posited name, as when one calls out to a person and says "O Zayd!"—and it is said that he named him; and if he says "O Abū Bakr!" it is said that he used his agnomen [*kannāhu:* the *kunya* is a name formed by combining the prefix *Abū* (father) or *Umm* (mother) with the name of the child]. The term "naming" is common to the positing of the name and the mention of the name, though the likelier is that it is worthier [truer] of the positing than of the mention.

19 Name and naming and named are analogous to motion and moving and mover and moved, and these are four different names indicating different notions [meanings, things]. "Motion" indicates a moving from a place to a place; and "moving" indicates the production [causing] of this motion; and "mover" indicates the agent of the motion; and "moved" indicates the thing in which the motion is along with its proceeding [issuing] from an agent—and not like "that which is in motion" [*al-mutaḥarrik*], which indicates only the place [*maḥall:* substrate] in which the motion is, without indicating the agent [i.e. that there is an agent]. If the meanings of these words are now clear, one should consider whether it can be said of them that one of them is identified with another, or it must be said that it is other than [distinct from] it.

20 This will be understood only through knowledge of "the other" [diversity] and of "it is it" [identity]. Our saying "it is it" is used in three ways. *One way* is like one's saying: *"al-khamr* [wine] is *al-ᶜuqār* [wine]," and *"al-layth* [lion] is *al-ʾasad* [lion]." This takes place in the case of everything which is one in itself, but has two synonymous names the meaning of which does not differ at all, nor it is dissimilar by any addition or lack, but only their letters are different. The likes of these names are called "synonymous."

21 [p. 22] *The second way* is like one's saying "The *ṣārim* [sharp sword] is the sword [*al-sayf*]," and "The *muhannad* [sword made of Indian steel] is the sword [*al-sayf*]"—*and* this differs from the previous case [Para. 20]. For these names have different meanings and are not synonymous, because *al-ṣārim* indicates the sword in so far as it is cut-

ting, while *al-muhannad* indicates the sword in so far as it has a relation to India, and the sword [*al-sayf*] indicates sword in an absolute way without any allusion to anything else. But the synonymous differ only in their letters and are nor dissimilar by any addition or lack. So let us call this kind [genus] "interpenetrating" since "the sword" enters into the meaning of the three words, though some of them indicate along with it an addition.

22 *The third way* is that one say "Snow is white [and] cold; so the white and the cold are one, and the white is the cold—and this is the most improbable [farfetched, farthest out] of the ways. That comes down to the oneness of the posited qualified by two qualities and means that a single individual [essence] is qualified by whiteness and coldness. In general, our saying "It is it" indicates a plurality which in some way has a oneness. For if there were no oneness, one could not say "It is it, one [that is, identically]," and so long as there were no plurality, there would be no "It is it" [identity], for the latter is an allusion [a pointing to] two things.

23 The name cannot be the named in the first way [synonyms—Para. 20]. For the meaning of the named is other than the meaning of the name, since we have shown that the name is an indicating word and the named is something indicated and may be other than a word; and because the name is Arabic and Persian and Turkish, and the named may not be such; and in asking about the name one says: "What is it?" whereas in asking about the named one may say: "Who is it?" . . . [p. 23] . . . and the name may be a figure of speech, but not the named; and the name may be changed, but not the named..

24 The name cannot be the named in the second way [Para. 21] . . . be-

25 cause this would necessitate that the naming and the namer and the named and the name all be one and the same—a foolhardy statement example of motion, moving, etc. . . . [p. 24] . . . each of the terms has a proper and distinct meaning..

26 The third way [Para. 22] not applicable to the name and the named,

27 or to the name and the naming . . . [p. 25]. . . .

28 The third view [Para. 9—"a third group"] is the farthest from the right and the most confused unless it be interpreted in a certain way—but then the name and the named are clearly different . . . long discussion [Paras. 29–48; pp. 26–35] on the use of certain of God's Names; and answers to difficulties drawn from the Qur'ān.

49 This is enough, really too much, but given to show the way to deal with such problems.

[pp. 36–38]

Chapter Two

Explanation of Names Close to One Another in Meaning: Are They Synonyms Indicating Only One Meaning, or Must Their Meanings Differ?

50 In the case of God's Names such names are not synonyms. Examples:

54 difference between al-Ghāfir, al-Ghafūr and al-Ghaffār: must be considered as three Names. The first indicates only "pardoning"; the second indicates "multiplicity of pardoning in relation to multiplicity of sins"; the third indicates multiplicity by way of repeated pardoning. Other examples: al-Ghanī and al-Malik; al-ᶜAlīm and al-Khabīr; alᶜAẓīm and al-Kabīr. In general there is no synonymity in the Names included in the Ninety-Nine, because the latter are intended, not for their letters or pronunciation, but for their semantic contents and meanings.

[pp. 39–41] Chapter Three

On the One Name Which Has Different Meanings

55 It is common in relation to them, e.g. *mu'min* [believing, and, affording
57 security or protection]. But it is not predicated of each of its "objects named" as the general is of its objects named. Difference possible in legal and linguistic usages. Case of *al-Salām*. . . . The meaning more indicative of perfection and praise is the one to be preferred.

[pp. 42–59] Chapter Four

Explanation of the Fact That the Servant's Perfection and Happiness Lie in Putting on the Moral Qualities of God Most High and Adorning Himself with the Meanings of His Attributes and His Names as Far as He Conceivably Can

58 Know that one whose only portion [lot] of the meanings of the Names of God—Great and Glorious!—is that he hears the words and understands its linguistic explanation and positing, and believes with his heart that the meaning exists in God Most High, is luckless in his lot and of low rank and cannot rightly boast of what he has acquired. For such things are shared by many, and while they possess a certain relative excellence, are still a clear defect in relation to the acme of perfection. For the good deeds of the righteous are the bad deeds of the intimates [close friends of God, Saints]. The lots [portions] of the intimate respecting the Names of God Most High are three [kinds].

59 *The first lot* is the knowledge of these meanings by way of revelation and direct vision [*al-mukāshafa wa l-mushāhada* [cf. Notes 55 and 183 to my Translation of the *Munqidh*] so that their realities become manifest to them by proof in which error cannot be and God's being qualified by them is disclosed to them in a manner which, in clarity and distinctness [plainness], is analogous to the certainty a man has of his interior qualities which he perceives by direct experience of his interor, not by any exterior sensation. How great a difference there is between this and the belief acquired from parents and teachers by servile conformism and persistence in it, even though it be accompanied by dialectical and *kalām* proofs!

60 *The second* lot is their high regard for [thinking great] what is disclosed to them regarding the Attributes of splendor in a way such that their high regard gives rise to their desire [*shawq*] to be qualified by these Attributes so far as they can be, in order thereby to draw close to the True [God] qualitatively, not spatially, and so to acquire from that qualification a likeness to the Angels brought close to God—Great and Glorious! It is inconceivable that the heart be filled with high regard for an Attribute and esteeming it radiant without an ensuing yearning for that Attribute and a passionate love of that perfection and splendor and an avid desire of being adorned by that quality, if that be possible for the one who has a high regard for its perfection. And if it cannot be [attained] in its perfection, there arises the yearning for the amount possible of it—no doubt about it!

61 One will be devoid of this yearning only for one of two reasons: either because of the weakness of the knowledge and certainty that the quality known belongs to the qualities of splendor and perfection, or because the heart is filled with and absorbed in another yearning. Thus when a disciple sees the perfection of his master in knowledge there is aroused in him a yearning to resemble and imitate him—unless, for example, he is filled with [totally preoccupied with] hunger: for his interior's absorption with the yearning for food may prevent the arousing of the yearning for knowledge. [p. 44] Therefore one who contemplates [looks into] the Attributes of God Most High ought in his heart to be devoid of the desire for anything other than God—Great and Glorious! For knowledge is the seed of yearning, but [only] so long as it encounters a heart free of the thorny growths of the passions: so if it be not free, the seed will not flourish [be productive].

62 *The third* lot is striving to acquire what is possible of those qualities, and to be changed [molded] by them and to be adorned with their beauties. By this the servant becomes "divine" [Lordly], i.e. close to the Lord Most High, and by this he becomes a companion [associate] of the heavenly host of the Angels, for they are on the carpet of proximity [to God]. So one who inclines to a likeness respecting their qualities obtains something of their proximity commensurate with what he obtains of their qualities which bring them close to the True—Exalted He!

63 *If you say:* Seeking proximity to God—Great and Glorious!—by quality [attribute] is something obscure and hearts almost recoil from accepting it or believing it. So give a fuller explanation to break [down] the force [violence] of the rejection of those who reject it, for this would be like something disapproved of [rejected] by the majority unless you were to disclose its true meaning. *I say:* It is not unknown to you, or to one who has developed [grown, progressed] a little from the rank of the common ulema, that existents are divided into perfect and imperfect—and the perfect is nobler than the imperfect. However much [whenever] the degrees of perfection differ, and the ultimate perfection is restricted to one, so that only he possesses absolute perfection and the other existents do not possess an absolute perfection but rather possess perfections differing from each other in relation [relatively], then undoubtedly the most perfect of them is closer to Him Who possesses absolute perfection—I mean a closeness in rank and degree, not in perfection.

64 Furthermore, existents are divided into animate and inanimate. And you know that the animate is nobler and more perfect than the inanimate, and that the degrees of the animate are three: that of angels, that of men, [p. 45] and that of beasts. That of beasts is the lowest in that very life in which is its nobility, for the animate is the perceptive and the active—and the beast is imperfect in perception and action, since its perception is limited to sensation and its action is motivated only by passion [appetite] and anger [irascibility]. . . .

65 The degree of the angel is the highest, because closeness and distance have no effect on his perception and he is exempt from passion and anger, his only motive for action being to seek to draw near to God—Great and Glorious!

66 Man's degree is intermediate between those two, as though he is composed of "angelic-ness' and "beast-ness." The latter is dominant in him at first, until the light of reason [*al-ᶜaql*] illumines him and enables him to act freely in the kingdom of the heavens and the earth. At first, also, he is mastered by passion and anger, until there appears in him the desire to seek perfection . . . and by conquest of passion and anger he acquires a likeness to the angels. So, too, by weaning his soul from sensibles and "imaginables" he acquires another likeness to the angels . . . and his imitation of the angels in perception

and actions brings him close to the angel, and the angel is close to God—and the close to the close is close.

67 *If you say:* The literal meaning of what you say points to the affirmation of a resemblance between the servant and God, but it is known of God by revelation and by reason that "there is nothing like Him" [42.9/II] and that nothing resembles Him, *I say:* Once you know the likeness [resemblance] denied of God, you know that He has no like, but it must not be thought that sharing in any Attribute [quality] entails likeness.

68 [p. 47] Do you not see that two contraries are like one another, yet between them is an extreme distance, while they share in many qualities. For example, black and white share in being an accident, and being a color, and being perceived by sight, etc.? Do you think that one who says that God is existing not in a substrate, and that He is hearing, seeing, knowing, willing, speaking, living, powerful, acting, and that man also is like that, has likened and affirmed a like? Not at all! The matter is not so. Were it so, all creatures would be like [God], at least in the affirmation of existence, and this would suggest resemblance. On the contrary, likeness is an expression for sharing in species and essence [*al-māhiyya:* quiddity]. For even though the horse be very clever, it will not be "a like" of man, because it is opposed to him in species, but it will simply resemble him in cleverness, which is accidental [*ᶜāriḍa*] [and] outside the quiddity constituting the essence [*dhāt*] of "humanity" [man-ness].

69 The peculiar divine property is that God is a being [existent] necessarily existing of Himself, from Whom there exists everything the existence of which is possible according to the best ways [modes] of order and perfection. It is inconceivable that there can be any sharing at all in this peculiar property, but likeness to it occurs. The servant's being compassionate [and] patient [and] grateful does not entail likeness, as his being hearing, seeing, knowing, powerful, living [and] acting. On the contrary [Nay more], I say: The peculiar divine property belongs only to God and only God knows it, and it is inconceivable that anyone know it save Him or one who is His like; but since He has no like, no other knows it. The truth, therefore, is what al-Junayd—God's mercy upon him!—said when he remarked: "Only God knows God." Therefore He gave His greatest [most exalted] creatures only a Name by which He veiled him [Himself] and said: "Praise [glorify] the name of thy Lord Most High" [87.1]. [This may all be in the citation from Junayd] So, by God, no other than God knows God in this life and the next. And it was said to Dhū l-Nūn when he was at death's door: "What do you crave [desire]?" He said: "To know Him before I die, if only for an instant." Now this confuses [would muddle] the hearts of most of the weak and makes [would make] them think [suggest to them] the doctrine [assertion] of negation and "divesting" [God of His Attributes: *al-taᶜṭīl*]—and that because of their inability to understand this discourse [to understand what you say].

70 I also say: Were one to say "I know only God," he would be truthful; and were he to say "I do not know God," he would be truthful. Of course negation and affirmation cannot be true simultaneously—but when the mode [way] of speaking differs, truth in both is conceivable. It is like one's saying to another "Do you know The Upright [*al-Ṣiddīq*], Abū Bakr?" And the other replies: "Can he be someone unknown, or can there conceivably be in the world one who does not know him, given the fame and renown of his name?"—and he is truthful. And were it said to another: "Do you know him [Abū Bakr]?" and he were to reply: "And who am I that I should know al-Ṣiddīq? Far from it! Only al-Ṣiddīq knows al-Ṣiddīq. . . ," [p. 49]] he would also be truthful. . . . Thus must be understood the assertion of him who says "I know God" and that of him who says "I do not know God."

71 If you were to show some ordered [tidy] handwriting to an intelligent person and to say: "Do you know its writer?" and he were to say "No," he would be truthful. And were he to say "Yes. Its writer is a person living, powerful, hearing, seeing, with a sound hand and with a knowledge of the art of writing—and if I know all this about him, how do I not know him?" he would also be truthful. But the former answer would be truer and more correct, for he does not really know him, but simply knows that orderly writing requires such a writer. Similarly, all creatures know only that this ordered and well-made world requires a Maker-Manager [Planner, Director] Who is living, knowing and powerful.

72 This [latter] knowledge has two extremities [aspects, sides]. One of them pertains [refers] to the world and its meaning [*ma^{c}lūmihi:* notion, semantic content] and its need for a manager [director, planner], and the other pertains to God—Great and Glorious!—and its semantic content is names derived from attributes which do not enter into the reality and essence [quiddity] of the essence. For we have shown that when one points to something and says "What is it?" the mention of the derived names is not at all an answer. . . . [p. 50] The knowledge of a thing is the knowledge of its reality and its essence, not the knowledge of its derived names. . . .

73 *If you say:* Our declaration that He [God] is the necessarily existent from Whom alone exists all that can possibly exist is an expression of His reality and His definition—and we indeed know this, *I say:* Not at all! It merely denies that He has a cause and relates actions to Him and is simply names and attributes and relationships.

74 *If you say:* What, then, is the way to knowledge of Him? *I say:* If a child or one impotent were to say to us: "What is the way to knowledge of the pleasure of sexual intercourse and the perception of its reality?" we would say: There are two ways. One is for us to describe it to you so that you may know it; the other is for you to be patient until the natural impulse of passion appears in you, then for you to practice sexual intercourse so that its pleasure may appear in you and you will know it—and this second way is the sure way leading to true knowledge.

75 The first way [description] can lead only to suggestion and comparison

76 with pleasure he knows, e.g. food, drink, sweetmeats—and this is quite inadequate [p. 51]—eg. sweetness of sugar or sweetmeats—not a real likeness, but misleading. . . .

77 Similarly, there are two ways to the knowledge of God, one inade-

78 quate and the other closed. The inadequate is the mention of God's Names and Attributes and comparison with what we know of ourselves as living, knowing, powerful, etc. This is even more inadequate than the comparison of the pleasure of sexual intercourse with that of eating sweetmeats . . . and ends with saying "Nothing is like Him" [42.9/11] . . . [p. 52] . . . comparison of the divine Attributes with ours is insufficient, because the real likeness must be denied and only a sharing in names remains. . . .

79 The second way—and this is closed—is that the servant wait until he comes to have all the divine Attributes and becomes a "Lord"—[p. 53] and this is something impossible for a creature and closed to all save God.

80 Therefore it is impossible for anyone except God to truly know God.

81 Nay more, only the Prophet can know the Prophet, and furthermore, one can know the reality of death and of the Garden and the Fire [Heaven and Hell] only after death and entrance into the Garden or the Fire. It is impossible to make one understand in this life the pleasures of the Garden and the pains of the Fire. Comparisons are inadequate: we can only say "Eye has not seen nor ear heard [p. 54] nor has it occurred to the heart of a

man" [cf. 1 Cor 2:9]. Likenesses must be denied—and this a fortiori regarding the knowledge of God. . . .

82 The ultimate knowledge of the "knowers" [*al-ᶜārifīn*—Sufi overtone, "gnostics"] of God is that they are powerless to know Him, and that their knowledge really is that they do not know Him, and that they cannot know Him, and that only God can know God. . . . then they know Him, i.e. they have reached the limit of the creature regarding knowledge of God.

83 Abū Bakr alluded to this when he said: "Powerlessness to attain perception is a perception"; and this is what Muḥammad meant by his assertion: "I reckon no praise of You like Your own praise of Yourself."

84 [p. 55] *If you say:* By what, then, do the ranks of the Angels and the Prophets and the Friends [Saints] differ in knowledge of God, if knowledge of Him is inconceivable? *I say:* You indeed know that there are two ways to knowledge. One is the true way, but it is closed to all save God Himself. . . .

85 The second way—knowledge of His Attributes and His Names—is open to creatures, and in it their ranks differ. One who knows that God is, in general, knowing and powerful is not like one who sees the marvels of His signs in the kingdom of the heavens and the earth and the creation of spirits and bodies and becomes cognizant of the wonders of His domain and the marvels of His making in the details and fine points of His wisdom and governance and becomes qualified with the angelic qualities which bring one close to God: between them is a great and incalculable distance, and in details and quality the Prophets and the Saints differ.

86 You will understand this only by an example "while God's is the highest likeness [Blachère: la Représentation Auguste]" [16.62/60]. You know that a pious and perfect man like al-Shāfiᶜi, for example, was known by his own porter and by al-Muzanī [a disciple of al-Shāfiᶜi who propagated his doctrine; d. 878]. The porter knew him to be learned in the Law and a writer on it and a director of God's creatures in a general way. But al-Muzanī's knowledge of him was not like that of the porter, but rather a knowledge embracing the details of his qualities and his learning. Moreover, one learned in ten kinds of sciences is not really known by his disciple [p. 56] who has acquired only one kind, to say nothing of his servant who has learned nothing of his sciences. He who has learned one science really knows only a tenth of him, if he so equals him in that science that he does not fall short of him. If he does fall short of him, he really knows what he falls short in only by name and general suggestion, viz. he knows that his master knows something other than what *he* knows. Thus you should know that the difference of creatures in the knowledge of God is commensurate with what is revealed to them of the objects of His knowledge—Great and Glorious He!—and the marvels of His power and the wonders of His signs in this life [world] and the next.

87 The knowledge of God [possessed by] the Angels and Spirits [*malakūt:* kingdom ?] is greater and their knowledge approaches that of God Most High. *If you say:* If they do not know the reality of His Essence and the knowledge of it be impossible, do they know [His] Names and Attributes with a perfect, true knowledge? *We say:* Far from it! That also is known perfectly and really only by God—Great and Glorious! For if we know that an essence is knowing, we know something vague [ambiguous] the reality of which we do not know, but we know that it has the attribute of knowledge. And if the attribute of knowledge is known to us truly, our knowledge that He is knowing is a perfect knowledge of the reality of this attribute—otherwise no [it is not]. But no one knows the reality

of the knowledge of God—Great and Glorious!—save one who possesses the like of His knowledge; but only He possesses that—so no one else knows Him. Another knows him simply by comparison with the knowledge of himself, as we adduced in the example of the comparison with sweetmeats [Paras. 75–76]. The knowledge of God—Great and Glorious!—does not at all resemble the knowledge of creatures, so the creatures' knowledge of Him is not perfect and true, but rather suggestive and comparative.

88 Do not be surprised at this, for I say: Only the sorcerer [magician] himself knows the sorcerer [p. 57], or a sorcerer like him or superior to him. One who does not know sorcery [magic] and its reality and essence [quiddity] knows of the sorcerer only his name, and knows that he has a knowledge and a special quality, without knowing what that knowledge is, since he does not know what the sorcerer knows, and without knowing what that special quality is. To be sure, he knows that that special property, though vague, belongs to the genus of the cognitions, and that its fruit is changing hearts and altering the qualities of individuals and scrutiny [detection of qualities] and the separation of spouses [introducing discord between the married]; but he is excluded from the knowledge of the reality of sorcery. And one who does not know the reality of sorcery does not know the reality of the sorcerer, because the latter is one who possesses the special quality of sorcery. The purport [meaning] of the name "sorcerer" is that it is a name derived from a quality [attribute]. If that quality be unknown, the name [the sorcerer] is unknown, and if it be known, it [he] is known. What is known of sorcery by someone other than the sorcerer is a general description far from the essence [quiddity], viz. that it belongs to the genus of the cognitions, for the name of knowledge is applied to it.

89 Similarly, the purport, in our view, of the power of God—Great and Glorious!—is that it is a quality [description] [and] its fruit and effect is the existence of things. The name "power" is applied to it because it resembles our power the way the pleasure of sexual intercourse resembles that of sweetmeats. But all this is apart from the reality of that power. To be sure, the more the servant comprehends the details of the objects of [God's] power and the marvels of [His] making in the kingdom of the heavens [and the earth], the ampler is his portion of the knowledge of the Attribute of power, because the fruit indicates the fruitful [producer of fruit], just as, the more the disciple comprehends the details of his master's lore and his writings, the more perfect is his knowledge of him and the greater his esteem of him.

90 To this comes down the difference of the knowledge of the "knowers." It is susceptible of an unending difference, because what a man cannot know of the objects of God's knowledge is infinite [limitless]. So also what God can do is infinite, though what enters into [actual] existence is finite. [p. 58] But man's power respecting knowledges has no limit. To be sure, what emerges into existence is different in multiplicity and paucity, and in it difference appears. It is like the difference among men in the power they acquire by wealth through property. One man possesses a dānaq [or: *dāniq*—sixth of a dirham] and [or?] a dirham [drachma], and another thousands. So it is with knowledge [cognitions], nay but the difference in knowledge is greater, because cognoscibles are limitless whereas the chattels of property are bodies, and bodies are finite and limit cannot conceivably be denied of them.

91 Hence you indeed know how creatures differ in the seas of the knowledge of God—Great and Glorious!—and that that has no limit. You also know that he who said "No other than God knows God" was indeed truthful, and that he who said "I know only God" was also truthful. For there is in existence only God and His works—Great and Glorious

He! So when one considers His works in so far as they are His works, and his consideration is limited to that [?], and he does not see that as heaven and earth and tree, but as His doing [making], his knowledge does not exceed [go beyond] the Presence [Majesty] of Divinity and he can say "I know only God, and I see only God—Great and Glorious!"

92 If one were to imagine a person who sees only the sun and its light diffused in the horizons [remote countries], it would be correct for him to say "I see only the sun," for the light emanating from it belongs to its totality [and] is not outside of it. Everything in existence is a light from the lights of the eternal Power and one of its effects. And as the sun is the source of the light emanating on everything illuminated, so also the meaning [notion] for which expression is inadequate [which is inexpressible], and it is of necessity expressed by "the eternal Power," is the source of the existence [being] emanating on [flooding] every existent. [p. 59] So in existence there is only God—Great and Glorious! And the "knower" can rightly say "I know only God."

93 One of the wonders is that a man say "I know only God" and be truthful, and also say "Only God knows God" and also be truthful—but the former in one way and the latter in another. If contradictory things were false when the ways of consideration differ, the Most High's declaration would not be true: "And you did not cast, when you cast, but God cast [8.17]. But it is truthful because the casting has two regards: it is ascribed to the servant in one of them, and to the Lord Most High in the second—so there is no contradiction in it.

94 Let us grasp the bridle of explanation, for we have indeed waded into the depth [abyss] of a shoreless sea. The likes of these mysteries ought not to be vulgarized by depositing them in [entrusting them to] books. And since this has come about accidentally and unintentionally, let us desist from it and return to the explanation of the meanings of God's fairest Names in detail.

[p. 61]

SECTION TWO

On the Aims

[pp. 63–162]

Chapter One

On the Explanation of the Meanings of the Ninety-nine Names of God

95 [This is the Chapter translated by R. C. Stade. It begins with a Tradition attributed to Abū Hurayra: "The Apostle of God—God's blessing and peace upon him!—said: God—Great and Glorious!—has nine and ninety Names, one hundred minus one: He is Odd [i.e. single, unique] and loves the odd; whoso enumerates them will enter the Garden." (Then follows the enumeration of the ninety-nine Names.) I shall give the list, and will translate Ghazālī's comments on the first few by way of example; all the comments will be found in Stade's work.]

96 1—As for his saying *Allāh* [God], it is the Name of the True Existent [Being], Who unites [combines, comprehends] the Attributes of Divinity, the qualified by the Qualities of Lordship, the unique possessor of true Existence [Being]. For every existent [being] other than He does not merit [claim, is not entitled to] existence by its essence [of itself], but simply derives existence from Him. So it, with respect to its essence [itself], is

perishing [perishable], but from the aspect [side] adjacent to Him it is existent. So every existent [being] is perishable except His Face [Countenance: metonymy for "Him—cf. 28.88]. The more likely [explanation] is that it [Allāh], in indicating this meaning [explained above], is analogous to the proper names [nouns], and everything which has been said about its derivation and definition is arbitrariness [aberration, inaccuracy] and affectation [studiedness, forcing].

97 *Note* [*fā'ida*]: Know that this Name, of the nine and ninety, is the greatest of the Names of God—Great and Glorious! For it denotes the Essence combining [comprehending, uniting] all the Divine Attributes without exception, whereas all the other individual Names denote only individual meanings, such as [a] knowledge or [a] power or [an] action or something else. Also because it is the most proper [peculiar, specific] of the Names, since no one can apply it to another either truly [literally] or figuratively, whereas by the other Names another may be named [denominated], e.g. the Powerful and the Knowing and the Merciful etc. So for these two reasons it is likely [clear ?] that this Name is the greatest of these Names.

98 *Precision* [*daqīqa:* detail, particular, fine point]: It is conceivable that the creature may be qualified by something of all the other Names so that the Name may be applied to [predicated of] him, e.g. the Merciful and the Knowing and the Indulgent [Forbearing] and the Patient and the Very Grateful, etc.; but the Name is applied to it [creature] in another way different from its predication of God—Great and Glorious! As for the meaning of this Name, it is peculiar [proper: to God] in a special sense, [and] it is inconceivable that there be any sharing in it either figuratively or truly [literally]. Because of this specialness all the other Names are described as being "the Name of God [Allāh]"—Great and Glorious!—and are defined [explained] in relation to Him [It—Allāh]. So one says: the Patient and the Very Grateful and the King and the Compeller [Almighty] are among the Names of God [Allāh]—Great and Glorious! But one does not say: Allāh is among the Names of the Very Grateful and the Patient. For that [Allāh], inasmuch as it is more indicative of the Essence of the divine meanings and more peculiar to them, is [p. 65] better known [more celebrated, renowned] and more manifest [distinct]; hence there is no need to define it by something else, but others are defined in relation to it.

99 *Remark* [*tanbīh:* admonition, counsel, alerting]: The creature's [man's] portion [lot, share in] respecting this Name ought to be *al-ta'alluh* [becoming Godlike, deification, divinization, "putting on" God]. By this I mean that his heart and ardor [ambition] be wholly engaged by [immersed in, claimed completely by] God—Great and Glorious! He sees none but Him, attends to no other, hopes [in] and fears only Him. How could it be otherwise when it has been understood from this Name that He is the True, Real Existent [Being], and everything else is transient [ephemeral, evanescent] and perishing and null [nothing, worthless] except through Him. So man first of all sees himself as the first thing perishing and worthless, just as the Apostle of God—God's blessing and peace upon him!—saw himself when he said: "The truest verse uttered by the Arabs is the statement of Labid:

> Sorely everything except God is worthless,
> And every happiness [comfort] without doubt is fleeting."

100 2 and 3—*The Merciful, the Compassionate* [al-raḥmān, al-raḥīm]: two Names derived from "mercy" [*al-raḥma*]. Mercy requires [calls for] an object of mercy" [*marḥūm:* a "mercified"], and there is no such object save that it is needy [in need, in

want]. One because of whom the need of the needy is satisfied without any design [intent] and will [volition, desire] and concern [solicitude] for the needy is not called [named] "compassionate." And one who wishes to satisfy a needy man's need but does not satisfy it, if he be able to satisfy it, is not called "compassionate"; for if [his] wish were fulfilled, he would satisfy the need. But if he be powerless [to satisfy the need], he may be called "compassionate" with regard to the graciousness [sensitivity] which affects [influences] him, but it [he?] is imperfect [faulty, defective]. Perfect mercy [*al-raḥma al-tāmma*] is simply the pouring forth of good upon the needs and one's [God's?] will for them out of concern for them. And general [inclusive, all-embracing] mercy [*al-raḥma al-ᶜāmma*] is that which includes [encompasses] the deserving and the undeserving. The mercy of God—Great and Glorious!—is perfect and all-embracing. It is perfect in so far as He wills to fulfill the needs of the needy and [actually] fulfills them. It is all-embracing in so far as it comprehends the deserving and the undeserving, and embraces this life and the afterlife, and includes necessities and needs and the advantages [privileges] outside of them. So He is in truth the Absolute Merciful [*al-raḥīm al-muṭlaq*].

101 *Precision:* Mercy is not devoid of a painful empathy [sympathy, sensitiveness] which befalls [afflicts] the merciful [compassionate] and moves him to satisfy the need of the object of mercy. But the Lord—Praised and Exalted He!—is deemed far above that. So perhaps you will think that to be a defect [an imperfection] is the meaning [notion, concept] of mercy. Know, then, that that is a perfection and not an imperfection in the meaning of mercy. That it is not an imperfections [is clear] from the fact [standpoint] that the perfection of mercy is by the perfection of its fruit. So long as the need of the needy is fulfilled perfectly, the object of mercy has no share in the suffering and affliction of the merciful, but the suffering of the merciful is simply due to the weakness and imperfection of his soul. And its weakness adds nothing respecting the aim of the needy after his need is perfectly satisfied. And that it is a perfection in the meaning of mercy is that one who is compassionate out of sensitiveness [sympathy] and suffering, almost as good as intends by his action the removal of the pain of sympathy from himself [his soul] and will have had a regard for himself and will have exerted himself for a personal end—and that diminishes [detracts from] the perfection of the meaning of mercy. Rather the perfection of mercy is that his regard be for [be directed toward] the object of mercy for the latter's sake, not for the sake of finding ease [repose, rest] from the pain of sympathy.

102 *Note:* Al-Raḥmān is more specific [particularized] than Al-Raḥīm, and for that reason no one other than God—Great and Glorious!—is named by it, whereas al-raḥīm may be applied to other than God. So from this viewpoint it [Al-Raḥmān] is close to the Name of God Most High which functions like a proper name [i.e. Allāh], though this [Al Raḥmān] is certainly derived from *al-raḥma* [mercy]. For that reason God—Great and Glorious!—united [joined] the two of them and said: "Pray to [call upon] God [Allāh], or pray to the Merciful [al-Raḥmān]: Whichever you pray to, He has [possesses] the Fairest Names" [17.110]. From this aspect, and inasmuch as we have forbidden [barred, declared impossible] synonymity in the enumerated Names, it follows necessarily that one must distinguish between the meanings of the two Names. To be exact, the meaning of Al-Raḥmān is a kind of mercy beyond creatures' objects of power, and it [this mercy] is connected with the beatitude of the afterlife. So Al-Raḥmān is He Who is compassionate toward servants [men] [p. 67], first by creation [of them], and secondly by guidance to the Faith and the causes of happiness, and thirdly by making [them] happy in the afterlife, and fourth by granting [them] the favor of looking at [beholding] His gracious [noble, eminent, precious] Face.

103 *Remark:* The servant's [man's] portion of the Name Al-Raḥmān is that he be merciful to God's heedless servants and turn them from the way of heedlessness to God—Great and Glorious!—by admonition [preaching] and counsel, gently and not harshly, and that he look upon sinners [the disobedient] with the eye of mercy, not that of contempt, and that every sin taking place in the world be like his own personal sin so that he spares no effort to remove [do away with] it as far as he can out of mercy [compassion] for that sinner lest he be exposed to God's wrath and merit being far from God's presence [vicinity].

104 And his portion of the Name Al-Raḥīm is that he leave no want of a needy person without trying to satisfy it to the best of his ability, and abandon no poor person in his neighborhood and his town without undertaking to care for him and to drive away his need either by his own wealth [property], or by his repute [rank], or by striving for him through intercession with another. If he is unable to do all that, then he will help him by [private] prayer [*duᶜāʾ*], or by manifesting grief because of his need, out of compassion and sympathy for him, so that he is, as it were, a sharer of his in his hurt and his need.

105 *A question and its Answer:* [pp. 67–70; Paras. 105–10] Here Ghazālī
110 attacks the perennial problem of evil: How can God be Merciful and Compassionate and "the most merciful of the merciful" [7.150/151; 12.64 and 92; 21.83]? One who is merciful tries to remove every pain, etc. which he can. God can remove all suffering, sickness, pain, grief, etc.—yet this world is full [brim-full] of such things.

Ghazālī answers this objection at some length. Basically his answer is that God allows evil for the sake of the good that results—and every evil has in it a good. A fond mother tries to spare her child the ordeal of cupping [bleeding], but the good father has it done because it will really benefit the child. A diseased hand is amputated to save the whole body. God Himself said: "My mercy outstrips [takes precedence Over] My wrath" [cf. 9.15]. You may think of an evil in which there is no good, or that the good is possible without the evil. Your thinking is awry. No one can know such an evil: you are like the child who regards cupping as an unmitigated evil, or like a stupid person who does not realize that the just killing of a man, as punishment, promotes the general good. So also your thinking that the good is possible without the evil is faulty: this is a very abstruse matter incomprehensible to most men. So doubt not that God is truly "the most merciful of the merciful": herein there is a mystery which the Law forbids to be divulged: be content with prayer and seek not divulging.

You would have made heard had you called out to one living:
But the one you called out to has no life!

Such is the status of the majority. But you, my brother for whom this explanation is intended, are, I think, seeking insight into [are aware of ?] God's mystery concerning predestination [*al-qadar*] and have no need of these adulterations [coatings] and remarks.

111 4—*The King* [*al-malik*]: This is He Who, in His Essence and His Attributes, has no need [is independent] of every existent, while every existent has need of Him. Nay more, nothing is independent of Him in anything: not in its essence, nor in its attributes, nor in its existence, nor in its duration. Rather the existence of everything is from Him, or from what is from Him. So everything other than He belongs to Him in its essence and attributes, and He is independent of everything [has no need of anything]. This, then, is the King absolutely.

112 *Remark:* The servant [a man] cannot conceivably be an absolute king, for he is not independent of anything. For he always is in need of God Most High, even though he be independent of others. And it is inconceivable that everything have need of him: on the contrary, most existents are independent of him. But when it is conceivable that he is independent of some things and that some things are not independent of him, he has a "touch" ["dash"] of the King.

113 The king, among servants [men], is he who is possessed [ruled] only by God Most High, nay but he is independent of everything save God—Great and Glorious! Along with that he rules his kingdom in such fashion that in it his soldiers [troops] and subjects obey him. But his proper [special] kingdom is his heart and his soul [*qālab, qālib:* form, mold]. His soldiers are his appetite and his anger and his desire, and his subjects are his tongue, his two eyes, his two hands and all his other members [organs]. When he rules them, not they him, and they obey him, not he them, he indeed attains the rank of king in his world. And if there be joined to him his independence of all men, and all men need him in their present and future life, he is the king in the world of the earth.

114 [p. 71] That [just mentioned] is the rank of the Prophets—God's blessings on them all! For, regarding guidance to the afterlife, they are independent of everyone save God—Great and Glorious!—and every one needs them. In this sovereignty they are followed by the ulema [learned, "doctors"], who are the heirs of the Prophets [a Tradition: cf. Wensinck, *Handbook,* p. 234]; and their [ulema] sovereignty [kingship] is commensurate with their power to guide men and their own independence of seeking guidance.

115 By these attributes the servant [a man] approximates the Angels in their attributes, and by them he draws close to God Most High. This sovereignty [kingship] is a gift from the True King in Whose Kingship there is no "doubling" [*mathnawiyya:* reservation?; i.e. it is unique.] One of the "knowers" [Sufis] spoke the truth when one of the princes said to him: "Ask me your need [for what you need]." He replied: "Do you say this to me, when I have two servants who are your masters?" He said: "Who are they?" He replied: "Greed [covetousness] and passion [caprice, whim]: I have indeed mastered them, but they have mastered you; and I rule them, but they rule you." And someone said to one of the Shaykhs [Masters: of Sufism]: "Counsel me." He replied: "Be a king in this life [and] thou will be a king in the afterlife—i.e. cut off your need and your passion [appetite] from this life, for sovereignty [kingship] is in freedom and independence. [I now list the remaining Names of God, each followed by Stade's translation and that of Asín Palácios.]

5—al-Quddūs: The Most Holy One; Santísimo.

6—al-Salām: the Sound One; Salud.

7—al-Muʾmin: The Author of Safety and Security; Protector.

8—al-Muhaymin: The Protector and Guardian; Vigilante.

9—al-ʿAzīz: The Incomparable and Unparalleled One; Precioso.

10—al-Jabbār: The One Who Compels His Creatures to Do as He Wills; Enérgico.

11—al-Mutakabbir: The One Supreme in Pride and Greatness; Soberano.

12, 13, 14—al-Khāliq, al-Bāriʾ, al-Muṣawwir: The Creator, The Maker, The Fashioner; Inventor, Creador y Formador.

15—al-Ghaffār: The Very Forgiving One; Indulgente.

16—al-Qahhār: The Dominating One; Victorioso.

17—al-Wahhāb: The One Who Gives Freely, without Thoughts of Compensation; Donador.

18—al-Razzāq: The One Who Provides All Sustenance; Proveedor.
19—al-Fattāḥ: He Who Opens All Things; Revelador.
20—al-ᶜAlīm: The Omniscient One; Conocedor.
21, 22—al Qābiḍ al-Bāsiṭ: The One Who Withholds and Provides the Means of Subsistence as He Wills; Entristecedor y Consolador.
23, 24—al-Khāfiḍ al-Rāfiᶜ: The One who Abases the Unbeliever and Exalts the Believer; Humillador y Exaltador.
25, 26—al-Muᶜizz al-Mudhill: The One Who Raises to Honor and Abases; Ennoblecedor y Envilecedor.
27—al-Samīᶜ: The All-Hearing One; Oidor.
28—al-Baṣīr: The All-Seeing One; Vidente.
29—al-Ḥakam: The Arbiter; Providente.
30—al-ᶜAdl: The Just One; Justo.
31—al-Laṭīf: The Subtle One; Bondadoso.
32—al-Khabīr: The All-Cognizant One; Sagaz.
33—al-Ḥalīm: The Nonprecipitate and Forbearing One; Manso.
34—al-ᶜAẓīm: The Great One; Grande.
35—al-Ghafūr: The Most Forgiving One; Perdonador.
36—al-Shakūr: The One Who Expresses Thankfulness by Rewarding Bounteously; Agradecidor.
38—al-Kabīr: The Grand One; Magnifico.
39—al-Ḥafīz: The Preserver; Conservador.
40—al-Muqīt: He Who Is Cognizant and Capable of Providing His Creation with Everything It Needs; Alimentador.
41—al-Ḥasīb: He Who Satisfies the Needs of All Creation; Suficiente.
42—al-Jalīl: The Sublime One; Majestuoso.
43—al-Karīm: The Selflessly Generous One; Generoso.
44—al-Raqīb: The One Who Watches All; Guardián.
45—al-Mujīb: The One Who Responds to Every Need; Complaciente.
46—al-Wāsiᶜ: The One Whose Capacity Is Limitless; Inmenso.
47—al-Ḥakīm: The Ultimately Wise One; Sabio.
48—al-Wadūd: The Objectively Loving One; Amoroso.
49—al-Majīd: The Most Glorious One; Noble.
50—al-Bāᶜith: The Quickener; Resucitador.
51—al-Shahīd: The One Who Witnesses and Knows Everything Manifest; Testigo.
52—al-Ḥaqq: The Real One; Verdad.
53—al-Wakīl: The Ultimate and Faithful Trustee; Abogado.
54, 55—al-Qawī al-Matīn: The Perfectly Strong and Firm One; Fuerte y Robusto.
56—al-Walī: The Patron; Amigo.
57—al-Ḥamīd: The Ultimately Praiseworthy One; Alabado.
58—al-Muḥṣī: The Absolute Reckoner; Comprehendor.
59, 60—al-Mubdīᵓ al-Muᶜīd: The Originator and Restorer; Productor y Reproductor.
61, 62—al Muḥyī al-Mumīt: The One Responsible for Both Life and Death; Vivificador y Mortificador.
63—al-Ḥayy: The Absolutely Percipient One; Vivo.
64—al-Qayyūm: The Self-Subsisting One; Subsistente.
65—al-Wājid: He Who Has No Needs; Perfecto.

66—al-Mājid: The Glorified One; Ilustre.
67—al-Wāḥid [Stade: al-Aḥad; cf. Shehadi, p. 63, n. (5)]; He Who is Uniquely One; Uno.
68—al-Ṣamad: He to Whom One Turns in Every Exigency; Fin.
69, 70—al-Qādir al-Muqtadir: He Who Acts, Or Does Not Act, as He Pleases; Libre y Poderoso.
71, 72—al-Muqaddim wa l-Muʾakhkhir: The One Who Causes Men to Be Both Near to and Distant from Him; Aproximador y Alejador.
73, 74—al-Awwal al-Ākhir: He Who Is Both First and Last; Primero y Ultimo.
75, 76—al-Ẓāhir al-Bāṭin: The Manifest and Hidden One; Manifesto y Oculto.
77—al-Barr: The Dutiful One; Bueno.
78—al-Tawwāb: He Who Constantly Turns Man to Repentance; Clemente.
79—al-Muntaqim: The Avenger; Vengador.
80—al-^{c}Afw [^{c}Afū]: The One Who Erases Sin; Absolvedor.
81—al-Raʾūf: The Very Indulgent One; Benévolo.
82—Mālik al-Mulk: The One Who Has Perfect Power over His Kingdom; Emperador.
83—Dhū l-Jalāl wa l-ʾIkrām: The One Possessed of Majesty and Honour; Digno de gloria y honor.
84—al-Wālī: He Who Has Charge over All; Gobernador.
85—al-Muta^{c}ālī: The Highly Exalted One; Sublime.
86—al-Muqsiṭ: The Ultimately Equitable One; Juez equitativo.
87—al-Jāmi^{c}: He Who Combines All Things in the Universe to Accomplish His Purposes; Reunidor.
88, 89—al-Ghanī al-Mughnī: The Rich, the Enriching One; Rico y Enriquecedor.
90—al-Māni^{c}: He Who Repels Those Things Detrimental to His Creation; Defensor.
91, 92—al-Ḍārr al-Nāfi^{c}: He Who is Responsible for Both Good and Evil; Causa del bien y del mal.
93—al-Nūr: The Light; Luz.
94—al-Hādī: The Guide; Guía.
95—al-Badī^{c}: The Matchless, Unequaled One; Innovador.
96—al-Bāqī: The Everlasting One; Eterno.
97—al-Wārith: The Inheritor; Heredero.
98—al-Rashīd: The Absolutely Judicious Guide; Director.
99—al-Ṣabūr: He Who Times All Things Perfectly; Paciente.

A Conclusion to This Chapter and a Disclaimer [Plea, Excuse]

343 Know that what has prompted me to give these remarks [admonitions, counsels, comments] following these Names and Attributes is the declaration of the Apostle of God—God's blessings and peace upon him!—"Put on [clothe yourself with, don] the virtues [the excellent qualities] of God Most High," as well as his saying: "God has nine and ninety virtues: whosoever puts on one of them will surely enter the Garden [Heaven]." Certain sayings [words] passed by the Sufis from tongue to tongue hint at what we have mentioned, but in a manner which would suggest to the uninitiated something of the notion of indwelling [inhabitation] and identification [union]. But that is not to be thought of in the case of an intelligent person, to say nothing of those distinguished [characterized] by [gifted with] the prerogatives of mystical visions [insights].

344 I actually heard the Master Abū ᶜAlī al-Fārmadhī relate of his Master Abū l-Qāsim al-Kurkānī—God hallow his face!—that the latter said: "The nine and ninety Names become qualities of the servant who follows the path [of perfection, i.e. the Sufi] while he is still in the way and not yet arrived." This citation of his is true [correct] if by it Abū l-Qāsim meant something in accordance with what we have adduced—and nothing other than that is to be suspected of him. But the pronouncement smacks of figure and metaphor. For the meanings of the Names [the notions expressed by, or contained in, the Names] are the Attributes of God Most High—and His Attributes do not [cannot] become an attribute of another. Rather it means that one [the Sufi] acquires for himself something resembling those qualities, just as one says: So-and-so has acquired the knowledge of his master; but the actual knowledge of the master is not acquired by the disciple, but rather the like of the master's knowledge.

345 If anyone thinks that what is meant by it is not what we have mentioned, this is decidedly false. For I [would] say: The statement [claim, assertion] of one who declares that the meanings [notions] contained in the Names of God—Praised and Glorified He!—have become qualities of his admits of only two interpretations. Either he means by it those very Attributes themselves, or the like of them. If he means by it the like of them, then he must mean by it the like of them absolutely and in every respect, or he must mean by it the like of them regarding the name and the sharing in the general notion of the Attributes, but not in the intrinsic essences of the notions [contained in the Names]. These, then, are two divisions. Now if he means by them the very Attributes themselves, then it must come about either by way of the passage [transference] of the Attributes from the Lord to the creature, or not by such passage. If it be not by passage, then it must be either by the identification of the creature [servant, man, Sufi] with the essence of the Lord to the point [degree] that they are one and the same [identical] and His Attributes are his [creature's], or it must be by the way of indwelling [inhabitation]. And these are three divisions, viz, passage [transfer], identification, and indwelling.

346 So there are five divisions, of which one division is the correct one, viz, that the creature really possesses certain elements of the Attributes which resemble them in general and share the name with them, but they are not perfectly [totally, exactly] like them—as we have mentioned in the remarks.

347 As for *the second division,* viz. that the creature possesses the likes of the Attributes really and truly, it is impossible [absurd]. For in God's totality is that He possesses a comprehensive [all-embracing] knowledge of all the cognoscibles to the degree that "there does not escape Him an atom in the earth and in the heavens" [cf. 10.62/61], and a single [unique, individual] power which extends to all the created things to the point that He is truly the Creator "of the earth and the heavens and of what is between them" [a Qurᵓānic phrase—cf. e.g. 5.20—21/17/18], And how can this conceivably be true of anyone other than God Most High? How can a creature be the Creator of the heavens and the earth and of what is between them, when he himself belongs to the totality of what is between them—so how could he be the Creator of himself? Furthermore, if these Attributes were possessed by two creatures, each of them would be the Creator of his fellow so that each would be the Creator of him who had created him. All that is a farcical collection of absurdities!

348 As for *the third division,* viz. the transfer of the divine Attributes themselves, it is also impossible. For attributes cannot separate themselves from [quit] their subjects. This is not peculiar to the eternal Essence: it is even inconceivable that the very knowledge of Zayd be transferred to ᶜAmr; nay more, the only subsistence of attributes is in specific

subjects. [That is so] because the transfer would entail the emptiness of what suffered the transfer, and hence it would entail the stripping of the Essence from Which the divine Attributes would be transferred so that the later would be stripped of divinity and of its Attributes: that is also patently impossible.

349 As for *the fourth division,* viz. identification, that is even more patently false, because a speaker's assertion that the creature becomes the Lord is a statement which is self-contradictory, nay but the Lord— Praised and Glorious He!—must be deemed too holy to have the tongue utter in His regard such absurdities. We say unequivocally that a speaker's assertion that one thing becomes another is absolutely impossible. For we declare that, if Zayd be understood [conceived] alone, and ᶜAmr alone, then it be asserted that Zayd has become ᶜAmr and has become identified with him, then, at the identification, either both of them must be existent, or both of them must be nonexistent, or Zayd must be existent and ᶜAmr nonexistent, or vice versa: no division beyond the four is possible.

350 If both are existent, then the essence [substance, individuality] of one of the two has not become the essence of the other, but the essence of each one of the two is existent: at most only their locus is identical, and this does not entail identification; for knowledge and volition and power may be united in one and the same essence and their substrates not be distinct without power being knowledge or volition and without part having become identified with part.

351 And if both are nonexistent, then they have not become identified but have ceased to exist [have vanished, disappeared] and the incipient may be a third thing. And if one of the two is nonexistent and the other existent, then there is no identification, since the existent cannot be identified with the nonexistent.

352 Identification of two things is absolutely impossible. This is true of essences which resemble one another, to say nothing of those which differ. For it is impossible that this black become that black, just as it is impossible that this black become that white or that knowledge. And the dissimilarity between the creature and the Lord is greater than that between black and knowledge.

353 So the principle of identification is false. Whenever one speaks of identification [identification is predicated] and declares "This is identified with this," it can only be by way of the extension and allowance proper to the usage of the Sufis and the poets. For in order to make what is said more pleasing to minds they follow the way of metaphorical usage, as the poet says: "I am the one I love, and the one I love is I." That is the poet's interpretation, for he does not mean thereby that he is really the beloved, but it is as though he were, because his interest is as absorbed by the beloved as it is by himself; so he expresses that state by "identifitation" through [poetic] license.

354 In the same way one ought to interpret the utterance of Abū Yazīd [al-Bisṭāmi, d. 261/875]—God have mercy upon him!—when he said: "I sloughed off [shed] myself as the snake sloughs off [sheds] its skin: then I looked, and behold, I was He!" It means that whenever one casts off his soul's passions [desires] and love of them and concern with them there remains in him no room for other than God and no eagerness for other than God—Praised and Exalted He! If only God's majesty and beauty dwell in a heart so that it is absorbed in Him, it becomes as though it were He, but it is not He in reality. There is a difference between our saying "as though it were He" and our saying "it is He." But by our saying "it is He" can be expressed our saying "as though it were He," just as the poet sometimes says "As though I were whom I love," and sometimes "I am whom I love." This is a slippery place, for one whose foot is not firmly planted in rational matters may not dis-

cern for himself one from the other. Then he will look at the perfection of his own essence, once it has been adorned by what gleams in it of the finery [ornament] of the Truth [God], and will consequently think that he is He, and so he will say 'I am the Truth" [famous utterance of al-Ḥallāj, d. 309/922—cf. Annotated Bibliography under Massignon].

355 Such a man commits the same error as that of the Christians: when the latter see that [the finery of the Truth] in the Christ, Jesus— God's peace upon him!—they say: "He is the true God!" Even more it is the same as the error of a man who looks at a mirror in which is impressed [reflected] an image colored with his own coloration and thinks that that image is the image of the mirror and that that color is the color of the mirror. Not at all! Rather the mirror has no color in itself. Its function is to receive the images of colors in such fashion that it appears to superficial observers that that is the image of the mirror, so much so that when a child sees a man in the mirror he thinks that the man [really] is in the mirror. Similarly, the heart is in itself empty of images and forms. Its forms are simply the receiving of the meanings [abstractions, ideas, notions, "las esencias ideales," "intentiones"] of the forms and images and realities. So what subsists [dwells] in it is as though identified with it—not that it is *really* identified with it. If one unfamiliar with glass and wine were to see a glass. containing wine, he would not comprehend their distinction and would say at one time "There is no wine," and at another time "There is no glass," as the poet put it when he said:

Clear the glass and clear the wine
So they are alike and the matter unclear;
So it seems there is wine and no cup,
And it seems there is a cup and no wine.

356 The utterance of the one of them who said: "I am the Truth" either has the same meaning as that of the poet's declaration "I am whom I love, and he whom I love is I," or he indeed erred in that, as the Christians erred in their supposition of the identification [union] of the divinity with the humanity. Abū Yazīd's utterance—God have mercy on him!—if he really said it, "Glory to me! How great is my dignity!" either was uttered by him in the form of a quotation from God—Mighty and Glorious!—as, had he been heard to say "There is no God but I: so worship me!" [20.14], it would have been interpreted as a quotation, or he would have seen the perfection of his share of the Attribute of holiness, according to what we have reported regarding the ascension by knowledge above things imagined and sensed and by zeal above passions and pleasures, and so he announced the holiness of his own soul and said: "Glory to me!" and he would have seen the greatness of his dignity in comparison with that of the generality of creatures and said: "How great is my dignity!" knowing all the while that his holiness and greatness in dignity were in comparison with that of creatures and completely unproportioned to the holiness of the Lord—Exalted and All Holy!—and the greatness of His dignity.

357 And he may have uttered this phrase in his [mystical] intoxication and under the influence of his ecstatic rapture. For his return to sobriety and mental equilibrium would entail guarding his tongue from [such] suspect utterances, whereas the state of [mystical] intoxication may not suffer that. If you go beyond these two interpretations to "identification," that is decidedly impossible. One should not have such a high regard for the ranks of men as to believe in the impossible: rather men ought to be known by the truth, not the truth by men [ef. Para. 53 of my translation of the *Munqidh*].

358 As for *the fifth division,* viz. indwelling [inhabitation], it may conceivably [be affirmed in two ways]: that one affirms that the Lord— Blessed and Exalted!—dwells in [descends into] the creature, or that the creature dwells in [descends into] the Lord—Exalted the Lord of Lords above the claim of the unjust! Even if this were true, "identification" would not be entailed, nor that the creature be qualified by the Attributes of the Lord. For the attributes of the "indweller" do not become the attributes of the "dwelt in," but remain the attribute of the "indweller," as was the case [before the indwelling]. But just how indwelling is impossible can be understood only after the meaning [notion, concept] of indwelling is understood. For isolated [single, individual] meanings [notions], when they are not perceived by the process of simple apprehension [*al-taṣawwur*—concept, conception, representation], cannot understandably be denied and affirmed. So if one does not know the meaning of indwelling, whence can he know whether indwelling is existent or impossible?

359 We therefore say: Two things are understood by indwelling. *One of them* is the proportion [relationship] between a body and its locus in which it is—and that can be only between two bodies: hence that is impossible regarding what is free of the notion of corporeality. *The second* is the proportion [relationship] between an accident and a substance. For the subsistence of the accident is in the substance, and this may be expressed by [saying] that it indwells [inheres] in it—and that is impossible for what has its subsistence in itself. So make no mention of the Lord—Exalted and Blessed!—in this connection, for it is impossible for anything which has its subsistence in itself to indwell [inhere] in what has its subsistence in itself, save by way of the propinquity which occurs between bodies. Hence indwelling is inconceivable between two creatures [men, servants]—how, then, is it conceivable between the creature and the Lord?

360 If indwelling and transfer and identification and being qualified by the likes of the Attributes of God—Praised and Exalted He!—in a real way are [all] false, there remains for their assertion no meaning except what we have indicated in the remarks. That prohibits the categorical affirmation that the meanings of the Names of God Most High become descriptions [qualifications] of the creature, except by a kind of limitation [reservation] devoid of deception: otherwise the unrestricted use of this expression would be misleading.

361 *if you say:* What, then, is the meaning of his [Fārmadhī's] statement that the creature, despite his being qualified by all of that, is in the way and not yet arrived? What means "being in the way"? And what means arriving" [*al-wuṣūl:* attaining, reaching]? *Then know* that "being in the way" is the refining [polishing, burnishing] of moral qualities and of actions and of cognitions—and that is a preoccupation with the building of the exterior and the interior. In all that the creature is diverted by himself from his Lord—Praised and Exalted He!—being preoccupied with the purification of his interior that he may prepare himself for "arriving." And "arriving" is simply that there is disclosed to him the true state of the Truth. So if he considers his knowledge, he knows only God, and if he considers his ambition [aspiration, eager desire], he has no aspiration other than God. Thus he will be totally preoccupied with His totality [all of Him], in sight and desire [seeing and desiring], without attending in that to himself, so that he may build up his exterior by [acts of] worship, or his interior by moral cultivation. All that is "purity"—and this is the beginning. And the culmination [end] is simply that he slough off himself completely and strip himself [become stripped] for Him, so that he will, as it were, be He—and that is "arriving."

362 *If you say:* The words [expressions] of the Sufis are based on mystical visions revealed to them in the stage of friendship [with God]. But reason [man's intellect] fails to [is unable to] grasp that, whereas what you have mentioned is an exercise of the intellectual wares. *Know that* there cannot appear [be manifest] in the stage of friendship anything which reason judges to be impossible. To be sure, there can be manifest what reason fails [to grasp] in the sense that one cannot grasp it by reason alone. An example would be that there can be disclosed [revealed] to a friend [of God] that so-and-so will die tomorrow: and that cannot be perceived by the wares of reason—nay but reason is incapable of perceiving it. But it cannot be disclosed that God—Praised and Exalted He!—tomorrow will create the like of Himself, for reason declares that impossible, and it is not a case of reason's being unable [to grasp] it. More farfetched than this is that a man say: God—Great and Glorious!—will make me become Himself, i.e. I shall become He," because it means that I am an incipient and God—Exalted and Blessed!—will make me preeternal, and that I am not the Creator of the heavens and the two earths [upper and lower worlds ?], but God will make me the Creator of the heavens and the two earths.

363 This [latter statement] is the meaning of [Bisṭāmī's] utterance "I looked, and lo! I was He," if it be not interpreted. One who believes in the like of this has indeed been stripped of his native wit and finds indistinguishable what he knows and what he does not know. So let him believe that a "friend" [of God] may have it revealed to him that the Law [*al-Sharīʿa*] is untrue [false], and that, if it was true, God has changed it into untrue and has made all the utterances of the Prophet a lie. One who says it is impossible for the true to be changed into a lie says that simply through the use of reason's wares. For the changing of the true into a lie is not more unlikely than the changing of an incipient into [some thing] preeternal, and of a creature into [the] Lord. One who cannot distinguish between what reason declares impossible and what reason can attain is too contemptible [base, mean, vile] to be spoken to—so he should be left alone with his ignorance!

Chapter Two

Explanation of How These Many Names Come Back to [Are Reducible to] One Essence and Seven Attributes, according to the Doctrine of the Partisans of the Sunria [pp. 172–74]

Chapter Three

Explanation of How All That Is Reducible to One and the Same Essence according to the Doctrine of the Muʿtazilites and the Philosophers [pp. 175–77]

[p. 179]

SECTION THREE

On the Consequents and Complements It Contains Three Chapters

Chapter One

Explanation of the Fact That the Names of God Most High, with Respect to Positive Determination [al-tawqīf], Are Not Limited to Ninety-nine [pp. 181–83]

Chapter Two

Explanation of the Benefit of the Enumeration and Specification by [as] Ninety-nine
In This Chapter There Are Reflections [Considerations] on [Several] Matters: So Let Us Present It in the Form of Questions [pp. 184–91]

Chapter Three

Are the Names and Attributes Applied to [Predicated of] God—Great and Glorious!—Based on Positive Determination, or Are They Possible [Allowable] by Way of Reason? [pp. 192–96]

[End of the *Maqṣad*]

[p. 179]

APPENDIX V

Kitāb Sharḥ ᶜAjāʾib al-Qalb

THIS is the book referred to by Ghazālī in Para. 98 of my translation. There is a complete German translation of the book [cf. Annotated Bibliography]. I have used the Arabic text in the undated edition of Dār al-Maᶜrifa li l-Ṭibāᶜa wa l-Nashr, Beyrouth.

I consider this book to be one of the most important parts of the *Iḥyāʾ*, Ghazālī's chef d'oeuvre. To give a complete translation here would take up a disproportionate space. So I have contented myself with some selections, in themselves, I believe, very important. These include the first four sections of the book and the eighth section, the latter being, in many ways, the highlight of the whole book and a kind of peak in all the writings of Ghazālī.

I have often thought of attempting a complete and coherent English translation of the entire *Iḥyāʾ*. I fear, however, that my health and strength and years will not allow me to complete that most attractive enterprise. Here, at least, is a sample, and I hope the future will allow me to do more—*Allāh karīm!*

[*Introduction*]

In the Name of God Most Gracious and Beneficent!

1 Praise be to God! Hearts and minds are too baffled to grasp His glory. Eyes and looks are perplexed about the source of the radiance of His lights. He is perfectly aware of the innermost secret thoughts and what is concealed in consciences. In the governance of His realm He has no need of counselor or helper. He is the upsetter [converter] of hearts, the ready pardoner of misdeeds, the veiler of vices and the dispeller [or: comforter] of sorrows! And the abundance of God's blessings and peace be upon the chief of God's emissaries, the unifier of Religion, the eradicator of the godless, and upon the good and pure members of his household!

2 *Now then:* Man's title to honor and the excellence by which he excels most creatures is due to his predisposition for the knowledge of God—Praised be He! In this life this knowledge is man's beauty and perfection and glory; in the afterlife it will be his equipment and his treasure [stores]. Man is predisposed for this knowledge simply by reason of his heart, not because of any of his other members. It is the heart which knows God, which draws near to God, which strives for God, which speeds toward God and which discloses what is in and with God. The other members are simply subordinates and servants and instruments which the heart employs and uses as a master uses a slave and a shepherd uses his flock and a craftsman uses a tool.

3 It is the heart which is acceptable to God, if it be free from what is not God, and which is veiled from God when it is immersed in what is not God. It is the heart which is accountable and spoken to and censurable. It is the heart which is rendered happy by closeness to God and which prospers [thrives] when He chastens [praises ?] it and which is disappointed [frustrated] and distressed [wretched] when He disgraces [dishonors] it and seduces [corrupts: *dassā*]. It is the heart which really is the obeyer of God Most High: the acts of worship dispersed among the [other] members are simply its lights. And it is the heart which disobeys and rebels against God Most High: the vile deeds spreading in the organs are simply its effects [signs, marks, impressions, actions]. By its darkness and luminosity the good qualities and shortcomings of the exterior are made visible, for every vessel is moistened by what is in it.

4 The heart it is which, if a man knows it, he indeed knows himself, he indeed knows his Lord. It is also the heart which, if a man does not know it. he indeed knows not himself: and if he knows not himself, he indeed knows not his Lord—and one who knows not his heart is even more ignorant of other things. For most men know not their hearts and themselves, since their selves have been made inaccessible to them, because God intervenes between a man and his heart. His intervention is by preventing him from seeing it and attentively regarding it and knowing its attributes and the manner of its changeableness between two of the Merciful's fingers, and how at one time it may fall to "the lowest of the low" [95.5] and drop [be reduced] to the horizon of the devils, and how at another it may rise to the highest of the heights [cf. 83.18] and ascend to the world of the Angels closest to God. The man who knows not his heart, so that he may watch it attentively and supervise it and be on the watch for those treasures of the Kingdom which appear regarding it and in it, is one of those of whom God Most High has said: "(who) forgot God, and so He caused them to forget their souls; those—they are the ungodly" [59.19]. Knowledge of the heart and of the true meaning of its qualities is the root of religion and the foundation of the way of those who follow the path [*al-sālikīn*].

5 Since, in the first half of this book, we finished our study [consideration] of the acts of worship and the practices which take place in the members—and this is exterior knowledge [the science of the exterior]—and promised that we would explain in the second half the destructive and the saving qualities which take place in the heart—and this is interior knowledge [the science of the interior]—we must preface this with two books: a book explaining the marvels of the qualities and morals [habits, manners] of the heart, and a book on how to exercise [train] the heart and refine its morals. Then, after that, we shall plunge into a detailed presentation [study] of the things which lead to perdition and of those which lead to salvation.

6 Let us now relate, of the explanation of the marvels of hearts, following the method of giving examples, what can readily be understood—for the clear statement of the heart's marvels and secrets which belong to the totality of the world of the Kingdom is something most minds are too dull to grasp.

ELUCIDATION [EXPOSITION] ONE

The Meaning of al-Nafs, al-Rūḥ, al-Qalb, al-ᶜAql, and What Is Intended by These Names

7 Know that these four names are used in these chapters. Among the outstanding ulema there are few who fully understand these names and the difference of their meanings

and their definitions and the things designated [denominated] by them. The source of most errors is ignorance of the meaning of these names and of their being common to different designates. On the meaning of these names we shall explain what concerns our purpose.

8 The first word [term, expression] is *al-qalb.* It is an expression for two things. *One of them* is the flesh, pinelike in shape, lodged in the left side of the breast. It is special flesh and has within it a hollow [cavity]. In that cavity there is black [dark-colored] blood which is the source and origin of the *rūḥ.* But we do not now intend to explain its shape and quality, since that is the business of physicians and not the concern of religious aims. This *qalb* is found in beasts, and it is even found in a dead body. When we use the word *qalb* in this book we do not mean that. For that is a lump of flesh having no value. It belongs to the material and visible world, for beasts perceive it by the sense of sight, to say nothing of man.

9 *The second thing* [designated by *qalb*] is something subtle, divine and spiritual, which has a relation to this corporeal *qalb.* That subtle thing is the essence [true nature] of a man. In man it is what perceives, knows. is aware [cognizant], is spoken to, punished, blamed and responsible. It has a connection with the corporeal *qalb,* and the minds of most men have been baffled in [trying to] grasp the mode of the connection. For its connection with it resembles the connection of accidents with bodies and of qualities with the qualified, or the connection of the user of a tool with the tool, or the connection of something in a place with the place. Explaining that is something we are wary of for two reasons: one is that it is connected with the sciences [lore] of revelation [*al-mukāshafa*]—and our aim in this book is only the sciences [lore] of conduct [behavior—*al-muᶜāmala*]. The other is that verifying [pinpointing] it calls for divulging the secret [mystery] of the *rūḥ*—and that is something which was not discussed by the Apostle of God—God's blessings and peace be upon him!—so it is not for anyone else to discuss it. Our aim, when we use the word *qalb* in this book. is that we mean by it this subtle thing; and our purpose is to speak of its qualities and states, not of its real meaning [nature] in itself: the science of behavior [conduct] requires knowledge of its qualities and states, but it does not require speaking of its real nature [essence].

10 The second word is *al-rūḥ.* In what is related to the sort of aim we have this also is an expression for two things. One is a subtle body the source of which is the cavity of the corporeal heart. It then spreads, by means of the arteries, to the other parts of the body. Its coursing is in the body, and the emanation [flowing] of the lights of life and sensation and sight and hearing and smell from it to [into] the members resembles the emanation of light from a lamp which is rotated [moved in a circle] in the corners of a house. For it does not reach a part of the house but that the latter is illuminated [lit] by it. Life is comparable [analogous] to the light occurring on the walls, and the *rūḥ* is analogous to the lamp. And the diffusion and movement of the *rūḥ* in the interior is analogous to the movement of the lamp in the parts of the house in virtue of the moving action of its mover. When physicians used the word *rūḥ* they mean thereby this sense. It is a subtle vapor brought to maturity by the heat of the heart. But explaining it is not a part of our purpose, since it is the concern of physicians who treat bodies. But the aim of religious physicians who treat the heart so that it may be driven [carried, given over] to the proximity of the Lord of the Worlds has no connection at all with the explanation of *this rūḥ.*

11 The second thing [designated by *rūḥ*] is the subtle thing in man which is knowing and perceptive. It is what we explained about one of the meanings of *qalb.* It is also what God Most High meant by His utterance: "Say: The Spirit is of the bidding [Blachère:

l'Ordre; the Command] of my Lord" [17.87/85]. This is a marvelous divine bidding [command] of which most minds and understandings are unable to grasp the real meaning.

12 The third word is *al-nafs.* This also is common to several things, two of which have to do with our purpose. One of them is that it means the thing [*maᶜnan*] which unites the irascible and concupiscible power in man, as will be explained. This usage is that which prevails among the Sufis. For they mean by *nafs* the principle [*aṣl*] which unites [links] the reprehensible qualities of a man. They affirm: One must strive [fight] against the *nafs* and break [shatter] it. To this is the allusion in the Prophet's utterance—Peace be upon him!—"Your worst enemy is your *nafs* which is between your two sides." The second thing [designated by *nafs*] is the subtle thing which we have spoken of and which in reality is the man. It is man's soul and self [*dhāt*]. But it is characterized by different qualities according to the difference of its states. When it is tranquil under the command [it is in tranquil subjection to God's command ?] and free from agitation because of the opposition of the passions, it is called 'the soul at peace" [serene, tranquil, quiet, at ease]. God Most High said of its like: "O soul at peace, return to thy Lord, well pleased, well pleasing!" [89.27–28]. But the *nafs* in the first sense cannot conceivably return to God Most High. since it is far removed [banished, exiled] from God and belongs to the party of Satan.

13 If it is not perfectly tranquil, but gets involved in resisting and opposing the concupiscible *nafs,* it is called "the reproachful soul" [Blachère: qui sans trêve censure; and cf. his note; censorious], because it reproaches its possessor when he falls short in the worship [service] of his Master. God Most High said: "No! I swear by the reproachful soul" [75.2]. But if it leaves off opposing and yields and submits to the exigency [demand] of the passions and the requirements of Satan, it is called "the soul inciting to evil." God Most High said, reporting of Joseph—Peace be upon him!—or of the wife of the Governor: "Yet I claim not that my soul was innocent—surely the soul of man incites to evil" [12.53]. It also may be said that the meaning of "inciting to evil" is the *nafs* in the first sense. Hence the soul in the first sense is most severely to be reprehended, but in the second sense it is praiseworthy because it is the *nafs* of man, i.e. his self and his real nature which knows God Most High and [all] the other knowables [cognoscibles].

14 The fourth word is *al-ᶜaql.* This also is a common expression for different things which we have mentioned in the Book of Knowledge [Book I of the *Iḥyāʾ*]. Two of all these things have to do with our purpose. One of them is that it may be used to mean knowledge of the true natures of things, thus being a term for the quality of the knowledge which resides in the *qalb.* The second is that it may be used to mean that which perceives [grasps] cognitions [*al-ᶜulūm*], thus being the *qalb,* viz. that subtle thing. We know that every knower has in himself an existence [a being: *wujūd*] which is a principle [*aṣl*] subsisting in itself, and knowledge is a quality residing in it—and the quality is distinct from the qualified. *Al-ᶜaql* may be used to mean the quality of the knower, and it may be used to mean the locus [*maḥall:* substrate] of the perception, i.e. the perceiver. This is the meaning of his [Muḥammad's] statement—God's blessing and peace be upon him!—"The first thing created by God was *al-ᶜaql.*" For knowledge is an accident which cannot conceivably have been the first thing created. On the contrary, the locus must have been created before it or with it. Also, because one cannot address it [knowledge]—and in the Tradition [we have] "The Most High said to it: Approach, and it approached, then He said to it: Turn back, and it turned back . . . the Tradition" [Cf. Fans, *The Book of Knowledge,* p. 222].

15 Hence it has been disclosed to you that the meanings of these names exist: viz. the corporeal *qalb,* and the corporeal *rūḥ,* and the concupiscible soul [*nafs*], and knowledges [*al-ᶜulūm*]. These are four meanings to which the four words are applied. And there is a fifth meaning, viz. the subtle thing belonging to man which knows and perceives. All four of the words apply in turn to it. So the meanings are five and the words four, each of them used to express two things. But for most ulema the difference and application of these words are obscure. Hence you see them discussing ideas [*khawāṭir:* thoughts] and saying: This is the idea of the *ᶜaql,* and this is the idea of the *rūḥ,* and this is the idea of the *qalb,* and this is the idea of the *nafs.* But the one considering does not know the difference of the meaning of these names. So to remove the veil from that, we have first presented the explanation of these names. Where the word *qalb* occurs in the Qurᵓān and the Sunna it means the thing in man which understands and knows the meaning [nature] of things. It may be alluded [referred] to by the *qalb* which is in the breast, because between that subtle thing and the body of the *qalb* there is a special connection. For even though that subtle thing is connected with the rest of the body and uses it. yet it is connected with it by means of the *qalb.* So its first connection is with the *qalb,* which, as it were, is its locus and its kingdom and its world and its mount [riding animal]. For that reason Sahl al-Tustarī likened the heart [*qalb*] to a throne and the breast to a chair [seat]. He said "The *qalb* is the throne and the breast is the seat." But let it not be thought that he considered it to be the Throne of God and His Seat—for that is impossible [absurd]. Rather he meant thereby that it is the kingdom of man and the first [primary] channel of his governance and conduct. So the two of them in relation to man are like the Throne and the Seat in relation to God Most High. Also, this likening [analogy] is correct only from certain aspects; but the explanation of that also is not consonant with our purpose, and therefore let us pass over it.

ELUCIDATION [EXPOSITION] TWO

The Soldiers of the Heart

16 God Most High has said: "None knows the hosts of thy Lord but He" [74.34/31]. So God—Praised be He!—has, in hearts and spirits and other worlds [creatures] enlisted [recruited, mobilized] soldiers the real nature and detailed number of which nobody knows but He. We shall now indicate some of the soldiers of the heart, for this has to do with our purpose.

17 The heart has two sorts of soldiers [*junūd:* troops, hosts, armies, minions, myrmidons], one seen by the eyes, and one seen only by the inner eyes. The heart is like a king, and the soldiers are like servants and helpers—this is the meaning of "soldiers." The heart's soldiers visible to the eye are hand, foot, eye, ear, tongue and the other organs, exterior and interior. For they all serve the heart and are subject to it, while it has them at its disposal and [frequently] has recourse to them. They were created with a natural disposition [propensity] for obeying the heart and cannot oppose or disobey it. When it commands the eye to open, it opens; when it commands the foot to move, it moves; when it commands the tongue to speak, and is firmly decided on it, it speaks—and so of all the other organs. The subjection of the organs and senses to the heart resembles in a way the subjection of the Angels to God Most High. For they have a natural disposition for obedience and cannot oppose God, nay more they cannot resist God whatever He commands

them, but they do what they are commanded. They [organs and Angels] differ in only one thing. This is that the Angels—Peace be upon them! know their obedience and their compliance [submission], whereas the eyelids obey the heart in opening and shutting by way of subjection without having any information [intelligence ?] about themselves and their obedience to the heart.

18 The heart needs these soldiers simply because of its need for a mount and provisions for its journey for which it was created, viz. the journey to God—Praised be He!—and traversing the way stations to the meeting with Him: and for this hearts have been created. God Most High has said: "I have not created jinn and mankind except to serve Me" [51.5ff]. The heart's mount is simply the body and its provisions knowledge. The causes [means] which bring it to the provisions and enable it to supply itself with them are right [virtuous] action. The servant [creature] cannot arrive at God—Praised be He!—so long as he does not dwell in the body and does not leave behind this life [world]. For the lowest [nearest] way station must be traversed to arrive at the furthest [most distant] way station. This life [world] is the plantation of the afterlife [a Tradition from Muḥammad], and it is one of the way stations of guidance. It is called *dunyā* because it is the closer [*adnā*] of the two grades [*manzilatayn:* way stations, dwellings ?]. So the heart is compelled to find provisions in this world. And the body is its mount with which it arrived in this world. Hence the heart must care for and maintain the body; and it maintains the body simply by getting for it suitable nourishment and other things, and by repelling from it the destructive things incompatible with it.

19 In order to get nourishment for the body the heart needs two soldiers, one interior, i.e. appetite [desire, passion], and the other exterior, i.e. the hand and the organs which fetch the nourishment. So in the heart are created the appetites [desires] which it needs, and there are created the organs which are the tools [instruments] of the appetites. In order to repel destructive things two soldiers are needed. One is interior, i.e. anger [irascibility], by which it repels destructive things and takes revenge upon enemies. The other is exterior, i.e. the band and foot by which it effects what anger demands. All that has to do with external matters. So the members are to the body like weapons, etc. Furthermore, so long as one who needs nourishment does not know the nourishment, the appetite and fondness for nourishment will be of no use to him. So he needs, for such knowledge, two [types of] soldiers. One is interior, viz. the perception of hearing and sight and smelling and touching and tasting. The other is exterior, viz. eye and ear and nose, et al. Detailed discussion of the need for these and how there is wisdom in them would be lengthy and many tomes would not contain it. We have indicated a bit of it in the "Book of Gratitude" [Bk. II of Fourth Quarter of *Iḥyāᵓ*]—so be content with that.

20 So all the soldiers of the heart are confined to three sorts. One sort is instigating and inciting [urging], either to getting the useful and suitable, like appetite [desire], or to repelling the harmful and incompatible, like anger [irascibility]. The instigating sort may be designated by *al-irāda* [the will]. The second sort is what moves the members to acquire these aims. It is designated by *al-qudra* [power], and includes soldiers scattered about in all the members, especially the muscles and tendons [sinews]. The third sort is the perceptive which gets to know [uncovers] things like spies. These are the power [faculty] of seeing and hearing and smelling and tasting and touching which are scattered about in specific members. This sort is designated by *al-ᶜilm wa l-idrāk* [knowledge and perception]. Along with each of these interior soldiers there are exterior soldiers, viz. the members made up of fat and flesh and nerves and blood and hones,

which are prepared as tools of these soldiers. For the power of snatching [Or: striking] is simply by the fingers, and that of sight by the eye, and so for the other powers [faculties]. We shall not discuss the exterior soldiers, I mean the members, because they belong to the material and visible world, but we shall now discuss only the invisible soldiers that support them.

21 This third sort, i.e. what is perceptive in this totality, is divided into what is lodged in exterior positions—viz. the five senses, i.e. hearing, sight, smell, taste, and touch—and what is lodged in interior positions, viz. the cavities of the brain. These are also five. For after seeing a thing a man shuts his eye and perceives its image [form: *ṣūra*] in himself: this is the imagination [*al-khayāl*]. Then that image stays with the man by reason of something which preserves it: this is the preserving [conserving, memory] soldier. Then the man reflects on what he remembers and joins part of it to another part, then recalls and returns to what he has forgotten, then unites a group of concepts of sensibles in his imagination by means of a sense [perception ?] common to the sensibles. So in [man's] interior there is a common sense ["sensus communis"], and the imagination, and thought [reflection], and recalling [remembrance], and preservation [memory]. Had not God created the power of preservation and reflection and recall and imagination, the brain would be devoid of this just as the hand and the foot are. These powers are also interior soldiers and their places are also interior. These are the divisions of the soldiers of the heart. To explain that by using examples so that weak minds would grasp it would be lengthy. The aim of such a book as this is that it be helpful to the strong and outstanding ulema. However we shall endeavor to make the weak understand by means of giving examples so that it may be close to [accessible to] their understandings [minds].

ELUCIDATION [EXPOSITION] THREE

Examples of the Heart's [*Relation to*] *Its Interior Soldiers*

22 Know that the soldiers of anger [irascibility] and appetite [concupiscence] may be entirely submissive to the heart. That would help it on its path which it is following, and their companionship on the journey which occupies it would be a good thing. But they may also oppose it wilfully and recalcitrantly to the point of dominating and enslaving it: in this lies its perdition and its being cut off from its journey on which depends its attainment of eternal happiness.

23 But the heart has other soldiers: knowledge and wisdom and thought [reflection], as will be explained. And it has the right [duty] to appeal for aid to this [kind of soldier], for the latter is of God Most High's party against the other two soldiers [anger and desire]—because they may be affiliated with the party of Satan. If the heart omits the appeal for aid and empowers over itself the soldiers of anger and desire [appetite] it will surely perish and will incur a most evident loss. That is the state of most men, for their intellects have become subject to their appetites in seeking out stratagems for satisfying appetite, whereas the appetite ought to be subject to their intellects regarding what reason requires. We shall bring this close to your understanding by means of three examples.

24 *The first example* is that we say: A man's soul in his body—by "soul" I mean the subtle thing already mentioned—is like a king in his city and his kingdom. For the body is the soul's kingdom, its world and residence [abode] and city. Its members and powers are in the position of craftsmen and workmen. Its intellectual, reflective power is like a

sincere counselor and a wise minister. Its appetite is like the lowly [vile] slave who brings food and supplies to the city. Its anger and violence [ardor] are for it like the chief of police.

25 The slave who brings provisions is very untruthful, cunning, deceptive and wicked [vicious] and represents himself in the guise of a sincere adviser, but underneath his advice there is appalling evil and lethal poison. His habit and wont is opposing the counselor-minister in his views and measures to such an extent that there is not an hour free from his opposition and resistance. Just as the ruler in his kingdom, when, in his measures [plans], he invokes the aid of his minister, counsulting him and discarding the suggestion of his wicked slave, concluding from the latter's suggestion that the right [course of action] is the opposite of the slave's view, [and] his chief of police educates [refines ?] him and conducts him to his minister and makes [the latter] his counselor, and he on his part makes him master of this wicked slave and of his followers and helpers, so that the slave is ruled, not ruling, and commanded and managed, not a commander and manager,—[then] all is well in his country and because of that justice is in good order,

26 so also [going back to "Just as" of preceding Para.] the soul, when it seeks help from *al-ʿaql* [reason, intellect] and disciplines the ardor of anger [irascibility] and makes the latter master over appetite [concupiscence] and seeks the help of one against the other, at one time by reducing the degree and extravagance [excess] of anger by its opposition and promotion of appetite, and at another by curbing and subduing appetite by making anger and ardor its master and by censuring its demands, [then] the soul's powers [faculties] are in equilibrium and its morals are good. But he who turns from this path is like him of whom God Most High has said: "Hast thou seen him who has taken his caprice to be his god, and God has led him astray out of a knowledge" [45.22/23]. And the Most High has said: "and followed his lust. So the likeness of him is as the likeness of a dog; if thou attackest it, it lolls its tongue out, or if thou leavest it, it lolls its tongue out" [7.175/176]. And God—Mighty and Glorious!—has said of him who forbids the soul its caprice: "But as for him who feared the Station of his Lord and forbade the soul its caprice, surely Paradise shall be the refuge" [79.40/41]. How to battle these soldiers and to make one master another, will come in the Book of the Exercise [Askesis] of the Soul [the Book following this book], if God Most High wills,

27 *The second example:* Know that the body is like a city and the *ʿaql*—I mean what perceives—in man is like a king governing it, and man's perceptive faculties—such as the exterior and interior senses—are like the king's soldiers and helpers, and his members are like his subjects, and the soul inciting to evil, which is appetite and anger, is like an enemy who opposes the king in his kingdom and strives to ruin his subjects. So man's body is like a *ribāṭ* [caravansary] and *thaghr* [frontier post], and his soul is like one residing and stationed in it. If he battles his enemy and routs him and forces him to what he [the victor] wants, he is subsequently praised when he returns to the cultivated region as God Most High has said: "God has preferred in rank those who struggle with their possessions and their selves over the ones who sit at home" [4.97/95]. But if he loses his frontier post and neglects his subjects he will subsequently be blamed and vengeance will be exacted in his regard with God and on the Day of the Resurrection he will be told: "O wicked shepherd, you have eaten the flesh and drunk the milk and have not sheltered the stray [lost sheep] nor set [the bones of] the fractured: today I shall be revenged upon you—as has come down in the Tradition. To this battle is the allusion in his utterance—God's blessings and peace be upon him!—"We have come back from the Lesser *Jihād* [Holy War] to the Greater *Jihād.*"

28 *The third example:* The likeness of *al-ᶜaql* [reason, intelligence] is the likeness of a horseman hunting for prey. His desire is like his horse, and his anger is like his dog. When the horseman is skillful and his steed well trained and his dog disciplined and schooled, he is deserving of success. But when he is clumsy and his steed unruly and his dog mordacious, so that his steed does not hasten beneath him submissively nor is his dog easily obedient to his signal, then he deserves to be destroyed—to say nothing of his attaining what he seeks. The clumsiness of the horseman is like a man's ignorance and scanty wisdom and dim discernment, and the unruliness of the steed is like the domination of desire, especially desire related to the belly and to sexual pleasure, and the mordacity of the dog is like the dominion and mastery of anger—we ask God graciously to grant us good guidance!

ELUCIDATION [EXPOSITION] FOUR

The Special Quality of Man's Heart

29 Know that all we have spoken of has been bestowed by God on all the animals other than man. For animals also have desire and anger and the external and internal senses. Thus a sheep sees a wolf with its eye and knows its hostility by its *qalb* and flees from it: that is interior perception. But let us speak of what is peculiar to man's heart and because of which he has an immense dignity and is worthy of closeness to God Most High. This comes down to *knowledge* and *will.*

30 The *knowledge* is knowledge of worldly and other-worldly matters and of intellectual truths—for these are things beyond sensibles and the animals do not share with man in them. Nay more, the universal and necessary cognitions belong to the special qualities [properties] of the intellect. For a man judges that one and the same individual cannot conceivably be in two places at one time, and this is a judgment by him about every individual. But it is clear that he has sensibly perceived only some individuals. So his judgment about all individuals is superadded to what sense perceives. If you understand this regarding obvious and necessary knowledge, it is even more obvious in the case of speculative matters.

31 The *will:* when a man perceives intellectually the consequences of something and the advantageous way to deal with it, there springs from his essence [*dhāt*] a desire [*shawq*] for the advantageous aspect and for busying himself with its causes and willing it. This differs from the *irāda* [will, volition] of appetite [*al-shahwa*] and the *irāda* of animals and can even be contrary to appetite. For appetite has an aversion for bloodletting [venesection] and cupping, but the intellect [reason] wills it and seeks it and spends money freely for it. And appetite has a liking for sweet foods in time of illness, but the intelligent man is conscious in himself of a warner against them [something chiding away from them]—and that is not the warner of appetite. Had God created the intellect apprised of the consequences of things, and not created this spur [inciter] which moves the members according to the demand of the judgment of reason, the judgment of reason would truly be wasted [lost].

32 Man's heart, then, is specially characterized by a knowledge and a will not found in the other animals, and not even found in the child at the beginning of his natural constitution [*al-fiṭra:* original disposition], but it comes to be in him only after he reaches the age of reason [after puberty]. But appetite and anger and the external and internal senses

are present in the case of the child. Moreover, the child experiences *two stages* [phases, steps] in coming to have these cognitions in himself. *One is* that his heart comes to contain all the necessary and primary cognitions, such as the knowledge of the impossibility and the possibility of the things that are patently impossible and possible. But speculative cognitions about them are not present, but have become possible and close to possibility and occurrence. The child's state with reference to cognitions is like that of a writer who knows of writing only the inkwell and the pen and the detached letters, not the combined: such a person is near to writing, but has not yet reached it.

33 The *second stage* is that he come to have the cognitions acquired by experiences and thought [reflection] and that they be as though stored up in him. Then, when he wishes, he returns [refers] to them. His state is then that of one skilled in writing. For the latter is said to be a writer, even though he is not practicing writing by his power to do so. This is the ultimate stage of humanity [human-ness]. But in this stage there are innumerable degrees in which men differ by reason of plurality and paucity of cognoscibles, and nobility and baseness of cognoscibles and the way of acquiring them. For they are acquired by some hearts by a divine inspiration by way of direct revelation, and by some men by learning and acquisition; and they may come quickly, and may come slowly. At this level there is a difference in the positions [stations] of the ulema and the philosophers [wise: *ḥukamāᵓ*] and the Prophets and the Saints, and the degrees of progress in it are unlimited, since the cognoscibles of God—Praised be He!—are infinite. The ultimate rank is that of the Prophet to whom are revealed all, or most of, the truths without any acquisition or effort [trouble, pains], by a divine disclosure in the quickest time. By this happiness each man approaches God Most High in nearness in concept and meaning [truth] and quality, not in space and distance. And the stairs [steps] of these stages are the stations of those journeying to God Most High, and there is no counting of those stations.

34 Each wayfarer knows only his own station which he has reached in his journey: he knows it and knows what station is behind him. But he does not have an encompassing knowledge of the reality of what is before him. He may, however, believe in it with a faith in the unseen [invisible], just as we believe in prophecy and the Prophet and believe in his existence, but the reality of prophecy is known only by the Prophets; and just as the foetus [embryo] does not know the state of the infant, and the infant does not know the state of the one arrived at the use of reason, and the necessary cognitions that are opened to the latter, and the one arrived at the use of reason does not know the state of the [mature] reasoning one and what speculative cognitions the latter has acquired, so also the [mature] reasoner does not know what God has opened to His Saints and His Prophets of the privileges of His grace and His mercy. "Whatsoever mercy God opens to men, none can withhold" [35.2]. This mercy is freely given by virtue of goodness and generosity on the part of God Most High—Praised be He!—and is not withheld from anyone. But it appears only in hearts putting themselves in the way of the gusts of God Most High's mercy—as he said—God's blessing and peace be upon him!—"Your Lord, in the days of your lifetime, sends forth gusts of grace: do you then put yourselves in the way of them!" And "putting oneself in the way of them" is done by purifying the heart and cleansing it from the badness and turbidity resulting from blameworthy morals [habits], as will be explained.

35 To this goodness is the allusion in his statement—God's blessing and peace be upon him!"—"God descends every night to the lowest heaven and says: Is there a suppliant that I may answer his prayer?" also in his utterance—Blessing and peace upon him!—

citing his Lord—Mighty and glorious!—"The just have long yearned to meet Me, and I yearn even more intensely to meet them!"; and in the Most High's [reported] saying: "Whoso approaches Me a span [an inch ?], I approach him a cubit," All that is an indication that the lights of cognitions are not veiled from hearts because of any stinginess or withholding on the part of the Giver—Exalted He far above stinginess and holding back!—but they are veiled because of badness and turbidity and preoccupation on the part of hearts. For hearts are like vessels: so long as the latter are filled with water, air cannot enter them. So hearts preoccupied by anything else than God cannot be entered by the knowledge of God Most High's glory. To this is an allusion in his statement—God's blessing and peace be upon him!—"Were it not that the devils swarm about the hearts of the sons of Adam, they would look at [direct their attention to] the kingdom of heaven." From all this it is clear that the special quality of man is knowledge and wisdom.

36 The noblest kind of knowledge is the knowledge of God and His attributes and His acts. In this lies the perfection of man; and in its perfection is his happiness and his fitness for propinquity to the Presence of Glory and Perfection. The body is the soul's mount; the soul is the place of knowledge; and knowledge is the thing purposed by man and his special quality for the sake of which he is created. And just as the horse shares with the ass in the power to bear burdens but is specially distinguished from the ass by the property of attacking and retreating in battle and by beauty of form, and the horse is created for that special quality so that if the latter is obstructed [becomes inactive, is put out of action] in it, it descends to the low rank of the ass—so also man shares with the ass and the horse in some things and differs from them in others which are his special quality. And that special quality belongs to the qualities of the Angels who are brought close to the Lord of the Worlds. Man is in a rank between beasts and Angels. For man, in so far as he feeds and procreates, is a plant; and in so far as he senses and moves voluntarily, he is an animal; and with reference to his form and stature he is like a picture painted on a wall: but his special quality is simply the knowledge of the realities of things.

37 One who uses all his members and powers [faculties] by way of calling on their help for knowledge and action has become like the Angels. So he deserves to join [unite] with them and is worthy of being called "angel" and "divine"—as God Most High has reported of the female companions of Joseph in His utterance: "This is no mortal: he is no other but a noble angel" [12.31]. He who directs his ambition to pursuing bodily pleasures, eating as the cattle eat, has sunk to the low level of the beasts and become either simple like an ox, or greedy like a pig, or voracious like a dog or a cat, or malicious [rancorous] like a camel, or proud [haughty, overweening] like a leopard [tiger], or sly [artful] like a fox—or he combines all of that like a rebellious devil.

38 There is not one of the members or the senses but that its help can be invoked on the path leading to God Most High—and some of that will be explained in the "Book of Gratitude" [Book II of the Fourth Quarter]. One who so uses it will be victorious: but one who turns from that will incur loss and be frustrated. The sum of happiness in that is that man make the meeting with God Most High his goal, and the House of the afterlife his abode, and this life his inn [stopping place], and the body his mount, and the members his servants. And let it dwell—I mean that in a man which perceives—in a heart which is in the midst of its kingdom like a king, and it will make the imaginative power which is in the forefront of the brain act as its postmaster for the reports of the sensibles will be gathered with him. and it will make the conserving power which resides in the posterior part of the brain act as its treasurer, and it will make the tongue act as its interpreter, and it will

make the moving members act as its secretaries [scribes], and it will make the five senses act as its spies each one put in charge of the reports of one of the regions [areas]: the eye charged with the world of colors, and the hearing charged with the world of sounds, and smell with the world of odors, and so for the rest of them.

39 For they are entrusted with reports which they gather [collect] from these worlds and convey [channel] to the imaginative faculty which is like the postmaster. The post master hands them over to the treasurer, i.e. the conserving power. And the treasurer presents them to the king, and the king takes from them what he needs for the governance of his kingdom and completing his journey in which he is engaged and subduing his enemy by whom he is afflicted, and repelling the brigands who would cut off his journey. If he does that he will be successful, happy and grateful for the bounty [grace] of God; but if he neglects all this, or makes use of it, but in deference to his enemies, viz. appetite and anger and the other worldly pleasures, or in the building of his way rather than his way station [i.e. seeking performance in this life rather than passage]—for this life is his way which he must traverse, whereas his homeland and abode is the afterlife—he will be forsaken [disappointed], wretched, ungrateful for the bounty of God Most High, wasteful of the soldiers of God Most High, aiding the enemies of God, inciting to the forsaking of God's party, and he would merit loathing [hatred] and isolation [banishment] in the final destiny and the life to come—We take refuge with God from that!

40 Kaᶜb al-Aḥbār alluded to the example we have cited when he said: "I entered where ᶜĀᵓisha was—God be pleased with her!—and said: Man's eyes are a guide and his ears a quelling and his tongue an interpreter and his hands wings and his feet a post[ing] and his heart a king: and if the king is good, his soldiers are good. And ᶜĀᵓisha said 'So I have heard the Apostle of God—God's blessing and peace be upon him!—say.'" And ᶜAli—God be pleased with him!—said in proposing a likeness of hearts: "God Most High has in His earth vessels which are [men's] hearts: the dearest of them to the Most High is the tenderest [gentlest, most sensitive] and the serenest [purest] and the firmest [hardest]." Then he explained this and said: "The firmest of them in religion, and the serenest in certainty and the tenderest concerning the brethren." This is an allusion to the Most High's utterance: "hard against the unbelievers, merciful one to another" [48.29], and to the Most High's utterance "the likeness of His Light is as a niche wherein is a lamp" [24.35]—said Abū [Ubayy] ibn Kaᶜb—God be pleased with him!—It means: the likeness of the light of the believer and of his heart; and to the Most High's utterance: 'or they are as shadows upon a sea obscure" [24.40]—the likeness of the hypocrite's heart. Said Zayd ibn Aslam about the Most High's utterance: "in a guarded tablet" [85.22]: that is, the heart of the believer. And Sahl said: The likeness of the heart and breast is the likeness of the Throne and the Seat [Chair]. These are the likenesses of the heart.

ELUCIDATION [EXPOSITION] FIVE

Ensemble of the Qualities of the Heart and Examples of It

41 Know that man, in his constitution and structure [composition, makeup] takes [has] as companions four flaws [defects]. So there come together in him four kinds of qualities. These are: the feral [predatory], the beastly [animal], the diabolic [satanic], and the divine [lordly]. To the extent that he makes anger his master, he practices the acts of

beasts of prey, such as enmity and hatred and assailing people with blows and curses. And to the extent that appetite dominates him, he practices the acts of beasts, such as greediness and covetousness and lust et al. And to the extent that there is in his soul a divine *ᵓamr* [bidding, command]—as God Most High has said: "Say: The Spirit is of the bidding of my Lord" [17.87/85]—he claims for himself lordship [*al-rubūbiyya:* divinity] and loves mastery and superiority [the upper hand] and being favored and monopolizing [autocracy in] all matters and sole leadership and escape from the noose of servitude and lowliness and he desires familiarity with all sciences—nay but he claims for himself knowledge [*ᶜilm*] and gnosis [*maᶜrifa*] and the grasp [comprehension] of the real meanings [essences] of things: he rejoices when he is linked with learning and grieves when he is linked with ignorance. Comprehension of all truths and the appropriation by subjugation of all creatures are among the qualities of lordship [divinity]—and in man there is a desire for that. And inasmuch as man is distinguished, with regard to beasts, by discernment, but at the same time shares with them in anger and appetite, there results in him a devilishness [diabolicalness]. So he becomes evil [wicked], using [his] discernment to devise [contrive] varieties of evil and attaining [his] purpose by cunning [craftiness] and artifice [wile] and deception and manifests evil in the form of good: and these are the mores of [the] devils.

42 In every man there is a mixture of these four principles—I mean the divine and the diabolical and the feral and the beastly—and all that is collected in the heart, as though the total in a man's skin is a pig, a dog, a devil, a wise man. The pig is appetite: for a pig is not reproached because of its color or shape or form, but because of its greed and covetousness and avidity. The dog is anger: for the rapacious beast of prey and the mordacious dog are not dog and beast of prey because of form and color and shape, but rather the spirit [essence] of the meaning of "beast-of-prey-ness" is voracity and hostility [aggression] and mordacity—and in man's interior are the voracity and rage [fury] of the beast of prey and the greed and lust of the pig. So the pig invites by greed to the vile and the abominable, and the beast of prey by anger to injustice and wrongdoing. And the devil continually stirs up the desire of the pig and the anger of the beast of prey and seduces [tempts, goads] one by the other and presents to them in a favorable light that for which they have a natural propensity.

43 The wise one, which is the model of the intellect [reason] is charged with repelling the craftiness and cunning of the devil by revealing his deception through its piercing insight and radiant and clear light. It is also charged with breaking the greed of this pig by making the dog its master. For the vigor of appetite is broken by anger and the voracity of the dog is controlled by making the pig its master and rendering the dog subject under its mastership. If [the wise one] does that and is capable of it, the matter is in equilibrium and justice appears in the kingdom of the body and all proceeds on the straight path; but if he is unable to dominate them, they dominate and use him [as a servant] so that he is continually seeking out stratagems and carefully thinking [reflecting] in order to satiate the pig and please the dog, and he will always be in the service of dog and pig. [Ghazālī goes on to describe at length that such is the sorry lot of most men so long as most of their ardor concerns the belly and sexual pleasure and competing with enemies. Service of the pig and the dog lead to all sorts of vices; so also worship of the devil. But if all is under the sway of the divine quality, all goes well and it leads to all the virtues. He then likens the heart to a mirror surrounded by all these influences and describes their effect on it. . . .]

ELUCIDATION SIX

The Likeness of the Heart, Especially in Its Relationship to the Cognitions [Knowledges].

ELUCIDATION SEVEN

The State [Condition] of the Heart in Its Relationship to the Divisions of Knowledges [Cognitions], Rational [Intellectual] and Religious, Secular [Worldly] and Salvific [Otherworldly]

ELUCIDATION [EXPOSITION] EIGHT

Exposition of the Difference between Ilhām and Taᶜallum and the Difference between the Way [Method] of the Sufis in Discovering the Truth and That of the Reasoners

44 Know that the cognitions which are not necessary, but simply come to be in the heart in certain states [*al-aḥwāl*], differ in the way they come to be. At times they surprise the heart as though cast into it from where it knows not; and at times they are acquired by way of inference [argumentation, reasoning] and the process of learning [*al-taᶜallum*]. That which comes to be neither through acquisition nor the artifice [expedient] of proof, is called "inspiration" [*ilhām*]; and that which eventuates through inference is called "learning" [reflection, consideration, contemplation] and "intelligence" [reasoning, seeing].

45 The knowledge which suddenly falls into the heart with no artifice or learning process or effort on a man's part is divided into what a man does not know how and whence it came to be in him, and that of which he is simultaneously [concomitantly] aware of the cause from which he derived that knowledge, i.e. the Angel who cast it into his heart. The former is called an "inspiration" or a "puffing" [gusting] into the mind, and the latter is called a "revelation" and is peculiar to the Prophets. The former is peculiar to the Saints and the pure, whereas what precedes it—i.e. what is acquired through inference—is peculiar to the savants [learned].

46 What can truly be said of it [*ilhām*] is that the heart is predisposed for the disclosure in it of the Supreme Reality [Truth] present in all things. Interposition between It and them is due simply to one of the five causes previously mentioned [in Elucidation Six: (1) defect in the heart, e.g. an infant; (2) the tarnish of sins and the rust of the passions; (3) all that distracts from the quest for the Truth; (4) prejudices; (5) ignorance of where the sought is to be found]. These are like a veil lowered and interposing between the mirror of the heart and the Preserved Tablet on which is engraven all that God has decreed until the Day of the Resurrection. The irradiation of the realities of cognitions from the mirror of the Tablet into the mirror of the heart resembles the impressson of an image from one mirror on another facing it.

47 The veil between the two mirrors is removed sometimes by hand and at other times it goes away because of the blowing of winds which move it. Thus the winds of [divine] graces [favors] may blow and the veils are raised from the eyes of hearts and there is disclosed in them some of what is written on the Guarded Tablet. That sometimes occurs during sleep and what will be in the future is known. The complete lifting of the

veil takes place at death when by it the covering is lifted. But it may also be lifted during wakefulness to the point that the veil is removed by a hidden grace from God Most High and there shines in hearts from behind the curtain of the invisible some of the wonders of knowledge, at times like the swift lightning, and again with a limited sequence, but its abiding is extremely rare.

48 So inspiration does not differ from acquisition in the knowledge itself, or in its place [substrate] or in its cause. But it does differ from it from the standpoint of the withdrawal of the veil, for that is not by a man's choice. Nor does revelation differ from inspiration in any of that, but rather in the seeing of the Angel who conveys the knowledge. For the knowledge comes to be in our hearts through mediation of the Angels: to this is the allusion in God Most High's utterance: "It has not been given to a man that God speak to him save by [direct] revelation or from behind a veil or by His sending a messenger who, by His leave, reveals what He wills" [42.50–51].

49 Now that you are acquainted with this, know that the preference of the men of *taṣawwuf* [the Sūfīs] is for inspirational rather than for instructional ["learning-process"] cognitions. Hence they are not intent on the study of a science and the acquisition of what authors have written and the investigation of the teachings and proofs set forth. Rather they affirm that the [right] way is to give preference to spiritual combat and eradicating blameworthy qualities and cuttting off all attachments [to creatures] and applying oneself with the utmost ardor to God Most High. Whenever that eventuates, it is God Who takes care and charge of His servant's heart by enlightening it with the lights of knowledge. And when God takes charge of the heart's affairs His mercy floods it and His light shines in it and man's heart is dilated and there is disclosed to him the mystery of the Kingdom and there is lifted from the face of his heart by the favor of the [divine] mercy the veil concealing God's glory and there gleams in it the realities of the divine things. The only requirement for man is to dispose himself by simple purification and to furnish ardor along with a sincere will and total yearning and continual lying in wait for the mercy which God Most High will open to him.

50 To the Prophets and the Saints the matter was disclosed and light poured forth into their hearts, not by study and the writing of books, but by abstinence in worldly things and freeing themselves from attach ments to them and emptying their hearts of preoccupations and devoting themselves most ardently to God Most High. He who belongs to God, God belongs to him.

51 They claim that the way to that is first of all the entire cutting off of worldly attachments and emptying the heart of them, and the sundering of the concern for family and property and offspring and fatherland and learning and power and fame; much more bringing one's heart to a state in which it is indifferent to the existence and nonexistence of everything. Then one retires alone with himself to some nook [cell ?] and confines himself to the religious duties and offices [rituals; or supererogatory exercises of piety]. He sits with heart empty and attention concentrated, his reflection not dispersed by any recital of the Qurᵓān or any exegetic consideration or any book of Tradition or anything else. Rather he exerts himself that nothing may occur to his mind save God Most High.

52 And after he sits down in seclusion he unceasingly says with his tongue "Allāh, Allāh" without interruption concomitantly with the presence of his heart until he finally reaches a state in which he gives up moving his tongue and sees the word as though it were flowing on his tongue. Then he patiently endures it until its trace disappears from his tongue and he finds his heart steadily applied to remembrance [of God—*al-dhikr*].

Then he perseveres in this until there is effaced from his heart the image and letters of the expression and the form of the word, and the meaning of the word remains bare in his heart, present in it as though cleaving to it and not parting from it.

53 He has a freedom of choice until he reaches this terminus and a freedom to seek to prolong this state by repelling the whisperings [of Satan], but he has no freedom in seeking to attract the mercy of God Most High. Rather, by what he does he becomes exposed [open] to the gusts of God's mercy and it remains for him only to await the mercy which God will open to him as He opened it to the Prophets and Saints by this way.

54 At this point, if his will is sincere and his intention [ardor] pure and his perseverance proper [good], and he is not pulled by his passions or distracted by inner concern with worldly attachments, the gleams of the Truth will shine in his heart. In its beginning it will be like the rapid lightning and will not remain. Then it will return and it may tarry. And if it returns, it may remain, and it may be snatched away. And if it remains, it may, or may not be, prolonged. And the likes of it may be manifested in close succession, and it may be limited to a single kind [specimen]. The abodes [way stations] of God Most High's Saints in it are innumerable just as the difference of their natural diposition and character cannot be reckoned. This way definitely comes down to sheer purification on your part and purgation and burnishing, then to readiness and waiting, nothing more.

55 The reasoners and those given to reflection do not deny the existence and possibility of this way and its leading to this end on rare occasions: for it is the most frequent of the states of the Prophets and the Saints. But they find this way rugged and its fruit slow to come and the union of its requirements unlikely. They allege that the effacement of attachments to such a degree is almost impossible and if on occasion it occurs its abiding is even more improbable. For the least temptation and fugitive thought disturb the heart—and the Apostle of God—God's blessing and peace be upon him!—said: "The believer's heart is more unstable than the pot in its boiling." He also said—[God's] best blessing and peace upon him!—"The believer's heart is between two of the Merciful's fingers."

56 And in the course of this spiritual combat [say the reasoners] one's temperament may be impaired [adversely affected] and his mind confused and his body may sicken. And if there has been no prior exercise and refining [training] of the soul by the realities of the sciences, there cling to the heart vicious [corrupt, idle] imaginings [phantasmi] with which the soul is at ease for a long period until life passes and is finished before one achieves success in such matters. How many a Sufi has followed this way, and then remained in the grip of a single imagining [phantasm] for twenty years; Had he indeed first mastered the sciences [become a master of knowledge] the dubious nature of that imagining would have been disclosed to him straightaway. Hence applying oneself to the way of learning is surer and closer to the goal.

57 They [the reasoners] also allege that the case of the Sufi is like that of the man who would refrain from learning the science of *fiqh* [jurisprudence] and allege "that the Prophet—God's blessing and peace be upon him!—did not learn that but became a *faqīh* [jurisprudent] by means of revelation and inspiration without repetition and notetaking. And I also may be brought to that by [spiritual] exercises and perseverance. Who thinks that [they say] wrongs himself and wastes his life; nay, he is like one who gives up the way of earning [his livelihood] and farming in the hope of lighting upon some treasure—that is possible, but extremely unlikely: so also is this. They also say: First of all one simply must acquire what the learned have acquired and understand what they have said; thereafter there will be no harm in waiting for what has nor been disclosed to all the learned, and it may be discovered thereafter by the spiritual combat.

ELUCIDATION NINE

Explanation of the Difference between the Two Positions [*Levels*] *by a Sensible Example* [*actually Ghazālī used two examples*]

ELUCIDATION TEN

Explanation of Revealed Texts Witnessing to the Soundness of the Sufis' Method in Acquiring Knowledge Not by the Learning Process and Not by the Accustomed Method [*Ghazālī also draws on stories*]

ELUCIDATION ELEVEN

Explanation of Satan's Overcoming the Heart by Means of wasāwis [*Temptations, Whisperings, Suggestions, Insinuations*] *and of the Meaning of "Temptation"* [*waswasa*] *and the Reason for Its Victory*

ELUCIDATION TWELVE

Detailed Explanation of Satan's Avenues [*Entrances*] *to the Heart*

ELUCIDATION THIRTEEN

Explanation of What the Servant Is Censured [*Blamed*] *for of Hearts' Temptations* [*wasāwis*] *and Solicitude and Thoughts and Intentions, and What It Is Forgiven and Is Not Censured For*

ELUCIDATION FOURTEEN

Explanation of Whether or Not It Is Conceivable That Temptations [*wasāwis*] *Be Entirely Cut Off during Remembrance* [*of God: al-dhikr; also the exercise so called. Ghazālī cites five opinions. At any rate one will never long be free of temptations*].

ELUCIDATION FIFTEEN

Explanation of the Rapidity of the Changing of Hearts, and the Division of Hearts Respecting Change and Stability

Annotated Bibliography

Note: This Bibliography is by no means exhaustive. It contains the books, mostly in English and French, which I think may be of some assistance to readers who may be inclined to seek further enlightenment about a very great man and his work. It also contains most of the works which I have found helpful. Not every item requires comment, and I have tried to be brief in most of my comments.

1. ABD-EL-JALIL, J.-M. *Autor de la Sincérité d'Al-Gazzālī.* Vol. I. pp. 57–72. Damascus: Mélanges Louis Massignon, 1956. An article containing a useful, and corrective, discussion of the following item.
2. AL-BAQARI, ᶜABD AL-DĀᵓIM. *Iᶜtirāfāt al-Ghazālī, aw kayfa ᶜarrakha al-Ghazālī nafsahu.* Cairo, 1943. Very critical of Ghazālī, and unjustly so, as the previous item points out.
3. ANAWATI, G. C., and GARDET, LOUIS [abhr. AGth]. *Introduction à la Théologie Musulmane. Essai de théologie comparée.* Paris: Librairie Philosophique, J. Vrin. 1948. An excellent general work with a strong Thomist bent. The item by Gardet listed below is the Second Part. A Third Part, by Père Anawati, has not yet appeared.
4. ANAWATI, G. C., and GARDET, Louis. *Mystique musulmane. Aspects et tendances, expériences et techniques.* Paris: Librairie Philosophique, J. Vrin, 1961. A fine work on Islamic mysticism [Sufism]. Excellent chapters on *dhikr,* and some translated texts.
5. ANAWATI, G. C. and LAUGIER DE BEAURECUEIL, SERGE. *La preuve de l'existence de Dieu chez Ghazālī.* In M.I.D.E.O. [Mélanges: Institut Dominicain d'Études Orientales du Caire], III (1959).
6. ARBERRY, ARTHUR JOHN. *Revelation and Reason in Islam.* London: George Allen and Unwin Ltd., 1957. The Forwood Lectures for 1956, Delivered in the University of Liverpool. Interesting remarks on Ghazālī, pp. 61–65, 108–11.
7. ———. *Sufism: An Account of the Mystics of Islam.* London, 1950. The best short account.
8. ———. *The Koran Interpreted.* London: George Allen and Unwin Ltd., 1955; New York: The Macmillan Company, 1967 (second printing). The best modern English translation of the book which is the heart and soul of Islam.
9. ARKOUN, MOHAMMED. *Essais sur la Pensée Islamique.* Paris: Éditions G.-P. Maisonneuve et Larose, 1973. Ch. VI—Révélation, Vérité et Histoire d'après l'oeuvre de Ġazālī, pp. 233–49. The new "sociological" approach with a lot of technical terminology.
10. ARNALDEZ, ROGER. *La Mystique Musulmane.* In *La Mystique et les Mystiques* (ed. Ravier, A., S.J.). Paris, 1965, pp. 571–646.

11. ASIN PALÁCIOS, MIGUEL. *Algazel, Dogmatica, moral y ascetica.* Zaragosa, 1901.
12. ———. *El justa medio en la creencia.* Madrid, 1929. A fine Spanish translation of Ghazālī's *al-Iqtiṣād fi l-Iᶜtiqād* by the great Spanish scholar.
13. ———. *La espiritualidad de Algazel y su sentido cristiano.* Madrid-Granada, 1934–1941. Four excellent volumes, with many texts.
14. BADAWĪ ᶜABD AL-RAḤMĀN. *Faḍāʾiḥ al-Bāṭiniyya.* Cairo, 1383/1964. A full edition. Cf. Appendix II.
15. BAGLEY, F. R. C. *Ghazālī's Book of Counsel for Kings.* London, 1964.
16. BAMMATE, HAIDAR. *Visages de l'Islam.* Paris: Payot Lausanne, 1958 (2d ed.; 1st ed. 1946). A brief, sympathetic account of Ghazālī, pp. 167–78.
17. BARBIER DE MEYNARD, M. C. [abbr. BM]. "Traduction nouvelle du traité de Ghazzali intitulée Le Préservatif de l'Erreur et notices sur las extases (des Soufis)." *Journal Asiatique,* VII Séria, Tome 9, Janvier 1877, pp. 5–93.
18. BAUER, HANS. *Islamische Ethik.* Four volumes, each a translation of a book of the *Iḥyāʾ*. Book II (1912), Book XII (1917), Book XIV (1912), Book XXXVII (1916) . Halle an der Saale.
19. BERCHER, LÉON. *L'obligation d'ordonner le bien et d'interdire le mal.* Tunis, 1961. Trans. of Book XIX of the *Iḥyāʾ*.
20. ———, and BOUSQUET, G. H. *La livre des bons usages en matière de mariage.* Paris, 1953. Trans. of Book XII of the *Iḥyā.*
21. BLACHÈRE, RÉGIS. *La Coran (al-Qor'ân).* Paris: G.-P. Maisonneuve—Max Besson Succr, 1957. In my opinion the best translation of the Qurʾān, with just the right amount of notes; in reading it one would do well to follow his chronological order of the Chapters. His *Introduction au Coran* is also very useful. Paris, 1959 (2e éd. partiellement refondue).
22. BOUSQUET, G. H. *Iḥyā' 'Ouloūm ed-Dīn ou Vivification des sciences de la foi. Analyse et Index.* Paris, 1955. A fine summary translation which will be very useful to anyone who desires a fairly detailed summary of Ghazālī's great work.
23. BOUYGES, MAURICE, S.J. *Essai de chronologie des oeuvres de al-Ghazali,* édité et mis à jour par Michel Allard, S.J. Beyrouth: Imprimerie Catholique, 1959. A very detailed effort to put Ghazalis work in chronological order.
24. CALVERLEY, EDWIN ELLIOTT. *Worship in Islam.* Being a translation with commentary of al-Ghazālī's Book of the *Iḥyāʾ* on the Worship. London, 1957 (Second Edition with corrections). A useful translation of Ghazālī's Book on the canonical Prayer.
25. CARRA DE VAUX, B. *Al-Ghazzālī.* Paris, 1902.
26. ———. *Al-Ghazzālī.* In *Penseurs de l'Islam,* t.IV, pp. 156–81. Paris, 1923.
27. ———. *Ghazzālī, le traité de la rénovatian des sciences religieuses.* Paris, 1891.
28. CHAHINE, OSMAN E. *L'Originalité créatrice de la philosophie musulmane.* Librairie d'Amérique et d'Orient. Paris: Adrien Maisonneuve, 1972. On Ghazālī, pp. 103–77: Theory of Knowledge, Notion of Certitude, the God of the *Tahāfut.*
29. CHELHOT, VICTOR, S.J. *al-Qisṭās al-Mustaqīm* (French translation and Introduction). Institut Français de Damas. *Bulletin d'Études Orientales,* Tome XV, Années 1955–1957, Damas, 1958.
30. ———. *al-Qisṭās al-Mustaqīm* (Arabic text and Introduction). I used Father Chelhot's books in my preparation of Appendix III.
31. CORBIN, HENRI. *Histoire de la philosaphie islamique.* Première partie. Des origines jusqu'à la mort d'Averroës (1198) avec la collaboration de Seyyad Hossein Nasr et

Osman Yahya. Paris: Gallimard, 1964. A lively work which emphasizes Iranian influences and the "prophetic" philosophy.

32. CRAGG, KENNETH. *The Event of the Qur'ān. Islam in Its Scripture.* London: George Allen and Unwin Ltd., 1971.

33. ———. *The Mind of the Qur'ān. Chapters in Reflection.* London: George Allen and Unwin Ltd., 1973. This and the preceding item form a splendid and very perceptive introduction to Islam and its great "Book" by a scholar who felicitously combines learning and spirituality.

34. AL-DAYLAMĪ, MUḤAMMAD IBN AL-ḤASAN. *Die Geheimlehre der Baṭiniten nach der Apologie-Dogmatik des Hauses Muhammad,* herausgegeben von R. Strothmann. *Bibliotheca Islamica,* Bd. II, Leipzig-Istanbul, 1939.

35. DUNYĀ, SULAYMĀN. *Fayṣal al-tafriqa bayn al-Islam wa 1-zandaqa.* Cairo, 1381/1961. Cf. Appendix I.

36. ECKMANN, KARL FRIEDRICH. *Die Wunder des Herzens.* Trans. of Book XXI of the *Iḥyā'*. Cf. Appendix V

37. *L'Élaboration de l'Islam.* Colloque de Strasbourg, June 1959. II. Francesco Gabrieli: *La "Zandaqa" au Ier siècle abbasside,* pp. 23–38. Paris: Presses Universitaires de France, 1961.

38. *Encyclopaedia of Islam* [abbr. EI(l) and EI(2)]. London-Leyden, 1934; Second Edition, London-Leyden, 1960–.

39. FAKHRY, MAJID. *A History of Islamic Philosophy.* New York and London: Columbia University Press, 1970. A readable and well-documented general account.

40. ———. *Islamic Occasionalism. And Its Critique by Averroes and Aquinas.* London: George Allen and Unwin Ltd., 1958.

41. FARIS, NABIH AMIN. *The Book of Knowledge.* Being a translation with notes of Kitāb al-ᶜIlm of al-Ghazālī's Iḥyā' ᶜUlūm al-Dīn [Book I of the *Iḥyā'*]. Lahore: Sh. Muhammad Ashraf, 1962 (Second revised edition, 1966).

42. ———. *The Foundations of the Articles of Faith.* Being a translation with notes of the Kitāb qawāᶜid al-aqā'id of al-Ghazzālī's Iḥyā' ᶜUlūm al-Dīn [Book II of the *Iḥyā'*]. Lahore, 1963.

43. ———. *The Mysteries of Almsgiving.* A translation from the Arabic with notes of the Kitāb Asrār al-Zakāh of al-Ghazzālī's Iḥyā' ᶜUlūm al-Dīn [Book V of the *Iḥyā'*]. Beirut: The American University of Beirut, 1966.

44. ———. *The Mysteries of Fasting.* Being a translation with notes of the Kitāb Asrār al-Ṣawm of al-Ghazzālī's Iḥyā' ᶜUlūm al-Dīn [Book VI of the *Iḥyā'*]. Lahore: Sh. Muhammad Ashraf, 1968.

45. ———. *The Mysteries of Purity.* English translation of the Kitāb Asrār al-Tahārah of al-Ghazzālī's Iḥyā' ᶜUlūm al-Dīn [Book III of the *Iḥyā'*]. Lahore: Sh. Muhammad Ashraf, 1966.

46. FIELD, CLAUDE. *Al-Ghazzali: The Alchemy of Happiness.* Translated from the Hindustani (Wisdom of the East Series). Lahore: Sh. Muhammad Ashraf, 1964 (repr. 1971).

47. ——— *The Confessions of Al-Ghazzali.* Translated for the first time into English [abbr. F] (Wisdom of the East Series). London, 1909. Lahore: Sh. Muhammad Ashraf, n.d. Omits section on the Bāṭinites.

48. FRICK, HEINRICH. *Ghazālī's Selbstbiographie: Ein Vergleich mit Augustins Konfessionen.* Leipzig, 1919. Comparisons are always insidious. I am somewhat prejudiced, but Augustine's is by far a greater book.

49. FURLANI, GIUSEPPE. "Dr. J. Obermann, Der philos. und religiöse Subjektivismus Ghazālīs" (Recensione). *Revista trimestrale di studi filosofici e religiosi,* vol. III, no. 3, pp. 340–53. Perugia, 1922. Cf. item by Obermann, below.
50. GAIRDNER, W. H. TEMPLE. *Al-Ghazzali's Mishkāt Al-Anwār ("The Niche for Lights").* A Translation with Introduction. Lahore: Sh. Muhammad Ashraf, 1952 [London, 1924, 1915].
51. GARDET, LOUIS. *Dieu et la destinée de l'homme.* Études Musulmanes IX. Paris: Librairie Philosophique, J. Vrin, 1967.
52. GHAZALI. *Al-Munqidh.* Ed. M. M. Jābir, Cairo, n.d. Ed. ᶜAbd al-Ḥalīm Maḥmūd, Cairo 1388/1968 (6th printing). Ed. J. Ṣalibā and K. ᶜAyyād, Beirut, 1967 (7th printing).
53. GIBB, H. A. R. *Mohammedanism. An Historical Survey.* OPUS 17 [Oxford Paperbacks University Series], Oxford, 1969. An excellent brief account by a fine scholar.
54. GOLDZIHER, IGNAZ. *Le dogme et la loi de l'Islam.* French trans. by Félix Arin of Goldziher's *Vorlesungen über den Islam,* Heidelberg, 1925 [1st ed. 1910]. Paris: Paul Geuthner, 1920 (Nouveau tirage, 1958).
55. ———. *Muhammedanische Studien.* Halle a.S., 1889–1890 (Neudruck, Hildesheim, 1961) English trans.: *Muslim Studies,* trans. by C. R. Barber and S. M. Stern. London: George Allen and Unwin Ltd., 1967 and 1971, 2 vols.
56. ———. *Streitschrift des Ġazdlf gegen die Bāṭinijja-Sekte.* Leiden: E. J. Brill, 1916.
57. GRUNEBAUM, GUSTAVE E. VON. *Medieval Islam.* Chicago, 1953.
58. HACHEM, HIKMAT. *Critère de l'Action.* A trans. of Ghazālī's *Mīzān al-ᶜAmal.* Paris: G.-P. Maisonneuve, 1945.
59. HOURANI, GEORGE F. "The Chronology of Ghazālī's Writings," in *Journal of the American Oriental Society* LXXIX (1959), 225–33.
60. JADAANE, FEHMI [abbn. Jadaane]. *L'Influence du Stoicisme sur la Pensée Musulmane.* Recherches: Tome XLI (Série 1: Pensée arabe et musulmane) Dar El-Machreq Éditeurs. Beyrouth: Imprimierie Catholique, 1968.
61. JABRE, C. M., FARID. *La biographie et l'oeuvre de Ghazālī reconsidérées à la lumière des Ṭabaqāt de Sobki,* in M.I.D.E.O. I (1954), 73–102.
62. ———. *Al-Munqidh min Aḍḍalāl (Erreur de Délivrance)* [abbr. J. (his translation) Ja (his Arabic text)]. *Collection Unesco d'Oeuvres Représentatives,* Série Arabe Commission Internationale pour la Traduction des Chefs-d'oeuvres. Beyrouth, 1959.
63. ———. *La notion de certitude selon Ghazālī dans ses origines psycholoqiques et historiques* [abbr. JC]. Paris, 1958.
64. ———. *La notion de la Ma'rifa chez Ghazālī* [abbr. JM]. Beyrouth, 1958. These two books by one of the best living Ghazālī scholars contain a great deal of useful information and discussion.
65. KAMALI, SABIH AHMAD. *Al-Ghazali's Tahāfut al-Falāsifah* [Incoherence of the Philosophers] [abbr. Kamali], Lahore: Pakistan Philosophical Congress, 1963, 2d. impr.; first published 1958. A fair translation of this work of Ghazālī.
66. FAZLUL KARIM, ALHAJ MAULANA. *Ghazali's Ihya Ulum-id-Din, or The Revival of Religious Learnings.* Dacca: F. K. Islam Mission, East Pakistan, 1971. Five volumes. An abridged translation from the Bengali in poor English.
67. LAMMENS, HENRI, S.J. *L'Islam: croyances et institutions.* Beyrouth: Imprimerie Catholique, 1943 (3rd ed. revue at augmentée) English trans. of the 1st ed.: *Islam,*

Beliefs and Institutions, by Sir E. D. Ross. London, 1920. One of the best short handbooks on Islam.

68. LAOUST, HENRI. *La politique de Ġazālī* (Bibliothèque d'Études Islamiques: tome premier). Paris: Paul Geuthner, 1970. A good background book.
69. ———. *Les schismes dans l'Islam. Introduction à une étude de la religion musulmane.* Paris: Payot, 1965.
70. LEEUWEN, A. TH. VAN. *Ghazālī als Apologeet van de Islam.* Leyden. 1947.
71. LEWIS, BERNARD. *The Assassins. A Radical Sect in Islam.* London: World University, Weidenfeld and Nicholson, 1970 (second impr. 1972). A very readable and reliable account.
72. MACDONALD, DUNCAN BLACK. *Development of Muslim Theology, Jurisprudence and Constitutional Theory.* New York: Charles Scribners Sons, 1903. A classic, somewhat outdated, but containing much interesting and useful material. Ch. IV of Part Thnee, pp. 215–42, is on Ghazālī.
73. ———. "Emotional Religion in Islam as affected by Music and Singing." Being a Translation of a Book of the *Iḥyā' ᶜUlūm ad-Dīn* of al-Ghazzālī with Analysis, Annotation and Appendices [Book XVIII of the *Iḥyā'*]. *Journal of the Royal Asiatic Society,* London, 1901–1902, pp. 195–252, 705–48, 1–28.
74. ———. "The Life of al-Ghazzālī, with Especial Reference to His Religious Experiences and Opinions." *Journal of the American Oriental Society* XX (1899), 71–132. An excellent article.
75. MAKDISI, GEORGE. "Ashᶜari and the Ashᶜarites in Islamic Religious History." *Studia Islamica* XVII (1962), 37–80; XVIII (1963), 19–39. A fundamental, groundbreaking article.
76. ———. "Muslim Institutions of Learning in Eleventh Century Baghdad." *Bulletin of the School of Oriental and African Studies* (BSOAS) XXII (1961), 1–56. Excellent background reading.
77. MCKANE, WILLIAM. *Al-Ghazālī's Book of Fear and Hope.* Book XXXIII of the *Iḥyā'*. Leiden, 1962.
78. MUBĀRAK, MUḤAMMAD ZAKĪ ᶜABD AL-SALĀM. *al-Akhlāq ᶜind al-Ghazālī.* Cairo, 1924 (?). A study of Ghazālī's Ethics.
79. MUCKLE, J. T., C.S.B., *Algazel's Metaphysics. A Mediaeval Translation* (Latin). Toronto: St. Michael's College, 1933.
80. MUNK, S. *Mélanges de philosophie juive et arabe.* Paris: Librairie Philosophique, J. Vrin, 1955 (nouvelle édition; orig. edition Paris, 1859).
81. NAKAMURA, KOJIRO. *Ghazali on Prayer.* Book IX of the *Iḥyā'* Tokyo, 1973.
82. NICHOLSON, REYNOLD A. *A Literary History of the Arabs.* London, 1907 (and reprinted since). A very readable and delightful classic.
83. ———. *The Mystics of Islam.* London: George Bell and Sons Ltd., 1914. Reprint, Chester Springs, Pa., 1962; Routledge and Kegan Paul Ltd., 1963, 1966, 1970, 1974; paper, 1975.
84. OBERMANN, J. *Der philosophische und religiöse Subjektivismus Ghazālīs. Ein Beitrag zum Problem der Religion.* Wien und Leipzig, 1921. Père Jabre (in the third item cited under his name), pp. 28–32, discusses this book at some length; and Wensinck (in item three under his name) refers to the "libre admirable d'Obermann qui étudie à fond la position théologique et philosophique du maître." Since this is probably the most serious, or at least weightiest, study we have of Ghazālī, I think it worthwhile to give the

reader excerpts from the reviews by (a) Wensinck and (b) by the celebrated Italian Orientalist Guiseppe Furlani, in *Rivista Trimestrale di Studi Filosofici e Religiosi,* vol. III (1922), no. 3, pp. 340–53 (cited above): (a) WENSINCK: In the introduction Obermann exposes the double aspect, philosophical and religious, of Ghazali's work, then gives an historical aperçu of Islamic thought up to Ghazali's time; finally be analyzes the very "development" of the master's personality. Obermann repeats the account of the doubts and their phases, and states that the more Ghazali seeks the truth, the more his confidence and personal conviction diminish. That meant that in Ghazali subjective certitude was inversely proportional to the mass of objective knowledge (cognitions) . Regarding religious knowledge in particular Ghazali perceives (discerns) that true religion is not an exterior belonging to Islam, as "objective" accomplishment of its precepts and teachings, but is "in the subjective purity and limpidity of the soul." (p. 20).

One is then engaged in the subjectivism of Ghazali under its double aspect, religious and philosophical.

(b) FURLANI: Fundamental motive of Ghazali's gnoseology is the doubt of the critic of knowledge, not that of the sceptic. Before all the question was *ḥaqīqat al-ᶜilm mā hiya?* [the essence of knowledge, what is it?], True Knowledge, *ᶜilm al-yaqīnī,* e.g. principle of contrast and of causality.

Of entirely different nature are metaphysics, doctrine of God's essence, of His attributes, of man's destiny, of the origin of the world—i.e., of all the questions which belong to the field of religious cognitions *(al-ᶜulūm al-dīniyya)*—in these there is great difference of opinion (not true knowledge).

Why this difference? Because their nature is different and the sources whence they come are different. True knowledge has its seat and origin in *ᶜaql* (intellect)—belief (Ital. *credenza*) in the *qalb* (heart). These are two different faculties and should remain different.

[Furlani then discusses Obermann's analysis of Ghazali's ideas in detail and sums up Obermann's study in this way:]

Ghazali is the apostle of *religiosità* and the enemy of religion exteriorized, systematized, organized in a church and that therefore became a *social religion.* He was always a convinced and faithful Muslim, but animated by a profound religious spirit: he fought strenuously against the two tendencies of Islam which in his time dominated all religious life: against the theologians, the *fuqahāʾ,* and against the mystics, the Sufis. The former had created Islamic law, and the latter had theologized feeling (ital.: *il sentimento).* . . . Neither of these two currents can satisfy our philosopher, who was in his time a theologian and a Sufi. The *faqīh,* too worldly and external, does not even touch the problem of religion, neither are the Sufis up to establishing the true science of religion (though Ghazali does not hide his sympathy for them and never definitely detached himself from them). He reproaches Sufis for not taking as basis of their doctrine the principles of human nature, but operating with vague and obscure concepts which are the fruits of states of mind and spiritual intonations which signify only the specific temperament of an individual. They do not occupy themselves with the religious life of others, are intent exclusively on their own salvation, and easily degenerate into "mysticism" and "mysterism."

These are the motives which led Ghazali to attempt a reform of religion, a vivification *(iḥyāʾ)* of the same—an interiorization—religion is not external but grounded in the very nature of man—man by nature is a religious being—specific organ of his *religiosità* is the *qalb* (not *nafs, ᶜaql)*—a kind of sixth sense constituting essence of man, his "*rabbānī*" part (lordly or sovereign, not "divinistisch" as Obermann says).

[Furlani concludes his review as follows:]

For Ghazālī the problem of religion is the problem of man: man is a being essentially religious. Hence his philosophy is subjective and "criticist." He belongs to the same group to which belong Socrates, Plato, il Cuzano, Malebranche, Galilei, Kant. His fight against *Kalām* and Aristotelianism is a fight against sensualism, materialism, rationalism and empiricism, traditionalism, utilitanianism, and ritualism. His characteristic is that he extended his subjectivism not only to philosophy, but also to religion. He raised to a science the historical *religiosità* of Islam through religious subjectivism. In this, as Obermann says, is the *eigentümlich historische Bedeutung* of the philosopher of Ṭūs.

Oberman's interpretation is correct in part—I admit that, so far as regards religion—the fundamental tendency of philosophy—he has hit the target, understanding it as subjectivistic. But in particular Obermann does not always respect the spirit of Ghazālī's thought. . . .

The philosophico-religious thought of Ghazali is not to be shown on the screen of Kantianism, but is to be studied in closest connection with Islamic thought and with Christian theology, the influence of which, though almost always indirect, was great. We can say that there is not a thought in Ghazali's science of religions of which we could not find copious comparisons in the Christian theologians of the Orient, Greek or Syriac.

"Il libro è però un po' prolisso. Sarebbero bastate cento pagine!"

85. PINES, SHLOMO. *The Guide of the Perplexed. Moses Maimonides.* Translated with an Introduction and Notes; an Introductory Essay by Leo Strauss. Chicago and London: University of Chicago Press, 1963 (2d impr., 1969). An excellent translation of this famous work.
86. POGGI, VINCENZO M., S.J. *Un Classico della Spiritualità Musulmana.* Rome: Libreria dell' Università Gregoriana, 1967. This is Father Poggi's doctoral thesis, and is certainly one of the finest studies we have on al-Ghazālī and the *Munqidh.* I am greatly indebted to Father Poggi and have drawn heavily on this excellent study of his.
87. PRETZL, OTTO. *Die Streitschrift des Ġazālī gegen die Ibāḥīja.* Im persischen Text herausgegeben und übersetzt (Sitzungsberichte der Bayrischen Akademie der Wissenschaften: Philosophisch-historische Abteilung-Jahrgang 1933, Heft 7) München, 1933.
88. RAHMAN, FAZLUR. *Islam.* New York: Holt, Rinehart and Winston, 1966 (1st ed.); Doubleday and Company, Inc., Anchor Books (paperback), 1968.
89. ———. *Prophecy in Islam. Philosophy and Orthodoxy.* London: George Allen and Unwin Ltd., 1958. These books are a penetrating study of Islam and a lucid exposition of the notion of Prophecy in Islam by a devout Muslim who is a learned scholar and independent thinker.
90. RIFĀᶜI, AḤMAD FARĪD. *(Ḥalqat) Al-Ghazālī,* 3 vols. Cairo, 1939. Selections from Ghazālī's works, including the *Munqidh.*
91. SCHIMMEL, ANNEMARIE. *Mystical Dimensions of Islam.* Chapel Hill: University of North Carolina Press, 1975. The best and most comprehensive modern account of Sufism by an author with a broad knowledge of her subject and sympathetic attitude to the spirituality of Islam.

92. SCHMÖLDERS, AUGUSTE. *Essai sur les écoles philosophiques chez les arabes et notamment sur la doctrine d'Alghazzali.* Paris: Firmis Didot Frères, 1842. One of the earliest translations of the *Munqidh* with a still-valuable introduction on Islamic philosophy and mysticism.
93. SHEHADI, FADLOU A. *Abū-Ḥāmid Al-Ghazālī: Al-Maqṣad Al-Asnā fi Sharḥ Maᶜānī Asmāᵓ Allāh Al-Ḥusnā.* Arabic Text, Edited with Introduction. Recherches: Nouvelle Série. A: Langue arabe at Pensée Islamique, Tome III. Beyrouth: Imprimerie Catholique, 1971.
94. ———. *Ghazālī's Unique and Unknowable God.* Leiden, 1964. A philosophical critical analysis of some of the problems raised by Ghazali's view of God as utterly unique and unknowable.
95. SMITH, JANE I. *An Historical and Semantic Study of the Term "Islām" as seen in the Sequence of Qurᵓān-Commentaries.* (Contains some comments on *Imān.)* Harvard Dissertations in Religion, vol. I. Missoula, Mont., 1975.
96. SMITH, MARGARET. "The Forerunner of al-Ghazālī," in *Journal of the Royal Asiatic Society.* London, 1936, pp. 65–78.
97. ———. *Al-Ghazālī the Mystic.* London: Luzac and Co., 1944.
98. ———. *An Early Mystic of Baghdad. A Study of the Life and Teaching of Ḥārith ibn Asad al-Muḥāsibī (781–857* A.D.) London, 1935.
99. ———. "Al-Risālat al-Laduniyya." By Abū Ḥāmid Muḥammad Al Ghazālī (450/1059– 505/1111). Translated by Margaret Smith. *Journal of the Royal Asiatic Society.* London, 1938. Part II—April, pp. 177–200; Part III—July, pp. 353–74. Margaret Smith's articles and books are valuable contributions to Ghazālī's thought and to the study of Islamic mysticism.
100. STADE, ROBERT CHARLES. *Ninety-nine Names of God in Islam.* Ibadan: Daystar Press, 1970. A translation of the major portion of Al-Ghazālī's *Al-Maqṣad Al-Asnā.*
101. SYED NAWAB ALI. *Some Moral and Religious Teachings of Ghazzali.* Lahore: Sh. Muhammad Ashraf, 1920 (2d ed., 1944; third reprint, 1960; fourth reprint, 1968). Contains extracts from the *Iḥyāᵓ* and *Minhāj al-ᶜĀbidīn.*
102. TIBAWI, A. L. "Al-Ghazālī's Tract on Dogmatic Theology," in *Islamic Quarterly,* vol. IX, Nos. 3–4, July–December 1965. Edited, translated, annotated, and introduced by A. L. Tibawi.
103. UMARUDDĪN, M. *The Ethical Philosophy of Al-Ghazzali.* Lahore: Sh. Muhammad Ashraf, 1962 (1st ed., 4 vols., 1949–51 Aligarh?)
104. AL-ᶜUTHMĀN, ᶜABD AL-KARĪM. *Sīrat al-Ghazālī wa-Aqwāl al-Mutaqaddimīn fīhi.* Damascus, 1960.
105. VAN DEN BERGH, SIMON. *Averroes' Tahāfut Al-Tahāfut* [VDB]. Vol. I—Translation; Vol. II—Notes. London: Luzac and Co. Ltd. [For the Trustees of the "E.J.W. Gibb Memorial Series"], 1969. An excellent translation with one volume of full and illuminating notes.
106. VECCIA VAGLIERI, LAURA, and RUBINACCI, ROBERTO. *Scritti Scelti di al-Ghazālī.* Torino: Unione Tipografico-Editrici Torinese, 1970. An excellent anthology of selections, very competently translated: *al-Munqidh,* well-chosen texts from the *Iḥyāᵓ,* and the complete *Mishkāt al-Anwār.*
107. WALZER, RICHARD. *Greek into Arabic. Essays on Islamic Philosophy.* Oriental Studies I. Oxford: Bruno Cassirer, 1962.

108. ———. *L'Eveil de la Philosophie Islamique.* Revue des Etudes Islamiques—hors série 1. Paris: Paul Geuthner, 1970. Excellent essays and lectures by the foremost authority on Islamic philosophy.
109. WATT, WILLIAM MONTGOMERY. "The Authenticity of the Works Attributed to al-Ghazālī." *Journal of the Royal Asiatic Society.* London, 1952, pp. 24–45.
110. ———. *Islamic Philosophy and Theology.* Islamic Survey I. Edinburgh: Edinburgh University Press, 1962. Best short introduction into this subject.
111. ———. *Muslim Intellectual: A Study of al-Ghazali.* Edinburgh: Edinburgh University Press, 1963. A good companion volume to the author's translation of the *Munqidh* (see next item).
112. ———. *The Faith and Practice of Al-Ghazālī.* London: George Allen and Unwin Ltd., 1953.
113. ———. *The Formative Period of Islamic Thought.* Edinburgh: Edinburgh University Press, 1973. The only work on a subject which is obscure and presents many problems.
114 WEHR, HANS. *Al-Ghazzālī's Buch vom Gottvertrauen: Das 35. Buch des Iḥyā'.* Halle, 1940.
115. WENSINCK, AREND JAN. *Concordance et indices de la tradition musulmane* [W Conc.]. Leiden, 1933.
116. ———. *A Handbook of Early Muhammadan Tradition* [Wensinck, *Handbook*]. Leiden, 1927.
117. ———. *La pensée de Ghazzālī.* Paris, 1940. An important, informative, and illuminative introduction into Ghazālī's thought.
118. WOLFSON, HARRY AUSTRYN. *The Philosophy of the Kalam* [WPK]. Cambridge, Mass., and London: Harvard University Press, 1976. The major modern work on the subject by an eminent scholar.
119. ZOLONDEK, LEON. *Iḥyā'*, Book XX (Bk. 10 of 2d Quart.). Leiden, 1963.
120. ZWEMER, SAMUEL M. *A Moslem Seeker after God: Showing Islam at Its Best in the Life and Teaching of Al-Ghazali, Mystic and Theologian of the Eleventh Century.* New York, Chicago, London and Edinburgh: Fleming H. Revill Company, 1920.

Addenda

76a. MASSIGNON, LOUTS. *Essai sur les origines du lexique technique de la mystique musulmane.* Paris, 1928.
76b. ———. *La Passion d'al-Ḥosayn ibn Mansour al-Hallaj, martyr mystique de l'Islam.* 2 vols. Paris, 1922.
These two books are classics. An English translation of 76b is in preparation.
lOOa. TRIMINGHAM, J. S. The Sufi Orders in Islam. Oxford: Oxford University Press, 1971.